Caesar

Selections from his COMMENTARII
DE BELLO GALLICO

Hans-Friedrich Mueller

Johannes Fridericus Molinarius

Bolchazy-Carducci Publishers, Inc.
Mundelein, Illinois USA

Editors: Donald E. Sprague, Bridget S. Dean

Contributing Editor: Laurel Draper

Design & Layout: Adam Phillip Velez

Proofreader: Gary K. Varney

Cartography: Mapping Specialists

Cover Image: Bust of Julius Caesar in the Kunsthistorisches Museum, Vienna, Austria. Wikimedia photo by Andrew Bossi.

Caesar
Selections from his *Commentarii De Bello Gallico*

Hans-Friedrich Mueller

AP is a registered trademark of the College Entrance Examination Board, which was not involved in the production of, and does not endorse, this product.

Bolchazy-Carducci Publishers, Inc.
1570 Baskin Road
Mundelein, Illinois 60060
www.bolchazy.com

Printed in the United States of America
2013
by United Graphics

Paperback: ISBN 978-0-86516-752-0
Hardbound: ISBN 978-0-86516-778-0

Library of Congress Cataloging-in-Publication Data

Caesar, Julius.
  [De bello Gallico]
  Selections from his Commentarii de bello gallico / Caesar ; by Hans-Friedrich Mueller.
    pages. cm.
  Includes bibliographical references.
   ISBN 978-0-86516-752-0 (paperback/perfect bound : alkaline paper) -- ISBN 978-0-86516-778-0
  (hardbound/casebound : alkaline paper) 1. Latin language--Readers. I. Mueller, Hans-Friedrich,
  1959- II. Title.
  PA6236.M84 2012
  478.6'421--dc23

                                                                      2012003872

Contents

—— List of Illustrations and Maps ——

Illustrations

Maps

— PREFACE AND INTRODUCTORY NOTES —

This book is designed as a reader for those passages from Julius Caesar's *Dē Bellō Gallicō* that have been adopted by the syllabus of the newly revised Advanced Placement course in Latin literature. As a convenience to teachers and students, we also provide an annotated translation of the required readings in English from Caesar's *Gallic War*, but we offer, above all, a detailed guide to the required selections in Latin. The selections in Latin prescribed by the AP syllabus include readings from Books One, Four, Five, and Six of Caesar's *Gallic War*.

Book One (1.1–7) introduces Gaul, its geography as well as its cultural and political features, and it presents the first conflict of Caesar's campaign, which Caesar describes not as the opening battle in a campaign to conquer all Gaul, but instead merely as an intervention, a sort of police action to safeguard the integrity of the Roman province of which he was governor.

Book Four (4.24–36.1) picks up four years later when Caesar appeared to have brought all Gaul under his effective military control. He felt secure enough to lead an expeditionary force to Britain, and Book Four tells the story of that first "invasion."

Book Five (5.24–48) presents a rather different picture. After Caesar secures his men in winter quarters at the end of a summer of campaigning (ancient armies generally did not fight in the winter), the previously conquered Belgic tribes rise in revolt and destroy one of Caesar's legions. Caesar's tense narrative describes what went wrong and how he repaired the situation.

Book Six (6.13–20) describes the Gauls and their customs in greater detail than did the brief introduction Caesar provided in Book One. Caesar paints a vivid picture of Celtic religious, social, and political institutions.

These selections provide good insight into Caesar's genre (*commentāriī*), his style as an author, the issues he faced as the governor of a province, his decision making as a general, and the culture of northern Europe before it was forcibly integrated into Greco-Roman cultural traditions. For each chapter of Book One only, we provide an introductory overview in English to help students find their way into the general flow of Caesar's narrative in Latin. The additional readings in English will help students flesh out their understanding of the more general shape of the war to conquer Gaul, but these Latin passages, which convey Caesar's thinking in his own Latin are well chosen to illustrate many of the crucial issues that defined Roman war and politics in Caesar's day, and which are truly comprehensible only if we understand the words and concepts used by the historical actors themselves.

How to Use This Reader

This book has been designed as a Latin reader. With this book in hand, students should be able to read efficiently, and then review intensively and with minimal wasted time, the selections from Caesar's *Gallic War* that appear on the new AP Latin syllabus. Those who know Clyde Pharr's magisterial edition of the first six books of Vergil's *Aeneid*, a continuing treasure for all students and teachers of Vergil, will recognize the model. Like its model, this reader is designed to guide students through the Latin text with minimal time lost to searching for vocabulary or through Latin grammars (not that such activities are a bad way to spend time—but students' time is limited, so we must use what time we have as effectively as possible). For students in search of additional information, we provide a complete vocabulary at the end of the volume. In addition, we offer this complete vocabulary as well as a grammatical and syntactical appendix online (www.bolchazy.com/extras/caesarappendix.pdf) so that students can have these resources available on their computers while reading the text. *The primary aim of this reader, however, is to supply enough information on each page to permit students to spend almost all the time that they devote to Caesar's Latin on those same pages where Caesar's Latin text appears.* How do we accomplish this?

Like Gaul, each page has been divided into three parts. Caesar's Latin text appears first. Words that appear in *italics* are familiar words and those that Caesar uses frequently. Because he uses them so frequently, these words have been printed on an extensible vocabulary sheet, "Familiar Words Frequently Used by Caesar," which students may pull out and keep open for every page (or until they have memorized these frequently appearing words). In the glossary, a dagger † follows the entry for these words on the pullout vocabulary list.

All vocabulary not italicized is provided immediately below the Latin passage. Below this list of vocabulary, students will find a running commentary on the text. The primary aim of the commentary is to help students understand the Latin text. We supply succinct, but relatively detailed, information about how the syntax of Caesar's sentences works. References to further grammatical and syntactical particulars (which can be found in the Online Appendix) also appear, but these references are made for the convenience of teachers and students. The references to this Online Appendix are not essential for following the text itself. What syntactical guidance is needed is supplied below the passage and on the same page. Finally, background information, notes on Caesarian style, and other relevant issues receive brief treatment, insofar as such commentary will help students understand and properly appreciate the Latin text. And, when students and/or teachers feel that students have adequately prepared the text, students may test their mettle with the unadorned and unannotated Latin text that we also provide on pp. 177–197.

A proper balance between too much and too little information in the confined space of a printed page is a delicate one. We have aimed for an *aurea mediocritās* (golden mean), but students and teachers will be the ultimate judges of whether we have hit or missed that mark. What we can say is that our only goal has been to provide a book that is useful, instructive, and pleasurable for all who care to become better acquainted with a pivotal historical figure and a classic of Roman prose—not to mention prepare effectively for the AP Latin exam.

A Note on the Same-page Vocabulary

In the same-page (or running) vocabulary on each page, the numbers 1, 2, and 4 indicate for regular verbs the conjugation to which the verb belongs, and that their principal parts are formed according to the patterns of the model verbs **laudō**, **moneō**, and **audiō**, respectively; or, if the verb is deponent, according to the patterns of **hortor**, **vereor**, and **partior** (see App. §73).

Words in *italics* in the entry are explanatory and are not part of the definition. Words in square brackets are the root(s) from which a word is derived or another closely related word.

The symbol • follows the last letter of the base or stem of the word. To this base, subsequent syllables are added, e.g., **abic•iō, -ere** = **abiciō, abicere** or **āc•er, -ris, -re** = **ācer, ācris, ācre.** (NB: In Caesar's day, nouns that ended in **-ius** and **-ium** regularly had a genitive **-ī**, rather than **-iī**, e.g., **auxil•ium, -ī.** For details, see App. §16, *c*.)

ACKNOWLEDGMENTS

T his book stands on the shoulders of nineteenth- and early twentieth-century textbooks.

The Latin text that appears in this edition has been prepared in close consultation with the following editions.

Renatus Du Pontet, ed. *C. Iulii Caesaris Commentariorum Pars Prior qua Continentur Libri VII De Bello Gallico cum A. Hirtii Supplemento.* Oxford: Clarendon Press, 1900.

Friedrich Kraner, ed. *C. Iulii Caesaris Commentarii De Bello Gallico.* 15th ed. rev. by W. Dittenberger. Berlin: Weidmann, 1890.

Carolus Nipperdeius [Karl Nipperdey], ed. *C. Iulii Caesaris Commentarii cum Supplementis A. Hirtii et Aliorum.* Leipzig: Breitkopfius et Haertelius, 1847.

T. Rice Holmes, ed. *C. Iulii Caesaris Commentarii Rerum in Gallia Gestarum VII; A. Hirti Commentarius VIII.* Oxford: Clarendon Press, 1914.

Macrons have been added in close consultation with the following editions.

Francis W. Kelsey, ed. *C. Iulii Caesaris Commentarii Rerum Gestarum: Caesar's Commentaries: The Gallic War, Books I-IV, with Selections from Books V-VII and from the Civil War: With an Introduction, Notes, a Companion to Caesar and a Vocabulary.* Boston, New York, & Chicago: Allyn and Bacon, 1918.

Arthur Tappan Walker, ed. *Caesar's Gallic War with Introduction, Notes, Vocabulary and Grammatical Appendix.*
Chicago & New York: Scott, Foresman, and Company,
1907.

Grammatical irregularities that appear in some, but not all, editions of
Caesar have been regularized. This text prints, for example, *eīs* (rather than
iīs) for the dative plural of *is, ea, id*, and the accusative plural of *fīnis* appears
as *fīnēs* (rather than *fīnīs*).

The vocabulary and grammatical Online Appendix were taken with
revisions from the edition of Arthur Tappan Walker cited above.

The Appendix: Figures of Speech containing grammatical and rhetorical figures was taken with revisions from the edition of Francis W. Kelsey
cited above.

The English translation of Books One, Six, and Seven of the *Gallic War*
is a revised version of

W. A. McDevitte and W. S. Bohn (translators). *Caesar's Commentaries.* Harper's Classical Library. Harper & Brothers:
New York, 1869.

In revising this literal translation, I aimed primarily to replace archaic
diction (e.g., "cavalry" for "horse") and to clarify sentence structure (e.g.,
by breaking up overly long sentences and by repeating explicitly the subjects and objects of many verbs—this may be clear enough in Latin, but
frequently becomes opaque in a literal English translation). Our revised
translation also uses Caesar's Latin names for the Gallic tribes rather than
our own more colloquial English equivalents (e.g., "Helvetii" rather than
"Helvetians," although I generally prefer the latter in my own commentary, which, of course, represents a modern voice rather than Caesar's,
hence the discrepancy).

The commentary itself also owes numerous debts of gratitude to these
as well as many other still informative and useful school editions of Caesar that survive in print and online.

I offer my public and sincere thanks to Lou and Marie Bolchazy, Don
Sprague, Bridget Buchholz, Jody Cull, Adam Velez, and Laurel De Vries
of Bolchazy-Carducci Publishers; two anonymous and helpful referees;
Christopher D. C. Choquette, my undergraduate research assistant at
Union College; and, above all, my wife Terri, who suffered many an ex-
tended absence as I worked to complete the manuscript. Any errors that

remain belong by right to me. I hope that readers will find the pages that follow useful, and perhaps even pleasurably instructive. And, if they do, they will have Caesar, his commentators, and the people I have just mentioned to thank for that useful pleasure and instruction.

HANS-FRIEDRICH MUELLER
Johannes Fridericus Molinarius
Union College
Schenectady, New York

GAIUS IULIUS CAESAR:
Politician, General, Author

Gaius Julius Caesar was born in 100 BCE, rising to become one of Rome's leading politicians and most successful generals as well as an accomplished orator and author of the first rank. After defeating his political opponents in a bitter civil war, Caesar reigned briefly as dictator before he was assassinated in 44 BCE. After his murder, the Roman Senate passed legislation declaring that Caesar had become a god. His impact on Rome's political and religious institutions was decisive and long lasting, and today his career still inspires both emulation and loathing, and we may trace the influence of Caesar's career in such founding documents of our own society as the Constitution of the United States.

This famous bust of Caesar presents an idealized portrait of the Roman leader. While portraits in the Republican period presented realistic representations, most of the portraits of Caesar present an idealized image.

CAESAR'S LIFE

Caesar was born in troubled times. Two names from this period are important: Marius (157–86 BCE) and Sulla (138–79 BCE). Marius reformed the Roman army to include the lower classes, he held an unprecedented seven consulships, his politics tended to support politicians opposed to the interests of the conservative aristocracy, and he was married to Caesar's aunt, Julia. Sulla was Marius's former lieutenant, a great general in his own right, and dictator in Rome when Caesar was in his teens. After Sulla won supreme authority in Rome (by twice marching his army on the city), he reorganized the Roman constitution to restore, as he saw it, the Roman Senate (which was populated by the conservative aristocracy) to its rightful and dominant place and to suppress the tribunes of the people, who often rallied Rome's common people to support legislation opposed by the aristocracy. Politicians who worked to achieve consensus in the Senate were called *optimātēs* ("the best men"). Those willing to bypass the Senate to pass legislation in the people's assemblies were called *populārēs* ("men of the people"). These were not political parties but represented a style of politics and a loose set of alliances with like-minded colleagues. In many ways, it would be best to avoid these overused terms altogether, but the Romans themselves used these terms, as do many older accounts of Roman history. According to this traditional (and now disfavored scheme), Sulla was *optimās*; Marius *populāris*, as was Caesar. We might also simply describe Sulla and Marius as political enemies, and Caesar was related to the Marian faction.

Another element in Sulla's initial plan for political renewal was "proscriptions." Proscriptions entailed writing the names of political enemies on lists that would be posted in public. Proscribed men could be hunted down and killed. Those who did the hunting and killing earned a right to a portion of the proscribed man's estate. Pompey the Great (although he had not yet earned the title) was, like Caesar, young at the time, and he profited from Sulla's proscriptions, earning

This bust of Pompey displayed in the Louvre Museum in Paris shows us Pompey the statesman rather than the teenage butcher, *adulēscentulus carnifex.*

the nickname "teenage butcher" (*adulēscentulus carnifex*). Caesar, on the other hand, because of his connection to Marius as well as his refusal to divorce—yes, he was already married in his teens—a wife whose family had been hostile to Sulla, barely escaped proscription, and eventually had to travel to the East until things became safer in Rome.

While in the East, Caesar, like many upper-class Roman youths, served in the entourage of a Roman official and participated in battle where he earned the "civic crown." The *corōna cīvica* was awarded to men who saved the lives of fellow citizens in battle. His biographers report that Caesar was also kidnapped by pirates, and that, after the ransom was collected and paid, he led an expedition to catch his former captors, personally overseeing their crucifixion. This episode illustrates the privileged status that upper-class Roman men—even very young ones—held across the Mediterranean world. After this adventure, Caesar went to Rhodes to study rhetoric (in Greek—upper-class Romans were generally bilingual) with Apollonius,

The seated Caesar is portrayed as an author holding a papyrus manuscript in his left hand. The nineteenth-century Parliament building in Vienna, Austria is a grand tribute to the classical tradition. On the two large ramps at the front of the building, this statue of Julius Caesar joins fellow Roman historians Tacitus, Titus, Livy, and Sallust as well as the Greek historians Thucydides, Polybius, Xenophon, and Herodotus.

who was at the time a star teacher. Cicero studied with Apollonius too, and Caesar, like Cicero, became by all accounts one of Rome's most accomplished orators.

In addition to military experience and work as a prosecutor in Rome's courts, Caesar's early career included numerous official posts, both military and civil. His elective posts included an aedileship in 65 BCE, notable for the games he put on (necessary for winning the favor of the voting public), as well as a somewhat scandalous election to Rome's chief priesthood in 63 BCE. Caesar's election as *pontifex maximus* was scandalous because Caesar was relatively young; because older, more established candidates, who had held the consulship, lost; and because Caesar had borrowed huge sums of money for the purpose of bribery. Politics at Rome were at this time hopelessly corrupt, and Caesar played the game well. Caesar had, in fact, borrowed so much money that, when he tried to leave for Spain, which was the province he was to govern in 61 BCE, his creditors went to court to prevent his departure. Caesar was able to depart only after Crassus, reputedly the richest man in Rome, as well as a successful politician and general in his own right, personally guaranteed Caesar's debts.

With the profits Caesar made governing in Spain (generals and soldiers shared in the profits derived from war, and Spain was inhabited by rebellious tribes), Caesar paid off his debts and prepared to run for election to the consulship. In this campaign, he was able to enlist the aid of two senior politicians, Pompey the Great and Crassus. Pompey and Crassus were enemies, but Caesar reconciled them and brokered a three-way alliance that would be mutually beneficial. The alliance, which they called "friendship" (amīcitia), had no legal standing. It is frequently called the "first triumvirate," but this term implies an official commission sanctioned by the state. Even if its public impact was profound, their amīcitia was, from a legal point of view, private. Pompey also married Caesar's daughter Julia. (Upper-class Roman marriages were strategic and political, although affection played a role sometimes too—especially after the fact.) After his election to the consulship in 59 BCE, Caesar used constitutionally dubious methods (e.g., physically preventing his colleague in the consulship, Bibulus, from participating, so that he could not veto proceedings) to pass legislation that would benefit his "friends."

At the end of his consulship, in addition to Illyricum (located on the Adriatic coast opposite northern Italy), Caesar received a proconsulship in the two Gauls, which, at the time, consisted of Cisalpine or Nearer Gaul (northern Italy) and Transalpine or Farther Gaul (the Mediterranean coast of what is now France). His initial command was for a period of five years, but, after he became involved in the conquest of the remainder of Gaul (roughly corresponding to what is now the rest of France), Caesar realized that it would take him longer than five years to accomplish the task. He was able to renew his alliance with Crassus and Pompey in 56 BCE and to complete the conquest of Gaul by 50 BCE. In the process, Caesar flooded Roman markets with slaves, acquired fabulous wealth, dispensed many political favors, won the fierce devotion of his soldiers, and increased the size of his army.

Roman politics had in the meantime entered into a critical phase. Caesar's daughter, Julia, who was married to Pompey (by all accounts, despite the political nature of their marriage, the two actually loved each

— ROMAN WORLD IN CAESAR'S DAY —

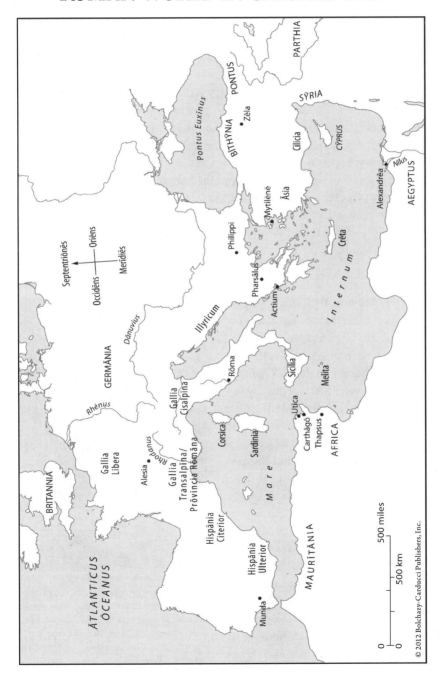

PARTHIA

BITHYNIA PONTUS

SYRIA

Pontus Euxinus

Zēla

Cilicia

CYPRUS

Myrtilēnē

Ăsia

Alexandrēa • Nīlus

AEGYPTUS

Philippī

Crēta

Septentriōnēs — Oriēns

Occidēns — Merīdiēs

Pharsālus

Actium

I n t e r n u m

Illyricum

Dānuvius

GERMĀNIA

Rōma

Sicilia

Melita

Rhēnus

Gallia
Cisalpīna

Corsica

Sardinia

Ūtica

Carthāgō
Thapsus

AFRICA

Gallia
Lībera

Alesia • • Rhod anus

Gallia
Transalpīna/
Prōvincia Rōmāna

M a r e

BRITANNIA

Hispānia
Citerior

MAURĪTĀNIA

ĀTLANTICUS
ŌCEANUS

Hispānia
Ulterior

Munda •

500 miles

500 km

© 2012 Bolchazy-Carducci Publishers, Inc.

0

0

other) died in childbirth in 54 BCE. Crassus was defeated in Parthia in 53 BCE and died in battle. Parthia ruled a territory roughly corresponding to what is now Iraq and Iran. The defeat was humiliating for Rome. After these events, Pompey began drifting into a closer alliance with leaders in the Roman Senate who were opposed to Caesar. Before his political alliance with Pompey fell apart, Caesar had been led to believe that he could celebrate a triumph (or military victory parade) in Rome as well as run for a second consulship. Instead, after winning Pompey over to their side, leading senators felt powerful enough to ruin Caesar's career, which, constitutionally speaking, they were entitled to do. They ordered Caesar to lay down his command, while, at the same time, allowing Pompey to retain his. Caesar refused to obey, so the Senate declared that Caesar was an outlaw. Caesar hesitated for a day, and then, crossing the Rubicon, the small river that divided his province from Italy proper, he invaded Italy in the middle of winter on January 10th, having uttered the famous words (if we can believe Suetonius *Divus Iulius* 32): *iacta ālea est* ("the die has been cast" [the Romans played with one *die*; we generally play with two or more *dice*]).

Pompey and the Senate appear to have been taken by surprise. They fled to Greece. Caesar secured Italy and then moved operations to Greece where he defeated Pompey at Pharsalus in 48 BCE. Pompey fled to Egypt (still independent under the Ptolemies), where he was assassinated. Caesar arrived in Egypt too late to engage Pompey but became involved in a local dispute over who had the right to rule in Egypt. Caesar supported Cleopatra over her brother. Because he arrived with so few soldiers, Caesar was at times in real danger, but he eventually prevailed. After settling affairs in Egypt (and allegedly fathering a child with Cleopatra), Caesar moved on to the East where, in 47 BCE, he penned his famous report

One of the best preserved temples in Egypt, the Ptolemaic Temple dedicated to Hathor and Horus the Elder in Abydos contains relief sculptures completed after Cleopatra's suicide. This panel shows Cleopatra flanked by her son Caesarion. Symbolically, they stand before the Egyptian gods Isis and Osiris.

from Zela: *vēnī, vīdī, vīcī* ("I came, I saw, I conquered"). But the civil war was not yet over. He had to fight senatorial armies in North Africa (46 BCE) and then in Spain (45 BCE).

After a bitter civil war, Caesar was faced with the task of reestablishing constitutional government. He had in the interim been named dictator, and, in 44 BCE, he was named dictator for life. On the other hand, Caesar originally invaded Italy on the grounds that he was defending elected leaders (tribunes) who had supported him, but had, along with himself, been declared outlaws by the Senate. He also argued that he was defending his soldiers' interests as well as the honors that he had been promised and that he had earned. Dictatorship was convenient. It allowed Caesar to hold office continuously without the necessity of annual election. The rest of the machinery of government ran as usual, but Caesar controlled who could have what post. There is some evidence that he wished to become king, to establish his rule on the basis of his own divinity, or both, but this remains far from settled.

During his short rule in Rome, Caesar began urban improvements that included a renovation of the Curia, the Roman Senate house (Domitian's restoration depicted). Coinage from the period shows acroteria celebrating the victory over Gaul mounted on the building's roof. Behind the Curia, he began the forum of Julius Caesar whose temple to Venus Genetrix celebrated his divine origin traced back to Aeneas, son of Venus and legendary ancestor of Romulus, the founder of Rome.

Caesar did not possess sole rule for long, so it is impossible to say what his long-term plans were. During his short-lived administration, however, he attempted to settle economic affairs by relieving, but not abolishing, debt. This satisfied neither debtors nor creditors. He also reformed the calendar. With only modest adjustments, we still use Caesar's calendar today, including an interesting anomaly. Logic dictated that the new year should begin on the day after the winter solstice (the shortest day of the year), but Roman religion required delay. We live with that delay to this day as well as with a month that still bears Caesar's name: July.

Another political policy contributed to Caesar's early demise. After his victory in the civil war, Caesar, unlike Sulla, preferred to forgive, rather than proscribe, his enemies, reckoning that people who owed their very lives to him would demonstrate future gratitude. He was wrong in this calculation, as many of those whom he forgave joined the successful conspiracy to assassinate him. The conspirators struck during a meeting of the Senate on March 15 (the Ides), 44 BCE—the eve of Caesar's planned departure for Parthia where he hoped to avenge Crassus's humiliating defeat.

Shakespeare's play *Julius Caesar* made the phrase "Beware the Ides of March" a well-known admonition. As Caesar heads to the Theater of Pompey where the Senate was meeting on the Ides of March, a soothsayer tries to warn him.

CAESAR'S LEGACY

After Caesar's murder, another round of civil war erupted, but not before the Senate declared that Caesar was a god. In his will, Caesar had adopted his great-nephew, Gaius Octavius (the son of his sister's daughter), who adopted Caesar's name, as did every subsequent Roman emperor. Caesar's name eventually passed into other languages too with the meaning of "emperor," such as *Kaiser* in German and *czar* in Russian. Caesar worship was transformed into emperor worship, and this worship of the emperors after they died and while they lived became an important element of

Roman administrative policy during the empire. This element of Roman religion eventually involved the Roman government in conflict with Jews and early Christians.

But Caesar's legacy goes beyond his calendar, his supposed divinity, and his name. The people of Gaul became Roman, and their descendants speak a form of Latin to this day. Caesar's example has also attracted imitators for thousands of years, and, in North America, fear of such would-be imitators haunted the framers of the U.S. Constitution. Whether or not Caesar had the moral right to attack Pompey and the Senate, from a legal perspective, Caesar trampled on Rome's constitution, which, as the framers of our constitution correctly diagnosed, had allowed him to acquire vast and virtually unchecked military power. Partly in reaction to this case study, a complex system of checks and balances was established in the United States to prevent any single individual from usurping supreme constitutional authority on Caesar's model.

Caesar is in every respect truly a pivotal historical figure. His career marks the final ruin of the Roman Republic, and his dictatorship served as the prelude to a constitutional reorganization that inaugurated the Roman Empire under his adoptive great-nephew Octavius (who became Augustus). We still reckon time by Caesar's reformed calendar, and our constitution continues to protect us from those who might otherwise try to imitate him. But why should we read Caesar's prose in Latin?

CAESAR AS AN AUTHOR

Caesar wrote many works that do not survive, apart from some fragments, including a work on Latin grammar, *Dē analogiā*, which is an especially bitter loss for Latin teachers, but Latin students too—because Caesar did not like exceptions to grammatical rules.

Caesar's literary fame rests on his surviving "commentaries" on the Gallic and Civil Wars: *Commentāriī dē bellō Gallicō* and *Commentāriī dē bellō cīvīlī* (most likely not the original title). The first seven books of the *Gallic War* were composed by Caesar. Aulus Hirtius supplemented the work after Caesar's death, contributing an eighth book. Caesar also wrote the three books of the *Civil War*. These books were supplemented as well with books (authorship uncertain) on events in Egypt (the *Alexandrian War*), North Africa (the *African War*), and Spain (the *Spanish War*).

What were *commentāriī*? Roman governors and generals wrote official reports, which they sent to the Senate. Caesar's actual reports to the Senate are not what we read today. We read reports modeled on the genre of those reports. Why would Caesar have chosen a genre that imitated such reports? Caesar was the politician who, during his consulship, first published "minutes" or "proceedings of the Senate" (*acta Senātūs*), much to the resentment of the conservative aristocracy, who preferred to settle matters among themselves without public scrutiny. When Caesar departed for Gaul, he probably chose *commentāriī* as a genre to publicize his accomplishments among as wide a public as possible in a format that made it appear as if he were sharing his official reports to the Senate with all Roman citizens. Caesar was also absent from Rome for nine years. His "dispatches" on the Gallic War would have been devoured by a public eager for news, and would have been promoted by Caesar's political allies. Similarly, Caesar's "reports" on the civil war were likely crucial in presenting Caesar's side in this bitterly divisive conflict. When were these books published? How were they published? Did they appear serially or as a complete work? Were there revisions along the way? The answers to all these questions remain disputed. We do have testimony, however, that, although the genre was in general conceived of as providing the raw materials for historians, Caesar's *commentāriī* were considered so polished that they dissuaded competitors from attempting to rewrite his accounts, especially of his Gallic campaigns.

Caesar's style has often been praised for its distinctive qualities. He tells his stories logically, clearly, and without obscure Latin vocabulary. If readers compare his prose to his contemporary Cicero or to the later historian Livy, they will soon perceive why Caesar's style is called "plain." His sentences, artfully constructed though they are, do not become involved in the complex syntax of subordinate and relative clauses (a style called "periodic"). His use of rhetorical devices is more subtle. He writes as a dispassionate observer, as opposed to the outraged orator or the emotional and moralizing historian.

Caesar also demotes himself to the third person. Much has been written on this topic, but one must consider his original audience at Rome: a public eagerly listening to reports about the progress of the Gallic war. Texts were often read aloud to larger groups who gathered to listen. If we compare, "When Caesar was informed of this, he decided to . . ." to "When I heard this, I reckoned I should . . . ," we can observe that the third person would seem more natural in reporting the great general's accomplishments in the wilds of Gaul to a larger audience. Even upper-class "readers" frequently employed slaves to read texts to them out loud. If Caesar were not writing letters to people personally, the first person would have been jarring. Why would Caesar be speaking to them directly, especially if they were in a group, and he was so far away in Gaul? With the help of the third person, the focus of the reports was more squarely on Caesar's actions rather than his authorship, and their plain and unemotional style lent them a seeming objectivity. How could they not be true? And Caesar does use the first person from time to time, but when he speaks as an author, not when he is telling a story in which he is another character, even though we know that he is the most important character in his own story!

Caesar's *commentāriī* have seduced many readers over thousands of years with their seemingly objective authority. A cursory glance, however, at the bitterly partisan times in which they appeared quickly reveals what was at stake for Caesar: his reputation, his public career, and even his life, as the subsequent civil war and Caesar's murder amply demonstrate.

Caesar's view of the world is a pleasure to read, and his prose is convincing. *Caveat lector* (reader beware). Critically aware study of his texts will reap even richer harvests.

The Chain of Command: Caesar as General and the Roman Army

Commander-in-Chief

Caesar, who had been consul in 59 BCE, arrived in his province as a proconsul, that is, a magistrate who came in place of (*prō*) a consul. A proconsul enjoyed the executive power of a Roman consul within his assigned sphere of operation, his *prōvincia* or province. Roman Gaul, however, was at the edge of the Roman world, and Caesar's province was protected by the Roman army. As governor, Caesar also served as commander-in-chief or leader (*dux*) or—after he won a victory, and was hailed as such—commander (*imperātor*) of the army. Who served in this army? Whole books are written on this topic, but we can sketch the basic principles here, and we will begin with the chain of command, and work our way from Caesar to subordinate officers to infantry and beyond.

Caesar enjoyed almost unlimited authority as a general. His power to punish enemies, for example, included execution, selling them into slavery, or, as his general Aulus Hirtius in his supplementary book on the Gallic War writes, chopping off the hands of those who had rebelled. Roman citizens had the right to appeal and were not supposed to be put to death without trial. The rules were different in the army. There was no appeal, and Caesar had the right, as general, to order the execution of deserters, thieves, and other criminals. Although the power of life and death dramatically illustrates Caesar's authority, it does not offer a comprehensive or representative view. Generals do not lead by killing their men. Caesar exercised his authority judiciously, and he lets us know throughout his narrative how important the health and safety of his men were to him. Almost like the CEO of a large corporation, the *dux* had to build cities (camps), supply that city with food and other necessities, find new markets to fund profit-sharing (plunder), make travel arrangements (e.g., invade), manage hostile takeovers (battle), and negotiate contracts (treaties), as well as supervise and direct operations in the heat of battle.

The job was a difficult one, and Caesar's men depended on Caesar to look out for their interests. For Rome too, of course, Caesar also protected the safety and integrity of his province in a hostile and brutal world (as cruel as the Romans may seem to us—and they were—their enemies were no less cruel, rapacious, and violent). How did he manage these operations that involved thousands? We have touched on one key component, Caesar's authority or *imperium*, i.e., his right to give orders. The other key is obedience to authority and clear chains of command. *Fidēs* (loyalty or trust) was a key Roman virtue, and one that Caesar prized and rewarded. Just as soldiers require a general they can trust and in whom they have confidence, so also a general requires men who are loyal and upon whom he could rely. Hierarchy—and the Roman army raised hierarchy to the level of an art—was a two-way street, and we will be able to observe the important role trust and loyalty play in Caesar's narrative: from foreign allies (who frequently lack the quality) and Roman infantry (who possess it in abundance) to officers. (For other moral and military qualities of the Roman army, see the section below on centurions.)

Lieutenants

Let us review the ranks. Caesar, the commander-in-chief, relied heavily on his subordinate commanders or generals. Traditionally, we call them "lieutenants" in English, but the term in Latin is *lēgātus* or legate, that is, someone to whom Caesar delegates authority, and, when Caesar is not present, these legates represent the highest authority over whatever legion Caesar has placed them. Caesar mentions them frequently, as the legions were generally not all in one place or even close to each other, and communications were slow. These legates were powerful and important men in their own right, and some were better than others. Caesar blames his lieutenants for disasters (as he does in the selections from Book Five), but he singles them out for praise too. Caesar's most famous lieutenant (who would later turn against Caesar and fight on Pompey's side during the Civil War that began immediately after the Gallic War) was Labienus. Caesar frequently relies on him, and he is generous with his praise. Also mentioned frequently are Cicero (the brother of the more famous orator) and the sons of Crassus (Caesar's great patron and political ally).

The Officer Class

These names will serve to illustrate another important point about the officer class. Elite officers were from the highest social, political, and economic classes at Rome. Roman politics followed generals wherever they went, and Roman generals were, of course, also politicians. Politicians have favors to confer and favors to repay, and the Roman army was full of posts not just for relatives of men as famous and powerful as Crassus and Cicero, but also for younger men and other hangers-on of the upper classes more generally, who joined the armies of powerful politician-generals in search of training, political connections, and profit. These lesser officers were not always particularly helpful, as they were not infrequently liable to panic. Caesar mentions such men from time to time, but generally as a group or class.

Another important officer was the *quaestor* or quartermaster, who was in charge of money and supplies. Generals had to bring large amounts of cash (which they carried in chests) to pay troops and purchase supplies. Maintaining a sufficient supply of grain (Romans preferred bread to meat) was a constant concern. It is perhaps not surprising that, like the general himself, the *quaestor* was accompanied by a bodyguard (*cohors praetōria*) of elite soldiers, generally from the upper classes (yet another job opportunity for aspiring young men as well as political patronage for the general).

Each legion had six military tribunes (*tribūnī mīlitum*) who could be put in charge of groups or detachments of various sizes. This rank offered Caesar an additional opportunity for political appointments and personal favors.

Despite the political nature of many appointments, it would be a mistake to conclude that Rome's officer class lacked competent and dedicated men. Motivations, experience, talent, and luck varied from individual to individual. Caesar looked for competence, and he put many men to efficient use. He also used them as a sounding board. It was standard Roman practice for generals to seek advice from their advisory council (*consilium*) on important decisions or major points of strategy. Although Caesar does not talk about his own discussions, he does share discussions that took place in the councils of his legates.

Centurions

Below the elite officer class, we find the men and leaders who did most of the fighting, and the men on whom Caesar frequently relied, especially in the heat of battle. Men of the lowest social classes could aspire to this rank, as one earned one's post by meritorious service. There was a hierarchy among this rank of officers as well, but, in general, centurions (something like a captain) or *centuriōnēs* (also *ordinēs*) commanded the basic unit of the Roman legion, the century (*ordō*) or company. (See the discussion below for the organization of the legion.) Centurions were veteran soldiers who had proven their qualities in battle. The word in Latin for character and moral quality is *virtūs*—literally, "manliness"—and centurions embodied that value in its most elemental sense. They tended to be brave, loyal, self-sacrificing, disciplined leaders of the common soldiers. They were the heart—the core—of the Roman army, and Caesar frequently singles them out for praise. He depended on them.

The Infantry

In Caesar's day, Roman legions were staffed entirely by Roman citizens. Common enlisted men (*mīlitēs*) served in the Roman infantry. They fought on foot, hence also the term foot soldiers (*peditēs* and *peditātus*). These men were either volunteers or conscripts. Volunteers signed up for a term of twenty years. In return, they received a steady job, an income, a pension, and profit-sharing (plunder). All male Roman citizens, however, between the ages of 17 and 45 were also subject to the draft or conscription at any time, and, as you will read, when Caesar needed more troops, he conducted a levy (*dīlectus*). Caesar was an industrious recruiter, and he increased the size of his army dramatically over the ten years of the Gallic campaign. This would enable him to take on Pompey and the Roman Senate in the subsequent Civil War.

The Legion

How many men were there and how were they organized? Numbers varied over time, but during the Gallic War, one legion (*legiō*) had about 3,600 troops. Each legion was divided into ten cohorts (*cohortēs*). Each cohort had three maniples (*manipulī*). Each maniple had two centuries or companies (*ordinēs*). These subsets within the legion allowed the general to control the movement of formations with some precision, even in the heat of battle, through the chain of command.

If we do the math:

    1 legion = 3,600 men

    10 cohorts of 360 men

    30 maniples of 120 men

    60 centuries of 60 men

Looking at it another way:

    1 legion = 10 cohorts

    1 cohort = 3 maniples

    1 maniple = 2 centuries

    1 century = 60 men

Each legion was called by a number, and Caesar's favorite legion was the tenth. When Caesar arrived in his province, there were four experienced legions (*legiōnēs veterānae*). He immediately conscripted two more legions, and would continue to levy troops as the war dragged on. If you have kept up with the math, you will realize that Caesar had over twenty thousand legionary soldiers at his disposal soon after he arrived in Gaul. He had other fighting men too, but, before we turn to them, let us return to organization.

Communications

Each legion had an eagle (*aquila*), which was carried on a long pole by an eagle-bearer (*aquilifer*). A legion also had standards (*signa*), carried by a standard-bearer (*signifer*), for each maniple. These standards were an important element in military communications as well as important for maintaining spirit and discipline within the legion and its individual units. A legion followed its eagle and treated its eagle, which was stored in a shrine, with religious reverence. It was beyond shameful to lose an eagle. Eagles were, morever, Jupiter's special bird, and Jupiter was the chief god of the Roman state. And, if we imagine the noise and confusion of battle, we quickly grasp one of the principal practical purposes of standards. They too involved emblems carried atop long poles. Soldiers could see the standard above people's heads, and, by following their assigned standards, would know in what direction to proceed, even if they could not hear commands. Other means of nonverbal communication included flags (*vexillae*) and trumpets (*tubae*). Communication was a challenge.

This statue of Claudius, the fifth of Caesar's successors in the Julio-Claudian dynasty of emperors, depicts several important Roman symbols—the crown of laurel leaves, the fasces in his left hand and the libation plate in his right, and the *aquila*. The eagle was associated with Jupiter and as a symbol came to represent the imperial power of Rome and subsequently the Holy Roman Empire. One tradition states that Caesar wore the laurel crown so as to hide his baldness. Roman emperors were regularly hailed as "Caesar."

To keep up more complex lines of communication, Caesar employed a variety of messengers and letters, sometimes written in code. Patrols on horseback (*explōrātōrēs*) were sent out to keep a close watch on local surroundings. Scouts and spies (*speculātōrēs*) were employed where less conspicuous observation was required.

Non-Roman Troops

Caesar also employed foreign soldiers. Auxiliary troops (*auxilia*) were trained in the same fashion as the Roman infantry. They were often placed at the end of the battle lines or wings (*ālae*). More specialized troops included light-armed soldiers, slingers (*funditōrēs*), who used slingshots, archers (*sagittāriī*), and, more spectacularly, cavalry (*equitēs* or *equitātus*). Each legion had a cavalry contingent of about two to three hundred. These foreign mercenaries hailed primarily from Spain and Germany, but Caesar also employed Gallic cavalry.

Non-Combatants

The army would not have been complete without a large support staff. These included camp slaves (*cālōnēs*), muleteers (*mūliōnēs*), traders (*mercātōrēs*), who sold goods to the soldiers and purchased plunder from them, and engineers (*fabrī*), who helped build siegeworks, ships, bridges, and more.

Baggage

Caesar frequently mentions baggage (*impedīmenta*). The army had to bring tents, weapons, food, cash (which was heavy), building materials, cooking utensils, supplies, and an entourage that included a menagerie of animals.

Soldiers carried their own equipment. The army also had wagons and mules. After taking a city by storm, the army would acquire plunder, which could consist of things, but also people, whom they could sell as slaves to the traders for cash, but then they would have to carry the cash. You will frequently read, however, about measures taken to protect the baggage as well as how enemy troops aimed at plundering the Romans' baggage. Baggage also could hinder the effectiveness of a legion. It slowed them down, and they worried about losing it.

A Male Microcosm of Rome

A Roman army was a highly complex operation, and was much like a Roman city (if Roman cities had been populated only by adult men). A knowledge of its basic outlines will help readers appreciate the challenges, successes, and failures of Caesar's campaigns.

An Overview of the Gallic War

Rome rose over centuries from a small city-state to an imperial power that dominated an area larger than the continental United States—all of the Mediterranean and much of Northern Europe. Caesar's conquest of Gaul represents a part toward the conclusion of that larger story of conquest. This addition to Rome's empire is, however, especially fascinating for several reasons. We have the public professions of the man who decided on the invasion, and who found the means to pursue the war for almost nine years until the job was finished. This war also played a crucial role in the development of Caesar's career, and thus, in a sense, in the revolution that would soon overwhelm the Roman Republic. Let us review briefly this war both as it is described by Caesar and in the context of Caesar's larger career.

As we outlined above, Caesar arrived in his "Gallic provinces" (i.e., northern Italy and the Mediterranean coast along what is now the south of France) in 58 BCE, the year after his consulship of 59 BCE. By some reports, his first inclination was to win further military glory in Illyricum (territory along the Adriatic coast opposite Italy and corresponding to northern Albania and parts of the former Yugoslavia). Why? Military glory provided immense political capital in Roman politics, and Caesar's goal was to remain a powerful political force at Rome. For this reason, he required military glory to match his son-in-law Pompey's, and he also needed a great deal more cash. This is not an element of Roman politics that receives as much discussion, but, even if it is tawdry, it was essential. Roman politics for reasons we cannot describe in detail here required enormous sums of money (suffice it to say that political support could be purchased), and, for the ancient entrepreneur, war could be extremely profitable as well as a source of publicity and glory. Conquered cities and villages could be plundered for their material goods, of course, but another rich source of wealth was the local population, who could be sold into slavery. Soldiers and generals shared in the profits. In the modern world, plundering is a war crime and slavery is a crime against humanity, and rightly so, but the ancient world had very different and much harsher rules. Wherever the Roman army went, slave traders followed. These traders would buy and sell other goods too, of course, but the slave trade was an immense source of profit. The Roman army was in many respects a mercantile operation. Caesar, because he was ambitious, needed a war, if not in Illyricum, then in Gaul.

Were there no constraints on ambitious generals? There were, in fact, many: legal, religious, and moral. Romans attributed their military success to their devotion to the gods, to their moral code (the *mōs māiōrum* or "customs of their ancestors"), and their laws. The Romans did not fight aggressive wars, as that would be unjust. They did not aim to conquer and enslave their neighbors. That would violate the "law of nations" (*ius gentium*; a primitive equivalent of international law).

How in the world then did Rome end up with an empire? That is the age-old question, and it has many answers. Historians disagree. By way of partial answer, we can look at the situation at the beginning of Caesar's governorship of Roman Gaul. In Book One of his *Dē Bellō Gallicō*, Caesar tells us that the Helvetii wished to move from their homes in a territory that corresponds to what is now Switzerland to other Gallic territories that were outside Roman territory. How did that affect Rome? At first the Helvetii asked whether Caesar would permit them to pass through Roman territory on their way to non-Roman territory. Caesar said no. The Helvetii then tried to emigrate by another route through non-Roman territory. Even though these events took place on non-Roman territory, Caesar used them to justify an incursion with his army into non-Roman territory in order to prevent the Helvetii from emigrating. Why? The migration of the Helvetii represented a danger for Roman territory. Caesar explains this at greater length in the AP selections from Book One, but the main point is clear. Caesar first enters Gaul in order to deal with a relatively minor local threat to Roman territory on the grounds that he was thereby protecting Roman interests. Caesar's war was (in this presentation) not aggressive; it was defensive.

All Roman wars were justified in similar terms, and this is why historians disagree. Some historians agree with the Roman point of view while others sympathize with the people the Romans conquered. Caesar himself tells us nothing of politics in Rome or Rome's larger strategic interests, and he certainly does not tell us that he aims to enrich himself and his allies for the sake of his future political career. That would have been crass, morally offensive, and illegal. Did Caesar perhaps protect Rome from a real threat? Indeed, Rome's neighbors were hardly pacifists devoted to peace, love, and harmony. Gauls as well as the Germanic tribes who were continually infiltrating Gaul from across the Rhine were fierce and warlike people. What does all this say about Caesar's character? The question is well worth discussing, as few people are entirely good or entirely evil, and Caesar was, it is safe to assume, no exception to this general rule. Caesar likely combined Rome's interests with his own on the basis of traditional Roman thinking about defense and in the context of Roman politics as it existed in Caesar's day. Leaders who can combine their own interests with the interests of larger groups generally stand a better chance of success than those who are purely self-seeking. In the final analysis, however, the burden of accounting for Caesar's motivations falls on his modern readers because Caesar presents the war in his *commentāriī* as a simple series of events. Each campaign leads naturally from the previous campaign.

Let us turn then to that series of events, as Caesar describes them in the *Dē Bellō Gallicō*. After our survey, we can place this war in the context of Caesar's subsequent career and assess its impact for Caesar and for Rome.

> I. In Book One, Caesar arrives in his province in 58 BCE to discover that the Helvetii are on the move. Caesar leads his army into non-Roman Gallic territory and, after defeating the Helvetii in battle, compels them to return to their homes on the grounds that their otherwise vacant lands would be an open invitation for Germans (an even more warlike and dangerous people) to settle on the vacated territory that is just across the border from the Roman Province. After this action, Caesar calls an assembly of the Gauls and receives a number of complaints about a German leader, Ariovistus, who has brought his followers across the Rhine into Gallic territory. Caesar campaigns against Ariovistus and thus "frees" the Gauls from German oppression.

Caesar's Campaigns

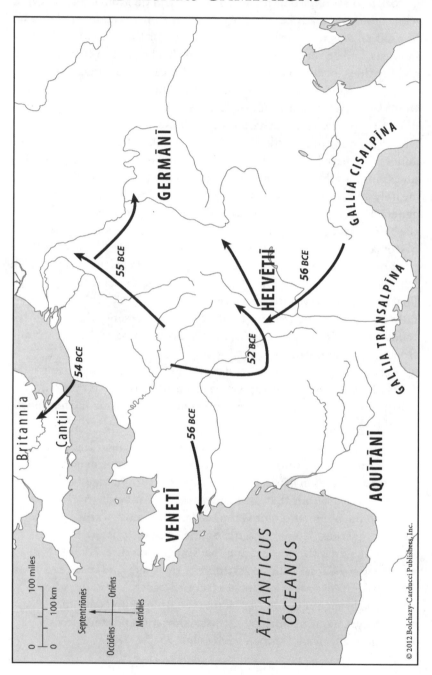

GERMĀNĪ

GALLIA CISALPĪNA

55 BCE

HELVĒTĪ

56 BCE

52 BCE

GALLIA TRANSALPĪNA

54 BCE

Britannia

Cantiī

56 BCE

AQUĪTĀNĪ

VENETĪ

ĀTLANTICUS ŌCEANUS

100 miles

100 km

Septentriōnēs

Occidēns — Oriēns

Merīdiēs

0

0

Here we observe another common method the Romans used to justify intervention. Rome defended friends against their friends' enemies. Caesar thus becomes a significant force in the politics of non-Roman Gaul. Moreover, he does not leave Gaul but instead establishes winter quarters (ancient armies generally did not fight in winter when it was difficult to secure supplies) in Gallic territory. The invasion of Gaul has thus been launched and the military occupation of Gaul has begun. The next seven books will describe what it took to finish the job.

II. In Book Two, which relates the events of 57 BCE, Caesar campaigns against Belgic tribes in northern Gaul, thus extending his military power and political sway. At Rome, the Senate decrees fifteen days of prayers and sacrifices to the immortal gods in thanks for Caesar's successes.

III. Book Three covers events from 57 through 56 BCE. Various campaigns throughout Gaul continue to extend and solidify Caesar's effective military control over the whole territory.

Ehrenbreitstein, the Prussian castle-fortress, at Koblenz, the confluence of the Rhine and the Moselle rivers, hosts the local museum of history. Depicted is a faithful reconstruction of a Roman pile driver, one of the tools the Romans used to build bridges. In building a bridge across the Rhine, Caesar knew the psychological impact of demonstrating Rome's superior technology.

IV. By 55 BCE, military affairs seem fairly secure throughout Gaul, so, as Book Four describes, Caesar moves his military operations across the Rhine into German territory. This expedition is designed as a lesson to German leaders that Roman armies can hurt them in their own territory. The bridge that Romans built across the Rhine was another demonstration of their superior abilities. After this demonstration of Roman strength against the Germans, Caesar decides to sail to Britain and has a fleet built for this purpose. The fleet is damaged by a storm, but, after inflicting some defeats on local Britons, Caesar manages to repair the loss of his ships and to transport his troops safely back to the mainland. These expeditions against Germans and Britons were more spectacular than practical from a local military point of view, but they were effective in building Caesar's political popularity at Rome. The Senate this time decreed twenty days of prayers and sacrifices to the immortal gods in thanks for Caesar's military successes.

V. In Book Five, which describes the events of 54 BCE, Caesar begins to experience setbacks. His second expedition to Britain is again marred by trouble with storms as well as some difficult fighting. The troops acquit themselves well, however, and Caesar manages to transport them to the mainland for winter. But, after the troops have been dispersed to widely separated winter quarters, Belgic tribes rise in revolt and manage to destroy one Roman legion before Caesar can come to the relief of others.

VI. In Book Six, which describes the events of 53 BCE, there are continued revolts among the Gauls. Caesar also describes the customs, political organization, and religion of Gauls and Germans.

VII. Troubles continue in Book Seven, which describes the events of 52 BCE. Caesar calls it a "conspiracy," but the Gauls gather as a people and select Vercingetorix as the leader of their united effort to drive the Romans, their camps, and their armies from Gallic territory. The Gauls fight desperately for freedom. Even Caesar recognizes this, and respects them as he fights to conquer them. This struggle culminates in the siege of a city called Alesia. Eventually, Alesia and Vercingetorix submit to Caesar. At Rome, the Senate decrees another twenty days of prayers and sacrifices to the immortal gods in thanks for Caesar's military successes.

VIII. The capitulation of Alesia represents the dramatic turning point of the war, but the work of conquest was not entirely done. Book Eight describes the military operations that continue in 51 and 50 BCE to suppress the revolt finally and completely. This book was not written by Caesar, however, but by one of his lieutenants, Aulus Hirtius.

The bronze statue of Caesar in military dress stands in front of the first-century Porta Palatina in Turin, Italy. Caesar is joined by a similar statue of his grand-nephew Caesar Augustus. Ancient Turin, *Augusta Taurīnōrum*, was part of Cisalpine Gaul.

We have surveyed in a few short paragraphs a difficult war that lasted almost nine years. Caesar won that war and, immediately after completing it, marched his armies on Rome in January 49 BCE, thus beginning the war against his own government that would eventually lead to his dictatorship. We have already sketched this chronology in the paragraphs above. A question that we may ask after our brief survey of the Gallic War is how Caesar's conquest of Gaul fits into the larger context of his life and career. The conquest of Gaul was crucial and the consequences are difficult to overstate. Caesar emerged from this war with a loyal, well-trained, and substantially larger army. Caesar also emerged from this war a fabulously wealthy man who had throughout its duration used the wealth that he had acquired to purchase friends, allies, and influence in Roman politics. Caesar's well-publicized victories had also bought tremendous political capital among the people of Rome and Italy. Romans liked winners, and they admired Caesar's victories over the warlike peoples of the North. Caesar was the hero of the day among many, even when he marched his army against Rome's government. The war in Gaul transformed Caesar from a leading politician into one of the two dominant military and political leaders of Rome. The war in Gaul transformed Caesar into a colossus: Caesar had become Pompey's near equal, and Caesar had become strong enough to challenge Pompey and the Senate. The result was the Roman Civil War. The conquest of Gaul was central to Caesar's subsequent success against his enemies, and thus, in no small measure, a contributing factor to the final destruction of the Republic.

Select Bibliography for Further Reading:

Badian, E. *Roman Imperialism in the Late Republic*. 2nd rev. ed. Oxford: Blackwell, 1968.

Balsdon, J.P.V.D. *Julius Caesar: A Political Biography*. New York: Athenaeum, 1967.

Canfora, Luciano. *Julius Caesar: The People's Dictator*. Translated by Marian Hill and Kevin Windle. Edinburgh: Edinburgh University Press, 2007.

Flower, Harriet I., ed. *The Cambridge Companion to the Roman Republic*. Cambridge: Cambridge University Press, 2004.

Gelzer, Matthias. *Caesar: Politician and Statesman*. Translated by Peter Needham. Cambridge, MA: Harvard University Press, 1968.

Goldsworthy, Adrian Keith. *Caesar: Life of a Colossus*. New Haven: Yale University Press, 2006.

———. *The Complete Roman Army*. New York: Thames & Hudson, 2003.

———. *The Roman Army at War: 100 BC–AD 200*. Oxford: Clarendon Press, 1996.

Griffin, Miriam, ed. *A Companion to Julius Caesar*. Chichester, UK, and Malden, MA: Wiley-Blackwell, 2009.

Kleiner, Diana E. E. *Cleopatra and Rome*. Cambridge, MA: Belknap Press of Harvard University Press, 2005.

Mehl, Andreas. *Roman Historiography: An Introduction to its Basic Aspects and Development*. Translated by Hans-Friedrich Mueller. Chichester, UK, and Malden, MA: Wiley-Blackwell, 2011.

Meier, Christian. *Caesar: A Biography*. Translated by David McLintock. New York: Basic Books, 1982.

Mommsen, Theodor. *A History of Rome*. Translated by William Purdie Dickson. London: R. Bentley, 1894.

Parenti, Michael. *The Assassination of Julius Caesar: A People's History of Ancient Rome*. New York: New Press, 2003.

Riggsby, Andrew M. *Caesar in Gaul and Rome: A War in Words*. Austin: University Press of Texas, 2006.

Rosenstein, Nathan and Robert Morstein-Marx, eds. *A Companion to the Roman Republic*. Oxford and Malden, MA: Blackwell Publishing, 2006.

Seager, Robin. *Pompey the Great: A Political Biography*. 2nd ed. Malden, MA: Blackwell Publishing, 2002.

Syme, R. *The Roman Revolution*. Oxford: Oxford University Press, 1939.

Tatum, W. Jeffrey. *Always I Am Caesar*. Oxford and Malden, MA: Blackwell Publishing, 2008.

Taylor, Lily Ross. *Party Politics in the Age of Caesar*. Berkeley: University of California Press, 1961.

———. *The Divinity of the Roman Emperor*. Middletown, CN: The American Philological Association, 1931.

Weinstock, Stefan. *DIVUS JULIUS*. Oxford: Clarendon Press, 1971.

Welch, Kathryn and Anton Powell, eds. *Julius Caesar as Artful Reporter: The War Commentaries as Political Instruments*. London: Duckworth, 1998.

Wyke, Maria. *Julius Caesar: A Life in Western Culture*. Chicago: University of Chicago Press, 2008.

Wyke, Maria, ed. *Julius Caesar in Western Culture*. Oxford and Malden, MA: Blackwell Publishing, 2002.

Yavetz, Zwi. *Julius Caesar and his Public Image*. Ithaca, New York: Cornell University Press, 1983.

Signs and Abbreviations

§ = section

† = word appears in the high-frequency word list.

abbr. = abbreviation

abl. = ablative

acc. = accusative

adj. = adjective

adv. = adverb

App. = Appendix

BC = Bellum Cīvile

BG = Bellum Gallicum

card. = cardinal

cf. = cōnfer (*i.e.,* compare)

comp. = comparative

conj. = conjunction

dat. = dative

def. = defective

dim. = diminutive

e.g. = exemplī grātiā (*i.e.,* for example)

etc. = *et cētera* (*i.e.,* and so on)

f. = feminine

freq. = frequentative

fut. = future

gen. = genitive

i.e. = id est (*i.e.,* that is)

imperat. = imperative

impers. = impersonal

impf. = imperfect

ind. = indicative

indecl. = indeclinable

indef. = indefinite

inf. = infinitive

infs. = infinitives

interrog. = interrogative

m. = masculine

n. = neuter

nom. = nominative

num. = numeral

obs. = obsolete

ord. = ordinal

p., pp. = page, pages

part. = participle

pass. = passive

perf. = perfect

pl. = plural

plupf. = pluperfect

poss. = possessive

prep. = preposition

preps. = prepositions

pres. = present

pron. = pronoun

rel. = relative

reflex. = reflexive

sc. = scīlicet (*i.e.,* supply)

sing. = singular

superl. = superlative

C. IVLI CAESARIS
COMMENTARIORUM
DE BELLO GALLICO
LIBER PRIMVS

Caesar DĒ BELLŌ GALLICŌ 1.1–7:
Caesar Describes Gaul and Begins the War

C aesar begins his work with a famous sentence about the ethnic geography of Gaul, a territory corresponding roughly to what is today modern France. Today, of course, most inhabitants of France speak French, a form of modern Latin. In Caesar's day, the territory was primarily inhabited by Celts (or Kelts) who spoke their own Celtic languages and dialects. Caesar must introduce his audience to the territory in which he will spend the better part of a decade campaigning. Did Gaul (whether they wanted it or not) need Roman protection from more savage Germanic invaders farther east? Were Caesar's foes (both Gallic and, potentially, German) formidable? Who were these Gauls who lived beyond Roman rule, as opposed to the Gauls who had, according to traditional Roman chronology, sacked Rome in 390 BCE, or who, in Caesar's day, lived under Roman administration along the Mediterranean coast or in northern Italy? These are the questions Caesar will answer. The geography and topography set the context for the people who lived there and for the general who would spend the next eight years conquering them. The Gauls fought hard for their freedom and independence. Caesar and his men fought harder.

GAUL

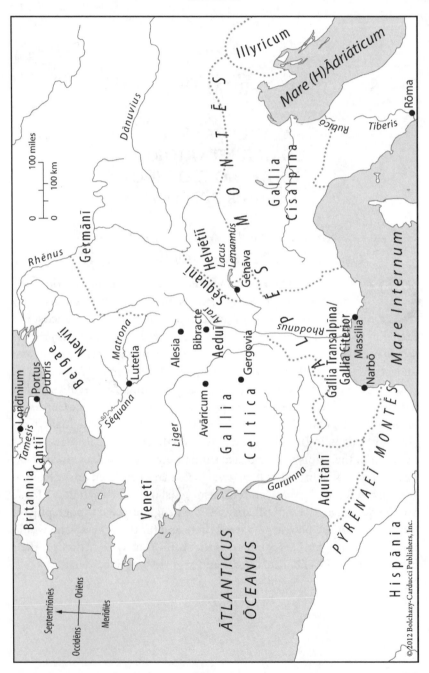

Caesar Dē Bellō Gallicō 1.1:
A Lesson in Geography and Ethnography

[1.1] *Gallia est omnis* dīvīsa *in partēs trēs, quārum ūnam* incolunt *Belgae, aliam* Aquītānī, *tertiam quī ipsōrum* linguā Celtae, *nostrā Gallī* appellantur. *Hī omnēs* linguā, īnstitūtīs, lēgibus *inter sē* differunt.

---

appell•ō, -āre, 1, call, name.

Aquītān•ī, -ōrum, *m.*, the Aquitani *or* Aquitanians (*a people located on the Atlantic coast above the Pyrenees, the mountains that separate the Iberian peninsula from Gaul*).

Celt•ae, -ārum, *m.*, the Celts *or* Kelts, the Celtae.

commentāri•us, -ī, *m.* [**commentor,** consider], notebook, journal; report; commentary.

differō, differre, distulī, dīlātum [**ferō,** carry. App. §81], scatter, spread; put off, defer; be different, differ.

dī•vidō, -videre, dīvīsī, dīvīsum, divide, distribute, separate.

Gallic•us, -a, -um, *adj.* [**Gallia,** Gaul], pertaining to Gaul *or* the Gauls, Gallic.

incol•ō, -ere, -uī, — [**colō,** cultivate], inhabit, dwell in.

īnstitūt•um, -ī, *n.*, established plan *or* principle; custom, institution, habit.

lēx, lēgis, *f.*, law, statute.

lib•er, -rī, *m.*, book, work, treatise.

lingu•a, -ae, *f.*, language, tongue.

---

1. Gallia: Gaul or the territories known today as France and northern Italy. From the Roman perspective, the Alps divided Gaul on "this side (*cis*) of the Alps" from the Gaul that was "across (*trans*) the Alps": *Gallia Cisalpīna* vs. *Gallia Transalpīna*. Another Gaul was the area beyond the Alps, but along the Mediterranean, which the Romans frequently called *Prōvincia* or "the Province." To this day, the French call the area "Provence." Caesar refers in this passage to the part of Gaul not yet under Roman rule.

omnis: "as a whole"; that is, if one looks at the entire territory, one finds three major ethnic groups among which territory has been "distributed."

1–2. partēs . . . incolunt: note the ellipsis (which is to leave out something that can be supplied from context) of the words *pars* and *incolunt* in the rest of the sentence: **quārum** (*partium*) **ūnam** (*partem*) **incolunt Belgae, aliam** (*partem incolunt*) **Aquītānī, tertiam** (*partem incolunt*), etc.

2. quī = *eī quī.*

linguā: abl. of means; see App. §143.

2–4. linguā, īnstitūtīs, lēgibus: abl. of respect or specification; see App. §149. Caesar does not use a conj. in this list. This is common in Latin, and is called ASYNDETON. Feel free to supply an "and" in your translation.

3. nostrā: again, ellipsis, this time of **linguā.**

5 *Gallōs ab* Aquītānīs Garumna *flūmen, ā Belgīs* Matrona *et*
Sēquana dīvidit. *Hōrum omnium* fortissimī *sunt Belgae,*
proptereā *quod ā* cultū *atque* hūmānitāte *prōvinciae longissimē*
absunt, minimē*que ad eōs* mercātōrēs saepe commeant *atque*
ea quae ad effēminandōs animōs *pertinent* important,
10 *proximīque sunt Germānīs, quī* trāns Rhēnum incolunt,
quibuscum continenter *bellum gerunt.*

---

absum, abesse, āfuī, — [**sum,** be. App.
§78], be away, be distant, be lacking.
anim•us, -ī, *m.,* mind; character; spirit,
soul; courage.
Aquītān•ī, -ōrum, *m.,* the Aquitani *or*
Aquitanians (*a people located on the*
Atlantic coast above the Pyrenees, the
mountains that separate the Iberian
peninsula from Gaul).
commeō, 1 [**meō,** go], go back and forth;
with **ad,** resort to, visit.
continenter, *adv.* [**continēns,** continuous],
continually.
cult•us, -ūs, *m.* [**colō,** cultivate], civilization;
lifestyle; dress; religious worship.
dī•vidō, -videre, dīvīsī, dīvīsum, divide,
distribute, separate.
effēminō, 1 [**ex + fēmina,** woman], make
effeminate, weaken.
fort•is, -e, *adj.,* strong, brave.
Garumn•a, -ae, *m.,* the Garumna *or*
Garonne, *a river that formed the boundary*
between Aquitania and Celtic Gaul.

hūmāni•tās, -tātis, *f.* [**hūmānus,** human],
humanity, culture, refinement.
importō, 1 [**in + portō,** carry], carry *or*
bring in, import.
incol•ō, -ere, -uī, — [**colō,** cultivate],
inhabit, dwell in.
Matron•a, -ae, *m.,* the *river* Matrona, *now*
called the Marne.
mercāt•or, -ōris, *m.* [**mercor,** trade],
merchant, trader.
minimē, *adv.* [**minimus,** least], least, very
little; not at all.
proptereā, *adv.* [**propter,** because of], on
this account; **proptereā quod,** because.
saepe, *adv.,* often, frequently.
Sēquan•a, -ae, *m.,* the *river* Sequana, *now*
called the Seine. *It flows across much of*
northern Gaul, and, more famously today,
flows through Paris.
trāns, *prep. with acc.,* across, beyond, over.

---

5. Garumna flūmen: flūmen agrees with
and is in apposition to **Garumna;** see App.
§95, *b.*

5–6. Gallōs . . . dīvidit: Caesar achieves
his terse style in large measure through the
ease with which Latin writers can, thanks
to the clarity of Latin inflection, use ellipsis.
You will need to supply *Gallōs, flūmen,* and
dīvidit where appropriate to make sense of
the grammar.

6. dīvidit: sing., because verb agrees with
each river separately.

Hōrum: partitive gen.; see App. §101.

7. prōvinciae: Caesar appears to argue
that proximity to a sophisticated and refined

lifestyle (**cultū atque hūmānitāte**) makes
men less warlike. The main city in the Province was Massilia (now Marseilles), originally
a Greek colony, and the merchants who operated from this base had much to sell (wine,
for example) that could shift men's thoughts
from war to pleasure. Caesar looks ahead to
his narrative about fighting Germans, whom
he reckons even more warlike than the Gauls.

7–8. quod . . . absunt: for the indicative
mood, as Caesar gives his own reason, see
App. §244.

8. minimē . . . saepe: employing the figure
of speech called LITOTES, Caesar negates "often" with "least," hence "very seldom."

Quā dē causā Helvētiī quoque *reliquōs Gallōs virtūte* praecēdunt,
quod ferē cotīdiānīs *proeliīs cum Germānīs* contendunt, *cum aut
suīs fīnibus eōs* prohibent *aut ipsī in eōrum fīnibus bellum gerunt.*

15 *Eōrum ūna pars, quam Gallōs* obtinēre *dictum est,* initium *capit
ā flūmine Rhodanō, continētur* Garumnā *flūmine,* Ōceanō,

---

con•tendō, -tendere, -tendī, -tentum
[**tendō**, stretch], push forward, hasten;
march; fight; maintain.
cotīdiān•us, -a, -um, *adj.* [**cotīdiē**, daily],
daily; customary.
Garumn•a, -ae, *m.,* the Garumna *or*
Garonne, *a river that formed the boundary
between Aquitania and Celtic Gaul.*
init•ium, -ī, *n.* [**ineō,** go into], beginning,
commencement, origin; edge *of a country,*
borders.

ob•tineō, -tinēre, -tinuī, -tentum [**teneō**,
hold], hold, retain, possess, maintain;
acquire.
Ōcean•us, -ī, *m.,* the ocean.
prae•cēdō, -cēdere, -cessī, -cessum [**cēdō,**
go], go before; surpass, excel.
prohibeō, 2 [**habeō,** hold], keep from,
prevent, prohibit; keep out *or* away from;
guard.
quoque, *conj., following the word
emphasized,* also, too, likewise.

---

12. Quā dē causā: *conjunctio relativa:* the
rel. is used as a conj., and the phrase is thus
equivalent to *et dē eā causā;* see App. §173.

virtūte: abl. of respect or specification.

12–14. Helvētiī ... suīs ... ipsī: the reflex.
suīs refers to the subject, i.e., the Helvetii, and
ipsī, the intensive pron., serves to remind
readers that the Helvetii remain the subject.

13. proeliīs: abl. of means, but "in battles,"
because preps. do not map neatly from language to language. Work to adjust your translation to respect English idioms and rules.

13–14. Germānīs ... eōs ... eōrum: Caesar uses the non-reflex. pron. **eōs** and **eōrum**
to refer to the Germans because they are *not*
the subject.

14. suīs fīnibus: abl. of separation; see
App. §134.

15. Eōrum: poss. gen.; see App. §99.

Eōrum ūna pars: partitive gen. (in reference, presumably, to all the parts belonging to all of the various Gauls previously

mentioned). Most readers find the rest of
this chapter vague; harsh critics have gone
further. A map helps to some extent, but difficulties remain. Some scholars believe that the
rest of this chapter was not actually written by
Caesar, but inserted by someone who thought
we needed more geography, and some texts
even omit the section altogether.

quam ... Gallōs: quam is the direct object
and **Gallōs** is the subject of the inf. **obtinēre;**
see App. §123. The whole phrase in turn is the
subject of the impers. verb **dictum est;** see
App. §266. The syntax is difficult to parse, but
the meaning is clear: "which it has been said
the Gauls possess."

16. ā flūmine: the river forms a boundary
"from which" the writer imagines that the
territory begins, but experiment with other
prep. in English, e.g., "at," "on," "along," "on
the side of," etc. Look at the map: using the
river as your guide, how would you describe
the geography?

finibus Belgārum, attingit *etiam ab* Sēquanīs *et Helvētiīs flūmen Rhēnum,* vergit *ad* septentriōnēs. *Belgae ab* extrēmīs *Galliae finibus* oriuntur, *pertinent ad* īnferiōrem *partem flūminis Rhēnī,* spectant *in* septentriōnem *et* orientem sōlem. Aquītānia *ā* Garumnā *flūmine ad* Pȳrēnaeōs montēs *et eam partem* Ōceanī *quae est ad* Hispāniam *pertinet;* spectat *inter* occāsum sōlis *et* septentriōnēs.

20

Aquītān•ia, -ae, *f.,* Aquitania. *Southwestern Gaul between the Garonne River and the Pyrenees Mountains (which separate the Iberian peninsula from Gaul).*

atting•ō, -ere, attigī, attactum [ad + tangō, touch], touch *or* border on, reach, extend to, arrive at, attain.

extrēm•us, -a, -um, *adj.* [*superl. of* **exterus.** App. §44], outermost, farthest; the farthest part of.

Garumn•a, -ae, *m.,* the Garumna *or* Garonne, *a river that formed the boundary between Aquitania and Celtic Gaul.*

Hispāni•a, -ae, *f.,* Hispania, Spain.

īnfer•us, -a, -um, *adj.,* low, below; *comp.:* **īnferior,** lower, inferior.

mōns, montis, *m.,* mountain; mountain range.

occās•us, -ūs, *m.* [**occidō,** fall, happen], falling down, setting; *with* **sōlis,** sunset; the west.

Ōcean•us, -ī, *m.,* the ocean.

orior, orīrī, ortus sum, arise, begin, spring up; be born, descend; **oriēns sōl,** the rising sun, sunrise; the east.

Pȳrēnae•us, -a, -um, *adj.,* Pyreneian; **Pȳrēnaeī montēs,** the Pyrenaei *or* the Pyrenees Mountains.

septentriōn•ēs, -um, *m.* [**septem,** seven + **triōnēs,** plough oxen], *the seven plough oxen, the stars of the Great Bear (Big Dipper), hence* the North.

Sēquan•us, -a, -um, *adj.,* of *or* belonging to the **Sequani;** *pl. as noun,* **Sēquanī,** the Sequani.

sōl, sōlis, *m.,* the sun; **ad occidentem sōlem,** toward the setting sun *or* west; **ad orientem sōlem,** toward the rising sun *or* east.

spectō, 1 [*frequentative of* **speciō,** see], look at, regard; face.

verg•ō, -ere, —, —, look *or* lie toward, be situated.

---

17. ab Sēquanīs et Helvētiīs: again, the writer conceives of the territory beginning "from" territory that belongs to the Sequani and Helvetii on the other side of the border, but experiments with other preps.

19. ad īnferiōrem . . . Rhēnī: toward the mouth of the Rhine.

20. in septentriōnem et orientem sōlem: northeast.

22–23. inter occāsum sōlis et septentriōnēs: northwest.

Caesar DĒ BELLŌ GALLICŌ 1.2: The Conspiracy of Orgetorix, Leader among the Helvetians

Caesar introduces Orgetorix, a leader among the Helvetians, his conspiracy, and the Helvetians' desire to leave their own territory for new dwelling places. Caesar will eventually decide that they must be stopped, enter Gallic territory, and thus begin a war that will take another eight years to complete. Caesar likely did not expect the war to last so long. His command was initially for only five years, and he later had to negotiate for more time to finish the job. But Caesar does not explain any of this at the beginning. His focus is instead on one people at a specific time at the beginning of his governorship, and his actions on behalf of Rome in reference to this event. He writes as if he allows us to read his report to the Senate. The focus of the narrative is quite narrow, and does not take up the issue of a larger war. The larger war will instead be presented as flowing quite naturally in a chain of events from this first event. Caesar's narrative presents Caesar as someone who reacts effectively to events in the moment, as opposed to someone who shapes his reaction to smaller events for a larger strategic purpose. In this way, Caesar avoids the larger and much more important issue: his motivation and justification for the conquest of Gaul.

Lake Geneva , called *Lacus Lemannus* in Caesar's day, and the surrounding mountains proved a formidable challenge for the Helvetians in their quest to move westward.

[1.2] *Apud Helvētiōs longē* nōbilissimus *fuit et* dītissimus
Orgetorīx. Is Marcō Messālā, *et* Marcō Pūpiō Pīsōne cōnsulibus
rēgnī cupiditāte inductus coniūrātiōnem nōbilitātis *fēcit et*
cīvitātī persuāsit ut dē fīnibus suīs cum omnibus cōpiīs exīrent:

5　　perfacile *esse, cum virtūte omnibus* praestārent, *tōtīus Galliae*
imperiō potīrī.

---

coniūrāti•ō, -ōnis, *f.* [**coniūrō**, swear], a
swearing together; plot, conspiracy.
cōn•sul, -sulis, *m.*, consul, *one of the two*
chief magistrates elected annually at Rome.
cupidi•tās, -tātis, *f.* [**cupidus**, eager],
eagerness, desire, greed.
dīves, dīvitis, *adj.*, rich, wealthy. *Superl.*:
dītissimus.
ex•eō, -īre, -iī, ītum [**eō**, go. App. §84], go
from, leave.
imper•ium, -ī, *n.* [**imperō**, order], right
to command; authority; jurisdiction;
supreme military command.
in•dūcō, -dūcere, -dūxī, -ductum [**dūcō,**
lead], lead *or* draw on; induce; influence,
instigate; cover.
Marc•us, -ī, *m.*; **Messāl•a, -ae,** *m.*, Marcus
Valerius Messala, *consul in 61* BCE.

Marc•us, -ī, *m.*; **Pīs•ō, -ōnis,** *m.*, Marcus
Pupius Piso Calpurnianus, *consul with*
Messala in 61 BCE.
nōbil•is, -e, *adj.* [**nōscō**, know], well-
known, distinguished; of noble birth.
nōbili•tās, -tātis, *f.* [**nōbilis**, well-known],
fame; noble birth, rank; the nobility.
perfacil•is, -e, *adj.* [**facilis**, easy], very easy.
potior, 4 [**potis**, powerful], become master
of, get control *or* possession of, obtain,
capture.
prae•stō, -stāre, -stitī, -stātum [**stō**, stand],
stand *or* place before; show, exhibit,
supply; be superior, excel, surpass.
Pūpi•us, -ī, *m., see* **Pīsō.**

---

1. nōbilissimus: predicate nom.; see App.
§§156–157.
2. Messālā et . . . Pīsōne cōnsulibus: abl.
absolute; see App. §150. Consuls served for
just one year, so their names were used to
identify the year in which events occurred.
This conspiracy, thus dated to 61 BCE, began
three years before Caesar arrived in Gaul.
3. rēgnī: objective gen.; see App. §98.
Gauls did not have kings, so Orgetorix aims
at leadership and power.
coniūrātiōnem: according to Caesar (but
how did he know?), Orgetorix aims to convince the Helvetians to emigrate with himself
as their leader.
4. cīvitātī: dat. indirect object with an intransitive verb; see App. §115.
ut . . . exīrent: subjunctive in a substantive
clause of purpose (or indirect command); see
App. §228, *a.* This is an example of SYNESIS
(breaking strict grammatical rules for the

sake of sense), as Caesar follows the sing. state
(or tribe) with a pl. verb that must refer to the
people in that state; see App. §301, *h.*
omnibus cōpiīs: this means everybody,
the entire population: men, women, children.
5. cum . . . praestārent: "since they were
superior in manliness"; subjunctive in a causal clause; see App. §239.
virtūte: abl. of respect or of specification;
see App. §149.
omnibus: dat. with compound verb; see
App. §116, I.
tōtīus Galliae: in other words, ironically
enough, Orgetorix wanted to do what Caesar
eventually did: conquer all of Gaul.
5–6. perfacile esse . . . potīrī: indirect
statement dependent on **persuāsit**; see App.
§266.
6. imperiō: abl. with a special deponent
verb; see App. §145.

Id hōc facilius eīs persuāsit, quod undique *locī* nātūrā *Helvētiī*
continentur: ūnā ex parte flūmine Rhēnō lātissimō *atque*
altissimō, *quī agrum Helvētium ā Germānīs* dīvidit; *alterā ex*
10   *parte* monte Iūrā altissimō, *quī est inter* Sēquanōs *et Helvētiōs;*
tertiā lacū Lemannō *et flūmine Rhodanō, quī prōvinciam*
nostram ab Helvētiīs dīvidit.

---

alt•us, -a, -um, *adj.*, high, deep.
dī•vidō, -videre, dīvīsī, dīvīsum, divide,
   distribute, separate.
Iūr•a, -ae, *m.*,the Jura *mountains which*
   stretched from the Rhine to the Rhone,
   separating the Helvetians from the Sequani.
lac•us, -ūs, *m.*, lake.
lāt•us, -a, -um, *adj.*, wide, broad, extensive.
Lemann•us, -ī (*often with* **lacus**), *m.*, Lake
   Lemannus, Lake Leman, *or* Lake Geneva.

mōns, montis, *m.*, mountain; mountain
   range.
nātūr•a, -ae, *f.* [**nāscor**, be born], nature;
   character.
Sēquan•us, -a, -um, *adj.*, of *or* belonging
   to the Sequani; *pl. as noun*, **Sēquanī,** the
   Sequani.
undique, *adv.* [**unde**, whence], on all sides,
   everywhere.

---

7. Id: i.e., his plan of action.
hōc: abl. of cause; see App. §138.
locī: gen. of possession; see App. §99.
nātūrā: abl. of means; see App. §143.

7–8. quod . . . continentur: the Helvetii felt
boxed in, and, because Caesar himself provides
this analysis, he uses the indicative mood in a
causal clause to let readers know that he is not
merely reporting someone else's analysis; see
App. §244.

   8–11. ūnā ex parte . . . flūmine Rhodanō:
another geography lesson; Caesar describes
territory that corresponds roughly to territory today occupied by Switzerland.

9. ā Germānīs: abl. of separation; see App.
§134.
9–10. alterā ex parte: "on the second side."
   11. tertiā: ellipsis of *ex parte*; "on the third
side."
   11–12. prōvinciam nostram: Roman territory is just across the border. Is the conspiracy
a danger to Rome? Later in Book One, Caesar
will argue that the Germans would occupy
Helvetian territory, if it were left empty, and
Germans, as we learned at the beginning, were
more warlike than Gauls. Readers are left to
draw their own conclusions, but Caesar's prose
guides their thoughts.

Hīs rēbus fīēbat ut et minus lātē vagārentur *et minus facile*
fīnitimīs *bellum* īnferre *possent; quā ex parte hominēs* bellandī
15   cupidī *magnō* dolōre adficiēbantur. *Prō multitūdine autem*
hominum et prō glōriā *bellī atque* fortitūdinis angustōs *sē fīnēs*
habēre arbitrābantur, quī in longitūdinem *mīlia passuum*
CCXL, *in* lātitūdinem CLXXX patēbant.

---

ad•ficiō, -ficere, -fēcī, -fectum [ad +
   faciō, do], affect, inspire; **magnō dolōre**
   afficere, to annoy greatly.
angust•us, -a, -um, *adj.* [**angō,** squeeze],
   compressed, narrow.
bellō, 1, wage war.
CCXL, *sign for* **ducentī et quadrāgintā,**
   two hundred forty (*see also* App. §47).
CLXXX, *sign for* **centum et octōgintā,** one
   hundred eighty (*see also* App. §47).
cupid•us, -a, -um, *adj.* [**cupiō,** desire],
   eager, desirous.
dol•or, -ōris, *m.* [**doleō,** grieve], grief,
   distress, pain, anguish.
fīnitim•us, -a, -um, *adj.* [**fīnis,** limit],
   bordering on, neighboring.

fortitūd•ō, -inis, *f.* [**fortis,** brave], bravery,
   courage.
glōri•a, -ae, *f.,* glory, reputation.
īn•ferō, īnferre, intulī, illātum [**ferō,**
   carry. App. §81], carry into, import,
   inflict, cause, produce; cast into.
lātē, *adv.* [**lātus,** wide], widely, extensively.
lātitūd•ō, -inis, *f.* [**lātus,** wide], width,
   extent, breadth.
longitūd•ō, -inis, *f.* [**longus,** long], length,
   extent; long duration.
pate•ō, -ēre, -uī, —, lie *or* be open, be
   passable; extend.
vagor, 1 [**vagus,** roaming], roam around,
   wander.

---

13. Hīs ... fīēbat: "as a result of these fac-
tors"; *lit.* "by means of these things it (*note the*
impers. construction) happened that."

   ut ... vagārentur: subjunctive in a substantive clause of result; see App. §229, *b.*

   14. quā ex parte: "and for this reason"; *con-*
junctio relativa: the rel. is used as a conj., and
the phrase is thus equivalent to *et dē eā parte;*
see App. §173, *a.*

   bellandī: gerund used with the objective
gen.; see App. §§ 287, 291.

   14–15. hominēs ... cupidī: "as people
(**hominēs,** not *virī*) eager for waging war."
Caesar will eventually attack all the Helvetians, not just the men.

   16. angustōs ... fīnēs: "narrow boundaries" = "too small a territory."

   sē: acc. subject of the inf. **habēre;** see App.
§123.

   fīnēs: acc. object of the inf. **habēre;** see
App. §124.

   17. arbitrābantur: How does Caesar know
all this? Caesar tells the story from his own
point of view and for his own purposes, but
he would have had reports from Gallic spies,
traders, defectors, and, after his victory,
prisoners.

   mīlia: acc. of extent of space; see App.
§130.

Caesar DĒ BELLŌ GALLICŌ 1.3: Orgetorix Puts his Plan into Action

Orgetorix is persuasive. The Helvetians decide to emigrate. Caesar calls Orgetorix a conspirator, yet the kinds of things he does (send delegations to negotiate alliances, use his near relations in marriage alliances) are precisely the kinds of things Caesar and other Roman politicians did too. On the other hand, Roman leaders considered themselves superior both to their fellow citizens and certainly to foreigners. Rules and standards of judgment were different for different classes and peoples. What was good for Caesar was not necessarily acceptable conduct for foreigners.

Switzerland's pride in its Helvetian heritage is evident in both its coinage and its stamps on which HELVETIA serves as the nation's identification. The twenty-franc coin shows the personification of Helvetia with the Alps in the background. The stamp celebrates the 2,000th anniversary of Vindonissa. It displays the face of a Roman brick imprinted with the head of Gaul, the sign of Legion X, Caesar's favorite legion.

[1.3] *Hīs rēbus* adductī *et* auctōritāte *Orgetorīgis* permōtī
cōnstituērunt ea quae ad proficīscendum pertinērent comparāre,
iūmentōrum *et* carrōrum *quam maximum numerum* coemere,
sēmentēs *quam maximās facere, ut in itinere cōpia frūmentī*
5   suppeteret, *cum proximīs cīvitātibus* pācem *et* amīcitiam
cōnfirmāre.

---

ad•dūcō, -dūcere, -dūxī, -ductum [**dūcō,**
lead], lead to; induce, influence.
amīciti•a, -ae, *f.* [**amīcus,** friend], friendship.
auctōri•tās, -tātis, *f.* [**auctor,** producer],
influence, authority.
carr•us, -ī, *m.,* cart, wagon.
co•emō, -emere, -ēmī, -ēmptum [**emō,**
buy], buy, buy up.
comparō, 1 [**parō,** prepare], prepare;
acquire, prepare for.
cōnfirmō, 1 [**firmō,** strengthen], establish,
strengthen, encourage, console; declare.

iūment•um, -ī, *n.* [**iungō,** join, yoke], yoke
or pack animal.
pāx, pācis, *f.,* peace treaty, truce, peace,
favor.
per•moveō, -movēre, -mōvī, -mōtum
[**moveō,** move], move thoroughly; incite;
influence.
sēment•is, -is, *f.* [**sēmen,** seed], sowing.
sup•petō, -petere, -petīvī, -petītum [**sub**
+ **petō,** seek, obtain], be near; be in store,
be supplied.

---

2. ad proficīscendum: gerund with **ad** to
express purpose; see App. §§287, 293.

cōnstituērunt: the main verb whose
meaning is completed by the many (complementary) infs. that appear in this sentence.

3. iūmentōrum: partitive gen.; see App.
§101.

quam maximum numerum: "as large a
number as possible"; "as many... as possible."

4–5. ut . . . suppeteret: subjunctive in a
clause of purpose; see App. §225, *a,* 3.

5. cum . . . cīvitātibus: abl. of accompaniment; see App. §140.

5–6. pācem et amīcitiam cōnfirmāre:
The Helvetii, who plan to move with their
entire families, appear to wish to make their
move peacefully. Caesar, by branding their
plans a "conspiracy" and by portraying them
as warlike by nature, makes these efforts appear ominous.

> *Ad eās rēs* cōnficiendās biennium *sibi* satis *esse dūxērunt; in*
> *tertium annum* profectiōnem lēge cōnfirmant. *Ad eās rēs*
> cōnficiendās *Orgetorīx* dēligitur. *Is sibi* lēgātiōnem *ad cīvitātēs*
> 10   suscēpit. *In eō itinere persuādet* Casticō, Catamantaloedis fīliō,
> Sēquanō, *cuius* pater *rēgnum in* Sēquanīs *multōs annōs*

---

bienn•ium, -ī, *n.* [**bis,** twice + **annus,** year], two years.
Castic•us, -ī, *m.,* Casticus, *an important man among the Sequani.*
Catamantaloed•is, -is, *m.,* Catamantaloedis, *a leader among the Sequani before Caesar's day.*
cōn•ficiō, -ficere, -fēcī, -fectum [**faciō,** make], make *or* do thoroughly, complete, finish.
cōnfirmō, 1 [**firmō,** strengthen], establish, strengthen, encourage, console; declare.
dē•ligō, -ligere, -lēgī, -lēctum [**legō,** choose], pick out, choose.

fīl•ius, -ī, *m.,* son.
lēgāti•ō, -ōnis, *f.* [**lēgō,** delegate], embassy; commission.
lēx, lēgis, *f.,* law, statute.
pat•er, -ris, *m.,* father.
profecti•ō, -ōnis, *f.* [**proficīscor,** set out], a setting out; start, departure.
satis, *adv., and indecl. adj. and noun, as adj.,* sufficient.
Sēquan•us, -a, -um, *adj.,* of *or* belonging to the Sequani; *pl. as noun,* **Sēquanī,** the Sequani.
sus•cipiō, -cipere, -cēpī, -ceptum [**su(b)s** + **capiō,** take], take up; undertake; begin.

---

7. Ad ... rēs cōnficiendās: gerundive with **ad** to express purpose (compare **ad proficīscendum** in the previous sentence); see App. §§288, 293. The prep. **ad** governs **rēs,** which is modified by the verbal adj. or gerundive **cōnficiendās.** Translating literally, however, which would give us "for the purpose of these things necessary to be completed," yields a phrase that cannot be considered English, and makes little (if any) sense. For this reason, we generally translate the pass. verbal adj. (or gerundive) as if it were an active verbal noun (gerund) that takes as its object the noun that it actually modifies as an adjective with pass. meaning, i.e., "for the purpose of completing these things." Confused? The problem is in English. The Latin is perfectly clear!
biennium: 60–59 BCE.
sibi: dat. with **satis esse;** see App. §116, II.
dūxērunt: "they considered." This is a common meaning of **dūcō.** As a verb of thinking, it introduces indirect statement.

8. tertium annum: 58 BCE, and, bad luck for them, the year Caesar arrived just across the border as governor.
lēge: the Helvetii pass a law in public assembly. Their plans are methodical and public, and they have entered into peace treaties with neighboring peoples.
cōnfirmant: historical pres. (a rhetorical device that makes readers witnesses to the events described by the author); see App. §190, a.
9–10. sibi ... suscēpit: dat. with compound verb; see App. §116, I.
10. Casticō: dat. indirect object with special verb; see App. §115.
11. Sēquanō: dat. in apposition with **fīliō;** see App. §95, b.
annōs: acc. of extent of time; see App. §130.

obtinuerat *et ā* senātū *populī Rōmānī* amīcus appellātus *erat,*
ut rēgnum in cīvitāte suā occupāret, *quod* pater *ante habuerat;*
item*que* Dumnorīgī Aeduō, frātrī Dīviciācī, *quī eō tempore*
15   prīncipātum *in cīvitāte* obtinēbat *ac* maximē plēbī *acceptus*
erat, ut idem cōnārētur *persuādet eīque* fīliam *suam in*
mātrimōnium *dat.*

Aedu•us, -a, -um, *adj.,* of the Aedui; *as a*
  noun: an Aeduan; *pl. as a noun:* the Aedui.
amīc•us, -ī, *m.* [amō, love], friend.
appellō, -āre, 1, call, name.
cōnor, 1, try, attempt.
Dīviciāc•us, -ī, *m.,* Diviciacus, *a leader of*
  the Aedui, friendly to the Romans. Caesar
  pardons Dumnorix at his request.
Dumnor•ix, -īgis, *m.,* Dumnorix, *a leader*
  of the Aeduans, brother of Diviciacus,
  son-in-law of Orgetorix, enemy of Caesar,
  and leader of the anti-Roman party. Caesar
  orders his execution in 54 BCE when he tries
  to escape.
fīli•a, -ae, *f.,* daughter.
frāt•er, -ris, *m.,* brother.

item, *adv.,* in like manner, so, also, just so.
magis, *adv. comp.* [from **magnus,** large],
  more, rather; *superl.:* **maximē,** especially.
mātrimōn•ium, -ī, *n.* [māter, mother],
  marriage.
ob•tineō, -tinēre, -tinuī, -tentum [teneō,
  hold], hold, retain, possess, maintain.
occupō, 1 [ob + capiō, take], take
  possession of, seize; engage.
pat•er, -ris, *m.,* father.
plēbs, plēbis, *or* **plēbēs, plēbēī,** *f.,*
  populace, common people.
prīncipāt•us, -ūs, *m.* [prīnceps, chief],
  chief place; chief authority, leadership.
senāt•us, -ūs, *m.* [senex, old], *a body of old*
  men, senate; especially, the Roman Senate.

---

12. senātū: abl. of agent; see App. §137.

amīcus: an honorary and formal title
conferred by the Roman Senate. Remember,
though, that in the world of Roman politics,
less powerful friends were expected to show
deference to more powerful friends.

13. rēgnum: "absolute authority in the
state." In other words, the envoys aim to convince leaders sympathetic with Orgetorix's
plan to take over the government in their tribes.
This would not mean establishing formal king-
ships, but somehow dominating the machinery of government. For an example of how this
worked at Rome, you may compare the alliance
of Caesar, Crassus, and Pompey (the so-called
first triumvirate). They did not become kings,
but they were powerful enough to control government policy through their "friendship."

ut . . . occupāret: subjunctive in a substantive clause of purpose (or indirect command); see App. §228, *a.*

14. Aeduō: The Aedui were rivals of the
Sequani.

quī = Dumnorix.

tempore: abl. of time when; see App. §152.

15. prīncipātum: "first place in leadership," but not a formal post.

plēbī: dat. with the adj. **acceptus;** see App.
§122. Would-be tyrants often turned to the
common people when they wished to take
power from fellow aristocrats.

16. ut idem cōnārētur: i.e., that he too
should aim at **rēgnum.**

eī: dat. indirect object with transitive verb;
see App. §114.

16–17. fīliam . . . dat: marriage was a part
of politics. Caesar similarly made his alliance
with Pompey much more secure when, in 59
BCE (the year of his consulship), Caesar gave
Pompey his daughter Julia in marriage. The
histories that survive tell us primarily about
the political activities of men. They are much
less talkative about the crucial roles that
women played in the private sphere.

Perfacile *factū esse illīs* probat cōnāta perficere, proptereā *quod*
ipse suae cīvitātis imperium obtentūrus *esset*: *nōn esse* dubium
20   quīn *tōtīus Galliae plūrimum Helvētiī possent; sē suīs cōpiīs*
suōque exercitū illīs rēgna conciliātūrum cōnfirmat.

---

conciliō, 1 [concilium, assembly], bring
together; gain *or* win over, secure.
cōnfirmō, 1 [firmō, strengthen], establish,
strengthen, encourage, console; declare.
cōnor, 1, try, attempt.
dubi·us, -a, -um, *adj.*, uncertain, doubtful.
imper·ium, -ī, *n.* [imperō, order], right
to command; authority; jurisdiction;
supreme military command, highest
official power.
ob·tineō, -tinēre, -tinuī, -tentum [teneō,
hold], hold, retain, possess, maintain;
acquire.

perfacil·is, -e, *adj.* [facilis, easy], very easy.
per·ficiō, -ficere, -fēcī, -fectum [faciō,
make, do], finish; build; accomplish.
probō, 1 [probus, good], approve;
demonstrate.
proptereā, *adv.* [propter, because of], on
this account; proptereā quod, because.
quīn, *conj.* [quī, who *or* how + ne, negative],
that not, but that; *after negative words of*
doubt or hindrance, but that, that.

---

18. Perfacile factū ... perficere: Caesar
deploys ASSONANCE and ALLITERATION to
suggest a rhetorical argument.

factū: supine; "very easy to do."

18–19. proptereā quod ... obtentūrus
esset: a causal clause: "inasmuch as he was
going to take over supreme authority in his
own state." The mood is subjunctive because
the clause is subordinate in indirect statement; see App. §269. Note also the sequence
of tenses. Although **probat** is pres. in form,
it is an historical pres., and thus introduces
secondary (or past tense) sequence.

19–20. nōn ... quīn: indirect statement
after **probat.** "He proved to them that there
was no doubt that...."

20–21. sē ... illīs ... conciliātūrum:
supply *esse*, which is routinely omitted from
fut. inf.

21. illīs = Casticus and Dumnorix.

exercitū: armies were often used by those
who aimed to take over governments to
achieve *rēgnum* or absolute authority. When
Caesar was still very young, Sulla had marched
his army on Rome, and Caesar would himself,
in 49 BCE, use his legions against the Senate.

Hāc ōrātiōne adductī *inter sē* fidem *et* iūs iūrandum *dant et regnō* occupātō *per trēs* potentissimōs *ac* firmissimōs *populōs totīus Galliae sēsē* potīrī *posse* spērant.

---

ad•dūcō, -dūcere, -dūxī, -ductum [**dūcō,** lead], lead to; induce, influence.

fid•ēs, -eī, *f.,* [**fīdō,** confide], faith; trustworthiness; allegiance, protection; pledge.

firm•us, -a, -um, *adj.,* strong, stable, vigorous.

iūs iūrandum, iūris iūrandī, *n.* [**iūs,** right + **iūrō,** swear], an oath.

occupō, 1 [**ob** + **capiō,** take], take possession of, seize; engage.

ōrāti•ō, -ōnis, *f.* [**ōrō,** speak], speech, argument.

pot•ēns, -entis, *adj.* [*pres. part. of* **possum,** be able], powerful, influential.

potior, 4 [**potis,** powerful], become master of, get control *or* possession of, obtain, capture.

spērō, 1 [**spēs,** hope], hope, hope for, anticipate.

---

22. Hāc ōrātiōne: abl. of means.

inter sē: "among themselves" = "to one another."

iūs iūrandum: "oath." Oaths were especially sacred in the ancient world, as sharp-eyed sky-gods hated perjurers. Secret oaths were a hallmark of conspiracy.

23. regnō occupātō: "after they had seized control"; abl. absolute; see App. §150.

per trēs . . . populōs = the Helvetii, the Sequani, and the Aedui.

24. totīus Galliae: gen. with **potīrī;** see App. §111.

Caesar Dē Bellō Gallicō 1.4:
Downfall and Death of Orgetorix

Although the Helvetii had publicly approved Orgetorix's plan by passing legislation, his conspiracy to take control of the state was apparently less pleasing. "An informer" brings the conspiracy to light. Orgetorix is put on trial. Orgetorix disappears under mysterious circumstances. Was it suicide? Caesar implies that the Helvetii liked Orgetorix's ideas, but did not wish to submit to Orgetorix's domination of the state.

Nineteenth-century France saw a strong interest in the country's Gallic and Roman heritage. This interest spurred a series of illustrations such as this group of Gallic Warriors by Emile Wattier and published in Magasin Pittoresque.

[1.4] *Ea rēs est Helvētiīs per* indicium ēnūntiāta. Mōribus *suīs Orgetorīgem ex* vinculīs *causam dīcere coēgērunt*; damnātum poenam sequī oportēbat, *ut* ignī cremārētur.

---

cremō, 1, burn.
damnō, 1 [**damnum,** damage], declare guilty, sentence, condemn.
ē•nūntiō, 1 [**nūntiō,** announce], report, declare, disclose.
ign•is, -is, *m.,* fire.
indic•ium, -ī, *n.,* [**indicō,** disclose], disclosure, information; **per indicium,** through informers.

mōs, mōris, *m.,* manner, custom, practice; *pl.*: customs, habits.
oport•et, -ēre, -uit, —, *impers.,* it is necessary.
poen•a, -ae, *f.,* punishment, penalty.
sequor, sequī, secūtus sum, follow; accompany; *with* **poena,** be inflicted.
vincul•a, -ae, *f.* [**vinciō,** bind], chain.

---

1. Ea rēs: the plot, the conspiracy, "this affair."

Helvētiīs: dat. with a pass. verb; see App. §114, *c.*

per indicium: "by an informer," but, literally, "through information (provided by an informer)."

Mōribus: abl. of accordance; see App. §142, *a.* Caesar frequently reports on foreign customs. Such reports are interesting, but would presumably also help Roman readers imagine Caesar's opponents as non-Roman.

2. ex vinculīs: "in chains," because preps. do not map well from language to language, and "out of" chains would not be English.

damnātum: equivalent to "if condemned"; see App. §283.

3. ut . . . cremārētur: in apposition with **poenam** to explain the result of a condemnation (the idea of result also explains the subjunctive mood). In Caesar's day, Romans did not execute people by burning them alive. Caesar provides another example of his opponents' savagery.

> *Diē cōnstitūtā causae* dictiōnis *Orgetorīx ad* iūdicium *omnem*
> 5   *suam* familiam, *ad hominum mīlia* decem, undique *coēgit, et*
> *omnēs* clientēs obaerātōs*que suōs, quōrum magnum numerum*
> *habēbat, eōdem* condūxit; *per eōs nē causam dīceret sē* ēripuit.

---

cliēns, clientis, *m., f.* [**clueō,** hear, obey],
    client, vassal, dependent, retainer.
con•dūcō, -dūcere, -dūxī, -ductum [**dūcō,**
    lead], lead *or* bring together, assemble,
    conduct; hire.
decem (X), *indecl. card. num.,* ten.
dicti•ō, -ōnis, *f.* [**dīcō,** say], speaking,
    pleading.
ē•ripiō, -ripere, -ripuī, -reptum [**rapiō,**
    seize], take away; rescue.

famili•a, -ae, *f.,* household (*including*
    slaves); retinue (*including all dependents*);
    family.
iūdic•ium, -ī, *n.* [**iūdex,** judge], trial;
    opinion.
obaerāt•us, -a, -um, *adj.* [**aes,** money], in
    debt; *as a noun:* debtor.
undique, *adv.* [**unde,** whence], on all sides,
    everywhere.

---

4. Diē ... dictiōnis: "on the day set for trying (pleading) the case."
    causae: objective gen.; see App. §98.
    5. familiam: the whole household, in-
cluding men, women, children, both slaves
and the free. The task of such "families" was
generally to weep, wail, and show support for
the accused in an effort to win the sympathy
of jurors and judges.
    ad: "toward (the number of)," hence "about."
    6. clientēs: less powerful men who de-
pended on a great man for protection and
patronage. In return for previous favors, the
great man would rely on his clients' gratitude
to ensure they did his bidding when he called
on them to support him. Political life worked
this way in Rome too. Favors were not free,
and those who accepted the most favors (like

those who borrowed the most money) were
the most dependent and least free.
    obaerātōs: those monetarily indebted to
Orgetorix, who had thus become his slaves.
    7. per eōs: "with their help." The prep.
per is routinely used to express the people
"through," "with," or "by" whose assistance
another decision-making agent accomplishes
some task. They may perform the action of the
verb, but they follow directions. When the
people who accomplish the task also make
their own decisions, the correct prep. is *ab*,
which is the prep. used to express personal
agency. In this instance, the multitudes acted
on behalf of Orgetorix, who directed their actions. He worked "through" them.
    nē ... dīceret: subjunctive in a clause of
(negative) purpose; see App. §225, b.

Cum cīvitās ob *eam rem* incitāta *armīs* iūs *suum* exsequī
cōnārētur *multitūdinemque hominum ex agrīs* magistrātūs
10   *cōgerent, Orgetorīx* mortuus *est; neque* abest suspīciō, *ut Helvētiī*
arbitrantur, quīn *ipse sibi mortem* cōnscīverit.

---

absum, abesse, āfuī, — [**sum,** be. App.
    §78], be away, be lacking *or* free from.
cōnor, 1, try, attempt.
cōn•scīscō, -scīscere, -scīvī, -scītum
    [**scīscō,** resolve], resolve upon; **sibi**
    mortem conscīscere, commit suicide.
ex•sequor, -sequī, -secūtus sum [**sequor,**
    follow], follow out, enforce.
incitō, 1 [**citō,** put in motion], set in
    motion; excite, urge on; exasperate.
iūs, iūris, *n.,* human law; power, authority.
    Compare: **fās,** divine law.

magistrāt•us, -ūs, *m.* [**magister,** master],
    public office, magistracy; public official,
    magistrate.
morior, morī, mortuus sum [**mors,** death],
    die.
ob, *prep. with acc.,* on account of, for.
quīn, *conj.* [**quī,** who *or* how + **ne,** negative],
    that not, but that; *after negative words of*
    doubt or hindrance, but that, that, from;
    to.
suspīci•ō, -ōnis, *f.* [**suspicor,** suspect],
    suspicion, distrust; surmise.

8–10. Cum ... cōnārētur ... -que ...
cōgerent: "while the state was attempting
... and the magistrates were rounding up."
Subjunctive in a temporal clause; see App.
§§240, 242, *a.*
    10. ut: with the indicative, **ut** generally
means "as" or "when."

10–11. neque abest . . . quīn . . .
cōnscīverit: "nor was the suspicion lacking
... but that he contrived death for himself,"
i.e., "they suspected . . . that he committed
suicide."

Caesar DĒ BELLŌ GALLICŌ 1.5:
The Helvetii Attempt to Move West

Although the original author of the plan has died, the Helvetii still attempt to put his plan into effect. They burn villages, farms, food, possessions—everything that they cannot bring with them. And they persuade many of their near neighbors to do the same thing. From Caesar's perspective, this mass migration represents a threat to his province. Crowds can be volatile, and this crowd included thousands upon thousands of warlike men.

Václav Hollar, a native of Bohemia, spent much of his adult life in England where he served in the court of the Earl of Arundel. A prolific illustrator, Hollar's corpus includes over 2,700 etchings covering subjects from everyday life to illustrations for Homer and Vergil's poems. In this etching, Hollar recreates a set of Roman legionary standards.

[1.5] Post *eius mortem* nihilō *minus Helvētiī id quod cōnstituerant facere* cōnantur, *ut ē finibus suīs* exeant. Ubi iam *sē ad eam rem* parātōs *esse arbitrātī sunt,* oppida *sua omnia, numerō ad* duodecim, vīcōs *ad* quadringentōs, *reliqua* prīvāta aedificia

5   incendunt; *frūmentum omne,* praeterquam *quod sēcum* portātūrī *erant,* combūrunt,

---

aedifi•cium, -cī, *n.* [**aedificiō,** build], building, house.

comb•ūrō, -ūrere, -ussī, -ustum [con + ūrō, burn], burn up.

cōnor, 1, try, attempt.

duodecim, *card. num. and adj.* [**duo,** two + **decem,** ten], twelve.

ex•eō, -īre, -iī, -ītum [eō, go. App. §84], go from, leave.

iam, *adv.,* now; **ubi iam,** as soon as.

in•cendō, -cendere, -cendī, -cēnsum, set fire to, burn; inflame, excite.

nihilō, *adv.,* by no means; **nihilō minus,** nevertheless.

oppid•um, -ī, *n.,* fortified town, town.

parō, 1, prepare; acquire.

portō, 1, carry, transport, bring, take.

post, *prep. with acc.,* behind, after.

praeterquam, *adv.,* besides, except.

prīvāt•us, -a, -um, *adj.,* private.

quadringent•ī, -ae, -a, *card. num. adj.,* four hundred.

ubi, *adv.* when.

vīc•us, -ī, *m.,* village, hamlet.

---

1. nihilō: used adverbially, but more properly an abl. of degree of difference; see App. §148.

2. cōnantur: historical pres.; see App. §190, *a.*

ut . . . exeant: "that is, to depart . . . "; a substantive clause of purpose in apposition with **id.**

ad eam rem: "for this undertaking."

3. numerō: abl. of respect or specification; see App. §149.

ad: "about," "around," "approximately."

3–4. oppida . . . vīcōs . . . aedificia: another example of ASYNDETON (which is quite common in Latin). The Helvetii do not plan on returning. Are these the actions of a people bent on the conquest of all Gaul? And, as Caesar will later point out, the Germans were ready to move in, which may well have been the real reason the Helvetii were so bent on finding a new place to live in western Gaul. In fact, it has even been argued that the Helvetii were on the march to help the Aedui, the very people whom Caesar (as a justification to continue his intervention in Gaul) claims that he defends against Ariovistus and the Germans.

5. sēcum = *cum* + *sē*; see App. §52, *a.*

> *ut* domum reditiōnis *spē* sublātā parātiōrēs *ad*
> *omnia perīcula* subeunda *essent; trium* mēnsum molita cibāria
> *sibi quemque* domō efferre *iubent.* Persuādent Rauracīs *et*
> Tulingīs *et* Latobrīgīs fīnitimīs, *utī eōdem ūsī cōnsiliō* oppidīs
> 10   *suīs vīcīsque* exustīs *ūnā cum eīs proficīscantur,* Bōiōsque, *quī*
> trāns *Rhēnum* incoluerant *et in agrum* Nōricum trānsierant
> Nōrēiam*que* oppugnārant, *receptōs ad sē* sociōs *sibi* adscīscunt.

---

ad•scīscō, -scīscere, -scīvī, -scītum [ad + scīscō, approve], receive (*as allies*).

Bōi•ī, -ōrum, *m.,* the Boii, *a Celtic tribe in southern Germany and Cisalpine Gaul.*

cibāri•us, -a, -um, *adj.* [**cibus,** food], pertaining to food; **molita cibāria,** flour.

dom•us, -ūs (App. §29, *d.*), *f.,* house; home; native country.

efferō, efferre, extulī, ēlātum [ex + ferō, carry. App. §81], carry out *or* away.

ex•ūrō, -ūrere, -ussī, -ustum [con + ūrō, burn], burn up.

fīnitim•us, -a, -um, *adj.* [**fīnis,** limit], bordering on, neighboring.

incol•ō, -ere, -uī, — [colō, cultivate], inhabit, dwell in.

Latobrīg•ī, -ōrum, *m.,* the Latobrigi, *a Gallic tribe east of the Rhine.*

mēns•is, -is, *m.,* month.

mol•ō, -ere, -uī, -itum, grind.

Nōrēi•a, -ae, *f.,* Noreia, *a town in Noricum.*

Nōric•us, -a, -um, *adj.* pertaining to Noricum (*between the Danube and Alps*).

oppid•um, -ī, *n.,* fortified town, town.

oppugnō, 1 [**ob** + **pugnō,** fight], fight against, attack, besiege.

parō, 1, prepare; acquire.

Raurac•ī, -ōrum, *m.,* the Rauraci, *a people along the upper Rhine, north of the Helvetians.*

rediti•ō, -ōnis, *f.* [**redeō,** return], return.

soc•ius, -ī, *m.* [*compare* **sequor,** follow], companion, ally.

sub•eō, -īre, -iī, -itum [eō, go. App. §84], endure.

tollō, tollere, sustulī, sublātum, lift up; take on board; remove; destroy; elate.

trāns, *prep. with acc.,* across, beyond, over.

trāns•eō, -īre, -iī, -itum [eō, go. App. §84], cross; march through; migrate.

Tuling•ī, -ōrum, *m.,* the Tulingi, *a Gallic tribe east of the Rhine.*

vīc•us, -ī, *m.,* village, hamlet.

---

6. domum reditiōnis spē: "hope of returning home."

domum: acc. of place to which without prep.; see App. §131.

spē sublātā: abl. absolute.

6–7. ut ... essent: subjunctive in a rel. clause of purpose.

ad ... perīcula subeunda: gerundive with **ad** to express purpose; see App. §§288, 293.

7. trium mēnsum: "for three months"; gen. of measure of time; see App. §100.

8. sibi: dat. of reference; see App. §120.

domō: abl. of place from which without prep.; see App. §134, *a.*

8–9. Rauracīs et Tulingīs et Latobrīgīs: note here how POLYSYNDETON (the use of "many conjunctions") helps create the

appearance of larger numbers. The threat grows and grows and grows!

9. cōnsiliō: abl. with deponent verb **ūsī;** see App. §145.

9–10. utī ... proficīscantur: they persuaded their neighbors "to set out together with them" after effecting the same plan.

oppidīs ... exustīs: abl. absolute.

10. cum eīs: equivalent here to *sēcum.*

10–12. Bōiōs ... sociōs sibi adscīscunt: "they admit (or receive) the Boii as their allies" or, more literally, "as allies to themselves."

12. receptōs ... ad sē: literally: "(the Boii) having been admitted among themselves," but this is awkward English. English generally prefers a subordinate clause and the active: "after they had received (the Boii)."

Caesar Dē Bellō Gallicō 1.6:
On the Road(s)

The Helvetii are ready to set out for non-Roman territory in Western Gaul. They have two options. One route traverses gentler terrain through Roman territory (the Province). The alternative route passes through the Iura mountains. The terrain was more difficult, and the mountains were also inhabited by other warlike people. After considering their options, the Helvetii elect to gather on the border of the Roman province near Geneva on March 28, 58 BCE, in hopes of making their journey less arduous.

HELVETIAN ESCAPE ROUTES

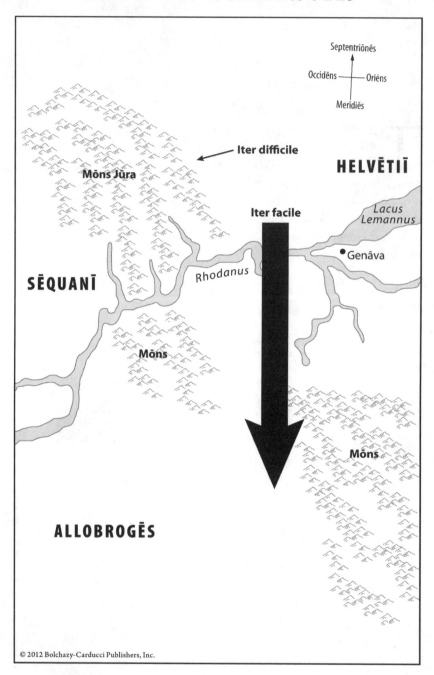

[1.6] *Erant* omnīnō *itinera duo, quibus itineribus* domō exīre
possent: ūnum per Sēquanōs, angustum *et* difficile, *inter*
montem Iūram *et flūmen Rhodanum,* vix *quā* singulī carrī
dūcerentur, mōns *autem* altissimus impendēbat, *ut facile*
5   perpaucī prohibēre *possent; alterum per prōvinciam nostram,*
multō facilius atque expedītius,

---

alt•us, -a, -um, *adj.,* high, deep.
angust•us, -a, -um, *adj.* [**angō,** squeeze],
   compressed, narrow.
carr•us, -ī, *m.,* cart, wagon.
difficil•is, -e, *adj.* [**facilis,** easy], difficult.
dom•us, -ūs (App. §29, *d.*), *f.,* house; home;
   native country.
ex•eō, -īre, -iī, -itum [**eō,** go. App. §84], go
   from, leave.
expedīt•us, -a, -um, *adj.* [*perf. part. of*
   expedio, set free], unimpeded; without
   baggage; light-armed.
im•pendeō, -pendēre, —, — [**in + pendeō,**
   hang], overhang, impend.
Iūr•a, -ae, *m.,* the Jura *mountains which*
   stretched from the Rhine to the Rhone,
   separating the Helvetians from the Sequani.

mōns, montis, *m.,* mountain; mountain
   range.
omnīnō, *adv.* [**omnis,** all], entirely, only.
perpauc•ī, -ae, -a [**paucī,** few], very few, but
   very few; *m. pl. as noun:* very few.
prohibeō, 2 [**habeō,** hold], keep from,
   prevent, prohibit.
Sēquan•us, -a, -um, *adj.,* of *or* belonging
   to the Sequani; *pl. as noun,* **Sēquanī,** the
   Sequani.
singul•ī, -ae, -a, *distributive num. adj.,* one
   each; one at a time, single.
vix, *adj.,* with difficulty, hardly.

---

1. Erant: "there were."

quibus itineribus: the antecedent of **quibus** is **itinera,** a word Caesar repeats within
the subordinate clause as **itineribus.** This was
not necessary, but it is not uncommon. How
does its repetition help make Caesar's meaning clearer and more specific? Would the
sentence sound the same without the second
itineribus?

domō: abl. of place from which without
the prep.; see App. §134, *a.*

1–2. quibus . . . possent: Subjunctive
mood in rel. clause of characteristic; see App.
§230.

2–5. ūnum . . . alterum: supply *iter* for
each, as each represents one of the two possible routes (**itinera duo**) with which they are,
taken together, in apposition; see App. §95, *b.*

3. vix: the normal place for an adv. is before the verb it modifies (here **dūcerentur**).
Putting it in front of the rel. pron. **quā** makes
it emphatic, thus lending more drama to Caesar's narrative.

4. dūcerentur: "they could (or would be
able to) be driven, dragged, or drawn." Subjunctive in a rel. clause of characteristic; see
App. §230, *c*; G.-L. §631, 2.

4–5. ut . . . possent: subjunctive in a clause
of result; see App. §226.

5. prohibēre: the reader will have to supply a direct object derived from the first part
of the sentence, e.g., *illōs, eōs, vel. sim.*

6. multō: abl. of degree of difference; see
App. §148.

proptereā *quod inter fīnēs*
Helvētiōrum et Allobrogum, *quī* nūper pācātī *erant, Rhodanus*
fluit *isque* nōnnūllīs *locīs* vadō trānsītur. Extrēmum oppidum
Allobrogum *est proximumque Helvētiōrum fīnibus* Genava.

10   *Ex eō* oppidō pōns *ad Helvētiōs pertinet.* Allobrogibus *sēsē* vel
persuāsūrōs, quod nōndum bonō animō *in populum Rōmānum
vidērentur, exīstimābant* vel *vī coāctūrōs ut per suōs fīnēs eōs* īre
paterentur.

Allobrog•ēs, -um, *m.*, the Allobroges, a
   Gallic people in the Roman Province.
anim•us, -ī, *m.*, mind; character; spirit,
   soul; courage.
bon•us, -a, -um, *adj.*, good, well-disposed;
   (*with* **animō**) friendly.
eō, īre, iī (īvī), itum (App. §84), go,
   proceed, march, pass.
extrēm•us, -a, -um, *adj.* [*superl. of* **exterus**.
   App. §44], outermost, farthest; the
   farthest part of.
fluō, fluere, flūxī, —, flow, run.
Genav•a, -ae, *f.*, Genava, *a city belonging
   to the Allobroges on the shores of Lacus
   Lemannus; now called* Geneva.
nōndum, *adv.* [**nōn** + **dum**], not yet.

nōnnūll•us, -a, -um, *adj.* [**nōn** + **nūllus**,
   none], some, several.
nūper, *adv.*, recently.
oppid•um, -ī, *n.*, fortified town, town,
   stronghold.
pācō, 1 [**pāx,** peace], subdue, pacify.
patior, patī, passus sum, endure, suffer;
   allow.
pōns, pontis, *m.*, bridge.
proptereā, *adv.* [**propter,** because of], on
   this account; **proptereā quod,** because.
trāns•eō, -īre, -iī, -itum [**eō,** go. App. §84],
   cross; march through; migrate.
vad•um, -ī, *n.*, ford, shallow.
vel, *conj.*, or; **vel . . . vel,** either . . . or.

---

7. nūper pācātī erant: the Romans had
two years earlier in 61 BCE made the area
"peaceful" by suppressing a violent struggle
for independence.

   8. nōnnūllīs locīs: "in a few places," "at
several points"; abl. of place where without
prep.; see App. §151, *b*.

   vadō trānsītur: "it is crossed by wading."
Wading through a shallow area along the
course of a river is called "fording a river."
The place where a river is shallow enough to
attempt this is called "a ford."

   8–9. Extrēmum . . . Genava: Caesar
speaks from the point of view of an Italian
looking north. Allobrogian Geneva (Genava),
which was, thanks to the efforts of the praetor
C. Pomptinus in 61 BCE, securely under Roman jurisdiction, was just across the border
from Helvetian territory.

   10. pōns: rather than ford the river, the
Helvetians would like to cross the bridge. Was
this unreasonable?

   **10–12. vel . . . persuāsūrōs . . . vel . . .
coāctūrōs:** *esse* has been omitted from each of
these fut. act. infs. in indirect statement dependent on a verb of thinking (**exīstimābant**);
see App. §269.

   11. nōndum bonō animō: because their
revolt had so recently and violently been
suppressed, the Allobroges seemed "not yet
well-disposed (or friendly) toward the Roman people." Abl. of quality or description;
see App. §141.

   12–13. ut . . . paterentur: subjunctive
mood in an indirect command, that is, a noun
clause that serves as the object of the infs.
persuāsūrōs *esse* and **coāctūrōs** *esse*. Other
names for the same phenomenon include
jussive noun clause, volitive substantive, and
substantive clause of purpose (which is the
more general classification).

15 *Omnibus rēbus ad* profectiōnem comparātīs *diem dīcunt, quā
    diē ad* rīpam *Rhodanī omnēs conveniant. Is diēs erat* a. d. V. Kal.
    Apr. Lūciō Pīsōne, Aulō Gabīniō cōnsulibus.

---

a. = **ante,** *adv.,* (1) before, above, previously;
(2) *prep. with acc.,* before, in front of, in
advance of.

Apr. = **Aprīl•is, -e,** *adj.,* of *(the month of)*
April.

Aul•us, -ī, *m.;* **Gabīn•ius, -ī,** *m.,* Aulus
Gabinius, *consul with Lucius Calpurnius
Piso in 58* BCE.

comparō, 1 [**parō,** prepare], prepare;
acquire, prepare for.

cōn•sul, -sulis, *m.,* consul.

d. = *diem.*

Kal., *abbr. for* **Kalend•ae, -ārum,** *f.,* the
Kalends, *the first day of the Roman month.*

Lūci•us, -ī, *m.;* **Pīs•ō, -ōnis,** *m.,* Lucius
Calpurnius Piso, *Caesar's father-in-law;
consul in 58* BCE.

profecti•ō, -ōnis, *f.* [**proficīscor,** set out], a
setting out; start, departure.

rīp•a, -ae, *f.,* bank *(of a stream).*

V, *sign for* **quīnque,** five *(see also* App. §47).

---

14. Omnibus . . . comparātīs: "after they
had gotten everything ready"; abl. absolute.

14–15. quā diē: abl. of time when; see
App. §152. Caesar repeats the antecedent
(i.e., **diem**) within the subordinate clause (as
diē). The repetition serves to make his meaning unambiguous and emphatic.

15. conveniant: subjunctive mood in a rel.
clause of purpose; see App. §225, *a.*

15–16. a. d. V. Kal. Apr. = *ante diem
quīntum Kalendās Aprīlēs.* This phrase represents what the Romans themselves said, and
is thus idiomatic, but, because the grammar
does not make sense, we cannot translate it
literally. The phrase means "on the fifth day
before the calends of April." If the Romans
had followed their own grammatical rules,
they would have written *diē quīntō ante*

Kalendās Aprīlēs. Another challenge for us
is the way they counted. It is not obvious that
five days before the calends (or first) of April
is 28 March. The Romans, however, included
the day from which they started counting,
and then counted backwards until they arrived at the number of days originally cited,
hence, in this case, here is how we count five
days before the first of April:1 April (day
1), 31 March (day 2), 30 March (day 3), 29
March (day 4), 28 March (day 5). To make it
even simpler, try counting backwards on the
five fingers of one hand, starting, of course,
with the first of April (seriously, no joke; it
works).

**16. Lūciō Pīsōne, Aulō Gabīniō cōn-
sulibus** = 58 BCE.

Caesar Dē Bellō Gallicō 1.7:
Caesar Rushes In

Caesar rushes to the vicinity of Geneva. The Helvetii send an embassy who requests permission to pass through the Province. Caesar tells them that he needs time to consider their request. This delaying tactic will allow Caesar to finish defensive fortifications before Caesar formally rejects their request. Caesar's lie or duplicity will have struck his Roman readers as smart statesmanship. Diplomats, generals, and politicians do not always speak the truth, especially when it is inconvenient or would give their opponents an advantage.

Trajan's Column, which towers over the remains of the Forum of Trajan in Rome, details his conquest of Dacia in the second century CE. The many relief panels of the column provide a comprehensive view of Roman military activities. The excerpted panels include the army on a march with the standards as well as a set of military construction scenes. Such images help us reconstruct Caesar's campaigns.

[1.7] *Caesarī cum id* nūntiātum *esset, eōs per prōvinciam nostram iter facere* cōnārī, mātūrat *ab* urbe *proficīscī et quam maximīs potest itineribus in Galliam* ulteriōrem contendit *et ad* Genavam *pervenit. Prōvinciae tōtī quam maximum potest mīlitum*

5   *numerum* imperat (*erat* omnīnō *in Galliā* ulteriōre *legiō ūna*), pontem, *quī erat ad* Genavam, *iubet* rescindī.

---

cōnor, 1, try, attempt.

con•tendō, -tendere, -tendī, -tentum [**tendō,** stretch], push forward, hasten; march; fight; insist.

Genav•a, -ae, *f.,* Genava, *a city belonging to the Allobroges on the shores of Lacus Lemannus; now called* Geneva.

imperō, 1 [**in** + **parō,** procure], demand from; requisition; command.

mātūrō, 1 [**mātūrus,** ripe], hurry, hasten.

nūntiō, 1 [**nūntius,** messenger], announce, report; order.

omnīnō, *adv.* [**omnis,** all], at all; altogether, only.

pōns, pontis, *m.,* bridge.

re•scindō, -scindere, -scidī, -scissum [**re** + **scindō,** cleave], cut down, destroy.

urbs, urbis, *f.,* city; *especially,* the city, *Rome.*

ulter•ior, -ius, *adj., comp.* [**ultrā,** beyond. App. §43], farther, more remote.

---

1. cum ... nūntiātum esset: subjunctive mood in a temporal clause; see App. §§240, 242, *a.*

id: "this thing" or (better) "this fact" is explained by the clause (**eōs ... cōnārī**) that is in apposition with it. This clause provides the actual information that was reported to Caesar.

eōs: acc. subject (see App. §123) of the inf. **cōnārī** in indirect statement; see App. §266.

2. ab urbe: "from Rome," the only *urbs* that never had to be named. Having just finished his consulship, Caesar was still in the vicinity of Rome preparing for his governorship.

2–3. quam maximīs potest itineribus: "by (day-)trips as long as he can (make them)." Although Caesar was known for traveling especially speedily, Plutarch *Caesar* 17 tells us that this trip took eight days, so about ninety miles a day. Travel was time-consuming in the ancient world.

3. Galliam ulteriōrem: "more remote (or farther) Gaul," which, from an Italian point of view, was Transalpine Gaul, i.e., Gaul on the other side of the Alps.

ad Genavam: "to the vicinity of Geneva"; see App. §131.

4. mīlitum: partitive gen. App. §101.

4–5. Prōvinciae ... imperat: "he enlisted from the province"; historical pres. Caesar orders the province to supply as many men as possible.

5. in Galliā: abl. of place where; see App. §151, *b.*

legiō: the tenth legion, which famously became Caesar's favorite.

6. pontem: Caesar takes no chances, and removes the bridge.

Ubi *dē eius adventū Helvētiī certiōrēs factī sunt, lēgātōs ad eum*
mittunt nōbilissimōs *cīvitātis, cuius* lēgātiōnis Nammēius *et*
Verucloetius prīncipem *locum* obtinēbant, *quī dīcerent sibi esse*
10   *in* animō *sine* ūllō maleficiō *iter per prōvinciam facere,* proptereā
quod aliud iter habērent nūllum: rogāre *ut eius* voluntāte *id sibi*
facere liceat. *Caesar, quod* memoriā *tenēbat* Lūcium Cassium
cōnsulem occīsum *exercitumque eius ab Helvētiīs* pulsum *et*

---

anim•us, -ī, *m.,* mind; feelings; character.

cōn•sul, -sulis, *m.,* consul.

lēgāti•ō, -ōnis, *f.* [**lēgō,** delegate], embassy.

licet, licēre, licuit *and* **licitum est,** *impers.,*
it is permitted.

Lūcius, -ī, *m.;* **Cass•ius, -ī,** *m.,* Lucius
Cassius Longinus, *consul in 107* BCE,
defeated and slain in battle by the Tigurini.

malefic•ium, -ī, *n.* [**malus,** evil + **faciō,** do],
mischief, harm.

memōri•a, -ae, *f.* [**memor,** mindful],
memory; **memoriā tenēre,** remember.

Nammē•ius, -ī, *m.,* Nammeius, *a Helvetian*
noble and envoy.

nōbil•is, -e, *adj.* [**nōscō,** know], well-
known, distinguished; of noble birth.

nūll•us, -a, -um, *gen.* **nūllīus,** *adj.* [**ne-** +
ūllus, any], not any, no.

ob•tineō, -tinēre, -tinuī, -tentum [**teneō,**
hold], hold, retain, possess; acquire.

oc•cīdō, -cīdere, -cīsī, -cīsum [**caedō,** cut],
cut down, kill.

pellō, pellere, pepulī, pulsum, defeat, rout.

prīn•ceps, -cipis, *adj.* [**prīmus,** first], chief,
first.

proptereā, *adv.* [**propter,** because of], on
this account; **proptereā quod,** because.

rogō, 1, ask.

ubi, *adv.* when.

ūll•us, -a, -um *gen.* **ūllīus** (App. §32), *adj.,* a
single, any.

Verucloeti•us, -ī, *m.,* Verucloetius, *a*
Helvetian envoy.

volun•tās, -tātis, *f.* [**volō,** wish], wish;
goodwill; consent.

---

7. certiōrēs factī sunt: "were made more
certain" = "were informed."

certiōrēs: predicate nom.; see App. §§156,
157.

8. nōbilissimōs: "the most renowned
men"; substantive use of the adj.

9. quī dīcerent: "who were saying (because they were sent for this purpose)," i.e.,
"whose assignment was to explain," subjunctive mood in a rel. clause of purpose.

9–10. sibi esse in animō: "that they had
in mind," "they intended"; indirect statement
dependent on **dīcerent.**

9. sibi: dat. of possession; see App. §117.

11. quod ... habērent: subjunctive mood
because a subordinate clause in indirect
statement.

rogāre: inf. dependent on **dīcerent** in indirect statement. Because it may be deduced
from the **sibi** that appeared earlier, Caesar has
ellipted the proper subject of the infinitive,

which would be *sē.* The style is thus clipped,
terse, matter-of-fact.

eius: "Caesar's"; because the reflexives
refer to the ambassadors who are the subject
of the main verb of speaking (i.e., **dīcerent**).

voluntāte: "in accordance with his prefer-
ence," i.e., "with his consent"; abl. of manner
without *cum;* see App. §142, *a.*

11–12. ut ... sibi ... liceat: "that it be permitted to them," i.e. "that they be allowed";
subjunctive in a substantive clause of purpose
(or indirect command); see App. §228, *a.*

12. tenēbat: indicative in a causal clause;
see App. §244. Notice also the use of the impf.
tense in this sentence. Caesar presents himself
in the midst of thought, thus inviting readers to
share his logic as he works through it.

13. ab Helvētiīs: abl. of agent; see App.
§137.

13–14. occīsum ... pulsum ... missum:
perf. pass. inf. (with the *esse* omitted) in indirect

sub iugum *missum,* concēdendum *nōn* putābat; *neque hominēs*
15   inimīcō animō, *datā* facultāte *per prōvinciam itineris faciendī,*
      temperātūrōs *ab* iniūriā *et* maleficiō *exīstimābat.*

---

anim•us, -ī, *m.,* mind; character; spirit,
    soul; courage.
con•cēdō, -cedere, -cessī, -cessum [cēdō,
    go], depart; grant; permit.
facul•tās, -tātis, *f.* [facilis, easy], power;
    opportunity; resources.
inimīc•us, -a, -um, *adj.* [in + amīcus,
    friendly], unfriendly, hostile.

iniūri•a, -ae, *f.* [in + iūs, right], wrong;
    injury, damage.
iug•um, -ī, *n.* [iungō, join], yoke; ridge, crest.
malefic•ium, -ī, *n.* [malus, evil + faciō, do],
    mischief, harm, injury.
putō, 1, think, consider, believe.
sub, *prep. with acc.,* under, beneath.
temperō, 1, refrain.

---

statement dependent on a verb of thinking
(**memoriā tenēbat**). Caesar recalls an event
more than half a century in the past. This may
strike modern readers as forced, but it is difficult to overestimate how seriously Romans
took the past. They treated remote events as
if they were quite recent, and typically used
events from the farther and nearer past to
make arguments about the present and for
the future. If it had been in Caesar's interest,
he could have neglected to remember the incident, of course, but, as Cassius's defeat helped
his argument (Romans were always eager to
avenge a loss), Caesar mentioned it precisely
because it would be effective in convincing
the audience at home that his aggression
against the Helvetians was justified.

14. sub iugum: "under the yoke." When
a victorious army wanted to humiliate a defeated enemy, they would set up a "yoke" or
low arch, which was constructed with spears.
They would then force the defeated army to
march "under the yoke." The defeated soldiers
would have to bend over to get underneath
(thus forcing them to bow down—another
sign of submission), and the victors would

line up to jeer and make fun of the defeated
soldiers. Although the Romans inflicted the
same punishment on others, they did not like
to lose, and they especially resented disrespectful behavior that did not acknowledge
Roman superiority.

concēdendum: a pass. periphrastic inf.
(with *esse* omitted) dependent on **putābat** in
indirect statement. The unexpressed subject
of the inf. is the Helvetians' request to pass
through Roman territory, hence "Caesar
was thinking that this (request) must not be
granted."

15. animō: abl. of quality or description;
see App. §141.

datā facultāte: "given the opportunity,"
i.e., "if they were given the opportunity"; conditional abl. absolute; see App. §150.

itineris faciendī: gerundive in the gen. to
express purpose; see App. §§288, 291.

16. temperātūrōs: a fut. active inf. (with
esse omitted) dependent on **exīstimābat** in
indirect statement. The subject is the word
hominēs, hence "Caesar was reckoning that
the people would (in the future) not refrain
from," etc.

> *Tamen, ut* spatium intercēdere *posset dum mīlitēs quōs*
> imperāverat *convenīrent, lēgātīs* respondit *diem sē ad*
> dēlīberandum sūmptūrum: *sī quid vellent, ad* Īd. Aprīl.
> 20   reverterentur.

Aprīl. = **Aprīl•is, -e,** *adj.,* of (*the month of*)
April.

dēlīberō, 1 [**lībra,** balance], weigh well;
consider, deliberate.

Īd., *abbr.* of **Īd•ūs, -uum,** *f. pl.,* the Ides: *the*
15th of March, May, July, and October, and
the 13th of other months.

imperō, 1 [**in** + **parō,** procure], demand
from; order, instruct, rule.

inter•cēdō, -cēdere, -cessī, -cessum
[**cēdō,** go], go *or* come between,
intervene; pass.

re•spondeō, -spondēre, -spondī,
-sponsum [**re** + **spondeō,** promise],
reply, answer.

re•vertor, -vertī, -versus sum [**re** + **vertō,**
turn], turn back, come back, return.

spat•ium, -ī, *n.,* space; period *or* length *of*
time.

sūmō, sūmere, sūmpsī, sūmptum [**sub** +
emō, take], take; assume.

17–18. dum mīlitēs . . . convenīrent:
"while the soldiers were assembling" or "until
the soldiers arrived." Because Caesar shared
his thoughts about avenging Rome's humiliating defeat of 107 BCE as well as his assessment of how dangerous the Helvetians were,
he invites us, as readers, to view his less than
honest response to the ambassadors as crafty
diplomacy rather than dishonest dealing.

18. diem: Caesar does specifically say "one
day" (*ūnum diem*), so we may infer that he
planned on taking whatever time he needed.
Roman governors, whose power within their
provinces was almost absolute, acted when it
suited them. One of the most basic ways to
demonstrate one's power over others is to
make them wait.

18–19. sē . . . sūmptūrum: "that he would
take"; fut. active inf. (with *esse* omitted) dependent on **respondit** in indirect statement.
The subject of the inf., **sē,** refers to Caesar, the
unexpressed subject of the main verb.

ad dēlīberandum: gerund with **ad** to express purpose; see App. §§287, 293.

19. sī quid vellent: "if they wanted something." After **sī,** *aliquid* drops the "*ali*"; see
App. §174.

ad Īd. Aprīl.: *ad Īdūs Aprīlēs,* i.e., 13
April.

20. reverterentur: "they should return";
subjunctive mood in indirect statement to
represent a command. When the ambassadors were with Caesar, he said directly to
them (something like): "If you want something, return on the Ides of April!" (*sī quid*
vultis, ad Īdūs Aprīlēs revertiminī!) Reported
as a past event, this became (in indirect statement): "(Caesar) responded . . . that, if they
wanted something, they should return on
the Ides of April." For more on the use of the
subjunctive mood to represent commands in
indirect statement, see App. §267.

Aftermath

This story does not end well for the Helvetians. Caesar eventually denied them permission to cross through Roman territory, so they then attempted to take the more difficult route north, which did not pass through Roman territory. Caesar considered this too dangerous to permit (because they would still be close to Roman territory), and this argument provided a pretext or, depending on your perspective, a legitimate reason for invading non-Roman Gaul with a Roman army. Caesar defeated the Helvetians without too much effort, and slaughtered a large number of men, women, and children. Caesar compelled the survivors to return to their burnt fields and villages on the grounds that even more dangerous Germans would otherwise drift in to settle on the vacant territory. At all events, once Caesar had entered non-Roman Gaul, he did not leave until he had conquered the entire territory. This took another eight long years, probably much longer than Caesar had anticipated or hoped.

C. IVLI CAESARIS
COMMENTARIORUM
DE BELLO GALLICO
LIBER QUARTUS

Caesar Dē Bellō Gallicō 4.24–36.1:
Caesar's Invasion of Britain

C aesar's governorship began in 58 BCE with an incursion into Gaul to prevent the Helvetians from leaving their homes for new settlements in western Gaul. Once he was in Gaul, Caesar soon became more deeply involved in the various disputes of Gallic tribes with each other and in their disputes with neighboring peoples, especially the Germanic tribes pressing into Gaul from across the Rhine. At first, some Gallic tribes truly welcomed Caesar as a protector or were at least eager to enlist his assistance in their struggles against others. Caesar did not lack pretexts for pressing on with his conquests. In 57 BCE, Caesar moved north to fight the Belgae and to consolidate control of Gaul along the northern coast. Action in the north continued into 56 BCE as well as in the south in the region of Aquitania on the Atlantic coast north of Spain. By 55 BCE, the military situation in Gaul appeared secure. The only Gauls not under Roman rule or military domination were across the channel in Britain. For the first part of the summer of 55 BCE, Caesar fought against Germans who had initially been welcomed into Gaul by tribes no longer happy with the Romans. Caesar defeated them, and, when they fled across the Rhine, Caesar built a bridge, and crossed over with his troops to demonstrate that he had the ability to bring war to the Germans in their home territory, or, as he put it, "to fill the Germans with terror" (*ut Germānīs metum iniceret; BG* 4.19). The Gauls in Britain were another matter. Their freedom was, of course, a bad example in general, and they had sent aid to the Gauls on the

BRITISH INVASION

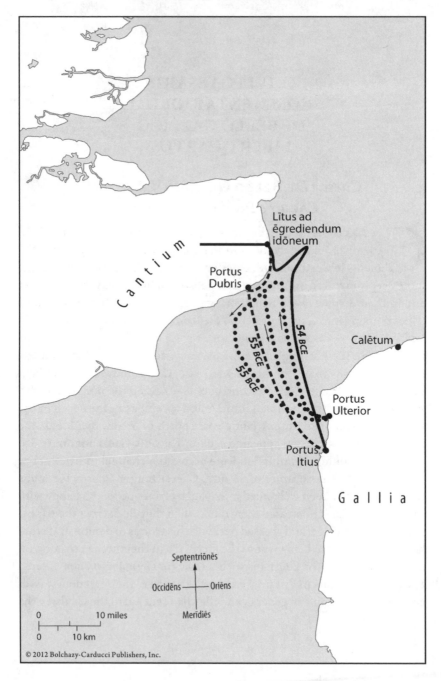

© 2012 Bolchazy-Carducci Publishers, Inc.

mainland during earlier battles against Caesar. Caesar also tells us that he could not gather clear information about the island. Caesar's expedition was thus partly reconnaissance and information-gathering.

Caesar's operations in 55 BCE yielded tremendous public relations benefits. To Romans at home, Germany and Britain were both remote and terrifying places. They were uncharted, unknown, dangerous, and populated—at least in the Roman imagination—by primitive savages. To reach Britain, Caesar had to cross the open sea, which was always a daunting prospect to the Roman imagination. To reach the Germans, he had to cross the Rhine, which he did by having a bridge constructed, thus showing off Roman engineering. Caesar's successes were duly reported and celebrated in Rome by Caesar's political allies and supporters. And so, despite his long absence from Rome, Caesar's fame and popularity kept growing. We should not forget too that the war Caesar fought in Gaul was enormously profitable. Slave dealing was an integral part of ancient warfare. "Merchants" (slave-dealers) traveled with the army. Tens of thousands of defeated Gauls were sold into slavery, and Caesar could use the profits from their sale to reward his soldiers and to buy loyalty and political support in Rome. Because the war in Gaul was to this extent also a business operation, Caesar's stated interest in learning more about the island of Britain may well have included reasons he would have been too diplomatic to state explicitly.

In this selection, we pick up the story just as Caesar and two legions have arrived in Britain aboard a fleet of some eighty ships. Caesar has brought the fleet as close to shore as the size of the ships will allow. The native inhabitants, however, have been watching the Roman ships from shore. They immediately attack. Their goal is to prevent Roman soldiers from establishing a beachhead. The fight is difficult for the Romans because they must fight while wading through water and waves. The native inhabitants, on the other hand, fight from dry land or after wading only a little way into the water.

Caesar DĒ BELLŌ GALLICŌ 4.24–36.1:
Caesar's Invasion of Britain

[4.24] *At* barbarī, *cōnsiliō Rōmānōrum cognitō* praemissō *equitātū et* essedāriīs, *quō* plērumque *genere in proeliīs ūtī cōnsuērunt, reliquīs cōpiīs* subsecūtī *nostrōs nāvibus* ēgredī prohibēbant.

---

barbar•us, -a, -um, *adj.*, foreign (*to Romans and Greeks*), uncivilized; *pl. as noun:* barbarians.

ē•gredior, -gredī, -gressus sum [**gradior**, step], come forth, depart; march out, make a sortie; disembark.

essedāri•us, -a, -um, *adj.* [**essedum,** war chariot], a soldier who fought from a two-wheeled British war chariot.

plērumque, *adv.* [**plērusque,** the greater part], mostly; very often.

prae•mittō, -mittere, -mīsī, -missum [**mittō,** send], send before *or* in advance.

prohibeō, 2 [**habeō,** hold], keep from, prevent, prohibit; keep out *or* away from; guard.

sub•sequor, -sequī, -secūtus [**sequor,** follow], follow closely.

---

1. cōnsiliō ... cognitō: abl. absolute; see App. §150. The native inhabitants knew what the Romans planned because they had been watching from shore.

1–2. praemissō equitātū et essedāriīs: abl. absolute; **praemissō** agrees with the word closest to it. Chariots were an archaic weapon and no longer in use on the continent.

2. quō ... genere: "which kind" (of warrior) or "a type (of warrior) that." If **genere** had stood outside the rel. clause, it would

have been in apposition with **equitātū et essedāriīs,** and thus served as the antecedent of **quō.** Instead, this appositional antecedent has been placed within the rel. clause. This is similar to Caesar's practice of repeating the antecedent within the rel. clause.

3. reliquīs cōpiīs: abl. of accompaniment with *cum* omitted (common in military phrases); App. §140.

nāvibus: abl. of separation without the prep.; App. §134.

5   *Erat* ob *hās causās summa* difficultās, *quod nāvēs* propter
magnitūdinem nisi *in* altō *cōnstituī nōn poterant, mīlitibus
autem,* ignōtīs *locīs,* impedītīs *manibus, magnō et gravī* onere
armōrum oppressīs simul *et dē nāvibus* dēsiliendum *et in*
flūctibus cōnsistendum *et cum hostibus erat pugnandum, cum*

10   *illī aut ex* āridō *aut* paulum *in* aquam prōgressī *omnibus*
membrīs expedītīs, nōtissimīs *locīs,* audācter *tēla* conicerent *et*
equōs īnsuēfactōs incitārent.

---

alt•us, -a, -um, *adj.,* high, deep.
aqua, -ae, *f.,* water.
ārid•us, -a, -um, *adj.* [**areō,** be dry], dry; *n.
as noun:* dry land.
audācter, *adv.* [**audāx,** bold], fearlessly,
daringly.
con•iciō, -icere, -iēcī, -iectum [co + iaciō,
throw. App. §7], hurl, throw, cast.
cōn•sistō, -sistere, -stitī, — [**sistō,** stand],
take a stand *or* position, keep one's
position, stand; stop, halt, remain, stay.
dē•siliō, -silīre, -siluī, -sultum [saliō,
jump], jump from, dismount.
difficul•tās, -tātis, *f.* [**difficilis,** difficult],
trouble, embarrassment.
expedīt•us, -a, -um, *adj.* [*perf. part. of*
expediō, set free], unimpeded; without
baggage; light armed.
flūct•us, -ūs, *m.* [**fluō,** flow], flood, wave.
ignōt•us, -a, -um, adv. [**in** + (g)nōtus,
known (**nōscō,** know)], unknown,
unfamiliar.
impediō, 4 [**in** + **pēs,** foot], *entangle the feet,*
obstruct, hinder, delay.

incitō, 1 [citō, put in motion], set in
motion; excite, urge on; exasperate.
īnsuēfact•us, -a, um, *adj.* [**suēscō,** become
accustomed, **faciō,** make], accustomed,
trained.
magnitūd•ō, -inis, *f.* [**magnus,** large], large
size.
membr•um, -ī, *n.,* limb.
nisi, *conj.,* [**ne-** + **sī,** if], if not, except, unless.
nōt•us, -a, -um, *adj.* [*perf. part. of* **nōscō,**
learn], known, well-known, familiar.
ob, *prep. with acc.,* on account of, for.
on•us, -eris, *n.,* burden; weight.
op•primō, -primere, -pressī, -pressus [ob
+ **premō,** press], press down, oppress;
destroy; surprise.
paulum, *adv.* [**paulus,** little], a little,
somewhat, slightly.
prō•gredior, -gredī, -gressus sum [**gradior,**
step], step *or* go forward, advance.
propter, *prep. with acc.* [**prope,** near], on
account of, because of.
simul, *adv.* at once, at the same time,
thereupon.

---

5. Erat: "there was."
hās causās: "the following reasons."
6. in altō: substantive use of the adj.
cōnstituī: "to be anchored."
6–8. mīlitibus ... dēsiliendum: "the soldiers had to jump down"; dat. of agent with
fut. pass. periphrastic; see App. §118, *a.*
7. ignōtīs locīs: "in an unfamiliar place";
abl. of place where without a prep.; see App.
§151, *b.* The phrase could also be construed
as an abl. absolute.

8–9. et . . . et . . . et: POLYSYNDETON; see
App. §301, *f.*
9–12. cum ... conicerent et ... incitārent:
"while they were . . . "; subjunctive mood in a
temporal clause; see App. §§240, 242, *a.*
10. ex āridō: "from (on) dry land"; substantive use of the adj.
11. nōtissimīs locīs: "on ground they
knew very well."
12. īnsuēfactōs: the horses were "trained"
to fight along and in the water.

> *Quibus rēbus nostrī* perterritī *atque huius* omnīnō *generis pugnae*
> imperītī, *nōn eādem* alacritāte *ac* studiō *quō in* pedestribus *ūtī*
> 15   *proeliīs cōnsuērant ūtēbantur.*

---

alacrit•ās, -ātis, *f.,* [**alacer,** lively],
    enthusiasm, eagerness.
imperīt•us, -a, -um, *adj.* [**in + perītus,**
    experienced], inexperienced, unskilled,
    ignorant.
omnīnō, *adv.* [**omnis,** all], at all; altogether,
    only.

pedest•er, -ris, -re, *adj.* [**pēs,** foot], on foot,
    pedestrian.
per•terreō, 2 [**terreō,** frighten], frighten
    thoroughly.
stud•ium, -ī, *n.* [**studeō,** be zealous],
    eagerness; devotion; pursuit.

---

13. Quibus = *et hīs;* see App. §173, *a.*
generis: objective gen. with **imperītī;** see
App. §98.
    14. eādem: agrees with the nearest noun;
see App. §157, 1.

quō: agrees with the nearest antecedent.
    in pedestribus: "on foot," i.e., "in infantry
battles (on land)."
    15. ūtēbantur: "were showing."

[4.25] *Quod* ubi *Caesar* animadvertit, *nāvēs longās, quārum et*
speciēs *erat* barbarīs inūsitātior *et* mōtus *ad ūsum* expedītior,
paulum removērī *ab* onerāriīs *nāvibus et* rēmīs incitārī *et ad*
latus apertum *hostium cōnstituī atque* inde fundīs, sagittīs,
5   tormentīs *hostēs* prōpellī *ac* submovērī *iussit; quae rēs magnō*
ūsuī nostrīs fuit.

---

animad•vertō, -vertere, -vertī, -versum
[**animus**, mind + **ad** + **vertō**, turn], turn
the mind to; notice.
aper•iō, -īre, -uī, -tum, open, expose.
barbar•us, -a, -um, *adj.*, foreign (*to Romans
and Greeks*), uncivilized; *pl. as noun:*
barbarians.
expedīt•us, -a, -um, *adj.* [*perf. part. of*
expediō, set free], unimpeded; without
baggage; light-armed.
fund•a, -ae, *f.*, sling.
incitō, 1 [**citō**, put in motion], set in
motion; excite, urge on; exasperate.
inde, *adv.*, from that place; then.
inūsitāt•us, -a, -um, *adj.* [**in** + **ūsitātus**,
usual], unusual, startling.
lat•us, -eris, *n.*, side; wing *or* flank *of an
army.*
mōt•us, -ūs, *m.* [**moveō**, move], movement;
uprising, disturbance.

onerāri•us, -a, -um, *adj.* [**onus**, load],
equipped for loads; *with* **nāvis**, transport,
freight ship.
paulum, *adv.* [**paulus**, little], a little,
somewhat, slightly.
pro•pellō, -pellere, -pulī, -pulsum [**pellō**,
drive], put to flight, rout; drive back.
re•moveō, -movēre, -mōvī, -mōtum
[**moveō**, move], move back *or* away,
withdraw.
rēmus, -ī, *m.*, oar.
sagitt•a, -ae, *f.*, arrow.
speci•ēs, -eī, *f.* [**speciō**, see], sight;
appearance.
sub•moveō, -movēre, -mōvī, -mōtum
[**moveō**, move], drive away.
torment•um, -ī, *n.* [**torqueō**, twist], means
of twisting; an engine *or* machine *for*
hurling missiles, *e.g., catapults and ballista.*
ubi, *adv.*, when.

---

1. Quod ubi: equivalent in sense to *et ubi
id*; **quod** refers to all that was just described;
conjunctio relativa; see App. §173, *a.*

animadvertit: indicative in a temporal
clause after **ubi.**

2. inūsitātior: "less familiar," hence
"more startling" and more likely to disorient
the Britons who were familiar with barges
("transports"), but not the technological wiz-
ardry of boats with rudders and oars.

mōtus . . . expedītior: "whose movement
was more unimpeded for use (i.e., in the practice of sailing)."

4. latus apertum: "exposed flank or side."
4–5. fundīs, sagittīs, tormentīs: "with
slingshots, arrows, catapults"; ASYNDETON,
which underscores Caesar's efficient decision
making; see App. §§301, *a.*

5. quae rēs: "and this maneuver."

6. ūsuī nostrīs fuit: "was of great use (i.e,
very advantageous) for us"; double dat. with
the verb *sum*; dat. of purpose (**ūsuī**) and dat.
of reference (**nostrīs**); see App. §§119–120.

Nam et nāvium figūrā *et* rēmōrum mōtū *et* inūsitātō *genere*
tormentōrum permōtī barbarī *cōnstitērunt ac* paulum modo
pedem rettulērunt. *Atque nostrīs mīlitibus* cūnctantibus,
10   maximē propter altitūdinem maris, *quī* decimae *legiōnis*
aquilam *ferēbat*, obtestātus deōs, *ut ea rēs legiōnī* fēlīciter
ēvenīret,

---

altitūd•ō, -inis, *f.* [altus, high, deep], depth.
aquil•a, -ae, *f.*, an eagle; a military standard
   (*the* aquila *was the main standard of the*
   legion).
barbar•us, -a, -um, *adj.*, foreign (*to Romans*
   and Greeks), uncivilized; *pl. as noun*:
   barbarians.
cūnctor, 1, delay, hesitate, be reluctant.
decim•us, -a, -um [decem, ten], *ord. num.*,
   adj., tenth.
de•us, -ī (*nom. pl.*: diī; *dat. pl.*: dīs), *m.*, god.
ē•veniō, -venīre, -vēnī, -ventum [veniō,
   come], turn out, result.
fēlīciter, *adv.* [fēlīx, happy], happily,
   fortunately.
figūr•a, -ae, *f.* [fingō, form], form, shape.
inūsitāt•us, -a, -um, *adj.* [in + ūsitātus,
   usual], unusual, startling.
magis, *adv. comp.* [from magnus, large],
   more, rather; *superl.*: maximē, especially.
mare, maris, *n.*, sea.
modo, *adv.* [modus, measure], *with measure*
   or limit; only; just, at least, but; *of time*,
   just now.

mōt•us, -ūs, *m.* [moveō, move], movement;
   uprising, disturbance.
obtestor, 1 [testor, witness], call to witness;
   beseech, entreat.
paulum, *adv.* [paulus, little], a little,
   somewhat, slightly.
per•moveō, -movēre, -mōvī, -mōtum
   [moveō, move], move thoroughly; incite.
pēs, pedis, *m.*, the foot, a foot; pedem
   referre, retreat.
propter, *prep. with acc.* [prope, near], on
   account of, because of.
referō, referre, rettulī, relātum [re + ferō,
   carry. App. §81], report; pedem referre,
   go back, retreat.
rēmus, -ī, *m.*, oar.
torment•um, -ī, *n.* [torqueō, twist], means
   of twisting; an engine *or* machine *for*
   hurling missiles, e.g., catapults and ballista.

7–8. figūrā et . . . mōtū et . . . genere . . .
permōtī: "scared by the shape . . . and the
movement . . . and the type"; POLYSYNDETON,
which underscores the many things put into
efficient action by Caesar that frightened the
"barbarians"; see App. §301, *f.*
   8. paulum modo: "just a little"; much effort for small progress, but Caesar effectively
places the reader in the midst of the action.
   9. nostrīs . . . cūnctantibus: abl. absolute;
see App. §150.
   10. altitūdinem: "depth." The ships could
not be brought very close to shore because of
their size, and the men were hesitant to jump
fully armed into relatively deep water, especially while under fire from the shore.

quī: the antecedent is the unexpressed
subject of inquit (line 12), i.e., the *aquilifer*
(standard-bearer) who carries the legion's
"eagle" (*aquila*) into battle, so translate *is quī.*
   11. aquilam: a legion's standard was considered a protective god, and received religious worship. Soldiers were deeply devoted
to their "eagle," and jealously guarded it.
   deōs: soldiers preferred to have the gods on
their side. *Fēlīcitās* is what the gods bestowed
on those whom they favored: the happiness
that comes from success and good fortune.
   12. ēvenīret: volitive subjunctive in a
substantive clause of purpose (or indirect
command) after obtestātus; see App. §228, *a.*

"Dēsilīte," inquit, "commīlitōnēs, nisi *vultis* aquilam
hostibus prōdere; egō certē meum *reī pūblicae atque* imperātōrī
officium praestiterō." *Hoc cum* vōce *magnā dīxisset, sē ex nāvī*
15　　prōiēcit *atque in hostēs* aquilam *ferre coepit. Tum nostrī*
cohortātī *inter sē, nē tantum* dēdecus admitterētur, ūniversī
ex nāvī dēsiluērunt. *Hōs* item *ex proximīs prīmī nāvibus cum*
cōnspexissent, subsecūtī *hostibus* appropinquārunt.

---

ad•mittō, -mittere, -mīsī, -missum [mittō,
　send], admit; commit; incur.
appropinquō, 1 [ad + propinquus, near],
　come near, approach.
aquil•a, -ae, *f.,* an eagle; a military standard.
certē, *adv.* [**certus,** certain], certainly; at
　least.
cohortor, 1 [co + **hortor,** encourage],
　encourage greatly, cheer, animate.
commīlitō, -ōnis, *m.* [**mīles,** soldier],
　fellow soldier, comrade.
cōn•spiciō, -spicere, -spexī, -spectum
　[**speciō,** look], look at, discern, perceive.
dē•decus, -oris, *n.* [**decus,** honor],
　dishonor, disgrace.
dē•siliō, -silīre, -siluī, -sultum [**saliō,**
　jump], jump from, dismount.
ego, meī (App. §51), *first pers. pron.,* I, me.
imperāt•or, -ōris, *m.* [**imperō,** order],
　commander-in-chief, general.

inqu•am, -is, -it, say.
item, *adv.,* in like manner, so, also, just so.
me•us, -a, -um, *poss. adj.* [*of the pron.* **egō,**
　my, mine.
nisi, *conj.* [**ne-** + **sī,** if], if not, except, unless.
offic•ium, -ī, *n.,* allegiance, duty; business.
prae•stō, -stāre, -stitī, -stātum [**stō,** stand],
　stand *or* place before; show, exhibit,
　supply; be superior, excel, surpass.
prōd•ō, -dere, -didī, -ditum [**dō,** give],
　give forth, reveal; betray; hand down.
prō•iciō, -icere, -iēcī, -iectum [**iaciō,**
　throw. App. §7], throw forward *or* away;
　reject, give up; **sē prōicere,** cast oneself;
　jump.
sub•sequor, -sequī, -secūtus [**sequor,**
　follow], follow closely.
ūnivers•us, -a, -um, *adj.* [**unus,** one +
　vertō, turn], all together, whole.
vōx, vōcis, *f.,* voice; shout; word.

---

14. praestiterō: the fut. perf. emphasizes
that at least the speaker, as opposed to his audience (whose enthusiasm is in doubt), will
have discharged his duties.

vōce: abl. of manner; see App. §142.

dīxisset: subjunctive in a temporal clause
with **cum.**

16. inter sē: "each other" or "one another";
see App. §166.

tantum dēdecus: the loss of their "eagle."

admitterētur: volitive subjunctive in a
substantive clause of purpose (or indirect
command) after **cohortātī.**

17. cum: although it generally belongs at
the beginning of its clause, by delaying **cum,**

Caesar increases the drama of the scene. Note
too the INTERLOCKED WORD ORDER. The
"first men" (i.e., the men up front with a view
of the action) on the closest ships, who catch
sight of them (i.e., the men following the standard bearer), are in this sentence surrounded
by the ships and the adj. that modifies them.
Compare how much flatter a more standard
word order would be: *cum ex proximīs nāvibus
prīmī hōs item cōnspexissent,* etc.

18. appropinquārunt = *appropinquā-
vērunt.*

[4.26] *Pugnātum est ab utrīsque* ācriter. *Nostrī tamen, quod
neque ōrdinēs* servāre *neque* firmiter īnsistere *neque* signa
subsequī *poterant atque alius aliā ex nāvī quibuscumque* signīs
occurrerat *sē* adgregābat, magnopere perturbābantur; *hostēs*
5   vērō, nōtīs *omnibus* vadīs, ubi *ex* lītore *aliquōs* singulārēs *ex
nāvī* ēgredientēs cōnspexerant, incitātīs *equīs* impedītōs
adoriēbantur, *plūrēs* paucōs circumsistēbant, *aliī ab* latere
apertō *in* ūniversōs *tēla* coniciēbant.

ācriter *adv.* [ācer, sharp], sharply, fiercely.
adgregō, 1 [ad + grex, flock] *unite in a flock;*
    assemble; join, attach.
ad•orior, -orīrī, -ortus sum [orior, arise],
    rise against, attack.
aper•iō, -īre, -uī, -ertum, open, expose.
circum•sistō, -sistere, -stitī, — [sistō,
    stand], surround.
con•iciō, -icere, -iēcī, -iectum [co + iaciō,
    throw. App. §7], hurl, throw, cast.
cōn•spiciō, -spicere, -spexī, -spectum
    [speciō, look], look at, discern, perceive.
ē•gredior, -gredī, -gressus sum [gradior,
    step], come forth, depart; march out,
    make a sortie; disembark.
firmiter, *adv.* [firmus, firm], firmly.
impediō, 4 [in + pēs, foot], obstruct,
    hinder, delay.
incitō, 1 [citō, put in motion], set in
    motion; excite, urge on; exasperate.
īn•sistō, -sistere, -stitī, — [sistō, stand],
    stand upon; stand firm, take a stand.
lat•us, -eris, *n.,* side; wing *or* flank *of an army.*

līt•us, -eris, *n.,* beach, shore.
magnopere, *adv.* [magnus, large + opus,
    work], greatly.
nōt•us, -a, -um, *adj.* [*perf. part. of* nōscō,
    learn], known, well-known, familiar.
oc•currō, -currere, -currī, -cursum [ob +
    currō, run], meet; happen upon; come to.
pauc•ī, -ae, -a, *adj.,* few; *as noun:* few *persons
    or things.*
perturbō, 1 [turbō, disturb], disturb
    greatly, throw into confusion; terrify.
servō, 1, save, preserve; maintain; guard.
sign•um, -ī, *n.,* signal; standard.
singulār•is, -e, *adj.* [singulī, one each], one
    at a time; single; remarkable.
sub•sequor, -sequī, -secūtus [sequor,
    follow], follow closely.
ubi, *adv.* when, where.
ūnivers•us, -a, -um, *adj.* [unus, one +
    vertō, turn], all together, whole.
vad•um, -ī, *n.,* ford, shallow.
vērō, *adv.* [vērus, true], truly; but, however.

---

1. Pugnātum est: impers. use of a personal
verb in the pass.; see App. §87, *d.*

2. ōrdinēs servāre: "keep to their ranks"
or "preserve their formations."

3. alius aliā ex nāvī: "one man from another ship" is Latin's idiomatic way of saying
in the sing. what we generally say in the pl.:
"various men from different ships." The sing.
verbs that follow agree, of course, with alius,
so you will have to adjust your translation
there too to get the general sense. On the
other hand, each man was doing this individually, so you can also try translating with
the sing. for a more literal translation.

3–4. quibuscumque signīs occurrerat:
"with whatever standards they (he) had 'run
into' or happened upon."

4. sē adgregābat: "they (he) would attach
themselves (himself) in formation."

5. singulārēs: "one at a time."

5–6. ubi . . . cōnspexerant: "whenever
they had caught sight."

6. incitātīs equīs: abl. absolute, attendant
circumstances; see App. §§142, *b;* 150.

7. adoriēbantur: "they would repeatedly
attack"; see App. §191, *a.*

8. ūniversōs: "the whole group (of
Romans)."

10

15

> *Quod cum* animadvertisset *Caesar,* scaphās *longārum nāvium,*
> item speculātōria nāvigia *mīlitibus* complērī *iussit, et quōs*
> labōrantēs cōnspexerat, *hīs* subsidia submittēbat. *Nostrī,* simul
> in āridō *cōnstitērunt, suīs omnibus* cōnsecūtīs, *in hostēs* impetum
> *fēcērunt atque eōs in* fugam *dedērunt; neque longius* prōsequī
> *potuērunt, quod equitēs* cursum *tenēre atque* īnsulam *capere nōn*
> *potuerant.*

---

animad•vertō, -vertere, -vertī, -versum
 [animus, mind + ad + vertō, turn], turn
 the mind to; notice.
ārid•us, -a, um, *adj.* [āreō, be dry], dry; *n.*
 as noun: dry land.
com•pleō, -plēre, -plēvī, -plētum [*obs.:*
 pleō, fill], fill up; complete; cover.
cōn•sequor, -sequī, -secutus sum [sequor,
 follow], follow up; reach.
cōn•spiciō, -spicere, -spexī, -spectum
 [speciō, look], look at, discern, perceive.
curs•us, -ūs, *m.* [currō, run], speed; course;
 voyage.
fug•a, -ae, *f.*, flight; in fugam conicere *or*
 dare, put to flight.
impet•us, -ūs, *m.*, attack; force, vehemence.
īnsul•a, -ae, *f.*, island.

item, *adv.*, in like manner, so, also, just so.
labōrō, 1 [labor, toil], work hard; labor, be
 hard pressed.
nāvig•ium, -ī, *n.* [nāvigō, sail], ship.
prō•sequor, -sequī, -secūtus sum [sequor,
 follow], follow; pursue.
scaph•a, -ae, *f.*, skiff, boat.
simul, *adv.* at once, at the same time,
 thereupon.
speculātōri•us, -a, -um, *adj.* [speculātor,
 spy], scouting.
sub•mittō, -mittere, -mīsī, -missum
 [mittō, send], send, send to the
 assistance of.
subsid•ium, -ī, *n.* [subsideō, sit near *or* in
 reserve], reserve force; help.

---

9. Quod cum: equivalent in sense to *et cum id*; *conjunctio relativa*; see App. §173, *a.*

 scaphās: small boats that were carried on the warships (*longae nāvēs*).

 10. speculātōria nāvigia: "spy craft"; smaller boats for reconnaissance that could move more quickly and in shallow water.

 quōs: the rel. comes before its antecedent **hīs**, which makes sense chronologically.

 10–11. iussit . . . cōnspexerat . . . submittēbat: perf. . . . plupf. . . . impf.; as always, Caesar's use of tense is precise: "he commanded" after "he had seen," and then "he was sending help."

 11. simul = *simul atque.*

11–12. Nostrī . . . suīs omnibus: "our (men) . . . all their (comrades)."

 13. longius: "very far." We are taught to use "rather" with comparatives and "very" with superlatives, but try both, and decide which makes more sense in context. Such rules are guidelines, not immutable laws.

 14. cursum tenēre: "hold their course." The cavalry were following separately.

 īnsulam capere: "reach the island." The failure of the cavalry to arrive will impede Caesar's military operations because cavalry traditionally chase and kill retreating enemies. If one's enemies escape, they can later regroup and fight again.

Hoc ūnum ad prīstinam fortūnam *Caesarī* dēfuit.

---

dē•sum, -esse, -fuī, — [**sum,** be. App. §66],
be lacking, be absent from, fail.
fortūn•a, -ae, *f.* [**fors,** chance], fortune,
chance, opportunity, condition; success,
property. *All* fortuna *was the domain of*

the goddess Fortuna, *a deity Caesar and his
troops cultivated with great devotion.*
prīstin•us, -a, -um, *adj.* [*from* **prior,**
former], former; previous.

---

16. Hoc ūnum: "this one thing," i.e., the
ability to pursue the fleeing Britons.

prīstinam fortūnam: Caesar's "luck,"
or good fortune, was well-established and
long-standing. Like most Roman generals,
he would have attributed such success to
special divine favor. The phrase also turns
what was in fact a very difficult landing into
something of a success in the eyes of the
reader. The whole sequence draws us in, so
that we admire Caesar's quick thinking and
his soldiers' bravery. We take their side, and
are relieved when they finally make it relatively safely to shore. A more matter-of-fact
presentation of a difficult landing might otherwise have led a skeptical reader in Rome
to ask whether Caesar, perhaps with better
planning, could have found a way to land
without immediately coming under attack
from a watchful enemy!

[4.27] *Hostēs proeliō* superātī, simul *atque sē ex* fugā *recēpērunt,*
statim *ad Caesarem lēgātōs dē* pāce *mīsērunt;* obsidēs *datūrōs*
quaeque imperāsset *factūrōs sēsē* pollicitī *sunt. Ūnā cum hīs*
lēgātīs Commius Atrebās vēnit, *quem* suprā dēmōnstrāveram
5   *ā Caesare in Britanniam* praemissum.

Atre•bās, -bātis, *m.,* an Atrebatian; *pl.* the
Atrebates.
Com•mius, -mī, *m.,* Commius, *a leader of*
the Atrebates. He was loyal to Caesar until
52 BCE *when he led troops in support of the*
general Gallic revolt.
dēmōnstrō, 1 [**mōnstrō,** show], point out,
explain, describe; declare.
fug•a, -ae, *f.,* flight.
imperō, 1 [**in + parō,** procure], demand
from; order, instruct, rule.
ob•ses, -idis, *m. and f.* [**obsideō,** blockade],
hostage; pledge, security.

pāx, pācis, *f.,* peace treaty, truce, peace, favor.
polliceor, 2 [**prō + liceor,** bid, offer], offer,
promise.
prae•mittō, -mittere, -mīsī, -missum
[**mittō,** send], send before *or* in advance.
simul, *adv.,* at once, at the same time,
thereupon; **simul atque,** as soon as.
statim, *adv.* [**stō,** stand], immediately.
superō, 1 [**super,** over], go over; be superior
to, conquer; remain.
suprā, *adv.,* before.
veniō, venīre, vēnī, ventum, come, arrive,
go, advance.

---

2. lēgātōs dē pāce: "negotiators for (the
terms of a) peace (treaty)." In addition to
"peace," *pāx* signifies the cessation of armed
conflict, i.e., a "truce," according to the stipu-
lations of an agreement, which we might call
a "pact."
    2–3. datūrōs . . . factūrōs: fut. infs. without
esse in indirect statement with **pollicitī sunt:**
"they promised that they (**sēsē**) would," etc.
    4. Commius: Caesar had earlier sent
Commius to the Britons as an envoy, but they
arrested him on arrival. After their defeat, the
Britons hope that, by returning Commius to
Caesar, they will gain better terms.
    dēmōnstrāveram: uncharacteristically,
Caesar uses the first person. Why? He writes
as an author, explaining that he has mentioned Commius earlier in his narrative.
When, on the other hand, Caesar the author
tells a story in which Caesar the general plays
a role, Caesar the author describes Caesar
the general, as he does all the characters in
his seemingly objective narrative, in the third
person.

Hunc illī ē nāvī ēgressum, *cum ad eōs* ōrātōris modō *Caesaris*
mandāta dēferret, comprehenderant *atque in* vincula coniēcerant;
tum proeliō factō remīsērunt *et in petendā* pāce *eius reī* culpam
in multitūdinem contulērunt *et* propter imprūdentiam *ut*
10   ignōscerētur *petīvērunt.*

**com·prehendō, -prehendere, -prehendī,
-prehēnsum [prehendō (= prendō),**
seize], lay hold of, seize, arrest.
cōn·ferō, -ferre, contulī, collātus [ferō,
bring. App. §81], collect, carry; ascribe
to; compare.
con·iciō, -icere, -iēcī, -iectum [co + iaciō,
throw. App. §7], throw; put.
culp·a, -ae, *f.*, blame, fault, guilt.
dē·ferō, -ferre, -tulī, -lātum [ferō, carry.
App. §81], carry, take; report; bring
before; bestow.
ē·gredior, -gredī, -gressus sum [gradior,
step], come forth, depart; march out,
make a sortie; disembark.
ig·nōscō, -nōscere, -nōvī, -nōtum [in
+ (g)nōscēns, knowing (*from* nōscō,
know)], forgive, pardon.

imprudenti·a, -ae, *f.* **[imprūdēns,**
imprudent], ignorance, indiscretion.
mandāt·um, -ī, *n.* **[mandō,** command],
order; message.
mod·us, -ī, *m.*, measure, quantity, size;
manner, method.
ōrāt·or, -ōris, *m.* **[ōrō,** speak], speaker;
ambassador, envoy.
pāx, pācis, *f.*, peace treaty, truce, peace,
favor.
propter, *prep. with acc.* **[prope,** near], on
account of, because of.
re·mittō, -mittere, -mīsī, -missum [mittō,
send], send *or* dispatch back, return;
release, relax, give up.
vincul·a, -ae, *f.* **[vinciō,** bind], chain.

---

6. ōrātōris modō: Commius made a formal presentation of Caesar's demands in his role as Caesar's envoy. Instead of preparing an answer, the Britons arrested him.
8. petendā: gerundive; see App. §§288, 294.
eius reī: Commius's mistreatment.
9. multitūdinem: the envoys blame the lower classes, whose desires they claim their leaders were unable to resist or deny.

imprūdentiam: in addition to passing the blame, the envoys also claim that British leaders were ignorant.
10. ignōscerētur: subjunctive in a substantive clause of purpose with **petīvērunt;** see App. §228, *a.*

Caesar questus *quod, cum* ultrō *in continentem lēgātīs missīs*
pācem *ab sē petīssent, bellum sine causā* intulissent, ignōscere
imprūdentiae *dīxit* obsidēs*que* imperāvit; *quōrum illī partem*
statim *dedērunt, partem ex* longinquiōribus *locīs* arcessītam
15   paucīs *diēbus sēsē datūrōs dīxērunt.* Intereā *suōs* remigrāre
in agrōs iussērunt, prīncipēs*que* undique *convenīre et sē*
cīvitātēsque suās Caesarī commendāre *coepērunt.*

---

arcess•ō, -ere, -īvī, -ītum, summon, send
for, invite.
commendō, 1 [**mandō,** entrust], entrust,
surrender.
ig•nōscō, -nōscere, -nōvī, -nōtum [in
+ (g)**nōscēns,** knowing (*from* **nōscō,**
know)], forgive, pardon.
imperō, 1 [**in** + **parō,** procure], demand
from; order, instruct, rule.
imprudenti•a, -ae, *f.* [**imprūdēns,**
imprudent], ignorance, indiscretion.
īnferō, īnferre, intulī, illātum [**ferō,** carry.
App. §81], carry into, import, inflict,
cause, produce; cast into.
intereā, *adv.,* in the meantime, meanwhile.
longinqu•us, -a, -um, *adj.* [**longus,** long],
distant, remote; long.

ob•ses, -idis, *m. and f.* [**obsideō,** blockade],
hostage; pledge, security.
pauc•ī, -ae, -a, *adj.,* few; *as noun:* few *persons*
or things.
pāx, pācis, *f.,* peace treaty, truce, peace,
favor.
prīn•ceps, -cipis, *adj.* [**prīmus,** first], first;
as noun, chief *or* leader.
queror, querī, questus sum, complain,
bewail, lament.
re•migrō, 1 [**migrō,** move, migrate], move
back, return.
statim, *adv.* [**stō,** stand], immediately.
ultrō, *adv.,* voluntarily; besides, moreover.
undique, *adv.* [**unde,** whence], on all sides,
everywhere.

---

11. quod: when **quod** introduces a causal
clause, the clause can take either the subjunctive or the indicative. The indicative
represents the speaker's own reasoning; the
subjunctive someone else's or a change in attitude in the speaker toward his own reasoning.
11–12. cum . . . petīssent: "although . . .
they (were the ones who) had requested." Even
before Caesar sailed with eighty ships to their
island, the Britons were well aware of Caesar's
many victories in Gaul. As a precaution, they
had sent envoys to the continent to arrange a
"treaty" (*pāx*) with the victorious general.
11–13. Caesar . . . dīxit . . . imperāvit
(que): HYPERBATON; see App. §301, *f.*
12. bellum sine causā intulissent: Caesar
arrived in Britain with warships and soldiers;
yet Caesar claims that the British waged un-
provoked war on him.
12–13. ignōscere . . . dīxit: the envoys
gain their request.

13. imprūdentiae: dat. indirect object
with an intransitive verb; see App. §115.
obsidēs: these hostages for good behavior
would have included close relatives of the
British leaders.
14–15. partem . . . arcessītam: "because
some had been summoned . . . "; the part.
takes the place of a subordinate clause; see
App. §283.
15. datūrōs: fut. inf. with *esse* omitted in
indirect statement.
suōs: "their people."
16. convenīre: "assemble"; at a place determined by Caesar for their formal surrender.
17. commendāre: "entrust"; Latin uses
terms that suggest reciprocal personal rela-
tionships, although what they are actually doing is submitting to Caesar's superior military
power in formal surrender.

[4.28] *Hīs rēbus* pāce cōnfirmātā, post *diem* quārtum *quam est in Britanniam* ventum *nāvēs* XVIII, *dē quibus* suprā dēmōnstrātum *est, quae equitēs* sustulerant, *ex superiōre* portū lēnī ventō solvērunt.

---

cōnfirmō, 1 [**firmō,** strengthen], establish, strengthen, encourage, console; declare.

dēmōnstrō, 1 [**mōnstrō,** show], point out, explain, describe; declare.

lēn•is, -e, *adj.,* gentle, mild, smooth.

pāx, pācis, *f.,* peace treaty, truce, peace, favor.

port•us, -ūs, *m.,* harbor, haven, port.

post, *prep. with acc.,* behind, after.

quārt•us, -a, -um, *adj., ord. num.* [**quattuor,** four], fourth.

solvō, solvere, solvī, solūtum, loosen, untie; *with or without* **nāvēs,** set sail.

suprā, *adv.* before.

tollō, tollere, sustulī, sublātum, lift up; take on board; remove; destroy.

veniō, venīre, vēnī, ventum, come, arrive, go, advance; *pass. often impers. as* **ventum est,** they came, it came, etc.

vent•us, -ī, *m.,* wind.

XVIII, *sign for* **duodēvīgintī,** eighteen (*see also* App. §47).

---

1. Hīs rēbus: "these terms" or "conditions"; i.e., hostages, assembly in Caesar's camp, and formal submission.

post diem quārtum quam = *diē quartō postquam;* the construction is idiomatic and not entirely grammatical as an attempt at a literal translation will soon demonstrate and, because Romans included both the day from which they began counting (we do not do

this) as well as the day on which they stopped counting (we do this as well), we have to subtract one day, hence: "on the third day after" or "three days after."

2. suprā: See *BG* 4.22–23 where Caesar describes how he separated the fleet into two contingents.

3. superiōre portū: a port on the mainland.

5   *Quae cum* appropinquārent *Britanniae et ex castrīs vidērentur,*
      tanta tempestās subitō coorta *est ut* nūlla *eārum* cursum
      tenēre posset, sed aliae eōdem unde *erant profectae* referrentur,
      aliae ad īnferiōrem *partem* īnsulae, *quae est* propius sōlis
      occāsum, *magnō suō cum perīculō* dēicerentur; *quae tamen*
10   ancorīs iactīs *cum* flūctibus complērentur, necessāriō adversā
      nocte in altum prōvectae continentem *petiērunt.*

---

advers•us, -a, -um, *adv.* [perf. part. of
  advertō, turn to], turned against;
  opposite; adverse, unfavorable.
alt•us, -a, -um, *adj.,* high, deep; *n. as noun:*
  the deep, the sea.
ancor•a, -ae, *f.,* anchor; **in ancorīs,** at
  anchor.
appropinquō, 1 [**ad + propinquus,** near],
  come near, approach.
com•pleō, -plēre, -plēvī, -plētum [*obs.:*
  pleō, fill], fill up; complete; cover.
contin•ēns, -entis, *adj.* [**contineō,** hold
  together], continuous, unbroken; *as noun,*
  continent.
co•orior, -orīrī, -ortus sum [**orior,** rise],
  arise, spring up, break out.
curs•us, -ūs, *m.* [**currō,** run], speed; course;
  voyage.
dē•iciō, -icere, -iēcī, -iectum [**iaciō,** throw.
  App. §7], cast down; dislodge; kill;
  disappoint.
flūct•us, -ūs, *m.* [**fluō,** flow], flood, wave.
iaciō, iacere, iēcī, iactum, throw, cast, hurl.
īnfer•us, -a, -um, *adj.,* low, below; *comp.:*
  īnferior, lower, inferior.

īnsul•a, -ae, *f.,* island.
necessāriō, *adv.* [*abl. of* **necessārius,**
  necessary], necessity, of necessity,
  unavoidably.
nūll•us, -a, -um, *gen.* **nūllīus,** *adj.* [**ne-** +
  ūllus, any], not any, no; *as noun:* no one,
  none.
occās•us, -ūs, *m.* [**occidō,** fall, happen],
  falling down, setting; *with* **sōlis,** sunset;
  the west.
propius, *adv. and prep. with acc.* (App. §122,
  b.) [**prope,** near], nearer.
prō•vehō, -vehere, -vexī, -vectum [**vehō,**
  carry], carry forward; *pass.,* be carried
  forward, sail.
referō, referre, rettulī, relātum [**re** + **ferō,**
  carry. App. §81], bear, carry back, report.
sōl, sōlis, *m.,* the sun; **ad occidentem
  sōlem,** toward the setting sun *or* west; **ad
  orientem sōlem,** toward the rising sun
  or east.
subitō, *adv.* [**subitus,** sudden], suddenly.
tempes•tās, -tātis, *f.* [**tempus,** time], time,
  season; weather, storm.
unde, *adv.,* from which place, whence.

---

5. Quae = *et illae; conjunctio relativa;* see
App. §173, *a.*
  7. posset: subjunctive in a clause of result;
see App. §226.
  7–8. aliae ... aliae: "some (ships) ... other
(ships)."
  8. īnferiōrem partem īnsulae: "the lower
part of the island," i.e., the southern coast of
Britain.
  propius: "nearer to" or "toward" with acc.;
see App. §122, *b.*
  8–9. sōlis occāsum: "setting of the sun,"
i.e., west.

  9. dēicerentur: "were tossed" by the waves
and wind.
  quae tamen = *quae nāvēs tamen.*
  10. ancorīs iactīs: "although they cast
their anchors."
  complērentur: subjunctive with **cum** in a
temporal clause.
  10–11. adversā nocte: "with night opposed"; i.e., despite the danger of (sailing at)
night. See also PERSONIFICATION in App.
§302, *h.*

[4.29] *Eādem nocte accidit ut esset* lūna plēna, *quī diēs* maritimōs
aestūs *maximōs in* Ōceanō efficere *cōnsuēvit, nostrīsque id erat*
incognitum. *Ita ūnō tempore et longās nāvēs, quibus exercitum*
trānsportandum cūrāverat, *quāsque Caesar in* āridum
5   subdūxerat, aestus complēverat, *et* onerāriās, *quae ad* ancorās
erant dēligātae, tempestās adflīctābat, *neque* ūlla *nostrīs*
facultās *aut* administrandī *aut* auxiliandī *dabātur.*

---

administrō, 1 [**minister,** servant], serve,
attend, wait upon; manage, guide.
ad•flictō, 1 [*freq.* of **afflīgō**], strike
repeatedly, harass; oppress, vex
aest•us, -ūs, *m.,* heat, boiling, surging, tide;
minuente aestū, at ebb tide.
ancor•a, -ae, *f.,* anchor; **in ancorīs,** at
anchor.
ārid•us, -a, -um, *adj.* [**āreō,** be dry], dry; *n.*
as noun: dry land.
auxilior, 1 [**auxilium,** help], help, give aid,
assist, render assistance.
com•pleō, -plēre, -plēvī, -plētum [*obs.:*
pleō, fill], fill up; complete; cover.
cūrō, 1 [**cūra,** care], take care of, provide
for.
dēligō, 1 [**ligō,** bind], bind *or* tie down,
fasten, moor.
ef•ficiō, -ficere, -fēcī, -fectum [**faciō,**
make], make *or* do completely; cause.

facul•tās, -tātis, *f.* [**facilis,** easy], power;
opportunity; resources.
incognit•us, -a, -um, *adj.* [**in** + **cognitus,**
known], unknown.
lūn•a, -ae, *f.,* the moon.
maritim•us, -a, -um, *adj.* [**mare,** sea], of the
sea; on the sea.
Ōcean•us, -ī, *m.,* the ocean.
onerāri•us, -a, -um, *adj.* [**onus,** load],
equipped for loads; *with* **nāvis,** transport,
freight ship.
plēn•us, -a, -um, *adj.* [**pleō,** fill], full, whole,
complete.
sub•dūcō, -dūcere, -dūxī, -ductum [**dūcō,**
lead], lead.
tempes•tās, -tātis, *f.* [**tempus,** time], time,
season; weather, storm.
trānsportō, 1 [**portō,** carry], carry across *or*
over, bring over, convey, transport.
ūll•us, -a, -um, *adj.,* a single, any.

---

1. nocte: abl. of time when; see App. §152.
lūna plēna: scholars have used this astro-
nomical fact to calculate the night: 30–31
August 55 BCE. This means that Caesar must
have landed in Britain on 27 August ("four
days" earlier, counting from the 30th according to Roman methods).
2. aestūs: the tide that is increased in
strength by a full moon is called a "spring
tide" (this has nothing to do with the season,
but instead with the surging or rising of the
water; compare a spring of water).
2–3. nostrīs ... incognitum: "unknown
. . . to our men"; Caesar does not scold his
men for their ignorance, but, of course, he
does not mention that he too was ignorant
of the local tides, not to mention the effect of
the full moon on them. Caesar is a master at
shifting blame away from himself.

3. ūnō tempore: abl. of time when; §152.
quibus: abl. of means; §143.
4. exercitum trānsportandum: "for the
conveyance of his army"; gerundive of purpose after the verb **cūrāverat.**
4–5. quās ... subdūxerat: Caesar lets us
know that he, as a prudent commander, had
taken precautions by dragging the warships
onto the beach.
5–6. quae ... dēligātae: the transport
ships had not been dragged ashore; they were
left anchored close to shore.
6–7. neque ūlla nostrīs facultās: note
how the men, not Caesar (who had taken
insufficient precautions), are the ones who
had no opportunity to manage or render assistance in this situation.

Complūribus *nāvibus* frāctīs, *reliquae cum essent* fūnibus,
ancorīs *reliquīsque* armāmentīs āmissīs *ad* nāvigandum
10   inūtilēs, *magna, id quod* necesse *erat accidere, tōtīus exercitūs*
perturbātiō *facta est. Neque* enim *nāvēs erant aliae quibus*
reportārī *possent, et omnia* deerant *quae ad* reficiendās *nāvēs*
erant *ūsuī, et, quod omnibus* cōnstābat hiemārī *in Galliā*
oportēre, *frūmentum in hīs locīs in* hiemem prōvīsum *nōn erat.*

ā·mittō, -mittere, -mīsī, -missum [**mittō,**
send], send away, dismiss; let go; lose.
ancor·a, -ae, *f.,* anchor; **in ancorīs,** at
anchor.
armāment·a, -ōrum, *n. pl.* [**armō,** arm],
implements, gear; tackle *or* rigging (*of a*
ship).
complūr·ēs, -a, *adj.* [**plūs,** more], several,
many; a great many.
cōn·stō, -stāre, -stitī, -statum [**stō,** stand],
stand firm; depend on; be complete; cost;
impers.: it is evident *or* known.
dē·sum, -esse, -fuī, — [**sum,** be. App. §66],
be lacking, be absent from, fail.
enim, *conj.,* in fact, really; for; **sed enim,** but
in fact, however.
frangō, frangere, frēgī, frāctum, break,
wreck; crush, discourage.
fūn·is, -is, *m.,* rope, cable.

hiemō, 1 [**hiems,** winter], pass the winter,
winter.
hiem·s, -is, *f.,* wintertime, winter.
inūtil·is, -e, *adj.* [**in** + **ūtilis,** useful],
useless, disadvantageous.
nāvigō, 1 [**nāvis,** ship] set sail, sail.
necesse, *indecl. adj.,* necessary, unavoidable,
indispensable.
oport·et, -ēre, -uit, —, *impers.,* it is
necessary *or* proper.
perturbāti·ō, -ōnis, *f.* [**perturbō,** disturb],
disturbance, disorder, confusion.
prō·videō, -vidēre, -vīdī, -vīsum [**videō,**
see], see beforehand, foresee; care for,
provide.
re·ficiō, -ficere, -fēcī, -fectum [**re** + **faciō,**
make], repair.
reportō, 1 [**re** + **portō,** carry], carry *or*
bring back, convey.

---

8. reliquae: i.e., *nāvēs;* by moving "the remaining (ships)" outside the **cum** clause, Caesar places them in more dramatic contrast with
those that had been shattered. Note too that
the clause also ends with an adj. (**inūtilēs**) in
agreement with the ellipted ships.

8–9. fūnibus . . . āmissīs: abl. absolute,
causal; see App. §150.

9. ad nāvigandum: gerund plus **ad** to express purpose; see App. §§287, 293.

10. id quod: in reference to the great disturbance; **id** is in apposition with the whole
clause, and serves as the antecedent of **quod.**

necesse: when things go wrong, Caesar
is not at fault (at least in Caesar's narrative).

11–12. quibus . . . possent: "of the type
by means of which," etc.; subjunctive in a rel.
clause of characteristic.

12. ad reficiendās nāvēs: gerundive with
ad to express purpose; see App. §§288, 293.

12–13. quae . . . erant: the rel. clause explains what was meant by the indefinite antecedent (**omnia**); see App. § 231.

13. ūsuī: dat. of purpose; see App. §119.

omnibus . . . cōnstābat: "it was obvious to
everyone." But who gave the orders?

14. in hiemem: "for the winter."

prōvīsum nōn erat: this clause lacks an
abl. of agent (*ā Caesare,* for example).

[4.30] *Quibus rēbus cognitīs*, prīncipēs *Britanniae, quī* post
*proelium ad Caesarem convēnerant, inter sē collocūtī, cum
equitēs et nāvēs et frūmentum Rōmānīs* deesse intellegerent
et paucitātem *mīlitum ex castrōrum* exiguitāte *cognōscerent*,
5   *quae hōc erant etiam* angustiōra *quod sine* impedīmentīs *Caesar
legiōnēs* trānsportāverat, optimum *factū esse dūxērunt* rebelliōne
factā frūmentō commeātūque *nostrōs* prohibēre *et rem in* hiemem
prōdūcere,

---

angust•us, -a, -um, *adj.,* [**angō,** squeeze],
compressed, narrow.
bon•us, -a, -um, *adj.,* good, well-disposed;
superl., **optimus** (App. §42).
commeāt•us, -ūs, *m.* [**commeō,** go back
and forth], voyage; provisions.
de•sum, -esse, -fuī, — [**sum,** be. App. §66],
be lacking, be absent from, fail.
exigui•tās, -tātis, *f.* [**exiguus,** scanty],
scantiness, shortness.
hiem•s, -is, *f.,* wintertime, winter.
impedīment•um, -ī, *n.* [**impediō,** hinder],
hindrance; *pl.*: baggage, baggage train.
intel•legō, -legere, -lēgī, -lēctum [**inter +
legō,** choose, select], select; understand;
perceive; find out.

pauci•tās, -tātis, *f.* [**paucus,** few], fewness,
small number.
post, *prep. with acc.,* behind, after.
prīn•ceps, -cipis [**prīmus,** first], chief, first;
as noun, chief *or* leader.
prō•dūcō, -dūcere, -dūxī, -ductum [**dūcō,**
lead], lead out; prolong.
prohibeō, 2 [**habeō,** hold], keep from, keep,
restrain, prevent, prohibit; keep out *or*
away from; protect, guard.
rebelli•ō, -ōnis, *f.* [**rebellō,** renew war],
renewal of war, rebellion, revolt.
trānsportō, 1 [**portō,** carry], carry across
or over, bring over, convey, transport.

---

1. prīncipēs Britanniae: "the chiefs of
the British tribes"; subject of **dūxērunt.** After they realize that Caesar has lost his ships,
their attitude shifts from defense to offense.

2–4. cum . . . cognōscerent: subjunctive
in a causal clause.

3. et . . . et: polysyndeton; see App.
§301,*f.*

5. quae hōc . . . angustiōra: "which (the
antecedent is the n. pl. **castra**) was even
smaller *because of the following* (*fact*)"; **hōc** anticipates **quod,** which explains why the camp
was so small. Abl. of cause; see App. §138.

6. optimum factū: "the best thing to do";
for the supine in the abl. with adj., see App.
§§296, 510.

6–7. rebelliōne factā: "if they were to
rebel"; abl. absolute, equivalent to a condition; see App. §150.

7. frūmentō commeātūque: abl. of separation (similarly **reditū** below); see App.
§134.

rem: ongoing negotiations with Caesar
about the surrender of hostages, etc.

10
quod hīs superātīs *aut* reditū interclūsīs nēminem
posteā *bellī* īnferendī *causā in Britanniam* trānsitūrum
cōnfīdēbant. Itaque rūrsus coniūrātiōne *factā* paulātim *ex
castrīs discēdere et suōs* clam *ex agrīs* dēdūcere *coepērunt.*

---

clam, *adv.,* secretly.
cōn•fīdō, -fīdere, -fīsī, -fīsum [**fīdō,** trust.
   App. §74], rely on, feel confident, hope.
coniūrāti•ō, -ōnis, *f.* [**coniūrō,** swear], a
   swearing together; plot, conspiracy.
dē•dūcō, -dūcere, -dūxī, -ductum [**dūcō,**
   lead], lead down; bring, conduct.
īn•ferō, īnferre, intulī, illātum [**ferō,**
   carry. App. §81], carry into, import,
   inflict, cause, produce; cast into.
inter•clūdō, -clūdere, -clūsī, -clūsum
   [**claudō,** shut], shut *or* cut off.
itaque, *conj.* [**ita,** so], and so, therefore.
nēmō, *acc.* **nēminem,** *m. and f.* [**ne-** +
   homō, human being], no one, nobody.

paulātim, *adv.* [**paulus,** little], little by little,
   by degrees, gradually.
posteā, *adv.* [**post,** after], after this,
   afterward.
redit•us, -ūs, *m.* [**redeō,** return], returning,
   return.
rūrsus, *adv.* [*for* **reversus,** *from* **revertō,**
   turn back], again, back, anew; in turn.
superō, 1 [**super,** over], go over; be superior
   to, conquer; remain.
trāns•eō, -īre, -iī, -itum [**eō,** go. App. §84],
   cross; march through; migrate.

---

8. hīs ... interclūsīs: another abl. absolute
equivalent to a conditional; see App. §150.
   9. bellī īnferendī causā: gerundive with
causā to express purpose; see App. §§288,
291.
   trānsitūrum: fut. inf. without *esse* in indirect statement dependent on **cōnfīdēbant.**
   10. rūrsus coniūrātiōne factā: "having
renewed by oaths their mutual loyalty"; abl.
absolute; see App. §150. Because they oppose him, Caesar brands the British chiefs
"conspirators." Because they plan in secret

and take religious oaths, the term is objec-
tively true. Of course, Caesar likely failed
to broadcast his military plans publicly in
advance of operations. Did Caesar's men
take oaths to obey him? Were he and his staff
"conspirators"?
   10–11. ex castrīs: the British leaders had
gathered in Caesar's camp to deliver hostages
and make formal submission. They began to
slip away.
   11. suōs: "their men."

[4.31] *At Caesar,* etsī nōndum *eōrum cōnsilia cognōverat, tamen et ex* ēventū *nāvium suārum et ex eō quod* obsidēs *dare* intermīserant *fore id quod accidit* suspicābātur. Itaque *ad omnēs* cāsūs subsidia comparābat. *Nam et frūmentum ex agrīs*
5   cotīdiē *in castra* cōnferēbat *et, quae gravissimē* adflīctae *erant nāvēs, eārum* māteriā *atque* aere *ad reliquās* reficiendās ūtēbātur *et quae ad eās rēs erant ūsuī ex* continentī comparārī *iubēbat.*

---

ad•flīgō, -flīgere, -flīxī, -flīctum, strike against; overthrow; damage, injure.

aes, aeris, *n.,* copper.

cās•us, -ūs, *m.* [**cadō,** fall], accident, chance, misfortune.

comparō, 1 [**parō,** prepare], prepare; acquire, prepare for.

cōn•ferō, -ferre, contulī, collātus [**ferō,** bring. App. §81], collect, carry; ascribe to; compare.

contin•ēns, -entis, *adj.* [**contineō,** hold together], continuous, unbroken; *as noun,* continent.

cotīdiē, *adv.* [**quot,** how many + **diēs,** day], daily, every day.

etsī, *conj.* [**et** + **sī,** if], even if, although.

ēvent•us, -ūs, *m.* [**ēveniō,** turn out], outcome, issue, result, consequence.

inter•mittō, -mittere, -mīsī, -missum [**mittō,** send], send between; intervene, separate; cease; delay, neglect; let pass.

itaque, *conj.* [**ita,** so], and so, therefore.

māteri•a, -ae, *f.,* material; wood, timber.

nōndum, *adv.* [**nōn** + **dum**], not yet.

ob•ses, -idis, *m. and f.* [**obsideō,** blockade], hostage; pledge, security.

re•ficiō, -ficere, -fēcī, -fectum [**re** + **faciō,** make], repair.

subsid•ium, -ī, *n.* [**subsideō,** sit near *or* in reserve], reserve force; help.

suspicor, 1 [**suspiciō,** suspect], suspect, distrust; surmise.

---

2. ex ēventū: "from the fate."

ex eō quod: "from this (fact) that"; **quod** introduces a substantive clause; see App. §248, *a.*

3. fore = *futūrum esse* in indirect statement dependent on **suspicābātur.**

quod accidit: "what actually happened."

4. comparābat: Caesar tells us that he analyzed the situation, and then took all possible precautions. Caesar takes credit for superior leadership when he can.

frūmentum: grain could be harvested only when it was ripe, and bread was the main staple in a soldier's diet.

5–6. quae ... nāvēs, eārum (*nāvium*) ... **reliquās** (*nāvēs*): the ships (the proper antecedent with **eārum**) have been brought into the subordinate clause to round it off rhetorically, and ellipted twice from the main clause. To make the meaning clearer in English, translate *eārum nāvium, quae* ....

7. quae ... ūsuī: we may supply an ellipted **ea** in the acc. (and hence subject of the pass. complementary inf. **comparārī**) to serve as the antecedent of **quae.**

Itaque, *cum summō* studiō *ā mīlitibus* administrārētur, XII
nāvibus āmissīs, *reliquīs ut* nāvigārī commodē *posset* effēcit.

---

administrō, 1 [**minister,** servant], serve,
attend, wait upon; manage, guide.

ā•mittō, -mittere, -mīsī, -missum [**mittō,**
send], send away, dismiss; let go; lose.

commodē, *adv.* [**commodus,** convenient],
conveniently; readily, easily, fitly; **satis
commodē,** to great advantage, very easily.

ef•ficiō, -ficere, -fēcī, -fectum [**faciō,**
make], make *or* do completely, complete,
construct; cause, render.

itaque, *conj.* [**ita,** so], and so, therefore,
accordingly.

nāvigō, 1 [**nāvis,** ship] set sail, sail.

stud•ium, -ī, *n.* [**studeō,** be zealous],
eagerness; devotion; pursuit.

XII, *sign for* **duodecim,** twelve (*see also* App.
§47).

---

8. summō studiō: abl. of manner; see App.
§142.

cum ... administrārētur: subjunctive in
a causal clause.

8–9. XII ... āmissīs: "although we lost
twelve ships"; abl. absolute; see App. §150.

9. reliquīs (*nāvibus*): abl. of means; see
App. §143.

ut ... posset: subjunctive in a clause of
result; see App. §226.

[4.32] *Dum ea geruntur, legiōne ex* cōnsuētūdine *ūnā*
frūmentātum *missā, quae* appellābātur septima, *neque* ūllā *ad
id tempus bellī* suspīciōne interpositā, *cum pars hominum in
agrīs* remanēret, *pars etiam in castra* ventitāret, *eī quī prō* portīs
5   *castrōrum in* statiōne *erant* Caesarī nūntiāvērunt pulverem
maiōrem *quam* cōnsuētūdō *ferret in eā parte vidērī quam in
partem legiō iter fēcisset.*

---

appellō, -āre, 1, call, name.
cōnsuētūd•ō, -inis, *f.* [**cōnsuēscō,** become
   accustomed], habit, custom, practice;
   "lifestyle."
frūmentor, 1 [**frūmentum,** grain], get
   grain, forage.
inter•pōnō, -pōnere, -posuī, -positum
   [**pōnō,** put], interpose; allege; cause.
maior, māius, *adj.* [*comp. of* **magnus,** large],
   larger; older, elder.
nūntiō, 1 [**nūntius,** messenger], announce,
   report; order.
port•a, -ae, *f.,* gate.
pulv•is, -eris, *m.,* dust.

re•maneō, -manēre, -mānsī, -mānsum [**re**
   + **maneō,** remain], stay behind, remain.
septim•us, -a, -um, *ordinal num., adj.,*
   seventh.
stati•ō, -ōnis, *f.* [**stō,** stand], standing;
   sentries, outposts; **in statiōne esse,** be
   on guard.
suspīci•ō, -ōnis, *f.* [**suspicor,** suspect],
   suspicion, distrust; surmise.
ūll•us, -a, -um *gen.* **ūllīus** (App. §32), *adj.,* a
   single, any.
ventitō, 1 [*frequentative of* **veniō,** come],
   keep coming, resort; go back and forth,
   visit.

---

1. geruntur: historical pres.; see App.
§190, *a.*
2. frūmentātum: supine in the acc. to express purpose; see App. §295.
2–3. neque ūllā ... suspīciōne: Caesar just
told us above that he knew exactly what was
going to happen because of the disaster to his
ships and the small size of his camp, but now he
tells us that his men were suspecting nothing.
On the other hand, if they had been suspicious,
their inattentiveness to security would have re-
flected badly on Caesar's leadership.

4. ventitāret: "repeatedly came" (with
the grain they were harvesting); freq. form
of *veniō.*
5. pulverem: acc. subject of the inf.
vidērī in indirect statement dependent on
nūntiāvērunt.
6. quam cōnsuētūdō ferret: "than regular operations would produce"; subjunctive
because the clause is subordinate in indirect
statement.
6–7. quam in partem: "in which direction."

Caesar id quod erat suspicātus *aliquid* novī *ā* barbarīs initum
cōnsilī, cohortēs quae in statiōnibus *erant sēcum in eam partem*
10   *proficīscī, ex reliquīs duās in* statiōnem *cohortēs* succēdere, *reliquās*
armārī *et* cōnfestim *sēsē* subsequī *iussit. Cum paulō longius*
ā castrīs prōcessisset, *suōs ab hostibus premī atque* aegrē *sustinēre*
et cōnfertā *legiōne ex omnibus partibus tēla* conicī animadvertit.

---

ae•ger, -gra, -grum, *adj.,* sick, ill.
animad•vertō, -vertere, -vertī, -versum
[**animus,** mind + **ad** + **vertō,** turn], turn
the mind to; notice.
armō, 1 [**arma,** arms], arm, equip; *pass.*
arm oneself; **armātus,** *perf. part., as adj.,*
armed; **armātī,** *as noun,* armed men.
barbar•us, -a, -um, *adj.,* foreign (*to Romans*
and Greeks), uncivilized; *pl. as noun:*
barbarians.
cōnfert•us, -a, -um, *adj.* [*perf. part. of*
cōnferciō, crowd together], dense, thick,
compact, stuffed.
cōnfestim, *adv.,* hastily, at once, immediately.
con•iciō, -icere, -iēcī, -iectum [**co** + **iaciō,**
throw. App. §7], hurl, throw, cast.
in•eō, -īre, -iī, -itum [**eō,** go. App. §84], go
into; enter upon, begin; **inīre cōnsilium,**
form a plan; **inīre ratiōnem,** make an
estimate, decide; **inīre grātiam,** gain
favor; **inīre numerum,** enumerate.

nov•us, -a, -um, *adj.,* new, novel; unusual,
fresh; **rēs novae,** a change of government,
revolution; *superl.:* **novissim•us, -a, -um,**
latest, last; *as noun or with* **agmen,** those
in the rear, the rear.
paulō, *adv.* [**paulus,** little], a little,
somewhat, slightly.
prō•cēdō, -cēdere, -cessī, -cessum [**cēdō,**
go], go forth *or* forward, proceed, advance.
stati•ō, -ōnis, *f.* [**stō,** stand], standing;
sentries, outposts; **in statiōne esse,** be
on guard.
sub•sequor, -sequī, -secūtus [**sequor,**
follow], follow closely.
suc•cēdō, -cēdere, -cessī, -cessum [**cēdō,**
go], go *or* come under; come up to, come
up, advance, be next to; succeed, take the
place of; succeed, prosper.
suspicor, 1 [**suspīciō,** suspect], suspect,
distrust; surmise.

---

8. Caesar id quod erat suspicātus:
"Caesar, having suspected (in advance) this
(thing) which was (happening)," namely,
that, etc. The key to understanding the syntax here is to realize that **Caesar** is the subject
of **iussit,** that **suspicātus** modifies **Caesar** as
an adj., and that **id,** which is the antecedent
of the subordinate clause **quod erat,** is in
apposition with the indirect statement that
depends on **suspicātus.**
    8–9. aliquid . . . initum (*esse*) **cōnsilī:** in-
direct statement dependent on **suspicātus,**
and the clause with which **id** is in apposition.
aliquid novī . . . cōnsilī = "some new plan";
indef. n. acc. with the partitive gen.; see App.
§101.
    9. in statiōnibus: "on guard duty" in dif-
ferent areas (e.g., at the four gates), hence pl.

10. reliquās: supply *cohortēs.*
    10–11. proficīscī . . . succēdere . . . armārī
. . . subsequī: complementary infs. dependent on **iussit.**
    12. prōcessisset: subjunctive in a tempo-
ral clause.
    12–13. suōs . . . premī atque . . . sustinēre
et . . . tēla . . . conicī: indirect statement dependent on **animadvertit.** Note that the conj.
atque binds the two infs. that have **suōs** as
their subject, whereas **conicī,** which has **tēla**
as its subject, is joined to the list with **et.**
    13. cōnfertā legiōne: "because the le-
gion was crowded together"; abl. absolute;
see App. §150. Their crowding made them an
easy target for British spears.

Nam quod omnī ex reliquīs partibus dēmessō *frūmentō pars*
15   *ūna erat reliqua,* suspicātī *hostēs* hūc *nostrōs esse* ventūrōs
noctū in silvīs dēlituerant; *tum* dispersōs dēpositīs *armīs*
in metendō occupātōs subitō adortī paucīs *interfectīs reliquōs*
incertīs *ōrdinibus* perturbāverant, simul *equitātū atque* essedīs
circumdederant.

---

ad•orior, -orīrī, -ortus sum [**orior**, arise],
rise against, attack.
circum•dō, -dare, -dedī, -datum [**dō**, put],
put around, encompass, surround.
dē•litēscō, -litēscere, -lituī, — [**latēscō,**
inceptive of **lateō,** lie hidden], hide
oneself, lurk.
dē•metō, -metere, -messuī, -messum
[**metō,** reap], mow, reap.
dē•pōnō, -pōnere, -posuī, -positum
[**pōnō,** put], lay down; deposit.
di•spergō, -spergere, -spersī, -spersum
[**spargō,** scatter], scatter, disperse.
essed•um, -ī, *n., a two-wheeled war* chariot
used by the Britons.
hūc, *adv.* [*from* **hic,** this], to this place,
hither, here; against these, to these.
incert•us, -a, -um, *adj.* [**in + certus,**
decided], undecided, uncertain,
untrustworthy; indefinite; disordered.

metō, metere, messuī, messum, mow,
harvest, reap.
occupō, 1 [**ob + capiō,** take], take
possession of, seize; engage.
pauc•ī, -ae, -a, *adj.,* few; *as noun:* few *persons
or things.*
perturbō, 1 [**turbō,** disturb], disturb
greatly, throw into confusion; terrify.
silv•a, -ae, *f.,* forest, woods, a wood.
simul, *adv.* at once, at the same time,
thereupon.
subitō, *adv.* [**subitus,** sudden], suddenly.
suspicor, 1 [**suspīciō,** suspect], suspect,
distrust; surmise.
veniō, venīre, vēnī, ventum, come, arrive,
go, advance.

---

14. omnī . . . frūmentō: abl. absolute; see
App. §150.
15. hūc . . . ventūrōs: indirect statement
dependent on **suspicātī,** which modifies
hostēs, the subject of **dēlituerant.**
16. dēpositīs armīs: "after they put down
their weapons"; abl. absolute; see App. §150.
16–17. dispersōs . . . occupātōs: supply
eōs (= *nostrōs,* our men); acc. dir. object of
adortī, a perf. part. in agreement with the

unexpressed subject of **perturbāverant,** i.e.,
the **hostēs** mentioned earlier.
17. metendō: gerund; see App. §§288, 294.
paucīs interfectīs: "after a few had been
killed"; abl. absolute; see App. §150.
18. incertīs ōrdinibus: "because their
ranks were disordered"; abl. absolute; see
App. §150.
19. circumdederant: supply *reliquōs* as
the direct object, which has been ellipted.

[4.33] *Genus hoc est ex* essedīs *pugnae. Prīmō per omnēs partēs* perequitant *et tēla* coniciunt *atque ipsō* terrōre *equōrum et* strepitū rotārum *ōrdinēs* plērumque perturbant *et, cum sē inter equitum* turmās īnsinuāvērunt, *ex* essedīs dēsiliunt *et*
5   pedibus proeliantur.

---

con•iciō, -icere, -iēcī, -iectum [co + iaciō, throw. App. §7], hurl, throw, cast.

dē•siliō, -silīre, -siluī, -sultum [saliō, jump], jump from, dismount.

essed•um, -ī, *n., a two-wheeled war* chariot *used by the Britons.*

īnsinuō, 1 [sinuō, wind], wind into; make one's way into, penetrate.

perequitō, 1 [equitō, ride], ride around, ride about, ride through.

perturbō, 1 [turbō, disturb], disturb greatly, throw into confusion; terrify.

pēs, pedis, *m.,* the foot, a foot; **pedibus,** on foot.

plērumque, *adv.* [plērusque, the greater part], mostly, generally; very often.

proelior, 1 [proelium, battle], join *or* engage in battle.

rot•a, -ae, *f.,* wheel.

strepit•us, -ūs, *m.* [strepō, make a noise], noise, rattle, uproar.

terr•or, -ōris, *m.* [terreō, frighten], fright, alarm, panic, terror.

turm•a, -ae, *f.,* troop *or* squadron *of about thirty cavalrymen.*

---

1. ex essedīs: the prepositional phrase modifies **pugnae:** "fighting from chariots." The chariots were built for two, a driver and a fighter. The driver would deliver the fighter where he was needed, pull back, and stand ready to rush in again if the fighter needed to escape quickly. The chariots provided speed and mobility.

2. equōrum: subjective gen.; see App. §98.

2–3. terrōre ... et strepitū: abl. of means; see App. §143.

3–4. cum ... īnsinuāvērunt: "whenever," etc.; **cum** with the indicative in a clause of repeated action; see App. §241, *b.*

Aurīgae *interim* paulātim *ex proeliō* excēdunt *atque ita* currūs
collocant ut, sī illī ā multitūdine hostium premantur, expedītum
ad suōs receptum *habeant. Ita* mōbilitātem *equitum,* stabilitātem
peditum *in proeliīs* praestant, *ac* tantum *ūsū* cotīdiānō *et*
10   exercitātiōne efficiunt *utī in* dēclīvī *ac* praecipitī *locō* incitātōs
equōs sustinēre et brevī moderārī *ac* flectere *et per* tēmōnem
percurrere *et in* iugō īnsistere *et sē* inde *in* currūs citissimē
recipere cōnsuērint.

---

aurīg•a, -ae, *m.,* charioteer.
brev•is, -e, *adv.,* short, brief, transitory.
citō, *adv.,* quickly, speedily. *Comp.:* **citius;**
   superl.: **citissimē.**
cotīdiān•us, -a, -um, *adj.* [**cotīdiē,** daily],
   daily; customary.
curr•us, -ūs, *m.,* chariot.
dēclīv•is, -e, *adj.* [**clīvus,** a slope], sloping
   downward, declining; *n. pl. as noun:*
   slopes.
ef•ficiō, -ficere, -fēcī, -fectum [**faciō,**
   make], make *or* do completely, complete,
   construct; cause, render.
ex•cēdō, -cēdere, -cessī, -cessum [**cēdō,**
   go], go out, go away, withdraw, retire.
exercitāti•ō, -ōnis, *f.* [*frequentative of*
   exercitō, *from* **exerceō,** exercise],
   exercise, training, practice, experience.
expedīt•us, -a, -um, *adj.* [*perf. part. of*
   expediō, set free], unimpeded; without
   baggage; light-armed.
flectō, flectere, flexī, flectum, bend, turn,
   direct.
incitō, 1 [**citō,** put in motion], set in
   motion; excite, urge on; exasperate.
inde, *adv.,* from that place; then.

īn•sistō, -sistere, -stitī, — [**sistō,** stand],
   stand upon; stand firm, take a stand.
iug•um, -ī, *n.* [**iungō,** join], yoke.
mōbili•tās, -tātis, *f.* [**mōbilis,** movable],
   activity, speed, mobility.
moderor, 1 [**modus,** limit], manage, govern,
   control, guide.
paulātim, *adv.* [**paulus,** little], little by little,
   by degrees, gradually.
ped•es, -itis, *m.* [**pēs,** foot], foot soldier; *pl.:*
   infantry.
per•currō, -currere, -currī, -cursum
   [**currō,** run], run along *or* over.
prae•ceps, -cipitis, *adj.* [**caput,** head],
   headlong; steep, precipitous.
prae•stō, -stāre, -stitī, -stātum [**stō,** stand],
   stand *or* place before; show, exhibit,
   supply; be superior, excel, surpass.
recept•us, -ūs, m. [**recipiō,** take in], retreat,
   refuge; shelter.
stabili•tās, -tātis, *f.* [**stabilis,** firm],
   firmness, steadiness.
tantum, *adv.* [**tantus,** so great], so much, so,
   so far; only, merely.
tēm•ō, -ōnis, *m.,* pole (*of a wagon*).

---

7. sī ... premantur: subjunctive in a condition dependent on a subjunctive in a result
clause (**ut ... habeant**); see App. §274. Compare App. §251.

10–13. utī ... cōnsuērint: subjunctive in
a clause of result.

11. brevī (*tempore*) abl. of time within
which; see App. §152.

13. cōnsuērint: contracted forms are
common in the perfect.

**11–13. sustinēre et . . . moderārī ac
flectere et ... percurrere et ... īnsistere et
... recipere:** complementary infs. dependent
on **cōnsuērint.** POLYSYNDETON; see App.
§301, *f.* Note that **ac** joins two infs. as a close
pair with **brevī** as their adv.

[4.34] *Quibus rēbus* perturbātīs *nostrīs,* novitāte *pugnae, tempore* opportūnissimō *Caesar* auxilium *tulit: namque eius adventū hostēs* cōnstitērunt, *nostrī sē ex* timōre *recēpērunt. Quō factō, ad* lacessendum *hostem et ad* committendum *proelium*
5   aliēnum *esse tempus arbitrātus suō sē locō continuit et* brevī *tempore* intermissō *in castra legiōnēs* redūxit.

---

aliēn•us, -a, -um, *adj.* [alius, other], of *or* belonging to another; unfamiliar; unfavorable.

auxil•ium, -ī, *n.* [augeō, increase], help; *pl.,* reinforcements.

brev•is, -e, *adv.,* short, brief, transitory.

com•mittō, -mittere, -mīsī, -missum [mittō, send], join, do; allow; entrust; proelium committere, join *or* begin battle.

cōn•stō, -stāre, -stitī, -stātum [stō, stand], stand firm; stand still; stop.

inter•mittō, -mittere, -mīsī, -missum [mittō, send], send between; intervene, separate; cease, discontinue; delay, neglect, omit; let pass.

lacess•ō, -ere, -īvī, -ītum, arouse, harass, provoke, irritate, attack.

novi•tās, -tātis, *f.* [novus, new], newness; strangeness, novelty.

opportūn•us, -a, -um, *adj.,* fit, opportune, lucky, suitable; favorable, advantageous.

perturbō, 1 [turbō, disturb], disturb greatly, throw into confusion; terrify.

re•dūcō, -dūcere, -dūxī, -ductum [dūcō, lead], lead back; draw back; extend back.

tim•or, -ōris, *m.* [timeō, fear], fear, alarm, dread.

---

1. Quibus rēbus = *et eīs rēbus,* i.e., the Britons' way of fighting from chariots; abl. of means; for *conjunctio relativa;* see App. §173, *a.*

perturbātīs nostrīs: abl. absolute; see App. §150.

novitāte pugnae: in apposition with **rēbus** by way of further explanation (and excuse); abl. of cause; see App. §138. The insertion of this phrase seems awkward, and has led some scholars to reject it.

2. tempore opportūnissimō: abl. of time when; see App. §152.

3. adventū: abl. of cause; see App. §138. Note that Caesar represents his appearance as changing the whole tide of the battle.

3–4. Quō factō = *et eō factō (conjunctio relativa);* "and even though (all) this was accomplished" by Caesar's arrival on the scene; abl. absolute; see App. §150.

4. lacessendum . . . committendum: gerundives with **ad** to express purpose; see App. §§288, 293.

5. aliēnum esse tempus: indirect statement dependent on **arbitrātus.**

suō . . . locō: abl. of place where without a prep.; see App. §151, *b.*

5–6. brevī . . . intermissō: abl. absolute; see App. §150.

Dum haec geruntur, nostrīs omnibus occupātīs *quī erant in agrīs reliquī discessērunt.* Secūtae *sunt* continuōs complūrēs *diēs* tempestātēs, *quae et nostrōs in castrīs continērent et hostem ā* pugnā prohibērent.

10

---

complūr•ēs, -a, *adj.* [**plūs,** more], several, many; a great many.
continu•us, -a, -um, *adj.* [**contineō,** hold together], holding together, unbroken, uninterrupted, continuous.
occupō, 1 [**ob + capiō,** take], take possession of, seize; engage.

prohibeō, 2 [**habeō,** hold], keep from, prevent, prohibit; keep out *or* away from; guard.
sequor, sequī, secūtus sum, follow; accompany; follow *in point of time.*
tempes•tās, -tātis, *f.* [**tempus,** time], time, season; weather, storm.

---

7. Dum haec geruntur: "while these things occur," i.e., "meanwhile."
nostrīs . . . occupātīs: abl. absolute; see App. §150. Caesar's men have been very busy with ship repair, foraging, guard duty, and fighting.
quī: if one construes **reliquī** as part of the subordinate clause, the antecedent is an ellipted *eī,* subject of **discessērunt.** On the other hand, we may also construe **reliquī** as the subject of **discessērunt,** and thus the antecedent of **quī.**

8. reliquī: "the remaining men." Were these men *Rōmānī* who were still in the fields after having been caught by surprise or *hostēs* who left because the Romans retreated into their camp? *Hostēs* are more likely as **reliquī** ("the rest of them") stands in contrast with **nostrīs** ("our men").
9–10. quae . . . prohibērent: rel. clause of characteristic equivalent to a clause of result; see App. §230, *a.*
10. pugnā: abl. of separation; see App. §134.

Interim barbarī nūntiōs *in omnēs partēs* dīmīsērunt
paucitātem*que nostrōrum mīlitum suīs* praedicāvērunt *et
quanta* praedae *faciendae atque in* perpetuum *suī* līberandī
facultās *darētur, sī Rōmānōs castrīs* expulissent,
15   dēmōnstrāvērunt. *Hīs rēbus* celeriter *magnā multitūdine*
peditātūs *equitātūsque coāctā ad castra* vēnērunt.

---

barbar•us, -a, -um, *adj.,* foreign (*to Romans
and Greeks*), uncivilized; *pl. as noun:*
barbarians.
celeriter, *adv.* [**celer,** swift], quickly,
rapidly, speedily. *Comp.*: **celerius;** *superl.*:
celerrimē (App. §40).
dēmōnstrō, 1 [**mōnstrō,** show], point out,
explain, describe; declare.
dī•mittō, -mittere, -mīsī, -missum [**mittō,**
send], send away, dismiss; break up; let
go, let pass, give up.
ex•pellō, -pellere, -pulī, -pulsum [**pellō,**
drive], drive out, drive forth, expel.
facul•tās, -tātis, *f.* [**facilis,** easy], power;
opportunity; resources.
līberō, 1 [**līber,** free], make *or* set free,
release, deliver.

nūntius, -ī, *m.,* messenger; message, news,
report.
pauci•tās, -tātis, *f.* [**paucus,** few], fewness,
small number.
peditāt•us, -ūs, *m.* [**pedes,** foot soldier],
foot soldiers, infantry.
perpetu•us, -a, -um, *adj.,* continuous; *n. as
noun in the phrase* **in perpetuum,** forever.
praed•a, -ae, *f.,* booty, plunder, spoil.
prae•dīcō, 1 [**dīcō,** proclaim], proclaim
publicly *or* before others; declare, report,
tell of.
veniō, venīre, vēnī, ventum, come, arrive,
go, advance.

---

12. suīs: "their people"; i.e., their fellow
Britons.
13–14. quanta . . . facultās darētur: subjunctive in an indirect question; see App.
§262. This clause represents the apodosis
(or conclusion) of a condition in direct statement. The sequence is secondary (past) after
praedicāvērunt.
**praedae faciendae . . . suī līberandī
facultās:** gerundive in the gen. to express
purpose; see App. §§288, 291.
14. sī Rōmānōs castrīs expulissent: this
protasis (if-clause) of a fut. condition appears
within an indirect question in secondary
sequence after **praedicāvērunt.** The original condition would have been something
like: *tanta . . . facultās dabitur, sī Rōmānōs . . .
expulerimus* (future more vivid). In other

words, "such a great opportunity . . . will exist, if we expel the Romans . . . " (note that in
American English we use the pres. tense to
represent something that will be completed
before some other action in the future; Latin
uses the fut. perf.). In secondary sequence
this becomes (in American English): "they
proclaimed what a great opportunity would
exist, if they expelled the Romans." "Will"
becomes "would" and "expel" becomes
"expelled." In Latin, further complications
arise from a greater sensitivity to tense
combined with robust rules for the use of
the subjunctive.
15. Hīs rēbus: "by means of these
speeches."
15–16. magnā . . . coāctā: abl. absolute;
see App. §150.

[4.35] *Caesar, etsī idem quod superiōribus diēbus acciderat fore*
vidēbat, ut, sī essent hostēs pulsī, celeritāte perīculum effugerent,
tamen nactus equitēs circiter XXX, *quōs* Commius Atrebās, *dē*
quō ante dictum est, sēcum trānsportāverat, legiōnēs in aciē
5   *prō castrīs cōnstituit.* Commissō *proeliō* diūtius *nostrōrum*
mīlitum impetum *hostēs ferre nōn potuērunt ac* terga vertērunt.

---

aci•ēs, -ēī (*old gen.* aciē), *f.,* battle line.
Atre•bās, -bātis, *m.,* an Atrebatian; *pl.* the
    Atrebates.
com•mittō, -mittere, -mīsī, -missum [mittō,
    send], join; do; allow; entrust; **proelium**
    committere, join *or* begin battle.
Com•mius, -mī, *m.,* Commius, *a leader of*
    the Atrebates. He was loyal to Caesar until
    52 BCE *when he led troops in support of the*
    general Gallic revolt.
diū, *adv.,* for a long time; **diūtius,** longer,
    too long, very long.
ef•fugiō, -fugere, -fūgī, — [fugiō, flee], flee
    from, run away, escape.

etsī, *conj.* [et + sī, if], even if, although.
impet•us, -ūs, *m.,* attack; force, vehemence.
nancīscor, nancīscī, nactus sum, get,
    obtain possession of; meet with, find.
pellō, pellere, pepulī, pulsum, defeat, rout.
trānsportō, 1 [portō, carry], carry across
    or over, bring over, convey, transport.
terg•um, -ī, *n.,* the back; **terga vertere,** to
    flee; **post tergum** *or* **ab tergō,** in the rear.
vertō, vertere, vertī, versum, turn, turn
    around; **terga vertere,** flee.
XXX, *sign for* **trīgintā,** thirty (*see also* App.
    §47).

1–5. Caesar... cōnstituit: before we find
out that "Caesar decided" to draw up his legions in battle formation in front of the camp,
we encounter all the complications that fac-
tored into this decision. The placement of the
subject at the beginning of the sentence and
the main verb at the end is dramatic. Separating words that belong together is called
HYPERBATON; see App. §301, *f.*

    1. idem... fore = *idem... futūrum esse;*
"the same thing would happen"; indirect
statement dependent on **vidēbat.**

    2. ut... effugerent: a clause of result in
apposition with **idem** to explain what that
"same thing" was.

    sī essent... pulsī: plupf. subjunctive in
an if-clause dependent on a subjunctive in

a result clause in secondary sequence. This
represents indirectly in the past what, in the
present, would have been a future more vivid
condition in Caesar's direct thought, something like: *sī erunt... pulsī,... effugient* or "if
they are routed, they will escape."

    3. equitēs: cavalry were essential for pur-
suing the enemy in retreat. The cavalry could
chase them, and kill them, while they were
disorganized. Otherwise, they could run away,
regroup, and return for another battle.

    3–4. quōs... trānsportāverat: Commius
had been sent with his own squad of cavalry
ahead of the main force.

    5. Commissō proeliō: abl. absolute; see
App. §150.

Quōs tantō spatiō secūtī *quantum* cursū *et vīribus* efficere
potuērunt, complūrēs *ex eīs* occīdērunt, deinde *omnibus longē*
lātē*que* aedificiīs incēnsīs *sē in castra* recēpērunt.

[4.36.1] *Eōdem diē lēgātī ab hostibus missī ad Caesarem dē* pāce
vēnērunt.

---

aedifi•cium, -cī, *n.* [aedificiō, build],
  building, house.
complūr•ēs, -a, *adj.* [plūs, more], several,
  many; a great many.
curs•us, -ūs, *m.* [currō, run], speed;
  course; voyage.
deinde, *adv.* [dē + inde, from there, thence],
  then, next, after this, thereupon.
ef•ficiō, -ficere, -fēcī, -fectum [faciō,
  make], make *or* do completely, complete,
  construct; cause, render.
in•cendō, -cendere, -cendī, -cēnsum, set
  fire to, burn; inflame, excite.

lātē, *adv.* [lātus, wide], widely, extensively;
  longō lātēque, far and wide.
oc•cīdō, -cīdere, -cīsī, -cīsum [caedō, cut],
  cut down, kill.
pāx, pācis, *f.,* peace treaty, truce, peace,
  favor.
sequor, sequī, secūtus sum, follow, pursue;
  accompany.
spat•ium, -ī, *n.,* space, distance; period *or*
  length *of time.*
veniō, venīre, vēnī, ventum, come, arrive,
  go, advance.

---

7. Quōs = *et eōs.*
  cursū et vīribus: abl. of means; see App.
§143.
  7–8. tantō spatiō . . . quantum . . . efficere potuērunt: "for as great a distance as
they could accomplish . . ."; abl. of the route

or way (i.e., the means); see App. §144: more
literally, "by *or* along so great a distance," etc.
  8–9. omnibus . . . incēnsīs: abl. absolute;
see App. §150.
  4.36.1 Eōdem diē: "on the very same day";
abl. of time when; see App. §152.

What Caesar Accomplished in Britain

Caesar's show of force and strength convinced the British leaders to return to negotiations. Caesar doubles the number of hostages that the Britons are required to submit, and good weather soon permits him to depart from Britain in the ships that his men were able to salvage. Caesar thus conveys his men to winter quarters on the mainland with his dignity and military reputation intact. In fact, the report that Caesar submitted about this expedition led the Senate to decree twenty days of public prayer in thanks to the gods (a *supplicātiō*). As students of Caesar's narrative and rhetorical style, we have some insight into why the Senate may have reacted so favorably to what they read and heard.

C. IVLI CAESARIS
COMMENTARIORUM
DE BELLO GALLICO
LIBER QUINTUS

Caesar Dē Bellō Gallicō 5.24–5.48:
The Revolt of the Belgic Tribes

Despite the difficulties Caesar experienced in his first expedition to Britain, because his conquest of Gaul seemed secure, Caesar decided to attempt a second expedition to Britain the next summer in 54 BCE. Again, Caesar experienced some military success before he returned to the mainland toward the end of the summer campaigning season. He then sent the men to their winter quarters, and this is when trouble began. Because of a drought (and thus a smaller than usual harvest), he has to spread the army out over a larger geographical area. Because it is divided into smaller units, the Roman army appears more vulnerable to the native inhabitants, and the Belgic tribes in northeastern Gaul decide to take advantage of the opportunity to revolt. In the passages that follow, you will read about Caesar's ultimately successful operations to suppress this revolt against Roman rule. Although most of the action takes place while Caesar is not present, Caesar remains a force throughout the narrative, on the one hand, of course, because he tells the story, but, even if we put that obvious fact aside, Caesar is mentioned frequently. Ambiorix, a leader of the Eburones, leads an attack on the winter quarters commanded by Quintus Titurius Sabinus and Lucius Aurunculeius Cotta, after which he promises them safe passage from his people's territory. Ambiorix's speech is part of an elaborate plan to lure the Romans into an ambush, but Caesar puts praises of Caesar into Ambiorix's speech. Caesar also inserts knowing and disparaging remarks about Sabinus into

WINTER QUARTERS

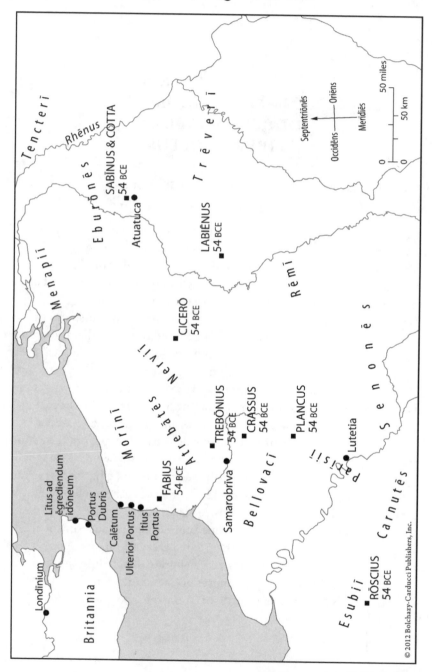

the narrative, so that readers will blame not Caesar, but Caesar's lieutenants, for the disaster. The conduct of Sabinus and Cotta is also compared
unfavorably with the conduct of the lieutenant Quintus Tullius Cicero,
when Ambiorix tries the same trick at his camp. Finally, we see Caesar
rush to rescue Cicero's camp after Caesar gets word of the attacks on
winter quarters. Even military setbacks contribute—at least in Caesar's
narrative—to a portrait of Caesar as the consummate military leader.
And, in the end, Caesar did reestablish military control.

Caesar DĒ BELLŌ GALLICŌ 5.24–5.48:
The Revolt of the Belgic Tribes

[5.24] Subductīs *nāvibus* conciliōque *Gallōrum* Samarobrīvae
perāctō, *quod eō annō frūmentum in Galliā* propter siccitātēs
angustius prōvēnerat, *coāctus est* aliter *ac superiōribus annīs*
exercitum in hībernīs collocāre legiōnēsque in plūrēs cīvitātēs
5   distribuere. *Ex quibus ūnam in* Morinōs *dūcendam* Gāiō Fabiō
lēgātō dedit, alteram in Nerviōs Quīntō Cicerōnī, *tertiam in*
Esubiōs Lūciō Rosciō; quārtam *in* Rēmīs *cum* Titō Labiēnō

---

aliter, *adv.* [alius, other], otherwise; **aliter**
  ... **ac**, otherwise ... than.
angust•us, -a, -um, *adj.*, [angō, squeeze],
  compressed, narrow.
concil•ium, -ī, *n.*, assembly, gathering,
  council.
dis•tribuō, -tribuere, -tribuī, -tribūtum
  [tribuō, assign], assign, divide.
Esubi•ī, -ōrum, *m.*, the Esubii, *a people in*
  northwestern Gaul.
Gā•ius, -ī, *m.*; Fab•ius, -ī, *m.* Gaius Fabius,
  one of Caesar's lieutenants.
Lūci•us, -ī, *m.*; Rōsc•ius, -ī, *m.*, Lucius
  Roscius, *one of Caesar's lieutenants.*
Morin•ī, -ōrum, *m.*, the Morini. *A Belgic*
  people on the seacoast.
per•agō, -agere, -ēgī, -āctum [agō, lead],
  lead through; complete, finish.
propter, *prep. with acc.* [prope, near], on
  account of, because of.
prō•veniō, -venīre, -vēnī, -ventum [veniō,
  come], come forth, grow.

quārt•us, -a, -um, *adj., ord. num.* [quattuor,
  four], fourth.
Quīnt•us, -ī, *m.*; Cicer•ō, -ōnis, *m.*,
  Quintus Tullius Cicero, *brother of the*
  more famous orator and consul of 63 BCE,
  Marcus Tullius Cicero. Quintus *served as*
  one of Caesar's legates.
Rēm•us, -a, -um, *adj.*, belonging to *or* one
  of the Remi; *pl. as noun,* Rēmī, *m.*, the
  Remi, *a Belgic people along the Axona*
  (Aisne) whose main city was Durocortorum
  (now Reims).
Samarobrīv•a, -ae, *f.*, Samarobriva (*now*
  Amiens), *a city belonging to the Ambiani*
  on the river Samara (Somme).
sicci•tās, -tātis, *f.* [siccus, dry], drought.
sub•dūcō, -dūcere, -dūxī, -ductum [dūcō,
  lead], draw up; with nāvēs, beach.
Tit•us, -ī, *m.*; Labiēn•us, -ī, *m.*, Titus Atius
  Labienus, *Caesar's most trusted lieutenant*
  in the Gallic War.

1–2. Subductīs nāvibus conciliōque ...
perāctō: abl. absolutes; see App. §150.
  1. conciliō: Caesar routinely called assemblies and compelled Gallic leaders to attend.
Caesar used these meetings to requisition
cavalry and supplies from the various tribes
as well as to gather information and to gauge
the general mood among the Gauls. In light of
subsequent events, we may note that, despite
appearances, the conquest of Gaul was, from
the perspective of the Gauls themselves, not
yet a "done deal." They soon rose in revolt.
  2–3. annō ... annīs: abl. of time; see App.
§152.

5. Ex quibus ūnam = **Ex quibus** *quattuor*
legiōnibus **ūnam** *legiōnem*; ELLIPSIS, see App.
§301, *c.*
  dūcendam: the fut. pass. part. agrees with
ūnam (*legiōnem*), the direct object of **dedit**,
to express purpose; see App. §285, II, *b.* The
next two clauses will ellipt part. and verb as
well.
  7–8. quārtam ... hiemāre iussit: Caesar shifts construction; **quārtam** *legiōnem*
is the acc. subject of the complementary inf.
hiemāre. See App. §277.

in cōnfīniō Trēverōrum hiemāre *iussit. Trēs in* Bellovacīs
collocāvit: hīs Marcum Crassum quaestōrem *et* Lūcium
10   Munātium Plancum *et* Gāium Trebōnium *lēgātōs* praefēcit.
Ūnam legiōnem, quam proximē trāns Padum cōnscrīpserat,
et cohortēs V *in* Eburōnēs, *quōrum pars maxima est inter*
Mosam *ac* Rhēnum, *quī* sub imperiō *Ambiorīgis et* Catuvolcī
erant, mīsit.

Bellovac•ī, -ōrum, *m.,* the Bellovaci (*a
Belgic people*).

Catuvolc•us, -ī, *m.,* Catuvolcus, *a leader
among the the Eburones who eventually
poisons himself when things go badly for
him.*

cōnfīn•ium, -ī, *n.* [**fīnis,** boundary],
common boundary, neighborhood.

cōn•scrībō, -scrībere, -scrīpsī, -scrīptum
[**scrībō,** write], enroll, enlist.

Eburōn•ēs, -um, *m.,* the Eburones, *a Belgic
people who in 54 BCE destroyed troops
under the command of Sabinus and Cotta.
Afterwards, Caesar almost exterminated
them.*

Gā•ius, -ī, *m.;* **Trebōn•ius, -ī,** *m.,* Gaius
Trebonius, *one of Caesar's lieutenants.*

hiemō, 1 [**hiems,** winter], pass the winter,
winter.

imper•ium, -ī, *n.* [**imperō,** order], right
to command; authority; jurisdiction;
supreme, highest official power.

Lūci•us, -ī, *m.;* **Munāt•ius, -ī,** *m.;* **Planc•us,
-ī,** *m.,* Lucius Munatius Plancus, *a
lieutenant of Caesar.*

Marc•us, -ī, *m.;* **Crass•us, -ī,** *m.,* Marcus
Licinius Crassus, *son of Caesar's powerful
ally, served as one of Caesar's quaestors
after his brother Publius left Gaul.*

Mos•a, -ae, *m.,* the *river* Mosa, *now called
the Meuse or the Maas.*

Pad•us, -ī, *m.,* the Padus *river,* the Po, *the
biggest river in northern Italy.*

prae•ficiō, -ficere, -fēcī, -fectum [**faciō,**
make], make before, put in command of.

proximē, *adv.* [**proximus,** last], last; lately,
recently.

quaest•or, -ōris, *m.* [**quaerō,** seek], a
quaestor; (1) at Rome, an annually elected
official in charge of state revenues; (2) in
the Roman army, a quartermaster in charge
of money and supplies, and sometimes
employed in commanding troops.

sub, *prep. with abl.,* under, beneath.

trāns, *prep. with acc.,* across, beyond, over.

Trev•ir, -erī, *m.,* one of the Treveri; *pl.*
Treverī, the Treveri, *a Belgic people near
the Rhine.*

V, *sign for* **quīnque,** five (*for ord. and
distributive numbers, see* App. §47).

---

8. Trēs = Trēs *legiōnēs.*

9. hīs = hīs *legiōnibus.* Dat. indirect object
with a compound verb; see App. §116.

quaestōrem: in apposition with Crassus;
see App. §95, *b.*

10. lēgātōs: in apposition with Munatius
Plancus and Trebonius; see App. §95, *b.*

11. proximē: Caesar lets us know that
these are new recruits.

trāns Padum: from the perspective of
Rome, Cisalpine Gaul in northern Italy was
on the "other side" of the Po River.

12. cohortēs: it is not clear to which legion
these five cohorts belonged. Some scholars
argue that Caesar wants us to know that he
sent some experienced soldiers along with the
new legion.

15   *Hīs mīlitibus* Quīntum Titūrium Sabīnum *et* Lucium
       Aurunculēium Cottam *lēgātōs* praeesse *iussit. Ad hunc* modum
       distribūtīs *legiōnibus facillimē* inopiae frūmentāriae *sēsē* medērī
       posse exīstimāvit. Atque hārum tamen omnium legiōnum hīberna
       praeter *eam, quam* Lūciō Rōsciō *in* pācātissimam *et* quiētissimam
20   *partem dūcendam dederat, mīlibus passuum* centum *continēbantur.*
       Ipse intereā, quoad *legiōnēs collocātās* mūnīta*que hīberna*
       cognōvisset, in Galliā morārī *cōnstituit.*

---

centum, (C.), *indecl. card. num.,* one
  hundred.
dis•tribuō, -tribuere, -tribuī, -tribūtum
  [**tribuō,** assign], assign, divide, distribute.
frūmentāri•us, -a, -um, *adj.* [**frūmentum,**
  grain], of *or* pertaining to grain.
inopi•a, -ae, *f.* [**inops,** needy], need, lack,
  poverty; lack of provisions, hunger.
intereā, *adv.,* in the meantime, meanwhile.
Lūci•us, -ī, *m.;* **Aurunculēi•us, -ī,** *m.;*
  Cott•a, -ae, *m.,* Lucius Aurunculeius
  Cotta, *one of Caesar's lieutenants.*
Lūci•us, -ī, *m.;* **Rōsc•ius, -ī,** *m.,* Lucius
  Roscius, *one of Caesar's lieutenants.*
medeor, medērī, —, cure, remedy.
mod•us, -ī, *m.,* measure, quantity, size;
  manner, method; **ad hunc modum,** in
  this way.

moror, 1 [**mora,** a delay], delay, hinder;
  linger, hang back.
mūniō, 4, defend with a wall, fortify.
pācō, 1 [**pāx,** peace], subdue, pacify;
  pācātus, *perf. part. as adj.:* peaceful.
prae•sum, -esse, -fuī, — [**sum,** be. App.
  §77], be before *or* over, be in command
  of, rule over, be at the head of.
praeter, *prep. with acc.* [**prae,** before],
  before; past; except.
quiēt•us, -a, -um, *adj.,* in repose,
  undisturbed, peaceful, calm, quiet.
Quīnt•us, -ī, *m.;* **Titūr•ius, -ī,** *m.;*
  Sabīn•us, -ī, *m.,* Quintus Titurius
  Sabinus, *one of Caesar's lieutenants.*
quoad, *adv.* [**quō,** where? + **ad,** to], to
  where; as long as, as far as; till, until.

---

15. mīlitibus: dat. indirect object with a
compound verb; see App. §116.

**15–16. Titūrium Sabīnum et ... Aurun-
culēium Cottam:** Caesar introduces the lieutenants who are responsible for the safety of
the soldiers entrusted to them, and who will,
in the narrative that follows, bear blame for
the disaster.

17. distribūtīs legiōnibus: abl. absolute;
see App. §150.

inopiae frūmentāriae: dat. with an intransitive verb **medērī;** see App. §115.

18. hīberna: nom. subject of the verb
continēbantur.

19. eam = eam *legiōnem.*

20. mīlibus ... centum: "within one hundred miles" of one another. This may have
been an underestimate.

21. Ipse = *Caesar* **Ipse.**

collocātās mūnītaque = collocātās *esse*
mūnītaque *esse;* infs. in indirect statement
dependent on **cognōvisset.**

22. cognōvisset: subjunctive in a temporal clause; see App. §234.

morārī: Caesar tells us that he decided to
stay in Gaul until his men were safely in their
winter quarters because, as it turned out, they
soon came under deadly attack. Caesar thus
anticipates and neutralizes potential accusa-
tions that his generalship put Roman soldiers
in harm's way.

[5.25] *Erat in* Carnutibus *summō locō* nātus Tasgetius, *cuius*
maiōrēs *in suā cīvitāte rēgnum* obtinuerant. *Huic Caesar prō eius*
virtūte atque in sē benevolentiā, *quod in omnibus bellīs* singulārī
eius operā *fuerat* ūsus, maiōrum *locum* restituerat. *Tertium* iam
5   *hunc annum* rēgnantem inimīcī *multīs* palam *ex cīvitāte*
auctōribus *interfēcērunt.* Dēfertur *ea rēs ad Caesarem.*

---

auctor, -is, *m.* [**augeō,** increase], one
who produces, creates, *or* originates;
promoter, instigator, advisor, author.

benevolenti•a, -ae, *f.* [**bene,** well + **volō,**
wish], goodwill, kindness.

Carnut•ēs, -um, *m.,* the Carnutes (*a people*
in central Gaul).

dē•ferō, -ferre, -tulī, -lātum [**ferō,** carry.
App. §81], carry, take; report; confer.

iam, *adv.,* now; already, at last; indeed, even.

inimīc•us, -a, -um, *adj.* [**in** + **amīcus,**
friendly], unfriendly, hostile; *as a noun:*
personal enemy; *as opposed to* **hostis,**
public enemy.

maior, maius, *adj.* [*comp. of* **magnus,**
large], larger; older; *as noun:* **maiōres,**
ancestors.

nāscor, nāscī, nātus sum, be born, be
produced; rise, spring up, be raised; be
found.

ob•tineō, -tinēre, -tinuī, -tentum [**teneō,**
hold], hold, retain, possess, maintain;
acquire.

oper•a, -ae, *f.* [**opus,** work], work, exertion;
service; pains, attention.

palam, *adv.,* openly, publicly.

rēgnō, 1 [**rēgnum,** royal power], reign, rule.

re•stituō, -stituere, -stituī, -stitūtum [**re**
+ **statuō,** set up], set up again, rebuild,
renew, restore.

singulār•is, -e, *adj.* [**singulī,** one each], one
at a time; single; remarkable.

Tasget•ius, -ī, *m.,* Tasgetius, *a leader among*
the Carnutes.

---

1. summō locō: "highest rank"; abl. of
source or origin; see App. §135.

3. in sē: to use a prepositional phrase to
modify a noun is not common in classical
Latin, but, as this phrase demonstrates, not
impossible.

4. operā: abl. with a special deponent verb;
see App. §145,

maiōrum locum: Caesar had restored
Tasgetius to the supreme authority his ancestors had held, but apparently lost. Why?
Because Tasgetius was useful to Caesar. Note
how Caesar feels that it is his right to dictate
to the tribes who their leaders will be. Could
this be perhaps one source of their unhappi-
ness with Roman rule?

4–5. Tertium . . . annum: acc. of extent of
time; see App. §130.

5. hunc = Tasgetius.

rēgnantem: Latin uses a part. where we
would use a subordinate clause. Although a
pres. part., **rēgnantem** should be translated
as "who was ruling," because we translate in
reference to the tense of the main verb. See
App. §205.

5–6. multīs . . . auctōribus: abl. absolute;
see App. §150. Note the numbers and the
openness of the assassination. Tasgetius was
unpopular among his own people.

Ille veritus, *quod ad plūrēs pertinēbat, nē cīvitās eōrum* impulsū
dēficeret, Lūcium Plancum *cum legiōne ex* Belgiō celeriter *in*
Carnutēs *proficīscī iubet* ibique hiemāre *quōrumque* operā
10   *cognōverat* Tasgetium *interfectum, hōs* comprehēnsōs *ad sē
mittere. Interim ab omnibus lēgātīs* quaestōribus*que, quibus
legiōnēs* trādiderat, *certior factus est in hīberna perventum
locumque hībernīs esse* mūnītum.

Belg•ium, -gī, *n.,* the territory belonging to
   the Belgae.
Carnut•ēs, -um, *m.,* the Carnutes (*a people
   in central Gaul*).
celeriter, *adv.* [**celer,** swift], quickly,
   rapidly, speedily. *Comp.,* **celerius;** *superl.,*
   celerrimē (App. §40).
**com•prehendō, -prehendere, -prehendī,
   -prehēnsum** [**prehendō** (= **prendō**),
   seize], lay hold of, seize, arrest.
dē•ficiō, -ficere, -fēcī, -fectum [**faciō,**
   make], fail, desert, fall away, revolt.
hiemō, 1 [**hiems,** winter], pass the winter,
   winter.
ibi, *adv.,* there, in that place.
impuls•us, -ūs, *m.* [**impellō,** impel],
   impulse, instigation.

Lūci•us, -ī, *m.;* **Planc•us, -ī,** *m.,* Lucius
   Munatius Plancus, *a lieutenant of
   Caesar.*
mūniō, 4, defend with a wall, fortify.
oper•a, -ae, *f.* [**opus,** work], work, exertion;
   service; pains, attention; **dare operam,**
   give attention, take pains.
quaest•or, -ōris, *m.* [**quaerō,** seek], a
   quaestor.
Tasget•ius, -ī, *m.,* Tasgetius, *a leader among
   the Carnutes.*
trā•dō, -dere, -didī, -ditum [**trāns** + **dō,**
   give], give over; entrust; teach.
vereor, verērī, veritus sum, revere; fear,
   dread, be afraid of.

---

7. plūrēs: "a large number of people" because the assassination took place openly and
involved many conspirators.
   impulsū: abl. of cause; see App. §138.
   7–8. veritus . . . nē . . . dēficeret: subjunctive in a fear clause; see App. §228, 6.
   9. quōrum: the rel. anticipates its antecedent **hōs.**
   10. interfectum (*esse*): perf. inf. in indirect
statement dependent on **cognōverat.**
   comprehēnsōs: "after they had been
rounded up and arrested"; the perf. part. is
equivalent here to a subordinate clause; see
App. §283.
   11. mittere: complementary inf. dependent on **iubet;** see App. §275.

12. perventum: perf. inf. (with *esse* omitted) in indirect statement dependent on **certior factus est** (*Caesar*). In direct speech,
"*perventum est*" is impers., hence the lack of
an acc. subject here.
   13. hībernīs: dat. of purpose or reference;
see App. §§119–120. Some editors delete the
word as unnecessary.
   mūnītum: this narrative is heading toward
disaster. Note how carefully Caesar informs
his readers that he, Caesar, had taken all due
precautions. Will this help deflect blame from
Caesar to his subordinates?

[5.26] *Diēbus circiter* XV, *quibus in hīberna ventum est,*
initium repentīnī tumultūs *ac* dēfectiōnis ortum *est ab*
Ambiorīge et Catuvolcō; *quī, cum ad fīnēs rēgnī suī* Sabīnō
Cottaeque praestō *fuissent frūmentumque in hīberna*
5 comportāvissent, Indutiomārī Trēverī nūntiīs impulsī *suōs*
concitāvērunt subitō*que* oppressīs lignātōribus *magnā manū*
ad castra oppugnātum vēnērunt.

Catuvolc•us, -ī, *m.,* Catuvolcus, *a leader*
among the the Eburones who eventually
poisons himself when things go badly for him.
comportō, 1 [**portō,** carry], carry together,
collect, bring.
concitō, 1 [**citō,** put in motion], stir up,
rouse, instigate, incite.
dēfecti•ō, -ōnis, *f.* [**dēficiō,** fail], falling
away, desertion, revolt.
im•pellō, -pellere, -pulī, -pulsum [**pellō,**
drive], drive *or* urge on, incite, instigate,
impel.
Indutiomār•us, -ī, *m.,* Indutiomarus, *a*
leader of the Treveri, rival to Cingetorix,
and hostile to Caesar.
init•ium, -ī, *n.* [**ineō,** go into], beginning,
commencement, origin; edge *of a country,*
borders.
lignāt•or, -ōris, *m.* [**lignum,** wood], one
sent to gather wood, wood-forager.
nūntius, -ī, *m.,* messenger; message, news,
report.
op•primō, -primere, -pressī, -pressus [**ob**
+ **premō,** press], press down, oppress;
destroy; surprise.

oppugnō, 1 [**ob** + **pugnō,** fight], fight
against, attack, besiege.
orior, orīrī, ortus sum, arise, begin, spring
up; be born, descend.
praestō, *adv.,* at hand, ready; *with* **sum,**
meet.
repentīn•us, -a, -um, *adj.* [**repēns,** sudden],
sudden, unexpected, hasty.
Sabīn•us, -ī, *m.,* Quintus Titurius Sabinus,
one of Caesar's lieutenants.
subitō, *adv.* [**subitus,** sudden], suddenly.
Trēv•ir, -erī, *m.,* one of the Treveri; *pl.*
Trēverī, the Treveri, *a Belgic people near*
the Rhine.
tumult•us, -ūs, *m.* [**tumeō,** swell], uproar,
confusion, disorder, tumult; uprising,
insurrection.
veniō, venīre, vēnī, ventum, come, arrive,
go, advance.
XV, *sign for* **quīndecim,** fifteen (*see also*
App. §47).

---

1. Diēbus circiter XV, quibus: "within
about fifteen days, during which . . . ," i.e.,
"about fifteen days, after . . . "; abl. of time, see
App. §152.
3. Ambiorīge et Catuvolcō: "Ambiorix
and Catuvolcus" were leaders of a nearby
tribe, the Eburones, and were thus responsible for providing Caesar's occupying army
with supplies for the winter.
3–4. Sabīnō Cottaeque: When we first
meet Caesar's lieutenants in action, they
have just completed the duty of meeting with

local leaders to ensure sufficient supplies for
the winter.
5. Indutiomārī Trēverī nūntiīs: "Indutiomarus the Treveran's messages" must
have been convincing, as Ambiorix and Catuvolcus immediately stopped assisting the
Romans, and instead attacked them.
6. magnā manū: abl. of accompaniment
with *cum* omitted; see App. §140.
7. oppugnātum: "to attack"; after a verb
of motion, the supine is used in the acc. to
express purpose; see App. §295.

Cum celeriter *nostrī arma cēpissent* vāllum*que* ascendissent
atque ūnā ex parte Hispānīs *equitibus* ēmissīs equestrī
10   *proeliō superiōrēs fuissent,* dēspērātā *rē hostēs suōs ab*
oppugnātiōne redūxērunt. *Tum suō* mōre conclāmāvērunt,
utī aliquī ex nostrīs ad colloquium prōdīret: *habēre sēsē, quae*
dē rē commūnī dīcere vellent, quibus rēbus contrōversiās minuī
posse spērārent.

---

a•scendō, -scendere, -scendī, -scēnsum
  [ad + scandō, climb], climb up, ascend,
  mount, climb.
celeriter, *adv.* [celer, swift], quickly,
  rapidly, speedily. *Comp.*: celerius; *superl.*:
  celerrimē (App. §40).
collo•quium, -quī, *n.* [colloquor, talk
  together], talking together; conference,
  parley, interview.
conclāmō, 1 [clāmō, shout], shout out, call
  aloud, yell.
dēspērō, 1 [spērō, hope], despair, be
  hopeless, lack confidence; dēspērātus,
  perf. part.: despaired of; *as adj.*: desperate.
ē•mittō, -mittere, -mīsī, -missum [mittō,
  send], let go, send out *or* forth, release;
  hurl, discharge; drop.

eques•ter, -tris, -tre, *adj.* [eques,
  horseman], of *or* belonging to a
  horseman, equestrian, of cavalry, cavalry.
Hispān•us, -a, um, *adj.*, Spanish.
minuō, minuere, minuī, minūtum
  [minus, less], lessen, impair, diminish;
  settle (contrōversiās).
mōs, mōris, *m.*, manner, custom, practice.
prod•eō, -īre, -iī, -itum [prō + eō, go, App.
  §84], come forth, go forward.
re•dūcō, -dūcere, -dūxī, -ductum [dūcō,
  lead], lead back; draw back; extend back.
spērō, 1 [spēs, hope], hope, hope for,
  anticipate.
vāll•um, -ī, *n.* [vāllus, palisade], wall
  or rampart *of earth set with palisades;*
  entrenchments, earthworks.

---

8. nostrī: "our men." Caesar gives credit
for the quick response not to his lieutenants,
Sabinus and Cotta, but to the soldiers.

**8–10. Cum ... cēpissent ... ascendissent
... fuissent:** subjunctive in a causal clause;
see App. §§238–239.

9. Hispānīs equitibus ēmissīs: "after the
Spanish cavalry were sent out"; abl. absolute;
see App. §150. Who sent the cavalry out?
Again, Caesar does not give credit to the local lieutenants.

10. suōs: "their men."

11. mōre: abl. of manner; see App. §142, *a.*

12. utī ... prōdīret: volitive subjunctive
in a substantive clause of purpose (or indirect
command) after conclāmāvērunt; see App.
§228, *a.*

aliquī: nom. sing. subject of prōdīret;
see App. §62; the adj. is sometimes used for
the pron.

habēre: inf. in indirect statement dependent on conclāmāvērunt; see App. §266.

13. quibus rēbus: "by means of which
(proposed parley about) matters (of common interest)."

[5.27] *Mittitur ad eōs colloquendī causā* Gāius Arpīnēius, *eques Rōmānus,* familiāris Quīntī Titūrī, *et* Quīntus Iūnius *ex* Hispāniā *quīdam, quī* iam *ante* missū *Caesaris ad Ambiorīgem* ventitāre *cōnsuērat; apud quōs Ambiorīx ad hunc* modum

5 locūtus *est: sēsē prō Caesaris in sē* beneficiīs *plūrimum eī* cōnfitērī dēbēre, *quod eius* operā stīpendiō līberātus *esset, quod* Aduātucīs, finitimīs *suīs,* pendere *cōnsuēsset, quodque eī*

Aduātuc•ī, -ōrum, *m., a people in Belgic Gaul and neighbors of the Eburones,* the Aduatici.
benefi•cium, -cī, *n.,* [**bene,** well + **faciō,** do], benefit, favor, kindness, good deed.
cōn•fiteor, -fitērī, -fessus sum [**fateor,** confess], acknowledge, confess.
dēbeō, 2 [**dē** + **habeō,** have], owe; *with inf.:* ought, must.
familiār•is, -e, *adj.* [**familia,** household], personal, private; *as noun:* intimate friend.
finitim•us, -a, -um, *adj.* [**finis,** limit], bordering on, neighboring.
Gā•ius, -ī, *m.;* **Arpīnēius, -ī,** *m.,* Gaius Arpineius, *an equestrian in Caesar's army.*
Hispāni•a, -ae, *f.,* Hispania, Spain.
iam, *adv.,* now; already, at last; indeed.

līberō, 1 [**līber,** free], make *or* set free; release, deliver.
loquor, loquī, locūtus sum, speak, talk, converse.
miss•us, -ūs, *m.* [**mittō,** send], a sending; **missū Caesaris,** sent by Caesar.
mod•us, -ī, *m.,* measure; manner, method; **ad hunc modum,** in this way.
oper•a, -ae, *f.* [**opus,** work], work; service.
pendō, pendere, pependī, pēnsum, weigh, weigh out; weigh out *money,* pay, pay out.
Quīnt•us, -ī, *m.;* **Titūr•ius, -ī,** *m.,* Quintus Titurius Sabinus, *one of Caesar's lieutenants.*
Quīnt•us, -ī, *m.;* **Iun•ius, -ī,** *m.,* Quintus Junius, *a Spaniard in Caesar's army.*
stīpend•ium, -ī, *n.,* tax, tribute.
ventitō, 1 [*frequentative of* **veniō,** come], go back and forth, visit.

---

1. colloquendī causā: gerundive with **causā** to express purpose; see App. §§288, 291.

4. apud quōs: "and in the presence of these men," i.e., the envoys, Arpineius and Junius.

5. locūtus est: this verb introduces Ambiorix's entire speech, which will be related in indirect statement down to "**Hāc ōrātiōne habitā discēdit Ambiorīx,**" i.e., the last sentence before 5.28. Note also that the many subordinate clauses embedded in this speech will thus take the subjunctive; see App. §269.

prō Caesaris in sē beneficiīs: "in respect of the benefits bestowed by Caesar on himself (i.e, Ambiorix)." Note the force of the subjective gen. Caesar *did* things for Ambiorix that *benefited* Ambiorix. See App. §98. Note also that Ambiorix absolves Caesar of blame for the attack. None of what follows will be Caesar's fault.

sēsē: acc. subject (referring to Ambiorix) of the inf. **cōnfitērī** in indirect statement dependent on **locūtus est.**

5–6. eī . . . dēbēre = *sē Caesarī . . . dēbēre.* The inf. **dēbēre** depends in indirect statement on **cōnfitērī.** The proper subject **sē,** i.e., Ambiorix, has been ellipted because it is easily understood from the emphatic **sēsē** at the beginning of the clause. "Ambiorix spoke as follows: he confessed that he owed, etc."

6. eius operā = *Caesaris operā.*

7. quodque eī = *quodque Ambiorīgī.* If native speakers slavishly followed the grammatical rules we learn in class, we would expect **sibi,** rather than **eī,** but, with the insertion of Caesar's name as the agent of the pass. verb, **eī** makes it clear that Caesar returned the sons to Ambiorix, not to himself.

> *et* filius *et* frātris filius *ab Caesare* remissī *essent, quōs* Aduātucī
> obsidum *numerō missōs apud sē in* servitūte *et* catēnīs *tenuissent;*
10   *neque id, quod fēcerit dē oppugnātiōne castrōrum, aut* iūdiciō *aut*
> voluntāte *suā fēcisse, sed* coāctū *cīvitātis, suaque esse* eiusmodī
> imperia, *ut nōn minus habēret* iūris *in sē multitūdō quam ipse in*
> *multitūdinem.* Cīvitātī porrō *hanc fuisse bellī causam, quod*
> repentīnae Gallōrum coniūrātiōnī resistere *nōn potuerit.*

Aduātuc•ī, -ōrum, *m., a people in Belgic Gaul and neighbors of the Eburones,* the Aduatici.
catēn•a, -ae, *f.,* chain, fetter.
coāct•us, -ūs, *m.* [**cōgō,** compel], compulsion.
coniūrāti•ō, -ōnis, *f.* [**coniūrō,** swear], a swearing together; plot, conspiracy.
eiusmodī, of such a sort *or* kind, such.
fīl•ius, -ī, *m.,* son.
frāt•er, -ris, *m.,* brother.
imper•ium, -ī, *n.* [**imperō,** order], right to command; authority; highest official power.
iūdic•ium, -ī, *n.* [**iūdex,** judge], judicial proceedings, trial; opinion, judgement; **iūdiciō,** by design, purposely.
iūs, iūris, *n.,* (human) law, justice; rights; power, authority.

ob•ses, -idis, *m. and f.* [**obsideō,** blockade], hostage; pledge, security.
porrō, *adv.,* farther on; furthermore, then.
re•mittō, -mittere, -mīsī, -missum [**mittō,** send], send *or* dispatch back, return; release, relax, give up.
repentīn•us, -a, -um, *adj.* [**repēns,** sudden], sudden, unexpected, hasty.
re•sistō, -sistere, -stitī, — [**sistō,** stand], stand back, remain behind, halt, stand still; withstand, resist, oppose.
servit•ūs, -ūtis, *f.* [**servus,** slave], slavery, servitude.
volun•tās, -tātis, *f.* [**volō,** wish], wish; goodwill; consent.

---

8. ab Caesare: the rules tell us to expect *ā* before a consonant, but the manuscripts do not show complete regularity; compare *ab cēterīs* in 5.30.

8–9. Aduātucī . . . apud sē: within the subordinate clause, **sē** refers to the **Aduātucī,** who are the subject of the verb **tenuissent.**

9. obsidum numerō missōs: "(who had been) sent as part of a contingent of hostages." The part. takes the place of a subordinate clause; see App. §283.

10. dē oppugnātiōne: "in regard to the, etc."

10–11. iūdiciō . . . voluntāte . . . coāctū: abl. of cause; see App. §138.

11. fēcisse: again, we have to supply a **sē** (referring to Ambiorix) as the acc. subject of

an inf. in indirect statement dependent on **locūtus est.**

11–12. sua . . . imperia: "his commands" or "his authority"; n. pl. acc. subject of the inf. **esse** in indirect statement.

12. ut . . . habēret: subjunctive in a substantive clause of result; see §229.

minus . . . iūris: "less authority"; partitive gen.; see App. § 101.

in sē . . . quam ipse = *in Ambiorīgem . . . quam Ambiorīx.*

13. Cīvitātī porrō: Note the prominent placement of *cīvitās,* underscored by *porrō.* Having explained why he himself joined the attack, Ambiorix moves on to explain why his people have joined the attack.

potuerit: the subject is *cīvitās.*

15   *Id sē facile ex* humilitāte *suā* probāre *posse, quod nōn* adeō *sit*
imperītus *rērum ut suīs cōpiīs populum Rōmānum* superārī *posse*
cōnfīdat. *Sed esse Galliae commūne cōnsilium: omnibus hībernīs*
Caesaris oppugnandīs *hunc esse dictum diem, nē quā legiō alterae*
legiōnī subsidiō venīre *posset. Nōn facile Gallōs Gallīs* negāre

20   *potuisse,* praesertim *cum dē* recuperandā *commūnī* lībertāte
cōnsilium initum *vidērētur.*

---

adeō, *adv.,* to such an extent, so much, so very, so; in fact.

cōn·fīdō, -fīdere, -fīsī, -fīsum [**fīdō,** trust. App. §74], rely on, feel confident, hope.

humili·tās, -tātis, *f.* [**humilis,** low], humility, lowness; weakness.

imperīt·us, -a, -um, *adj.* [**in** + **perītus,** experienced], inexperienced, unskilled, ignorant.

in·eō, -īre, -iī, -itum [**eō,** go. App. §84], go into; **inīre cōnsilium,** form a plan.

līber·tās, -tātis, *f.* [**līber,** free], freedom, liberty, independence.

negō, 1, say no, refuse, say no to.

oppugnō, 1 [**ob** + **pugnō,** fight], fight against, attack, besiege.

praesertim, *adv.,* particularly, especially.

probō, 1 [**probus,** good], approve; demonstrate.

recuperō, 1, recover, regain.

subsid·ium, -ī, *n.* [**subsideō,** sit near *or* in reserve], reserve force; help.

superō, 1 [**super,** over], be superior to, surpass; conquer, master, overcome.

veniō, venīre, vēnī, ventum, come, arrive, go, advance.

---

15. sē: the reflexive refers back to the subject of **locūtus est,** i.e., Ambiorix, and serves as the acc. subject of **posse.**

    probāre: complementary inf. with **posse;** see App. §175.

    16–17. ut . . . cōnfīdat: subjunctive in a substantive clause of result; see App. §§226–227.

    17. Galliae . . . cōnsilium: subjective gen.; see App. §98.

    17–18. omnibus . . . oppugnandīs: dat. of purpose; see App. §119.

    18. quā: "any"; see App. §174.

    alterae: an older form of *alterī;* compare regular forms in App. §32. Caesar also uses *nūllō* for the dat. of *nūllus* in 6.13.1.

    18–19. nē . . . posset: subjunctive in a clause of purpose; see App. §225.

    19. legiōnī: dat. of reference; see App. §120.

    subsidiō: dat. of purpose; see App. §119.

    Gallōs: acc. subject of **potuisse** in indirect statement.

    Gallīs: dat. indirect object with the sometimes intransitive verb **negāre;** see App. §117.

    20. recuperandā: gerundive; see App. §§288, 294.

    21. cōnsilium initum (*esse*) **vidērētur:** "a plan appeared to have been formed."

Quibus quoniam *prō* pietāte satisfēcerit, *habēre* nunc *sē*
ratiōnem officī *prō* beneficiīs *Caesaris*: monēre, orāre
Titūrium *prō* hospitiō, *ut suae ac mīlitum salūtī* cōnsulat.
25   *Magnam manum Germānōrum* conductam *Rhēnum* trānsīsse;
hanc adfore bīduō.

---

adsum, adesse, adfuī [**sum**, be, App. §77],
be near, be present, be at hand, appear.
benefi·cium, -cī, *n.* [**bene**, well + **faciō**, do],
benefit, favor, kindness, good deed.
bīdu·um, -ī, *n.* [**bis**, twice + **diēs**, day],
space *or* period of two days.
con·dūcō, -dūcere, -dūxī, -ductum [**dūcō**,
lead], lead *or* bring together, assemble,
conduct; hire.
cōnsul·ō, -ere, -uī, -tum, take counsel,
consult, consider; *with dat.*: take counsel
for, consider the interests of, take care
for; spare.
hospit·ium, -ī, *n.* [**hospes**, host *or* guest],
the reciprocal relationship that exists
between a host and a guest; friendship,
hospitality.
moneō, 2, warn, advise, instruct, order.
nunc, *adv.,* now, at present, at this time.
offic·ium, -ī, *n.,* allegiance, duty; business.
ōrō, 1 [**ōs**, mouth], speak; beseech, entreat.

pie·tās, -tātis, *f.* [**pius**, loyal], loyalty,
devotion.
quoniam, *conj.* [**cum** (= **quom**), since +
iam, now], since now, since, inasmuch as,
because, whereas.
rati·ō, -ōnis, *f.* [**reor**, reckon], reckoning,
account, estimate; design, plan, strategy,
science; method, arrangement; cause,
reason; regard, consideration; condition,
state of affairs; manner, way; condition,
terms; *in pl.,* transactions.
satis·faciō, -facere, -fēcī, -factum [**satis**,
enough + **faciō**, make], make *or* do
enough for; give satisfaction, satisfy;
make amends, apologize, ask pardon.
Titūr·ius, -ī, *m.,* Quintus Titurius Sabinus,
one of Caesar's lieutenants.
trāns·eō, -īre, -iī, -itum [**eō**, go. App. §84],
go across *or* come over, cross; march
through, pass through; move, migrate; *of
time,* pass by.

---

22. Quibus: *conjunctio relativa*: the rel. is
used as a conj., and the phrase is thus equivalent to *et eīs* (*Gallīs*); see App. §173, *a*. Dat.
indirect object with the intransitive verb
satisfēcerit; see App. §117. Now that Ambiorix has satisfied the Gauls, he may thus
consider once more what he owes Caesar.
Again, Caesar has done everything right.
   sē: acc. subject (referring to Ambiorix)
of the inf. **habēre** in indirect statement after
locūtus est.
   23. (*sē*) **monēre,** (*sē*) **orāre:** the ellipted
subject of these infs. (note the ASYNDETON;
see App. §301, *a*) may be inferred from the
previous clause. On ELLIPSIS, see App. §301, *c*.
   24. Titūrium: acc. direct object of the
infs. **monēre, orāre.** Ambiorix lies to Titurius
(a.k.a., Sabinus; Caesar uses both names), and

Titurius will be deceived. Caesar carefully
steers blame away from himself.
   25. manum: acc. subject of the inf.
trānsīsse, which takes **Rhēnum** as its direct
object. Ambiorix plays the German card, as
the Romans feared Germans more than they
did Gauls.
   conductam: "hired," i.e., *mercēde* ("with
pay"), hence "mercenary." Large, mercenary
gangs of Germans did not fight for free. The
Romans hired Germans too, of course, and
Gauls, we should not forget, fought in the Roman cavalry.
   26. bīduō: abl. of time within which; see
App. §152.
   adfore: *fore* = *futurus esse,* the fut. active
inf. of *esse.*

Ipsōrum esse cōnsilium, velintne priusquam fīnitimī sentiant
ēductōs ex hībernīs mīlitēs aut ad Cicerōnem aut ad Labiēnum
dēdūcere, quōrum alter mīlia passuum circiter quīnquāgintā,
30   alter paulō amplius ab eīs absit. Illud sē pollicērī et iūre iūrandō
cōnfirmāre tūtum iter per fīnēs datūrum.

---

absum, abesse, āfuī, — [**sum,** be. App.
§78], be away, be distant, be lacking.
amplē, adv. [**amplus,** large], largely; comp.:
amplius, more, farther.
cōnfirmō, 1 [**firmō,** strengthen], establish,
strengthen, encourage, console; declare.
dē•dūcō, -dūcere, -dūxī, -ductum [**dūcō,**
lead], lead down; bring, conduct.
ē•dūcō, -dūcere, -dūxī, -ductum [**dūcō,**
lead], lead out, lead forth; draw (a sword).
fīnitim•us, -a, -um, adj. [**fīnis,** limit],
bordering on, neighboring.
iūs iūrandum, iūris iūrandī, n. [**iūs,** right +
iūrō, swear], an oath.
Labiēn•us, -ī, m., Titus Atius Labienus,
Caesar's most trusted lieutenant in the
Gallic War. During the Civil War, Labienus

fought on Pompey's side, and died in battle
against Caesar in Munda (in Spain) in 45
BCE.
paulō, adv. [**paulus,** little], a little,
somewhat, slightly.
polliceor, 2 [**prō** + **liceor,** bid, offer], offer,
promise.
priusquam or **prius . . . quam,** conj., sooner
than, before; until.
quīnquāgintā (L), card. num. adj., indecl.,
fifty.
sentiō, sentīre, sēnsī, sēnsum, perceive,
be aware of, notice, experience, undergo;
realize, know; decide, judge; sanction,
adhere to.
tūt•us, -a, -um, adj. [**tueor,** protect],
protected, safe, secure.

---

27. Ipsōrum (Rōmānōrum) **esse cōnsilium:** "the most advisable plan is up to
them" or "theirs to decide"; subjective gen.
(see App. §98), as the Romans *themselves* will
have to *consider* what course of action is most
advisable in this situation. Ambiorix "helpful-
ly" suggests two possibilities, both of which
will lead to ambush.

velintne: subjunctive in an indirect question (see App. §§262–264) within indirect
statement (see App. §269).

28. ēductōs ex hībernīs mīlitēs: this
whole phrase serves as the direct object of
the complementary inf. **dēdūcere.**

ad Cicerōnem aut ad Labiēnum: Caesar
pointedly names the very lieutenants who
will not be taken in by such tricks.

30. eīs: Titurius and his men.

Illud: acc. direct object of the infs.
pollicērī and **cōnfirmāre.**

sē: acc. subject (referring to Ambiorix) of
the infs. **pollicērī** and **cōnfirmāre** in indirect statement after **locūtus est.**

31. datūrum: fut. inf. with *esse* omitted in
indirect statement in apposition with **illud**
to explain what Ambiorix promises. Note
that the subject of this inf., *sē* (referring to
Ambiorix), has been ellipted because it can
be supplied easily from the beginning of the
sentence.

Quod cum faciat, et cīvitātī sēsē cōnsulere, *quod hībernīs* levētur,
et Caesarī prō eius meritīs grātiam referre. *Hāc* ōrātiōne habitā
discēdit Ambiorīx.

---

cōnsul•ō, -ere, -uī, -tum, take counsel,
  consult, consider; *with dat.*: take counsel
  for, consider the interests of, take care
  for; spare.
grāti•a, -ae, *f.* [grātus, pleasing], favor,
  goodwill, gratitude, esteem, influence,
  popularity; grātiās agere, thank;
  grātiam referre, to return a favor.
hab•eō, -ēre, -uī, -itum, have, hold; deliver
  (*with* ōrātiōnem)

levō, 1 [levis, light], lighten, ease, relieve.
merit•um, -ī, *n.* [mereor, deserve], service,
  desert, merit; favor, kindness, benefit.
ōrāti•ō, -ōnis, *f.* [ōrō, speak], a speech,
  address.
referō, referre, rettulī, relātum [re + ferō,
  carry. App. §81], bear, carry back, report;
  grātiam referre, show one's gratitude,
  make a requital.

---

32. Quod cum faciat: "And, because he
(i.e., Ambiorix) does this" or "by doing this."
On the causal use of *cum*, see App. §283.

Quod = *et id*; see App. §173, *a.*

sēsē: acc. subject (referring to Ambiorix)
of the inf. cōnsulere, and, by way of ellipsis,
also of referre.

hībernīs: abl. of separation; see App. §134.

33. Caesarī . . . referre: Caesar keeps his
own merits, benefits, and planning before the
reader in his representation of Ambiorix's
speech. We are left with the impression that
Caesar's actions, whatever may follow, were
beyond reproach—even his enemies confess
as much!

Hāc ōrātiōne habitā: the abl. absolute
punctuates the conclusion of a rather long
speech entirely in indirect statement!

[5.28] Arpīnēius *et* Iūnius, *quae* audierunt, *ad lēgātōs* dēferunt. *Illī* repentīnā *rē* perturbātī, etsī *ab hoste ea dīcēbantur, tamen nōn* neglegenda *exīstimābant* maximē*que hāc rē* permovēbantur, *quod cīvitātem* ignōbilem *atque* humilem Eburōnum *suā* sponte
5   *populō Rōmānō bellum facere* ausam vix *erat* crēdendum. Itaque *ad cōnsilium rem* dēferunt *magnaque inter eōs* exsistit *contrōversia.*

Arpīnēius, -ī, *m.*, Gaius Arpineius, *an equestrian in Caesar's army.*
aud•eō, -ēre, ausus sum (App. §74), dare, risk, venture.
audiō, 4, hear, hear of.
crēd•ō, -ere, -idī, -itum, believe; entrust.
dē•ferō, -ferre, -tulī, -lātum [**ferō,** carry. App. §81], carry, take; report; bring before; bestow.
Eburōn•ēs, -um, *m.,* the Eburones, *a Belgic people who in 54* BCE *destroyed troops under Sabinus and Cotta. Afterward, Caesar almost exterminated them.*
etsī, *conj.* [**et** + **sī,** if], even if, although.
ex•sistō, -sistere, -stitī, — [**sistō,** stand], stand *or* come forth, appear, arise; ensue.
humil•is, -e, *adj.* [**humus,** the ground], *on the ground;* low, humble, abject, weak.

ignōbil•is, -e, *adj.* [**in** + (**g**)**nōbilis,** well-known], unknown, undistinguished.
itaque, *conj.* [**ita,** so], and so, therefore.
Iūn•ius, -ī, *m.,* Quintus Junius, *a Spaniard who served in Caesar's army.*
maximē, *superl. adv.* [**magnus,** large], especially.
neg•legō, -legere, -lēxī, -lēctum [**neg** + **legō,** choose], not heed, disregard.
per•moveō, -movēre, -mōvī, -mōtum [**moveō,** move], move thoroughly; incite.
perturbō, 1 [**turbō,** disturb], disturb greatly, throw into confusion; terrify.
repentīn•us, -a, -um, *adj.* [**repēns,** sudden], sudden, unexpected, hasty.
spontis, *gen. and* **sponte,** *abl.* (*obs. nom.* **spōns**), *f.,* of one's own accord, willingly.
vix, *adj.,* with difficulty, hardly.

---

1. quae: the implied antecedent, *ea* ("those things"), is omitted.

audierunt: indicative because the clause is subordinate to a principal clause in direct statement.

lēgātōs: i.e., Sabinus (a.k.a. Titurius) and Cotta (a.k.a. Aurunculeius). How will they handle the situation?

2. Illī ... perturbātī = *lēgātī,* i.e., Sabinus (a.k.a. Titurius) and Cotta.

etsī ... dīcēbantur: Caesar lets us know that the lieutenants are not as bright as Caesar, who, Caesar thus suggests, would not have been taken in by Ambiorix's story.

2–3. tamen nōn neglegenda: indirect statement dependent on **exīstimābant.** The acc. subject of the pass. periphrastic inf. (with *esse* omitted) must be supplied from the previous clause: *ea.*

4. sponte: abl. of manner or accordance; see App. §142, *a.*

4–5. cīvitātem ... ausam: indirect statement dependent on **erat crēdendum.** Note that Caesar once again omits *esse* from the perf. active inf. of the semi-deponent verb *audeō.*

6. cōnsilium: it was customary for Roman leaders, generals, and lieutenants to decide all matters of importance in consultation with colleagues, although the man in charge would bear ultimate responsibility for his choice. Even a father (or head of household) was expected to consult senior family members before exercising his rights as *pater familiās.* The authority figure seeks advice (or counsel) from an advisory group.

Lūcius Aurunculēius complūrēs*que* tribūnī *mīlitum et prīmōrum*
ōrdinum centuriōnēs *nihil* temerē agendum *neque ex hībernīs*
iniussū *Caesaris discēdendum exīstimābant*: quantāsvīs *magnās*
10   *cōpiās etiam Germānōrum sustinērī posse* mūnītīs *hībernīs*
docēbant: *rem esse* testimōniō, *quod prīmum hostium* impetum
multīs ultrō vulneribus illātīs fortissimē *sustinuerint*: *rē*
frūmentāriā *nōn premī*; intereā *et ex proximīs hībernīs et ā*

---

ag•ō, -ere, ēgī, actum, set in motion; do,
    transact; discuss, speak.
centuri•ō, -ōnis, *m.* [centum, hundred],
    centurion, *the commander of the century,*
    a unit corresponding to one-sixtieth of a
    legion.
complūr•ēs, -a, *adj.* [plūs, more], several,
    many; a great many.
doceō, docēre, docuī, docitum, show,
    teach, instruct, inform.
fort•is, -e, *adj.,* strong, brave.
frūmentāri•us, -a, -um, *adj.* [frūmentum,
    grain], of *or* pertaining to grain; rēs
    frūmentāria, grain supply, provisions.
impet•us, -ūs, *m.,* attack; force, vehemence.
īn•ferō, īnferre, intulī, illātum [ferō,
    carry. App. §81], carry into, import,
    inflict, cause, produce; cast into.
iniussū, *abl. of* iniussus, -ūs, *m.* [iūbeō,
    order], without command *or* order.
intereā, *adv.,* in the meantime, meanwhile.

Lūci•us, -ī, *m.;* Aurunculēi•us, -ī, *m.,*
    Lucius Aurunculeius Cotta, *one of*
    Caesar's lieutenants.
mūniō, 4, defend with a wall, fortify.
quant•usvīs, -avīs, -umvīs, *adj.* [quantus,
    as great as + vīs, you wish], as great
    (large, much, etc.) as you wish, however
    great.
temerē, *adv.,* rashly, blindly, without good
    reason.
testimōn•ium, -ī, *n.* [testor, be a witness],
    testimony, evidence, proof.
tribūn•us, -ī, *m.* [tribus, tribe], tribune;
    tribūnus plēbis, *at Rome, a magistrate*
    elected by the people voting in tribes,
    originally to defend the interests of the
    plebs; tribūnus mīlitum *or* mīlitāris, a
    military tribune.
ultrō, *adv.,* voluntarily; besides, moreover.
vuln•us, -eris, *n.,* a wound.

7–8. Lūcius . . . centuriōnēs: Caesar gives
us a clear picture of who took part in a military council and the frank discussion and debate that was customary.

8–9. agendum neque . . . discēdendum:
pass. periphrastic infs. (without *esse*) in indirect
statement dependent on **exīstimābant**. The
subject of **agendum** (*esse*), **nihil**, may serve as
the subject of the impers. **discēdendum** (*esse*)
as well, but, in order to translate the phrase
into English, it will be best to render the verb
actively and its subject as an adv.: "they should
by no means depart."

10. cōpiās: acc. subject of **posse** in indirect statement dependent on **docēbant**.
    hībernīs: abl. of means; see App. §143.
    11. rem esse testimōniō (*id*), **quod:** "the
thing for proof was (this, namely) that . . . "
or, more idiomatically, "proof of this was the
fact that . . . ."
    testimōniō: dat. of purpose; see App.
§119.
    13. premī: this inf. in indirect statement
lacks an acc. subject; we may supply *sē* referring back to the main speakers as well as to
everyone in the Roman camp.

Caesare conventūra subsidia: postrēmō *quid esse* levius *aut*

15   turpius, *quam* auctōre *hoste dē summīs rēbus capere cōnsilium?*

---

auctor, -is, *m.* [**augeō,** increase], one
who produces, creates, *or* originates;
promoter, instigator, advisor, author.
lev·is, -e, *adj.* light (*in weight*), slight; light-
minded, silly, fickle, inconstant.
postrēmō, *adv.* [**postrēmus,** last], finally,
at last.

subsid·ium, -ī, *n.* [**subsideō,** sit near *or* in
reserve], reserve force; help.
turp·is, -e, *adj.,* ugly, unseemly; shameful,
disgraceful, dishonorable.

---

14. conventūra: fut. active inf. (with *esse*
omitted) in indirect statement dependent on
docēbant; the acc. subject is **subsidia.**

14–15. quid esse … quam … capere: for
the retention of the inf. in a rhetorical question in indirect statement, see App. §268, II.

15. auctōre hoste: "on the authority of an
enemy"; abl. absolute; see App. §150.

summīs rēbus: "matters of life and death."

[5.29] Contrā *ea* Titūrius sērō *factūrōs* clāmitābat, *cum*
maiōrēs *manūs hostium* adiūnctīs *Germānīs convēnissent aut*
cum aliquid calamitātis *in proximīs hībernīs esset acceptum.*
Brevem cōnsulendī *esse* occāsiōnem. *Caesarem arbitrārī*
5   *profectum in* Italiam; *neque* aliter Carnutēs *interficiendī* Tasgetī
cōnsilium fuisse captūrōs, neque Eburōnēs, *sī ille* adesset, *tantā*
contemptiōne *nostrī ad castra* ventūrōs *esse.*

---

ad•iungō, -iungere, -iūnxī, -iūnctum
[**iungō**, join], attach, join to, unite, add.
adsum, adesse, adfuī [**sum**, be, App.
§77], be near, be present, be at hand,
appear.
aliter, *adv.* [**alius**, other], otherwise.
brev•is, -e, *adv.*, short, brief, transitory.
calami•tās, -tātis, *f.*, disaster, misfortune,
defeat.
Carnut•ēs, -um, *m.*, the Carnutes (*a people
in central Gaul*).
clāmitō, 1 [*frequentative of* **clāmō**, cry out],
cry out repeatedly, exclaim.
cōnsul•ō, -ere, -uī, -tum, take counsel,
consult, consider; *with dat.*: take counsel
for.
contempti•ō, -ōnis, *f.* [**contemnō**, despise],
disdain, contempt.

contrā, *adv. and prep. with acc.*: (1) *as adv.*:
against him *or* them; on the other hand.
Eburōn•ēs, -um, *m.*, the Eburones, *a Belgic
people who in 54* BCE *destroyed troops
under Sabinus and Cotta. Afterward,
Caesar almost exterminated them.*
Itali•a, -ae, *f.*, Italy, *generally Italy below
Cisalpine Gaul.*
maior, māius, *adj.* [*comp. of* **magnus**, large],
larger.
occāsi•ō, -ōnis, *f.* [**occidō**, fall, happen],
occasion, opportunity.
sērō, *adv.*, late, too late.
Tasget•ius, -ī, *m.*, Tasgetius, *a leader among
the Carnutes.*
Titūr•ius, -ī, *m.*, Quintus Titurius Sabinus,
one of Caesar's lieutenants.
veniō, venīre, vēnī, ventum, come, go.

---

1. ea: "these arguments."
    sērō factūrōs: "that they would be acting
too late," i.e., *sē* **sērō factūrōs** *esse*; the ellipted acc. subject *sē* refers to everyone involved
in the conversation, hence the pl. fut. active
inf. dependent on **clāmitābat** in indirect
statement.
    clāmitābat: Titurius (a.k.a. Sabinus) "shouts
over and over again." The verbal suffix -**itō**
makes verbs freq. Caesar's unflattering portrait
of Sabinus suggests that he was not assessing
the situation rationally. This verb of speaking
(or screaming) introduces another long speech,
and Sabinus's rant in indirect statement runs
through the remainder of the chapter.
    cum: "after"; see App. §§238, 242.
    2. adiūnctīs Germānīs: abl. absolute; see
App. §150.
    3. calamitātis: partitive gen; see App.
§101, *a.*
    4. cōnsulendī: gerund; see App. §287.

Caesarem: acc. subject of the inf. **profectum** (*esse*) in indirect statement dependent
on **arbitrārī**.
    arbitrārī: supply *sē* to serve as the subject
of this inf. in indirect statement dependent on
clāmitābat, whose subject, of course, is Titurius (a.k.a. Sabinus), the irrational screamer
who is delivering this speech.
    5. interficiendī: gerundive; see App.
§§288, 291.
    **5–7. neque Carnutēs ... fuisse captūrōs,
neque Eburōnēs, sī ille adesset, ... ventūrōs
esse:** "if Caesar had been nearby, neither would
the Carnutes have adopted ... nor would the
Eburones be approaching," etc. For contrary to
fact conditions in indirect statement, see App.
§272; compare §§ 252, *b*; 254.
    7. contemptiōne: abl. of manner; see App.
§ 142.
    nostrī: "for us"; objective gen.; see App.
§98.

> *Nōn hostem* auctōrem, *sed rem* spectāre: subesse *Rhēnum;*
> *magnō esse Germānīs* dolōrī Ariovistī *mortem et superiōrēs*
> 10 *nostrās victōriās;* ārdēre *Galliam* tot contumēliīs *acceptīs* sub
> *populī Rōmānī* imperium redāctam *superiōre* glōriā *reī* mīlitāris
> exstīnctā.

---

ard•eō, -ēre, arsī, arsum, burn, blaze, be
  inflamed, be eager.
- **Ariovist•us, -ī,** *m.,* Ariovistus, a Germanic
  king.
auctor, -is, *m.* [**augeō,** increase], one
  who produces, creates, *or* originates;
  promoter, instigator, advisor, author.
contumēli•a, -ae, *f.,* affront, indignity,
  insult; injury, violence.
dol•or, -ōris, *m.* [**doleō,** grieve], grief,
  distress, pain, anguish.
ex•stinguō, -stinguere, -stīnxī, -stīnctum,
  put out, quench; destroy.
glōri•a, -ae, *f.,* glory, reputation.
imper•ium, -ī, *n.* [**imperō,** order], right
  to command; authority; jurisdiction;
  supreme, highest official power.

mīlitār•is, -e, *adj.* [**mīles,** soldier], of a
  soldier, military, martial; **rēs mīlitāris,**
  military matters, warfare, the science of
  war.
red•igō, -igere, -ēgī, -āctum [**red-** + **agō,**
  put in motion], bring back, bring under;
  render, make; reduce.
spectō, 1 [*frequentative of* **speciō,** see], look
  at, regard; face.
sub, *prep. with acc.,* under, beneath.
sub•sum, -esse, -fuī, — [**sum,** be. App.
  §77], be under *or* below, be near *or* close
  at hand.
tot, *indecl. adj.,* so many.

---

8. spectāre: supply *sē* (referring to Titurius Sabinus) as the acc. subject of this inf.
  9. magnō . . . dolōrī: dat. of purpose; see
App. §119.
  Germānīs: dat. of reference; see App. §120.
  Ariovistī mortem: Caesar defeated Ariovistus in 58 BCE, which is described in Book
One. How he may have died in the interim,
however, is unclear.
  10. Galliam: acc. subject of **ārdēre** in indirect statement.

10–11. Galliam . . . redāctam: "Gaul,
which, after suffering so many violent as-
saults, was subjugated under the military
authority of the Roman people," etc. As is
so often the case, we use subordinate clauses
where Latin prefers an abl. absolute and a
part. See App. §286.
  11–12. superiōre glōriā . . . exstīnctā:
another abl. absolute; see App. §150.

Postrēmō *quis hōc sibi persuādēret, sine certā rē Ambiorīgem*
ad eiusmodī *cōnsilium* dēscendisse? *Suam* sententiam *in*
15   *utramque partem esse* tūtam: *sī nihil esset* dūrius, nūllō *cum*
perīculō ad proximam legiōnem perventūrōs; sī Gallia omnis cum
Germānīs cōnsentīret, *ūnam esse in celeritāte* positam *salūtem.*

---

cōn•sentiō, -sentīre, -sēnsī, -sēnsum
[**sentiō,** feel], *think together*: agree,
combine.
dē•scendō, -scendere, -scendī, -scēnsum
[**scandō,** climb], climb down, go down,
descend; have recourse (*to*), resort.
dūr•us, -a, -um, *adj.*, hard, rough, harsh,
difficult, dangerous; severe, inclement.
eiusmodī, of such a sort *or* kind, such.
nūll•us, -a, -um, *gen.* **nullīus,** *adj.* [**ne-** +
ūllus, any], not any, no.
pōnō, pōnere, posuī, positum, place, put,
place over; lay down, set aside; station,

post; regard, consider; make, build; *with*
in *and the abl.*, depend on, *in addition to*
the above meanings.
postrēmō, *adv.* [**postrēmus,** last], finally,
at last.
sententi•a, -ae, *f.* [**sentiō,** think], way of
thinking, opinion, sentiment; purpose,
design, scheme, plan; decision, resolve;
verdict; sentence.
tūt•us, -a, -um, *adj.* [**tueor,** protect],
protected, safe, secure.

---

13. persuādēret: what was an indicative
verb in an interrog. sentence becomes subjunctive when represented in indirect statement; see App. §268.
   certā rē: "irrefutable proof."
   Ambiorīgem . . . dēscendisse: ind. statement dependent on **persuādēret.**
   14. suam sententiam: acc. subject of **esse**
in indirect statement dependent (because
we have moved on to a new argument) on
the verb **clamitābat** at the beginning of the

section, and thus **suam** refers to Titurius Sabinus's opinion.
   15–16. sī . . . sī: on conditions in indirect
statement, see App. §272.
   16. perventūrōs: fut. active inf. (without
esse) dependent on **sententia.** Why do we find
the m. pl.? The subject is ellipted, so we may
supply *sē,* but *sē* would here refer both to Titurius Sabinus and to everyone in the council
and camp.
   17. ūnam: "(their) only."

Cottae quidem *atque eōrum, quī* dissentīrent, *cōnsilium quem
habēre* exitum? *In quō sī nōn* praesēns *perīculum, at* certē
20   longinquā obsidiōne famēs *esset* timenda?

---

certē, *adv.* [**certus,** certain], certainly; at
  least.
Cott•a, -ae, *m.*, Lucius Aurunculeius Cotta,
  one of Caesar's lieutenants.
dis•sentiō, -sentīre, -sēnsī, -sēnsum
  [**sentiō,** feel], differ, disagree.
exit•us, -ūs, *m.* [**exeō,** go out], a going out,
  exit, passage; issue, result, end.
fam•ēs, -is, *f.*, starvation, hunger.
longinqu•us, -a, -um, *adj.* [**longus,** long],
  distant, remote; long.
obsidi•ō, -ōnis, *f.* [**obsideō,** blockade],
  siege, investment, blockade; peril,
  oppression.

prae•sum, -esse, -fuī, — [**sum,** be. App.
  §77], be before *or* over, be in command
  of, rule over, be at the head of; **praesēns,**
  pres. part. as adj.: present, in person; for
  the present.
quidem, *adv.,* indeed, at any rate, at least,
  truly; on the other hand; **nē ... quidem,**
  not even.
time•ō, -ēre, -uī, —, fear, be afraid of,
  dread; *with dat.*, be anxious about, be
  anxious for, dread; **nihil timēre,** have
  no fear.

---

18. Cottae ... cōnsilium: note the emphatic placement of Cotta and all those opposed to Titurius Sabinus at the beginning of the clause as well as the placement of the direct object, **cōnsilium,** before the interrog. adj. **quem.** We can almost hear Titurius Sabinus shouting in indirect statement!

18–19. quem habēre exitum: because the question was rhetorical (i.e., Titurius Sabinus

knows what answer he wants), the inf. is used in indirect statement rather than the subjunctive. See App. §268, II.

19. in quō: "in which case" (referring to the antecedent **exitum**).

20. obsidiōne: abl. of cause; see App. §138.

[5.30] *Hāc in utramque partem* disputātiōne *habitā, cum ā*
Cottā *prīmīsque ōrdinibus* ācriter resisterētur, "Vincite," inquit,
"sī ita vultis," Sabīnus, *et id* clāriōre vōce, *ut magna pars mīlitum*
exaudīret; *"neque is sum,"* inquit, *"quī gravissimē ex* vōbīs *mortis*
5　　*perīculō* terreat: *hī* sapient; *sī gravius quid acciderit, abs* tē
ratiōnem reposcent, *quī, sī per* tē liceat, perendinō *diē cum
proximīs hībernīs* coniūnctī *commūnem cum reliquīs bellī* cāsum
sustineant, *nōn* rēiectī *et* relēgātī *longē ab* cēterīs *aut* ferrō *aut*
fame intereant."

ācriter, *adv.* [**ācer,** sharp], sharply, fiercely.
cās•us, -ūs, *m.* [**cadō,** fall], accident,
　chance, misfortune.
cēter•ī, -ae, -a, *adj.,* the rest of.
clār•us, -a, -um, *adj.,* clear, loud.
con•iungō, -iungere, -iūnxī, -iūnctum
　[**coniungō,** join], join with *or* together,
　connect, unite, bind.
Cott•a, -ae, *m.,* Lucius Aurunculeius Cotta,
　one of Caesar's lieutenants.
disputāti•ō, -ōnis, *f.* [**disputō,** discuss],
　argument, discussion.
ego, meī (App. §51), *first pers. pron.,* I, me;
　pl. **nōs,** we, us, etc.
ex•audiō, 4 [**audiō,** hear], hear (*from a
　distance*).
fam•ēs, -is, *f.,* starvation, hunger.
ferr•um, -ī, *n.,* iron; tool; sword.
inqu•am, -is, -it, say.
inter•eō, -īre, -iī, -itum [**eō,** go], die.
licet, licēre, licuit *and* **licitum est,** *impers.,*
　it is permitted.

perendin•us, -a, -um, *adj.,* after tomorrow.
rati•ō, -ōnis, *f.* [**reor,** reckon], reckoning,
　account.
re•iciō, -icere, -iēcī, -iectum [**re** + **iaciō,**
　throw.], hurl *or* drive back, repel; cast
　down *or* off; drive off *or* out.
relegō, 1 [**re** + **legō,** delegate], send away,
　remove.
re•poscō, -poscere, —, — [**re** + **poscō,**
　demand], demand back, exact, ask for.
re•sistō, -sistere, -stitī, — [**sistō,** stand],
　stand back, remain behind, halt; resist,
　oppose.
Sabīn•us, -ī, *m.,* Quintus Titurius Sabinus,
　one of Caesar's lieutenants.
sap•iō, -ere, -īvī, —, be wise, understand.
terreō, 2, frighten, terrify.
tū, tuī (App. §51), *second pers. pron.,* you;
　pl. **vos.**
vincō, vincere, vīcī, victum, conquer,
　prevail; have one's way *or* desire.
vōx, vōcis, *f.,* voice; shout; word.

---

1. in utramque partem: Caesar refers to
Cotta's argument in favor of staying in the
camp versus Titurius Sabinus's in favor of ac-
cepting Ambiorix's promise of safe passage.

1–2. cum ... resisterētur: subjunctive in a
temporal clause; see App. §§237, 240.

2. Vincite: Caesar's sudden shift to direct
statement is the rhetorical equivalent to turning up the volume.

4. neque is sum, quī ... ex vōbīs: "nor am
I the one who ... among you," i.e., among the
men in this council; compare App. §101, *b.*

5. hī = *mīlitēs,* i.e., the soldiers who are not
in the council, but who are in the camp, and

can hear what Titurius Sabinus is saying—because he is shouting so loudly!

**6–9. quī, sī per tē liceat, ... sustineant,
nōn ... intereant:** future less vivid conditions; see App. §257. The protasis (if-clause)
has been ellipted from the second condition,
which is appended to the first apodosis (conclusion) with no conj. in ASYNDETON. The
second apodosis will be easier to translate,
if you repeat the ellipted *"quī, sī per tē liceat."*

7. cum reliquīs = *mīlitibus,* i.e., Caesar's
other soldiers in other camps.

8. ab cēterīs = *mīlitibus,* i.e., Caesar's other
soldiers in other camps.

[5.31] Cōnsurgitur *ex cōnsiliō*; comprehendunt *utrumque et
ōrant, nē suā* dissēnsiōne *et* pertināciā *rem in summum perīculum*
dēdūcant: *facilem esse rem,* seu maneant, seu *proficīscantur, sī
modo ūnum omnēs* sentiant *ac* probent; contrā *in* dissēnsiōne
5   nūllam *sē salūtem* perspicere. *Rēs* disputātiōne *ad* mediam
noctem perdūcitur.

---

com•prehendō, -prehendere, -prehendī,
-prehēnsum [prehendō (= prendō),
seize], lay hold of, seize, arrest.
cōn•surgō, -surgere, -surrēxī, -surrectum
[surgō, rise], arise together, arise in a
body, arise.
contrā, *adv. and prep. with acc.*: (1) *as adv.*:
against him *or* them; on the other hand;
contrā atque, contrary to what; (2) *as
prep.*, against, contrary to; opposite, facing.
dē•dūcō, -dūcere, -dūxī, -ductum [dūcō,
lead], lead down; bring, conduct.
disputāti•ō, -ōnis, *f.* [dispūtō, discuss],
argument, discussion.
dissensi•ō, -ōnis, *f.* [dissentiō, think
differently], disagreement, dissension.
maneō, manēre, mānsī, mānsum, remain,
continue, abide, stay.
medi•us, -a, -um, *adj.*, in the middle of; in
the middle, intervening, intermediate;
locus medius utrīusque, a place midway
between the two.
modo, *adv.* [modus, measure], *with measure
or limit*; only; just, at least, but; *of time*,
just now.

nūll•us, -a, -um, *gen.* nūllīus, *adj.* [ne- +
ūllus, any], not any, no.
ōrō, 1 [ōs, mouth], speak; beseech, entreat.
per•dūcō, -dūcere, -dūxī, -ductum [dūcō,
lead], lead through *or* along, conduct,
bring over, bring; construct, extend;
influence, win over; draw out, prolong.
per•spiciō, -spicere, -spexī, -spectum
[speciō, look], look *or* see through; view,
examine, inspect; perceive, realize, learn,
find out, ascertain.
pertināci•a, -ae, *f.* [pertineō, hold onto],
obstinacy, stubbornness, pertinacity.
probō, 1 [probus, good], approve;
demonstrate.
sentiō, sentīre, sēnsī, sēnsum, perceive,
be aware of, notice, experience, undergo;
realize, know; decide, judge; sanction,
adhere to.
sīve *and* seu, *conj.* [sī + ve, or], or if, if;
or; whether; sīve ... sīve, either ... or,
whether ... or, to see if ... or.

---

1. Cōnsurgitur: "they stand up as a group"
is preferable to a literal translation of this
typically Latin impers. construction of an
intransitive verb; see App. §181.

comprehendunt utrumque: "they clasp
(the hands) of each," i.e., of Titurius Sabinus
and Aurunculeius Cotta.

2. rem: "the current situation" or "state of
affairs."

2–3. nē ... dēdūcant: volitive subjunctive
in a substantive clause of negative purpose
(or indirect command) after ōrant; see App.
§227.

4. ūnum: "one thing," i.e., "the same
thing." The soldiers want their commanders
to agree.

5–6. ad mediam noctem: night was a no-
toriously bad time for deliberations. Military
necessity sometimes required nocturnal deliberation, but in Rome the civil government
always broke off deliberations at sunset, and
did not resume deliberations until after sunrise. Midnight also represented the end of the
Roman day.

Tandem *dat Cotta* permōtus *manūs*: superat sententia Sabīnī.
Prōnūntiātur *prīmā* lūce itūrōs. Cōnsūmitur vigiliīs *reliqua*
pars noctis, cum sua quisque mīles circumspiceret, *quid sēcum*
10   portāre *posset, quid ex* īnstrūmentō *hībernōrum relinquere*
       cōgerētur.

---

circum•spiciō, -spicere, -spexī, -spectum
[speciō, look] look (*around*) for *or* at,
consider, examine.

cōn•sūmō, -sūmere, -sūmpsī, -sūmptum
[sūmō, take], *take together* or *all at once*:
devour, consume, destroy; use up, waste,
pass.

eō, īre, iī (īvī), itum (App. §84), go,
proceed, march, pass.

īnstrūment•um, -ī, *n.* [īnstruō, build],
tool, apparatus, equipment.

lūx, lūcis, *f.*, light, daylight; prīmā lūce, at
dawn.

per•moveō, -movēre, -mōvī, -mōtum
[moveō, move], move thoroughly; incite;
influence.

portō, 1, carry, transport, bring, take.

pro•nūntiō, 1 [nūntiō, announce],
announce, give out publicly, tell, relate,
report, say; give orders; *with* sententia,
pronounce.

Sabīn•us, -ī, *m.*, Quintus Titurius Sabinus,
one of Caesar's lieutenants.

sententi•a, -ae, *f.* [sentiō, think], way of
thinking, opinion, sentiment; purpose,
design, scheme, plan; decision, resolve;
verdict; sentence.

superō, 1 [super, over], go over; be superior
to, conquer; remain.

tandem, *adv.*, at last, at length, finally; *in
interrog. clauses to add emphasis, as* quid
tandem, what then?

vigili•a, -ae, *f.* [vigil, awake], wakefulness,
watching; a watch, *one of the four equal
divisions of the night, used by the Romans in
reckoning time and organizing guard duty.*

---

7. dat Cotta ... manūs: Aurunculeius Cotta, the junior officer, "gives up," i.e., he lifts his
hands in surrender.

8. itūrōs = *omnēs* itūrōs *esse.*

9. cum ... circumspiceret: "while"; see
App. §234.

sua: "his things," i.e., his possessions. As
the heavy baggage train that later gets in their
way will demonstrate, the soldiers tried to
take along as much as possible.

9–11. quid ... posset, quid ... cōgerētur:
indirect questions; see App. §262.

Omnia excōgitantur, quārē *nec sine perīculō* maneātur, *et*
languōre *mīlitum et* vigiliīs *perīculum* augeātur. *Prīmā* lūce sīc
ex castrīs proficīscuntur, ut quibus esset persuāsum nōn ab hoste,
15   *sed ab homine* amīcissimō *Ambiorīge cōnsilium datum, longissimō*
agmine *maximīsque* impedīmentīs.

---

agm•en, -inis, *n.* [**agō,** move], *a moving*
body; a marching column; army; **in**
agmine, on the march; **prīmum**
agmen, the vanguard *(those in front);*
novissimum *or* **extrēmum agmen,** the
rear *(those in back).*
amīc•us, -ī, *m.,* [**amō,** love], friend.
auge•ō, -ēre, auxī, auctum, increase,
augment, enhance, add to.
excōgitō, 1 [**cōgitō,** think], think out,
contrive, devise, invent.
impedīment•um, -ī, *n.* [**impediō,** hinder],
hindrance, obstacle; *pl.*: baggage,
baggage-train *(including pack animals).*
langu•or, -ōris, *m.,* weakness, faintness.

lūx, lūcis, *f.,* light, daylight; **prīmā lūce,** at
dawn.
maneō, manēre, mānsī, mānsum, remain,
continue, abide, stay.
quārē, *adv.* [**quī,** which + **rēs,** thing],
(1) *interrog.,* why? wherefore? for
what reason? (2) *rel.,* on this account,
therefore, wherefore.
sīc, *adv.,* so, thus, in this manner; **sīc . . . ut,**
so . . . that; so . . . as.
vigili•a, -ae, *f.* [**vigil,** awake], wakefulness,
watching; a watch, *one of the four equal*
divisions of the night, used by the Romans in
reckoning time and organizing guard duty.

---

12. Omnia: "all sorts of reasons."
  nec sine perīculō: LITOTES, see App.
§301, *g.*
  12–13. quārē . . . maneātur, . . . augeātur:
"why they would remain (in that place) . . . ,
(why) danger would be increased . . . ."
  13. languōre . . . et vigiliīs: abl. of cause;
see App. §138.
  13–14. sīc . . . proficīscuntur ut (*eī*) **quibus**
esset persuāsum: "thus . . . they set out as (do
those) who had been convinced"; **ut** introduces

the comparisons; **quibus** introduces a rel.
clause of characteristic (see App. §230).
  15. sed (*proficīscuntur ut eī quibus*) **. . .**
(*esset*) **datum:** "but instead (they set out
like those to whom) had been granted," etc.
Latin requires that the reader keep ellipted
phrases in mind to construe the syntax. Such
ellipsis helps keep Caesar's thought terse,
compressed, and pointed.
  15–16. longissimō . . . impedīmentīs:
abls. of manner without *cum;* see App. §142.

[5.32] *At hostēs*, posteāquam *ex* nocturnō fremitū vigiliīs*que*
dē profectiōne *eōrum* sēnsērunt, *collocātīs* īnsidiīs bipertītō *in*
silvīs opportūnō *atque* occultō *locō ā mīlibus passuum circiter*
duōbus Rōmānōrum adventum exspectābant, *et cum sē* maior
5   *pars* agminis *in magnam* convallem dēmīsisset, *ex utrāque parte*
eius vāllis subitō *sē* ostendērunt novissimōs*que premere et*
prīmōs prohibēre ascēnsū *atque* inīquissimō *nostrīs locō proelium*
committere *coepērunt.*

---

agm•en, -inis, *n.* [**agō,** move], *a moving*
body; a marching column; army.
ascēns•us, -ūs, *m.* [**ascendō,** climb up],
ascent, approach, climbing up.
bipertītō, *adv.* [**bis,** twice + **partior,** divide],
in two parts *or* divisions, in two ways.
com•mittō, -mittere, -mīsī, -missum
[**mittō,** send], join; **proelium**
committere, join *or* begin battle.
convall•is, -is, *f.* [**vallis,** valley], enclosed
valley, defile.
dē•mittō, -mittere, -mīsī, -missum [**mittō,**
send], send, thrust *or* let down; **sē**
dēmittere, come *or* get down, descend.
exspectō, 1 [**spectō,** look at], look out for,
await, expect.
fremit•us, -ūs, *m.*, confusion, noise, uproar.
inīqu•us, -a, -um, *adj.* [**in** + **aequus,** even,
just], uneven; unfair; disadvantageous.
īnsidi•ae, -ārum, *f. pl.* [**sedeō,** sit], ambush;
treachery; artifice, trick, crafty device.
maior, maius, *adj.* [*comp. of* **magnus,** large],
larger.
nocturn•us, -a, -um, *adj.* [**nox,** night], at
night, nocturnal, nightly.

nov•us, -a, -um, *adj.*, new; *superl.*:
novissim•us, -a, -um, latest, last; *as noun*
or with **agmen,** those in the rear, the rear.
occultō, 1 [**occultus,** secret], hide, keep
secret, conceal.
opportūn•us, -a, -um, *adj.*, fit, opportune,
lucky, suitable; favorable, advantageous.
os•tendō, -tendere, -tendī, -tentum [**obs**
+ **tendō,** stretch], *stretch before;* present,
show, bring into view, reveal.
posteāquam, *adv.* [**posteā,** afterward +
quam, than], after.
profecti•ō, -ōnis, *f.* [**proficīscor,** set out], a
setting out; start, departure.
prohibeō, 2 [**habeō,** hold], keep from,
prevent; keep out *or* away from; guard.
sentiō, sentīre, sēnsī, sēnsum, perceive, be
aware of, notice.
silv•a, -ae, *f.*, forest, woods, a wood.
subitō, *adv.* [**subitus,** sudden], suddenly.
vall•ēs, is, *f.*, a valley
vigili•a, -ae, *f.* [**vigil,** awake], wakefulness,
watching; a watch.

---

1. hostēs: the nom. pl. subject of the many
pl. verbs in this sentence is placed first, and
rather far from the verbs this subject governs.
See App. §302, *f.*, on HYPERBATON.

2. collocātīs īnsidiīs: abl. absolute.

2–3. bipertītō . . . opportūnō atque
occultō locō: abl. of place where without *in*.

3–4. ā mīlibus passuum circiter duōbus:
"about two miles away."

4–6. cum sē . . . dēmīsisset, . . . sē
ostendērunt: each reflexive (*sē*) refers to

the subject of the verb of which it is itself
the direct object. Note too that Caesar helps
his readers by using a sing. verb to refer to
the "greater part of the (Roman) column,"
which makes it impossible to construe the
pl. **ostendērunt** as referring to anyone other
than the enemy.

7. ascēnsū atque . . . locō: abl. of separation; see App. §134.

nostrīs: "for our men"; dat. of reference;
see App. §120.

[5.33] *Tum* dēmum Titūrius, *quī nihil ante* prōvīdisset,
trepidāre *et* concursāre *cohortēsque* dispōnere, *haec tamen
ipsa* timidē *atque ut eum omnia* dēficere *vidērentur; quod*
plērumque *eīs accidere cōnsuēvit, quī in ipsō* negōtiō *cōnsilium*
5   *capere cōguntur. At* Cotta, *quī* cōgitāsset *haec posse in itinere
accidere atque ob eam causam* profectiōnis auctor *nōn fuisset,*

---

auctor, -is, *m.* [**augeō,** increase], one
who produces, creates, *or* originates;
promoter, instigator, advisor, author.

cogitō, 1 [**co + agitō,** consider], consider
thoroughly *or* carefully, ponder, reflect;
think, purpose, plan.

concursō, 1 [*frequ. of* **concurrō,** run], run
about.

Cott•a, -ae, *m.,* Lucius Aurunculeius Cotta,
one of Caesar's lieutenants.

dē•ficiō, -ficere, -fēcī, -fectum [**faciō,**
make], fail, desert, fall away, revolt.

dēmum, *adv.,* at length, at last, finally.

dis•pōnō, -pōnere, -posuī, -positum
[**pōnō,** put], place apart, place about;
distribute, arrange, station.

negōt•ium, -ī, *n.* [**neg- + ōtium,** leisure],
concern, business, undertaking; trouble,

difficulty, labor; **negōtium dare,** employ,
direct; **quid negōtī,** what business; **nihil
negōtī,** no difficulty.

ob, *prep. with acc.,* on account of, for.

plērumque, *adv.* [**plērusque,** the greater
part], mostly, generally; very often.

profecti•ō, -ōnis, *f.* [**proficīscor,** set out], a
setting out; start, departure.

prō•videō, -vidēre, -vīdī, -vīsum [**videō,**
see], see beforehand, foresee; care for,
provide.

timidē, *adv.* [**timidus,** fearful], fearfully,
cowardly, timidly.

Titūr•ius, -ī, *m.,* Quintus Titurius Sabinus,
one of Caesar's lieutenants.

trepidō, 1, hurry about in alarm; shake with
fear; *pass.,* be disturbed *or* in confusion.

---

1. quī ... prōvīdisset: "since he ... "; subjunctive because the rel. clause is causal; see
App. §243.

2. trepidāre et concursāre ... dispōnere:
historical infs., which may be translated as
past tense verbs: "Titurius ... hurried about
in fearful confusion," etc.; see App. §281.
Another way to translate them is as if they
depended on **coepit,** i.e., "Titurius ... (began
to) hurry about in fearful confusion," etc. Caesar portrays Titurius Sabinus as completely
incompetent.

2–3. haec tamen ipsa timidē: this phrase
refers in apposition to what Titurius finally
began to do, and describes the fearful manner
in which he did "these very things."

3. atque ut: "and as if" or "and with the
result that."

eum: acc. direct object of the complementary inf. **dēficere.**

omnia: nom. pl. subject of **vidērentur.**

quod = *id quod,* a clause in apposition to
the result clause that further explains why
everything was going wrong for Titurius
Sabinus.

5. At Cotta: This is the third time in a row
that Caesar begins with the subject. Compare
the previous two sentences: **At hostēs** in 5.32
and **Tum dēmum Titūrius** above. Caesar effectively brings our focus sharply onto the
three main "characters" in the unfolding
tragedy. See also HYPERBATON, App. §302,*f.*

5–6. quī cōgitāsset ... atque ... fuisset:
"since he ... "; subjunctive because the rel.
clause is causal; see App. §243.

nūllā *in rē commūnī salūtī* deerat *et in* appellandīs
cohortandīs*que mīlitibus* imperātōris *et in pugnā mīlitis*
officia praestābat. *Cum* propter longitūdinem agminis
10   *minus facile omnia per sē obīre et, quid quōque locō faciendum*
esset, prōvidēre *possent, iussērunt* prōnūntiāre, *ut* impedīmenta
relinquerent atque in orbem cōnsisterent.

---

agm•en, -inis, *n.* [**agō,** move], *a moving*
body; a marching column; army; **in**
agmine, on the march; **prīmum**
agmen, the vanguard *(those in front);*
novissimum *or* **extrēmum agmen,** the
rear *(those in back).*
appellō, -āre, 1, call, name.
cohortor, 1 [**co + hortor,** encourage],
encourage greatly, cheer, animate.
cōn•sistō, -sistere, -stitī, — [**sistō,** stand],
take a stand *or* position, keep one's
position, stand, form *(when soldiers make*
a formation); stop, halt, remain, stay; *(of*
ships) lie at anchor; consist in, depend *or*
rest on.
dē•sum, -esse, -fuī, — [**sum,** be. App. §66],
be lacking, be absent from, fail.
impedīment•um, -ī, *n.* [**impediō,** hinder],
hindrance, obstacle; *pl.*: baggage,
baggage-train *(including pack animals).*
imperāt•or, -ōris, *m.* [**imperō,** order],
commander-in-chief, general.

longitūd•ō, -inis, *f.* [**longus,** long], length,
extent; long duration.
nūll•us, -a, -um, *gen.* **nūllīus,** *adj.* [**ne-** +
ūllus, any], not any, no.
ob•eō, -īre, -iī, -itum [**eō,** go. App. §84], go
to *or* towards; perform, attend to.
offic•ium, -ī, *n.*, allegiance, duty; business.
orb•is, -is, *m.*, orb, ring, circle; **orbis**
terrārum, the word.
prae•stō, -stāre, -stitī, -stātum [**stō,** stand],
stand *or* place before; show, exhibit,
supply; be superior, excel, surpass.
prō•nūntiō, 1 [**nūntiō,** announce],
announce, give out publicly, tell, relate,
report, say; give orders; *with* **sententia,**
pronounce.
propter, *prep. with acc.* [**prope,** near], on
account of, because of.
prō•videō, -vidēre, -vīdī, -vīsum [**videō,**
see], see beforehand, foresee; care for,
provide.

---

7. **salūtī:** dat. of purpose; see App. §119.
7–8. **et . . . et . . . :** Cotta fulfilled in this
sentence the duties *both* of a commander *and*
of a soldier.
in . . . mīlitibus: on the gerundive construction, see App. §§288, 294.
8. **imperātōris:** supply *officia praestābat,*
which has been ellipted. English does not generally allow this kind of "gapping" in advance.
See App. §301, *c.*
10. **per sē:** "on their own" or "by themselves."
9–11. **Cum . . . possent:** subjunctive in a
causal clause; see App. §238.

quid: one may construe the whole clause
as the object of **prōvidēre.** For the insertion
of an explanatory phrase into the syntax of a
sentence, see PARENTHESIS in App. §301, *e.*
11. **iussērunt prōnūntiāre:** "they ordered
(everyone) to pass the word along." Some
manuscripts have the pass. **prōnūntiārī,**
which is only slightly easier to construe: "they
ordered the word to be passed along."
11–12. **ut . . . cōnsisterent:** volitive subjunctive in a substantive clause of purpose
(or indirect command); see App. §§227–228.

Quod cōnsilium etsī *in* eiusmodī cāsū reprehendendum *nōn
est, tamen* incommodē *accidit: nam et nostrīs mīlitibus spem*
15   minuit *et hostēs ad pugnam* alacriōrēs effēcit, *quod nōn sine
summō* timōre *et* dēspērātiōne *id factum vidēbātur.* Praetereā
accidit, quod fierī necesse *erat, ut* vulgō *mīlitēs ab* signīs
discēderent, quae quisque eōrum cārissima *habēret, ab*
impedīmentīs *petere atque* arripere properāret, clāmōre *et*
20   flētū *omnia* complērentur.

---

ala•cer, -cris, -cre, *adj.,* lively, eager, active,
  ready, joyous, "fired up."
arrip•iō, -ere, -uī, arreptum [ad + rapiō,
  seize], take *or* seize hurriedly.
car•us, -a, -um, *adj.,* dear, precious.
cās•us, -ūs, *m.* [cadō, fall], accident,
  chance, misfortune; **cāsū,** by chance.
clām•or, -ōris, *m.* [clamō, cry out], outcry,
  noise, shouting, clamor.
com•pleō, -plēre, -plēvī, -plētum [*obs.:*
  pleō, fill], fill up; complete; cover.
dēspērāti•ō, -ōnis, *f.* [dēspērō, despair],
  despair, hopelessness.
ef•ficiō, -ficere, -fēcī, -fectum [faciō,
  make], make *or* do completely, complete,
  construct; cause, render.
eiusmodī, of such a sort *or* kind, such.
etsī, *conj.* [et + sī, if], even if, although.
flēt•us, -ūs, *m.* [fleō, weep], weeping,
  lamentation.
impedīment•um, -ī, *n.* [impediō, hinder],
  hindrance, obstacle; *pl.:* baggage,
  baggage-train (*including pack animals*).

incommodē, *adv.* [incommodus,
  inconvenient], inconveniently.
minuō, minuere, minuī, minūtum
  [minus, less], lessen, impair, diminish;
  settle (controversiās); **minuente aestū,**
  the tide ebbing.
necesse, *indecl. adj.,* necessary, unavoidable,
  indispensable.
praetereā, *adv.* [praeter, beyond], beyond
  this, besides, furthermore.
properō, 1 [properus, quick], hasten,
  hurry.
**re•prehendō, -prehendere, -prehendī,
  -prehēnsum** [prehendō (= prendō),
  seize], hold back; criticize, blame,
  censure.
sign•um, -ī, *n.,* signal; standard; **ab signīs
  discēdere,** withdraw from the ranks.
tim•or, -ōris, *m.* [timeō, fear], fear, alarm,
  dread.
vulgō, *adv.* [vulgus, the crowd], commonly,
  everywhere.

---

13. Quod cōnsilium = *et id cōnsilium; conjunctio relativa;* see App. §173, *a.*

15. nōn sine: LITOTES; see App. §302, *g.*

15–16. quod . . . vidēbātur: a causal clause
with the indicative; see App. §243.

16. factum: perf. pass. inf. with *esse*
omitted in indirect statement dependent on
vidēbātur.

**17–20. ut . . . discēderent, . . . properāret,
. . . complērentur:** subjunctives in substantive clauses of result or fact; see App. §§224,

229, *a.* The *ut* is ellipted before the second and
third verbs, and the phrases are connected
without a conj. (ASYNDETON; see App. §301,
a.). Note also that each verb has a different
subject. This harsh syntax seems to mirror the
confusion in the ranks that Caesar describes.

18. quae . . . habēret: the omitted antecedent is *ea.*

habēret: the unexpressed subject is
quisque (from the subordinate clause introduced by **quae**).

[5.34] *At* barbarīs *cōnsilium nōn* dēfuit. *Nam* ducēs *eōrum tōtā* aciē prōnūntiāre *iussērunt, nē quis ab locō discēderet: illōrum esse* praedam *atque illīs* reservārī quaecumque *Rōmānī* relīquissent: proinde *omnia in victōriā* posita *exīstimārent.*

---

aci•ēs, -ēī *(old gen.* aciē), *f.,* sharp point *or* edge *of a weapon;* sharp *or* keen sight, glance; a line *(as forming an edge),* battle line; **prima,** the vanguard; **media,** the center; **novissima,** the rear(guard).

barbar•us, -a, -um, *adj.,* foreign *(to Romans and Greeks),* uncivilized; *pl. as noun:* barbarians.

dē•sum, -esse, -fuī, — [sum, be. App. §66], be lacking, be absent from, fail.

dux, ducis, *m.* [dūco, lead], leader, commander, general; guide.

pōnō, pōnere, posuī, positum, place, put, place over; lay down, set aside; station, post; regard, consider; make, build; *with*

castra, pitch; *pass.:* be situated; *with* in and the abl., depend on, *in addition to the above meanings.*

praed•a, -ae, *f.,* booty, plunder, spoil.

proinde, *adv.,* hence, accordingly, therefore.

pro•nūntiō, 1 [nūntiō, announce], announce, give out publicly, tell, relate, report, say; give orders; *with* **sententia,** pronounce.

quīcumque, quaecumque, quodcumque, *indef. (or generalizing) rel. pron.,* whoever, whatever; whosoever, whatsoever, any . . . whatever; everyone who, everything that.

reservō, 1 [re + servō, save, keep], keep back, save up, reserve.

---

1. barbarīs: dat. of reference; see App. §120.

2. tōtā aciē: "along the whole battle line"; abl. of place where; see App. §151, *b.*

quis = *aliquis;* see App. §174.

3. illīs reservārī (*ea*) **quaecumque:** we may supply *ea* both as the unexpressed acc. subject of the inf. **reservārī** in indirect statement after **prōnūntiāre** and as the antecedent to **quaecumque.** Note also that the baggage

the men brought got in their way and served as an incentive to their enemies.

4. posita: perf. pass. inf. with *esse* omitted in indirect statement dependent on **exīstimārent.**

exīstimārent: subjunctive in indirect statement dependent on the speech implied by the inf. **prōnūntiāre** (back at the beginning of the sentence!).

5   *Erant et virtūte et* studiō *pugnandī* parēs; *nostrī,* tametsī *ab*
duce *et ā* fortūnā dēserēbantur, *tamen omnem spem salūtis in*
virtūte pōnēbant, *et* quotiēns *quaeque cohors* prōcurrerat, *ab eā*
parte magnus numerus hostium cadēbat.

---

cad•ō, -ere, cecidī, cāsum, fall; fall in
battle, be killed, die.

dē•serō, -serere, -seruī, -sertum [**serō,**
entwine, join], disjoin; abandon, desert,
forsake; **dēsertus,** *perf. part. as adj.*:
deserted, solitary.

dux, ducis, *m.* [**dūcō,** lead], leader,
commander, general; guide.

fortūn•a, -ae, *f.* [**fors,** chance], fortune,
chance, opportunity, condition; success,
property.

pār, paris, *adj.,* equal, like, similar; equal
to, a match for; *with words of number and*
quantity, the same; **pār atque,** the same
as.

pōnō, pōnere, posuī, positum, place, put,
place over; lay down, set aside; station,

post; regard, consider; make, build; *with*
castra, pitch; *pass.*: be situated; *with* **in**
and the abl., depend on, *in addition to the*
above meanings.

prō•currō, -currere, -currī, -cursum
[**currō,** run], run *or* rush forward, rush
out, charge.

quotiēns, *adv.* [**quot,** how many?], (1)
interrog., how many times? how often? (2)
rel., as often as.

stud•ium, -ī, *n.* [**studeō,** be zealous],
eagerness; devotion; pursuit.

tametsī, *conj.* [**tamen,** however + **etsī,** even
if], although, though, notwithstanding.

---

5. et virtūte et studiō: ablatives of respect; see App. §149.

　pugnandī: gerund; see App. §291.

　nostrī: "our men." Note that Caesar may
cast all blame for the disaster on others, but he
does not blame his men. The men were brave;
their misfortune was to be led by idiots.

5–8. Erant ... dēserēbantur ... pōnēbant
... cadēbat: Note the many impf. verb forms
used to describe ongoing action in the past.

　7–8. quotiēns . . . prōcurrerat, . . .
cadēbat: Note Caesar's careful sequencing
of time through the combination of plupf.
and impf.

Quā rē animadversā *Ambiorīx* prōnūntiārī *iubet, ut* procul *tēla*

10   coniciant neu propius accēdant *et, quam in partem Rōmānī*
impetum *fēcerint,* cēdant (levitāte *armōrum et* cotīdiānā
exercitātiōne *nihil hīs* nocērī *posse*), rūrsus *sē ad* signa *recipientēs*
īnsequantur.

---

ac•cēdō, -cēdere, -cessī, -cessum [ad +
cēdō, go], approach, come near to, arrive
at, come to; to be added.
animad•vertō, -vertere, -vertī, -versum
[**animus,** mind + ad + **vertō,** turn], turn
the mind to; notice.
cēd•ō, -ere, cessī, cessum, go, go away;
give way, yield, retreat.
con•iciō, -icere, -iēcī, -iectum [co + iaciō,
throw. App. §7], hurl, throw, cast.
cotīdiān•us, -a, -um, *adj.* [**cotīdiē,** daily],
daily; customary.
exercitāti•ō, -ōnis, *f.* [*frequentative of*
exercitō, *from* **exerceō,** exercise],
exercise, training, practice, experience.
impet•us, -ūs, *m.,* attack; force, vehemence.
īn•sequor, -sequī, -secūtus sum [sequor,
follow], follow up, follow after, follow
close behind, pursue.

levi•tās, -tātis, *f.* [**levis,** light], lightness;
fickleness, restlessness.
nēve (neu) (App. §188, *b.*) [nē + ve, or], and
not, nor.
noceō, nocēre, nocuī, nocitum, harm,
injure, hurt; **nocēns,** *pres. part. as noun:*
guilty person.
procul, *adv.,* far off, from afar, in the
distance, at a distance.
pro•nūntiō, 1 [**nūntiō,** announce],
announce, give out publicly, tell, relate,
report, say; give orders; *with* **sententia,**
pronounce.
propius, *adv. and prep. with acc.* (App. §122,
b.) [**prope,** near], nearer.
rūrsus, *adv.* [*for* **reversus,** *from* **revertō,**
turn back], again, back, anew; in turn.
sign•um, -ī, *n.,* signal; standard; **signa
īnferre,** advance to the attack.

---

9. Quā rē animadversā = *et eā rē animadversā*; see App. §173, *a.*; abl. absolute; see
App. §150.

   iubet: note the sudden shift to the pres.
tense as we approach the height of the battle;
see App. §190, *a.*

   9–13. ut ... accēdant et ... īnsequantur:
two volitive subjunctives in substantive
clauses of purpose (or indirect command)
after **prōnūntiārī;** see App. §228.

10. quam in partem = *in eam partem, in
quam.* Caesar frequently puts what should be
the antecedent inside the rel. clause.

   11–12. levitāte ... posse: indirect statement dependent on the inf. **prōnūntiārī,**
which, although it governs the volitive substantive **ut** clause, also represents a verb of
speaking, hence the parenthetical indirect
speech, which might otherwise seem difficult to justify.

[5.35] *Quō* praeceptō *ab eīs* dīligentissimē observātō, *cum*
quaepiam *cohors ex* orbe excesserat *atque* impetum *fēcerat*,
hostēs vēlōcissimē refugiēbant. *Interim eam partem* nūdārī
necesse erat et ab latere apertō *tēla recipī.* Rūrsus *cum in eum*
5 *locum* unde *erant* ēgressī revertī *coeperant, et ab eīs quī* cesserant
et ab eīs quī proximī steterant *circumveniēbantur;* sīn *autem*
locum tenēre vellent, nec virtūtī locus relinquēbātur, neque ab tantā
multitūdine coniecta *tēla* cōnfertī vītāre *poterant.*

---

aper•iō, -īre, -uī, -ertum, open, expose.
cēd•ō, -ere, cessī, cessum, go, go away;
give way, yield, retreat.
cōnfert•us, -a, -um, *adj.* [*perf. part. of*
cōnferciō, crowd together], dense, thick,
compact, stuffed.
con•iciō, -icere, -iēcī, -iectum [co + iaciō,
throw. App. §7], hurl, throw, cast.
dīligenter, *adv.* [**dīligēns,** careful],
carefully; with exactness, pains, *or* care.
ē•gredior, -gredī, -gressus sum [gradior,
step], come forth, depart; march out,
make a sortie; disembark.
ex•cēdō, -cēdere, -cessī, -cessum [cēdō,
go], go out, go away, withdraw, retire.
impet•us, -ūs, *m.,* attack; force, vehemence.
lat•us, -eris, *n.,* side; wing *or* flank *of an army.*
necesse, *indecl. adj.,* necessary, unavoidable,
indispensable.
nūdō, 1 [**nūdus,** bare], strip, uncover, make
bare *or* naked, expose.

observō, 1 [**servō,** give heed], observe,
mark, watch; regard, obey; celebrate.
orb•is, -is, *m.,* orb, ring, circle; **orbis**
terrārum, the world.
prae•ceptum, -ī, *n.* [**praecipiō,** instruct],
instruction, injunction, command.
quispiam, quidpiam *and* **quispiam,**
quaepiam, quodpiam, *indef. pron.* (App.
§62), anyone, any.
re•fugiō, -fugere, -fūgī, -fugitum [re +
fugiō, flee], flee back, retreat; escape.
re•vertor, -vertī, -versus sum [re + vertō,
turn], turn back, come back, return.
rūrsus, *adv.* [*for* reversus, *from* **revertō,**
turn back], again, back, anew; in turn.
sīn, *conj.,* if however, but if.
stō, stāre, stetī, stātum, stand, abide by.
unde, *adv.,* from which place, whence.
vēl•ōx, -ōcis, *adj.,* swift, rapid, speedy.
vītō, 1, avoid, shun, evade, escape.

---

1. Quō ... observātō = *et eō ... observātō;*
see App. §173, *a.;* abl. absolute; see App. §150.
1–2. cum ... fēcerat: clause of repeated
action with the ind.; see App. §241, *b.*
3. partem: acc. subject of the pres. pass.
inf. **nūdārī,** which is itself the nom. subject
of **erat;** see App. §§276–278.
4. recipī: supply *necesse erat,* which has
been ellipted.
5. erant: the unexpressed subject will be
the Roman soldiers who attempt to attack.

6. eīs = *hostibus.*
sīn autem: "but if, on the other hand"; i.e.,
in contrast to what was just described.
7. vellent: impf. subjunctive in a past contrary to fact condition; see App. §254, *a.* They
may have tried to maintain their ground, but
they could not. It was too hard.
virtūtī: dat. of purpose; see App. §119.
8. cōnfertī: nom. pl. in agreement with the
unexpressed subject of **poterant,** i.e., the Roman soliders.

Tamen tot incommodīs cōnflīctātī, *multīs* vulneribus *acceptīs*
10   resistēbant *et magnā parte diēī* cōnsūmptā, *cum ā prīmā*
      lūce *ad* hōram octāvam *pugnārētur, nihil quod ipsīs esset*
      indignum committēbant.

com•mittō, -mittere, -mīsī, -missum
  [mittō, send], join; commit (*a crime*), do;
  allow; entrust.
cōnflīctō, 1 [*frequentative of* cōnflīgō],
  strike together; *in the pass.*: be distressed.
cōn•sūmō, -sūmere, -sūmpsī, -sūmptum
  [sūmō, take], *take together or all at once*:
  devour, consume, destroy; use up, waste,
  pass.
hōr•a, -ae, *f.*, hour. *There were twenty-four*
  hours in the Roman day, but they divided
  those hours into twelve hours of light and
  twelve hours of darkness (between sunrise
  and sunset). Except at the equinoxes, the
  hours were thus not of equal length, and
  varied according to the season.

incommod•um, -ī, *n.* [incommodus,
  inconvenient], inconvenience,
  disadvantage, trouble; disaster, defeat,
  loss, injury.
indign•us, -a, -um, *adj.* [in + dignus,
  worthy], unworthy, disgraceful.
lūx, lūcis, *f.*, light, daylight; prīmā lūce, at
  dawn.
octāv•us, -a, -um, *adj., ord. num. adj.* [octō,
  eight], eighth.
re•sistō, -sistere, -stitī, — [sistō, stand],
  stand back, remain behind, halt, stand
  still; withstand, resist, oppose.
tot, *indecl. adj.*, so many.
vuln•us, -eris, *n.*, a wound.

9. cōnflīctātī: nom. pl. in agreement with
the unexpressed subject of resistēbant, i.e,
the Roman soldiers.
    multīs . . . acceptīs: abl. absolute; see App.
§150.
    10. magnā . . . cōnsūmptā: abl. absolute;
see App. §150.

11. ad hōram octāvam: daylight was divided into twelve equal hours, noon was the sixth
hour, and the twelfth hour was sunset, so the
eighth hour would represent midafternoon.
    quod . . . esset: rel. clause of characteristic;
see App. §230.
    ipsīs: dat. of reference; see App. §120.

Tum Titō Balventiō, *quī superiōre annō prīmum* pīlum *dūxerat,*
virō fortī *et magnae* auctōritātis, *utrumque* femur trāgulā

15 trāicitur; Quīntus Lūcānius, *eiusdem ōrdinis,* fortissimē
pugnāns, dum circumventō filiō subvenit, *interficitur;* Lūcius
Cotta *lēgātus omnēs cohortēs ōrdinēsque* adhortāns *in* adversum
ōs fundā vulnerātur.

---

adhortor, 1 [**hortor,** encourage], encourage, incite.

adversus, *prep. with acc.* [**adversus,** turned against], opposite to, against.

auctori•tās, -tātis, *f.* [**auctor,** producer], influence, authority.

fem•ur, -oris *or* **-inis,** *n.,* the thigh.

fīl•ius, -ī, *m.,* son.

fort•is, -e, *adj.,* strong, brave.

fund•a, -ae, *f.,* slingshot.

Lūci•us, -ī, *m.;* **Cott•a, -ae,** *m.,* Lucius Aurunculeius Cotta, *one of Caesar's lieutenants.*

ōs, ōris, *n.,* mouth; face, countenance.

pīl•us, -ī, *m.,* century *of soldiers;* **prīmus pīlus,** first century *of a legion;* **prīmī pīlī**

centuriō *or* **prīmipīlus,** the centurion of the first century, the chief centurion.

Quīnt•us, -ī, *m.;* **Lūcān•ius, -ī,** *m.,* Quintus Lucanius, *a centurion.*

sub•veniō, -venīre, -vēnī, -ventum [**veniō,** come], come *or* go to help, aid, succor.

Tit•us, -ī, *m.;* **Balven•tius, -tī,** *m.,* Titus Balventius, *one of Caesar's centurions.*

trāgul•a, -ae, *f.,* a javelin, spear, *or* dart *used by the Gauls.*

tra•iciō, -icere, -iēcī, -iectum [**iaciō,** throw. App. §7], hurl across; pierce, transfix.

vulnerō, 1 [**vulnus,** wound], wound.

---

14. magnae auctōritātis: gen. of description; see App. §100.

16. circumventō: "who had been surrounded"; the part. takes the place of a subordinate clause; see App. §283.

17–18. in adversum ōs: "directly in the face."

[5.36] *Hīs rēbus* permōtus Quīntus Titūrius, *cum* procul
Ambiorīgem suōs cohortantem cōnspexisset, interpretem
suum Gnaeum Pompēium *ad eum mittit* rogātum *ut sibi
mīlitibusque* parcat. *Ille* appellātus respondit: *sī velit sēcum*
5   *colloquī,* licēre; spērāre *ā multitūdine* impetrārī *posse, quod ad
mīlitum salūtem pertineat; ipsī* vērō *nihil* nocitum īrī, *inque eam
rem sē suam* fidem interpōnere.

---

appellō, -āre, 1, call, name, call by name.
cohortor, 1 [co + **hortor,** encourage],
   encourage greatly, cheer, animate.
cōn·spiciō, -spicere, -spexī, -spectum
   [**speciō,** look], look at, discern, perceive.
eō, īre, -iī (īvī), itum (App. §84), go,
   proceed, march, pass.
fid·ēs, -eī, *f.* [**fīdō,** confide], faith; pledge;
   trustworthiness; allegiance, protection.
Gnae·us, -ī, *m.;* **Pompē·ius, -ī,** *m.,* Gnaius
   Pompeius, *an interpreter who served under
   Quintus Titurius Sabinus.*
impetrō, 1, obtain (*by request*), accomplish;
   impetrāre ā (ab), gain permission from.
inter·pōnō, -pōnere, -posuī, -positum
   [**pōnō,** put], interpose; **fidem
   interpōnere,** pledge.
interpr·es, -etis, *m. or f.,* interpreter;
   mediator.

licet, licēre, licuit *and* **licitum est,** *impers.,*
   it is permitted.
noceō, nocēre, nocuī, nocitum, harm,
   injure, hurt.
parcō, parcere, pepercī, parsus [**parcus,**
   frugal], be frugal; spare, do not harm.
per·moveō, -movēre, -mōvī, -mōtum
   [**moveō,** move], move thoroughly;
   influence.
procul, *adv.,* far off, from afar, in the
   distance, at a distance.
Quīnt·us, -ī, *m.,* Quintus; **Titūr·ius, -ī,** *m.,*
   Titurius Sabinus, *Caesar's lieutenant.*
**re·spondeō, -spondēre, -spondī,
   -sponsum** [re + **spondeō,** promise],
   reply, answer.
rogō, 1, ask.
spērō, 1 [**spēs,** hope], hope, anticipate.
vērō, *adv.* [**vērus,** true], truly; but, however.

---

2. suōs cohortantem: "who was encouraging his men"; the part. takes the place of a
subordinate clause; see App. §283.

3. suum: "his" in reference not to Ambiorix,
but to the subject of the verb that governs the
direct object (**interpretem ... Pompēium**) of
the verb **mittit,** i.e., Titurius Sabinus.

   ad eum = *Ambiorīgem.*

   rogātum: "in order to request"; on this use
of the supine, see App. §295.

4. sī velit: a condition in indirect statement; see App. §272.

5. licēre: Caesar has omitted the subject of
the inf. in indirect statement after **respondit.**
We may supply *id.*

   spērāre: supply *sē* as the acc. subject referring to the unexpressed subject of **respondit,**
i.e., Ambiorix.

   multitūdine = Ambiorix's men, whom he
claims not to be able to control against their will.

posse: again, Caesar omits an acc. subject
in indirect statement, so we may supply an
id, which will also serve as the antecedent of
quod. The effect of so much ellipsis is quite
clipped.

6. ipsī = *Titūriō Sabīnō;* dat. of reference;
see App. §120.

   nihil nocitum īrī: "no harm would be
done"; note the use in indirect statement
of the fut. pass. inf., a form Latin teachers
customarily tell their students not to worry
about because they will never see it—except,
of course, when they do, so enjoy! See also
App. §205, *b.*

7. sē: note the late, and thus rather dramatic, appearance of the previously ellipted
acc. subject. Latin can "gap" in advance. This
is something English speakers rarely do.

> *Ille cum* Cottā sauciō commūnicat, *sī videātur, pugnā ut*
> excēdant *et cum Ambiorīge ūnā colloquantur:* spērāre *ab eō dē*
> 10   *suā ac mīlitum salūte* impetrārī *posse.* Cotta *sē ad* armātum
> *hostem* itūrum negat *atque in eō* persevērat.

---

armō, 1 [**arma**, arms], arm, equip; *pass.*, arm oneself; **armātus**, *perf. part., as adj.*, armed; **armātī**, *as noun*, armed men.

commūnicō, 1 [**commūnis**, common], make common, communicate, impart, share.

Cott•a, -ae, *m.*, Lucius Aurunculeius Cotta, one of Caesar's lieutenants.

eō, īre, iī (īvī), itum (App. §84), go, proceed, march, pass.

ex•cēdō, -cēdere, -cessī, -cessum [**cēdō**, go], go out, go away, withdraw, retire.

impetrō, 1, obtain (*by request*), accomplish, succeed in obtaining (*one's request*); **impetrāre ā (ab)**, gain permission from, persuade.

negō, 1, say no, refuse, say . . . not.

persevērō, 1, persist, persevere.

sauci•us, -a, -um, *adj.*, wounded.

spērō, 1 [**spēs**, hope], hope, hope for, anticipate.

---

8. Ille = *Titūrius Sabīnus.*

sī videātur: "whether it seemed appropriate"; indirect question; see App. §264, *b.*

pugnā: abl. of separation; see App. §134.

9. spērāre: some manuscripts supply a *sē* to serve as the acc. subject of the inf. in indirect statement after **commūnicat.** Supply one as well, even if we do not print one.

ab eō = *ab Ambiorīge.*

10. posse: because its complementary inf. **impetrārī** is pass., supply the equivalent of *id* as the unexpressed acc. subject of **posse** in indirect statement dependent on **spērāre.**

11. itūrum: fut. active inf. without *esse* in indirect statement dependent on **negat.**

in eō: "in this (refusal)."

[5.37] Sabīnus *quōs in* praesentiā tribūnōs *mīlitum* circum
sē habēbat et prīmōrum ōrdinum centuriōnēs *sē* sequī *iubet et,*
cum propius *Ambiorīgem* accessisset, *iussus arma* abicere
imperātum *facit suīsque ut idem faciant* imperat. *Interim, dum*
5   *dē* condiciōnibus *inter sē* agunt *longiorque* cōnsultō *ab*
Ambiorīge īnstituitur sermō, paulātim *circumventus interficitur.*

---

abic•iō, -ere, abiēcī, abiectum [iaciō,
    throw. *See* §App. 7.], throw away *or*
    down; hurl.
ac•cēdō, -cēdere, -cessī, -cessum [ad +
    cēdō, go], approach, come near to, arrive
    at, come to; to be added.
ag•ō, -ere, ēgī, actum, set in motion,
    drive (*animals*); move forward, advance
    (*military works*); do, transact, carry on
    (*business*); discuss, speak.
centuri•ō, -ōnis, *m.* [**centum,** hundred],
    centurion, *the commander of the century,*
    a unit corresponding to one-sixtieth of a
    legion.
circum, *prep. with acc.* [**circus,** circle],
    around, about, near.
condici•ō, -ōnis, *f.,* condition, state;
    agreement, stipulation, terms.
cōnsult•um, -ī, *n.* [**cōnsulō,** take counsel],
    result of deliberation; decree, enactment,
    decision; plan.
imperō, 1 [**in + parō,** procure], demand
    from; order, instruct, rule.

īn•stituō, -stituere, -stituī, -stitūtum
    [**statuō,** set up], set up *or* put in order,
    draw up; train, educate; procure, prepare;
    build, construct; begin, determine,
    decide upon, adopt; **īnstitūtus,** *perf.*
    part. as adj. (*in addition to the definitions*
    above): usual, customary; finished.
paulātim, *adv.* [**paulus,** little], little by little,
    by degrees, gradually.
prae•senti•a, -ae, *f.* [**praesum,** be present],
    presence; the present moment; **in**
    praesentiā, for the present; then.
propius, *adv. and prep. with acc.* (App. §122,
    b.) [**prope,** near], nearer.
Sabīn•us, -ī, *m.,* Quintus Titurius Sabinus,
    one of Caesar's lieutenants.
sequor, sequī, secūtus sum, follow, pursue;
    accompany.
serm•ō, -ōnis, *m.,* conversation, interview,
    speech.
tribūn•us, -ī, *m.* [**tribus,** tribe], tribune;
    tribūnus mīlitum *or* **mīlitāris,** a
    military tribune.

1–2. quōs . . . tribūnōs . . . habēbat et
. . . centuriōnēs . . . sequī iubet: what we
might expect as the antecedent of **quōs**
(i.e., **tribūnōs**) has been placed inside the
rel. clause (as a direct object of **habēbat**).
The reader may thus supply an ellipted *eōs*
to serve both as the antecedent of **quōs** and
as one of the two acc. subjects of **sequī** (the
complementary inf. of **iubet**). But the reader
should also be aware that what comes after
et might also be construed with **habēbat** as a
direct object rather than with **sequī** as an acc.
subject, in which instance *eōs* would serve as
our only subject of **sequī** (unless, that is,
one construed the whole clause introduced

by **quōs** as the subject without supplying
what seems ellipted to us). In all events, the
simplest strategy will be to supply *eōs* before
quōs, and to enjoy the subtle puzzles of Latin
syntax. See also PARENTHESIS, App. §301, *e.*
    4. imperātum: "what had been command-
ed"; see App. §283.
    5. cōnsultō: abl. of accordance (manner);
see App. §142, *a.*
    5–6. longior . . . sermō: HYPERBATON;
see App. §302, *f.*
    agunt . . . interficitur: note the shift to the
historical pres. (App. §190, *a*) at the climax
of the action.

Tum vērō *suō* mōre *victōriam* conclāmant *atque* ululātum
tollunt impetūque *in nostrōs factō ōrdinēs* perturbant. Ibi
Lūcius Cotta *pugnāns interficitur cum maximā parte mīlitum.*
10   *Reliquī sē in castra recipiunt* unde *erant* ēgressī. *Ex quibus*
Lūcius Petrosidius aquilifer, *cum magnā multitūdine hostium*
premerētur, aquilam intrā vāllum prōiēcit; *ipse prō castrīs*
fortissimē *pugnāns* occīditur.

---

aquil•a, -ae, *f.,* an eagle; a military standard.
aquili•fer, -ferī, *m.* [aquila, eagle + ferō,
carry] standard-bearer.
conclāmō, 1 [clāmō, shout], shout out, call
aloud, yell.
ē•gredior, -gredī, -gressus sum [gradior,
step], come forth, depart; march out,
make a sortie; disembark.
fort•is, -e, *adj.,* strong, brave.
ibi, *adv.,* there, in that place.
impet•us, -ūs, *m.,* attack; force, vehemence.
intrā, *prep. with acc.* [inter, between],
within, inside, into.
Lūci•us, -ī, *m.;* Cott•a, -ae, *m.,* Lucius
Aurunculeius Cotta, *one of Caesar's*
lieutenants.
Lūci•us, -ī, *m.;* Petrosid•ius, -ī, *m.,* Lucius
Petrosidius, *a standard-bearer in Caesar's*
army.

mōs, mōris, *m.,* manner, custom, practice.
oc•cīdō, -cīdere, -cīsī, -cīsum [caedō, cut],
cut down, kill.
perturbō, 1 [turbō, disturb], disturb
greatly, throw into confusion; terrify.
prō•iciō, -icere, -iēcī, -iectum [iaciō,
throw. App. §7], throw forward *or* away;
throw, cast.
tollō, tollere, sustulī, sublātum, lift up,
elevate, raise.
ululāt•us, -ūs, *m.,* yell, shriek.
unde, *adv.,* from which place, whence.
vāll•um, -ī, *n.* [vāllus, palisade], wall
or rampart *of earth set with palisades;*
entrenchments, earthworks.
vērō, *adv.* [vērus, true], truly; but, however.

---

8. impetū . . . factō: abl. absolute; see App.
§150.
   nostrōs: "our men."
9. parte: abl. of accompaniment; see App.
§140.
   mīlitum: partitive gen.; see App. §101.
10. Ex quibus = *et ex eīs* (see App. §173, *a;*
and, for the use of ex, §101, *a*).
11. magnā multitūdine: although it consisted of human beings, the crowd did not
make its own decisions. Rather than abl. of
agent, we thus find an abl. of manner; see App.
§142. One might also argue for abl. of means,
but then we would need to think of Ambiorix

employing the crowd as his instrument or tool,
but Ambiorix is absent from the narrative at
this point. We focus instead on individual Roman soldiers adrift in a sea of troubles.
   11–12. cum . . . premerētur: subjunctive
in a causal clause; see App. §§238–239.
   12. aquilam: the standard-bearer protects
the eagle as best he can and to the death. Such
an event would have signalled to a Roman
audience the utmost dedication and bravery
that Romans expected from their soldiers.
Even in disastrous defeat, Caesar paints a
portrait that will make his Roman readers
proud to be Roman.

Illī aegrē *ad noctem oppugnātiōnem sustinent; noctū ad ūnum*
15   *omnēs* dēspērātā *salūte sē ipsī interficiunt.* Paucī *ex proeliō* ēlapsī
        incertīs *itineribus per* silvās *ad* Titum Labiēnum *lēgātum in*
        hīberna perveniunt atque eum dē rēbus gestīs certiōrem faciunt.

---

ae•ger, -gra, -grum, *adj.*, sick, ill.
dēspērō, 1 [spērō, hope], despair, be
    hopeless, lack confidence; dēspērātus,
    perf. part.: despaired of; *as adj.*: desperate.
ē•lābor, -lābī, -lāpsus sum [lābor, slip], slip
    away, escape.
incert•us, -a, -um, *adj.* [in + certus,
    decided], undecided, uncertain,
    untrustworthy; indefinite; disordered.

pauc•ī, -ae, -a, *adj.*, few; *as noun:* few *persons*
    or things.
silv•a, -ae, *f.*, forest, woods, a wood.
Tit•us, -ī, *m.*; Labiēn•us, -ī, *m.*, Titus Atius
    Labienus, *Caesar's most trusted lieutenant*
    in the Gallic War. During the Civil War,
    Labienus fought on Pompey's side, and
    died in battle against Caesar in Munda (in
    Spain) in 45 BCE.

---

14. Illī = *mīlitēs Rōmānī.*
ad ūnum: "to a man."
15. dēspērātā salūte: abl. absolute; see
App. §150.
sē . . . interficiunt: unlike moderns (who
almost universally condemn it), Romans
sometimes admired suicide. Roman religion
did not forbid the practice, and Romans
themselves assessed its moral value according to the context in which it occurred. To
choose death over slavery and the inevitable
humiliation of their status as Roman soldiers
would have been considered an honorable
choice, although even Caesar cannot avoid
representing this as what it was: a total disaster and humiliating defeat. What Caesar

could do in his narrative, he did: he excused
himself, he praised his soldiers, and he placed
all the blame squarely on Titurius Sabinus,
and, to a lesser extent, on Aurunculeius Cotta, who gave way to Sabinus.
Paucī: *i.e., mīlitēs.*
16. Titum Labiēnum: because Titus Labienus knew what happened to Sabinus and
Cotta, any actions he subsequently took will,
in Caesar's readers' minds, be less the result of
Labienus's superior military skills and more
the result of his better information. Cicero,
on the other hand, will have to face the same
dilemma that Sabinus and Cotta confronted.
17. dē rēbus gestīs: "about what had
happened."

[5.38] *Hāc victōriā* sublātus *Ambiorīx* statim *cum equitātū in* Aduātucōs, *quī erant eius rēgnō* fīnitimī, *proficīscitur; neque noctem neque diem* intermittit peditātum*que* subsequī *iubet.*

Aduātuc•ī, -ōrum, *m., a people in Belgic Gaul and neighbors of the Eburones,* the Aduatici.

fīnitim•us, -a, -um, *adj.* [**fīnis,** limit], bordering on, neighboring.

inter•mittō, -mittere, -mīsī, -missum [**mittō,** send], send between; intervene, separate; cease, discontinue; delay, neglect, omit; let pass.

peditāt•us, -ūs, *m.* [**pedes,** foot soldier], foot soldiers, infantry.

statim, *adv.* [**stō,** stand], immediately.

sub•sequor, -sequī, -secūtus [**sequor,** follow], follow closely.

tollō, tollere, sustulī, sublātum, lift, elevate; elate.

---

1. Ambiorīx: after ordering his infantry to follow as quickly as possible, Ambiorix rushes ahead with his cavalry first to the Aduatuci in an effort to extend and support similar efforts against other Roman encampments. After his visit to the Aduatuci, he will go to the Nervii.

Rē dēmōnstrātā Aduātucīsque concitātīs posterō diē in Nerviōs
5   pervenit hortāturque, nē suī in perpetuum līberandī atque
ulcīscendī Rōmānōs prō eīs quās accēperint iniūriīs occāsiōnem
dīmittant: interfectōs esse lēgātōs duōs magnamque partem
exercitūs interīsse dēmōnstrat; nihil esse negōtī subitō oppressam
legiōnem quae cum Cicerōne hiemet interficī; sē ad eam rem
10   profitētur adiūtōrem. Facile hāc ōrātiōne Nerviīs persuādet.

---

adiūt•or, -ōris, m. [adiuvō, aid], helper,
assistant, abettor.

Aduātuc•ī, -ōrum, m., a people in Belgic
Gaul, the Aduatici.

concitō, 1 [citō, put in motion], stir up,
rouse, instigate, incite.

dēmōnstrō, 1 [mōnstrō, show], point out,
explain, describe; declare.

dī•mittō, -mittere, -mīsī, -missum [mittō,
send], send away, dismiss; break up; let
go, let pass, give up.

hiemō, 1 [hiems, winter], pass the winter,
winter.

hortor, 1, exhort, encourage, incite, urge
strongly.

iniūri•a, -ae, f. [in + iūs, right], wrong;
outrage, damage, violence.

inter•eō, -īre, -iī, -itum [eō, go. App. §84],
perish, die.

līberō, 1 [līber, free], make or set free,
release, deliver.

negōt•ium, -ī, n. [neg- + otium, leisure],
concern, business, undertaking; trouble,

difficulty, labor; negōtium dare, employ,
direct; quid negōtī, what business; nihil
negōtī, no difficulty.

occāsi•ō, -ōnis, f. [occidō, fall, happen],
occasion, opportunity.

op•primō, -primere, -pressī, -pressus [ob
+ premō, press], press down, oppress;
destroy; surprise.

ōrāti•ō, -ōnis, f. [ōrō, speak], speech,
argument.

perpetu•us, -a, -um, adj., continuous; n. as
noun in the phrase in perpetuum, forever.

poster•us, -a, -um, adj. [post, after],
after, following, next; in m. pl. as
noun: posterity; superl.: postrēmus or
postumus, last.

pro•fiteor, -fitērī, -fessus sum [fateor,
confess], admit, acknowledge, declare,
offer.

subitō, adv. [subitus, sudden], suddenly.

ulcīscor, ulcīscī, ultus sum, avenge;
punish, take vengeance on.

---

4. Rē ... concitātīs: "After the news (of his
victory) was related and the Aduatuci were
stirred up." Note how the two abl. absolutes
connected by -que efficiently dispense with
Ambiorix's business among the Aduatuci; see
App. §150.

diē: abl. of time; see App. §152.

5–7. nē ... dīmittant: volitive subjunctive
in a substantive clause of desire or purpose (or
indirect command); see App. §228.

5–6. suī ... līberandī atque ulcīscendī
Rōmānōs ... occāsiōnem: "opportunity for
liberating themselves . . . and punishing the
Romans . . . ." The syntax is harsh, combin-
ing a gerundive (līberandī) with a gerund
(ulcīscendī) that takes a direct object; see

App. §§287–289. Note also the HYPERBA-
TON; see App. §302, f.

6. eīs ... iniūriīs: HYPERBATON within
HYPERBATON; see App. §302, f.

8. nihil ... negōtī: "not a difficult task";
gen. of the whole; see App. §101.

9. hiemet: subjunctive in indirect statement; see App. §269.

sē: acc. subject of the infinitive esse (which
has been ellipted, and thus must be supplied) in indirect statement dependent on
profitētur.

10. ōrātiōne: abl. of means; see App. §143.

Nerviīs: dat. object of an intransitive verb;
see App. §115.

[5.39] Itaque cōnfestim dīmissīs nūntiīs *ad* Ceutronēs,
Grudiōs, Levācōs, Pleumoxiōs, Geidumnōs, *quī omnēs* sub
*eōrum imperiō sunt, quam maximās manūs possunt cōgunt et
dē* imprōvīsō *ad Cicerōnis hīberna* advolant nōndum *ad eum*
5   fāmā *dē Titūrī morte* perlātā. *Huic* quoque *accidit, quod fuit*
necesse, *ut* nōnnūllī *mīlitēs, quī* lignātiōnis mūnītiōnis*que
causā in* silvās *discessissent,* repentīnō *equitum adventū*
interciperentur.

---

advolō, 1 [**volō,** fly], fly to *or* against, rush
on *or* at.

Ceutron•ēs, -um, *m.,* the Ceutrones: (1)
a Belgic people subject to the Nervii or (2)
*a people living in the eastern part of the
Roman Province.*

cōnfestim, *adv.,* hastily, at once, immediately.

dī•mittō, -mittere, -mīsī, -missum [**mittō,**
send], send in different directions, send
away, send off.

fām•a, -ae, *f.* [**fārī,** to speak], common talk,
rumor, report, reputation, fame.

Geidumn•ī, -ōrum, *m.,* the Geidumni, *a
people of Belgic Gaul, clients of the Nervii.*

Grudi•ī, -ōrum, *m.,* the Grudii, *a Belgic
people near the Nervii.*

imper•ium, -ī, *n.* [**imperō,** order], right
to command; authority; jurisdiction;
supreme, highest official power.

imprōvīsō, *adv.* [**imprōvīsus,** unforeseen],
unexpectedly, without warning.

inter•cipiō, -cipere, -cēpī, -ceptum [**ad +
capiō,** take], take *or* catch between (*one
point and another*); interrupt; intercept;
cut off.

itaque, *conj.* [**ita,** *so*], and so, therefore,
accordingly.

Levāc•ī, -ōrum, *m.,* the Levaci, a *Gallic tribe
between the rivers Marne and Moselle.*

lignāti•ō, -ōnis, *f.* [**lignum,** wood], the
procuring of wood, collecting of wood.

mūnīti•ō, -ōnis, *f.* [**mūniō,** fortify],
fortifying; fortification, rampart, works,
entrenchments.

necesse, *indecl. adj.,* necessary, unavoidable,
indispensable.

nōndum, *adv.* [**nōn + dum**], not yet.

nōnnūll•us, -a, -um, *adj.* [**nōn + nūllus,**
none], some, several.

nūntius, -ī, *m.,* messenger; message; news,
report.

per•ferō, -ferre, -tulī, -lātum [**ferō,** carry],
bear *or* carry through, convey; deliver;
announce, report; submit to, endure,
suffer.

Pleumoxi•ī, -ōrum, *m.,* the Pleumoxii.

quoque, *conj., following the word
emphasized,* also, too, likewise.

repentīn•us, -a, -um, *adj.* [**repēns,** sudden],
sudden, unexpected, hasty.

silv•a, -ae, *f.,* forest, woods, a wood.

sub, *prep. with abl., of position,* under,
beneath.

**1–2. cōnfestim dīmissīs nūntiīs . . .
Geidumnōs:** abl. absolute; see App. §150.

3. eōrum = *Nerviōrum.*

quam maximās manūs possunt: "armed
forces as large as possible"; see App. §161, *a*;
PARENTHESIS; see App. §301, *e*.

4–5. nōndum . . . fāmā . . . perlātā: abl.
absolute; see App. §150.

5. Huic = *Quīntō Tulliō Cicerōnī,* the commander of the winter quarters (and the orator
Marcus's brother).

quod = *id, quod.*

6–8. ut . . . interciperentur: subjunctive
in a substantive clause of result (see App.
§229, *b*) in apposition with "that which was
necessary" by way of further explanation.

6–7. quī . . . discessissent: subjunctive in a
rel. clause of purpose; see App. §225, 1.

10　　His circumventīs magnā manū Eburōnēs, Nerviī, Aduātucī atque
hōrum omnium sociī et clientēs legiōnem oppugnāre incipiunt.
Nostrī celeriter ad arma concurrunt, vāllum cōnscendunt.
Aegrē is diēs sustentātur, quod omnem spem hostēs in celeritāte
pōnēbant atque hanc adeptī victōriam in perpetuum sē fore
victōrēs cōnfīdēbant.

---

ad•ipīscor, -ipīscī, -eptus sum, attain to,
gain.

Aduātuc•ī, -ōrum, m., a people in Belgic
Gaul, the Aduatici.

ae•ger, -gra, -grum, adj., sick, ill.

celeriter, adv. [celer, swift], quickly,
rapidly, speedily. Comp.: celerius; superl.:
celerrimē (App. §40).

cliēns, clientis, m., f. [clueō, hear, obey],
client, vassal, dependent, retainer.

con•currō, -currere, -cursī, -cursum
[currō, run], run or rush together; hurry,
run, rush; run to the rescue; come, gather.

cōn•fīdō, -fīdere, -fīsī, -fīsum [fīdō, trust.
App. §74], rely on, feel confident, hope.

cōn•scendō, -scendere, -scendī, -scēnsum
[scandō, climb], climb, mount; go on
board, embark.

Eburōn•ēs, -um, m., the Eburones, a Belgic
people who in 54 BCE destroyed troops
under the command of Sabinus and Cotta.
Afterward, Caesar almost exterminated
them.

in•cipiō, -cipere, -cēpī, -ceptum [ad
+ capiō, take], undertake; begin,
commence.

oppugnō, 1 [ob + pugnō, fight], fight
against, attack, besiege.

perpetu•us, -a, -um, adj., continuous; n. as
noun in the phrase in perpetuum, forever.

pōnō, pōnere, posuī, positum, place, put,
place over; lay down, set aside; station,
post; regard, consider; make, build; with
castra, pitch; pass.: be situated; with in
and the abl., depend on, in addition to the
above meanings.

soc•ius, -ī, m. [compare sequor, follow],
companion, ally.

sustent•ō, 1 [freq. of sus-tineō, hold up],
sustain; hold out; withstand.

vāll•um, -ī, n. [vāllus, palisade], wall
or rampart of earth set with palisades;
entrenchments, earthworks.

vict•or, -ōris, m. [vincō, conquer],
conqueror, victor; as adj., victorious.

---

9. Hīs: "these (Roman soldiers in Cicero's
winter encampment)."

Hīs circumventīs: abl. absolute; see App.
§150.

manū: abl. of means; see App. §143.

11. Nostrī: "our men."

12. diēs: Caesar personifies the day when
it was actually the soldiers who had to sustain

the fight for an entire day; PERSONIFICATION
see App. §302, h.

13. hanc adeptī victōriam: "if they gained
this victory"; see App. §283.

fore: fore is an alternative form for futurus
esse, the fut. active inf. of esse.

[5.40] *Mittuntur ad Caesarem* cōnfestim *ab Cicerōne litterae*
magnīs prōpositīs praemiīs, *sī* pertulissent: obsessīs *omnibus viīs*
missī intercipiuntur. *Noctū ex* māteriā, *quam* mūnītiōnis *causā*
comportāverant, *turrēs* admodum CXX excitantur incrēdibilī
5 *celeritāte; quae* deesse operī *vidēbantur,* perficiuntur.

---

admodum, *adv.* [**modus,** measure], *literally:*
up to the measure; very much, very; *with*
numbers, fully; *with negative,* at all.
comportō, 1 [**portō,** carry], carry together,
collect, bring.
cōnfestim, *adv.,* hastily, at once, immediately.
CXX, *sign for* **centum et vīgintī,** one
hundred twenty (*see also* App. §47).
dē•sum, -esse, -fuī, — [**sum,** be. App. §66],
be lacking, be absent from, fail.
excitō, 1 [**citō,** rouse], construct (*towers*).
incrēdibil•is, -e, *adj.* [**in + crēdibilis,**
believable], unbelievable, incredible,
unlikely; extraordinary.
inter•cipiō, -cipere, -cēpī, -ceptum [**ad +**
capiō, take], take *or* catch between (*one*
point and another); interrupt; intercept;
cut off.
māteri•a, -ae, *f.,* wood, timber.
mūnīti•ō, -ōnis, *f.* [**mūniō,** fortify],
fortifying; fortification, rampart, works,
entrenchments.

ob•sideō, -sidēre, -sēdī, -sessum [**sedeō,**
sit], sit in the way of, obstruct, besiege,
blockade.
op•us, -eris, *n.,* work, labor; military work
or works, fortifications, defenses; a work
of engineering or architecture; **nātūrā et**
opere, by nature and art.
per•ferō, -ferre, -tulī, -lātum [**ferō,** carry],
bear *or* carry through, convey, deliver;
announce, report; submit to, endure,
suffer.
per•ficiō, -ficere, -fēcī, -fectum [**faciō,**
make, do], finish; build; accomplish.
praem•ium, -ī, *n.,* distinction, prize,
reward.
prō•pōnō, -pōnere, -posuī, -positum
[**pōnō,** put], place *or* put forward,
present, offer; relate, tell of, explain;
purpose, propose; expose.

---

2. magnīs ... praemiīs: abl. absolute; see
App. §150. The rewards were offered not to
Caesar, but to messengers, who are not mentioned, but who are the obvious choice for
carrying messages. Caesar keeps the narrative
clipped by omitting what would have been obvious to his readers.

sī (*nūntiī eās litterās*) **pertulissent:** plupf.
subjunctive in the protasis (if-clause) of a condition in indirect statement that represents
what would have been a fut. perf. ind. in a
future more vivid condition in direct statement; see App. §256.

obsessīs ... viīs: abl. absolute; see App.
§150.

3. missī: "those (messengers who had
been) sent"; see App. §283.

4–5. incrēdibilī celeritāte: abl. of manner; see App. §142.

5. quae = *et ea, quae.*

operī: dat. with a compound verb; see
App. §116.

Hostēs posterō *diē multō* maiōribus *coāctis cōpiīs castra*
oppugnant, fossam complent. *Eādem* ratiōne, *quā* prīdiē, *ab*
nostrīs resistitur. *Hoc idem reliquīs* deinceps *fit diēbus*. Nūlla
pars nocturnī *temporis ad* labōrem intermittitur; *nōn* aegrīs,
10   *nōn* vulnerātīs facultās quiētis *datur*.

---

ae•ger, -gra, -grum, *adj.,* sick, ill.

com•pleō, -plēre, -plēvī, -plētum [*obs.*:
  pleō, fill], fill up; complete; cover.

deinceps, *adv.,* one after the other, in turn,
  successively.

facul•tās, -tātis, *f.* [**facilis,** easy], power;
  opportunity; resources.

foss•a, -ae, *f.* [*perf. part. of* **fodiō,** dig],
  trench, ditch, *which was dug around a*
  Roman camp.

inter•mittō, -mittere, -mīsī, -missum
  [**mittō,** send], cease, discontinue; delay,
  neglect, omit; let pass.

lab•or, -ōris, *m.,* toil, effort, striving,
  hardship.

maior, maius, *adj.* [*comp. of* **magnus,** large],
  larger.

nocturn•us, -a, -um, *adj.* [**nox,** night], at
  night, nocturnal, nightly.

nūll•us, -a, -um, *gen.* **nūllīus,** *adj.* [**ne-** +
  ūllus, any], not any, no.

oppugnō, 1 [**ob** + **pugnō,** fight], fight
  against, attack, besiege.

poster•us, -a, -um, *adj.* [**post,** after],
  after, following, next; *in m. pl. as*
  noun: posterity; *superl.:* **postrēmus** *or*
  postumus, last.

prīdiē, *adv.* [**diēs,** day], on the day before.

qui•ēs, -ētis, *f.,* quiet, rest, repose.

rati•ō, -ōnis, *f.* [**reor,** reckon], plan,
  strategy; method; manner, way.

re•sistō, -sistere, -stitī, — [**sistō,** stand],
  stand back, remain behind, halt, stand
  still; withstand, resist, oppose.

vulnerō, 1 [**vulnus,** wound], wound.

---

6. multō . . . cōpiīs: "after they had gathered far larger forces"; abl. absolute; see App. §150.

7. quā prīdiē (*resistitur*)**:** the verb has been ellipted from the subordinate clause, but can be supplied from the main clause. Unlike Latin, English generally does not permit such "gapping" in advance.

8. reliquīs . . . diēbus: "on all the other days"; abl. of time; see App. §152.

10. vulnerātīs: "to those (who had been) wounded"; see App. §283.

Quaecumque *ad proximī diēī oppugnātiōnem* opus *sunt noctū*
comparantur; *multae* praeustae sudēs, *magnus* mūrālium
pīlōrum *numerus* īnstituitur; *turrēs* contabulantur, pinnae
lōrīcae*que ex* crātibus attexuntur. *Ipse Cicerō, cum* tenuissimā
15   valētūdine *esset,* nē nocturnum quidem *sibi tempus ad* quiētem
relinquēbat, ut ultrō *mīlitum* concursū *ac* vōcibus *sibi* parcere
cōgerētur.

---

at•texō, -texere, -texuī, -textum [ad + **texō,** weave], weave on.

comparō, 1 [**parō,** prepare], prepare; acquire, prepare for.

concurs•us, -ūs, *m.* [**concurrō,** run], a running together, attack, onset; collision.

contabulō, 1 [**tabula,** board], floor over, build in multiple stories, build up.

crāt•es, -is, *f.,* wickerwork.

īn•stituō, -stituere, -stituī, -stitūtum [**stātuō,** set up], set up *or* put in order; procure, prepare; build, construct.

lōrīc•a, -ae, *f.,* coat of mail; parapet, breastwork; deflective wall *or* screen (*for a tower*).

mūrāl•is, -e, *adj.* [**mūrus,** wall], pertaining to a wall, mural; **mūrāle pīlum,** mural javelin, *a heavy javelin that was thrown from the top of a wall.*

nē ... quidem (*enclosing the emphatic word*), not even.

nocturn•us, -a, -um, *adj.* [**nox,** night], at night, nocturnal, nightly.

opus, *indecl. noun, n.* [*cf.* **opus,** work, deed], need, necessity; **opus est,** it is necessary, there is need, *the thing needed is expressed either by the nom. or the abl.* (App. §146).

parcō, parcere, pepercī, parsus [**parcus,** frugal], be frugal *or* economical; spare, do not injure *or* harm.

pīl•um, -ī, *n.,* heavy javelin, pike.

pinn•a, -ae, *f.,* feather; battlement, parapet.

prae•ūrō, -ūrere, -ussī, -ustum [**ūrō,** burn], burn in front *or* at the end.

quīcumque, quaecumque, quodcumque, *indef.* (*or generalizing*) *rel. pron.,* whoever, whatever; whosoever, whatsoever, any ... whatever; everyone who, everything that.

quidem, *adv.,* indeed, at any rate, at least, truly; on the other hand; **nē ... quidem,** not even.

qui•ēs, -ētis, *f.,* quiet, rest, repose.

sud•is, -is, *f.,* heavy beam, pile, stake.

tenu•is, -e, *adj.,* slim, thin; slight, insignificant; delicate.

ultrō, *adv.,* voluntarily; besides, moreover.

valētūd•ō, -inis, *f.* [**valeō,** be strong], health, poor health.

vōx, vōcis, *f.,* voice; shout; word; *pl.,* words, language, *variously translated according to context, as* entreaties, complaints, tales, etc.

---

11. Quaecumque = *et ea, quaecumque.*

12. praeustae: burning the wood made it harder.

13–14. īnstituitur ... contabulantur ... attexuntur: Caesar provides an extensive list of "whatever was necessary" that the legions manufactured at night. Note also the ASYNDETON; see App. §301, *a.*

14–15. cum ... esset: subjunctive in a concessive clause; see App. §238–239.

15. valētūdine: descriptive abl.; see App. §141.

16. concursū ac vōcibus: ablatives of means; see App. §143.

sibi: dat. object of an intransitive verb; see App. §115.

16–17. ut ... cōgerētur: subjunctive in a clause of result; see App. §226.

[5.41] Tunc ducēs prīncipēs*que Nerviōrum quī aliquem*
sermōnis aditum *causamque* amīcitiae *cum Cicerōne habēbant*
colloquī sēsē velle dīcunt. Factā potestāte *eadem quae Ambiorīx*
cum Titūriō ēgerat commemorant: *omnem esse in armīs Galliam;*
5   *Germānōs Rhēnum* trānsīsse; *Caesaris reliquōrumque hīberna*
oppugnārī. Addunt *etiam dē* Sabīnī *morte: Ambiorīgem*
ostentant fideī *faciendae causā.*

---

ad•dō, -dere, -didī, -ditum [dō, put], place
on, add.

adit•us, -ūs, *m.* [**adeō,** go to], approach,
means of approach, right to approach,
access.

ag•ō, -ere, ēgī, actum, set in motion,
drive (*animals*); move forward, advance
(*military works*); do, transact, carry on
(*business*); discuss, speak.

amīciti•a, -ae, *f.* [**amīcus,** friend],
friendship.

commemorō, 1 [**memorō,** call to mind],
remind one of; state, mention.

dux, ducis, *m.* [**dūcō,** lead], leader,
commander, general; guide.

fid•ēs, -eī, *f.* [**fīdō,** confide], faith;
trustworthiness; allegiance, protection;
pledge; **fidem facere,** convince *or* give a
pledge.

oppugnō, 1 [**ob** + **pugnō,** fight], fight
against, attack, besiege.

ostentō, 1 [*frequentative of* **ostendō,** show],
show frequently; show, exhibit.

potes•tās, -tātis, *f.* [**potēns,** powerful],
power, ability, authority; control, sway,
rule; chance, opportunity, possibility;
potestātem facere, grant permission,
give a chance.

prīn•ceps, -cipis [**prīmus,** first], chief, first;
as noun, chief *or* leader.

Sabīn•us, -ī, *m.,* Quintus Titurius Sabinus,
one of Caesar's lieutenants.

serm•ō, -ōnis, *m.,* conversation, interview,
speech.

Titūr•ius, -ī, *m.,* Quintus Titurius Sabinus,
one of Caesar's lieutenants.

trāns•eō, -īre, -iī, -itum [**eō,** go. App. §84],
cross; march through; migrate.

tunc, *adv.,* then, at that time, at this
juncture.

1–2. aliquem sermōnis aditum: "some
plausible grounds for an interview." The leaders of the Nervii will attempt to lure Cicero
into an ambush in the same way that Ambiorix tricked Sabinus.

    3. Factā potestāte: abl. absolute; see App.
§150.

    4. omnem . . . Galliam: acc. subject of
the inf. **esse** in indirect statement after **commemorant.** Note the HYPERBATON; see App.
§302, *f.*

    4–6. esse . . . trānsīsse . . . oppugnārī:
note the tense of the infs. The first and third
are present, and happening at that moment.
The second is perf., and has already taken
place. See App. §205.

    6. Addunt . . . dē: "they add (words) con-
cerning" or "about."

    7. fideī . . . causā: gerundive with **causā** to
express purpose; see App. §§288, 291.

Errāre *eōs dīcunt, sī* quicquam *ab hīs* praesidī spērent, *quī suīs*
rēbus diffīdant; *sēsē tamen hōc esse in Cicerōnem populumque*
10   *Rōmānum* animō, *ut nihil* nisi *hīberna* recūsent *atque hanc*
inveterāscere cōnsuētūdinem nōlint: licēre *illīs* incolumibus
per sē ex hībernīs discēdere et quāscumque *in partēs velint sine*
metū *proficīscī.*

---

anim•us, -ī, *m.,* mind; character; spirit,
soul; courage.
cōnsuētūd•ō, -inis, *f.,* [**cōnsuēscō,** become
accustomed], habit, custom, practice;
"lifestyle."
dif•fīdō, -fīdere, -fīsī, -fīsum [**fīdō,** trust.
App. §74], distrust, lack confidence,
despair.
errō, 1, wander; err, be mistaken.
incolum•is, -e, *adj.,* unhurt, uninjured, safe
and sound, unimpaired.
in•veterāscō, -veterāscere, -veterāvī,
-veterātum, grow old; become
established.
licet, licēre, licuit *and* **licitum est,** *impers.,*
it is permitted.
met•us, -ūs, *m.* [**metuō,** fear], fear, dread,
terror, anxiety, apprehension; **metū**
territāre, terrify, terrorize; **hōc metū** =
metū huius reī, from fear of this.

nisi, *conj.* [**ne-** + **sī,** if], if not, except, unless.
nōlō, nōlle, nōlui, — (App. §82) [**ne-** +
volō, wish], not wish, be unwilling;
refuse; *imp.* **nōlī** *or* **nōlīte,** *with inf.* (App.
§219), do not.
praesid•ium, -ī, *n.,* [**praesideō,** guard],
guard, garrison; safeguard, protection;
fortification, stronghold; help, aid; safety.
quīcumque, quaecumque, quodcumque,
indef. (*or generalizing) rel. pron.,* whoever,
whatever; whosoever, whatsoever, any . . .
whatever; everyone who, everything that.
quisquam, quicquam, *indef. pron.* (App.
§62), any, any person *or* thing.
recūsō, 1, refuse, reject; object to, make
objections, complain; *with* **perīculum,**
shrink from.
spērō, 1 [**spēs,** hope], hope, hope for,
anticipate.

---

8. dīcunt: this main verb of speaking introduces three principal thoughts in indirect
statement: **eōs** *(Rōmānōs)* **errāre, sēse esse,**
and *(id)* **licēre illīs** *(Rōmānīs).* The rest of the
subordinate clauses depend on these indirect
statements.
    quicquam . . . praesidī: partitive gen.; see
App. §101.
    9. rēbus: dat. indirect object of the intran-
sitive verb **diffīdant;** see App. §115.

9–10. hōc . . . animō: descriptive abl.; see
App. §141.
    10–11. ut . . . recūsent atque . . . nōlint:
subjunctives in a clause of result; see App.
§226. The subjects of both verbs are the
Nervii.
    12. per sē: "on their (i.e., Nervian)
authority."

Cicerō ad haec ūnum modo respondit: *nōn esse* cōnsuētūdinem
15 *populī Rōmānī accipere ab hoste* armātō condiciōnem: *sī ab
armīs discēdere velint, sē* adiūtōre *ūtantur lēgātōsque ad Caesarem
mittant;* spērāre *prō eius* iūstitiā, *quae petierint,* impetrātūrōs.

---

adiūt•or, -ōris, *m.* [**adiuvō,** aid], helper,
assistant, abettor.
armō, 1 [**arma,** arms], arm, equip; *pass.*,
arm oneself; **armātus,** *perf. part., as adj.*,
armed; **armātī,** *as noun,* armed men.
condici•ō, -ōnis, *f.*, condition, state;
agreement, stipulation, terms.
cōnsuētūd•ō, -inis, *f.*, [**cōnsuēscō,** become
accustomed], habit, custom, practice;
"lifestyle."
impetrō, 1, obtain (*by request*), accomplish,
succeed in obtaining (*one's request*);

impetrāre ā (ab), gain permission from,
persuade.
iūstiti•a, -ae, *f.* [**iūstus,** just], justice, fair
dealing, uprightness.
modo, *adv.* [**modus,** measure], *with measure
or limit;* only; just, at least, but; *of time,*
just now.
**re•spondeō, -spondēre, -spondī,
-sponsum** [**re** + **spondeō,** promise],
reply, answer.
spērō, 1 [**spēs,** hope], hope, hope for,
anticipate.

---

14. Cicerō: Quintus Cicero, the brother of
the famous orator and consul of 63 BCE, is sin-
gled out for praise as a true Roman. Note too
how he replies with "just one answer" (**ūnum
modo**) to their "various points" (**haec**), although "this one answer" is then elaborated.

15–16. sī . . . velint: a general condition
in indirect statement. See App. §§253, 272.

16. adiūtōre: "as helper"; in apposition
with **sē.** See App. §97.

17. spērāre: supply *sē* (referring to Cicero)
as the subject of this inf. in indirect statement
after **respondit.**

18. eius = *Caesaris.*

quae: supply *ea* as the unexpressed
antecedent.

petierint = *petīverint.* See App. §72.

impetrātūrōs: this fut. active inf. with
esse omitted depends in indirect statement
on **spērāre.** Its subject (*eōs Nerviōs*) has been
omitted. Its object is the unexpressed antecedent *ea* of **quae petierint.**

[5.42] *Ab hāc spē* repulsī *Nerviī* vāllō pedum IX *et* fossā pedum XV *hīberna* cingunt. *Haec et superiōrum annōrum cōnsuētūdine ab* nōbīs *cognōverant et, quōs* clam *dē exercitū habēbant* captīvōs, *ab eīs* docēbantur; *sed* nūllā ferrāmentōrum *cōpiā quae esset ad*

5   *hunc ūsum* idōnea, gladiīs caespitēs circumcīdere, *manibus* sagulīs*que* terram exhaurīre *vidēbantur.*

---

caesp•es, -itis, *m.*, sod, turf.

captīv•us, -a, -um, *adj.* [**capiō**, take], prisoner, captive.

cing•ō, -ere, cīnxī, cīnctum, encircle, surround, invest, encompass; man (*a wall*).

circumcīd•ō, -ere, -ī, circumcīsum [**circum**, around + **caedō**, cut], cut around, cut off, cut; isolate.

clam, *adv.*, secretly.

cōnsuētūd•ō, -inis, *f.*, [**cōnsuēscō**, become accustomed], habit, custom, practice; "lifestyle."

doceō, docēre, docuī, docitum, show, teach, instruct, inform.

ego, meī (App. §51), *first pers. pron.*, I, me; *pl.* **nōs,** we, us, etc.

ex•hauriō, -haurīre, -hausī, -haustum [**hauriō**, drain], draw out, empty.

ferrāment•um, -ī, *n.* [**ferrum**, iron], an iron tool *or* implement.

foss•a, -ae, *f.* [*perf. part. of* **fodiō**, dig], trench, ditch.

glad•ius, -ī, *m.*, sword.

idōne•us, -a, -um, *adj.*, fit, suitable, adapted.

IX, *sign for* **novem,** nine (*see also* App. §47).

nūll•us, -a, -um, *gen.* **nūllīus,** *adj.* [**ne-** + **ūllus,** any], not any, no.

pēs, pedis, *m.*, the foot, a foot.

re•pellō, -pellere, -pulī, -pulsum [**pellō**, drive], bear *or* drive back, repel, repulse.

sagul•um, -ī, *n.* [*dim. of* **sagum**, coat], a small coat; military cloak.

terr•a, -ae, *f.*, earth, land, soil, ground; region, district; **terrae** (*pl.*) *and* **orbis terrārum,** the world.

vāll•um, -ī, *n.* [**vāllus**, palisade], wall *or* rampart *of earth set with palisades;* entrenchments, earthworks.

XV, *sign for* **quīndecim,** fifteen (*see also* App. §47).

---

2. cingunt: after their trick fails, the Nervii begin to besiege the Roman camp.

Haec: "these things," i.e., how to dig a trench and build an earthen wall or rampart.

3–4. quōs . . . captīvōs . . . ab eīs: the antecedent of **quōs** is **eīs.** By placing the rel. clause before its antecedent, Caesar emphasizes the role Roman captives had in instructing the Nervii.

4. nūllā . . . cōpiā: abl. absolute; see App. §150.

quae esset: subjunctive in a rel. clause of characteristic. See App. § 230.

5–6. gladiīs . . . manibus sagulīsque: ablatives of means; see App. §143.

Quā quidem *ex rē hominum multitūdō cognōscī potuit: nam
minus* hōrīs *tribus mīlium* pedum XV *in* circuitū mūnītiōnem
perfēcērunt *reliquīsque diēbus turrēs ad* altitūdinem vāllī, falcēs
10   testūdinēs*que, quās īdem* captīvī docuerant, parāre *ac facere
coepērunt.*

---

altitūd•ō, -inis, *f.* [**altus,** high, deep],
    height, depth.
captīv•us, -a, -um, *adj.* [**capiō,** take],
    prisoner, captive.
circuit•us, -ūs, *m.* [**circumeō,** go around],
    a going around; a winding path;
    circumference, circuit.
doceō, docēre, docuī, docitum, show,
    teach, instruct, inform.
falx, falcis, *f.,* sickle, pruning hook; hook
    (*for pulling down walls*).
hōr•a, -ae, *f.,* hour.
mūnīti•ō, -ōnis, *f.* [**mūniō,** fortify],
    fortifying; fortification, rampart, works,
    entrenchments.
parō, 1, prepare; acquire; get ready for.
per•ficiō, -ficere, -fēcī, -fectum [**faciō,**
    make, do], finish; build; accomplish.

pēs, pedis, *m.,* the foot, a foot.
quidem, *adv.,* indeed, at any rate, at least,
    truly; on the other hand; **nē . . . quidem,**
    not even.
testūd•ō, -inis, *f.,* tortoise; shed; a *testudo,
    a column of men, holding their shields
    overlapped above their heads (which made
    them look like a giant tortoise).*
vāll•um, -ī, *n.* [**vāllus,** palisade], wall
    or rampart *of earth set with palisades;*
    entrenchments, earthworks.
XV, *sign for* **quīndecim,** fifteen (*see also*
    App. §47).

---

7. Quā . . . ex rē = *et ex eā rē; conjunctio
relativa;* see App. §173, *a.*

8. hōrīs: abl. of comparison; see App. §139.
9. diēbus: abl. of time when; see App. §152.

Avid enthusiasts of Roman warfare and military techniques regularly gather to reenact those
maneuvers. Depicted is a group of Roman soldier reenactors using their shields to create a
testudo formation.

[5.43] Septimō *oppugnātiōnis diē maximō* coortō ventō
ferventēs fūsilī *ex* argillā glandēs fundīs *et* fervefacta iacula
in casās, *quae* mōre Gallicō strāmentīs *erant* tēctae, iacere
coepērunt. Hae celeriter ignem comprehendērunt *et* ventī
5   magnitūdine *in omnem locum castrōrum* distulērunt.

---

argill•a, -ae, *f.*, white clay.
cas•a, -ae, *f.*, hut, barrack.
celeriter, *adv.* [celer, swift], quickly,
    rapidly, speedily. *Comp.*: celerius; *superl.*:
    celerrimē (App. §40).
com•prehendō, -prehendere, -prehendī,
    -prehēnsum [prehendō (= prendō),
    seize], lay hold of, seize, arrest, catch
    (*fire*).
co•orior, -orīrī, -ortus sum [orior, rise],
    arise, spring up, break out.
differō, differre, distulī, dīlātum [ferō,
    carry. App. §81], scatter, spread; put off,
    defer; be different, differ.
ferve•faciō, -facere, -fēcī, -factum [ferveō,
    be red hot + faciō, make], heat, melt.
ferv•ēns, -entis, *adj.* [*pres. part. of* ferveō,
    be red hot], heated, glowing, hot.
fund•a, -ae, *f.*, sling.

fūsil•is, -e, *adj.* [fundō, pour], liquid,
    molten.
Gallic•us, -a, -um, *adj.* [Gallia, Gaul],
    pertaining to Gaul *or* the Gauls, Gallic.
glān•s, -dis, *f.*, acorn; ball, slug *of lead.*
iaciō, iacere, iēcī, iactum, throw, cast, hurl.
iacul•um, -ī, *n.* [iaciō, throw], javelin,
    spear, dart.
ign•is, -is, *m.*, fire.
magnitūd•ō, -inis, *f.* [magnus, large], large
    size; violence (venti).
mōs, mōris, *m.*, manner, custom, practice.
septim•us, -a, -um, *ord. num. adj.* [septum,
    seven], seventh.
strāmentum, -ī, *n.*, covering; straw, thatch;
    pack-saddle.
tegō, tegere, tēxī, tēctum, cover, hide;
    protect, defend.
vent•us, -ī, *m.*, wind.

---

1. Septimō . . . diē: abl. of time when; see
App. §152.

   maximō . . . ventō: abl. absolute; see App.
§150.

   2. ferventēs fūsilī ex argillā glandēs: "hot
balls of molten white clay." The separation of
the **ferventēs** from the noun it modifies is
useful, as the arrangement assists readers in
understanding the whole clause as one of the
objects of **iacere.**

3. mōre: abl. of accordance (manner); see
App. §142, *a.*

   strāmentīs: abl. of means; see App. §143.

   4. Hae = *casae*, i.e., the men's barracks.

   5. magnitūdine: abl. of cause; see App.
§138.

   distulērunt: supply *ignem* (from the first
clause) as the direct object.

Hostēs maximō clāmōre sīcutī partā iam *atque* explōrātā *victōriā turrēs* testūdinēs*que* agere *et* scālīs vāllum ascendere *coepērunt.*

---

ag•ō, -ere, ēgī, actum, set in motion, drive (*animals*); move forward, advance (*military works*); do, transact, carry on (*business*); discuss, speak.

a•scendō, -scendere, -scendī, -scēnsum [**ad** + **scandō,** climb], climb up, ascend, mount, climb.

clām•or, -ōris, *m.* [**clāmō,** cry out], outcry, noise, shouting, clamor.

explōrō, 1, search *or* find out, investigate, spy out, reconnoiter.

iam, *adv.,* now; already, at last; indeed.

pariō, parere, peperī, partum, bring forth; gain, acquire, win.

scāl•ae, -ārum, *f.* [**scandō,** climb], stairs; scaling ladder.

sīcut *or* **sīcutī,** *adv.* [**sīc,** so + **ut**(**ī**), as], so as, just as, just as if.

testūd•ō, -inis, *f.,* tortoise; shed; a *testudo, a column of men, holding their shields overlapped above their heads (which made them look like a giant tortoise).*

vāll•um, -ī, *n.* [**vāllus,** palisade], wall *or* rampart *of earth set with palisades;* entrenchments, earthworks.

---

6. maximō clāmōre: abl. of manner; see App. §142.

partā ... victōriā: abl. absolute; see App. §150.

7. turrēs testūdinēsque agere: the Nervii have built wooden towers which they can roll up to the Roman walls and they also have protective "tortoise shells" which they can use to protect their advancing troops. Soldiers could form "shells" on the fly by holding their shields over their heads and overlapping them with the shields of those next to them or they could also build light "roofs" which they could carry over their heads. At all events, the Nervii have learned Roman techniques rather well.

At tanta mīlitum virtūs atque ea praesentia animī *fuit, ut,*
cum undique flammā torrērentur *maximāque tēlōrum*
10   *multitūdine premerentur suaque omnia* impedīmenta *atque*
omnēs fortūnās cōnflagrāre intellegerent, *nōn* modo
dēmigrāndī *causā dē* vāllō dēcēderet nēmō, *sed* paene nē
respiceret quidem quisquam, *ac tum omnēs* ācerrimē
fortissimē*que pugnārent.*

āc•er, -ris, -re, *adj.,* sharp [App. §36].
anim•us, -ī, *m.,* mind; character; spirit,
  soul; courage.
cōnflagrō, 1 [**flagrō,** burn], burn, be on fire.
dē•cēdō, -cēdere, -cessī, -cessum [**cēdō,**
  go], go from *or* away, depart, withdraw,
  leave, forsake; die.
dē•migrō, 1 [**migrō,** move, migrate], move
  from, move away, step away (for a short
  time).
flamm•a, -ae, *f.,* fire, blaze.
fort•is, -e, *adj.,* strong, brave.
fortūn•a, -ae, *f.* [**fors,** chance], fortune,
  chance, opportunity, condition; success,
  property.
impedīment•um, -ī, *n.* [**impediō,** hinder],
  hindrance, obstacle; *pl.*: baggage,
  baggage-train (*including pack animals*).
intel•legō, -legere, -lēgī, -lēctum [**inter +**
  legō, choose, select], select; understand;
  perceive; find out.
modo, *adv.* [**modus,** measure], *with measure*
  or limit, only; just, at least, but; *of time,*
  just now; **nōn modo . . . sed etiam,** not
  only, . . . but also.

nē . . . quidem (*enclosing the emphatic word*),
  not even.
nēmō, *acc.* **nēminem,** *m. and f.* [**ne- +**
  homō, human being], no one, nobody.
paene, *adv.,* nearly, almost.
prae•senti•a, -ae, *f.* [**praesum,** be present],
  presence; the present moment; **in**
  praesentiā, for the present; then.
quidem, *adv.,* indeed, at any rate, at least,
  truly; on the other hand; **nē . . . quidem,**
  not even.
quisquam, quicquam, *indef. pron.* (App.
  §62), any, any person *or* thing.
re•spiciō, -spicere, -spexī, -spectum [**re**
  + speciō, look], look back; look at, take
  notice of; consider, regard.
torreō, torrēre, torruī, tostum, scorch,
  burn.
undique, *adv.* [**unde,** whence], on all sides,
  everywhere.
vāll•um, -ī, *n.* [**vāllus,** palisade], wall
  or rampart *of earth set with palisades;*
  entrenchments, earthworks.

8–14. ut . . . dēcēderet . . . respiceret . . .
pugnārent: subjunctives in a (long) clause of
result; see App. §226.

  10–11. impedīmenta atque . . . fortūnās:
Roman soldiers did not fight for free. They
received pay, plunder, and bonuses, and they
kept their wealth with them. Similarly, a general had to carry a cash box with him to pay

the soldiers and to purchase supplies. The
fires that the Nervii kindled threatened to
destroy the soldiers' earthly possessions.

  12–13. paene nē respiceret quidem
quisquam: "hardly anyone looked back at
all," i.e., turned around to see whether his
belongings were on fire.

15   *Hic diēs nostrīs longē gravissimus fuit; sed tamen hunc habuit
      ēventum, ut eō diē maximus numerus hostium* vulnerārētur
      atque interficerētur, ut sē sub *ipsō* vāllō cōnstīpāverant
      recessum*que prīmīs* ultimī *nōn dabant.*

---

cōnstipō, 1, press *or* crowd closely.
ēvent•us, -ūs, *m.* [**ēveniō,** turn out],
      outcome, issue, result, consequence.
recess•us, -ūs, *m.* [**re + cēdō,** go], a going
      back, retreat; way out.
sub, *prep. with abl.,* under, beneath.
ultim•us, -a, -um, *adj., superl.* [**ultrā,**
      beyond. App. §43], farthest, most distant
      or remote; *as noun,* those in the rear.

vāll•um, -ī, *n.* [**vāllus,** palisade], wall
      or rampart *of earth set with palisades;*
      entrenchments, earthworks.
vulnerō, 1 [**vulnus,** wound], wound.

---

15. nostrīs: "for our men"; dat. of reference; see App. §120.
      16–17. ut . . . vulnerārētur atque interficerētur: subjunctives in a substantive clause of result; see App. §229, *b.*

17–18. ut . . . cōnstīpāverant (*et*) nōn dabant: "when (from the time) they had," etc. and "they were not," etc. Note the indicative mood of the verbs in this use of *ut* in a temporal clause.

Paulum quidem intermissā flammā *et quōdam locō turrī* adāctā
20   *et* contingente vāllum *tertiae cohortis* centuriōnēs *ex eō, quō*
stābant, *locō* recessērunt *suōsque omnēs* remōvērunt, nūtū
vōcibus*que hostēs, sī* introīre *vellent,* vocāre *coepērunt; quōrum*
prōgredī ausus *est* nēmō. *Tum ex omnī parte* lapidibus coniectīs
dēturbātī, *turrisque* succēnsa *est.*

---

ad•igō, -igere, -ēgi, -āctum [ad + agō,
   move], thrust, plunge, hurl (*of weapons*).
aud•eō, -ēre, ausus sum (App. §74), dare,
   risk, venture.
centuri•ō, -ōnis, *m.* [centum, hundred],
   centurion, *the commander of the century,
   a unit corresponding to one-sixtieth of a
   legion.*
con•iciō, -icere, -iēcī, -iectum [co + iaciō,
   throw. App. §7], hurl, throw, cast.
con•tingō, -tingere, -tigī, -tāctum [tangō,
   touch], touch; extend to; happen to.
dēturbō, 1 [turbō, disturb], drive off,
   dislodge.
flamm•a, -ae, *f.,* fire, blaze.
inter•mittō, -mittere, -mīsī, -missum
   [mittō, send], send between.
intrō•eō, -īre, -iī, -itum [intrō, within +
   eō, go. App. §84], go *or* come in, enter.
lap•is, -idis, *m.,* stone.
nēmō, *m. and f.* [ne- + homō, human
   being], no one, nobody.

nūt•us, -ūs, *m.* [nuō, nod], nod; sign,
   command.
paulum, *adv.* [paulus, little], a little,
   somewhat, slightly.
prō•gredior, -gredī, -gressus sum
   [gradior, step], step *or* go forward,
   advance.
quidem, *adv.,* indeed, at any rate, at least,
   truly; on the other hand.
re•cēdō, -cēdere, -cessī, -cessum [cēdō,
   go], go back, retire.
re•moveō, -movēre, -mōvī, -mōtum
   [moveō, move], move back *or* away,
   withdraw.
stō, stāre, stetī, statum, stand, abide by.
suc•cendō, -cendere, -cendī, -cēnsum, set
   on fire below, kindle, burn.
vāll•um, -ī, *n.* [vāllus, palisade], wall
   or rampart *of earth set with palisades;*
   entrenchments, earthworks.
vocō, 1 [vōx, voice], call, summon; invite.
vōx, vōcis, *f.,* voice, tone; cry, shout.

---

19. intermissā flammā: abl. absolute; see
App. §150.

   quōdam locō: abl. of place where; see
App. §.

   19–20. Paulum . . . cohortis: the beginning of the sentence provides background information through a string of abl. absolutes.
See the next notes for details.

   turrī adāctā et contingente: abl. absolute;
see App. §150.

   20–21. ex eō . . . locō: HYPERBATON; see
App. §302, *f.* By vacating the area near the
tower, the Romans can play a few tricks of
their own.

21. suōs . . . omnēs: "all their men."

   22. sī . . . vellent: because Caesar nar-
rates events in the past, what was originally
a fut. condition is represented by the impf.
subjunctive.

   22–23. quōrum . . . nēmō = *et nēmō eōrum;*
see App. §173, *a.* The HYPERBATON helps emphasize that absolutely none of the Nervii
dared to leave the protection of the tower.

   23. lapidibus: abl. of means; see App.
§143.

   coniectīs: we would more likely use a rel.
clause: "that had been hurled"; see App. §205.

[5.44] *Erant in eā legiōne* fortissimī *virī*, centuriōnēs, *quī*
prīmīs ōrdinibus appropinquārent, Titus Pullō *et* Lūcius
Vorēnus. *Hī* perpetuās *inter sē contrōversiās habēbant*, quīnam
anteferrētur, *omnibusque annīs dē locīs summīs* simultātibus
5   contendēbant. *Ex hīs* Pullō, *cum* ācerrimē *ad* mūnītiōnēs
pugnārētur, "quid dubitās," inquit, "Vorēne?

āc•er, -ris, -re, *adj.,* sharp [App. §36].
ante•ferō, -ferre, -tulī, -lātum [ferō, carry.
    App. §81], carry *or* bear before; prefer.
appropinquō, 1 [ad + propinquus, near],
    come near, approach.
centuri•ō, -ōnis, *m.* [centum, hundred],
    centurion, *the commander of the century,*
    a unit corresponding to one sixtieth of a
    legion.
con•tendō, -tendere, -tendī, -tentum
    [tendō, stretch], push forward, hasten;
    march; strive, contend, fight; insist.
dubitō, 1 [dubius, doubtful], be uncertain,
    doubt; hesitate, delay.
fort•is, -e, *adj.,* strong, brave.
inqu•am, -is, -it, say.
Lūci•us, -ī, *m.;* Vorēn•us, -ī, *m.,* Lucius
    Vorenus, *a centurion in Caesar's army in*
    the legion commanded by Cicero.

mūnīti•ō, -ōnis, *f.* [mūniō, fortify],
    fortifying; fortification, rampart, works,
    entrenchments.
perpetu•us, -a, -um, *adj.,* continuous;
    permanent; whole.
Pull•ō, -ōnis, *m.,* Titus Pullo, *a centurion*
    in Caesar's army in the legion commanded
    by Cicero.
quisnam, quidnam *and* quīnam,
    quaenam, quodnam, *interrog. pron.*
    (App. §61 *and a.*), who? which? what?
    who then? what in the world?
simul•tās, -tātis, *f.,* jealousy, rivalry.
Tit•us, -ī, *m.;* Pull•ō, -ōnis, *m.,* Titus Pullo,
    a centurion in Caesar's army in the legion
    commanded by Cicero.
Vorēn•us, -ī, *m.,* Lucius Vorenus, *a*
    centurion in Caesar's army in the legion
    commanded by Cicero.

1–2. quī ... appropinquārent: rel. clause
of characteristic; see App. §230. In other
words, Pullo and Vorenus were the sort of
centurions who were advancing toward the
rank of first centurion.

2–3. Titus Pullō et Lūcius Vorēnus: the
story of Pullo and Vorenus, which follows,
tells the tale of personal enemies who saved
each others' lives. The story is an entertaining
distraction from an otherwise dreary narrative of difficulties. It has also proved popular,
even inspiring, for example, characters with
the same names on a relatively recent televi-
sion program (HBO's *Rome*).

3–4. quīnam anteferrētur: subjunctive
in an indirect question; see App. §§209, 264.

4. locīs: "ranks" or "military honors," in
short, their respective places in the military
hierarchy.

summīs simultātibus: abl. of manner; see
App. §142.

6. inquit: this is the proper verb for in-
troducing direct speech, something Caesar
rarely does. By using direct speech as well as
the historical pres., Caesar renders the narrative especially lively and vivid.

Aut quem locum tuae probandae *virtūtis* exspectās? *Hic diēs dē nostrīs contrōversiīs* iūdicābit." *Haec cum dīxisset,* prōcēdit extrā mūnītiōnēs *quaeque pars hostium* cōnfertissima *est vīsa*

10   irrumpit. Nē Vorēnus quidem *tum sēsē* vāllō *continet, sed omnium* veritus exīstimātiōnem subsequitur.

---

cōnfert•us, -a, -um, *adj.* [*perf. part. of* cōnferciō, crowd together], dense, thick, compact, stuffed.

exīstimāti•ō, -ōnis, *f.* [exīstimō, estimate], judgement, opinion.

exspectō, 1 [spectō, look at], look out for, await, expect; wait to see; anticipate, apprehend.

extrā, *adv. and prep. with acc.,* out of, outside of, beyond, without.

ir•rumpō, -rumpere, -rūpsī, -rūptum [in + rumpō, break], break into, rush into; force a way into, storm.

iūdicō, 1 [iūdex, judge], pass judgement on, judge, sentence, decide, determine, think, consider.

mūnīti•ō, -ōnis, *f.* [mūniō, fortify], fortifying; fortification, rampart, works, entrenchments.

nē . . . quidem (*enclosing the emphatic word*), not even.

probō, 1 [probus, good], approve; demonstrate.

pro•cēdō, -cēdere, -cessī, -cessum [cēdō, go], go forth *or* forward, proceed, advance.

quidem, *adv.,* indeed, at any rate, at least, truly; on the other hand; nē . . . quidem, not even.

sub•sequor, -sequī, -secūtus [sequor, follow], follow closely.

tu•us, -a, -um, *adj., poss. adj.* [tū, you], your, yours.

vāll•um, -ī, *n.* [vāllus, palisade], wall *or* rampart *of earth set with palisades;* entrenchments, earthworks.

vereor, verērī, veritus sum, revere; fear, dread, be afraid of.

Vorēn•us, -ī, *m.,* Lucius Vorenus, *a centurion in Caesar's army in the legion commanded by Cicero.*

---

7. probandae: gerundive to express purpose; see App. §§288, 291.

  Hic diēs: PERSONIFICATION; see App. §302, *h.*

8. Haec = *haec verba.*

9. quaeque pars hostium = *in eam partem hostium,* quaeque pars hostium. As he does so often, Caesar has put what we would expect as the antecedent within the rel. clause, and then ellipted the antecedent altogether.

  10. vāllō: abl. of place where; see App. §151.

    11. omnium = *omnium mīlitum Rōmānōrum.*

Mediocrī spatiō *relictō* Pullō pīlum *in hostēs* immittit *atque*
ūnum ex multitūdine prōcurrentem trāicit; *quō* percussō *et*
exanimātō *hunc* scūtīs prōtegunt, *in hostem tēla* ūniversī
15   coniciunt *neque dant* regrediendī facultātem. Trānsfīgitur
scūtum Pullōnī *et* verūtum *in* balteō dēfīgitur. Āvertit *hic*
cāsus vāgīnam *et* gladium ēdūcere cōnantī dextram morātur
manum, impedītum*que hostēs* circumsistunt.

āvert•ō, -ere, -ī, āversum, [ab + vertō,
  turn], turn away from *or* away; repulse.
balte•us, -ī, *m.*, sword belt.
cās•us, -ūs, *m.* [cadō, fall], accident,
  chance, misfortune.
circum•sistō, -sistere, -stitī, —[sistō,
  stand], surround.
con•iciō, -icere, -iēcī, -iectum [co + iaciō,
  throw. App. §7], hurl, throw, cast.
cōnor, 1, try, attempt.
dē•fīgō, -fīgere, -fīxī, -fīxum [fīgō, fix],
  fix *or* fasten down, drive in, plant.
dext•er, -ra, -rum, *adj.*, on the right, right.
ē•dūcō, -dūcere, -dūxī, -ductum [dūcō,
  lead], lead out, lead forth; draw (*a sword*).
ex•animō, 1 [anima, breath], deprive of
  breath, render breathless, exhaust; kill.
facul•tās, -tātis, *f.* [facilis, easy], power;
  opportunity; resources.
glad•ius, -ī, *m.*, sword.
im•mittō, -mittere, -mīsī, -missum [mittō,
  send], direct toward *or* against.
impediō, 4 [in + pēs, foot], obstruct,
  hinder, delay.
mediocr•is, -e, *adj.* [medius, middle of],
  ordinary, moderate, average.

moror, 1 [mora, a delay], delay, hinder;
  linger, hang back.
per•cutiō, -cutere, -cutī, -cussum, strike
  or thrust through, slay, kill.
pīl•um, -ī, *n.*, heavy javelin, pike.
pro•currō, -currere, -currī, -cursum
  [currō, run], run forward, charge.
prō•tegō, -tegere, -tēxī, -tēctum [tegō,
  cover], cover, protect.
Pull•ō, -ōnis, *m.*, Titus Pullo, *a centurion in*
  Caesar's army.
re•gredior, -gredī, -gressus sum [gradior,
  step], withdraw, retire, retreat.
scūt•um, -ī, *n.*, shield, buckler.
spat•ium, -ī, *n.*, space, distance; period *or*
  length *of time.*
tra•iciō, -icere, -iēcī, -iectum [iaciō,
  throw. App. §7], hurl across; pierce.
trāns•fīgō, -fīgere, -fīxī, -fīxum [fīgō, fix],
  thrust *or* pierce through; transfix.
ūnivers•us, -a, -um, *adj.* [ūnus, one +
  vertō, turn], all together, whole.
vāgīn•a, -ae, *f.*, sheath, scabbard.
verūt•um, -ī, *n.*, dart, spear, javelin.

---

12. spatiō relictō: abl. absolute.

13. prōcurrentem: "who was running forward"; see App. §205.

13–14. quō percussō et exanimātō = *et*
eō, etc.; *conjunctio relativa* (App. §173, *a*) in
an abl. absolute (App. §150).

14. prōtegunt: the Nervii protect their
wounded comrade with their shields.

in hostem . . . ūniversī = **in hostem**
Pullōnem . . . **ūniversī** *Nerviī.* One must pay
attention to number (sing. = Pullo and pl. =
Nervii) as well as to context to sort out who
is doing what to whom. Note how the point of

view shifts, depending on who is the subject.
The pl. **hostēs** referred to the Nervii, but the
sing. **hostem** refers to Pullo.

16. Pullōnī: dat. of reference; see App.
§117.

17. cōnantī: "for him as he was attempting"; the part., which is dat. of reference (App.
§117), takes the place of a rel. clause (App.
§205). It is impossible to translate both literally and elegantly. We would be more likely to
say "(this accident) hinders *his* right hand *as*
he attempts, etc."

18. impedītum: "the entangled (man)."

Succurrit inimīcus *illī* Vorēnus *et* labōrantī subvenit. *Ad hunc*
20   *sē* cōnfestim *ā* Pullōne *omnis multitūdō* convertit: *illum* verūtō
arbitrantur occīsum. Gladiō comminus *rem gerit* Vorēnus *atque*
ūnō interfectō reliquōs paulum prōpellit; *dum* cupidius īnstat,
in locum dēiectus īnferiōrem concidit. *Huic* rūrsus *circumventō*
fert subsidium Pullō, *atque* ambō incolumēs complūribus
25   *interfectīs summā cum* laude *sēsē* intrā mūnītiōnēs *recipiunt.*

---

amb•ō, -ae, -a, *adj.,* both.
comminus, *adv.* [**manus,** hand], hand to
   hand, in close combat.
complūr•ēs, -a, *adj.* [**plūs,** more], several,
   many; a great many.
con•cīdō, -ere, -cīdī, —, [**cadō,** fall], fall
   down, fall.
cōnfestim, *adv.,* hastily, at once,
   immediately.
con•vertō, -vertere, -vertī, -versum
   [**verto,** turn], turn completely, turn
   around; turn, change.
cupid•us, -a, -um, *adj.* [**cupiō,** desire],
   eager, desirous.
dē•iciō, -icere, -iēcī, -iectum [**iaciō,** throw.
   App. §7], cast down; dislodge; kill;
   disappoint.
glad•ius, -ī, *m.,* sword.
incolum•is, -e, *adj.,* unhurt, uninjured.
īnfer•us, -a, -um, *adj.,* low, below; *comp.*:
   īnferior, lower, inferior.
inimīc•us, -a, -um, *adj.* [**in + amīcus,**
   friendly], unfriendly, hostile.
īn•stō, -stāre, -stitī, -statum [**stō,** stand],
   stand upon *or* near, be at hand, press on;
   threaten.
intrā, *prep. with acc.* [**inter,** between],
   within, inside, into.

labōrō, 1 [**labor,** toil], work hard; be
   troubled; labor, hard pressed.
laus, laudis, *f.,* praise, commendation;
   renown, popularity, glory.
mūnīti•ō, -ōnis, *f.* [**mūniō,** fortify],
   fortifying; fortification, rampart, works,
   entrenchments.
oc•cīdō, -cīdere, -cīsī, -cīsum [**caedō,** cut],
   cut down, kill.
paulum, *adv.* [**paulus,** little], a little,
   somewhat, slightly.
prō•pellō, -pellere, -pulī, -pulsum [**pellō,**
   drive], put to flight, rout; drive back.
Pull•ō, -ōnis, *m.,* Titus Pullo, *a centurion*
   in Caesar's army in the legion commanded
   by Cicero.
rūrsus, *adv.* [*for* **reversus,** *from* **revertō,**
   turn back], again, back, anew; in turn.
subsid•ium, -ī, *n.* [**subsideō,** sit near *or* in
   reserve], reserve force; help.
sub•veniō, -venīre, -vēnī, -ventum [**veniō,**
   come], come *or* go to help, aid, succor.
suc•currō, -currere, -cursī, -cursum
   [**currō,** run], run to help, aid, assist.
verūt•um, -ī, *n.,* dart, spear, javelin.
Vorēn•us, -ī, *m.,* Lucius Vorenus, *a*
   centurion in Caesar's army in the legion
   commanded by Cicero.

---

19. inimīcus illī Vorēnus et labōrantī
(i.e., *Pullōnī*): note the INTERLOCKED WORD
ORDER. Caesar constructs even simple sentences artfully.

   illī . . . et labōrantī: dat. indirect objects
of compound verbs; see App. §116.

   hunc = *Vorēnum.*

   20. illum = *Pullōnem.*

   21. occīsum: perf. active inf. (with *esse*) omitted in indirect statement after **arbitrantur.**

   rem gerit: "he carries on the fight."

   22. ūnō (*ex Nerviīs*) **interfectō:** abl. absolute; see App. §150.

   23. Huic . . . circumventō: "to the one (i.e.,
Vorenus) . . . who had been surrounded"; see
App. §205 on the use of the part. in place of
a rel. clause.

   24–25. complūribus interfectīs: abl. absolute; see App. §150.

   25. summā cum laude: abl. of manner; see
App. §142.

Sīc fortūna *in* contentiōne *et* certāmine *utrumque* versāvit, *ut*
alter alterī inimīcus auxiliō *salūtīque esset, neque* dīiūdicārī
posset, uter utrī virtūte anteferendus *vidērētur.*

---

ante•ferō, -ferre, -tulī, -lātum [**ferō,** carry.
App. §81], carry *or* bear before; prefer.
auxil•ium, -ī, *n.* [**augeō,** increase], help,
assistance, aid; *pl.,* auxiliary troops;
reinforcements.
certām•en, -inis, *n.* [**certō,** struggle], strife,
struggle, contest, combat.
contenti•ō, -ōnis, *f.* [**contendō,** strive],
striving, struggle, contest, dispute.
dīiūdicō, 1 [**iūdicō,** judge], decide.
fortūn•a, -ae, *f.* [**fors,** chance], fortune,
chance, opportunity, condition; success,
property.

inimīc•us, -a, -um, *adj.* [**in + amīcus,**
friendly], unfriendly, hostile; *as a noun*:
personal enemy, rival; *as opposed to*
hostis, *public* enemy.
sīc, *adv.,* so, thus, in this manner; **sīc . . . ut,**
so . . . that; so . . . as.
versō, 1, turn; deal with; *pass. as deponent,*
turn oneself; be, remain; engage in;
fight.

---

26. fortūna: Caesar perhaps elevates the
status of the event almost to a miracle by in-
voking *Fortūna,* one of his special goddesses
(or religious forces).

26–27. ut . . . esset: subjunctive in a substantive clause of result or fact; see App. §229.

27. alterī: dat. of reference; see App. §120.
Each was an enemy or rival "to the other," but
each also served as a help and deliverance "for
the other" (see the next note for the rest of this
"double dative" construction). The thought
is quite compressed in this phrase and in the
phrases that follow.

auxiliō salūtīque: datives of purpose; see
App. §119.

28. posset: the impers. subject is unexpressed. You may supply *id.*

uter . . . vidērētur: subjunctive in an indirect question; see App. §264.

utrī: dat. of reference; see App. §120.

virtūte: abl. of respect; see App. §149.

anteferendus: complementary pass. periphrastic inf. (without *esse*) with **vidērētur.**

[5.45] *Quantō erat in diēs gravior atque* asperior *oppugnātiō,
et* maximē *quod magnā parte* mīlitum cōnfectā vulneribus
rēs ad paucitātem dēfēnsōrum *pervēnerat, tantō* crēbriōrēs
litterae nūntiīque ad Caesarem mittēbantur; *quōrum pars*
5   dēprehēnsa in cōnspectū nostrōrum mīlitum cum cruciātū
necābātur. *Erat ūnus* intus *Nervius* nōmine Verticō, *locō* nātus
honestō, *quī ā prīmā* obsidiōne *ad Cicerōnem* perfūgerat
suamque eī fidem praestiterat.

---

asp•er, -era, -erum, *adj.,* rough, violent.

cōn•ficiō, -ficere, -fēcī, -fectum [faciō,
make], make *or* do thoroughly, complete,
finish; exhaust, weaken.

cōnspect•us, -ūs, *m.* [cōnspiciō, look at],
sight, view; presence.

crēb•er, -ra, -rum, *adj.,* thick, close,
repeated, numerous, frequent, at short
intervals. *Comp.:* **crēbrior;** *superl.:*
crēberrimus (App. §40).

cruciāt•us, -ūs, *m.* [cruciō, torture; **crux,**
cross *(used for crucifixion)*], torture,
torment.

dēfēnsor, -is, *m.* [dēfendō, defend],
defender, protector; *(means of)* defense.

**dē•prehendō, -prehendere, -prehendī,
-prehēnsum** [prehendō (= prendō),
seize], seize, capture, catch.

fid•ēs, -eī, *f.* [fīdō, confide], faith;
trustworthiness; allegiance, protection;
pledge.

honest•us, -a, -um, *adj.* [honōs, honor],
honorable, worthy, distinguished,
eminent.

intus, *adv.,* within, on the inside.

magis, *adv. comp.* [from **magnus,** large],
more, rather; *superl.:* **maximē,** especially.

nāscor, nāscī, nātus sum, be born, be
produced; rise, spring up, be raised; be
found.

necō, 1 [**nex,** death], put to death, kill,
murder.

nōm•en, -inis, *n.,* name, title; reputation,
prestige; **nōmine** *with gen.,* in the name
of, as; **suō nōmine,** on his *or* their own
account, personally.

nūntius, -ī, *m.,* messenger; message, news,
report.

obsidi•ō, -ōnis, *f.* [obsideō, blockade],
siege, investment, blockade; peril,
oppression.

pauci•tās, -tātis, *f.* [paucus, few], fewness,
small number.

per•fugiō, -fugere, -fūgī, -fugitum [fugiō,
flee], flee for refuge, take refuge; desert.

prae•stō, -stāre, -stitī, -stātum [stō,
stand], stand *or* place before; show,
exhibit, supply; be superior, excel,
surpass.

Vertic•ō, -ōnis, *m.,* Vertico, *a high-ranking
Nervian.*

vuln•us, -eris, *n.,* a wound.

**1–3. Quantō . . . gravior atque asperior
oppugnātiō . . . tantō crēbriōrēs:** "The
heavier and the more violent the assault . . .
the more frequent(ly)," etc.

2. maximē quod: "especially inasmuch as"
or "because."

parte . . . cōnfectā: abl. absolute; see App.
§150.

3. rēs: "the situation."

4. quōrum = *et eōrum* (*nūntiōrum*); *conjunctio relativa*; see App. §173, *a.*

5. dēprehēnsa: "who had been captured";
on the use of part. in place of rel. clauses, see
App. §205.

6. locō: abl. of source; see App. §135.

Hic servō *spē* lībertātis *magnīsque persuādet* praemiīs, *ut litterās*
10   *ad Caesarem* dēferat. *Hās ille in* iaculō illigātās effert *et Gallus*
inter Gallōs sine ūllā suspīciōne versātus *ad Caesarem pervenit.*
Ab eō dē perīculīs Cicerōnis legiōnisque cognōscitur.

---

dē•ferō, -ferre, -tulī, -lātum [ferō, carry.
App. §81], carry, take; report; bring
before; bestow.
efferō, efferre, extulī, ēlātum [ex + ferō,
carry. App. §81], carry out *or* away; raise;
make known; elate.
iacul•um, -ī, *n.* [iaciō, throw], javelin,
spear, dart.
illigō, 1 [ligō, bind], attach, hold together,
bind together.
liber•tās, -tātis, *f.* [līber, free], freedom,
liberty, independence.

praem•ium, -ī, *n.*, distinction, prize,
reward.
serv•us, -ī, *m.*, slave, servant.
suspīci•ō, -ōnis, *f.* [suspicor, suspect],
suspicion, distrust; surmise.
ūll•us, -a, -um *gen.* **ūllīus** (App. §32), *adj.*, a
single, any.
versō, 1, turn; deal with; *pass. as deponent,*
conduct oneself.

---

9. Hic = *Verticō,* a high-ranking Nervian.
servō: dat. indirect object of an intransitive verb; see App. §115.
9–10. ut . . . dēferat: volitive subjunctive
in a substantive clause of purpose (or indirect
command); see App. §228.
10. Hās = *litterās.*

illigātās: how was the letter bound to the
spear? Scholars have various theories that include splitting the wood and wrapping twine
around the letter.
ille = *servus.*
12. eō = *servō.*

[5.46] *Caesar acceptīs litterīs* hōrā *circiter* XI *diēī* statim nūntium *in* Bellovacōs *ad* Marcum Crassum quaestōrem *mittit, cuius* hīberna aberant *ab eō mīlia passuum* XXV; *iubet* mediā *nocte* legiōnem proficīscī celeriter*que ad sē* venīre. Exit *cum* nūntiō

5   Crassus. *Alterum ad* Gāium Fabium *lēgātum mittit, ut in* Atrebātium *fīnēs* legiōnem *addūcat, quā sibi iter faciendum* sciēbat.

---

absum, abesse, āfuī, — [**sum,** be. App. §78], be away, be distant, be lacking.

ad•dūcō, -dūcere, -dūxī, -ductum [**dūcō,** lead], lead to; induce, influence.

Atre•bās, -bātis, *m.,* an Atrebatian; *pl.,* the Atrebates.

Bellovac•ī, -ōrum, *m.,* the Bellovaci (*a Belgic people*).

celeriter, *adv.* [**celer,** swift], quickly, rapidly, speedily. *Comp.:* **celerius;** *superl.:* **celerrimē** (App. §40).

Crassus, -i, *m.,* Marcus Licinius Crassus, *son of Caesar's powerful ally, served as one of Caesar's quaestors after his brother Publius left Gaul.*

ex•eō, -īre, -iī, -itum [**eō,** go. App. §84], go from, leave.

Gā•ius, -ī, *m.;* **Fab•ius, -ī,** *m.,* Gaius Fabius, *one of Caesar's lieutenants.*

hōr•a, -ae, *f.,* hour.

Marc•us, -ī, *m.;* **Crassus, -ī,** *m.,* Marcus Licinius Crassus, *son of Caesar's powerful ally, served as one of Caesar's quaestors after his brother Publius left Gaul.*

medi•us, -a, -um, *adj.,* in the middle of; in the middle, intervening, intermediate; **locus medius utrīusque,** a place midway between the two.

nūntius, -ī, *m.,* messenger; message, news, report.

quaest•or, -ōris, *m.* [**quaerō,** seek], a quaestor, officer (for finances).

sciō, 4, distinguish; know, understand.

statim, *adv.* [**stō,** stand], immediately.

veniō, venīre, vēnī, ventum, come, arrive, go, advance.

XI, *sign for* **ūndecim,** eleven (*for ord. and distributive numbers, see* App. §47).

XXV, *sign for* **quīnque et vīgintī,** twenty-five (*see also* App. §47).

---

1. acceptīs litterīs: abl. absolute; see App. §150.

statim: note how Caesar depicts his actions. He had been unaware of the troubles. As soon as he finds out, he "immediately" acts.

XI = *ūndecimā;* because daylight was divided into twelve hours, the eleventh hour of the day would be late afternoon, about an hour before sunset. Remember too that it was already fall, so the sun would set early.

3. ab eō = *ab eō locō.*

mediā nocte: a midnight departure underscores Caesar's decisiveness.

4. celeriter: again, Caesar emphasizes the speed with which he acts.

cum nūntiō: i.e., "as soon as he got the message."

5. Alterum = *alterum nūntium.*

mittit: Caesar is once again the subject.

5–6. ut . . . addūcat: volitive subjunctive in a substantive clause of purpose (or indirect command); see App. §228.

6. sibi = *Caesarī;* dat. of agent; see App. §118.

faciendum: pass. periphrastic inf. (without *esse*) in indirect speech dependent on **sciēbat.** Caesar ordered Fabius to bring his legion to the area where he (Caesar) also had to go.

Scrībit Labiēnō, *sī reī pūblicae* commodō *facere posset, cum*
legiōne ad fīnēs Nerviōrum veniat. *Reliquam partem exercitūs,*
10   *quod* paulō aberat *longius, nōn* putat exspectandam; *equitēs*
circiter quadringentōs *ex proximīs hībernīs* colligit.

---

absum, abesse, āfuī, — [**sum,** be. App.
§78], be away, be distant, be lacking.
colligō, 1 [**conv + ligō,** bind], bind *or* fasten
together.
commod•um, -ī, *n.* [**commodus,**
convenient], convenience, interest,
advantage.
exspectō, 1 [**spectō,** look at], look out for,
await, expect; wait to see; anticipate,
apprehend.
Labiēn•us, -ī, *m.,* Titus Atius Labienus,

Caesar's most trusted lieutenant in the
Gallic War. During the Civil War, Labienus
fought on Pompey's side, and died in battle
against Caesar in Munda (in Spain) in 45
BCE.
paulō, *adv.* [**paulus,** little], a little,
somewhat, slightly.
putō, 1, think, consider, believe.
quadringent•ī, -ae, -a, *card. num. adj.,* four
hundred.
scrībō, scrībere, scrīpsī, scrīptum, write,
record *or* make mention *in writing.*

veniō, venīre, vēnī, ventum, come, arrive, go, advance.

---

8. reī pūblicae: dat. of reference; see App.
§120 and see the next note for the second part
of this "double dative" construction.

   commodō: dat. of purpose; see App. §119.
In other words, "if he was be able to act for the
benefit of the Republic, he should," etc.

   8–9. Scrībit ... sī ... posset, ... veniat: in
indirect speech, the verb of an if-clause (protasis) becomes subjunctive, but the conclusion
(apodosis) is represented with an acc. and
inf. construction (App. §272). We find after
scrībit, however, a subjunctive (*veniat*) in what
might have been the conclusion. This means

that, in direct speech, Caesar had instead
used an imperative, as commands are represented by the subjunctive in indirect speech.
In direct speech, Caesar would thus have
written: *sī ... poteris* (Latin uses the future
tense), ... *venī!* i.e., "if ... you can (English
uses the pres. tense), ... come!" In indirect
speech, this becomes, "he writes that, if ...
he could, ... he should come."

   10. exspectandam: pass. periphrastic inf.
(without *esse*) in indirect statement after **putat.** Caesar has in this paragraph assembled
his forces. See the map on p. 80 for the loca-
tions of the various winter camps.

[5.47] Hōrā *circiter tertiā ab* antecursōribus *dē* Crassī
adventū certior factus eō diē mīlia passuum XX prōcēdit.
Crassum Samarobrīvae praeficit *legiōnemque* attribuit,
quod ibi impedīmenta *exercitūs,* obsidēs *cīvitātum, litterās*
5   *pūblicās frūmentumque omne quod eō* tolerandae hiemis *causā*
dēvexerat *relinquēbat.* Fabius, *ut* imperātum *erat, nōn ita*
multum morātus *in itinere cum legiōne* occurrit.

---

antecurs•or, -ōris, *m.,* [**currō,** run],
    forerunner; *pl.,* vanguard, advance guard.
at•tribuō, -tribuere, -tribuī, -tribūtum
    [**ad** + **tribuō,** assign], assign, allot.
Crass•us, -ī, *m.,* Marcus Licinius Crassus,
    one of Caesar's officers.
dē•vehō, -vehere, -vexī, -vectum [**vehō,**
    carry], carry away, bring.
Fab•ius, -ī, *m.* Gaius Fabius, *one of Caesar's*
    lieutenants.
hiem•s, -is, *f.,* wintertime, winter.
hōr•a, -ae, *f.,* hour.
ibi, *adv.,* there, in that place.
impedīment•um, -ī, *n.* [**impediō,** hinder];
    pl.: baggage, baggage train (*including pack*
    animals).

imperō, 1 order, instruct.
moror, 1 [**mora,** a delay], delay, hinder;
    linger, hang back.
ob•ses, -idis, *m. and f.* [**obsideō,** blockade],
    hostage; pledge, security.
oc•currō, -currere, -currī, -cursum [**ob**
    + **currō,** run], meet; come to.
prae•ficiō, -ficere, -fēcī, -fectum [**faciō,**
    make], make before; put in command of.
prō•cēdō, -cēdere, -cessī, -cessum [**cēdō,**
    go], proceed, advance.
Samarobrīv•a, -ae, *f., the city* Samarobriva.
tolerō, 1, bear, endure; hold out.
XX, *sign for* **vīgintī,** twenty.

---

1. Hōrā . . . tertiā: as Romans divided daylight into twelve hours, the third hour would be halfway between dawn and noon, hence midmorning. Note too that Caesar says "approximately" (*circiter*). The measurement of time was not an exact science.

2. certior factus: "having been informed"; modifying the unexpressed subject of the verb **prōcēdit** —and hero of the story—Gaius Julius Caesar.

3. praeficit: do not forget that Caesar remains the unexpressed subject of this verb as well as the ones that follow. Caesar also continues to use the historical pres. as a rhetorical means to help his readers feel that they are eyewitnesses to Caesar's decisive actions.

4. impedīmenta: Caesar prudently stashes his army's baggage at Samarobriva. The alert reader will compare the actions of Titurius Sabinus's army.

obsidēs cīvitātum: "hostages from the (Gallic) tribes." Caesar collected the relatives

of the leaders of the various tribes he conquered. Their continued safety depended on the good behavior of Gallic leaders back home. Caesar does not describe such unpleasantries, but he was ruthless in inflicting punishments when he felt a show of force was necessary to restore or maintain obedience.

4–5. litterās pūblicās: "official papers." No army wants its correspondence, records, plans, etc., to fall into enemy hands.

5. eō: "to that place."

tolerandae . . . causā: gerundive construction to express purpose; see App. §289.

6. ut imperātum: Caesar reminds us that his subordinate acted according to Caesar's instructions. Caesar is in control.

6–7. nōn ita multum morātus: "thus having delayed not much," i.e., with very little delay.

7. occurrit: but whom did Fabius meet? Caesar, of course, who leaves his name out, thus emphasizing his unspoken presence.

Labiēnus interitū Sabīnī *et* caede *cohortium cognitā, cum omnēs*
ad eum Trēverōrum *cōpiae* vēnissent, veritus *nē, sī ex hībernīs*
10   fugae similem profectiōnem *fēcisset, hostium* impetum *sustinēre*
nōn posset, praesertim *quōs* recentī *victōriā* efferrī scīret, *litterās*
Caesarī remittit, *quantō cum perīculō legiōnem ex hībernīs*
ēductūrus *esset; rem gestam in* Eburōnibus perscrībit; docet
omnēs equitātūs peditātūs*que cōpiās* Trēverōrum *tria mīlia*
15   *passuum longē ab suīs castrīs* cōnsēdisse.

---

caed•ēs, -is, *f.* [**caedō,** cut], slaughter,
   massacre, murder.
cōn•sīdō, -sīdere, -sēdī, -sessum [**sīdō,** sit
   down], take a position.
doceō, docēre, docuī, docitum, show,
   teach, instruct, inform.
ē•dūcō, -dūcere, -dūxī, -ductum [**dūcō,**
   lead], lead out, lead forth; draw (*a sword*).
Eburōn•ēs, -um, *m.,* the Eburones.
efferō, efferre, extulī, ēlātum [**ex + ferō**];
   raise; make known; elate.
fug•a, -ae, *f.,* flight.
impet•us, -ūs, *m.,* attack; force, vehemence.
interit•us, -ūs, *m.,* destruction, death.
Labiēn•us, -ī, *m.,* Titus Atius Labienus,
   Caesar's most trusted lieutenant.
peditāt•us, -ūs, *m.* [**pedes,** foot soldier],
   foot soldiers, infantry.

per•scrībō, -scrībere, -scrīpsī, -scrīptum
   [**scrībō,** write], write out, report.
praesertim, *adv.,* particularly, especially.
profecti•ō, -ōnis, *f.,* a setting out;
   departure.
rec•ēns, -entis, *adj.,* recent, late.
re•mittō, -mittere, -mīsī, -missum, send
   back, return.
Sabīn•us, -ī, *m.,* Quintus Titurius Sabinus,
   one of Caesar's lieutenants.
sciō, 4, distinguish; know, understand.
simil•is, -e, *adj.,* like, similar.
Trev•ir, -erī, *m., pl.* **Treverī,** the Treveri.
veniō, venīre, vēnī, ventum, come, arrive,
   go, advance.
vereor, verērī, veritus sum, revere; fear,
   dread, be afraid of.

---

8. interitū . . . cognitā: abl. absolute.

8–13. Labiēnus . . . litterās Caesarī re-
mittit . . . : this simple statement represents
the first principal clause. What comes between Labienus and **remittit** represents the
background to the letter he sends to Caesar.
What follows the verb represents what Labienus described in his letter. Two more indicative verbs (**perscrībit** and **docet**) will help
elaborate the letter's contents.

9–10. sī . . . fēcisset: "if he had made," etc.,
plupf. subjunctive in implied indirect statement that represents an original fut. perf. in a
future more vivid condition (i.e., "if we (will
have) set out, we will not be able to sustain the
attack," etc.—this is the fear); see App. §256.

9–11. veritus nē . . . nōn posset: "afraid
that . . . he would not be able"; subjunctive in
a fear clause; see App. §228, *b.* Labienus, Caesar's best lieutenant, experiences legitimate

fear based on careful assessment of the military situation.

11. praesertim quōs = *praesertim eōrum*
hostium quōs. As Latin inflection makes it clear
that **quōs** refers to **hostium,** Caesar does not
need to supply an antecedent that readers can
infer from context. **quōs** itself serves as the acc.
subject of the inf. **efferrī** in indirect speech dependent on **scīret.** To put it into English: "especially since he knew that they," etc.

12–13. quantō cum perīculō . . . esset:
abl. of manner (App. §142) and an indirect
question that depends on the speech implied
by sending a letter to Caesar, which informs
Caesar "how dangerous it would be for him,"
etc., or, more literally, "with what great danger
(to himself) he would," etc.

13. rem gestam: "what happened" (literally: "the thing done"), i.e., the loss of Sabinus
and Cotta's legion.

[5.48] *Caesar cōnsiliō eius* probātō, etsī opīniōne *trium legiōnum* dēiectus *ad duās* redierat, *tamen ūnum commūnis salūtis* auxilium *in celeritāte* pōnēbat. Venit *magnīs itineribus in Nerviōrum fīnēs.* Ibi *ex* captīvīs *cognōscit, quae apud*
5   *Cicerōnem gerantur, quantōque in perīculō rēs sit. Tum cuidam ex equitibus Gallīs magnīs* praemiīs *persuādet utī ad Cicerōnem* epistolam dēferat.

---

auxil•ium, -ī, *n.* [**augeō,** increase], help, assistance, aid; *pl.*, auxiliary troops; reinforcements.

captīv•us, -a, -um, *adj.* [**capiō,** take], prisoner, captive.

dē•ferō, -ferre, -tulī, -lātum [**ferō,** carry. App. §81], carry, take; report; bring before; bestow.

dē•iciō, -icere, -iēcī, -iectum [**iaciō,** throw. App. §7], disappoint.

epistol•a, -ae, *f.,* letter, epistle.

etsī, *conj.* [**et + sī,** if], even if, although.

ibi, *adv.,* there, in that place.

opīni•ō, -ōnis, *f.* [**opīnor,** think], way of thinking; expectation.

pōnō, pōnere, posuī, positum, place, put, place over; lay down, set aside; station, post; regard, consider; *with* **in** *and the abl.,* depend on.

praem•ium, -ī, *n.,* distinction, prize, reward.

probō, 1 [**probus,** good], approve; demonstrate.

red•eō, -īre, -iī, -itum [**red- + eō,** go. App. §84], go *or* turn back, return.

veniō, venīre, vēnī, ventum, come, arrive, go, advance.

---

1. cōnsiliō ... probātō: abl. absolute; see App. §150.

2–3. ūnum commūnis salūtis auxilium: CHIASMUS; see App. §302, *c.*

3. celeritāte: one of Caesar's signature qualities as a general.

itineribus: abl. of manner; see App. §142.

4–5. quae ... gerantur, quantōque ... sit: subjunctives in indirect questions; see App. §264.

6–7. utī ... dēferat: volitive subjunctive in a substantive clause of purpose (or indirect command) after **persuādet;** see App. §228, *a.*

7. epistolam: Caesar uses the Greek word for letter, perhaps because he writes the letter using the Greek alphabet or perhaps because he does not want to use the Latin word *litterae* twice in a row with two different meanings (letter of the alphabet versus epistle).

> *Hanc* Graecīs cōnscrīptam *litterīs mittit, nē* interceptā
> epistolā *nostra ab hostibus cōnsilia cognōscantur. Sī* adīre *nōn*
> 10　*possit,* monet *ut* trāgulam *cum* epistolā *ad* āmentum dēligātā
> intrā mūnītiōnem *castrōrum* abiciat. *In litterīs* scrībit *sē cum*
> *legiōnibus profectum* celeriter adfore; hortātur *ut* prīstinam
> *virtūtem* retineat. *Gallus perīculum* veritus, *ut erat* praeceptum,
> trāgulam *mittit.*

---

abic•iō, -ere, abiēcī, abiectum [iaciō,
　　throw. *See* App. §7.], throw away *or* down;
　　hurl.
ad•eō, -īre, iī, -itum [eō, go. App. §84], go
　　to, approach, visit, assail, attack.
adsum, adesse, adfuī [sum, be, App. §77],
　　be near, be present, be at hand, appear.
āment•um, -ī, *n.,* strap *or* thong, *fastened to
　　the shaft of a javelin to aid its propulsion.*
celeriter, *adv.* [celer, swift], quickly,
　　rapidly, speedily. *Comp.:* **celerius;** *superl.:*
　　celerrimē (App. §40).
cōn•scrībō, -scrībere, -scrīpsī, -scrīptum
　　[scrībō, write], enroll, enlist; write.
dēligō, 1 [ligō, bind], bind *or* tie down,
　　fasten, moor.
epistol•a, -ae, *f.,* letter, epistle.
Graec•us, -a, -um, *adj.,* of *or* belonging
　　to the Greeks, Greek; *pl. as noun:* the
　　Greeks.
hortor, 1, exhort, encourage, incite, urge
　　strongly.

inter•cipiō, -cipere, -cēpī, -ceptum [ad +
　　capiō, take], take *or* catch between (*one
　　point and another*); interrupt; intercept;
　　cut off.
intrā, *prep. with acc.* [inter, between],
　　within, inside, into.
moneō, 2, warn, advise, instruct, order.
mūnīti•ō, -ōnis, *f.* [mūniō, fortify],
　　fortifying; fortification, rampart, works,
　　entrenchments.
praecept•um, -ī, *n.* [praecipiō, instruct],
　　instruction, injunction, command.
prīstin•us, -a, -um, *adj.* [*from* prior,
　　former], former; previous.
re•tineō, -tinēre, -tinuī, -tentum [re +
　　teneō, hold], retain, preserve, maintain.
scrībō, scrībere, scrīpsī, scrīptum, write,
　　record *or* make mention *in writing.*
trāgul•a, -ae, *f.,* a javelin, spear, *or* dart *used
　　by the Gauls.*
vereor, verērī, veritus sum, revere; fear,
　　dread, be afraid of.

8–9. nē . . . cognōscantur: subjunctive in
a clause of (negative) purpose; see App. §255.
　　interceptā epistolā: abl. absolute equivalent to a condition; see App. §150.
　　10–11. ut . . . abiciat: volitive subjunctive
in a substantive clause of purpose (or indirect
command) after **monet**; see App. §228, *a.*

　　11. litterīs: Does Caesar return to the
Latin word for letter or does he refer to the
Greek letters with which he composed his
thoughts?
　　12. adfore: *fore* is an alternative form for
futurus esse, the fut. active inf. of *esse.*

15   *Haec* cāsū *ad turrim* adhaesit *neque ab nostrīs* bīduō
     animadversa *tertiō diē ā quōdam mīlite* cōnspicitur, dēmpta
     ad Cicerōnem dēfertur. *Ille* perlēctam *in* conventū *mīlitum*
     recitat *maximāque omnēs* laetitiā adficit. *Tum fūmī*
     incendiōrum procul *vidēbantur; quae rēs omnem* dubitātiōnem
20   *adventūs legiōnum* expulit.

---

ad•ficiō, -ficere, -fēcī, -fectum [**ad** + **faciō,**
do], affect, fill, inspire.
ad•haereō, -haerēre, -haesī, -haesum
[**haereō,** stick], cling to, stick to.
animad•vertō, -vertere, -vertī, -versum
[**animus,** mind + **ad** + **vertō,** turn], turn
the mind to; notice.
bīdu•um, -ī, *n.* [**bis,** twice + **diēs,** day],
space *or* period of two days.
cās•us, -ūs, *m.* [**cadō,** fall], accident,
chance, misfortune; **cāsū,** by chance.
cōn•spiciō, -spicere, -spexī, -spectum
[**speciō,** look], look at, discern, perceive.
convent•us, -ūs, *m.* [**conveniō,** come
together], a coming together, meeting,
assembly; court.
dē•ferō, -ferre, -tulī, -lātum [**ferō,** carry.
App. §81], carry, take; report; bring
before; bestow.

dēmō, dēmere, dēmpsī, dēmptum [**dē** +
emō, take], take down, remove.
dubitāti•ō, -ōnis, *f.* [**dubitō,** doubt], doubt,
uncertainty; hesitation.
ex•pellō, -pellere, -pulī, -pulsum [**pellō,**
drive], drive out, drive forth, expel.
fūm•us, -ī, *m.,* smoke.
incend•ium, -ī, *n.* [**incendō,** burn], fire,
burning, conflagration.
laetiti•a, -ae, *f.* [**laetus,** joyful], joy,
rejoicing.
per•legō, -legere, -lēgī, -lēctum [**legō,**
read], read through, read.
procul, *adv.,* far off, from afar, in the
distance, at a distance.
recitō, 1, read aloud.

---

15. Haec = *tragula.*
15–16. bīduō . . . tertiō diē: abl. of time;
see App. §152.
17. dēfertur: the last word of the sentence
dramatically delivers the first word of the next
sentence. See CLIMAX; App. § 302, *d.*

perlēctam: i.e., *epistolam.* Cicero reads the
letter aloud *after* he had himself read it. See
App. §283.

Subdued, but Not Broken

Caesar goes on to defeat the Nervii and secure the winter camps. He will soon face further unrest. The Gauls did not give up their freedom without a fight. Just how bitterly they fought for their liberty you may explore in the translation of Book Seven, which is included at the end of this volume.

C. IVLI CAESARIS
COMMENTARIORUM
DE BELLO GALLICO
LIBER SEXTUS

Caesar DĒ BELLŌ GALLICŌ 6.13–20:
Caesar Surveys the Enemy

In this selection Caesar describes the customs and the religious practices of the Gauls. To Romans at home, Gaul was remote, and Caesar satisfies the natural curiosity of his audience by describing both how the Gauls are like Romans and how Gauls differ from Romans. Smart generals also study their enemy, as it provides a tactical advantage to know how your enemy is likely to behave in a given situation. Caesar thus demonstrates his qualities of leadership through his ethnographical knowledge. But Caesar also demonstrates with this description of Gallic customs his literary knowledge of the traditions and genre of ethnography going back to Herodotus. He mentions Greek authors on the topic, and thus shows his erudition and wide learning. By any measure, Caesar's literary performance is, as usual, an excellent one that was sure to impress readers at home.

The Gauls' alleged practice of human sacrifice has captured the popular imagination through the ages. Caesar's description has yielded such creative reconstructions as this image of Gallic wicker work with human victims. The 1973 British film *Wickerman*, inspired by Caesar's chronicle of Druid life, has attracted a devoted cult following.

Caesar DĒ BELLŌ GALLICŌ 6.13–20:
Caesar Surveys the Enemy

[6.13] *In omnī* Galliā eōrum hominum, quī aliquō sunt numerō atque honōre, genera sunt duo. Nam plēbēs paene servōrum habētur locō, quae nihil audet per sē, nūllō adhibētur cōnsiliō. Plērīque, cum aut aere aliēnō aut magnitūdine

5   tribūtōrum aut iniūriā potentiōrum premuntur, sēsē in servitūtem dicant nōbilibus; quibus in hōs eadem omnia sunt iūra, quae dominīs in servōs.

---

adhib•eō, -ēre, -uī, -itum [**habeō,** have], bring to, bring in, summon; employ, use.

aes, aeris, *n.,* copper; *anything made of copper,* coin, money; **aes aliēnum,** *someone else's money:* debt.

aliēn•us, **-a, -um,** *adj.* [**alius,** other], of *or* belonging to another; unfavorable.

aud•eō, -ēre, ausus sum (App. §74), dare, risk, venture.

dīcō, 1 [**dīcō,** say], give over, surrender.

domin•us, -ī, *m.,* master.

Galli•a, -ae, *f.,* Gaul.

hon•ōs, -ōris, *m.,* honor, regard, glory, distinction; honorable position, office.

iniūri•a, -ae, *f.* [**in + iūs,** right], wrong; outrage, damage, violence.

iūs, iūris, *n.,* law, justice; authority.

magnitūd•ō, -inis, *f.* [**magnus,** large], large size.

nōbil•is, -e, *adj.* [**nōscō,** know], well-known; of noble birth, noble.

nūll•us, -a, -um, *adj.* [**ne- + ūllus,** any], not any, no.

paene, *adv.* nearly, almost.

plēbs, plēbis, *or* **plēbēs, plēbēī,** *f.,* populace, common people.

pot•ēns, -entis, *adj.* [*pres. part. of* **possum,** be able], powerful, influential.

servit•ūs, -ūtis, *f.* [**servus,** slave], slavery.

serv•us, -ī, *m.,* slave, servant.

tribūt•um, -ī, *n.* [**tribuō,** render, pay], tribute, tax.

1–2. aliquō ... numerō atque honōre: descriptive abl.; see App. §141. But what does it mean to be "of any number and distinction"? Think about what it means to have "some portion" of a quality. These are men who exist in "considerable" numbers and who enjoy "significant" status.

2. plēbēs: the "common people" likely outnumbered the groups Caesar will describe, but they lacked distinction and political importance (*honōs*).

3. servōrum ... locō: "as slaves"; abl. of respect or specification; see App. §149.

nūllō: an older dat. form of *nūllus.* Many editions change the reading to the standard dat. *nūllī,* but it is good to keep in mind that the linguistic world is not as regular as grammars sometimes lead students to believe.

4. aere aliēnō: "debt" was a problem for many Romans, even upper-class Romans.

Does Caesar suggest to readers at Rome that the situation for debtors at Rome is better than it is in Gaul?

5. iniūriā potentiōrum: "by the violence of the powerful." The Gauls did not have an organized police force, public prosecutors, or an impartial judicial system. The only protection from powerful men was the protection of a powerful man.

6. nōbilibus: the "nobles" are distinguished men because they command wealth and other men. Indebted commoners surrender themselves to them because slavery is apparently a more attractive option than debt, taxes, and violence.

quibus: dat. of possession; see App. §117.

in hōs = *in plēbēs.*

7. quae: Caesar has omitted the verb *sunt* from the rel. clause.

> *Sed dē hīs duōbus generibus alterum est* Druidum, *alterum*
> *equitum. Illī rēbus dīvīnīs* intersunt, sacrificia *pūblica ac*
> 10   prīvāta prōcūrant, religiōnēs interpretantur: *ad hōs magnus*
> adulēscentium *numerus* disciplīnae *causā* concurrit, *magnōque*
> *hī sunt apud eōs* honōre.

---

adulēsc•ēns, -entis, *m.* [*pres. part. of*
   adolēscō, grow up], youth, young man.
con•currō, -currere, -cursī, -cursum
   [**currō,** run], run *or* rush together; hurry,
   run, rush; run to the rescue; come, gather.
disciplīn•a, -ae, *f.* [**discō,** learn], learning,
   discipline; instruction, teaching; system.
dīvīn•us, -a, -um, *adj.* [**dīvus,** divine], of
   the gods, divine, sacred.
Druid•ēs, -um, *m.,* the Druids, *the priests of*
   the Celts in Gaul and Britain.
hon•ōs, -ōris, *m.,* honor, regard, glory,
   distinction; honorable position, office.

interpretor, 1 [**interpres,** interpreter],
   interpret, explain, settle, handle.
inter•sum, -esse, -fuī, — [**sum,** be. App.
   §66], be *or* lie between, intervene; be
   present *at*, take part *in*.
prīvāt•us, -a, -um, *adj.,* private, individual.
prōcūrō, 1 [**cūrō,** care], care for, attend to.
religi•ō, -ōnis, *f.,* religion; *in pl.,* religious
   ceremonies, rites; superstitions.
sacrific•ium, -ī, *n.* [**sacer,** sacred + **faciō,**
   make], (animal) sacrifice.

---

8. Druidum: "the class (*genus*) of Druids."
Caesar omits *genus*, which the reader can supply from **generibus.**

9. equitum: "the class (*genus*) of cavalry";
i.e., men who can afford a horse. The class is
both social and military, as Gauls, like Romans in earlier times (this was no longer the
case in Caesar's day), had to supply their own
military equipment.

Illī = "the former men," i.e., the Druids.

rēbus dīvīnīs: "divine matters"; i.e., all
rites, ceremonies, etc., pertaining to proper
worship of the gods.

10. religiōnēs: "religious issues"; hence pl.

11–12. magnō . . . honōre: descriptive
abl.; see App. §141.

12. hī = *Druidēs.*

eōs = *adulēscentēs,* of course, but also
Gallōs more generally.

Nam ferē dē omnibus contrōversiīs pūblicīs prīvātīsque
cōnstituunt, et, sī quod est admissum facinus, *sī* caedēs *facta,*
15   *sī dē* hērēditāte, *dē fīnibus contrōversia est, īdem* dēcernunt,
praemia poenās*que cōnstituunt; sī quī aut* prīvātus *aut populus*
eōrum dēcrētō *nōn* stetit, sacrificiīs interdīcunt. *Haec* poena
apud eōs est gravissima.

---

ad•mittō, -mittere, -mīsī, -missum [mittō, send], admit; commit; incur.

caed•ēs, -is, *f.* [caedō, cut], slaughter, massacre, murder.

dē•cernō, -cernere, -crēvī, -crētum [cernō, separate; decide], decide, vote, decree.

dēcrēt•um, -ī, *n.* [dēcernō, decide], decision, decree, order.

facin•us, -oris, *n.* [faciō, do], deed; misdeed, outrage, crime.

hērēdi•tās, -tātis, *f.* [hērēs, heir], inheritance.

inter•dīcō, -dīcere, -dīxī, -dictum [dīcō, say], prohibit, exclude, forbid, interdict; **aquā atque ignī interdīcere,** *forbid the use of fire and water,* exile, banish.

poen•a, -ae, *f.,* punishment, penalty.

praem•ium, -ī, *n.,* distinction, prize, reward.

prīvāt•us, -a, -um, *adj.,* private.

sacrific•ium, -ī, *n.* [sacer, sacred + faciō, make], sacrifice.

stō, stāre, stetī, statum, stand, abide by.

13–14. dē . . . contrōversiīs . . . cōnstituunt: the Druids served as judges of civil matters as well as religious matters. For this reason too, they enjoyed great power and prestige, and would subsequently attract the jealous attention of later Roman emperors who suppressed them (but this will take place well after Caesar's day).

14. quod = *aliquod;* see App. §174.

facta: Caesar omits *est.*

15. dē hērēditāte: crimes like murder may be more spectacular, but most law concerns property, and inheritance is a good example.

īdem: "the same men," i.e., the Druids. See App. §58.

16. quī: "any (litigant)"; i.e., "any(one)," who appears before the Druids for judgement. See App. §62.

aut prīvātus aut populus: "either an individual or an (entire) tribe."

17. dēcrētō: "(according to the terms of) the decree"; abl. of attendant circumstances; see App. §142, *b.*

sacrificiīs: from (*animal*) sacrifices (*and the associated communal meals, hence society*); abl. of separation; see App. §134.

18. eōs = *Gallōs.*

20

Quibus ita est interdictum, *hī numerō* impiōrum *ac* scelerātōrum
habentur, hīs omnēs dēcēdunt, aditum sermōnem*que* dēfugiunt,
nē quid ex contāgiōne incommodī *accipiant, neque hīs petentibus*
iūs redditur *neque* honōs ūllus commūnicātur. *Hīs autem
omnibus* Druidibus praeest *ūnus, quī summam inter eōs habet*
auctōritātem. *Hōc* mortuō *aut sī quī ex reliquīs* excellit dignitāte

25

succēdit, *aut, sī sunt plūrēs* parēs, suffrāgiō Druidum,

---

adit•us, -ūs, *m.* [**adeō,** go to], approach,
right to approach, access.

auctori•tās, -tātis, *f.* [**auctor,** producer],
influence, authority.

commūnicō, 1 [**commūnis,** common],
make common, communicate, share.

contāgi•ō, -ōnis, *f.* [**contingō,** touch],
contact.

dē•cēdō, -cēdere, -cessī, -cessum [**cēdō,**
go], go from *or* away, leave, forsake.

dē•fugiō, -fugere, -fūgī, -fugitum [**fugiō,**
flee], flee from, run away, shun.

digni•tās, -tātis, *f.* [**dignus,** worthy],
(*personal*) merit, status, rank.

Druid•ēs, -um, *m.,* the Druids, *the priests of
the Celts in Gaul and Britain.*

ex•cellō, -cellere, —, —, excel, surpass.

hon•ōs, -ōris, *m.,* honor, regard, glory,
distinction; honorable position, office.

impi•us, -a, -um, *adj.* [**in** + **pius,** loyal],
without reverence for gods, parents, country:
ungodly, disrespectful, unpatriotic.

incommod•um, -ī, *n.* [**incommodus,**
inconvenient], inconvenience,
disadvantage, trouble; loss, injury.

inter•dīcō, -dīcere, -dīxī, -dictum [**dīcō,**
say], prohibit, exclude, forbid, interdict;

aquā atque ignī interdīcere, *forbid the
use of fire and water,* exile, banish.

iūs, iūris, *n.,* (human) law, justice; rights.
Compare: **fās,** divine law.

morior, morī, mortuus sum [**mors,** death],
die.

pār, paris, *adj.,* equal, like, similar; equal
to, a match for; *with words of number and
quantity,* the same.

prae•sum, -esse, -fuī, — [**sum,** be. App.
§77], be before *or* over, be in command
of, rule over, be at the head of.

red•dō, -dere, -didī, -ditum [**red-** + **dō,**
give], give back, return, restore; give *or*
return *something due or owed;* make *or*
cause to be; render.

scelerāt•us, -a, -um, *adj.* [**scelerō,** pollute],
accursed, infamous; *as noun,* criminal.

serm•ō, -ōnis, *m.,* conversation, interview,
speech.

suc•cēdō, -cēdere, -cessī, -cessum [**cēdō,**
go], go *or* come under; come up to, come
up, advance, be next to; succeed, take the
place of.

suffrāg•ium, -ī, *n.,* vote, ballot.

ūll•us, -a, -um, *gen.* **ūllīus** (App. §32), *adj.,*
a single, any.

---

19. Quibus . . . hī: "Those, upon whom a
prohibition has been placed," etc. The rel. **quibus** has been placed before its antecedent **hī**
for emphasis and to facilitate the sequence of
thought from the previous sentence.

   numerō: "in the number," i.e., "among" or
"as"; abl. of respect; see App. §149.

   20. hīs: dat. of reference; see App. §120. In
other words, all people shun these men.

   21. nē . . . accipiant: subjunctive in a clause
of (negative) purpose; see App. §225, *b.*

   quid . . . incommodī = *aliquid incommodī;*
"any trouble"; see App. §174 and, for the partitive gen., §101.

   21–22. petentibus iūs: "when they seek
justice"; see App. §283.

   24. Hōc mortuō: abl. absolute; see App.
§150.

   quī = *aliquī;* see App. §174.

   dignitāte: abl. of respect; see App. §149.

   25. parēs: parēs *dignitāte.*

nōnnumquam *etiam armīs dē* prīncipātū contendunt. *Hī certō annī tempore in fīnibus* Carnutum, *quae* regiō *tōtīus Galliae* media *habētur,* cōnsīdunt *in locō* cōnsecrātō. Hūc *omnēs* undique, *quī contrōversiās habent, conveniunt eōrumque* dēcrētīs

30   iūdiciīs*que* pārent. Disciplīna *in Britanniā* reperta *atque* inde *in Galliam* trānslāta *esse exīstimātur, et* nunc, *quī* dīligentius *eam rem cognōscere volunt,* plērumque *illō* discendī *causā proficīscuntur.*

Carnut•ēs, -um, *m.,* the Carnutes (*a people in central Gaul*).

cōnsecrō, 1 [**sacrō,** dedicate], dedicate, consecrate.

cōn•sīdō, -sīdere, -sēdī, -sessum [**sīdō,** sit down], settle; take a position.

con•tendō, -tendere, -tendī, -tentum [**tendō,** stretch], push forward, hasten; march; strive, contend, fight; insist.

dēcrēt•um, -ī, *n.* [**dēcernō,** decide], decision, decree, order.

dīligenter, *adv.* [**dīligēns,** careful], carefully; with exactness, pains, *or* care.

disciplīn•a, -ae, *f.* [**discō,** learn], learning, discipline; instruction, teaching; system.

discō, discere, didicī, —, learn, be taught.

hūc, *adv.* [*from* **hic,** this], to this place, hither, here; against these, to these.

inde, *adv.,* from that place; then.

iūdic•ium, -ī, *n.* [**iūdex,** judge], judicial proceedings, trial; opinion, judgement; **iūdicium facere,** express an opinion; **iūdiciō,** by design, purposely.

medi•us, -a, -um, *adj.,* in the middle of; in the middle, intervening, intermediate; **locus medius utrīusque,** a place midway between the two.

nōnnumquam, *adv.* [**nōn + numquam,** never], sometimes.

nunc, *adv.,* now, at present, at this time.

pāreo, 2, appear; obey, yield to, be subject to.

plērumque, *adv.* [**plērusque,** the greater part], mostly, generally; very often.

prīncipāt•us, -ūs, *m.* [**prīnceps,** chief], chief place *or* position; leadership.

regi•ō, -ōnis, *f.* [**regō,** keep straight], line, direction; quarter, region, country, territory, place.

reperiō, reperīre, repperī, repertum [**re + pariō,** procure], procure, find out, discover, ascertain; devise.

trāns•ferō, -ferre, -tulī, -lātum [**ferō,** carry. App. §81], carry *or* bring over, transfer.

undique, *adv.* [**unde,** whence], on all sides, everywhere.

---

26. armīs: their use of weapons underlines how different the Druids were from what we might think when we hear the word "priest," and it is also interesting to consider in light of what Caesar says about Druids in the next section: they were exempt from military duties.

27. tempore: abl. of time; see App. §152.

quae regiō: "which region"; Caesar has placed the antecedent inside the rel. clause. One may also translate, "a region, which."

28. locō cōnsecrātō: the "consecrated spot" was probably a sacred grove.

32. eam rem: i.e., the *disciplīna* or religious system of the Druids.

illō: "to that place," i.e., Britain.

[6.14] Druidēs *ā bellō* abesse *cōnsuērunt neque* tribūta *ūnā cum reliquīs* pendunt; mīlitiae vacātiōnem *omniumque rērum habent* immūnitātem. *Tantīs* excitātī praemiīs *et suā* sponte *multī in* disciplīnam *conveniunt et ā* parentibus propinquīs*que*
5   *mittuntur. Magnum* ibi *numerum* versuum ēdiscere *dīcuntur. Itaque annōs* nōnnūllī vīcēnōs *in* disciplīnā permanent.

---

absum, abesse, āfuī, — [**sum,** be. App. §78], be away, be lacking *or* free from.

disciplīn•a, -ae, *f.* [**discō,** learn], learning, discipline; instruction, teaching; system.

Druid•ēs, -um, *m.,* the Druids, *the priests of the Celts in Gaul and Britain.*

ē•discō, -discere, -didicī, — [**discō,** learn], learn thoroughly, learn by heart.

excitō, 1 [**citō,** rouse], call forth, excite, animate, arouse; erect, construct (*towers*); kindle (*fires*).

ibi, *adv.,* there, in that place.

immūni•tās, -tātis, *f.* [**in** + **mūnis,** burden], freedom from public burdens, duties, *or* taxes; exemption.

mīliti•a, -ae, *f.* [**mīles,** soldier], military service, warfare.

nōnnūll•us, -a, -um, *adj.* [**nōn** + **nūllus,** none], some, several; *pl. as noun:* some, several.

parēn•s, -tis, *m., f.* [**pariō,** bring forth], parent.

pendō, pendere, pependī, pēnsum, weigh, weigh out; weigh out *money,* pay, pay out; *with* **poenās,** suffer.

per•maneō, -manēre, -mānsī, -mānsum [**maneō,** remain], stay through *or* to the end, stay, remain; continue, persist.

praem•ium, -ī, *n.,* distinction, prize, reward.

propinqu•us, -a, -um, *adj.* [**prope,** near], near, neighboring, close at hand; *pl. as noun,* relatives.

spontis, *gen. and* **sponte,** *abl.* (*obs. nom.* **spōns**), *f.,* of one's own accord, willingly.

tribūt•um, -ī, *n.* [**tribuō,** render, pay], tribute, tax.

vacāti•ō, -ōnis, *f.* [**vacō,** be empty], exemption.

vers•us, -ūs, *m.* [**vertō,** turn], turning, verse, poetry.

vīcēn•ī, -ae, -a, *distributive num. adj.* [**vīgintī,** twenty], twenty each, twenty.

---

1. cōnsuērunt = *consuēvērunt;* see App. §72. Caesar uses this perf. tense verb with a pres. meaning; see App. §193, I, *a.*

3. Tantīs . . . praemiīs: "such great rewards": on the one hand, exemption from military duty, no taxes, no other public duties, and, on the other hand, considerable judicial and religious authority.

5. versuum: it is easier to memorize metrical texts. Sacred texts also frequently employ meter as a means to elevate the language.

6. annōs . . . vīcēnōs: acc. of time (see App. §130), and, in this instance, a long time. Perhaps the length of time required and the nature of one's studies (memorizing verses) dissuaded some students, despite the other advantages. On the other hand, one can see why family members were eager to have a Druid in the family!

Neque fās *esse exīstimant ea litterīs* mandāre, *cum in reliquīs ferē rēbus, pūblicīs* prīvātīs*que* ratiōnibus, Graecīs *litterīs ūtantur. Id* mihi *duābus dē causīs* īnstituisse *videntur, quod neque*
10   *in* vulgum disciplīnam efferrī *velint neque eōs, quī* discunt, *litterīs* cōnfīsōs *minus* memoriae studēre: *quod ferē plērīsque accidit, ut* praesidiō *litterārum* dīligentiam *in* perdiscendō *ac* memoriam remittant.

---

cōn•fīdō, -fīdere, -fīsī, -fīsum [fīdō, trust], rely on, feel confident; cōnfīsus, *perf. part. with pres. meaning:* relying on.

diligenti•a, -ae, *f.*, painstaking care.

disciplīn•a, -ae, *f.* [discō, learn], learning, discipline; instruction, teaching; system.

discō, discere, didicī, —, learn, be taught.

efferō, efferre, extulī, ēlātum [ex + ferō], carry away; raise; make known; elate.

egō, meī (App. §51), I, me; *pl.* nōs, we.

fās, *n., indeclin.*, divine law, religiously correct, right, proper, permissable. *Compare:* iūs, human law.

Graec•us, -a, -um, *adj.*, Greek.

īn•stituō, -stituere, -stituī, -stitūtum [statuō, set up], draw up; train; begin, decide upon, adopt.

mandō, 1 [manus, hand], entrust, commit; command.

memori•a, -ae, *f.* [memor, mindful], the faculty of memory; memory.

per•discō, -discere, -didicī, — [discō, learn], learn thoroughly, learn by heart.

praesid•ium, -ī, *n.* [praesideō, guard], protection; fortification; help, aid; safety.

prīvāt•us, -a, -um, *adj.*, private.

rati•ō, -ōnis, *f.*, [reor, reckon], reckoning, account; arrangement; state of affairs; *in pl.*, transactions.

re•mittō, -mittere, -mīsī, -missum [mittō], send back, return; release, give up.

stude•ō, -ēre, -uī, —, be eager; strive after, devote oneself to; accustom oneself to.

vulg•us, -ī, *n.*, the common people.

---

7. ea: "these things"; i.e., the subject matter of their studies.

7–8. cum . . . ūtantur: subjunctive in a concessive clause; see App. §§238–239.

8. Graecīs litterīs: abl. with the special deponent verb *ūtor*; see App. §145. The Gauls used the Greek alphabet to represent their own language. Eventually, they would adopt Roman letters and the Latin language.

9. mihi: Caesar speaks to us as an author, hence his use of the first person. When he describes his role in the action of an event, he uses the third person.

9–10. quod . . . velint: Caesar uses the subjunctive because he is presenting someone else's explanation; see App. §244. The implied subjects of velint are the *Druidēs*.

10. eōs: acc. subject of the complementary inf. studēre, which, like efferrī, depends on velint.

11. litterīs cōnfīsōs: "because they relied on written texts"; see App. §283 on the use

of participles in place of subordinate clauses. The Druids were hardly alone in arguing that literacy destroyed memory. Plato made similar arguments. Today you might hear people talk about calculators, computers, and the Internet in similar terms.

11–12. quod . . . accidit: we may supply an unexpressed antecedent id, and conclude that the phrase is in apposition to the previous explanation in order to supply supporting evidence. Alternatively, we may view quod as the equivalent of et id, i.e., *conjunctio relativa* (App. §173, *a*.). Note, however, the switch to the ind. mood, which is the equivalent of inserting "in fact." Caesar states what he thinks of (or knows) as fact in the ind.

12. in perdiscendō: see App. §§287, 294 on the use of the gerund.

12–13. ut . . . remittant: subjunctive in a clause of result; see App. §229.

15 *In prīmīs hoc volunt persuādēre, nōn* interīre animās, *sed ab aliīs* post *mortem* trānsīre *ad aliōs, atque hōc* maximē *ad virtūtem* excitārī putant metū *mortis* neglēctō. *Multa* praetereā *dē* sīderibus *atque eōrum* mōtū, *dē* mundī *ac* terrārum magnitūdine, *dē rērum* nātūrā, *dē* deōrum immortālium *vī ac* potestāte disputant *et* iuventūtī trādunt.

---

anim•a, -ae, *f.,* breath, life, soul.

de•us, -ī (*nom. pl.:* **diī;** *dat. pl.:* **dīs**), *m.,* god.

disputō, 1 [**putō,** reckon], discuss, debate about.

excitō, 1 [**citō,** rouse], call forth, excite, animate, arouse; erect, construct (*towers*); kindle (*fires*).

immortāl•is, -e, *adj.* [**in** + **mortālis,** mortal], not mortal, immortal, deathless.

inter•eō, -īre, -iī, -itum [**eō,** go. App. §84], perish, die.

iuvent•ūs, -ūtis, *f.* [**iūvenis,** young], period of youth, *from seventeen to forty-five years;* the youth, the young men.

magis, *adv. comp.* [from **magnus,** large], more, rather; *superl.:* **maximē,** especially.

magnitūd•ō, -inis, *f.* [**magnus,** large], large size .

met•us, -ūs, *m.* [**metuō,** fear], fear, dread, terror, anxiety, apprehension; **metū territāre,** terrify, terrorize; **hōc metū** = **metū huius reī,** from fear of this.

mōt•us, -ūs, *m.* [**moveō,** move], movement; uprising, disturbance.

mund•us, -ī, *m.,* world, universe.

nātūr•a, -ae, *f.* [**nāscor,** be born], nature; character.

neg•legō, -legere, -lēxī, -lēctum [**neg** + **legō,** choose, regard], not heed, not pay attention to, disregard, neglect.

post, *prep. with acc.,* behind, after.

potes•tās, -tātis, *f.* [**potēns,** powerful], power, ability, authority; control, sway, rule; chance, opportunity, possibility; **potestātem facere,** grant permission, give a chance.

praetereā, *adv.* [**praeter,** beyond], beyond this, besides, furthermore.

putō, 1, think, consider, believe.

sīd•us, -eris, *n.,* star; constellation.

terr•a, -ae, *f.,* earth, land, soil, ground; region, district; **terrae** (*pl.*) *and* **orbis terrārum,** the world.

trā•dō, -dere, -didī, -ditum [**trāns** + **dō,** give], give over; entrust; teach.

trāns•eō, -īre, -iī, -itum [**eō,** go. App. §84], cross; march through; migrate.

---

14. animās: this word serves as the acc. subject of the inf. **interīre** and as the unexpressed subject of the inf. **trānsīre.**

14–15. nōn . . . aliōs: these phrases are in apposition with **hoc,** the direct object of the complementary inf. **persuādēre,** and they serve to explain what "this" is that they wish to teach.

    ab aliīs . . . ad aliōs: "from some people . . . to other people."

    15. hōc: abl. of means; see App. §143.

    16. excitārī: this pass. inf. in indirect statement is dependent on **putant,** but lacks an acc.

subject. We might once again supply *animās,* but we could also simply supply a generic *hominēs,* in whose bodies the transmigrating souls reside until their next transmigration.

    metū . . . neglēctō: abl. absolute that serves to explain the reason why the doctrine promotes bravery; see App. §150.

    Multa: "many things," i.e., many doctrines or teachings. The Druids cover all subject areas.

[6.15] *Alterum genus est equitum. Hī, cum est ūsus atque*
aliquod bellum incidit (*quod ferē ante Caesaris adventum*
quotannīs *accidere* solēbat, *utī aut ipsī* iniūriās īnferrent
aut illātās prōpulsārent), *omnēs in bellō* versantur, *atque*
5   *eōrum ut quisque est genere cōpiīsque* amplissimus, *ita*
plūrimōs circum *sē* ambactōs clientēs*que habet. Hanc ūnam*
grātiam potentiam*que* nōvērunt.

---

ambact•us, -ī, *m.*, vassal.
ampl•us, -a, um, *adj.*, of large extent, large;
   illustrious, noble; generous, magnificent.
circum, *prep. with acc.* [**circus,** circle],
   around, about, near.
cliēns, clientis, *m., f.* [**clueō,** hear, obey],
   client, vassal, dependent, retainer.
grāti•a, -ae, *f.* [**grātus,** pleasing], favor,
   goodwill, gratitude, esteem, influence,
   popularity.
in•cidō, -cidere, -cidī, — [**ad + cadō,**
   fall], fall into *or* upon; fall in with, meet;
   happen, arise.
īnferō, īnferre, intulī, illātum [**ferō,** carry.
   App. §81], carry into, import, inflict,
   cause, produce; cast into.

iniūri•a, -ae, *f.* [**in + iūs,** right], wrong;
   outrage, damage, violence.
nōscō, nōscere, nōvī, nōtum, learn; **nōvī,**
   perf., have learned, *hence* know.
potenti•a, -ae, *f.* [**potēns,** powerful], chief
   power, supremacy.
propulso (1) [**propello,** drive forward], to
   drive off, repel
quotannīs, *adv.* [**quot,** as many as + **annus,**
   year], every year, yearly.
soleō, solēre, solitus sum (App. §74), be
   accustomed, be used *to.*
versō, 1, turn; deal with; *pass. as deponent,*
   turn oneself; be, remain; engage in; fight.

---

1. equitum: having dealt with Druids,
Caesar proceeds to the second important
class of men, the *genus equitum* or "class of
cavalry," i.e., the military order, against whom
he wages his battles.

   1–4. Hī . . . omnēs = *equitēs.* Note the HY-
PERBATON (App. 302, *f.*).

   1–2. cum est . . . atque . . . incidit: "whenever," etc.; see App. §241 on temporal *cum*
with the indicative.

   2. quod = *et id*; see App. §173, *a.*

   3–4. utī aut . . . īnferrent aut . . .
prōpulsārent: subjunctives in substantive
clauses of result; see App. §229.

   4. illātās = *iniūriās ab aliīs* **illātās.** The
reader is expected to supply such details
from the previous phrase. Latin style prefers terseness. English tends toward a fuller
explanation.

4–6. atque eōrum ut quisque est . . . , ita
. . . habet: "and in proportion as (**ut**) each is
. . . , in such proportion (**ita**) each of them has
. . . ." This is another example of ellipsis or gapping, but here in advance (something we do
not do in English). Before **eōrum,** we must
thus supply *quisque,* which also serves as the
unexpressed subject of **habet.**

   5. genere cōpiīsque: ablatives of respect;
see App. §149.

   6. ambactōs clientēsque: powerful men
are surrounded by crowds of men who obey
them. We saw a prime example of this with the
story of Orgetorix in the selections from the
first book of Caesar.

   6–7. Hanc . . . nōvērunt: "they know this
single influence and power"; i.e., the kind of
influence and power that derives from having
large groups of followers who obey.

[6.16] Nātiō *est omnis Gallōrum* admodum dēdita religiōnibus,
atque ob *eam causam, quī sunt* adfectī *graviōribus* morbīs *quīque
in proeliīs perīculīsque* versantur, *aut prō* victimīs *hominēs*
immolant *aut sē* immolātūrōs vovent administrīsque *ad ea*
5   sacrificia Druidibus *ūtuntur, quod, prō* vītā *hominis* nisi *hominis*
vīta reddātur, *nōn posse* deōrum immortālium nūmen plācārī
arbitrantur, pūblicēque *eiusdem generis habent* īnstitūta sacrificia.

---

adminis•ter, -trī, *m.* [minister, servant],
attendant, priest.

admodum, *adv.* [modus, measure], *literally:
up to the measure;* very much, very; *with
numbers,* fully; *with negative,* at all.

af•ficiō, -ficere, -fēcī, -fectum [ad + faciō,
do], do to, treat, affect; afflict.

dē•dō, -dere, -didī, -ditum [dō, give], give
up, give over, yield, surrender; devote; sē
dēdere, submit, surrender.

deus, -ī (*nom. pl.:* diī; *dat. pl.:* dīs), *m.,* god.

Druid•ēs, -um, *m.,* the Druids, *the priests of
the Celts in Gaul and Britain.*

immolō, 1, sacrifice.

immortāl•is, -e, *adj.* [in + mortālis,
mortal], not mortal, immortal,
deathless.

īn•stituō, -stituere, -stituī, -stitūtum
[statuō, set up], set up *or* put in order,
draw up; train, educate; procure, prepare;
build, construct; begin, determine,
decide upon, adopt.

morb•us, -ī, *m.,* illness, sickness, disease.

nāti•ō, -ōnis, *f.* [nāscor, be born], people,
tribe, nation.

nisi, *conj.,* [ne- + sī, if], if not, except, unless.

nūm•en, -inis, *n.,* divinity, god; divine force
or will.

ob, *prep. with acc.,* on account of, for.

plācō, 1, appease, please.

pūblicē, *adv.* [pūblicus, public], publicly, in
the name of the state, on behalf of the state.

red•dō, -dere, -didī, -ditum [red- + dō,
give], give back, return, restore; give *or*
return *something due or owed;* make *or*
cause to be; render.

religi•ō, -ōnis, *f.,* religion; *in pl.,* religious
ceremonies, rites; superstitions.

sacrific•ium, -ī, *n.* [sacer, sacred + faciō,
make], sacrifice.

versō, 1, turn; deal with; *pass. as deponent,*
turn oneself; be, remain; be engaged in;
fight.

victim•a, -ae, *f.,* victim; a sacrificial animal.

vīt•a, -ae, *f.* [*cf.* vīvō, live], life, lifestyle.

voveō, vovēre, vōvī, vōtum, vow.

---

1. dēdita religiōnibus: "devoted to religious ceremonies and superstitions." Among
educated Romans and Greeks, excessive re-
ligiosity was considered a sign of weakness.
The Romans took great care to worship the
gods correctly, but they were suspicious of
those who were unduly fearful or in awe of
the supernatural.

2. graviōribus morbīs: abl. of manner; see
App. §142.

4. immolātūrōs: fut. active inf. with *esse*
omitted in indirect statement dependent on
vovent.

4–5. administrīsque . . . Druidibus:
"Druids as officiating priests"; abl. with the
deponent verb *ūtor*; see App. §145.

5–6. nisi . . . reddātur: subjunctive in the
protasis (if-clause) of a condition in indirect
statement; see App. §272. Ancient religion
often operated on the principle of "like for
like."

6. nūmen: acc. subject of the inf. posse
in indirect statement dependent on arbitrantur. The clause expresses the conclusion
(apodosis) of a condition in indirect statement; see App. §272.

7. habent īnstitūta: "they have established"; for the use of the verb *habēre* with a
past part., see App. §286, *b.*

Aliī immānī magnitūdine simulācra *habent, quōrum* contexta
vīminibus membra vīvīs *hominibus* complent; *quibus* succēnsīs
10   *circumventī* flammā exanimantur *hominēs.* Supplicia *eōrum quī*
in fūrtō *aut in* latrōciniō *aut aliquā* noxiā *sint* comprehēnsī
grātiōra dīs immortālibus *esse arbitrantur; sed, cum eius generis*
cōpia dēficit, *etiam ad* innocentium supplicia dēscendunt.

---

com•pleō, -plēre, -plēvī, -plētum [*obs.:*
  pleō, fill], fill up; complete; cover.
com•prehendō, -prehendere, -prehendī,
  -prehēnsum [**prehendō** (= **prendō**),
  seize], lay hold of, seize, arrest.
con•texō, -texere, -texuī, -textum [**texō,**
  weave], weave *or* bind together, connect.
dē•ficiō, -ficere, -fēcī, -fectum [**faciō,**
  make], fail, be insufficient.
dē•scendō, -scendere, -scendī, -scēnsum
  [**scandō,** climb], climb down, go down,
  descend; have recourse (*to*), resort.
de•us, -ī (*nom. pl.:* **diī;** *dat. pl.:* **dīs**), *m.,* god.
ex•animō, 1 [**anima,** breath], deprive of
  breath, render breathless, exhaust; kill.
flamm•a, -ae, *f.,* fire, blaze.
fūrt•um, -ī, *n.,* theft.
grāti•a, -ae, *f.* [**grātus,** pleasing], favor,
  goodwill, gratitude, esteem, influence,
  popularity.
immān•is, -e, *adj.,* huge, immense.

immortāl•is, -e, *adj.* [**in** + **mortālis,**
  mortal], not mortal, immortal, deathless.
innoc•ēns, -entis, *adj.* [**in** + **nocēns,**
  harmful], not harmful, innocent.
latrōcin•ium, -ī, *n.* [**latrō,** robber], robbery,
  brigandage.
magnitūd•ō, -inis, *f.* [**magnus,** large], large
  size.
membr•um, -ī, *n.,* limb.
noxi•a, -ae, *f.,* crime, offense.
simulācr•um, -ī, *n.* [**simulō,** make like],
  image, statue.
suc•cendō, -cendere, -cendī, -cēnsum, set
  on fire below, kindle, burn.
supplic•ium, -ī, *n.* [**sub** + **plicō,** bend],
  humiliation; sacrificing; humble request
  or petition, supplication; punishment,
  penalty, torture.
vīm•en, -inis, *n.,* a bendable stick, wicker,
  switch, osier.
vīv•us, -a, -um, *adj.* [**vīvō,** live], alive, living.

---

8. immānī magnitūdine: abl. of description; see App. §141.

  simulācra: as the subordinate clause will explain, these "images" are made of wickerwork.

  9. quibus succēnsīs = *et eīs (simulacribus)*
succēnsīs; abl. absolute; see App. §150.

  10. exanimantur hominēs: how believ-
able is it that Druids oversaw executions and
sacrifices, in which human beings were enclosed in large wickerwork structures in human shape (*simulacra*), and then burnt alive?
When we execute criminals, we no longer
allow large audiences, but, in previous centuries, public hangings were attended by large
crowds. The Romans, of course, put on games

before crowds where condemned criminals
fought to the death or were killed by wild animals. "Human sacrifice," on the other hand,
was considered barbaric, even by Romans.

  Supplicia: acc. subject of the inf. **esse** in
indirect statement dependent on **arbitrantur.** Note too the HYPERBATON (App. §302,
f.) in relation to the predicate **grātiōra.**

  10–11. quī . . . sint comprehēnsī: subjunctive in a rel. clause of characteristic; see
App. §230.

  12. dīs: dat. with the adj. **grātiōra;** see
App. §122.

  12–13. eius generis cōpia: "a supply of
this kind," i.e., of criminally guilty victims.

[6.17] Deum maximē Mercurium colunt. *Huius sunt plūrima*
simulācra: hunc omnium inventōrem artium *ferunt, hunc*
viārum *atque itinerum* ducem, *hunc ad* quaestūs pecūniae
mercātūrās*que habēre vim maximam arbitrantur.* Post *hunc*
5   Apollinem *et* Mārtem *et* Iovem *et* Minervam.

Apoll•ō, -inis, *m., the god* Apollo.
ars, artis, *f.,* skill, art; *pl.* the arts.
colō, colere, coluī, cultum, cultivate, dwell
    in; honor, worship.
de•us, -ī (*nom. pl.*: **diī;** *dat. pl.*: **dīs),** *m.,* god.
dux, ducis, *m.* [**dūcō,** lead], leader,
    commander, general; guide.
invent•or, -ōris, *m.* [**inveniō,** find],
    inventor, author.
Iuppiter, Iovis, *n.* (App. §27), *m.,* Jupiter,
    chief god of the Roman state.
magis, *adv. comp.* [from **magnus,** large],
    more, rather; *superl.*: **maximē,** especially.
Mār•s, -tis, *m.,* Mars, the god of war.

mercātūr•a, -ae, *f.* [**mercor,** trade], a
    commercial enterprise, trade.
Mercur•ius, -ī, *m.,* Mercury, *a god especially*
    associated by the Romans with trade.
Minerv•a, -ae, *f., the goddess* Minerva, *who*
    was associated with wisdom and the liberal
    arts.
pecūni•a, -ae, *f.,* property, wealth; money.
post, *prep. with acc.,* behind, after.
quaest•us, -ūs, *m.* [**quaerō,** seek], gain,
    acquisition.
simulācr•um, -ī, *n.* [**simulō,** make like],
    image, statue.
vi•a, -ae, *f.,* way, road, route; journey, march.

---

1. Mercurium: the god Mercury was associated especially with business and shady
deals. Caesar often accuses the Gauls of not
living up to their promises. This aspect of
their religion would in the minds of Caesar's
readers tend to justify Caesar's opinion. It
was common for all ancient people to call
other people's gods by their own names. The
Romans called Greek gods by Roman names,
and the Greeks called Roman gods by Greek
names. Caesar applies the same principle to
the Celtic gods.

2. hunc = *Mercurium.* The first **hunc** is the
acc. subject of the unexpressed inf. *esse* in
indirect statement with **ferunt.** The second
hunc is likewise the acc. subject of an unexpressed *esse,* but on what verb of speaking
does this indirect statement depend? There
are three possibilities: **ferunt,** an unexpressed verb of speaking, or **arbitrantur.** The
third **hunc,** however, is the acc. subject of the
inf. **habēre** in indirect statement dependent
on **arbitrantur.** The repetition of *hunc* at the
beginning of each phrase is called ANAPHORA

(App. §302, *a.*) and the lack of conjunctions
ASYNDETON (App. §301, *a.*).

3. viārum . . . ducem: Mercury assisted
travelers.

3–4. quaestūs pecūniae mercātūrāsque:
again, Caesar emphasizes Mercury's mercantile interests. It is also worth mentioning that
politicians of senatorial rank (Caesar would
be included in this category) considered
businessmen decidedly of a lower class in
comparison with themselves. In our country
today, successful business leaders enjoy much
higher prestige than their counterparts did in
Rome. Caesar likely emphasizes Mercury's
status as the chief Celtic god as a way to signal
to his readers that Gauls have different values
from Romans.

4. Post hunc = *post Mercurium colunt.* Caesar has ellipted the verb, as he knows his readers will be able to supply it from the previous
sentence. Note the POLYSYNDETON; see App.
§301, *f.*: the chief god of the Roman state, Jupiter, is just one among many.

Dē hīs eandem ferē, quam reliquae gentēs, habent opīniōnem:
Apollinem morbōs dēpellere, Minervam operum *atque*
artificiōrum initia trādere, Iovem imperium caelestium
tenēre, Mārtem *bella* regere. *Huic, cum proeliō* dīmicāre
10   *cōnstituērunt, ea quae bellō cēperint* plērumque dēvovent:
cum superāvērunt, animālia *capta* immolant *reliquāsque rēs
in ūnum locum* cōnferunt.

---

anim•al, -ālis, *n.* [anima, breath], animal,
living (*and* breathing) creature.
Apoll•ō, -inis, *m., the god* Apollo.
arti•ficium, -ficī, *n.* [ars, art + faciō, make],
a trade, handicraft; artifice, trick.
caelest•is, -e, *adj.* [caelum, sky], *what is in
the sky,* heavenly, celestial; *pl. as noun:* the
gods (*who live in the sky*).
cōn•ferō, -ferre, contulī, collātus [ferō,
bring. App. §81.], collect, carry.
dē•pellō, -pellere, -pulī, -pulsum [pellō,
drive], drive from *or* away, ward off.
dē•voveō, -vovēre, -vōvī, -vōtum [voveō,
vow], consecrate, devote.
dīmicō, 1 [micō, brandish], fight, struggle,
contend.
gēns, gentis, *f.,* clan, tribe; people.
immolō, 1, sacrifice.
imper•ium, -ī, *n.* [imperō, order], right
to command; authority; jurisdiction;
supreme, highest official power.

init•ium, -ī, *n.* [ineō, go into], beginning,
commencement, origin; basic elements.
Iuppiter, Iovis, *n.* (App. §27), *m.,* Jupiter.
Mār•s, -tis, *m.,* Mars, *the god of war.*
Minerv•a, -ae, *f., the goddess* Minerva.
morb•us, -ī, *m.,* illness, sickness, disease.
opīni•ō, -ōnis, *f.* [opīnor, think], way
of thinking, opinion; impression;
expectation; reputation.
op•us, -eris, *n.,* work, labor; military work
or works, fortifications, defenses; a work
of engineering or architecture.
plērumque, *adv.* [plērusque, the greater
part], mostly, generally; very often.
regō, regere, rēxī, rēctum, keep straight;
guide, direct, control.
superō, 1 [super, over], go over; be superior
to, conquer; remain.
trā•dō, -dere, -didī, -ditum [trāns + dō,
give], give over; entrust; teach.

---

6. Dē hīs: i.e., *deīs.*

eandem ... opīniōnem: the indirect statement that follows depends on the speech
implied by an opinion. Note again the HYPER-
BATON (App. §302, *f.*). Caesar inserts the rel.
clause between the antecedent and the adj.
that modifies the antecedent.

quam: the verb *habent* has been ellipted
from the rel. clause.

9. Huic = *Martī.*

10. quae ... cēperint: subjunctive in a rel.
clause of characteristic (App. §230). Note,
however, the tense (perf.) because the subordinate clause depends on a principal clause
with a pres. tense verb (**dēvovent**). Others
have argued that the subjunctive derives

from implied indirect statement. However
you choose to explain the syntax, vowing a
portion of what one captured to the god who
assisted the endeavor was a common practice
in the ancient world. Especially during the
early Republic, Roman generals often vowed
temples to gods in the heat of battle, which
they subsequently paid for with a share of the
booty plundered from their conquered opponents. The victors paid for their promises to
the gods with property confiscated from the
defeated. The Gauls, however, did not construct temples. They simply handed Mars's
share over to him directly (as Caesar goes on
to describe).

> *Multīs in cīvitātibus hārum rērum* exstrūctōs tumulōs *locīs*
> cōnsecrātīs cōnspicārī licet; *neque* saepe *accidit, ut* neglēctā
> 15   quispiam religiōne *aut capta apud sē* occultāre *aut* posita
> tollere audēret, *gravissimumque eī reī* supplicium *cum* cruciātū
> *cōnstitūtum est.*

---

aud•eō, -ēre, ausus sum (App. §74), dare, risk, venture.

cōnsecrō, 1 [**sacrō,** dedicate], dedicate, consecrate.

cōnspicor, 1 [**speciō,** look], observe, discern, perceive.

cruciāt•us, -ūs, *m.* [**cruciō,** torture; **crux,** cross (*used for crucifixion*)], torture, torment.

ex•struō, -struere, -strūxī, -strūctum [**struō,** build], build *or* pile up; construct, build.

licet, licēre, licuit *and* **licitum est,** *impers.,* it is permitted.

neg•legō, -legere, -lēxī, -lēctum [**neg** + **legō,** choose, regard], not heed, not pay attention to, disregard, neglect.

occultō, 1 [**occultus,** secret], hide, keep secret, conceal.

pōnō, pōnere, posuī, positum, place, put, place over; lay down, set aside; station,

post; regard, consider; make, build; *with* **castra,** pitch; *pass.:* be situated; *with* **in** *and the abl.,* depend on, *in addition to the above meanings.*

quispiam, quidpiam *and* **quispiam, quaepiam, quodpiam,** *indef. pron.* (App. §62), anyone, any.

religi•ō, -ōnis, *f.,* religion; *in pl.,* religious ceremonies, rites; superstitions.

saepe, *adv.,* often, frequently.

supplic•ium, -ī, *n.* [**sub** + **plicō,** bend], humiliation; sacrificing; humble request *or* petition, supplication; punishment, penalty, torture.

tollō, tollere, sustulī, sublātum, lift up; take on board; remove; destroy.

tumul•us, -ī, *m.* [**tumeō,** swell], swelling; mound, hill.

---

13. hārum rērum: "of these things," i.e., that have been captured from defeated enemies.

   exstrūctōs: "that have been constructed"; the part. is used as a substitute for a subordinate clause; see App. §283.

   13–14. locīs cōnsecrātīs: abl. of place where; see App. §151.

   14–16. ut ... quispiam ... audēret: subjunctive in a substantive clause of result; see App. §228.

   14–15. neglēctā ... religiōne: "without regard for religious rules"; abl. absolute; see App. §150.

   15. capta: "things that have been captured"; i.e., in battle.

posita: "things that have been deposited"; i.e., in a pile for Mars, after having been captured in war.

   16. eī reī: there are at least two possibilities for construing this phrase. The simplest is to understand it as "for this crime," i.e., **eī** modifies **reī** as an adj. Another is to construe both words as dat., but the first as an indirect object and pron., i.e., "for him (**eī**)," referring to the "someone" (**quispiam**), who dared steal from Mars, and the second as a dat. of purpose, i.e., punishment "for the crime (**reī**)."

   cum cruciātū: abl. of manner; see App. §142.

[6.18] *Gallī sē omnēs ab* Dīte patre prōgnātōs praedicant *idque ab* Druidibus prōditum *dīcunt.* Ob *eam causam* spatia *omnis temporis nōn numerō diērum sed noctium* fīniunt; *diēs* nātālēs *et* mēnsum *et annōrum* initia sīc observant *ut noctem diēs*
5   subsequātur.

Dīs, Dītis, *m.,* Dis, the god Pluto, *god of the underworld.*

Druid•ēs, -um, *m.,* the Druids, *the priests of the Celts in Gaul and Britain.*

fīniō, 4 [**fīnis,** limit], limit, bound; determine, measure.

init•ium, -ī, *n.* [**ineō,** go into], beginning, commencement, origin; edge *of a country,* borders.

mēns•is, -is, *m.,* month.

nātāl•is, -e, *adj.* [**nāscor,** be born], pertaining to birth, natal; **diēs,** birthday.

ob, *prep. with acc.,* on account of, for.

observō, 1 [**servō,** give heed], observe, mark, watch; regard, obey; celebrate.

pat•er, -ris, *m.,* father.

prae•dicō, 1 [**dicō,** proclaim], proclaim publicly *or* before others; declare, report, tell of.

prōd•ō, -dere, -didī, -ditum [**dō,** give], give forth, reveal; betray; hand down.

prōgnāt•us, -a, -um, *adj.* [**nāscor,** be born], born; descended, sprung.

sīc, *adv.,* so, thus, in this manner.

spat•ium, -ī, *n.,* space, distance; period *or* length *of time.*

sub•sequor, -sequī, -secūtus [**sequor,** follow], follow closely; follow on.

---

1. ab Dīte patre: descent from Pluto, god of the underworld, may have various motivations. Many ancient peoples liked to think of themselves as "sprung from the Earth" or, to use the Greek term, autochthonous. Such claims provided religious and organic claims to the land people already occupied. How could anyone else claim it? On the other hand, all who live are descendants of the dead (even if some of our ancestors are still alive, as the ones who are still alive are descended, if we go far enough back, from the dead). The Romans, although they did not claim autochthony (their foundation legends were rather different—refugees from Troy, etc.), had a well-developed cult of departed ancestors, whom they called the *Dī Mānēs* ("divine souls").

sē … prōgnātōs: indirect statement (with *esse* omitted) dependent on **praedicant.**

2. prōditum: again, supply *esse.*

Ob eam causam: Father Dis was god of the underworld where it is dark.

3. nōn numerō diērum sed noctium: "not by the number of days, but by the number of

nights." Although we generally count days, we sometimes count nights as well, primarily when we stay at hotels. The Gauls began the new day at sunset. Day followed night. Other ancient peoples began the new day at dawn or at noon. The Romans were actually odd, inasmuch as they began their days at midnight. We follow Roman practice, but beginning at midnight does introduce oddities that Roman law and religion had to deal with, as the night of one legal and religious day was split into two parts: one part of night occurred after midnight and before dawn and the other after sunset and before midnight. On the other hand, Roman armies measured night as if it were continuous (which it is, of course, as we experience it) by dividing the hours of darkness into twelve equal hours.

4. initia: birthdays, months, and years all begin at night (sunset). One might imagine a Gaul singing "Happy birthnight to you," etc.

4–5. ut … subsequātur: subjunctive in a clause of result; see App. §230.

In reliquīs vītae īnstitūtīs *hōc ferē ab reliquīs* differunt, *quod suōs* līberōs, nisi *cum* adolēvērunt, *ut* mūnus mīlitiae *sustinēre possint,* palam *ad sē* adīre *nōn* patiuntur filiumque puerīlī aetāte *in pūblicō in* cōnspectū patris assistere turpe *dūcunt.*

---

ad•eō, -īre, -iī, -itum [eō, go. App. §84], go
   to, approach, visit, assail, attack.
ad•olēscō, -olēre, -olēvī, -ultum, grow up.
aet•ās, -ātis, *f.,* period of life, age.
as•sistō, -sistere, astitī, —[ad + sistō,
   stand], stand by *or* near.
cōnspect•us, -ūs, *m.* [conspiciō, look at],
   sight, view; presence.
differō, differre, distulī, dīlātum [ferō,
   carry. App. §81], scatter, spread; put off,
   defer; be different, differ.
fīl•ius, -ī, *m.,* son.
īnstitūt•um, -ī, *n.,* established plan *or*
   principle; custom, institution, habit.

līber•ī, -ōrum, *m.* [līber, free], *the non-slave
   members of a family or household*; children.
mīliti•a, -ae, *f.* [mīles, soldier], military
   service, warfare.
mūn•us, -eris, *n.,* duty, service, task; present.
nisi, *conj.* [ne- + sī, if], if not, except, unless.
palam, *adv.,* openly, publicly.
pat•er, -ris, *m.,* father.
patior, patī, passus sum, endure, suffer;
   allow.
puerīl•is, -e, *adj.* [puer, child], childish.
turp•is, -e, *adj.,* ugly, unseemly; shameful,
   disgraceful, dishonorable.
vīt•a, -ae, *f.* [*cf.* vīvō, live], life; lifestyle.

---

6. hōc: abl. of respect; see App. §149.
ab reliquīs: "from other people."
7. nisi cum: "except (unless) after."
7–8. ut ... possint: subjunctive in a clause
of result; see App. §230.
   8. patiuntur: the unexpressed subjects are
the *Gallī* in general and the *patrēs* in particular who are implied by the details of the next
clause. Readers of Latin prose must always be
alert for clues, as Caesar has a high opinion of
our ability to supply necessary details.

8–9. fīlium ... assistere: indirect statement dependent on **dūcunt.** These customs
were likely meant to seem strange to Romans,
as Roman youths had during the early Republic traditionally accompanied their fathers as
their fathers went about their business.
   puerīlī aetāte: abl. of description; see
App. §141.

[6.19] *Virī, quantās* pecūniās *ab* uxōribus dōtis nōmine
accēpērunt, tantās ex suīs bonīs aestimātiōne *factā cum* dōtibus
commūnicant. *Huius omnis* pecūniae coniūnctim ratiō *habētur*
frūctūsque servantur: *uter eōrum* vītā superārit, *ad eum pars*
5   *utrīusque cum* frūctibus *superiōrum temporum pervenit.*

---

aestimāti•ō, -ōnis, *f.* [aestimō, value],
    valuation, appraisal.
bon•us, -a, -um, *adj.*, good, well-disposed;
    as noun, bon•a, -ōrum, *n. pl.*, goods,
    property, estate.
commūnicō, 1 [commūnis, common],
    make common, communicate, impart,
    share.
coniūnctim, *adv.* [coniungō, join], jointly.
dōs, dōtis, *f.* [dō, give], a marriage present,
    dowry.
frūct•us, -ūs, *m.* [fruor, enjoy], fruit; profit,
    reward.
nōm•en, -inis, *n.*, name, title; reputation,
    prestige; nōmine *with gen.*, in the name
    of, as; suō nōmine, on his *or* their own
    account, personally.

pecūni•a, -ae, *f.*, property, wealth; money.
rati•ō, -ōnis, *f.* [reor, reckon], reckoning,
    account, estimate; design, plan, strategy,
    science; method, arrangement; cause,
    reason; regard, consideration; condition,
    state of affairs; manner, way; condition,
    terms; *in pl.*, transactions.
servō, 1, save, preserve; maintain; guard;
    reserve.
superō, 1 [super, over], be superior to,
    prevail; be left over; vītā superāre,
    survive.
ux•or, -ōris, *f.*, wife.
vīt•a, -ae, *f.* [*cf.* vīvō, live], life; lifestyle.

---

1. dōtis nōmine: "under a bond (or prom-
issory note) of dowry."

2. aestimātiōne factā: "after an appraisal
has been made"; abl. absolute; see App. §150.

3. commūnicant: "they mingle," i.e., husbands and wives pool equal shares of their resources when they form a household. Gauls,
like Romans, viewed marriage in practical
terms. Love often grew between husband
and wife (we have many grave inscriptions
testifying to marital affection), but love was
generally not a primary motivating factor.
Ancient peoples were more practical about
such matters than we generally are today.
Gallic custom on marital property would also
have been of comparative interest to Caesar's
Roman readers, as the most common form of

Roman marriage in Caesar's day stipulated
that the property belonging to husbands
and wives should be kept separate. For this
reason, husbands and wives were not even
supposed to give each other gifts, as such vol-
untary transfers would have "mingled" the
very property that was supposed to be kept
in separate accounts!

ratiō: economic relations between husband and wife are strictly regulated, as the
wider circles of their families have, of course,
an economic interest at stake. What happens,
for example, to the woman whose dowry has
been squandered by her husband? Strict account must be kept of what wealth each family
has contributed.

4. superārit = *superāverit*; see App. §72.

Virī in uxōrēs, sīcutī *in* līberōs, vītae necis*que habent*
potestātem; *et cum* pater familiae illūstriōre *locō* nātus
dēcessit, *eius* propinquī *conveniunt et, dē morte sī rēs in*
suspīciōnem vēnit, *dē* uxōribus *in* servīlem modum
10   quaestiōnem *habent et, sī* compertum *est,* ignī *atque omnibus*
tormentīs excruciātās *interficiunt.*

---

com•periō, -perīre, -perī, -pertum
  [**pariō,** procure], find out with certainty,
  discover, ascertain.
dē•cēdō, -cēdere, -cessī, -cessum [**cēdō,**
  go], go from *or* away, depart, withdraw,
  leave, forsake; die.
excruciō, 1 [**cruciō,** torture; **crux,** cross
  (*used for crucifixion*)], torture severely,
  torment.
famili•a, -ae, *f.,* household (*including slaves*);
  retinue (*including all dependents*); family.
ign•is, -is, *m.,* fire.
illūstr•is, -e, *adj.,* distinguished, illustrious.
līber•ī, -ōrum, *m.* [**līber,** free], *the non-
  slave members of a family or household*;
  children.
mod•us, -ī, *m.,* measure, quantity, size;
  manner, method.
nāscor, nāscī, nātus sum, be born, be
  produced; rise, spring up, be raised; be
  found.
nex, necis, *f.,* violent death, death,
  execution.
pat•er, -ris, *m.,* father; **pater familiae,**
  father *or* head of a household.

potes•tās, -tātis, *f.* [**potēns,** powerful],
  power, ability, authority; control, sway,
  rule; chance, opportunity, possibility;
  potestātem facere, grant permission,
  give a chance.
propinqu•us, -a, -um, *adj.* [**prope,** near],
  near, neighboring, close at hand; *pl. as
  noun,* relatives.
quaesti•ō, -ōnis, *f.* [**quaerō,** inquire],
  inquiry; examination, investigation.
servīl•is, -e, *adj.* [**servus,** slave], of *or* like a
  slave, slavish, servile.
sīcut *or* **sīcutī,** *adv.* [**sīc,** so + **ut(ī),** as], so as,
  just as, just as if.
suspīci•ō, -ōnis, *f.* [**suspicor,** suspect],
  suspicion, distrust; surmise.
torment•um, -ī, *n.* [**torqueō,** twist], means
  of twisting; an engine *or* machine *for
  hurling missiles;* device for torturing,
  hence, torture.
ux•or, -ōris, *f.,* wife.
veniō, venīre, vēnī, ventum, come, arrive,
  go, advance.
vīt•a, -ae, *f.* [*cf.* **vīvō,** live], life; lifestyle.

6–7. vītae necisque . . . potestātem: a
Roman father traditionally (again, more so
in earlier Roman history) held the power of
life and death over his children too. Roman
husbands in Caesar's day (unless they were
married by an archaic ceremony, which was
no longer popular) did not have similar authority over their wives. The Gauls thus offer Caesar's readers a glimpse into what life
might have been like among their more primitive ancestors.

   7. illūstriōre locō: abl. of source; see App.
§435.

   8. dē morte: the phrase has been put in
front of the if-clause for emphasis.

9. in servīlem modum: "through torture."
In Rome, the testimony of slaves was admis-
sible in court, only if it had been extracted
through torture, hence "through the method
applied to slaves."

   10. sī compertum est: "if it has been
proved," i.e., the suspicion has been ascertained to be true.

   11. excruciātās: "after the women have
been tortured." Note the gender of the part.,
which is being used in place of a subordinate
clause (see App. §283).

Fūnera *sunt prō* cultū *Gallōrum* magnifica *et* sūmptuōsa;
omniaque quae vīvīs cordī *fuisse arbitrantur in* ignem īnferunt,
etiam animālia, *ac* paulō suprā *hanc* memoriam servī *et* clientēs,
15 *quōs ab eīs* dīlēctōs *esse* cōnstābat, iūstīs fūneribus cōnfectīs
ūnā cremābantur.

---

anim•al, -ālis, *n.* [**anima,** breath], animal,
living (*and* breathing) creature.
cliēns, clientis, *m., f.* [**clēmēns,** gentle],
gentleness, kindness, mercy, clemency.
cōn•ficiō, -ficere, -fēcī, -fectum [**faciō,**
make], make *or* do thoroughly, complete,
accomplish, finish.
cōn•stō, -stāre, -stitī, -statum [**stō,** stand],
stand firm; depend on; be complete; cost;
impers.: it is evident *or* known.
cor, cordis, *n.,* heart.
cremō, 1, burn.
cult•us, -ūs, *m.* [**colō,** cultivate],
civilization; lifestyle; dress; religious
worship.
dī•ligō, -ligere, -lēgī, -lēctum [**legō,**
choose], choose *or* single out, esteem
highly, love.
fūn•us, -eris, *n.,* funeral.
ign•is, -is, *m.,* fire.
īnferō, īnferre, intulī, illātum [**ferō,**
carry. App. §81], carry into, import,
inflict, cause, produce; cast into; **in
equum īnferre,** mount on a horse; **causā
illātā,** making an excuse; **signa īnferre,**
advance the standards, attack.
iūst•us, -a, -um, *adj.* [**iūs,** right], in
accordance with law *or* right; lawful,
valid, just, fair; proper, regular; *with*
fūnera, appropriate, fitting, proper.
magnific•us, -a, -um, *adj.* [**magnus,** large +
faciō, make], magnificent, splendid.
memori•a, -ae, *f.* [**memor,** mindful],
memory; tradition.
paulō, *adv.* [**paulus,** little], a little,
somewhat, slightly.
paul•us, -a, -um, *adj.,* little; **paulum,** *as
noun*: a little; **post paulum,** soon after.
serv•us, -ī, *m.,* slave, servant.
sūmptuōs•us, -a, -um, *adj.* [**sūmptus,**
expense], expensive.
suprā, *prep. with acc.,* above; before.
vīv•us, -a, -um, *adj.* [**vīvō,** live], alive,
living.

---

12. prō cultū: "in proportion to their
(level of) civilization." Upper-class Gauls
were poor compared to upper-class Romans,
so their "expensive" funerals would not have
been so "lavish" by Roman standards.

13. quae vīvīs cordī fuisse: "which they
thought had been (dear) to their heart for
(them while) living," i.e., "which they believed the deceased had loved in life."

vīvīs: dat. of reference; see App. §120.
cordī: dat. of purpose; see App. §119.

14. paulō . . . memoriam: i.e., not too long
before living memory. Again, we find charges
of human sacrifice. We may note that Rome's
gladiatorial games, which included men fighting to the death, had origins in funeral games
staged on behalf of the deceased.

**14–16. animālia . . . servī et clientēs . . .
ūnā cremābantur:** "animals . . . slaves and
clients . . . were all burned at the same time
(together with the deceased)."

15. quōs . . . esse: indirect statement depe-
dent on **cōnstābat.**

iūstīs fūneribus cōnfectīs: "after the appropriate funeral ceremonies had been conducted"; abl. absolute; see App. §150.

[6.20] Quae cīvitātēs commodius *suam rem pūblicam*
administrāre *exīstimantur, habent* lēgibus sānctum, *sī quis*
quid dē rē pūblicā ā fīnitimīs rūmōre *aut* fāmā *accēperit, utī*
ad magistrātum dēferat nēve *cum quō aliō* commūnicet, *quod*
5   saepe *hominēs* temerāriōs *atque* imperītōs falsīs rūmōribus
terrērī *et ad* facinus impellī *et dē summīs rēbus cōnsilium capere*
cognitum est.

---

administrō, 1 [**minister,** servant], serve,
    attend, wait upon; manage, guide.
commodē, *adv.* [**commodus,** convenient],
    conveniently; readily, easily, fitly.
commūnicō, 1 [**commūnis,** common], make
    common, communicate, impart, share.
dē•ferō, -ferre, -tulī, -lātum [**ferō,** carry.
    App. §81], carry, take; report; bring
    before; bestow.
facin•us, -oris, *n.* [**faciō,** do], deed;
    misdeed, outrage, crime.
fals•us, -a, -um, *adj.* [*perf. part. of* **fallō,**
    deceive], false.
fām•a, -ae, *f.* [**fārī,** to speak], common talk,
    rumor, report, reputation, fame.
fīnitim•us, -a, -um, *adj.* [**fīnis,** limit],
    bordering on, neighboring.
im•pellō, -pellere, -pulī, -pulsum [**pellō,**
    drive], drive *or* urge on, incite, instigate,
    impel.

imperīt•us, -a, -um, *adj.* [**in** + **perītus,**
    experienced], inexperienced, unskilled,
    ignorant.
lēx, lēgis, *f.,* law, statute.
magistrāt•us, -ūs, *m.* [**magister,** master],
    public office, magistracy; public official,
    magistrate.
nēve (neu) (App. §188, *b.*) [**nē** + **ve,** or], and
    not, nor.
rūm•or, -ōris, *m.,* hearsay, report, rumor.
saepe, *adv.,* often, frequently.
sanciō, sancīre, sānxī, sānctus, make
    sacred; make binding, ratify, sanction;
sānct•us, -a, -um, *perf. part. as adj.,*
    sacred, inviolable; established.
temerāri•us, -a, -um, *adj.* [**temerē,** rashly],
    rash, imprudent, reckless.
terreō, 2, frighten, terrify.

---

1. Quae cīvitātēs = *et eae cīvitātēs* **quae.**
Caesar has put the antecedent inside the rel.
clause, thus ellipting the subject of **habent.**

2. habent lēgibus sānctum: "have made
(it) binding by laws"; for the use of the verb
habēre with a past part., see App. §286, *b.*

2–4. sī . . . accēperit, utī . . . commūnicet:
a condition in indirect statement that depends on the implied statement of the laws.
The if-clause (protasis), however, is followed
not by a conclusion (apodosis) represented
by an acc. and inf., but instead by a volitive
subjunctive in a substantive clause of purpose (or indirect command). Together, these
clauses represent what in direct statement
would have been an if-clause followed by a
command: "if you learn . . . , report," etc. We
may compare the pre-recorded antiterrorism

messages one hears on New York City's sub-
ways: "If you see something, say something!"

2–3. sī quis quid: "if anyone anything,"
etc.; see App. §174.

3. dē rē pūblicā: "concerning public affairs" or "the state." The Gauls did not have
a republic.

    rūmōre aut fāmā: abl. of means; see App.
§143.

4. cum quō aliō: "with anyone else"; see
App. §174.

5–6. hominēs . . . terrērī et . . . impellī et
. . . capere: indirect statement dependent on
cognitum est.

    dē summīs rēbus cōnsilium capere:
"make decisions about matters of life and
death."

Magistrātūs *quae vīsa sunt* occultant *quaeque esse ex ūsū*
iudicāvērunt *multitūdinī* prōdunt. *Dē rē pūblicā* nisi *per*
10   concilium loquī *nōn* concēditur.

---

con•cēdō, -cādere, -cessī, -cessum [cēdō,
   go], depart; grant; permit.
concil•ium, -ī, *n.*, assembly, gathering,
   council.
iudicō, 1 [**iūdex,** judge], pass judgement on,
   judge, sentence, decide, determine, think,
   consider.
loquor, loquī, locūtus sum, speak, talk,
   converse.

magistrāt•us, -ūs, *m.* [**magister,** master],
   public office, magistracy; public official,
   magistrate.
nisi, *conj.* [**ne-** + **sī,** if], if not, except, unless.
occultō, 1 [**occultus,** secret], hide, keep
   secret, conceal.
prōd•ō, -dere, -didī, -ditum [**dō,** give],
   give forth, reveal; betray; hand down.

---

8. quae: you may supply *ea* as an antecedent for each **quae**.

quae vīsa sunt: "(those things) which (to
them) seemed best (to be kept secret)." Caesar has ellipted both the antecedent of **quae**
and a form of *occultō* from the subordinate
clause, as the alert reader can deduce *occultārī*
from the verb **occultant** in the main clause.

quaeque: i.e., *et ea quae*.

9. prōdunt: public officials share only limited information with the common people.
Caesar's readers at home would presumably
have compared their public official Caesar,
who, while consul, had published the proceedings of the Senate, and who, while general, sends exciting reports. Caesar, unlike
the leaders of the Gauls, informs his people.

10. concilium: Gauls, like Romans for
that matter, were not free to assemble on their

own to discuss matters of public concern.
These assemblies would have been organized
by recognized leaders. Speech in such assemblies can be regulated and directed. The
right of citizens to assemble to discuss matters of public concern is, along with freedom
of speech, one of the most basic requirements
for a democratic and free society, and for precisely this reason, such rights are generally restricted in less free societies. Caesar implies
that Gauls lacked freedom of speech outside
organized assemblies. At the time Caesar
wrote, Romans may not have had the right
to assemble on their own in a politically organized way, but they did enjoy considerable
freedom of speech as individuals. That right
would, with the end of the Roman Republic,
soon be severely restricted as well.

From Strange to Stranger

After Caesar finishes his discussion of the customs and religion of the Gauls, he turns to the Germans. Caesar describes the Germans as even more primitive and alien than the Gauls. You will find the details in the translation of Book Six at the end of this volume. The insight into these ancient peoples, even if from a Roman point of view, is fascinating. The world was a very different place in the 50s BCE!

Complete Latin Readings

Book One
Caesar Dē Bellō Gallicō 1.1–1.6

[1.1] Gallia est omnis dīvīsa in partēs trēs, quārum ūnam incolunt Belgae, aliam Aquītānī, tertiam quī ipsōrum linguā Celtae, nostrā Gallī appellantur. Hī omnēs linguā, īnstitūtīs, lēgibus inter sē differunt. Gallōs ab Aquītānīs Garumna flūmen, ā Belgīs Matrona et Sēquana dīvidit. Hōrum omnium fortissimī sunt Belgae, proptereā quod ā cultū atque hūmānitāte prōvinciae longissimē absunt, minimēque ad eōs mercātōrēs saepe commeant atque ea quae ad effēminandōs animōs pertinent important, proximīque sunt Germānīs, quī trāns Rhēnum incolunt, quibuscum continenter bellum gerunt. Quā dē causā Helvētiī quoque reliquōs Gallōs virtūte praecēdunt, quod ferē cotīdiānīs proeliīs cum Germānīs contendunt, cum aut suīs fīnibus eōs prohibent aut ipsī in eōrum fīnibus bellum gerunt. Eōrum ūna pars, quam Gallōs obtinēre dictum est, initium capit ā flūmine Rhodanō, continētur Garumnā flūmine, Ōceanō, fīnibus Belgārum, attingit etiam ab Sēquanīs et Helvētiīs flūmen Rhēnum, vergit ad septentriōnēs. Belgae ab extrēmīs Galliae fīnibus oriuntur, pertinent ad īnferiōrem partem flūminis Rhēnī, spectant in septentriōnem et orientem sōlem. Aquītānia ā Garumnā flūmine ad Pȳrēnaeōs montēs et eam partem Ōceanī quae est ad Hispāniam pertinet; spectat inter occāsum sōlis et septentriōnēs.

[1.2] Apud Helvētiōs longē nōbilissimus fuit et dītissimus Orgetorīx. Is Marcō Messālā, et Marcō Pūpiō Pīsōne cōnsulibus rēgnī cupiditāte inductus coniūrātiōnem nōbilitātis fēcit et cīvitātī persuāsit ut dē fīnibus suīs cum omnibus cōpiīs exīrent: perfacile esse, cum virtūte omnibus praestārent, tōtīus Galliae imperiō potīrī. Id hōc facilius eīs persuāsit, quod

undique locī nātūrā Helvētiī continentur: ūnā ex parte flūmine Rhēnō
lātissimō atque altissimō, quī agrum Helvētium ā Germānīs dīvidit; alterā
ex parte monte Iūrā altissimō, quī est inter Sēquanōs et Helvētiōs; tertiā
lacū Lemannō et flūmine Rhodanō, quī prōvinciam nostram ab Helvētiīs
dīvidit. Hīs rēbus fiēbat ut et minus lātē vagārentur et minus facile fīnitimīs
bellum īnferre possent; quā ex parte hominēs bellandī cupidī magnō dolōre
adficiēbantur. Prō multitūdine autem hominum et prō glōriā bellī atque
fortitūdinis angustōs sē fīnēs habēre arbitrābantur, quī in longitūdinem
mīlia passuum CCXL, in lātitūdinem CLXXX patēbant.

[1.3] Hīs rēbus adductī et auctōritāte Orgetorīgis permōtī cōnstituērunt ea
quae ad proficīscendum pertinērent comparāre, iūmentōrum et carrōrum
quam maximum numerum coemere, sēmentēs quam maximās facere,
ut in itinere cōpia frūmentī suppeteret, cum proximīs cīvitātibus pācem
et amīcitiam cōnfirmāre. Ad eās rēs cōnficiendās biennium sibi satis esse
dūxērunt; in tertium annum profectiōnem lēge cōnfirmant. Ad eās rēs
cōnficiendās Orgetorīx dēligitur. Is sibi lēgātiōnem ad cīvitātēs suscēpit. In
eō itinere persuādet Casticō, Catamantaloedis filiō, Sēquanō, cuius pater
rēgnum in Sēquanīs multōs annōs obtinuerat et ā senātū populī Rōmānī
amīcus appellātus erat, ut rēgnum in cīvitāte suā occupāret, quod pater
ante habuerat; itemque Dumnorīgī Aeduō, frātrī Dīviciācī, quī eō tempore
prīncipātum in cīvitāte obtinēbat ac maximē plēbī acceptus erat, ut idem
cōnārētur persuādet eīque fīliam suam in mātrimōnium dat. Perfacile
factū esse illīs probat cōnāta perficere, proptereā quod ipse suae cīvitātis
imperium obtentūrus esset: nōn esse dubium quīn tōtīus Galliae plūrimum
Helvētiī possent; sē suīs cōpiīs suōque exercitū illīs rēgna conciliātūrum
cōnfirmat. Hāc ōrātiōne adductī inter sē fidem et iūs iūrandum dant et rēgnō
occupātō per trēs potentissimōs ac firmissimōs populōs tōtīus Galliae sēsē
potīrī posse spērant.

[1.4] Ea rēs est Helvētiīs per indicium ēnūntiāta. Mōribus suīs Orgetorīgem
ex vinculīs causam dīcere coēgērunt; damnātum poenam sequī oportēbat,
ut ignī cremārētur. Diē cōnstitūtā causae dictiōnis Orgetorīx ad iūdicium
omnem suam familiam, ad hominum mīlia decem, undique coēgit, et
omnēs clientēs obaerātōsque suōs, quōrum magnum numerum habēbat,
eōdem condūxit; per eōs nē causam dīceret sē ēripuit. Cum cīvitās ob eam
rem incitāta armīs iūs suum exsequī cōnārētur multitūdinemque hominum
ex agrīs magistrātūs cōgerent, Orgetorīx mortuus est; neque abest suspīciō,
ut Helvētiī arbitrantur, quīn ipse sibi mortem cōnscīverit.

[1.5] Post eius mortem nihilō minus Helvētiī id quod cōnstituerant facere cōnantur, ut ē fīnibus suīs exeant. Ubi iam sē ad eam rem parātōs esse arbitrātī sunt, oppida sua omnia, numerō ad duodecim, vīcōs ad quadringentōs, reliqua prīvāta aedificia incendunt; frūmentum omne, praeterquam quod sēcum portātūrī erant, combūrunt, ut domum reditiōnis spē sublātā parātiōrēs ad omnia perīcula subeunda essent; trium mēnsum molita cibāria sibi quemque domō efferre iubent. Persuādent Raurācīs et Tulingīs et Latobrīgīs fīnitimīs, utī eōdem ūsī cōnsiliō oppidīs suīs vīcīsque exustīs ūnā cum eīs proficīscantur, Bōiōsque, quī trāns Rhēnum incoluerant et in agrum Nōricum trānsierant Nōrēiamque oppugnārant, receptōs ad sē sociōs sibi adscīscunt.

[1.6] Erant omnīnō itinera duo, quibus itineribus domō exīre possent: ūnum per Sēquanōs, angustum et difficile, inter montem Iūram et flūmen Rhodanum, vix quā singulī carrī dūcerentur, mōns autem altissimus impendēbat, ut facile perpaucī prohibēre possent; alterum per prōvinciam nostram, multō facilius atque expedītius, proptereā quod inter fīnēs Helvētiōrum et Allobrogum, quī nūper pācātī erant, Rhodanus fluit isque nōnnūllīs locīs vadō trānsītur. Extrēmum oppidum Allobrogum est proximumque Helvētiōrum fīnibus Genava. Ex eō oppidō pōns ad Helvētiōs pertinet. Allobrogibus sēsē vel persuāsūrōs, quod nōndum bonō animō in populum Rōmānum vidērentur, exīstimābant vel vī coāctūrōs ut per suōs fīnēs eōs īre paterentur. Omnibus rēbus ad profectiōnem comparātīs diem dīcunt, quā diē ad rīpam Rhodanī omnēs conveniant. Is diēs erat a. d. V. Kal. Apr. Lūciō Pīsōne, Aulō Gabīniō cōnsulibus.

[1.7] Caesarī cum id nūntiātum esset, eōs per prōvinciam nostram iter facere cōnārī, mātūrat ab urbe proficīscī et quam maximīs potest itineribus in Galliam ulteriōrem contendit et ad Genavam pervenit. Prōvinciae tōtī quam maximum potest mīlitum numerum imperat (erat omnīnō in Galliā ulteriōre legiō ūna), pontem, quī erat ad Genavam, iubet rescindī. Ubi dē eius adventū Helvētiī certiōrēs factī sunt, lēgātōs ad eum mittunt nōbilissimōs cīvitātis, cuius lēgātiōnis Nammēius et Verucloetius prīncipem locum obtinēbant, quī dīcerent sibi esse in animō sine ūllō maleficiō iter per prōvinciam facere, proptereā quod aliud iter habērent nūllum: rogāre ut eius voluntāte id sibi facere liceat. Caesar, quod memoriā tenēbat Lūcium Cassium cōnsulem occīsum exercitumque eius ab Helvētiīs pulsum et sub iugum missum, concēdendum nōn putābat; neque hominēs inimīcō animō, dātā facultāte per prōvinciam itineris faciendī, temperātūrōs ab iniūriā et maleficiō exīstimābat. Tamen, ut spatium intercēdere posset dum mīlitēs quōs imperāverat convenīrent, lēgātīs respondit diem sē ad dēlīberandum sūmptūrum: sī quid vellent, ad Īd. Aprīl. reverterentur.

Book Four
Caesar Dē Bellō Gallicō 4.24–4.36.1

[4.24] At barbarī, cōnsiliō Rōmānōrum cognitō praemissō equitātū et essedāriīs, quō plērumque genere in proeliīs ūtī cōnsuērunt, reliquīs cōpiīs subsecūtī nostrōs nāvibus ēgredī prohibēbant. Erat ob hās causās summa difficultās, quod nāvēs propter magnitūdinem nisi in altō cōnstituī nōn poterant, mīlitibus autem, ignōtīs locīs, impedītīs manibus, magnō et gravī onere armōrum oppressīs simul et dē nāvibus dēsiliendum et in flūctibus cōnsistendum et cum hostibus erat pugnandum, cum illī aut ex āridō aut paulum in aquam prōgressī omnibus membrīs expedītīs, nōtissimīs locīs, audācter tēla conicerent et equōs īnsuēfactōs incitārent. Quibus rēbus nostrī perterritī atque huius omnīnō generis pugnae imperītī, nōn eādem alacritāte ac studiō quō in pedestribus ūtī proeliīs cōnsuērant ūtēbantur.

[4.25] Quod ubi Caesar animadvertit, nāvēs longās, quārum et speciēs erat barbarīs inūsitātior et mōtus ad ūsum expedītior, paulum removērī ab onerāriīs nāvibus et rēmīs incitārī et ad latus apertum hostium cōnstituī atque inde fundīs, sagittīs, tormentīs hostēs prōpellī ac submovērī iussit; quae rēs magnō ūsuī nostrīs fuit. Nam et nāvium figūrā et rēmōrum mōtū et inūsitātō genere tormentōrum permōtī barbarī cōnstitērunt ac paulum modo pedem rettulērunt. Atque nostrīs mīlitibus cūnctantibus, maximē propter altitūdinem maris, quī decimae legiōnis aquilam ferēbat, obtestātus deōs, ut ea rēs legiōnī fēlīciter ēvenīret, "Dēsilīte," inquit, "commīlitōnēs, nisi vultis aquilam hostibus prōdere; egō certē meum reī pūblicae atque imperātōrī officium praestiterō." Hoc cum vōce magnā dīxisset, sē ex nāvī prōiēcit atque in hostēs aquilam ferre coepit. Tum nostrī cohortātī inter sē, nē tantum dēdecus admitterētur, ūniversī ex nāvī dēsiluērunt. Hōs item ex proximīs prīmī nāvibus cum cōnspexissent, subsecūtī hostibus appropinquārunt.

[4.26] Pugnātum est ab utrīsque ācriter. Nostrī tamen, quod neque ōrdinēs servāre neque firmiter īnsistere neque signa subsequī poterant atque alius aliā ex nāvī quibuscumque signīs occurrerat sē adgregābat, magnopere perturbābantur; hostēs vērō, nōtīs omnibus vadīs, ubi ex lītore aliquōs singulārēs ex nāvī ēgredientēs cōnspexerant, incitātīs equīs impedītōs adoriēbantur, plūrēs paucōs circumsistēbant, aliī ab latere apertō in

ūniversōs tēla coniciēbant. Quod cum animadvertisset Caesar, scaphās
longārum nāvium, item speculātōria nāvigia mīlitibus complērī iussit, et
quōs labōrantēs cōnspexerat, hīs subsidia submittēbat. Nostrī, simul in
āridō cōnstitērunt, suīs omnibus cōnsecūtīs, in hostēs impetum fēcērunt
atque eōs in fugam dedērunt; neque longius prōsequī potuērunt, quod
equitēs cursum tenēre atque īnsulam capere nōn potuerant. Hoc ūnum ad
prīstinam fortūnam Caesarī dēfuit.

[4.27] Hostēs proeliō superātī, simul atque sē ex fugā recēpērunt, statim ad
Caesarem lēgātōs dē pāce mīsērunt; obsidēs datūrōs quaeque imperāsset
factūrōs sēsē pollicitī sunt. Ūnā cum hīs lēgātīs Commius Atrebās vēnit,
quem suprā dēmōnstrāveram ā Caesare in Britanniam praemissum.
Hunc illī ē nāvī ēgressum, cum ad eōs ōrātōris modō Caesaris mandāta
dēferret, comprehenderant atque in vincula coniēcerant; tum proeliō factō
remīsērunt et in petendā pāce eius reī culpam in multitūdinem contulērunt
et propter imprūdentiam ut ignōscerētur petīvērunt. Caesar questus quod,
cum ultrō in continentem lēgātīs missīs pācem ab sē petīssent, bellum sine
causā intulissent, ignōscere imprūdentiae dīxit obsidēsque imperāvit;
quōrum illī partem statim dedērunt, partem ex longinquiōribus locīs
arcessītam paucīs diēbus sēsē datūrōs dīxērunt. Intereā suōs remigrāre in
agrōs iussērunt, prīncipēsque undique convenīre et sē cīvitātēsque suās
Caesarī commendāre coepērunt.

[4.28] Hīs rēbus pāce cōnfirmātā, post diem quārtum quam est in Britanniam ventum nāvēs XVIII, dē quibus suprā dēmōnstrātum est, quae
equitēs sustulerant, ex superiōre portū lēnī ventō solvērunt. Quae cum
appropinquārent Britanniae et ex castrīs vidērentur, tanta tempestās subitō
coorta est ut nūlla eārum cursum tenēre posset, sed aliae eōdem unde erant
profectae referrentur, aliae ad īnferiōrem partem īnsulae, quae est propius
sōlis occāsum, magnō suō cum perīculō dēicerentur; quae tamen ancorīs
iactīs cum flūctibus complērentur, necessāriō adversā nocte in altum
prōvectae continentem petiērunt.

[4.29] Eādem nocte accidit ut esset lūna plēna, quī diēs maritimōs aestūs
maximōs in Ōceanō efficere cōnsuēvit, nostrīsque id erat incognitum. Ita
ūnō tempore et longās nāvēs, quibus exercitum trānsportandum cūrāverat,
quāsque Caesar in āridum subdūxerat, aestus complēverat, et onerāriās,
quae ad ancorās erant dēligātae, tempestās adflīctābat, neque ūlla nostrīs
facultās aut administrandī aut auxiliandī dabātur. Complūribus nāvibus

frāctīs, reliquae cum essent fūnibus, ancorīs reliquīsque armāmentīs
āmissīs ad nāvigandum inūtilēs, magna, id quod necesse erat accidere,
tōtīus exercitūs perturbātiō facta est. Neque enim nāvēs erant aliae quibus
reportārī possent, et omnia deerant quae ad reficiendās nāvēs erant ūsuī,
et, quod omnibus cōnstābat hiemārī in Galliā oportēre, frūmentum in hīs
locīs in hiemem prōvīsum nōn erat.

[4.30] Quibus rēbus cognitīs, prīncipēs Britanniae, quī post proelium
ad Caesarem convēnerant, inter sē collocūtī, cum equitēs et nāvēs et
frūmentum Rōmānīs deesse intellegerent et paucitātem mīlitum ex
castrōrum exiguitāte cognōscerent, quae hōc erant etiam angustiōra quod
sine impedīmentīs Caesar legiōnēs trānsportāverat, optimum factū esse
dūxērunt rebelliōne factā frūmentō commeātūque nostrōs prohibēre et rem
in hiemem prōdūcere, quod hīs superātīs aut reditū interclūsīs nēminem
posteā bellī īnferendī causā in Britanniam trānsitūrum cōnfīdēbant. Itaque
rūrsus coniūrātiōne factā paulātim ex castrīs discēdere et suōs clam ex agrīs
dēdūcere coepērunt.

[4.31] At Caesar, etsī nōndum eōrum cōnsilia cognōverat, tamen et ex
ēventū nāvium suārum et ex eō quod obsidēs dare intermīserant fore id
quod accidit suspicābātur. Itaque ad omnēs cāsūs subsidia comparābat.
Nam et frūmentum ex agrīs cotīdiē in castra cōnferēbat et, quae gravissimē
adflīctae erant nāvēs, eārum māteriā atque aere ad reliquās reficiendās
ūtēbātur et quae ad eās rēs erant ūsuī ex continentī comparārī iubēbat.
Itaque, cum summō studiō ā mīlitibus administrārētur, XII nāvibus
āmissīs, reliquīs ut nāvigārī commodē posset effēcit.

[4.32] Dum ea geruntur, legiōne ex cōnsuētūdine ūnā frūmentātum
missā, quae appellābātur septima, neque ūllā ad id tempus bellī suspīciōne
interpositā, cum pars hominum in agrīs remanēret, pars etiam in castra
ventitāret, eī quī prō portīs castrōrum in statiōne erant Caesarī nūntiāvērunt
pulverem maiōrem quam cōnsuētūdō ferret in eā parte vidērī quam in partem legiō iter fēcisset. Caesar id quod erat suspicātus aliquid novī ā barbarīs
initum cōnsilī, cohortēs quae in statiōnibus erant sēcum in eam partem
proficīscī, ex reliquīs duās in statiōnem cohortēs succēdere, reliquās armārī
et cōnfestim sēsē subsequī iussit. Cum paulō longius ā castrīs prōcessisset,
suōs ab hostibus premī atque aegrē sustinēre et cōnfertā legiōne ex omnibus partibus tēla conicī animadvertit. Nam quod omnī ex reliquīs partibus dēmessō frūmentō pars ūna erat reliqua, suspicātī hostēs hūc nostrōs

esse ventūrōs noctū in silvīs dēlituerant; tum dispersōs dēpositīs armīs in metendō occupātōs subitō adortī paucīs interfectīs reliquōs incertīs ōrdinibus perturbāverant, simul equitātū atque essedīs circumdederant.

[4.33] Genus hoc est ex essedīs pugnae. Prīmō per omnēs partēs perequitant et tēla coniciunt atque ipsō terrōre equōrum et strepitū rotārum ōrdinēs plērumque perturbant et, cum sē inter equitum turmās īnsinuāvērunt, ex essedīs dēsiliunt et pedibus proeliantur. Aurīgae interim paulātim ex proeliō excēdunt atque ita currūs collocant ut, sī illī ā multitūdine hostium premantur, expedītum ad suōs receptum habeant. Ita mōbilitātem equitum, stabilitātem peditum in proeliīs praestant, ac tantum ūsū cotīdiānō et exercitātiōne efficiunt utī in dēclīvī ac praecipitī locō incitātōs equōs sustinēre et brevī moderārī ac flectere et per tēmōnem percurrere et in iugō īnsistere et sē inde in currūs citissimē recipere cōnsuērint.

[4.34] Quibus rēbus perturbātīs nostrīs, novitāte pugnae, tempore opportūnissimō Caesar auxilium tulit: namque eius adventū hostēs cōnstitērunt, nostrī sē ex timōre recēpērunt. Quō factō, ad lacessendum hostem et ad committendum proelium aliēnum esse tempus arbitrātus suō sē locō continuit et brevī tempore intermissō in castra legiōnēs redūxit. Dum haec geruntur, nostrīs omnibus occupātīs quī erant in agrīs reliquī discessērunt. Secūtae sunt continuōs complūrēs diēs tempestātēs, quae et nostrōs in castrīs continērent et hostem ā pugnā prohibērent. Interim barbarī nūntiōs in omnēs partēs dīmīsērunt paucitātemque nostrōrum mīlitum suīs praedicāvērunt et quanta praedae faciendae atque in perpetuum suī līberandī facultās darētur, sī Rōmānōs castrīs expulissent, dēmōnstrāvērunt. Hīs rēbus celeriter magnā multitūdine peditātūs equitātūsque coāctā ad castra vēnērunt.

[4.35] Caesar, etsī idem quod superiōribus diēbus acciderat fore vidēbat, ut, sī essent hostēs pulsī, celeritāte perīculum effugerent, tamen nactus equitēs circiter XXX, quōs Commius Atrebās, dē quō ante dictum est, sēcum trānsportāverat, legiōnēs in aciē prō castrīs cōnstituit. Commissō proeliō diūtius nostrōrum mīlitum impetum hostēs ferre nōn potuērunt ac terga vertērunt. Quōs tantō spatiō secūtī quantum cursū et vīribus efficere potuērunt, complūrēs ex eīs occīdērunt, deinde omnibus longē lātēque aedificiīs incēnsīs sē in castra recēpērunt.

[4.36.1] Eōdem diē lēgātī ab hostibus missī ad Caesarem dē pāce vēnērunt.

Book Five
Caesar Dē Bellō Gallicō 5.24–5.48

[5.24] Subductīs nāvibus conciliōque Gallōrum Samarobrīvae perāctō, quod eō annō frūmentum in Galliā propter siccitātēs angustius prōvēnerat, coāctus est aliter ac superiōribus annīs exercitum in hībernīs collocāre legiōnēsque in plūrēs cīvitātēs distribuere. Ex quibus ūnam in Morinōs dūcendam Gāiō Fabiō lēgātō dedit, alteram in Nerviōs Quīntō Cicerōnī, tertiam in Esubiōs Lūciō Rosciō; quārtam in Rēmīs cum Titō Labiēnō in cōnfīniō Trēverōrum hiemāre iussit. Trēs in Bellovacīs collocāvit: hīs Marcum Crassum quaestōrem et Lūcium Munātium Plancum et Gāium Trebōnium lēgātōs praefēcit. Ūnam legiōnem, quam proximē trāns Padum cōnscrīpserat, et cohortēs V in Eburōnēs, quōrum pars maxima est inter Mosam ac Rhēnum, quī sub imperiō Ambiorīgis et Catuvolcī erant, mīsit. Hīs mīlitibus Quīntum Titūrium Sabīnum et Lucium Aurunculēium Cottam lēgātōs praeesse iussit. Ad hunc modum distribūtīs legiōnibus facillimē inopiae frūmentāriae sēsē medērī posse exīstimāvit. Atque hārum tamen omnium legiōnum hīberna praeter eam, quam Lūciō Rōsciō in pācātissimam et quiētissimam partem dūcendam dederat, mīlibus passuum centum continēbantur. Ipse intereā, quoad legiōnēs collocātās mūnītaque hīberna cognōvisset, in Galliā morārī cōnstituit.

[5.25] Erat in Carnutibus summō locō nātus Tasgetius, cuius maiōrēs in suā cīvitāte rēgnum obtinuerant. Huic Caesar prō eius virtūte atque in sē benevolentiā, quod in omnibus bellīs singulārī eius operā fuerat ūsus, maiōrum locum restituerat. Tertium iam hunc annum rēgnantem inimīcī multīs palam ex cīvitāte auctōribus interfēcērunt. Dēfertur ea rēs ad Caesarem. Ille veritus, quod ad plūrēs pertinēbat, nē cīvitās eōrum impulsū dēficeret, Lūcium Plancum cum legiōne ex Belgiō celeriter in Carnutēs proficīscī iubet ibique hiemāre quōrumque operā cognōverat Tasgetium interfectum, hōs comprehēnsōs ad sē mittere. Interim ab omnibus lēgātīs quaestōribusque, quibus legiōnēs trādiderat, certior factus est in hīberna perventum locumque hībernīs esse mūnītum.

[5.26] Diēbus circiter XV, quibus in hīberna ventum est, initium repentīnī tumultūs ac dēfectiōnis ortum est ab Ambiorīge et Catuvolcō; quī, cum ad fīnēs rēgnī suī Sabīnō Cottaeque praestō fuissent frūmentumque in hīberna comportāvissent, Indutiomārī Trēverī nūntiīs impulsī suōs concitāvērunt subitōque oppressīs lignātōribus magnā manū ad castra oppugnātum vēnērunt. Cum celeriter nostrī arma cēpissent vāllumque ascendissent atque ūnā ex parte Hispānīs equitibus ēmissīs equestrī proeliō superiōrēs fuissent, dēspērātā rē hostēs suōs ab oppugnātiōne redūxērunt. Tum suō mōre conclāmāvērunt, utī aliquī ex nostrīs ad colloquium prōdīret: habēre sēsē, quae dē rē commūnī dīcere vellent, quibus rēbus contrōversiās minuī posse spērārent.

[5.27] Mittitur ad eōs colloquendī causā Gāius Arpīnēius, eques Rōmānus, familiāris Quīntī Titūrī, et Quīntus Iūnius ex Hispāniā quīdam, quī iam ante missū Caesaris ad Ambiorīgem ventitāre cōnsuērat; apud quōs Ambiorīx ad hunc modum locūtus est: sēsē prō Caesaris in sē beneficiīs plūrimum eī cōnfitērī dēbēre, quod eius operā stīpendiō līberātus esset, quod Aduātucīs, fīnitimīs suīs, pendere cōnsuēsset, quodque eī et fīlius et frātris fīlius ab Caesare remissī essent, quōs Aduātucī obsidum numerō missōs apud sē in servitūte et catēnīs tenuissent; neque id, quod fēcerit dē oppugnātiōne castrōrum, aut iūdiciō aut voluntāte suā fēcisse, sed coāctū cīvitātis, suaque esse eiusmodī imperia, ut nōn minus habēret iūris in sē multitūdō quam ipse in multitūdinem. Cīvitātī porrō hanc fuisse bellī causam, quod repentīnae Gallōrum coniūrātiōnī resistere nōn potuerit. Id sē facile ex humilitāte suā probāre posse, quod nōn adeō sit imperītus rērum ut suīs cōpiīs populum Rōmānum superārī posse cōnfīdat. Sed esse Galliae commūne cōnsilium: omnibus hībernīs Caesaris oppugnandīs hunc esse dictum diem, nē qua legiō alterae legiōnī subsidiō venīre posset. Nōn facile Gallōs Gallīs negāre potuisse, praesertim cum dē recuperandā commūnī lībertāte cōnsilium initum vidērētur. Quibus quoniam prō pietāte satisfēcerit, habēre nunc sē ratiōnem officī prō beneficiīs Caesaris: monēre, ōrāre Titūrium prō hospitiō, ut suae ac mīlitum salūtī cōnsulat. Magnam manum Germānōrum conductam Rhēnum trānsīsse; hanc adfore bīduō. Ipsōrum esse cōnsilium, velintne priusquam fīnitimī sentiant ēductōs ex hībernīs mīlitēs aut ad Cicerōnem aut ad Labiēnum dēdūcere, quōrum alter mīlia passuum circiter quīnquāgintā, alter paulō amplius ab eīs absit. Illud sē pollicērī et iūre iūrandō cōnfirmāre tūtum iter per fīnēs datūrum. Quod cum faciat, et cīvitātī sēsē cōnsulere, quod hībernīs levētur, et Caesarī prō eius meritīs grātiam referre. Hāc ōrātiōne habitā discēdit Ambiorīx.

[5.28] Arpīnēius et Iūnius, quae audierunt, ad lēgātōs dēferunt. Illī repentīnā rē perturbātī, etsī ab hoste ea dīcēbantur, tamen nōn neglegenda exīstimābant maximēque hāc rē permovēbantur, quod cīvitātem ignōbilem atque humilem Eburōnum suā sponte populō Rōmānō bellum facere ausam vix erat crēdendum. Itaque ad cōnsilium rem dēferunt magnaque inter eōs exsistit contrōversia. Lūcius Aurunculēius complūrēsque tribūnī mīlitum et prīmōrum ōrdinum centuriōnēs nihil temerē agendum neque ex hībernīs iniussū Caesaris discēdendum exīstimābant: quantāsvīs magnās cōpiās etiam Germānōrum sustinērī posse mūnītīs hībernīs docēbant: rem esse testimōniō, quod prīmum hostium impetum multīs ultrō vulneribus illātīs fortissimē sustinuerint: rē frūmentāriā nōn premī; intereā et ex proximīs hībernīs et ā Caesare conventūra subsidia: postrēmō quid esse levius aut turpius, quam auctōre hoste dē summīs rēbus capere cōnsilium?

[5.29] Contrā ea Titūrius sērō factūrōs clāmitābat, cum maiōrēs manūs hostium adiūnctīs Germānīs convēnissent aut cum aliquid calamitātis in proximīs hībernīs esset acceptum. Brevem cōnsulendī esse occāsiōnem. Caesarem arbitrārī profectum in Ītaliam; neque aliter Carnutēs interficiendī Tasgetī cōnsilium fuisse captūrōs, neque Eburōnēs, sī ille adesset, tantā contemptiōne nostrī ad castra ventūrōs esse. Nōn hostem auctōrem, sed rem spectāre: subesse Rhēnum; magnō esse Germānīs dolōrī Ariovistī mortem et superiōrēs nostrās victōriās; ārdēre Galliam tot contumēliīs acceptīs sub populī Rōmānī imperium redāctam superiōre glōriā reī mīlitāris exstīnctā. Postrēmō quis hōc sibi persuādēret, sine certā rē Ambiorīgem ad eiusmodī cōnsilium dēscendisse? Suam sententiam in utramque partem esse tūtam: sī nihil esset dūrius, nūllō cum perīculō ad proximam legiōnem perventūrōs; sī Gallia omnis cum Germānīs cōnsentīret, ūnam esse in celeritāte positam salūtem. Cottae quidem atque eōrum, quī dissentīrent, cōnsilium quem habēre exitum? In quō sī nōn praesēns perīculum, at certē longinquā obsidiōne famēs esset timenda?

[5.30] Hāc in utramque partem disputātiōne habitā, cum ā Cottā prīmīsque ōrdinibus ācriter resisterētur, "Vincite," inquit, "sī ita vultis," Sabīnus, et id clāriōre vōce, ut magna pars mīlitum exaudīret; "neque is sum," inquit, "quī gravissimē ex vōbīs mortis perīculō terrear: hī sapient; sī gravius quid acciderit, abs tē ratiōnem reposcent, quī, sī per tē liceat, perendinō diē cum proximīs hībernīs coniūnctī commūnem cum reliquīs bellī cāsum sustineant, nōn rēiectī et relēgātī longē ab cēterīs aut ferrō aut fame intereant."

[5.31] Cōnsurgitur ex cōnsiliō; comprehendunt utrumque et ōrant, nē suā dissēnsiōne et pertināciā rem in summum perīculum dēdūcant: facilem esse rem, seu maneant, seu proficīscantur, sī modo ūnum omnēs sentiant ac probent; contrā in dissēnsiōne nūllam sē salūtem perspicere. Rēs disputātiōne ad mediam noctem perdūcitur. Tandem dat Cotta permōtus manūs: superat sententia Sabīnī. Prōnūntiātur prīmā lūce itūrōs. Cōnsūmitur vigiliīs reliqua pars noctis, cum sua quisque mīles circumspiceret, quid sēcum portāre posset, quid ex īnstrūmentō hībernōrum relinquere cōgerētur. Omnia excōgitantur, quārē nec sine perīculō maneātur, et languōre mīlitum et vigiliīs perīculum augeātur. Prīmā lūce sīc ex castrīs proficīscuntur, ut quibus esset persuāsum nōn ab hoste, sed ab homine amīcissimō Ambiorīge cōnsilium datum, longissimō agmine maximīsque impedīmentīs.

[5.32] At hostēs, posteāquam ex nocturnō fremitū vigiliīsque dē profectiōne eōrum sēnsērunt, collocātīs īnsidiīs bipertītō in silvīs opportūnō atque occultō locō ā mīlibus passuum circiter duōbus Rōmānōrum adventum exspectābant, et cum sē maior pars agminis in magnam convallem dēmīsisset, ex utrāque parte eius vāllis subitō sē ostendērunt novissimōsque premere et prīmōs prohibēre ascēnsū atque inīquissimō nostrīs locō proelium committere coepērunt.

[5.33] Tum dēmum Titūrius, quī nihil ante prōvīdisset, trepidāre et concursāre cohortēsque dispōnere, haec tamen ipsa timidē atque ut eum omnia dēficere vidērentur; quod plērumque eīs accidere cōnsuēvit, quī in ipsō negōtiō cōnsilium capere cōguntur. At Cotta, quī cōgitāsset haec posse in itinere accidere atque ob eam causam profectiōnis auctor nōn fuisset, nūllā in rē commūnī salūtī deerat et in appellandīs cohortandīsque mīlitibus imperātōris et in pugnā mīlitis officia praestābat. Cum propter longitūdinem agminis minus facile omnia per sē obīre et, quid quōque locō faciendum esset, prōvidēre possent, iussērunt prōnūntiāre, ut impedīmenta relinquerent atque in orbem cōnsisterent. Quod cōnsilium etsī in eiusmodī cāsū reprehendendum nōn est, tamen incommodē accidit: nam et nostrīs mīlitibus spem minuit et hostēs ad pugnam alacriōrēs effēcit, quod nōn sine summō timōre et dēspērātiōne id factum vidēbātur. Praetereā accidit, quod fierī necesse erat, ut vulgō mīlitēs ab signīs discēderent, quae quisque eōrum cārissima habēret, ab impedīmentīs petere atque arripere properāret, clāmōre et flētū omnia complērentur.

[5.34] At barbarīs cōnsilium nōn dēfuit. Nam ducēs eōrum tōtā aciē prōnūntiāre iussērunt, nē quis ab locō discēderet: illōrum esse praedam atque illīs reservārī quaecumque Rōmānī relīquissent: proinde omnia in victōriā posita exīstimārent. Erant et virtūte et studiō pugnandī parēs; nostrī, tametsī ab duce et ā fortūnā dēserēbantur, tamen omnem spem salūtis in virtūte pōnēbant, et quotiēns quaeque cohors prōcurrerat, ab eā parte magnus numerus hostium cadēbat. Quā rē animadversā Ambiorīx prōnūntiārī iubet, ut procul tēla coniciant neu propius accēdant et, quam in partem Rōmānī impetum fēcerint, cēdant (levitāte armōrum et cotīdiānā exercitātiōne nihil hīs nocērī posse), rūrsus sē ad signa recipientēs īnsequantur.

[5.35] Quō praeceptō ab eīs dīligentissimē observātō, cum quaepiam cohors ex orbe excesserat atque impetum fēcerat, hostēs vēlōcissimē refugiēbant. Interim eam partem nūdārī necesse erat et ab latere apertō tēla recipī. Rūrsus cum in eum locum unde erant ēgressī revertī coeperant, et ab eīs quī cesserant et ab eīs quī proximī steterant circumveniēbantur; sīn autem locum tenēre vellent, nec virtūtī locus relinquēbātur, neque ab tantā multitūdine coniecta tēla cōnfertī vītāre poterant. Tamen tot incommodīs cōnflīctātī, multīs vulneribus acceptīs resistēbant et magnā parte diēī cōnsūmptā, cum ā prīmā lūce ad hōram octāvam pugnārētur, nihil quod ipsīs esset indignum committēbant. Tum Titō Balventiō, quī superiōre annō prīmum pīlum dūxerat, virō fortī et magnae auctōritātis, utrumque femur trāgulā trāicitur; Quīntus Lūcānius, eiusdem ōrdinis, fortissimē pugnāns, dum circumventō fīliō subvenit, interficitur; Lūcius Cotta lēgātus omnēs cohortēs ōrdinēsque adhortāns in adversum ōs fundā vulnerātur.

[5.36] Hīs rēbus permōtus Quīntus Titūrius, cum procul Ambiorīgem suōs cohortantem cōnspexisset, interpretem suum Gnaeum Pompēium ad eum mittit rogātum ut sibi mīlitibusque parcat. Ille appellātus respondit: sī velit sēcum colloquī, licēre; spērāre ā multitūdine impetrārī posse, quod ad mīlitum salūtem pertineat; ipsī vērō nihil nocitum īrī, inque eam rem sē suam fidem interpōnere. Ille cum Cottā sauciō commūnicat, sī videātur, pugnā ut excēdant et cum Ambiorīge ūnā colloquantur: spērāre ab eō dē suā ac mīlitum salūte impetrārī posse. Cotta sē ad armātum hostem itūrum negat atque in eō persevērat.

[5.37] Sabīnus quōs in praesentiā tribūnōs mīlitum circum sē habēbat et prīmōrum ōrdinum centuriōnēs sē sequī iubet et, cum propius Ambiorīgem accessisset, iussus arma abicere imperātum facit suīsque ut idem faciant imperat. Interim, dum dē condiciōnibus inter sē agunt longiorque cōnsultō ab Ambiorīge īnstituitur sermō, paulātim circumventus interficitur. Tum vērō suō mōre victōriam conclāmant atque ululātum tollunt impetūque in nostrōs factō ōrdinēs perturbant. Ibi Lūcius Cotta pugnāns interficitur cum maximā parte mīlitum. Reliquī sē in castra recipiunt unde erant ēgressī. Ex quibus Lūcius Petrosidius aquilifer, cum magnā multitūdine hostium premerētur, aquilam intrā vāllum prōiecit; ipse prō castrīs fortissimē pugnāns occīditur. Illī aegrē ad noctem oppugnātiōnem sustinent; noctū ad ūnum omnēs dēspērātā salūte sē ipsī interficiunt. Paucī ex proeliō ēlapsī incertīs itineribus per silvās ad Titum Labiēnum lēgātum in hīberna perveniunt atque eum dē rēbus gestīs certiōrem faciunt.

[5.38] Hāc victōriā sublātus Ambiorīx statim cum equitātū in Aduātucōs, quī erant eius rēgnō fīnitimī, proficīscitur; neque noctem neque diem intermittit peditātumque subsequī iubet. Rē dēmōnstrātā Aduātucīsque concitātīs posterō diē in Nerviōs pervenit hortāturque, nē suī in perpetuum līberandī atque ulcīscendī Rōmānōs prō eīs quās accēperint iniūriīs occāsiōnem dīmittant: interfectōs esse lēgātōs duōs magnamque partem exercitūs interīsse dēmōnstrat; nihil esse negōtī subitō oppressam legiōnem quae cum Cicerōne hiemet interficī; sē ad eam rem profitētur adiūtōrem. Facile hāc ōrātiōne Nerviīs persuādet.

[5.39] Itaque cōnfestim dīmissīs nūntiīs ad Ceutronēs, Grudiōs, Levācōs, Pleumoxiōs, Geidumnōs, quī omnēs sub eōrum imperiō sunt, quam maximās manūs possunt cōgunt et dē imprōvīsō ad Cicerōnis hīberna advolant nōndum ad eum fāmā dē Titūrī morte perlātā. Huic quoque accidit, quod fuit necesse, ut nōnnūllī mīlitēs, quī lignātiōnis mūnītiōnisque causā in silvās discessissent, repentīnō equitum adventū interciperentur. Hīs circumventīs magnā manū Eburōnēs, Nerviī, Aduātucī atque hōrum omnium sociī et clientēs legiōnem oppugnāre incipiunt. Nostrī celeriter ad arma concurrunt, vāllum cōnscendunt. Aegrē is diēs sustentātur, quod omnem spem hostēs in celeritāte pōnēbant atque hanc adeptī victōriam in perpetuum sē fore victōrēs cōnfīdēbant.

[5.40] Mittuntur ad Caesarem cōnfestim ab Cicerōne litterae magnīs prōpositīs praemiīs, sī pertulissent: obsessīs omnibus viīs missī intercipiuntur. Noctū ex māteriā, quam mūnītiōnis causā comportāverant, turrēs admodum CXX excitantur incrēdibilī celeritāte; quae deesse operī vidēbantur, perficiuntur. Hostēs posterō diē multō maiōribus coāctis cōpiīs castra oppugnant, fossam complent. Eādem ratiōne, quā prīdiē, ab nostrīs resistitur. Hoc idem reliquīs deinceps fit diēbus. Nūlla pars nocturnī temporis ad labōrem intermittitur; nōn aegrīs, nōn vulnerātīs facultās quiētis datur. Quaecumque ad proximī diēī oppugnātiōnem opus sunt noctū comparantur; multae praeustae sudēs, magnus mūrālium pīlōrum numerus īnstituitur; turrēs contabulantur, pinnae lōrīcaeque ex crātibus attexuntur. Ipse Cicerō, cum tenuissimā valētūdine esset, nē nocturnum quidem sibi tempus ad quiētem relinquēbat, ut ultrō mīlitum concursū ac vōcibus sibi parcere cōgerētur.

[5.41] Tunc ducēs prīncipēsque Nerviōrum quī aliquem sermōnis aditum causamque amīcitiae cum Cicerōne habēbant colloquī sēsē velle dīcunt. Factā potestāte eadem quae Ambiorīx cum Titūriō ēgerat commemorant: omnem esse in armīs Galliam; Germānōs Rhēnum trānsīsse; Caesaris reliquōrumque hīberna oppugnārī. Addunt etiam dē Sabīnī morte: Ambiorīgem ostentant fideī faciendae causā. Errāre eōs dīcunt, sī quicquam ab hīs praesidī spērent, quī suīs rēbus diffīdant; sēsē tamen hōc esse in Cicerōnem populumque Rōmānum animō, ut nihil nisi hīberna recūsent atque hanc inveterāscere cōnsuētūdinem nōlint: licēre illīs incolumibus per sē ex hībernīs discēdere et quāscumque in partēs velint sine metū proficīscī. Cicerō ad haec ūnum modo respondit: nōn esse cōnsuētūdinem populī Rōmānī accipere ab hoste armātō condiciōnem: sī ab armīs discēdere velint, sē adiūtōre ūtantur lēgātōsque ad Caesarem mittant; spērāre prō eius iūstitiā, quae petierint, impetrātūrōs.

[5.42] Ab hāc spē repulsī Nerviī vāllō pedum IX et fossā pedum XV hīberna cingunt. Haec et superiōrum annōrum cōnsuētūdine ab nōbīs cognōverant et, quōs clam dē exercitū habēbant captīvōs, ab eīs docēbantur; sed nūllā ferrāmentōrum cōpiā quae esset ad hunc ūsum idōnea, gladiīs caespitēs circumcīdere, manibus sagulīsque terram exhaurīre vidēbantur. Quā quidem ex rē hominum multitūdō cognōscī potuit: nam minus hōrīs tribus mīlium pedum XV in circuitū mūnītiōnem perfēcērunt reliquīsque diēbus turrēs ad altitūdinem vāllī, falcēs testūdinēsque, quās īdem captīvī docuerant, parāre ac facere coepērunt.

[5.43] Septimō oppugnātiōnis diē maximō coortō ventō ferventēs fūsilī ex argillā glandēs fundīs et fervefacta iacula in casās, quae mōre Gallicō strāmentīs erant tēctae, iacere coepērunt. Hae celeriter ignem comprehendērunt et ventī magnitūdine in omnem locum castrōrum distulērunt. Hostēs maximō clāmōre sīcutī partā iam atque explōrātā victōriā turrēs testūdinēsque agere et scālīs vāllum ascendere coepērunt. At tanta mīlitum virtūs atque ea praesentia animī fuit, ut, cum undique flammā torrērentur maximāque tēlōrum multitūdine premerentur suaque omnia impedīmenta atque omnēs fortūnās cōnflagrāre intellegerent, nōn modo dēmigrāndī causā dē vāllō dēcēderet nēmō, sed paene nē respiceret quidem quisquam, ac tum omnēs ācerrimē fortissimēque pugnārent. Hic diēs nostrīs longē gravissimus fuit; sed tamen hunc habuit ēventum, ut eō diē maximus numerus hostium vulnerārētur atque interficerētur, ut sē sub ipsō vāllō cōnstīpāverant recessumque prīmīs ultimī nōn dabant. Paulum quidem intermissā flammā et quōdam locō turrī adāctā et contingente vāllum tertiae cohortis centuriōnēs ex eō, quō stābant, locō recessērunt suōsque omnēs remōvērunt, nūtū vōcibusque hostēs, sī introīre vellent, vocāre coepērunt; quōrum prōgredī ausus est nēmō. Tum ex omnī parte lapidibus coniectīs dēturbātī, turrisque succēnsa est.

[5.44] Erant in eā legiōne fortissimī virī, centuriōnēs, quī prīmīs ōrdinibus appropinquārent, Titus Pullō et Lūcius Vorēnus. Hī perpetuās inter sē contrōversiās habēbant, quīnam anteferrētur, omnibusque annīs dē locīs summīs simultātibus contendēbant. Ex hīs Pullō, cum ācerrimē ad mūnītiōnēs pugnārētur, "quid dubitās," inquit, "Vorēne? Aut quem locum tuae probandae virtūtis exspectās? Hic diēs dē nostrīs contrōversiīs iūdicābit." Haec cum dīxisset, prōcēdit extrā mūnītiōnēs quaeque pars hostium cōnfertissima est vīsa irrumpit. Nē Vorēnus quidem tum sēsē vāllō continet, sed omnium veritus exīstimātiōnem subsequitur. Mediocrī spatiō relictō Pullō pīlum in hostēs immittit atque ūnum ex multitūdine prōcurrentem trāicit; quō percussō et exanimātō hunc scūtīs prōtegunt, in hostem tēla ūniversī coniciunt neque dant regrediendī facultātem. Trānsfīgitur scūtum Pullōnī et verūtum in balteō dēfīgitur. Āvertit hic cāsus vāgīnam et gladium ēdūcere cōnantī dextram morātur manum, impedītumque hostēs circumsistunt. Succurrit inimīcus illī Vorēnus et labōrantī subvenit. Ad hunc sē cōnfestim ā Pullōne omnis multitūdō convertit: illum verūtō arbitrantur occīsum. Gladiō comminus rem gerit Vorēnus atque ūnō interfectō reliquōs paulum prōpellit; dum cupidius īnstat, in locum dēiectus īnferiōrem concidit. Huic rūrsus circumventō fert subsidium

Pullō, atque ambō incolumēs complūribus interfectīs summā cum laude sēsē
intrā mūnītiōnēs recipiunt. Sīc fortūna in contentiōne et certāmine utrumque
versāvit, ut alter alterī inimīcus auxiliō salūtīque esset, neque dīiūdicārī posset,
uter utrī virtūte anteferendus vidērētur.

[5.45] Quantō erat in diēs gravior atque asperior oppugnātiō, et maximē
quod magnā parte mīlitum cōnfectā vulneribus rēs ad paucitātem
dēfēnsōrum pervēnerat, tantō crēbriōrēs litterae nūntiīque ad Caesarem
mittēbantur; quōrum pars dēprehēnsa in cōnspectū nostrōrum mīlitum
cum cruciātū necābātur. Erat ūnus intus Nervius nōmine Verticō, locō
nātus honestō, quī ā prīmā obsidiōne ad Cicerōnem perfūgerat suamque eī
fidem praestiterat. Hic servō spē lībertātis magnīsque persuādet praemiīs,
ut litterās ad Caesarem dēferat. Hās ille in iaculō illigātās effert et Gallus
inter Gallōs sine ūllā suspīciōne versātus ad Caesarem pervenit. Ab eō dē
perīculīs Cicerōnis legiōnisque cognōscitur.

[5.46] Caesar acceptīs litterīs hōrā circiter XI diēī statim nūntium in
Bellovacōs ad Marcum Crassum quaestōrem mittit, cuius hīberna aberant
ab eō mīlia passuum XXV; iubet mediā nocte legiōnem proficīscī celerit-
erque ad sē venīre. Exit cum nūntiō Crassus. Alterum ad Gāium Fabium
lēgātum mittit, ut in Atrebātium fīnēs legiōnem addūcat, quā sibi iter faciendum sciēbat. Scrībit Labiēnō, sī reī pūblicae commodō facere posset, cum
legiōne ad fīnēs Nerviōrum veniat. Reliquam partem exercitūs, quod paulō
aberat longius, nōn putat exspectandam; equitēs circiter quadringentōs ex
proximīs hībernīs colligit.

[5.47] Hōrā circiter tertiā ab antecursōribus dē Crassī adventū certior factus eō diē mīlia passuum XX prōcēdit. Crassum Samarobrīvae praeficit
legiōnemque attribuit, quod ibi impedīmenta exercitūs, obsidēs cīvitātum,
litterās pūblicās frūmentumque omne quod eō tolerandae hiemis causā
dēvexerat relinquēbat. Fabius, ut imperātum erat, nōn ita multum morātus
in itinere cum legiōne occurrit. Labiēnus interitū Sabīnī et caede cohortium
cognitā, cum omnēs ad eum Trēverōrum cōpiae vēnissent, veritus nē, sī ex
hībernīs fugae similem profectiōnem fēcisset, hostium impetum sustinēre
nōn posset, praesertim quōs recentī victōriā efferrī scīret, litterās Caesarī
remittit, quantō cum perīculō legiōnem ex hībernīs ēductūrus esset; rem
gestam in Eburōnibus perscrībit; docet omnēs equitātūs peditātūsque
cōpiās Trēverōrum tria mīlia passuum longē ab suīs castrīs cōnsēdisse.

[5.48] Caesar cōnsiliō eius probātō, etsī opīniōne trium legiōnum dēiectus ad duās redierat, tamen ūnum commūnis salūtis auxilium in celeritāte pōnēbat. Venit magnīs itineribus in Nerviōrum fīnēs. Ibi ex captīvīs cognōscit, quae apud Cicerōnem gerantur, quantōque in perīculō rēs sit. Tum cuidam ex equitibus Gallīs magnīs praemiīs persuādet utī ad Cicerōnem epistolam dēferat. Hanc Graecīs cōnscrīptam litterīs mittit, nē interceptā epistolā nostra ab hostibus cōnsilia cognōscantur. Sī adīre nōn possit, monet ut trāgulam cum epistolā ad āmentum dēligātā intrā mūnītiōnem castrōrum abiciat. In litterīs scrībit sē cum legiōnibus profectum celeriter adfore; hortātur ut prīstinam virtūtem retineat. Gallus perīculum veritus, ut erat praeceptum, trāgulam mittit. Haec cāsū ad turrim adhaesit neque ab nostrīs bīduō animadversa tertiō diē ā quōdam mīlite cōnspicitur, dēmpta ad Cicerōnem dēfertur. Ille perlēctam in conventū mīlitum recitat maximāque omnēs laetitiā adficit. Tum fūmī incendiōrum procul vidēbantur; quae rēs omnem dubitātiōnem adventūs legiōnum expulit.

Book Six
Caesar DĒ BELLŌ GALLICŌ 6.13–6.20

[6.13] In omnī Galliā eōrum hominum, quī aliquō sunt numerō atque honōre, genera sunt duo. Nam plēbēs paene servōrum habētur locō, quae nihil audet per sē, nūllō adhibētur cōnsiliō. Plērīque, cum aut aere aliēnō aut magnitūdine tribūtōrum aut iniūriā potentiōrum premuntur, sēsē in servitūtem dicant nōbilibus; quibus in hōs eadem omnia sunt iūra, quae dominīs in servōs. Sed dē hīs duōbus generibus alterum est Druidum, alterum equitum. Illī rēbus dīvīnīs intersunt, sacrificia pūblica ac prīvāta prōcūrant, religiōnēs interpretantur: ad hōs magnus adulēscentium numerus disciplīnae causā concurrit, magnōque hī sunt apud eōs honōre. Nam ferē dē omnibus contrōversiīs pūblicīs prīvātīsque cōnstituunt, et, sī quod est admissum facinus, sī caedēs facta, sī dē hērēditāte, dē fīnibus contrōversia est, īdem dēcernunt, praemia poenāsque cōnstituunt; sī quī aut prīvātus aut populus eōrum dēcrētō nōn stetit, sacrificiīs interdīcunt. Haec poena apud eōs est gravissima. Quibus ita est interdictum, hī numerō impiōrum ac scelerātōrum habentur, hīs omnēs dēcēdunt, aditum sermōnemque dēfugiunt, nē quid ex contāgiōne incommodī accipiant, neque hīs petentibus iūs redditur neque honōs ūllus commūnicātur. Hīs autem omnibus Druidibus praeest ūnus, quī summam inter eōs habet auctōritātem. Hōc mortuō aut sī quī ex reliquīs excellit dignitāte succēdit, aut, sī sunt plūrēs parēs, suffrāgiō Druidum, nōnnumquam etiam armīs dē prīncipātū contendunt. Hī certō annī tempore in fīnibus Carnutum, quae regiō tōtīus Galliae media habētur, cōnsīdunt in locō cōnsecrātō. Hūc omnēs undique, quī contrōversiās habent, conveniunt eōrumque dēcrētīs iūdiciīsque pārent. Disciplīna in Britanniā reperta atque inde in Galliam trānslāta esse exīstimātur, et nunc, quī dīligentius eam rem cognōscere volunt, plērumque illō discendī causā proficīscuntur.

[6.14] Druidēs ā bellō abesse cōnsuērunt neque tribūta ūnā cum reliquīs pendunt; mīlitiae vacātiōnem omniumque rērum habent immūnitātem. Tantīs excitātī praemiīs et suā sponte multī in disciplīnam conveniunt et ā parentibus propinquīsque mittuntur. Magnum ibi numerum versuum ēdiscere dīcuntur. Itaque annōs nōnnūllī vīcēnōs in disciplīnā permanent. Neque fās esse exīstimant ea litterīs mandāre, cum in reliquīs ferē rēbus, pūblicīs prīvātīsque ratiōnibus, Graecīs litterīs ūtantur. Id mihi duābus dē causīs īnstituisse videntur, quod neque in vulgum disciplīnam efferrī velint neque eōs, quī discunt, litterīs cōnfīsōs minus memoriae studēre: quod ferē plērīsque accidit, ut praesidiō litterārum dīligentiam in perdiscendō ac memoriam remittant. In prīmīs hoc volunt persuādēre, nōn interīre animās, sed ab aliīs post mortem trānsīre ad aliōs, atque hōc maximē ad virtūtem excitārī putant metū mortis neglēctō. Multa praetereā dē sīderibus atque eōrum mōtū, dē mundī ac terrārum magnitūdine, dē rērum nātūrā, dē deōrum immortālium vī ac potestāte disputant et iuventūtī trādunt.

[6.15] Alterum genus est equitum. Hī, cum est ūsus atque aliquod bellum incidit (quod ferē ante Caesaris adventum quotannīs accidere solēbat, utī aut ipsī iniūriās īnferrent aut illātās prōpulsārent), omnēs in bellō versantur, atque eōrum ut quisque est genere cōpiīsque amplissimus, ita plūrimōs circum sē ambactōs clientēsque habet. Hanc ūnam grātiam potentiamque nōvērunt.

[6.16] Nātiō est omnis Gallōrum admodum dēdita religiōnibus, atque ob eam causam, quī sunt adfectī graviōribus morbīs quīque in proeliīs perīculīsque versantur, aut prō victimīs hominēs immolant aut sē immolātūrōs vovent administrīsque ad ea sacrificia Druidibus ūtuntur, quod, prō vītā hominis nisi hominis vīta reddātur, nōn posse deōrum immortālium nūmen plācārī arbitrantur, pūblicēque eiusdem generis habent īnstitūta sacrificia. Aliī immānī magnitūdine simulācra habent, quōrum contexta vīminibus membra vīvīs hominibus complent; quibus succēnsīs circumventī flammā exanimantur hominēs. Supplicia eōrum quī in fūrtō aut in latrōciniō aut aliquā noxiā sint comprehēnsī grātiōra dīs immortālibus esse arbitrantur; sed, cum eius generis cōpia dēficit, etiam ad innocentium supplicia dēscendunt.

[6.17] Deum maximē Mercurium colunt. Huius sunt plūrima simulācra: hunc omnium inventōrem artium ferunt, hunc viārum atque itinerum ducem, hunc ad quaestūs pecūniae mercātūrāsque habēre vim maximam arbitrantur. Post hunc Apollinem et Mārtem et Iovem et Minervam. Dē hīs eandem ferē, quam reliquae gentēs, habent opīniōnem: Apollinem morbōs dēpellere, Minervam operum atque artificiōrum initia trādere, Iovem imperium caelestium tenēre, Mārtem bella regere. Huic, cum proeliō dīmicāre cōnstituērunt, ea quae bellō cēperint plērumque dēvovent: cum superāvērunt, animālia capta immolant reliquāsque rēs in ūnum locum cōnferunt. Multīs in cīvitātibus hārum rērum exstrūctōs tumulōs locīs cōnsecrātīs cōnspicārī licet; neque saepe accidit, ut neglēctā quispiam religiōne aut capta apud sē occultāre aut posita tollere audēret, gravissimumque eī reī supplicium cum cruciātū cōnstitūtum est.

[6.18] Gallī sē omnēs ab Dīte patre prōgnātōs praedicant idque ab Druidibus prōditum dīcunt. Ob eam causam spatia omnis temporis nōn numerō diērum sed noctium fīniunt; diēs nātālēs et mēnsum et annōrum initia sīc observant ut noctem diēs subsequātur. In reliquīs vītae īnstitūtīs hōc ferē ab reliquīs differunt, quod suōs līberōs, nisi cum adolēvērunt, ut mūnus mīlitiae sustinēre possint, palam ad sē adīre nōn patiuntur fīliumque puerīlī aetāte in pūblicō in cōnspectū patris assistere turpe dūcunt.

[6.19] Virī, quantās pecūniās ab uxōribus dōtis nōmine accēpērunt, tantās ex suīs bonīs aestimātiōne factā cum dōtibus commūnicant. Huius omnis pecūniae coniūnctim ratiō habētur frūctūsque servantur: uter eōrum vītā superārit, ad eum pars utrīusque cum frūctibus superiōrum temporum pervenit. Virī in uxōrēs, sīcutī in līberōs, vītae necisque habent potestātem; et cum pater familiae illūstriōre locō nātus dēcessit, eius propinquī conveniunt et, dē morte sī rēs in suspīciōnem vēnit, dē uxōribus in servīlem modum quaestiōnem habent et, sī compertum est, ignī atque omnibus tormentīs excruciātās interficiunt. Fūnera sunt prō cultū Gallōrum magnifica et sūmptuōsa; omniaque quae vīvīs cordī fuisse arbitrantur in ignem īnferunt, etiam animālia, ac paulō suprā hanc memoriam servī et clientēs, quōs ab eīs dīlēctōs esse cōnstābat, iūstīs fūneribus cōnfectīs ūnā cremābantur.

[6.20] Quae cīvitātēs commodius suam rem pūblicam administrāre exīstimantur, habent lēgibus sānctum, sī quis quid dē rē pūblicā ā fīnitimīs rūmōre aut fāmā accēperit, utī ad magistrātum dēferat nēve cum quō aliō commūnicet, quod saepe hominēs temerāriōs atque imperītōs falsīs rūmōribus terrērī et ad facinus impellī et dē summīs rēbus cōnsilium capere cognitum est. Magistrātūs quae vīsa sunt occultant quaeque esse ex ūsū iudicāvērunt multitūdinī prōdunt. Dē rē pūblicā nisi per concilium loquī nōn concēditur.

——————— ENGLISH READINGS ———————

THE GALLIC WAR, by Julius Caesar

Translated by W. A. McDevitte and W. S. Bohn, from *Caesar's Commentaries*, in Harper's Classical Library, Harper & Brothers: New York, 1869; revised by Hans-Friedrich Mueller, 2011.

C *aesar held his tumultuous consulship in 59 BCE. In 58 BCE, he took up his duties as governor of Roman Gaul, which included districts in northern Italy (i.e., nearer or **cis**-Alpine Gaul) and, beyond the Alps, territory along the Mediterranean coast that now belongs to France (i.e., the Province, a.k.a. further or **trans**-Alpine Gaul). Many of the inhabitants in these territories were ethnically and linguistically related to the Gauls whose territory Caesar would soon invade. Caesar begins the book with a brief overview of Gaul's geography and inhabitants. He quickly moves on to describe political turmoil among the Helvetii, a people who inhabited territory in what is now Switzerland, and who thus lived just across the border from Roman jurisdiction. Rome had always taken an interest in its neighbors on the grounds that what was near to them was a legitimate security interest, and Caesar will be careful to explain why his intervention in non-Roman territory was undertaken to protect the safety of his province. He does not present what he does as the opening of a war to conquer all Gaul. Quite the contrary. Once he has entered Gaul, however, he soon finds another reason to continue the war. According to Caesar, Gallic tribes request his assistance in driving out another invader, Ariovistus, who crossed the Rhine from German territory with a large number of Germans. Another Roman principle was that Romans help their friends. Ariovistus's settlement in Gallic territory also represented another threat to Rome, and the Romans considered the Germans even more formidable and dangerous adversaries than the Gauls. At all events, after crossing into Gaul to deal with the Helvetii, Caesar will subsequently defeat Ariovistus and the Germans. The invasion of Gaul has begun!*

KEY TRIBES OF GAUL

Britannia

GERMĀNĪ

BELGAE

Sēquana

Matrona

Rhēnus

CELTAE

Lutetia
Parisiōrum

ĀTLANTICUS
ŌCEANUS

GALLIA

AEDUĪ

SĒQUANĪ

HELVĒTIĪ

AMBARRĪ

ALLOBROGĒS

Arar

Rhodanus

ALPĒS MONTĒS

*Gallia
Cisalpina*

*Gallia
Transalpīna/
Prōvincia*

Garumna

AQUĪTĀNĪ

PῩRĒNAEĪ MONTĒS

ĪTALIA

HISPĀNIA

Septentriōnēs

Occidēns —— Oriēns

Meridiēs

0   500 miles

0   500 km

© 2012 Bolchazy-Carducci Publishers, Inc.

BOOK 1 [58 BCE]

NB: Because BG 1.1–7 is covered in Latin in this book and in order to eliminate any temptation to peek at the translation during class, we do not provide the translation of these passages here. Instead, we offer a brief summary of each omitted chapter.

CHAPTER 1: CAESAR SURVEYS GAUL: GEOGRAPHY AND ETHNOGRAPHY

Caesar talks about the geographical and ethnographical features of Gaul. The area may represent a geographical unity, but Caesar divides it ethnographically into three distinct regions on the basis of language and culture.

CHAPTER 2: MEET THE HELVETII AND ORGETORIX, THE CONSPIRATOR

Caesar introduces the Helvetii, who lived just across the border from his Roman province. He also introduces Orgetorix, who, according to Caesar, has formed a conspiracy with the goal of conquering all of Gaul. As a first step, the Helvetii must leave their homes and move deeper into Gallic territory.

CHAPTER 3: THE SCHEME TO CONQUER GAUL

Orgetorix enlists allies among neighbors and conspires to take over his state.

CHAPTER 4: ORGETORIX ON TRIAL AND A MYSTERIOUS DEATH

The Helvetii discover the conspiracy and put Orgetorix on trial, but he dies before the trial can be concluded.

CHAPTER 5: EVEN WITHOUT ORGETORIX, THE HELVETII PROCEED ACCORDING TO THE PLAN

Despite the death of Orgetorix, the plan to emigrate from Helvetia proceeds. They stockpile provisions and continue to enlist allies.

CHAPTER 6: TWO WAYS TO LEAVE HELVETIA

Caesar explains that there are two possible routes for the Helvetii to emigrate. The easier route passes through Roman territory, the more difficult route through the territory of the Sequani.

CHAPTER 7: CAESAR TAKES ACTION

Caesar learns that the Helvetii are on the move and wish to pass through Roman territory. Caesar has the bridge across the Rhone torn down. Helvetian ambassadors visit Caesar, and request permission to pass through Roman territory. Caesar tells them that he will consider their request and that they should return on the Ides of April.

CHAPTER 8: CAESAR PREVENTS THE HELVETII FROM PASSING THROUGH ROMAN TERRITORY

Meanwhile, with the legion that he had with him and the soldiers who had assembled from the Province, Caesar built a nineteen-mile-long wall, to the height of sixteen feet, and a trench, from the Lake of Geneva (which flows into the river Rhone) to Mount Jura (which separates the territories of the Sequani from those of the Helvetii). When that work was finished, he distributed garrisons and well-fortified posts, in order that he might more easily intercept the Helvetii, if they attempted to cross over against his will. When the day came that he had appointed with the ambassadors and they returned to him, he stated that he could not, consistently with the custom and precedent of the Roman people, grant anyone passage through the Province; and he let them understand that, if they should attempt to use violence, he would oppose them. The Helvetii, disappointed in this hope, attempted to force a passage, some by means of a bridge of boats and numerous rafts constructed for the purpose; others, by the fords of the Rhone, where the river was shallowest, sometimes by day, but more frequently by night. Being kept at bay by the strength of our works, however, and by the concentration of the soldiers, and by the javelins, they desisted from this attempt.

CHAPTER 9: THE HELVETII DECIDE TO TRY THE ROUTE THROUGH NON-ROMAN TERRITORY

There was one other route, namely, through the territory of the Sequani. On account of its narrowness, however, they could not travel by this route without the consent of the Sequani. As they could not of themselves prevail on the Sequani, they sent ambassadors to Dumnorix the Aeduan, in order that, through his intercession, they might obtain their request. Dumnorix, by his popularity and generosity, had great influence among the Sequani, and was friendly to the Helvetii, because he had married the daughter of Orgetorix of the Helvetian state; and, incited by a lust for supreme authority, was eager for a revolution, and wished to have as many states as possible obligated to him by his kindness toward them. He, therefore, undertook the business and prevailed upon the Sequani to allow the Helvetii to march through their territories, and he arranged that they should give hostages to each other as a guarantee—the Sequani not to obstruct the Helvetii in their march, the Helvetii to pass through without crime and violence.

CHAPTER 10: CAESAR GATHERS HIS ARMY AND INVADES NON-ROMAN GAUL

Caesar was told that the Helvetii intended to march through the country of the Sequani and the Aedui into the territories of the Santones, which are not far distant from those boundaries of the Tolosates, which is a state in the Province. If this took place, he saw that it would be extremely dangerous for the Province to have warlike men, who were enemies of the Roman people, bordering upon an open and very fertile tract of country. For these reasons he appointed Titus Labienus, his lieutenant, to the command of the fortification that he had made. He himself proceeded to Italy by forced marches, and there levied two legions, and led out from winter quarters three legions, which were spending the winter near Aquileia, and with these five legions he marched rapidly by the nearest route across the Alps into Further Gaul. Here the Centrones and the Graioceli and the Caturiges, having taken possession of the higher elevations, attempted to obstruct the army in their march. After having routed these tribes in several battles, Caesar arrived in the territories of the Vocontii in the Further Province on the seventh day from Ocelum, which is the most remote town of the Nearer Province (in northern Italy). From this place, he led his army into the country of the Allobroges, and from the Allobroges to the Segusiavi. These people are the first beyond the Province on the opposite side of the Rhone.

CHAPTER 11: WEAKER TRIBES IN GAUL ASK CAESAR FOR PROTECTION AGAINST THE HELVETII

The Helvetii had by this time led their forces over through the narrow defile and the territories of the Sequani, and had arrived at the territories of the Aedui, and were ravaging their lands. The Aedui, as they could not defend themselves and their possessions against the Helvetii, sent ambassadors to Caesar to ask for assistance, pleading that, because they had at all times so well served the interests of the Roman people, their fields ought not to have been laid waste, their children carried off into slavery, their towns stormed, almost within sight of our army! At the same time the Ambarri, the friends and kinsmen of the Aedui, apprised Caesar that it was not easy for them, now that their fields had been devastated, to ward off the violence of the enemy from their towns. The Allobroges likewise, who had villages and possessions on the other side of the Rhone, fled for refuge to Caesar and assured him that they had nothing left except the soil of their land. Caesar, induced by these circumstances, decided that he should not wait until the Helvetii, after destroying all the property of his allies, arrived among the Santones.

Ancient coins are an invaluable source for reconstructing the ancient world. They provide insight into the material culture of the period as well as insight into the ideals and messages communicated by the coin's images. This coin shows the profile of a Gallic chieftain and, on the obverse, presumably his horse.

CHAPTER 12: CAESAR CONFRONTS THE HELVETII AND WINS A BATTLE

There is a river called the Saone (Arar), which flows through the territories of the Aedui and Sequani into the Rhone with such incredible slowness, that it cannot be determined by the eye in which direction it flows. The Helvetii were crossing this river by rafts and boats joined together. When Caesar was informed by spies that the Helvetii had already conveyed three-fourths of their forces across that river, but that the fourth part was left behind on the nearer side of the Saone, he set out from the camp with three legions during the third watch of the night, and came upon that division that had not yet crossed the river. Attacking them encumbered with baggage and not expecting him, he cut to pieces a great part of them. The rest took to flight, and concealed themselves in the nearest woods. The name of that canton [which was cut down] was called the Tigurine; for the whole Helvetian state is divided into four cantons. This single canton, having left their country, within the recollection of our fathers, had slain Lucius Cassius, the consul, and had made his army pass under the yoke [in 107 BCE]. Thus, whether by chance, or by the design of the immortal gods, that part of the Helvetian state that had brought a signal calamity upon the Roman people was the first to pay the penalty. In this action, Caesar avenged not only the public but also his own personal injuries, because the Tigurini had slain, in the same battle as Cassius himself, Cassius's lieutenant, Lucius Piso, the grandfather of Lucius Calpurnius Piso, Caesar's father-in-law.

Chapter 13: The Helvetii Negotiate with Caesar but Refuse to Back Down

After this battle was over, in order that he might be able to catch up with the remaining forces of the Helvetii, Caesar had a bridge put across the Saone, and then led his army over it. The Helvetii, confused by his sudden arrival, when they found that Caesar had accomplished in one day what they themselves had with the utmost difficulty accomplished in twenty, namely, the crossing of the river, sent ambassadors to him. At the head of the embassy was Divico, who had been commander of the Helvetii in the war against Cassius. He negotiated with Caesar, stating that if the Roman people would make peace with the Helvetii, they would go to that part of Gaul, and stay there wherever Caesar might appoint and desire them to be—but, if, on the other hand, Caesar persisted in persecuting them with war, he ought to remember both the ancient disgrace of the Roman people and the characteristic valor of the Helvetii. As to his having attacked one canton by surprise, at a time when those who had crossed the river could not bring assistance to their friends, he ought not on that account to ascribe very much credit to his own valor or despise the Helvetii. They had learned from their fathers and ancestors to rely more on valor than on trickery and ambush. For this reason, let Caesar not bring it to pass that the place where they were standing should acquire a name from the disaster of the Roman people and the destruction of their army or transmit the remembrance [of such a disaster to posterity].

Chapter 14: Caesar Replies with Harsh Demands of his own to the Helvetian Ambassadors

To these words Caesar replied that, for that reason, he felt less need to hesitate, because he kept in remembrance those circumstances that the Helvetian ambassadors had mentioned, and he felt all the more indignant about these events, to the extent that they had happened undeservedly to the Roman people. For, if they had been conscious of having done anything wrong, it would not have been difficult for them to be on their guard. For that very reason, however, they had been deceived, because neither were they aware that they had committed any offense, on account of which they should be afraid, nor did they think that they ought to be afraid without cause. But, even if he were willing to forget their former atrocity, could he also lay aside the remembrance of the recent injuries, in that they had, against his will, attempted to take a route through the Province by force, in that they had harassed the Aedui, the Ambarri, and the Allobroges? As to their so insolently boasting of their victory, and as to their being astonished that they had for such a long time committed their outrages with impunity, both these things pointed to the same conclusion, for the immortal gods generally allow those persons, whom they wish to punish for their guilt, to enjoy for a time a greater prosperity and longer impunity, in order that they may suffer all the more severely from a reverse of fortune. Although these things were true, yet, if the Helvetii gave hostages to Caesar, in order that he might be assured that they would do what they promised, and, provided they would give satisfaction to the Aedui for the outrages which the Helvetii had committed against the Aedui and their allies, and likewise to the Allobroges, Caesar would make peace with them.

Divico replied that the Helvetii had been so trained by their ancestors, that they were accustomed to receive, not to give hostages—of that fact the Roman people were witness. Having given this reply, he withdrew.

CHAPTER 15: THE HELVETII CONTINUE THEIR MARCH; CAESAR FOLLOWS.

On the following day, the Helvetii moved their camp from that place. Caesar did the same, and sent ahead all his cavalry, about four thousand in number (which he had drawn together from all parts of the Province and from the Aedui and their allies), to observe in what direction the enemy were heading in their march. The cavalry, having too eagerly pursued the enemy's rear, engaged in a battle with the cavalry of the Helvetii in a disadvantageous place, and a few of our men fell. The Helvetii, elated with this battle, because they had with five hundred cavalry repulsed so large a body of cavalry, began to face us more boldly, sometimes too from their rear to provoke our men by an attack. Caesar, however, restrained his men from battle, deeming it sufficient for the present to prevent the enemy from plundering, foraging, and destroying. They marched for about fifteen days in such a manner that there was not more than five or six miles between the enemy's rear and our vanguard.

CHAPTER 16: CAESAR HAS TROUBLE MAINTAINING HIS LINES OF SUPPLY

Meanwhile, Caesar kept daily importuning the Aedui for the grain that they had promised in the name of their state, for, in consequence of the coldness (Gaul, as mentioned earlier, is situated toward the north), not only was the grain in the fields not ripe, but there was not in store a sufficiently large quantity even of fodder for the animals. Besides, Caesar was unable to use the grain that he had conveyed in ships up the river Saone, because the Helvetii, from whose pursuit he was unwilling to desist, had diverted their march away from the Saone. The Aedui kept deferring from day to day, and saying that it was "being collected—brought in—on the road." When Caesar saw that they were putting him off too long, and that the day was close at hand on which he was supposed to distribute grain to his soldiers—having called together their chiefs, of whom he had a great number in his camp, among them Diviciacus and Liscus who was invested with the chief magistracy (whom the Aedui style "the Vergobretus," and who is elected annually and has the power of life and death over his countrymen)—he severely reprimanded them, because he was not assisted by them on so urgent an occasion, when the enemy was so close at hand, and when grain could neither be bought nor harvested from the fields, particularly as he had undertaken the war in large measure because he had been urged by their prayers. Much more bitterly therefore did Caesar complain of his being forsaken.

CHAPTER 17: LISCUS REVEALS A CONSPIRACY AMONG CAESAR'S ALLIES IN CAESAR'S CAMP

Then at length Liscus, moved by Caesar's speech, disclosed what he had until then kept secret: there were some whose influence with the people was very great, who, though private men, had more power than the magistrates themselves. These men by seditions and violent language were deterring the populace from contributing the grain that they were supposed to supply by telling them that, if they could no longer retain their supremacy in Gaul, it would be better to submit to the government of fellow Gauls than of

Romans, nor should they have any doubt that, if the Romans overpowered the Helvetii, they would obtain their freedom from the Aedui together with the remainder of Gaul.

By these very men, Liscus explained, were our plans and whatever was done in the camp, disclosed to the enemy. They could not be restrained by him, and, what was more, Liscus was well aware at how great a risk to himself that he, although compelled by necessity, had disclosed the matter to Caesar; and for that reason, he had remained silent as long as he could.

CHAPTER 18: CAESAR INTERROGATES LISCUS AND MAKES INQUIRIES INTO DUMNORIX'S CONDUCT

Caesar perceived that Liscus's speech implicated Dumnorix, the brother of Diviciacus. As he was unwilling, however, to discuss these matters while so many were present, he speedily dismissed the council, but detained Liscus. He inquired from Liscus when alone about the matters he had mentioned in the meeting. Liscus spoke more unreservedly and boldly. Caesar made inquiries on the same points privately of others, and discovered that it was all true, and that Dumnorix was the person, a man of the highest daring, in great favor with the people on account of his generosity, a man eager for a revolution. For a great many years Dumnorix had been in the habit of obtaining the contract for the collection of the customs and all the other taxes of the Aedui at a small cost, because, when he bid for the contract, no one dared to bid against him. By these means, he had both increased his own private property and amassed great means for giving largesses. He maintained constantly at his own expense and kept about his own person a great number of cavalry. Not only at home, but even among the neighboring states, he had great influence, and for the sake of strengthening this influence had given his mother in marriage among the Bituriges to the most noble and most influential man there. He had himself taken a wife from among the Helvetii, and had given his sister by the mother's side and his female relations in marriage into other states. He favored and wished well to the Helvetii on account of this connection. He hated Caesar and the Romans on his own account, because by their arrival his power was weakened, and his brother Diviciacus had been restored to his former position of influence and dignity. If anything were to happen to the Romans, he would entertain the highest hope of gaining the supreme authority by means of the Helvetii, but, under the government of the Roman people, he despaired not only of political rule, but even of that influence which he already had.

Caesar discovered too, on inquiring into the unsuccessful cavalry engagement, which had taken place a few days before, that the commencement of that flight had been made by Dumnorix and his cavalry (for Dumnorix was in command of the cavalry whom the Aedui had sent to aid to Caesar); and that by their flight the rest of the cavalry were dismayed.

CHAPTER 19: CAESAR SUMMONS DIVICIACUS, THE BROTHER OF DUMNORIX

After learning these circumstances, the most unequivocal facts confirmed these suspicions. Dumnorix had led the Helvetii through the territories of the Sequani. Dumnorix had arranged that hostages should be mutually exchanged. Dumnorix had done all these things, not only without any orders from Caesar and from his own state, but even without the Aedui knowing anything about it themselves. Dumnorix stood accused by the chief magistrate of the Aedui. Caesar considered that there was sufficient reason why he should either punish Dumnorix himself, or order the state to do so. One thing, however, stood in the way of all this—he had learned by experience his brother Diviciacus's very high regard for the Roman people, his great affection toward Caesar, Diviciancus's distinguished faithfulness, justice, and moderation. For this reason, Caesar was afraid lest, by the punishment of Dumnorix, he should hurt the feelings of Diviciacus. Therefore, before he attempted anything, he ordered Diviciacus to be summoned to him, and, when the ordinary interpreters had been withdrawn, conversed with him through Gaius Valerius Procillus, chief of the province of Gaul, an intimate friend of Caesar's, in whom he reposed the highest confidence in everything. At the same time, Caesar reminded Diviciacus of what was said about Dumnorix in the council of the Gauls, when he himself was present, and showed what each had said about Dumnorix privately in Caesar's own presence. Caesar asked and exhorted him, that, without offense to Diviciacus's feelings, he might either himself pass judgment on Dumnorix after trying the case, or else order the Aeduan state to do so.

CHAPTER 20: DIVICIACUS CRIES, CAESAR RELENTS, AND DUMNORIX RECEIVES A SCOLDING

Diviciacus, embracing Caesar, began to implore him with many tears not to pass any very severe sentence upon his brother; saying that he knew that those charges were true, and that nobody suffered more pain on that account than he himself did, for, at the time when he exercised

great power as well as influence at home and in the rest of Gaul and Dumnorix enjoyed very little of either on account of his youth, Dumnorix
had become powerful through his assistance. This power and strength
Dumnorix now used not only in diminishing Diviciacus's popularity,
but almost to his ruin. He, however, was influenced both by brotherly
affection and by public opinion. But, if anything very severe from Caesar should befall Dumnorix, no one would think that it had been done
without Diviciacus's consent, since he himself held such a distinguished
place in Caesar's friendship. From this circumstance, the affections of the
whole of Gaul would be estranged from Caesar. While he was, with tears,
begging these things of Caesar in many words, Caesar took Diviciacus's
right hand and comforted him. Caesar begged him to make an end of
entreating, and assured him that his regard for him was so great that, at
his desire and prayers, he forgave both the injuries of the Republic and his
private wrongs. Caesar summoned Dumnorix to himself. Caesar brought
in Dumnorix's brother. He pointed out what he censured in Dumnorix.
He laid before him what he perceived on his own, and what the state
complained of. He warned Dumnorix for the future to avoid all grounds
of suspicion. He said that he pardoned the past for the sake of his brother
Diviciacus. Caesar then set spies over Dumnorix that he might be able to
know what he did, and with whom he communicated.

Chapter 21: Caesar Pursues the Helvetii—at Night

On the same day, Caesar was informed by his scouts that the enemy had
encamped at the foot of a mountain eight miles from his own camp. He
sent persons to ascertain the nature of the mountain and to determine
what sort of ascent there was on every side. Word was brought back that it
was easy. During the third watch of the night, he ordered Titus Labienus,
his lieutenant with praetorian powers, to ascend to the highest ridge of
the mountain with two legions, and with those men as guides who had
examined the road. Caesar explained what his plan was. He himself during the fourth watch hastened to them by the same route that the enemy
had used, and he sent all the cavalry ahead. Publius Considius, who was
reputed to be very experienced in military affairs, and had been in the
army of Lucius Sulla, and afterward in that of Marcus Crassus, was sent
ahead with the scouts.

CHAPTER 22: DAY DAWNS, BUT CONSIDIUS'S PANIC ATTACK SPOILS THE PLAN

At daybreak, when the summit of the mountain was in the possession of Titus Labienus, and he himself was not further off than a mile and a half from the enemy's camp, nor, as he afterward ascertained from the captives, had either his arrival or that of Labienus been discovered, Considius, with his horse at full gallop, came up to him, and said that the mountain that Caesar had wanted Labienus to seize was in possession of the enemy. He had allegedly discovered this by the Gallic arms and ensigns he witnessed. Caesar led off his forces to the next hill, and drew them up in battle order. Labienus, because he had been ordered by Caesar not to come to an engagement unless Caesar's own forces were seen near the enemy's camp, in order that the attack upon the enemy might be made on every side at the same time, was, after having taken possession of the mountain, waiting for our men and refraining from battle. When, at length, the day was far advanced, Caesar learned through spies that the mountain was actually in possession of his own men, and that the Helvetii had meanwhile moved their camp. Considius, struck with fear, had reported to Caesar eyewitness testimony of things that he had not actually seen. On that day, Caesar followed the enemy at his usual distance, and pitched his camp three miles from theirs.

CHAPTER 23: CAESAR DIVERTS HIS COURSE TO MAINTAIN HIS LINE OF SUPPLIES

The next day (as there remained in all only two day's space until the time when he had to distribute grain to his army, and as he was not more than eighteen miles from Bibracte, by far the largest and best-stored town of the Aedui), Caesar thought that he should provide for a supply of grain. He thus diverted his march from the Helvetii and advanced rapidly to Bibracte. This circumstance was reported to the enemy by some deserters from Lucius Aemilius, a captain of the Gallic cavalry. The Helvetii, either because they thought that the Romans, struck with terror, were retreating from them, all the more so, inasmuch as the day before, although they had seized on the higher grounds, they had not joined battle or because they flattered themselves that they might cut off the Romans from provisions, altered their plan, changed their route, and began to pursue and to harass our men in the rear.

CHAPTER 24: THE HELVETII ATTACK

Caesar, when he observed this, drew off his forces to the next hill, and sent the cavalry to sustain the attack of the enemy. He himself, meanwhile, drew up on the middle of the hill a triple line of his four veteran legions in such a manner that he placed above him on the very summit the two legions, which he had lately levied in Nearer Gaul, and all the auxiliaries. He ordered the whole mountain to be covered with men, and at the same time the baggage to be brought together into one place, and the position to be protected by those who were posted in the upper line. The Helvetii, who had followed with all their wagons, collected their baggage into one place. They themselves, after they repulsed our cavalry and formed a phalanx, advanced up to our front line in very close order.

CHAPTER 25: CAESAR DESCRIBES THE BATTLE

Caesar removed out of sight first his own horse and then those of all the men, so that he might make the danger equal for everyone, and thus do away with the hope of flight. After encouraging his men, he joined battle. His soldiers, hurling their javelins from the higher ground, easily broke the enemy's phalanx. After they dispersed the phalanx, they made a charge on the Helvetii with drawn swords. The Gauls were very much hindered in the fight whenever several of their shields were, by one stroke of the Roman javelins, pierced through and pinned fast together. The point of the iron would bend upon impact, and, as a result, the Helvetii could neither pluck it out, nor, with their left hand entangled, fight with sufficient ease. For this reason, many of them, after an unsuccessful attempt to shake the javelin loose, chose rather to cast away the shield from their hand, and to fight with their person unprotected. At length, worn out with wounds, they began to give way, and, as there was in the neighborhood a mountain about a mile off, to flee in that direction. When they had reached the mountain, and our men were approaching, the Boii and Tulingi (who, with about 15,000 men, followed closely the enemy's line of march, and served as a guard to their rear) attacked our men on the exposed flank as they advanced in order to surround our men. Upon seeing this, the Helvetii, who had fled to the mountain, began to attack again and renew the battle. The Romans then shifted their formation, and advanced to the attack in two divisions: the first and second line to resist those who had been defeated and driven off the field; the third line to meet those who were just arriving.

CHAPTER 26: CAESAR DEFEATS THE HELVETII

In such fashion the contest was long and vigorously carried on with doubtful success. When the Helvetii could no longer withstand the attacks of our men, one division, as they had initially begun to do, fled to the mountain. The other division retreated to their baggage and wagons. During this entire battle, although the fight lasted from the seventh hour [i.e., early afternoon] to evening, no one could see an enemy with his back turned. The fight was carried on also at the baggage till late in the night, for the Helvetii had set wagons in the way as a rampart, and some, from the higher ground, kept throwing weapons upon our men as they approached, and others, from between the wagons and the wheels, kept hurling their lances and javelins from below, and wounding our men. After the fight had lasted for some time, our men gained possession of their baggage and camp. There the daughter and one of the sons of Orgetorix were captured. After the battle, about 130,000 persons remained alive. They marched incessantly during the whole of that night, and, after a march discontinued for no part of the night, arrived in the territories of the Lingones on the fourth day. Our men, meanwhile, stopped for three days, both to care for wounded soldiers and to bury the dead, and thus had not been able to follow them. Caesar sent letters and messengers to the Lingones with orders not to assist the Helvetii with grain or with anything else; and instructed the Ligones that, if they were to assist them, he would regard them in the same light as the Helvetii. After the three days' interval, Caesar began to follow the Helvetii himself with all his forces.

CHAPTER 27: TERMS FOR PEACE AND A NOCTURNAL ESCAPE

The Helvetii, compelled by their complete lack of supplies, sent ambassadors to Caesar to discuss surrender. The ambassadors met Caesar on the way and threw themselves at his feet. Speaking in suppliant tone, with tears they sued for peace. Caesar ordered them to await his arrival in the place where the Helvetii then were. The ambassadors obeyed his commands. When Caesar arrived at that place, he demanded hostages, their weapons, and the slaves who had deserted to them. While the Helvetii were searching for and collecting everything, after a night's interval, about 6,000 men of that canton which is called the Verbigene, whether, terrified by the fear that, after delivering up their arms, they would suffer punishment, or else induced by the hope of safety, because they supposed that, amid so vast a multitude of those who had surrendered themselves, their own escape might either be concealed or entirely overlooked, at nightfall departed out of the camp of the Helvetii, and hastened to the Rhine and the territories of the Germans.

CHAPTER 28: CAESAR SENDS THE HELVETII HOME

But when Caesar discovered this, he commanded the people through whose territory they had fled to hunt them down, and to bring them back again, if they wanted Caesar to acquit them of complicity. After these escapees had been brought back, Caesar treated them as enemies. All the other Helvetii, however, Caesar admitted to a surrender after they had delivered the hostages, weapons, and deserters. Caesar ordered the Helvetii, the Tulingi, and the Latobrigi to return home to the territories from which they had come. But, because they had destroyed their crops and there was at home no means to stave off famine, he commanded the Allobroges to let them have a plentiful supply of grain. Caesar also ordered them to rebuild the towns and villages that they had burned. This he did, chiefly, on this account, because he was unwilling that the country, from which the Helvetii had departed, should be left unoccupied. Otherwise, the Germans, who dwell on the other side of the Rhine, on account of the excellence of the lands, might cross over from their own territories into those of the Helvetii, and become neighbors to the province of Gaul and the Allobroges. Caesar granted the petition of the Aedui, that they might allow the Boii to settle in their own (i.e., in the Aeduan) territories, as the Boii were known to be of distinguished valor. The Aedui gave them farmlands, and they afterwards admitted them to the same state of rights and freedom as themselves.

CHAPTER 29: CAESAR'S MATH LESSON: WHAT IS THE DIFFERENCE BETWEEN 368,000 AND 110,000?

In the camp of the Helvetii, lists were found, drawn up in Greek characters, and were brought to Caesar, in which an estimate had been drawn up, name by name, of the number of Helvetii who had emigrated from their country, the number of those who were able to bear arms, and likewise the number of boys, of old men, and of women, separately. The total number of all Helvetii was 263,000; of Tulingi, 36,000; of Latobrigi, 14,000; of Rauraci, 23,000; of Boii, 32,000. The grand total of all these people amounted to 368,000. Of all these people, the number who could bear arms amounted to about 92,000. When, as Caesar had commanded, the census of those who returned home was taken, the number was found to be 110,000.

CHAPTER 30: GAUL NOTICES CAESAR'S VICTORY AND REQUESTS A MEETING

When the war with the Helvetii was concluded, ambassadors from almost all parts of Gaul, who were the leaders of the various states, assembled to congratulate Caesar. They stated that they were well aware that, although he had taken vengeance on the Helvetii in war for the old wrong done by the Helvetii to the Roman people, yet that event had turned out to be of benefit no less to the land of Gaul than of the Roman people, because the Helvetii, although their affairs were most prosperous, had abandoned their country with the design of waging war upon the whole of Gaul. They also aimed at seizing the government of Gaul, and at selecting, out of a great abundance, that spot for their own abode, which they should judge to be the most convenient and most productive of all Gaul, and they planned to hold the rest of the states as tributaries. The ambassadors requested that they might be allowed to proclaim an assembly of the whole of Gaul for a particular day, and to do that with Caesar's permission. They stated that they had some things, which, with the general consent, they wished to ask of Caesar. Caesar granted their request, and they appointed a day for the assembly, and ordained by an oath with each other, that their deliberations were to be disclosed only by those to whom this duty should be assigned by the general assembly.

CHAPTER 31: THE GAULS COMPLAIN ABOUT ARIOVISTUS AND THE GERMANS

When that assembly was dismissed, the same chiefs of states, who had before been to Caesar, returned. They asked that they might be allowed to discuss with him privately concerning their own safety and the safety of all. After they obtained their request, they all threw themselves in tears at Caesar's feet. They stated that they begged and earnestly desired no less that what they might say should remain secret than that they might obtain the things they wished for. For they saw that if a disclosure were made, they would be put to the greatest tortures.

Diviciacus the Aeduan spoke on their behalf, and he told Caesar that there were two parties in the whole of Gaul; that the Aedui stood at the head of one of the two parties, the Arverni at the head of the other. After the Aedui and Arverni had already been violently struggling with one another for dominance for many years, it happened that the Arverni and Sequani hired Germans as mercenaries. At first about 15,000 Germans crossed the Rhine.

But, after that, these wild and savage men fell in love with the lands and the refinement and the abundance of the Gauls. More Germans were then brought over, and now there were as many as 120,000 of them in Gaul. The Aedui and their dependents had repeatedly struggled in arms with these Germans. The Aedui had been routed, and had sustained a great calamity. They had lost all their nobility, all their senate, all their cavalry. Moreover, broken by such engagements and calamities, although they had formerly been very powerful in Gaul, on account of both their own valor and the Roman people's hospitality and friendship, they were now compelled to give the chief nobles of their state as hostages to the Sequani, and to bind their state by an oath that they would neither demand hostages in return nor supplicate aid from the Roman people nor refuse to be forever under the sway and empire of the Sequani.

Diviciacus also stated that he was the only one out of all the state of the Aedui who could not be prevailed upon to take the oath or to give his children as hostages. For this reason, he had fled from his state and had gone to the Senate at Rome to beseech aid, as he alone was bound neither by oath nor hostages. But a worse thing had befallen the victorious Sequani than the vanquished Aedui, for Ariovistus, the king of the Germans, had settled in their territories, and had seized a third of their land, which was the best in the whole of Gaul, and was now ordering them to depart from another third of their land, because a few months ago 24,000 Harudes had come to him, for whom room and settlements had to be provided. The consequence of this would be that in a few years they would all be driven from the territories of Gaul, and all the Germans would cross the Rhine, because neither the land of the Germans nor their standard of living was on a level comparable to the level enjoyed by the Gauls.

Moreover, as for Ariovistus, no sooner did he defeat the forces of the Gauls in a battle (which took place at Magetobria) than he began to lord it over them haughtily and cruelly, demanding as hostages the children of all the principal nobles, and wreaking on them every kind of cruelty, if everything was not done at his nod or pleasure. He was a savage, passionate, and reckless man, and his commands could no longer be borne. Unless there was some aid from Caesar and the Roman people, the Gauls would all be compelled to do the same thing that the Helvetii had done, namely, emigrate from their country, and seek another dwelling place, other settlements remote from the Germans, and try whatever fortune may fall to their lot. If these things were to be disclosed to Ariovistus, Diviciacus added, he had no doubt that Ariovistus would inflict the most severe punishment on all the hostages who were in his possession. He also said that Caesar could, either by his own influence and by that of his army, or by his recent victory, or by name of the Roman people, intimidate Ariovistus, so as to prevent a greater number of Germans from being brought over the Rhine, and could protect all of Gaul from the outrages of Ariovistus.

CHAPTER 32: THE SEQUANI ARE TOO TERRIFIED TO SPEAK AT ALL

When this speech had been delivered by Diviciacus, all who were present began with loud lamentation to beg for assistance from Caesar. Caesar noticed that the Sequani were the only people among all of them who did none of the things that the others did, but, with their heads bowed down, gazed on the earth in sadness. Wondering what was the reason of this conduct, Caesar asked them. No reply did the Sequani make, but silently continued in the same sadness. When he had repeatedly inquired of them and could not elicit any answer at all, the same Diviciacus the Aeduan answered that the fate of the Sequani was more wretched and grievous than that of the rest, on this account, because they alone did not dare, even in secret, to complain or supplicate aid. They shuddered at the cruelty of Ariovistus, even when he was absent, just as if he were present, for, despite everything, the rest of them were at least granted an opportunity to escape; but the Sequani, who had admitted Ariovistus within their territories, and whose towns were all in his power, were compelled to endure all tortures.

CHAPTER 33: CAESAR DECIDES THAT THE GERMANS ARE A THREAT TO HIS PROVINCE AND TO ITALY

Caesar, after learning these things, cheered the minds of the Gauls with his words, and promised that this affair would be an object of his concern. He told them that he had great hopes that Ariovistus, induced both by his kindness and by his power, would put an end to his oppression. After delivering this speech, Caesar dismissed the assembly. And, besides those statements, many circumstances led Caesar to think that this business ought to be considered and taken up by him, especially as he saw that the Aedui, whom the Senate had repeatedly called "brothers" and "cousins by blood," were held in slavery and subjection to the Germans, and he was aware that their hostages were with Ariovistus and the Sequani. This, in so mighty an empire as that of the Roman people, he considered a huge disgrace to himself and the Republic. Moreover, if the Germans should by degrees become accustomed to cross the Rhine, and a great body of them should settle in Gaul, Caesar saw that this would be dangerous to the Roman people. He also reckoned that wild and savage men, after they had conquered all Gaul, would not likely restrain themselves from invading the Province, and, after this, from marching into Italy (as the Cimbri and Teutones had done before them), particularly as the river Rhone was the sole barrier that separated the Sequani from our province. To prevent these events, Caesar thought he ought to work as speedily as possible. Moreover, Ariovistus, for his part, had assumed to himself such pride and arrogance that he appeared insufferable.

CHAPTER 34: ARIOVISTUS REFUSES CAESAR'S DEMAND FOR A CONFERENCE

Caesar therefore determined to send ambassadors to Ariovistus to demand that he name some intermediate spot for a conference between the two of them. He stated that he wished to discuss with him state business and matters of the highest importance to both of them. To this embassy Ariovistus replied that, if he himself had had need of anything from Caesar, he would have gone to Caesar; and that, if Caesar wanted anything from him, Caesar ought to come to him. Besides, neither did he dare go without an army into those parts of Gaul that Caesar controlled nor could he, without great expense and trouble, assemble his army in one place. Moreover, it appeared strange to him what business either Caesar or the Roman people at all had in his own part of Gaul, which he had conquered in war.

CHAPTER 35: CAESAR MAKES MORE DETAILED DEMANDS

When these answers were reported to Caesar, he sent ambassadors to Ariovistus a second time with this message: "Since, after having been treated with so much kindness by Caesar and the Roman people (inasmuch as he had, during Caesar's consulship [in 59 BCE], been styled 'king and friend' by the Senate), he makes this recompense to Caesar and the Roman people, namely, that, when invited to a conference, he refuses, and does not think that it concerns him to advise and inform himself about an object of mutual interest, these are the things that Caesar requires of him: first, that he no longer bring any body of men across the Rhine into Gaul; in the next place, that he restore the hostages, whom he took from the Aedui, and that he grant the Sequani permission to restore to the Aedui with his consent those hostages whom they have, and that he neither provoke the Aedui by outrage nor wage war upon them or their allies. If he should, as instructed, do this," Caesar stated that "he himself and the Roman people will entertain a perpetual feeling of favor and friendship toward him; but, if Caesar does not obtain his desires, he (inasmuch as, in the consulship of Marcus Messala and Marcus Piso [in 61 BCE], the Senate had decreed that whoever should have the administration of the province of Gaul should, as far as he could do so consistently with the interests of the Republic, protect the Aedui and the other friends of the Roman people), will not ignore the wrongs done to the Aedui."

CHAPTER 36: ARIOVISTUS MAKES AN ARROGANT REPLY TO CAESAR'S DEMANDS

To this Ariovistus replied that the right of war was that they who had conquered should govern those whom they had conquered in what manner they pleased. In that same manner, the Roman people were accustomed to govern the nations that they had conquered, not according to the dictates of anyone else, but according to their own discretion. If he, for his part, did not dictate to the Roman people as to the manner in which they were to exercise their right, he ought not to be obstructed by the Roman people in his right. The Aedui, inasmuch as they had tried the fortune of war, and had engaged in arms and been conquered, had become tributaries to him. Caesar was doing a great injustice in that, by his arrival, Caesar was reducing the value of Ariovistus's revenues. Ariovistus was not going to restore their hostages to the Aedui, but neither would he make war wrongfully either upon them or their allies, provided that they abided by that which had been agreed on, and paid their tribute annually. If the Aedui did not continue to do that, the Roman people's name of "brothers" would not help them in the least. As to Caesar's threatening him, that Caesar would not ignore the wrongs done to the Aedui, Ariovistus stated that no one had ever entered into a contest with Ariovistus without utter ruin to himself. Caesar might enter the lists whenever he chose. He would then experience what invincible Germans, well-trained as they were beyond all others in arms, who, for fourteen years, had not been beneath a roof, could achieve by their valor.

CHAPTER 37: MORE GERMANS AND A SPEEDY DEPARTURE

At the same time that this message was delivered to Caesar, ambassadors came from the Aedui and the Treviri. The Aedui complained that the Harudes, who had lately been brought over into Gaul, were ravaging their territories, and that they had not been able to purchase peace from Ariovistus, even by giving hostages.

The Treviri stated that a hundred cantons of the Suebi had encamped on the banks of the Rhine, and were attempting to cross it, and that the brothers Nasua and Cimberius commanded them. Greatly alarmed by these reports, Caesar thought that he ought to use all speed, for fear that, if this new band of Suebi should unite with the old troops of Ariovistus, Ariovistus might be less easily resisted. Having therefore, as quickly as he could, provided a supply of grain, Caesar hastened to Ariovistus by forced marches.

CHAPTER 38: CAESAR SEIZES VESONTIO (BESANÇON)

When Caesar had proceeded three days' journey, word was brought to him that Ariovistus was hastening with all his forces to seize Vesontio, which is the largest town of the Sequani, and that Ariovistus had already advanced three days' journey from his territories. Caesar thought that he ought to take the greatest precautions to prevent this, for there was in that town a most ample supply of everything that was useful for war. This town was also so well fortified by the nature of the ground as to afford a great facility for conducting a war, inasmuch as the river Doubs (Dubis) almost surrounds the whole town, as though it were traced round it with a pair of compasses. A mountain of great height shuts in the remaining space, which is not more than 600 feet, where the river leaves a gap, in such a way that the base of that mountain extend to the river's bank on either side. A wall built around it turns this mountain into a citadel, and connects it with the town. Caesar hastened to this place by forced marches by night and day, and, after having seized the town, stationed a garrison there.

CHAPTER 39: CAESAR'S TROOPS PANIC

Caesar halted for a few days at Vesontio for the sake of grain and provisions. As a result of inquiries made by our men and the reports of the Gauls and traders (who asserted that the Germans were men of huge stature, of incredible valor and practice in arms—that frequently they, on encountering them, could not bear even their gaze and the fierceness of their eyes), a great panic suddenly seized the whole army, and discomposed the minds and spirits of all in no slight degree. This alarm first arose among the tribunes of the soldiers, the prefects, and the rest, who had followed Caesar from the City [of Rome] out of motives of friendship, but had no great experience in military affairs. Some of them alleged one reason, some another, that they said made it necessary for them to depart. They requested that with Caesar's consent they might be allowed to withdraw. Some, influenced by shame, stayed behind, in order that they might avoid the suspicion of cowardice. These men, however, could neither compose their countenance nor even sometimes check their tears. But, hidden in their tents, they either bewailed their fate or lamented with their comrades the general danger. Wills were sealed everywhere throughout the whole camp.

By the expressions and cowardice of these men, even those who possessed extensive military experience, both soldiers and centurions, and those who were in command of the cavalry [as decurions], were gradually disconcerted. Such of them, as they wished to be considered less alarmed, said that they did not dread the enemy, but feared the narrowness of the roads and the vastness of the forests that lay between them and Ariovistus, or else that the supplies could not be brought up readily enough. Some even declared to Caesar that, when Caesar gave orders for the camp to be moved and the troops to advance, the soldiers would not obey the command, nor advance as a result of their fear.

CHAPTER 40: CAESAR HARANGUES THE TROOPS

When Caesar observed these things, he called a council, and summoned to it the centurions of all the companies. He severely reprimanded them, particularly, for supposing that it belonged to them to inquire or conjecture, either in what direction they were marching, or with what object. Ariovistus, during Caesar's consulship [in 59 BCE], had most anxiously sought after the friendship of the Roman people—why should anyone believe that Ariovistus would so rashly depart from his duty? For his part, Caesar was persuaded that, when his demands were known and the fairness of the terms considered, Ariovistus would reject neither Caesar's nor the Roman people's favor.

But, even if, driven on by rage and madness, Ariovistus should make war upon them, why were they so scared? Or why should they despair either of their own valor or of Caesar's zeal? A trial had been made of that enemy within our fathers' recollection, when, at the defeat of the Cimbri [101 BCE] and Teutones [102 BCE] by Gaius Marius, the army was regarded as having deserved no less praise than their commander himself. Further tests had been passed recently, too, in Italy, during the rebellion of the slaves [73–71 BCE], who had even been assisted to some extent by the experience and training that they had received from us. From these experiences, an opinion might be formed concerning the advantages that courage carries with it, inasmuch as the enemies whom the Romans had for some time ground-lessly feared when they were unarmed, they had afterward defeated when their enemies were well-armed and flushed with success.

In short, these Germans were the same men whom the Helvetii have generally vanquished in frequent encounters not only in their own territo-ries but also in German territories, and yet even the Helvetii have not been a match for our army. If the unsuccessful battle and flight of the Gauls were a source of worry and concern, they, if they made inquiries, might discover that, when the Gauls had been tired out by the long duration of the war, Ariovistus, after he had many months kept himself in his camp and in the marshes, and had given no opportunity for a battle, suddenly attacked the Gauls, who, by this time, had given up hope of a battle, and were scattered in all directions. Ariovistus was victorious more through stratagem and cunning than valor. But, though there had been room for such stratagem against savage and unskilled men, not even Ariovistus himself expected that our armies could be entrapped by trickery.

Those, on the other hand, who attributed their fear to a pretense about the deficiency of supplies and the narrowness of the roads, acted presump-tuously, as they seemed either to distrust their general's discharge of his duty or to dictate to him. Such matters were Caesar's concern. The Sequani, the Leuci, and the Lingones were to furnish the grain, and it was already ripe in the fields. As to the road, they would soon be able to judge it for themselves.

As to the report that the soldiers would not obey Caesar's command or advance, he was not at all disturbed by that. For Caesar knew that in all cases where an army had refused to obey their general's command, ei-ther fortune had deserted the general after some mismanaged affair or his greed had been clearly proved after the discovery of some crime. Caesar's personal integrity had been on display throughout his whole life, and his good fortune in the war with the Helvetii was equally apparent. Caesar would therefore immediately put into action what he had intended to put off till a more distant day, and would break his camp the next night, in the fourth watch, in order that he might ascertain, as soon as possible, whether a sense of honor and duty or whether fear had more influence with them.

But, even if no one else would follow, he would still go with the tenth le-gion alone, whose absolute loyalty was beyond suspicion. They would serve as his praetorian cohort [the elite troops who escorted the commanding general]. Caesar had greatly favored this legion, and in it, on account of its valor, he placed the greatest confidence.

Chapter 41: The Army's Mood Changes and Caesar Departs before Dawn

Upon the delivery of this speech, the minds of all were changed in a surprising manner, and all the men were inspired with the greatest zeal and enthusiasm for prosecuting the war. The tenth legion was the first to return thanks to Caesar, through their military tribunes, for his having expressed this most favorable opinion of them. They assured him that they were quite ready to prosecute the war. Then, the other legions endeavored, through their military tribunes and the centurions of the principal companies, to excuse themselves to Caesar. They told him that they had never felt either doubt or fear, or had supposed that deciding on the conduct of the war was their task and not their general's. He accepted their excuse, and had the road carefully reconnoitered by Diviciacus, because Caesar had the greatest faith in him above all others. There was a circuitous route of more than fifty miles that would allow Caesar to lead his army through open territory. And he then set out in the fourth watch, as he had said he would. On the seventh day, as he did not interrupt his march, he was informed by scouts that the forces of Ariovistus were only twenty-four miles away from ours.

Chapter 42: Ariovistus Agrees to a Parley, and Caesar Converts his Infantry into a Cavalry

Upon being apprised of Caesar's arrival, Ariovistus sent ambassadors to him, indicating that the conference that Caesar had earlier requested might now, as far as he was concerned, take place, since Caesar had approached nearer, and he considered that he might now meet without danger. Caesar did not reject the proposal and began to think that Ariovistus was now returning to a rational state of mind, as he spontaneously proffered what he had previously refused when Caesar had requested it. And, in light of his own and the Roman people's great favors toward Ariovistus, Caesar was also in great hopes that, in the end, Ariovistus would desist from his obstinacy after he learned Caesar's demands. The day of the conference was set for the fifth day after that.

Meanwhile, inasmuch as ambassadors were often sent back and forth between them, Ariovistus demanded that Caesar not bring any foot soldiers with him to the conference, because he was afraid of being ensnared by him through treachery. Both should come accompanied by cavalry, and he would not come on any other condition. Caesar, however, although he did not want the conference to be broken off by the pretense of an excuse, did not dare to trust his life to the cavalry, which consisted of Gauls. He therefore decided that it would be most expedient to take away from the Gallic cavalry all their horses, and to mount on their horses the legionary soldiers of the tenth legion, in whom he placed the greatest confidence, in order that he might have a bodyguard as trustworthy as possible, should there be any need for action. And when this was done, one of the soldiers of the tenth legion said (not without a touch of humor) that Caesar did more for them than he had promised: "he had promised to employ the tenth legion as his praetorian cohort; but he now converted them into equestrians."[1]

CHAPTER 43: CAESAR REITERATES HIS DEMANDS TO ARIOVISTUS AT THEIR CONFERENCE

There was a large plain, and in it a mound of earth of considerable size. This spot was at nearly an equal distance from both camps. To that place, as had been arranged, they came for the conference. Caesar stationed the legion, which he had brought with him on horseback, 200 paces from this mound. The cavalry of Ariovistus also took their stand at an equal distance. Ariovistus then demanded that they should confer on horseback, and that, besides themselves, each of them should bring ten men to the conference.

When they had come to the place, Caesar, in the opening of his speech, detailed his own and the Senate's favors toward Ariovistus. He had been styled "king," he had been styled "friend" by the Senate, and very considerable presents had been sent to him. Such honors, Caesar informed him, had fallen to the lot of few, and had usually been bestowed in consideration of important personal services. Ariovistus, although he had a just ground neither for an introduction to the Senate nor for the request, had obtained these honors through the kindness and generosity of Caesar and the Senate.

Caesar informed him too how old and how just were the grounds of connection that existed between the Romans and the Aedui, what decrees the Senate had passed in their favor, and how frequent and how honorable

---

1. *Equites* at Rome were a census class that originally indicated that those in it possessed enough wealth to buy their own horses. Such men had in earlier times formed the Roman cavalry. This was no longer the case in Caesar's day, as the cavalry consisted instead of foreigners. The soldier thus implies that, by putting the infantry on horses, and thus converting them into a cavalry, Caesar intends to reward them with the wealth that they would require for status as equestrians at Rome.

these decrees were; and how from time immemorial the Aedui had held supremacy over all Gaul, even before they had sought our friendship. It was the custom of the Roman people to desire not only that its allies and friends should lose none of their property, but also that they should be advanced in influence, dignity, and honor. Who then could endure that what they had brought with them to the friendship of the Roman people should be torn from them? Caesar then made the same demands that he had commissioned the ambassadors to make. Ariovistus was not to wage war either on the Aedui or their allies, and he should restore the hostages. If he could not send back to their country any of the Germans, he should at all events no longer permit any more of them to cross the Rhine.

CHAPTER 44: ARIOVISTUS REPLIES THAT CAESAR SHOULD LEAVE ARIOVISTUS'S PART OF GAUL

Ariovistus briefly replied to the demands of Caesar, but preached a great deal about his own virtues. He had crossed the Rhine, not of his own accord, but after he was invited and sent for by the Gauls. He would not have left home and family without great expectations and great rewards. He had settlements in Gaul that had been granted by the Gauls themselves. The hostages had been sent to him voluntarily. He took by right of war the tribute that conquerors are accustomed to impose on the conquered. He had not made war upon the Gauls, but the Gauls upon him. All the states of Gaul came to attack him and had encamped against him. All their forces had been routed and beaten by him in a single battle. If they chose to make a second trial, he was ready to encounter them again, but, if they chose to enjoy peace, it was unfair to refuse the tribute, which of their own free will they had paid up to that time.

The friendship of the Roman people ought to prove to him an ornament and a safeguard, not a detriment, and he had sought it with that expectation. But, if, through the Roman people, the tribute was to be discontinued, and those who paid it were to be seduced from him, he would renounce the friendship of the Roman people no less heartily than he had sought it. As to his leading over a host of Germans into Gaul, he was doing this in order to protect himself, not to attack Gaul. There was no evidence for hostile intent on his part: he had not come without being invited, and he did not make war, but merely warded it off.

He had come into Gaul before the Roman people. Never before this time had a Roman army gone beyond the frontiers of the province of Gaul. What did Caesar want? Why had he come into Ariovistus's domains? This was Ariovistus's province of Gaul, just as the other one was ours. Just as he would not be pardoned, if he were to make an attack upon our territories; so, likewise, we were unjust to obstruct him in exercising his rights. As for Caesar's saying that the Aedui had been styled "brothers" by the Senate, he was not so uncivilized nor so ignorant of affairs as not to know that neither had the Aedui in the very last war with the Allobroges rendered assistance to the Romans, nor had they received any assistance from the Roman people in the battles that they had been fighting with him and with the Sequani.

He had to feel suspicious that Caesar, although feigning friendship as the reason for his keeping an army in Gaul, was actually keeping it with the intention of crushing him. And, unless Caesar departed and withdrew his army from these parts, he would regard him not as a friend, but as a foe. And, if he should put Caesar to death, he would do what would please many of the nobles and leading men of the Roman people. He had assurance of this fact from them through their messengers, and he could purchase the favor and the friendship of them all by Caesar's death. But, if Caesar would depart, and resign to Ariovistus the free possession of Gaul, he would recompense Caesar with a great reward, and would bring to a close whatever wars Caesar wished to be carried on, without any trouble or risk to Caesar.

CHAPTER 45: CAESAR EXPLAINS WHY ROME, NOT ARIOVISTUS, HAS THE RIGHT TO DETERMINE POLICY IN GAUL

Many things were stated by Caesar to show why he could not let the business go, and that neither his practice nor the Roman people's would permit him to abandon most meritorious allies, nor did he deem that Gaul belonged to Ariovistus rather than to the Roman people. The Arverni and the Ruteni had been subdued in war by Quintus Fabius Maximus [in 121 BCE], but the Roman people had pardoned them and had not reduced them into a province or imposed a tribute upon them. And, if whoever had the most ancient claim was to be the standard—then the sovereignty of the Roman people in Gaul was the most just claim. If, on the other hand, the decree of the Senate was to be observed, then Gaul ought to be free, because the Romans, although they had conquered it in war, had permitted Gaul to enjoy its own laws.

CHAPTER 46: CAESAR BREAKS OFF THE CONFERENCE

While these things were being transacted in the conference, it was announced to Caesar that the cavalry of Ariovistus was approaching nearer the mound, and was riding up to our men, and casting stones and weapons at them. Caesar ended his speech and joined his men. He commanded them by no means to return fire upon the enemy. For, although he saw that an engagement with the cavalry would be without any danger to his chosen legion, he did not think that it was proper to engage. Otherwise, after the enemy had been routed, it might be said that they had been tricked by him while under the sanction of a conference. When it was reported among the common soldiers how arrogantly Ariovistus had behaved at the conference, and how he had ordered the Romans to quit Gaul, and how his cavalry had made an attack upon our men, and how this attack had broken off the conference, a much greater enthusiasm and eagerness for battle was infused into our army.

CHAPTER 47: ARIOVISTUS WANTS TO CONTINUE THE CONFERENCE, BUT ARRESTS CAESAR'S ENVOYS

Two days later, Ariovistus sent ambassadors to Caesar, to state that he wished to treat with him about those things they had begun to discuss between them, but had not been concluded, and to beg that Caesar would either again appoint a day for a conference or, if he were not willing to do that, that he would send one of his officers as an ambassador to him. There did not appear to Caesar any good reason for holding a conference, and all the more so as the day before the Germans could not be restrained from casting spears at our men. Caesar thought that it would be very dangerous to send to Ariovistus as ambassador one of his Roman officers, as this would expose the officer to savage men.

It seemed therefore most appropriate to send Gaius Valerius Procillus, the son of Gaius Valerius Caburus, a young man of the highest courage and accomplishments (whose father had been presented with the freedom of the City by Gaius Valerius Flaccus), both on account of his fidelity and on account of his knowledge of the Gallic language, which Ariovistus, by long practice, now spoke fluently, and because, in Procillus's case the Germans would have no motive for committing violence. As his colleague, Caesar sent Marcus Mettius, who had shared the hospitality of Ariovistus. Caesar commissioned them to learn what Ariovistus had to say, and to report back to him. But, when Ariovistus saw them before him in his camp, he cried out in the presence of his army: "Why have they come to me? To spy?" He stopped them when they tried to speak, and cast them into chains.

CHAPTER 48: ARIOVISTUS HARASSES CAESAR, BUT DOES NOT ENGAGE IN BATTLE

The same day he moved his camp forward and pitched under a hill six miles from Caesar's camp. The next day he led his forces past Caesar's camp, and encamped two miles beyond him in order to cut off Caesar from the grain and provisions that were to be conveyed to him from the Sequani and the Aedui. For five days in a row from that day, Caesar drew out his forces before the camp, and put them in battle order, so that, if Ariovistus was willing to engage in battle, an opportunity for him would not be lacking. Ariovistus kept his army in camp all this time, although he did engage daily in cavalry skirmishes.

The method of battle in which the Germans had practiced themselves was this: there were 6,000 cavalry and as many very active and coura-geous foot soldiers. Each of the horsemen selected one foot soldier out of the whole army for his own protection. They were constantly accom-panied by these foot soldiers in their engagements. The horsemen retired to them. The foot soldiers rushed forward in any emergency. If anyone, upon receiving a very severe wound, had fallen from his horse, they stood around him. If it was necessary to advance farther than usual or to retreat more rapidly, so great, from practice, was the foot soldiers' swiftness, that, supported by the manes of the horses, they could keep pace with the speed of the horses.

CHAPTER 49: CAESAR BUILDS A SECOND CAMP

When he perceived that Ariovistus kept himself in camp, Caesar, in order not any longer to be cut off from supplies, chose a convenient position for a camp beyond the place where the Germans had encamped, which was about 600 paces from them, and, after drawing up his army in three lines, he marched to that place. He ordered the first and second lines to be under arms; the third to fortify the camp. This place was, as has been stated, about 600 paces from the enemy. Ariovistus sent light troops to this place, about 16,000 men in number, with all his cavalry to intimidate our men, and to hinder them in their work of fortification. Nevertheless, Caesar, as he had initially planned, ordered two lines to drive off the enemy; the third to execute the work. The camp was fortified, and Caesar stationed there two legions and a portion of the auxiliaries. He then led back the other four legions into the larger camp.

CHAPTER 50: CAESAR DISCOVERS WHY ARIOVISTUS REFUSES TO FIGHT

The next day, according to his custom, Caesar led out his forces from both camps, and having advanced a little from the larger one, drew up his line of battle, and gave the enemy an opportunity of fighting. When he found that they did not even then come out from their entrenchments, he led back his army into camp about noon. Then at last Ariovistus sent part of his forces to attack the smaller camp. The battle was vigorously maintained on both sides till evening. At sunset, after many wounds had been inflicted and received, Ariovistus led back his forces into camp.

When Caesar inquired of his prisoners why Ariovistus did not come to an engagement, he discovered this to be the reason—that among the Germans it was the custom for their matrons to pronounce from lots and divination whether it was advantageous that the battle should be engaged in or not, and that the matrons had said that it was not the will of heaven that the Germans should conquer, if they engaged in battle before the new moon.

CHAPTER 51: CAESAR FORCES ARIOVISTUS TO ENGAGE IN BATTLE

The next day, Caesar left what seemed sufficient as a guard for both camps, and then drew up all the auxiliaries in sight of the enemy in front of the smaller camp. He employed these allied troops for appearance, because, in comparison with the number of the enemy, he was not very powerful in the number of legionary soldiers. He himself drew up his legions in three lines, and advanced to the camp of the enemy. Then at last the Germans were compelled to draw their forces out of camp. They disposed them canton by canton at equal distances: the Harudes, Marcomanni, Triboces, Vangiones, Nemetes, Sedusii, Suebi. And they surrounded their whole army with their chariots and wagons, so that no hope might be left in flight. On these chariots and wagons, they placed their women, who, with disheveled hair and in tears, entreated the soldiers, as they went forward to battle, not to deliver them into slavery to the Romans.

CHAPTER 52: CAESAR DESCRIBES THE BATTLE

Caesar appointed over each legion a lieutenant and a quaestor, so that every soldier might have witnesses of his valor. He himself began the battle at the head of the right wing, because he had observed that part of the enemy to be the least strong. Accordingly, our men, after the signal was given,

vigorously made an attack upon the enemy, but the enemy so suddenly and
rapidly rushed forward that there was no time for casting the javelins at
them. Our men therefore threw aside their javelins, and fought with swords
hand to hand. But the Germans, according to their custom, rapidly formed
a phalanx, and sustained the attack of our swords. Quite a few of our soldiers were discovered to be brave enough to leap upon the phalanx, and,
with their hands, they tore away the shields, and wounded the enemy from
above. Although the army of the enemy was routed on the left wing and
put to flight, they still pressed heavily on our men from the right wing, by
the great number of their troops. When he observed this, Publius Crassus,
a young man, who commanded the cavalry—as he was more disengaged
than those who were employed in the fight—sent the third line as a relief
to our men, who were in distress.

Chapter 53: The Romans Win the Battle and Caesar Finds his Envoys

After this, the engagement was renewed, and all the enemy turned their
backs, nor did they cease to flee until they arrived at the river Rhine, about
five miles from that place. There, some few, relying either on their strength,
attempted to swim over, or, finding boats, procured their safety. Among the
latter was Ariovistus, who, finding a small vessel tied to the bank, escaped
in it. Our cavalry pursued and slew all the rest of them.

Ariovistus had two wives, one a Suebian by birth, whom he brought
with him from home; the other a Norican, the sister of king Vocio, whom
he had married in Gaul (she had been sent for that purpose by her brother).
Both perished in that flight. Of their two daughters, one was killed, the
other captured.

Gaius Valerius Procillus, as he was being dragged by his guards in the
flight, and bound with a triple chain, fell into the hands of Caesar himself,
as he was pursuing the enemy with his cavalry. This circumstance indeed
gave Caesar no less pleasure than the victory itself, because he saw a man
of the first rank in the province of Gaul, his intimate acquaintance and
friend, rescued from the hand of the enemy, and restored to him, and because fortune had not at all diminished the joy and exultation of that day
as it might have by the destruction of his friend. Procillus related that, in
his own presence, the lots had been thrice consulted concerning his fate,
whether he should immediately be put to death by fire or be reserved for
another time: it was by the favor of the lots that he was uninjured. Marcus
Mettius too was found and brought back to Caesar.

CHAPTER 54: AFTERMATH AND WINTER QUARTERS

After news of this battle was reported beyond the Rhine, the Suebi, who had come to the banks of that river, began to return home, and when the Ubii, who dwelled nearest to the Rhine, perceived the alarm of the Suebi, they pursued them and slew a great number of them. Caesar, having concluded two very important wars in one campaigning season, conducted his army into winter quarters among the Sequani, a little earlier than the season of the year required. He put Labienus in charge of the winter quarters, and set out in person for Nearer Gaul to administer justice in his capacity as governor of the province.

BOOKS 2–5 [57–54 BCE]

In Book Two, which relates the events of 57 BCE, Caesar campaigns against Belgic tribes in northern Gaul, thus extending his military power and political sway. At Rome, the Senate decrees fifteen days of prayers and sacrifices to the immortal gods in thanks for Caesar's successes. Book Three covers events from 57 through 56 BCE. Various campaigns throughout Gaul continue to extend and solidify Caesar's effective military control over the entire territory. By 55 BCE, military affairs seem fairly secure throughout Gaul, so, as Book Four describes, Caesar moves his military operations across the Rhine into German territory. This expedition is designed as a lesson to German leaders: Roman armies can hurt them in their own territory. The bridge that the Romans built across the Rhine was another demonstration of their superior abilities.

After this demonstration of Roman power against the Germans, Caesar decides to sail to Britain, and has a fleet built for this purpose. The fleet is damaged by a storm, but, after inflicting some defeats on local Britons, Caesar manages to repair the loss of his ships and to transport his troops safely back to the mainland. These expeditions against Germans and Britons were more spectacular than practical from a local military point of view, but they were effective in building Caesar's political popularity at Rome. The Senate this time decreed twenty days of prayers and sacrifices to the immortal gods in thanks for Caesar's military successes. In Book Five, which describes the events of 54 BCE, Caesar begins to experience setbacks. His second expedition to Britain is again marred by trouble with storms as well as some difficult fighting. The troops acquit themselves well, however, and Caesar manages to transport them to the mainland for winter. But, after the troops have been dispersed to widely separated winter quarters, Belgic tribes rise in revolt and manage to destroy one Roman legion before Caesar can come to the relief of others.

BOOK 6 [53 BCE]

In Book Six, Caesar's troubles continue, as there are continued revolts among the Gauls. Caesar provides some narrative relief, however, from these difficulties by describing the customs, political organization, and religion of the Gauls (see AP Latin selections BG 6.13–20) and of the Germans.

CHAPTER 1: CAESAR DRAFTS TWO NEW LEGIONS AND BORROWS A THIRD LEGION FROM POMPEY THE GREAT

Caesar, because for many reasons he expected more serious resistance in Gaul, decided to have his lieutenants, Marcus Silanus, Gaius Antistius Reginus, and Titus Sextius, conduct a levy. At the same time, he asked the proconsul [for Spain], Gnaeus Pompey, inasmuch as he remained near the City invested with military command for the sake of the Republic, to order the men, whom he had while consul [in 55 BCE] levied by military oath in Cisalpine Gaul, to join their respective units, and to proceed to Caesar. Caesar considered this of great importance for the opinion that the Gauls would form regarding the future, namely, that the resources of Italy would appear so great that, even if the Romans sustained a loss in war, not only could they repair it in a short time, but they could likewise supply still larger forces. Pompey granted Caesar's request for the sake of the Republic and the claims of friendship, and Caesar's lieutenants quickly completed the levy. Three regiments were both formed and brought to Caesar before winter was over, and the number of the cohorts that he had lost under Quintus Titurius were doubled, thus enabling Caesar to teach the Gauls both by his quick efficiency and by the size of his forces what the discipline and the power of the Roman people could accomplish.

CHAPTER 2: ALLIANCES OF GERMAN TRIBES WITH AMBIORIX AND THREATS OF WAR FROM THE NERVII, ADUATUCI, AND MENAPII

After Indutiomarus was killed, as we stated, the government was conferred upon his relatives by the Treviri. They did not cease to importune the neighboring Germans and to promise them money: when they failed to entice those nearest them, they tried those farther away. Having found some states willing to accede to their wishes, they entered into a compact with them by a mutual oath, and they gave hostages as a security for the money. They associated themselves with Ambiorix by an alliance and confederacy. Caesar, on being informed of their acts, saw that war was being prepared on all sides. The Nervii, Aduatuci, and Menapii, with the addition of all the Germans on this side of the Rhine were all under arms. The Senones did not assemble according to his command, and were discussing measures with the Carnutes and the neighboring states. The Germans were tempted by frequent embassies from the Treviri. For all these reasons, Caesar thought that he ought to take measures for the war earlier than usual.

CHAPTER 3: CAESAR LAUNCHES A SURPRISE ATTACK AGAINST THE NERVII, AND MARCHES AGAINST THE SENONES

Accordingly, before winter ended, having combined the four nearest legions, Caesar marched unexpectedly into the territories of the Nervii, and, before they could either assemble or retreat, captured a large number of cattle and people, laid waste their lands, and, giving up the captives as booty to the soldiers, compelled the natives to enter into a surrender and give him hostages. After he speedily executed this business, Caesar again led his legions back into winter-quarters. He announced a council of Gaul for the beginning of the spring, as he had been accustomed to do. When representatives from all Gaul came, except from the Senones, the Carnutes, and the Treveri, he judged this to be the beginning of war and revolt. In order that he might appear to consider all things of less importance than that war, Caesar transferred the council to Lutetia among the Parisii. They were adjacent to the Senones, and had united their state to them during the memory of their fathers, but were thought to have no part in the present plot. After he proclaimed this from the tribunal, Caesar advanced the same day toward the Senones with his legions, and arrived among them by forced marches.

CHAPTER 4: THE SENONES AND CARNUTES SURRENDER

Acco, who had been the author of that enterprise, on being informed of Caesar's arrival, ordered the people to assemble in the towns. While attempting this, and before they could accomplish it, news was brought to them that the Romans were close at hand. Necessity compelled them to abandon their plan and to send ambassadors to Caesar for the purpose of imploring pardon. They approached him through the Aedui, whose state was from ancient times under the protection of Rome. Caesar readily granted them pardon, and received their excuse at the request of the Aedui, because he thought that the summer season was one for an impending war not for a judicial investigation. After demanding one hundred hostages, Caesar delivered the hostages to the Aedui to be held in custody by them. The Carnutes sent ambassadors and hostages to the same place, and employed the Remi (who were their patrons and protectors) as their mediators. The Carnutes received the same answers. Caesar concluded the council, and imposed a levy of cavalry on the states.

CHAPTER 5: CAESAR PLANS TO ATTACK THE TREVERI AND AMBIORIX, BUT FIRST ATTACKS THE MENAPII

After restoring tranquility to this part of Gaul, Caesar applied himself entirely, both in mind and soul, to the war with the Treviri and Ambiorix. He ordered Cavarinus to march with him with the cavalry of the Senones, lest any trouble should arise either from his hot temper or from the hatred of the state which he had incurred. After arranging these things, since he deemed it certain that Ambiorix would not fight a set battle, he considered his other plans carefully. The Menapii bordered on the territories of the Eburones, and were protected by one continuous extent of morasses and woods; and they alone out of Gaul had never sent ambassadors to Caesar to negotiate a treaty of peace. Caesar knew that a tie of hospitality existed between them and Ambiorix. He also discovered that the latter had entered into an alliance with the Germans through the Treviri. He thought that these auxiliaries ought to be detached from Ambiorix before he provoked Ambiorix to war; lest Ambiorix, despairing of safety, should either proceed to conceal himself in the territories of the Menapii, or should be driven to combine forces with the Germans beyond the Rhine. After he entered upon this resolution, Caesar sent the baggage of the whole army to Labienus in the territories of the Treviri, and ordered two legions to proceed to Labienus. He himself proceeded against the Menapii with five lightly-equipped legions. The Menapii, however, assembled no troops, as they relied on the defense of their position, and they retreated into the woods and morasses, and conveyed all their property there too.

CHAPTER 6: THE MENAPII SURRENDER TO CAESAR

Caesar divided his forces with Gaius Fabius, his lieutenant, and Marcus Crassus, his quaestor, and hastily constructed some bridges. He entered country of the Menapii in three divisions, burned their houses and villages, and captured a large number of cattle and people. Forced by these circumstances, the Menapii sent ambassadors to Caesar to sue for peace. Caesar, after receiving hostages, instructed them that he would consider them enemies if they should receive within their territories either Ambiorix or his ambassadors. After he settled these things, he left among the Menapii, Commius the Atrebatian, with some cavalry as a guard; he himself (i.e., Caesar) proceeded toward the Treviri.

CHAPTER 7: LABIENUS LEADS THE ATTACK ON THE TREVERI

While Caesar did these things, the Treviri, after assembling large forces of infantry and cavalry, were preparing to attack Labienus and the legion that was wintering in their territories. They were already not further distant from him than a journey of two days when they learned that two legions had arrived by the order of Caesar. They pitched their camp fifteen miles off, and resolved to await the support of the Germans. Labienus, having learned the design of the enemy, hoped that their rashness would afford some opportunity of engaging. After leaving a guard of five cohorts for the baggage, Labienus advanced against the enemy with twenty-five cohorts and a large body of cavalry, and, leaving the space of a mile between them, fortified his camp. There was between Labienus and the enemy a river difficult to cross, and with steep banks. Neither did he himself design to cross this river nor did he suppose the enemy would cross it. Their hope of assistance was daily increasing. Labienus openly said in a council that since the Germans were said to be approaching, he would not bring into uncertainty his own and the army's fortunes, and the next day would move his camp at early dawn. These words were quickly carried to the enemy, since out of so large a number of cavalry composed of Gauls, nature compelled some of them to favor the Gallic interests. Labienus, after he assembled the tribunes of the soldiers and principal centurions by night, stated what his plan was, and, in order that he might more easily lead the enemy to believe that he was filled with fear, he ordered the camp to be moved with greater noise and confusion than was usual among Romans. By such means he made his departure appear like a retreat. These things, also, since the camps were so near, were reported to the enemy by scouts before daylight.

CHAPTER 8: LABIENUS DEFEATS THE TREVERI

Scarcely had the rear advanced beyond the fortifications when the Gauls began to encourage one another not to cast from their hands the anticipated booty, as it was a tedious thing, while the Romans were panic-stricken, to be waiting for the aid of the Germans. They argued that their dignity did not permit them to fear to attack so small a band with such great forces, particularly when that band was retreating and encumbered with baggage.

Therefore, they did not hesitate to cross the river and give battle in a disadvantageous position. Labienus, suspecting that these things would happen, was proceeding quietly, and using the same pretense of a march, in order that he might entice them across the river. Then, having sent forward the baggage some short distance and having placed it on an eminence, he said, "Soldiers, you have the opportunity you have sought: you hold the enemy in an encumbered and disadvantageous position. Display to us, your leaders, the same valor you have often displayed to your general. Imagine that he is present and actually sees these exploits." At the same time, he ordered the troops to turn around toward the enemy and form a line of battle. Dispatching a few troops of cavalry as a guard for the baggage, he placed the rest of the cavalry on the wings. Our men, raising a shout, quickly threw their javelins at the enemy. The enemy, when, contrary to their expectation, they saw those whom they believed to be retreating, advance toward them with threatening banners, were not able to sustain even the charge, and, after being put to flight at the first onslaught, fled toward the nearest woods. Labienus pursued them with the cavalry. A large number were slain, and several taken prisoners. Labienus got possession of the state a few days later, as the Germans, who were coming to the aid of the Treviri, retreated to their homes after they were informed of their flight. The relatives of Indutiomarus, who had been the promoters of the revolt, accompanied them, and abandoned their own state with them. The supreme power and government were delivered to Cingetorix, who, as we have stated, remained firm in his allegiance from the beginning.

Chapter 9: Caesar Builds a Bridge across the Rhine, and Accepts the Submission of Some of Ambiorix's Allies

Caesar, after he came from the territories of the Menapii into those of the Treviri, resolved for two reasons to cross the Rhine: first, because they had sent assistance to the Treviri against him; and second, in order that Ambiorix might not have a place to retreat among them. Having decided on these matters, he began to build a bridge a little above that place where he had earlier conveyed over his army. Caesar made his plan known and put into effect, and the work was accomplished in a few days by the great exertion of the soldiers. Caesar left a strong guard at the bridge on the side of the Treviri, so that no disturbance would suddenly arise among them. He then led over the rest of the forces and the cavalry. The Ubii, who before had sent hostages and come to a capitulation, sent ambassadors to Caesar for the purpose of defending their conduct, and to assure him that they had neither sent auxiliaries to the Treveri from their state nor violated their allegiance. They entreated and beseeched him to spare them, lest, in his common hatred of the Germans, the innocent should suffer the penalty of the guilty, and they promised to give more hostages, if he desired them. After he investigated the case, Caesar found that the auxiliaries had been sent by the Suebi, so he accepted the apology of the Ubii, and made minute inquiries concerning the approaches and the routes to the territories of the Suebi.

CHAPTER 10: THE SUEBI REMAIN HOSTILE

In the meantime, Caesar was informed by the Ubii a few days later that the Suebi were drawing all their forces into one place, and were giving orders to those nations which were under their government to send auxiliaries of infantry and of cavalry. Having learned these things, Caesar provided for a supply of grain, selected a proper place for his camp, and commanded the Ubii to drive off their cattle and to carry away all their possessions from the countryside into the towns. Caesar hoped that the Suebi, because they were a barbarous and ignorant people, when harassed by the lack of provisions, might be brought to an engagement on disadvantageous terms. He ordered the Ubii to send numerous scouts among the Suebi, and learn what things were going on among them. They executed the orders, and, a few days later, reported that all the Suebi, after receiving certain intelligence concerning the arrival of the Roman army, had retreated with all their own forces and those of their allies, which they had assembled, to the utmost extremities of their territories. They also reported that there was a forest there of very great extent, which was called Bacenis; that this forest stretched a great way into the interior, and served as a natural barrier in defending the Cherusci from the injuries and incursions of the Suebi, and the Suebi from those of the Cherusci; and that the Suebi had decided to await the approach of the Romans at the entrance to this forest.

CHAPTER 11: CAESAR INTERRUPTS THE NARRATIVE TO DESCRIBE THE CUSTOMS OF THE GAULS AND GERMANS; GAUL IS DIVIDED INTO FACTIONS

Since we have come to this place, it does not appear to be foreign to our subject to lay before the reader an account of the manners of Gaul and Germany, and wherein these nations differ from each other. In Gaul there are factions not only in all the states, and in all the cantons and their divisions, but almost in each family. The leaders of these factions are those who, by general agreement, are considered to possess the greatest influence. The management of all affairs and measures depends upon these leaders' will and determination. And this seems to have been instituted in ancient times in order that no one of the common people should lack support against someone more powerful; for none of those leaders suffers his supporters to be oppressed and defrauded, and, if he does otherwise, he has no influence among his party. This same policy exists throughout the whole of Gaul; for all the states are divided into two factions.

CHAPTER 12: THE AEDUI AND SEQUANI ARE RIVALS IN GAUL

When Caesar arrived in Gaul, the Aedui were the leaders of one faction, the Sequani of the other. Because the Sequani were less powerful by themselves—inasmuch as the Aedui enjoyed the chief influence from of old among them, and their dependencies were great—they had united to themselves the Germans and Ariovistus, and had brought them over to their side by great payments and promises. And, having fought several successful battles and having slain all the nobility of the Aedui, they had so far surpassed them in power, that they brought over, from the Aedui to themselves, a large portion of their clients, and received from them the sons of their leading men as hostages, and compelled them to swear publicly on behalf of their state that they would enter into no design against them; and they held a portion of the neighboring land, which they seized on by force, and possessed the sovereignty of the whole of Gaul. Diviciacus, urged by this necessity, had proceeded to Rome to the Senate for the purpose of entreating assistance, and had returned without accomplishing his object. A change of affairs ensued on the arrival of Caesar. The hostages were returned to the Aedui, their old dependencies restored, and they acquired new dependents through Caesar (because those who had attached themselves to their alliance saw that they enjoyed a better state and a milder government). In all their other affairs, their influence and reputation were likewise increased, and, in consequence, the Sequani lost the sovereignty. The Remi succeeded to their place, and, as it was perceived that they equaled the Aedui in favor with Caesar, those, who on account of their old animosities could by no means coalesce with the Aedui, consigned themselves in clientship to the Remi. The latter carefully protected them. Thus they possessed both a new and suddenly acquired influence. Such was state of affairs then that the Aedui were considered by far the leading people, and the Remi held the second post of honor.

CHAPTERS 13–20: DESCRIPTION OF THE RELIGION AND CUSTOMS OF THE GAULS

Because BG 6.13–20 are covered in Latin in this book and in order to eliminate any temptation to peek at the translation during class, we do not provide the translation of these passages here. The Gauls, as you will read (or already have), are both similar to and different from the Romans. The Germans, on the other hand, are much stranger.

CHAPTER 21: THE GERMANS ARE MORE PRIMITIVE THAN GAULS

The Germans differ much from Gallic usages, for they have neither Druids to preside over religious ceremonies, nor do they pay great regard to sacrifices. They rank in the number of the gods those alone whom they can see, and by whose assistance they are obviously benefited, namely, the Sun, Fire, and the Moon. They have not heard of the other gods, even by report. Their whole life is occupied in hunting and in the pursuits of the military art. From childhood, they devote themselves to extreme effort and toughness. Those who have remained chaste for the longest time receive the greatest praise among their people. They think that growth is promoted, the physical powers are increased, and the muscles are strengthened by chastity. And they reckon having physical relations with a woman before the twentieth year among the most disgraceful acts. And there is no secrecy in such matters, because both sexes bathe together in the rivers, and they clothe themselves only with skins or small cloaks of deer's hides. A large portion of the body is in consequence of this naked.

CHAPTER 22: THE GERMANS NEITHER FARM NOR OWN PRIVATE PROPERTY

They do not pay much attention to agriculture, and a large portion of their food consists in milk, cheese, and meat. No one owns a fixed quantity of land or an individual plot. Instead, the magistrates and the leading men each year apportion to the tribes and families who have united together as much land as, and in the place where, they deem appropriate. And, in the year after that, they compel them to move somewhere else. For this custom, they offer many reasons. They thereby prevent the comforts of long-term settlement from seducing the people to exchange their passion for waging war for agriculture. People do not become eager to acquire extensive estates with the result that the more powerful drive the weaker from their possessions.

People do not construct their houses with too great a desire to avoid cold and heat. The desire for wealth does not grow strong, from which cause divisions and discords arise. And they keep the common people in a contented state of mind, as each sees his own wealth equal to that of the most powerful.

CHAPTER 23: GERMAN MILITARY LEADERSHIP, JUSTICE, AND HOSPITALITY

After laying waste to their frontiers, the various states consider it their greatest glory to have deserted territory as widely as possible around them. They consider this the real evidence of their manliness, that their neighbors are driven out of their lands and abandon them, and that no one dares to settle near them. At the same time, they think that they will on this account be all the more secure, because they have removed the fear of a sudden invasion. When a state either repels war waged against it, or wages war against another state, magistrates are chosen to preside over that war with an authority that extends to the power of life and death. In peace, there is no common magistrate. Instead, the chiefs of provinces and cantons administer justice and settle controversies among their own people. Robberies that are committed outside the boundaries of each state bear no infamy, and they assert that such robberies are committed for the purpose of disciplining their youth and of preventing sloth. And when any of their chiefs has stated in an assembly that he is going to be their leader, he says, "Let those who intend to follow me make a public declaration." Those who approve of both the enterprise and the man arise and promise their assistance and are applauded by the people. Those who have declined to follow him are considered deserters and traitors, and confidence in all matters is afterward refused them. Their religion does not permit them to violate the rules established for the treatment of guests. They defend from wrong those who have come to them for any reason whatsoever, and they esteem guests inviolable. The houses of all stand open to them, and food is freely shared.

CHAPTER 24: GAULS USED TO BE MORE WARLIKE THAN GERMANS, BUT GREW SOFT

And there was formerly a time when the Gauls excelled the Germans in manliness, and waged aggressive war on them, and, on account of the great number of their people and their lack of land, sent colonies across the Rhine. The Volcae Tectosages thus seized those parts of Germany that are the most fruitful, and lie around the Hercynian forest (which was, I see, known by report to Eratosthenes and some other Greeks who call it the Orcynian forest), and settled there. This nation to this day retains its position in these settlements, and has a very high reputation for justice and military merit. They still continue today in the same poverty, hardship, endurance as the Germans, and use the same food and dress. On the other hand, their proximity to the Province and knowledge of commodities from countries beyond the sea acquaints the Gauls with many things that promote luxury as well as civilization. Gradually accustomed to defeat, they have been beaten in many battles, and even they do not compare themselves to the Germans in manliness.

CHAPTER 25: THE HERCYNIAN FOREST

The breadth of this Hercynian forest, which has been referred to above, requires for a quick traveler a journey of nine days. For it cannot be otherwise calculated, nor are the Germans acquainted with the measure of roads. The forest begins at the frontiers of the Helvetii, Nemetes, and Rauraci, and extends in a straight line along the river Danube to the territories of the Daci and the Anartes. From this point, it bends to the left in a direction away from the river, and, owing to its extent, touches on the borders of many nations. Nor is there any person belonging to this part of Germany who claims that he either has reached the end of that forest, even if he had proceeded on a journey of sixty days, or has learned in what place the forest begins. It is certain that many kinds of wild beasts are produced in it, which have not been seen in other areas. I will next describe those animals that differ the most from other animals, and thus appear worthy of being committed to record.

CHAPTER 26: THE GERMAN REINDEER

There is an ox in the shape of a stag. Between its ears, a horn rises from the middle of the forehead, higher and straighter than those horns that are known to us. From the top of this, branches, like palms, stretch out a considerable distance. The shape of the female and of the male is the same; and the appearance and the size of their horns is the same.

CHAPTER 27: GERMAN ELKS

There are also animals called elks. Their shape and the varied color of their skins are much like goats, but they surpass goats a little in size, and are destitute of horns. They have legs without joints and ligatures. Neither do they lie down for the purpose of rest nor, if they have been thrown down by any accident, can they raise or lift themselves up. Trees serve as their beds. They lean themselves against them, and, thus reclining only slightly, they take their rest. When hunters have discovered from their tracks to what place they are accustomed to go, the hunters either undermine all the trees at the roots or cut into them so far that the upper part of the trees may appear to be left standing. When the elks have leaned on them according to their custom, they knock down the unsupported trees with their weight, and fall down along with the trees.

CHAPTER 28: THE GERMAN OX

There is a third kind animal, which is called the ure-ox (aurochs). These German oxen are a little below the elephant in size and of the appearance, color, and shape of a bull. Their strength and speed are extraordinary. They spare neither man nor wild beast whom they have espied. The Germans make great efforts to trap them in pits where they kill them. The young men harden themselves with this exercise, and practice themselves in this kind of hunting. Those who have slain the greatest number of these oxen, produce the horns in public to serve as evidence, and receive great praise. But not even if they are caught when they are very young can these oxen be accustomed to people, and tamed. The size, shape, and appearance of their horns differ much from the horns of our oxen. The Germans eagerly search for these horns, bind their tips with silver, and use them as cups at their most sumptuous entertainments.

CHAPTER 29: CAESAR CROSSES BACK OVER THE RHINE, SETS A GUARD OVER THE BRIDGE, AND SETS OUT AGAINST AMBIORIX

Caesar, after he discovered through the Ubian scouts that the Suebi had retired into their woods, feared a scarcity of grain, because, as we have observed above, all the Germans pay very little attention to agriculture. He thus resolved not to proceed any farther. On the other hand, in order not to free the barbarians completely from the fear of his return, and in order to delay their reinforcements, after leading his army back across, he broke down, to the length of 200 feet, the farther end of the bridge, which joined the banks of the Ubii, and, at the end of the bridge, he built towers four stories in height. He also stationeed a guard of twelve cohorts to defend the bridge, and he strengthened the place with considerable fortifications. He appointed Gaius Volcatius Tullus, a young man, over that fort and garrison.

He himself, when the grain began to ripen, set forth for the war against Ambiorix (through the forest Arduenna [Ardennes], which is the largest in all Gaul, and stretches from the banks of the Rhine and the borders of the Treviri to those of the Nervii, and extends for more than 500 miles). He sent Lucius Minucius Basilus ahead with the whole cavalry, to attempt whether he might gain any advantage by rapid marches and the advantage of time. He instructed him to forbid fires from being made in the camp, lest any indication of his approach be given at a distance. He told Basilus that he would follow immediately.

CHAPTER 30: AMBIORIX ESCAPES BASILUS AND THE CAVALRY

Basilus did as he was commanded. He performed his march rapidly, and even surpassed everyone's expectations. He surprised in the fields many, who were not expecting him. With the help of information from them, he advanced toward Ambiorix himself, to the place where he was said to be with a few cavalry. Fortune has great power, not only in other affairs, but also in the art of war. For, as it happened, by a remarkable chance, Basilus fell upon Ambiorix himself unguarded and unprepared, and the enemy witnessed Basilus's arrival before a report or any information about his arrival could be conveyed to them. It was thus an incident of extraordinary fortune that, although every implement of war which Ambiorix was accustomed to have about him was seized, and his chariots and horses surprised, yet he himself escaped death. This was accomplished, however, owing to the circumstance that his house was surrounded by a wood (as the dwellings of the Gauls generally are, as they mostly seek the neighborhood of woods and rivers for the purpose of avoiding heat). His attendants and friends withstood for a short time the attack of our cavalry in a narrow spot. While they were fighting, one of his followers mounted him on a horse. The woods sheltered him as he fled. Fortune thus played a large role in both his encounter with and his escape from danger.

CHAPTER 31: THE EBURONES CONDUCT GUERRILLA WARFARE, AND THEIR LEADER COMMITS SUICIDE

It is doubtful whether Ambiorix failed to assemble his forces from cool calculation (because he considered it safer not to engage in a battle) or whether, with the sudden arrival of our cavalry, he was prevented from doing so by a lack of time when he supposed the rest of our army was closely following the cavalry. It is certain, however, that he dispatched messengers throughout the country to order everyone to provide for his own safety. Some of them fled into the forest Arduenna [Ardennes]; some into the extensive morasses. Those who were nearest the ocean concealed themselves on the islands that the tides usually form. Many, departing from their territories, entrusted themselves and all their possessions to perfect strangers. Catuvolcus, king of half the Eburones, who had entered into the scheme together with Ambiorix, was then worn out by age, and thus unable to endure the fatigue either of war or flight. He cursed Ambiorix with every imprecation as the person who had been the contriver of that scheme, and he killed himself with the help of a yew-tree [whose berries are poisonous], of which there is a great abundance in Gaul and Germany.

CHAPTER 32: CAESAR PUTS CICERO IN CHARGE OF A LEGION TO GUARD THEIR EQUIPMENT

The Segni and Condrusi, who derive their descent from, and count as, Germans, and who dwell between the Eburones and the Treviri, sent ambassadors to Caesar to request that he not reckon them in the number of his enemies nor consider that all the Germans on this side of the Rhine made common cause. They claimed that they had formed no plans of war, and had sent no auxiliaries to Ambiorix. Caesar, having verified this fact by interrogating his prisoners, commanded them to send back to him any of the Eburones, who in their flight had sought refuge with them. If they sent these refugees back to him, he assured them that he would not harm their territories. Then, having divided his forces into three parts, he sent the baggage of all the legions to Aduatuca. This is the name of a fort that is nearly in the middle of the Eburones, and it was here that Titurius and Aurunculeius had been quartered for the winter. Among other reasons, Caesar had also selected this place because the fortifications of the previous year remained in place, and in order to spare the soldiers a great deal of work. As a guard for the baggage, he left the fourteenth legion, which was one of the three legions that he had recently levied in Italy and brought over. He placed Quintus Tullius Cicero in charge of that legion and camp and gave him 200 cavalry.

CHAPTER 33: CAESAR DIVIDES HIS ARMY INTO THREE PARTS

After dividing the army, he ordered Titus Labienus to proceed with three legions toward the ocean into those parts that border on the Menapii. He sent Gaius Trebonius with a like number of legions to lay waste that district that lies contiguous to the Aduatuci. He himself determined to go with the remaining three legions to the river Sambre, which flows into the Meuse, and to the most remote parts of Arduenna [Ardennes]. He had heard that Ambiorix had gone to this region with a few cavalry. When departing, he promised that he would return before the end of the seventh day, which was the day (as he was well aware) that grain was supposed to be distributed to the legion that was being left on guard duty. He directed Labienus and Trebonius to return by the same day, as long as they could do so with advantage to the interests of the Republic, so that they might all once again confer on strategy, share what they had discovered about the enemy's tactics, and be able to commence a different line of operations.

CHAPTER 34: THE GOING IS ROUGH, AND CAESAR TRIES TO PIT NEIGHBORING TRIBES AGAINST THE EBURONES

There was, as we have above observed, no regular army. Neither was there a town or garrison that could defend itself by arms. The people were instead scattered in all directions. Wherever either a hidden valley or a woody spot or a difficult morass furnished some hope of protection or security, individuals had dug in. These places were known to those who dwelled in the neighborhood, and the matter demanded a great deal of attention, not so much to protect the main body of the army (for no danger could threaten the army as a whole from those alarmed and scattered troops), as to preserve the lives of individual soldiers, although this too contributed in some measure to the safety of the entire army. The problem was that both the desire for booty was inducing many to venture too far, and the woods with their unknown and hidden routes would not allow them to go in large groups. If Caesar wanted to finish the business, and exterminate the race of these criminal people, various groups of men had to be sent in several directions and the soldiers had to be separated from each other. If, however, he wanted to keep the companies at their standards, as the established discipline and practice of the Roman army required, the locality itself protected the barbarians. Moreover, there was not lacking among them individuals with the daring to lay secret ambushes and attack scattered soldiers. Amid dangers of this sort, such precautions were taken as could be made through vigilance. As a result, although the spirits of all were burning to take revenge, rather than inflict injury at the cost of any loss to our soldiers, some opportunities of injuring the enemy were neglected. Caesar dispatched messengers to the neighboring states. With the prospect of booty, he invited all of them to join him in plundering the Eburones. He did this in order that the lives of Gauls rather than those of his legionary soldiers might be put at risk in the woods, and also, at the same time, in order that, by surrounding them with a large force, he might for such a crime annihilate the race of that people and name of their state. A large number from all quarters speedily assembled.

CHAPTER 35: RATHER THAN ATTACK THE EBURONES, THE SUGAMBRI DECIDE TO ATTACK CAESAR'S BAGGAGE

These things were going on in all parts of the territories of the Eburones, and the seventh day was drawing near. This was the day on which Caesar had intended to return to the baggage and the legion. Here it was possible to observe how powerful a role fortune plays in war, and what great disasters fortune can inflict. The enemy, as we related above, had been scattered and alarmed. There was no force that could have produced even a slight occasion of fear. The report extended beyond the Rhine to the Germans that the Eburones were being pillaged, and that all tribes were without distinction invited to the plunder. The Sugambri, who lived nearest to the Rhine, and by whom, as we mentioned above, the Tencteri and Usipetes were received after their retreat, collected 2,000 cavalry. They crossed the Rhine in ships and rafts thirty miles below the place where the bridge was built and the garrison left by Caesar. They arrived at the frontiers of the Eburones, surprised many who were scattered in flight, and got possession of a large number of cattle, of which barbarians are extremely covetous. Allured by booty, they advanced farther. Neither morass nor forest obstructed these men born amid war and depredations. They asked their prisoners where Caesar was. They learned that he had advanced farther, and that the whole army had departed. At this point, one of the prisoners said, "Why do you pursue such wretched and trifling plunder, when it is possible for you to acquire the greatest fortune possible? In three hours you can reach Aduatuca where the Roman army has deposited all its fortune; there is so small a garrison that not even the wall can be manned, nor does anyone dare to go beyond the fortifications." After this hope was presented to them, the Germans left in concealment the plunder they had acquired. They themselves hastened to Aduatuca, employing as their guide the same man by whose information they had learned these things.

CHAPTER 36: CICERO PERMITS FIVE COHORTS TO FORAGE FOR GRAIN

Cicero, who during all the preceding days had kept his soldiers in camp with the greatest exactness in accordance with Caesar's instructions, had not permitted even any of the camp-followers to go beyond the fortifications. On the seventh day, he was not sure whether Caesar would keep his promise about the number of days, because he heard that Caesar had proceeded farther, and no news concerning Caesar's return had been reported to him. He was being pressured at the same time by the comments of those who called his patience almost a siege, if, indeed, he would not permit anyone to go out of the camp. And, as there was no reason to expect any disaster that could inflict serious damage within three miles of the camp while nine legions and all the cavalry were under arms, and, inasmuch as the enemy were scattered and almost annihilated, Cicero sent five cohorts into the neighboring grain fields, between which and the camp only one hill intervened, for the purpose of foraging. Many soldiers of the legions had been left behind in the camp because they were sick, and many of these invalids had in the meantime recovered, so about 300 of them were sent together under one standard. A large number of camp slaves with a great number of beasts of burden, which had remained in the camp, were also granted permission to follow them.

CHAPTER 37: THE SUGAMBRI LAUNCH A SURPRISE ATTACK

At this very moment, the German cavalry by chance came up, and immediately, with the same speed with which they had advanced, attempted to force the camp at the Decuman gate, and they were not observed until they were just reaching the camp because of woods that obstructed the view on that side. As a result, the traders who had their booths along the rampart did not have an opportunity to retreat into the camp. Our men, not anticipating anything, were confused by the sudden affair, and the cohort on the outpost scarcely withstood the first attack. The enemy spread themselves out to the other sides to ascertain whether they could find any access. Our men with difficulty defended the gates. The location itself and our fortifications secured the other access points. There was a panic in the entire camp, and men asked one another the cause of the confusion. They could not readily determine in what directions the standards should be carried, nor where each man should report for duty. One would assert that the camp was already taken, another insisted that the enemy, who had destroyed the army and commander-in-chief, had arrived as conquerors. Most of the men formed strange superstitious ideas on the spot, and saw before their eyes the catastrophe of Cotta and Titurius, who had fallen in the same camp. Because such fears had induced such panic in everyone, the confidence of the barbarians was strengthened that there was in fact no garrison within, as they had heard from their prisoner. They attempted to force an entrance, and encouraged one another not to let so valuable a prize slip from their hands.

CHAPTER 38: BACULUS SAVES THE DAY (AND THE CAMP)

Because he was sick, Publius Sextius Baculus, who had led a principal century under Caesar (we have made mention of him in previous battles), had been left in the garrison. He had by now been without food for five days. Worried about his own safety and everyone else's, he went forth from his tent unarmed. He saw that the enemy was close at hand and that matters were in the utmost danger. He snatched weapons from those nearest, and stationed himself at the gate. The centurions of the cohort who were on duty followed him. For a short time, they sustained the fight together. Sextius fainted after receiving many wounds. With difficulty he was saved, and dragged away by the soldiers from hand to hand. After this interval, the others recovered enough courage to venture to take their place on the fortifications and to present the appearance of defenders.

CHAPTER 39: THE SUGAMBRI ATTACK THE COHORTS FORAGING FOR GRAIN

Meanwhile, after completing the foraging, our soldiers distinctly heard the shout. The cavalry hastened on ahead, and discovered how dangerous the situation was. But at this moment there was no fortification to receive them in their alarm. Those who had been enlisted most recently, and were unskilled in military discipline, turned their faces to the military tribune and the centurions. They waited to find out what orders they would give them. No one was so brave as not to be scared by the suddenness of the affair. The barbarians, catching sight of our standard in the distance, desisted from the attack. At first, they supposed that the legions, who, as they had learned from their prisoners, had moved farther off, had returned. Afterward, contemptuous of their small number, the barbarians attacked them on all sides.

CHAPTER 40: THE SUGAMBRI KILL MANY OF THE ROMANS

The camp-slaves ran off to the nearest hill. After they were speedily driven from this spot, they threw themselves among the standards and companies. They thus alarmed all the more the soldiers who were already frightened. Some proposed that they form a wedge and suddenly break through, inasmuch as the camp was so near, and, even if some part of them were surrounded and slain, they fully expected that at least the rest could be saved. Others argued that they should take their stand on a ridge, and all share the same fate. The veteran soldiers, who, as we mentioned, had set out together with the others under one standard, did not approve of this. Therefore, encouraging one another, they broke through the midst of the enemy, and, under the leadership of Gaius Trebonius, a Roman knight, who had been appointed over them, arrived in the camp safe to a man. The camp slaves and the cavalry followed close behind them with the same impetuosity, and were saved by the courage of the soldiers. Those, however, who had taken their stand on the ridge, were completely inexperienced in military matters. They could neither persevere in the resolution that they had approved, namely, to defend themselves from their higher position, nor imitate the vigor and speed, which they had observed to have availed others. Instead, attempting to reach the camp, they descended into an unfavorable situation. The centurions, some of whom had been promoted for their bravery from the lower ranks of other legions to higher ranks in this legion, in order that they would not forfeit the glory for military exploits that they had previously earned, fell together fighting most valiantly. The enemy were dislodged by the valor of the centurions, and some of the soldiers arrived safe in camp, contrary to their expectations; others perished, surrounded by the barbarians.

CHAPTER 41: THE ROMANS IN CICERO'S CAMP ARE TERRIFIED UNTIL CAESAR RETURNS

The Germans despaired of taking the camp by storm because they saw that our men had taken up their position on the fortifications. They then retreated beyond the Rhine with the plunder that they had deposited in the woods. So great was the panic that, even after the departure of the enemy, when Gaius Volusenus, who had been sent with the cavalry, arrived that night, he could not convince them that Caesar was close at hand with his army unhurt. Fear had so taken hold of everyone that they had almost lost their minds, and claimed that all the other forces had been destroyed, that the cavalry alone had arrived there by flight, and that, if the army were safe, the Germans would not have attacked the camp. Caesar's arrival removed this terror.

CHAPTER 42: CAESAR SCOLDS CICERO

Caesar, on his return, inasmuch as he was well aware of the casualties of war, complained only of one thing, namely, that the cohorts had been sent away from the outposts and garrison duty. He also pointed out that no opportunity ought to have been left for even the most trivial casualty. Fortune had revealed its great power in the sudden arrival of their enemy—and much greater power in turning the barbarians away from the very rampart and gates of the camp! Of all these events, it seemed the most surprising that the Germans, who had crossed the Rhine in order to plunder the territories of Ambiorix, were induced to attack the camp of the Romans, thus rendering Ambiorix a most acceptable service.

CHAPTER 43: CAESAR PURSUES THE EBURONES, BUT AMBIORIX ESCAPES

Caesar once again marched to harass the enemy, and, after collecting a large number of auxiliaries from the neighboring states, dispatched them in all directions. All the villages and all the buildings, as far the eye could see, were on fire. Plunder was being driven off from all parts. Not only was the grain being consumed by such great numbers of cattle and men, but it had also fallen to the earth, owing to the time of the year and the storms. It thus appeared likely that, if any had concealed themselves for the present, they would surely perish through lack of all necessities, when the army withdrew. And, as so large a body of cavalry had been dispatched in all directions, it frequently occurred that the prisoners declared that they had just then seen Ambiorix in flight, and that he had not yet passed out of sight. This raised the hope of catching up with him, and inspired limitless exertions among those who thought they could thereby acquire the highest favor with Caesar. Their zeal almost surpassed the limits imposed by nature, and success continually seemed almost within reach. But Ambiorix rescued himself through hiding-places and forests, and, concealed by the night, he made for other districts and territories with no greater guard than that of four horsemen, to whom alone he dared to entrust his life.

CHAPTER 44: CAESAR EXECUTES ACCO

After he devastated the country in this manner, Caesar led back his army with the loss of two cohorts to Durocortorum, a city of the Remi. He summoned a council of Gaul to assemble at that place, and he resolved to hold an investigation into the conspiracy of the Senones and Carnutes. After he pronounced a very severe sentence upon Acco, who had been the leader of that plot, he punished him according to the custom of our ancestors: he was beaten to death with wooden clubs. Some, fearing a trial, fled. Caesar declared these men outlaws, forbidding them fire and water. He stationed in winter quarters two legions at the frontiers of the Treviri, two among the Lingones, the remaining six at Agedincum in the territories of the Senones; and, having provided grain for the army, Caesar set out for northern Italy, as he had decided to administer justice in his capacity as governor of the province.

BOOK 7 [52 BCE]

Caesar may call it a "conspiracy," but the Gauls gather as a people, and select Vercingetorix as the leader of their united effort to drive the Romans, Roman camps, and Roman armies from Gallic territory. It is a war of liberation, and the Gauls fight desperately for freedom. Even Caesar recognizes this, and respects them as he fights to conquer them. The struggle culminates in the siege of a city called Alesia. Eventually, Alesia and Vercingetorix will submit to Caesar, and, at Rome, the Senate will decree another twenty days of prayers and sacrifices to the immortal gods in thanks for Caesar's military successes.

CHAPTER 1: CAESAR BLAMES UNREST IN GAUL ON POLITICAL UNREST IN ROME

Gaul was tranquil. Caesar, as he had planned, set out for Italy to administer justice in his capacity as governor of the province. There he received news of the murder of the tribune Publius Clodius Pulcher, and he was informed of the decree of the Senate that required all the youth of Italy to take the military oath. He thus decided to hold a levy throughout the entire province of Cisalpine Gaul. Report of these events was rapidly conveyed into Transalpine Gaul. The Gauls themselves added to the report, and invented what seemed to fit the situation, namely, that Caesar was detained by political unrest in the City, and could not, amid such violent dissensions, come to his army. Inspired by this opportunity, those who already before this occurrence resented their reduction beneath the dominion of Rome, began to organize their plans for war more openly and daringly. The leading men of Gaul convened councils among themselves in the woods and secluded places. They complained of the death of Acco. They pointed out that this fate could fall in turn on themselves. They bewailed the unhappy fate of Gaul, and by every sort of promise and reward they earnestly solicited some to begin the war, and assert the freedom of Gaul at the risk of their lives. They said that special care should be paid to this: Caesar ought to be cut off from his army before their secret plans were divulged—this would be easy, however, because neither would the legions in the absence of their general dare to leave their winter quarters nor could the general reach his army without a guard—finally, it was better to be killed in battle than fail to recover their ancient glory in war and the freedom that they had inherited from their ancestors.

CHAPTER 2: THE CARNUTES ARE THE FIRST TO REVOLT

While such themes were feverishly discussed, the Carnutes declared that they would refuse no danger for the sake of their common welfare, and they promised that they would be the first of all the Gauls to begin the war. Because, however, they could not under present circumstances guarantee by exchanging hostages among themselves that the matter would not be divulged, the Carnutes demanded that the military standards be brought together (by this means they make their most sacred obligations binding), and that solemn assurance be given to them by oath and a pledge of sacred honor that the Carnutes would not be deserted by the rest of the Gauls, if they began the war. All who were present unanimously praised the Carnutes, swore the oath, and, after setting a date for the business, departed from the assembly.

CHAPTER 3: THE CARNUTES MURDER LOCAL ROMAN CITIZENS

When the appointed day came, the Carnutes, under the command of two reckless and violent men, Cotuatus and Conconnetodumnus, met together at Cenabum, and murdered the Roman citizens who had settled there for the purpose of trading (one of whom was Gaius Fusius Cita, a distinguished Roman of equestrian status, who by Caesar's orders had presided over the grain supply), and plundered their property. The report quickly spread among all the states of Gaul, for, whenever a more important and remarkable event takes place, they transmit the intelligence through their lands and districts by a shout, which others then take up in turn, and pass along to their neighbors. This is what happened on this occasion as well, inasmuch as news of the things that were done at Cenabum at sunrise was heard in the territories of the Arverni before the end of the first watch [about three hours after sunset], a distance of more than a hundred and sixty miles.

CHAPTER 4: THE GAULS ELECT VERCINGETORIX AS THEIR LEADER

There in a similar fashion, Vercingetorix summoned together his dependents, and easily inflamed their spirits. Vercingetorix was a young man of the greatest authority, the son of Celtillus the Arvernian (who had held the supremacy over all Gaul, and had been put to death by his fellow-citizens for this very reason: because he had aimed at sovereign power).

After they learned his plan, they rushed to arms. Vercingetorix was, however, expelled from the town of Gergovia by his uncle Gobannitio and the rest of the nobles who were of opinion that such an enterprise ought not to be risked. Vercingetorix nevertheless did not desist, but held in the country a levy among poverty-stricken and criminal outcasts. Having collected such a body of troops, he brought over to his point of view whatever fellow-citizens he was able to approach. He exhorted them to take up arms on behalf of their general freedom, and, having assembled large forces, he drove from the state his opponents, who had expelled him a short time previously. Vercingetorix was saluted king by his partisans. He sent ambassadors in every direction. He adjured them to adhere firmly to their promise. He quickly attached to his interests the Senones, Parisii, Pictones, Cadurci, Turones, Aulerci, Lemovices, Andi, and all the others who border on the ocean. The supreme command was conferred on him by unanimous consent. On obtaining this authority, he demanded hostages from all these states. He ordered a fixed number of soldiers to be sent to him immediately. He determined what quantity of arms each state should prepare at home, and by what time. He paid particular attention to the cavalry. To the utmost vigilance, he added the utmost rigor of authority, and by the severity of his punishments brought over those who were wavering. Any offenders who committed a more serious crime he put to death by fire and with every sort of torture. For a lesser offense, he sent home the perpetrators with their ears cut off or one of their eyes gouged out, in order to make them an example to the rest, and to frighten others by the severity of their punishment.

CHAPTER 5: THE BITURIGES JOIN THE REVOLT

He quickly gathered an army through these punishments, and he sent Lucterius (a man the of utmost daring and one of the Cadurci) with part of his forces into the territory of the Ruteni. Vercingetorix himself marched in person into the country of the Bituriges. On his arrival, the Bituriges sent ambassadors to the Aedui, under whose protection they were, to solicit aid in order that they might more easily resist the forces of the enemy. The Aedui, following the advice of the lieutenants whom Caesar had left with the army, sent reinforcements of cavalry and infantry to support the Bituriges. After they came to the river Loire, which separates the Bituriges from the Aedui, they delayed there for a few days, and, not daring to cross the river, returned home, and sent back word to the lieutenants that they had returned because they feared the treachery of the Bituriges, who, as they found out, had formed a plan to surround them, if the Aedui crossed the river (the Bituriges were on one side and the Arverni on the other). Whether the Aedui did this for the reason which they alleged to the lieutenants or influenced by treachery, we thought that we should not state openly because we had no proof. On their departure, the Bituriges immediately united themselves to the Arverni.

CHAPTER 6: HOW WILL CAESAR GET TO HIS ARMY IN GAUL?

These affairs were announced to Caesar in Italy at a time when he had learned that political matters in the City had been brought back to a more tranquil state by the efforts of Gnaius Pompey. Caesar thus set out for Transalpine Gaul. After he had arrived there, he was at a great loss to know by what means he could reach his army. For, if he summoned the legions into the province, he was aware that during their march they would have to fight in his absence. He foresaw too that, if he himself attempted to reach the army, he would act without appropriate caution by entrusting his personal safety to Gallic tribes, even though they seemed pacified.

CHAPTER 7: LUCTERIUS THREATENS THE ROMAN PROVINCE

In the meantime, Lucterius the Cadurcan, having been sent into the country of the Ruteni, won over that state to the Arverni. He advanced into the country of the Nitiobriges and Gabali, received hostages from both nations, and, after assembling a numerous force, marched to make a descent on the Province in the direction of Narbo. Caesar, when this news was announced to him, thought that the march to Narbo ought to take precedence over all his other plans. When he arrived there, he encouraged the timid, and he stationed garrisons among the Ruteni in the province of the Volcae Arecomici and the country around Narbo, which was in the vicinity of the enemy. He ordered a portion of the forces from the Province and the recruits whom he had brought from Italy to rendezvous among the Helvii, who border on the territories of the Arverni.

CHAPTER 8: CAESAR BLOCKS LUCTERIUS

After these matters were arranged, Lucterius was checked, and forced to retreat, because he thought it was dangerous to enter the line of Roman fortifications. Caesar then marched into the country of the Helvii, although Mount Cevennes, which separates the Arverni from the Helvii, blocked the way with very deep snow, as it was the severest season of the year. Nevertheless, after clearing away the snow to a depth of six feet and opening the roads, Caesar reached the territories of the Arverni thanks to the infinite labor of his soldiers. The Averni were caught by surprise because they believed that Mount Cevennes defended them as if it were a wall (indeed, the paths at this season of the year had never before been passable even to individuals). Caesar ordered the cavalry to extend themselves as far as they could, and to strike as great a panic as possible into the enemy. These operations were speedily announced to Vercingetorix by rumor and his messengers. All the Arverni crowded around him in alarm, and solemnly entreated him to protect their property, and not to allow them to be plundered by the enemy, especially as he saw that the entire war had been transferred into their country. Vercingetorix was prevailed upon by their entreaties, and moved his camp from the country of the Bituriges in the direction of the Arverni.

Chapter 9: Caesar Manages to Return to his Legions. Vercingetorix Attacks Gorgobina.

Caesar delayed for two days in that place because he anticipated that, in the natural course of events, Vercingetorix would react in such a way. Caesar subsequently left the army under the pretense of levying recruits and cavalry. He placed Brutus, a young man, in command of these forces. He gave him instructions that the cavalry should range as extensively as possible in all directions, and told him that he would himself try not to be absent from the camp longer than three days. After making these arrangements, he proceeded to Vienna by forced marches, and arrived before his own soldiers expected him. He found there a fresh body of cavalry, which he had sent ahead to that place several days earlier. Then, marching incessantly night and day, he advanced rapidly through the territory of the Aedui into that of the Lingones, where two legions were spending the winter, in order that, if any plot affecting his own safety had been organized by the Aedui, he might defeat it by the rapidity of his movements. When he arrived there, he sent word to the rest of the legions, and gathered all his army in one place before news of his arrival could be announced to the Arverni. Vercingetorix, on hearing this development, led back his army into the country of the Bituriges, and, after marching from there to Gorgobina (a town of the Boii, whom Caesar had settled there after defeating them in the Helvetian war, and had rendered tributary to the Aedui), determined to attack it.

CHAPTER 10: CAESAR WORKS TO RETAIN ALLIES

This action presented great difficulty for Caesar in the selection of his plans. He was afraid that, if he confined his legions in one place for the remaining portion of the winter, all Gaul would revolt when the tributaries of the Aedui were subdued because it would then appear that Caesar was unable to protect his friends. On the other hand, if he drew his troops too soon out of their winter quarters, he might be distressed by the lack of supplies as a result of difficulties in transporting them. It seemed better, however, to endure every hardship than to lose the affections of all his allies by submitting to such an insult. He therefore impressed on the Aedui the necessity of supplying him with provisions, he sent ahead messengers to the Boii to inform them of his arrival, and he encouraged them to remain firm in their allegiance, and to resist the attack of the enemy with great resolution. Having left two legions and the baggage of the entire army at Agedincum, he marched to the Boii.

CHAPTER 11: CAESAR CAPTURES TWO TOWNS

On the second day, when he came to Vellaunodunum, a town of the Senones, he determined to attack it, in order not to leave an enemy in his rear, and to procure supplies of provisions more easily, and to draw a line of circumvallation around it in two days. On the third day, ambassadors were sent from the town to negotiate a surrender. Caesar ordered them to collect their weapons, bring out their cattle, and give him six hundred hostages. He left his lieutenant Gaius Trebonius to complete these arrangements. He himself set out with the intention of marching as soon as possible to Genabum, a town of the Carnutes. The Carnutes had at that time for the first time received news of the siege of Vellaunodunum. Inasmuch as they thought that the siege would be protracted for a longer time, they were preparing a garrison to send to Genabum for the defense of that town. Caesar arrived here in two days. After pitching his camp before the town, being prevented by the time of the day, he deferred the attack to the next day, and ordered his soldiers to prepare whatever was necessary for that enterprise. And, as a bridge over the Loire connected the town of Genabum with the opposite bank, Caesar was afraid that the inhabitants might escape by night from the town, so he ordered two legions to keep watch under arms. The people of Genabum came forth silently from the city before midnight, and began to cross the river. When this circumstance was announced by scouts, Caesar set fire to the gates, sent in the legions, whom he had ordered to be ready, and obtained possession of the town so completely that very few of the whole number of the enemy escaped being captured alive. Because the bridge and roads were narrow, the multitude was prevented from escaping. Caesar pillaged and burned the town, gave the booty of it to the soldiers, then led his army over the Loire, and marched into the territories of the Bituriges.

CHAPTER 12: CAESAR ATTACKS ANOTHER TOWN; VERCINGETORIX COMES TO THE AID OF THE TOWN

Vercingetorix, when he learned about the arrival of Caesar, desisted from his siege, and marched to meet Caesar. Caesar had begun to besiege Noviodunum, and, when ambassadors came from this town to beg him to pardon them and spare their lives, he ordered them to collect their weapons, to bring out their horses, and to give him hostages. He did this in order to accomplish the rest of his plans with the same rapidity as he had accomplished most of them. When part of the hostages were already delivered up, the rest of the terms were being performed, and a few centurions and soldiers were sent into the town to collect the weapons and horses, the enemy's cavalry, who had outstripped the main body of Vercingetorix's army, was seen at a distance. As soon as the townspeople saw them, and formed hopes of assistance, they raised a shout, began to take up arms, shut the gates, and line the walls. When the centurions in the town realized from the Gauls' signals that they were forming some new plot, they drew their swords, seized the gates, and withdrew all their men safely.

CHAPTER 13: CAESAR CAPTURES THE TOWN

Caesar ordered the horsemen to be led out of camp and began a cavalry action. Because his men were now distressed, Caesar sent to their aid about four hundred German cavalry, whom he had decided, at the outset, to keep with him. The Gauls could not withstand their attack, but were put to flight, and retreated to their main body after losing a great number of men. When they were routed, the townspeople, again intimidated, arrested those persons by whose exhortations they thought that the mob had been riled up, and they brought these instigators to Caesar, and surrendered themselves to him. After all this business was finished, Caesar marched to Avaricum (which was the largest and best fortified town in the territories of the Bituriges, and located in a most fertile tract of country) because he confidently expected that, after taking that town, he would reduce beneath his dominion the state of the Bituriges.

Chapter 14: Vercingetorix Advises the Bituriges to Pursue a Scorched Earth Policy

Vercingetorix, after sustaining so many losses in a row at Vellaunodunum, Genabum, and Noviodunum, summoned his men to a council. He impressed on them that the war had to be prosecuted on a very different system from the one they had previously adopted. They should instead by all means aim for the goal of preventing the Romans from foraging and procuring provisions. This was easy, he argued, because they themselves were well supplied with cavalry, and were likewise assisted by the season of the year. Forage could not be cut. The enemy would have to disperse, and look for it in the houses. The foragers could be destroyed every day by the cavalry. The interests of private property also had to be disregarded for the sake of the general safety. The villages and houses had to be burned over as much territory in every direction as the Romans appeared capable of scouring in their search for forage. An abundance of these necessaries could be supplied to themselves, however, because they would be assisted by the resources of those in whose territories the war would be waged. The Romans would either not be able to bear the deprivation or else they would advance a greater distance from their camp with considerable danger. It also made no difference whether they killed the Romans or stripped them of their baggage, since, if the baggage was lost, the Romans could not carry on the war. In addition to this, the towns should be burned that were not secured against every danger by their fortifications or natural advantages. There should be no places of retreat for their own countrymen that would allow them to decline military service, nor should they allow any vulnerable towns to stand that might allow the Romans to carry off abundance of provisions and plunder. If these sacrifices appeared heavy or galling, they should consider it much more distressing that their wives and children could be dragged off to slavery, and themselves slain: these were the evils that would necessarily befall the conquered.

Chapter 15: The Bituriges Burn their Towns, but Want to Defend Avaricum

This opinion was approved of by unanimous consent. More than twenty towns of the Bituriges were burned in one day. Conflagrations were beheld in every quarter, and, although everyone bore this with great regret, yet they laid before themselves this consolation: as the victory was certain, they could quickly recover their losses. There was a debate concerning Avaricum in the general council whether they should decide to burn or defend it. The Bituriges threw themselves at the feet of all the Gauls, and begged their countrymen not to compel them to set fire with their own hands to the most beautiful city of almost the whole of Gaul, which was both a protection and an ornament to the state. They insisted that they could easily defend it, owing to the nature of the ground. Because it was enclosed almost on every side by a river and a marsh, it had only one entrance, and that very narrow. Permission was granted to them at their earnest request. Vercingetorix had at first dissuaded them from it, but afterward conceded the point, owing to their entreaties and the compassion of the soldiers. A proper garrison was selected for the town.

CHAPTER 16: VERCINGETORIX PITCHES HIS CAMP AT AVARICUM

Vercingetorix followed closely upon Caesar by shorter marches, and selected for his camp a place defended by woods and marshes at a distance of fifteen miles from Avaricum. There he received intelligence from trusted scouts every hour in the day of what was going on at Avaricum, and ordered whatever he wished to be done. He closely watched all our expeditions for grain and forage, and whenever the foragers were compelled to go to a greater distance, he attacked them while they were dispersed, and inflicted severe losses upon them, although the evil was remedied by our men, as far as precautions could be taken, by going forth at irregular times and by different routes.

CHAPTER 17: CAESAR BESIEGES AVARICUM

Caesar pitched his camp on the side of the town that was not defended by the river and marsh, and had a very narrow approach (as we have mentioned). He began to employ protective sheds and to erect two towers, as the nature of the place prevented him from drawing a line of circumvallation. He never ceased to importune the Boii and Aedui for supplies of grain. The Aedui, because they were acting with no enthusiasm, did not aid him much. The Boii, as their resources were not great, quickly consumed what they had. The army was distressed by the severe scarcity of grain brought on by the poverty of the Boii and the apathy of the Aedui and the burning of the houses to such a degree that for several days the soldiers went without grain, and had to satisfy their extreme hunger with cattle driven from remote villages [Romans preferred bread to meat]. Nevertheless, no language was heard from the men that was unworthy of the majesty of the Roman people and their former victories. Moreover, when Caesar addressed the legions individually while they were at work, and said that he would raise the siege, if they felt the scarcity too severely, they unanimously begged him not to do so, insisting that they had served for several years under his command without ever submitting to insult and never abandoning an enterprise before they accomplished it. They would consider it a disgrace if they abandoned the siege after commencing it. It was better to endure every hardship than not to avenge the names of the Roman citizens who perished at Genabum by the treachery of the Gauls. They entrusted the same declarations to the centurions and military tribunes, so that through their officers their sentiments might be communicated to Caesar.

Chapter 18: Vercingetorix Harasses Caesar

When the towers had now been moved toward the walls, Caesar learned from the captives that Vercingetorix, after destroying the forage, had pitched his camp closer to Avaricum, and that he himself with his cavalry and light-armed infantry (who generally fought among the cavalry) had gone to lay an ambush in the area where he thought that our troops would come the next day to forage. On learning these facts, Caesar set out from the camp secretly at midnight, and reached the camp of the enemy early in the morning. They quickly learned of the arrival of Caesar from scouts, hid their carts and baggage in the thickest parts of the woods, and drew up all their forces in a high and open space. After this circumstance was announced, Caesar immediately ordered the baggage to be piled, and the arms to be prepared.

Chapter 19: Caesar Declines to Fight an Open Battle

There was a hill with a gentle ascent from its base. A dangerous and impass-able marsh not more than fifty feet wide surrounded it on almost every side. The Gauls, having broken down the bridges, posted themselves on this hill, confident in their position, and drew up in tribes according to their respective states. They held all the fords and passages of that marsh with trusted guards, and were determined, if the Romans attempted to force their way through the marsh, to overpower the Romans from the higher ground while they were stuck in the marsh. Whoever saw the proximity of the position would imagine that the two armies were prepared to fight on almost equal terms, but whoever examined accurately the disadvantage of position would discover that the enemy was showing off an empty pretense of courage. Caesar clearly pointed this out to his soldiers, who were indignant that the enemy could bear the sight of them at so short a distance, and were earnestly demanding the signal for action. Caesar explained with what great losses and the deaths of how many gallant men the victory would necessarily be purchased, and that, when he saw the soldiers so determined to decline no danger for his renown, he would have to be considered guilty of the utmost injustice, if he did not value their lives more than his personal safety. After he thus consoled his soldiers, he led them back on the same day to the camp, and determined to prepare the other things that were necessary for the siege of the town.

Chapter 20: The Gauls Blame Vercingetorix, who Defends his Strategy

Vercingetorix, when he had returned to his men, was accused of treason, because he had moved his camp closer to the Romans, because he had gone away with all the cavalry, because he had left such large forces without a commander, because, on his departure, the Romans had come at such a favorable time and with such dispatch; because all these circumstances could not have happened accidentally or without design; because he preferred holding the sovereignty of Gaul by the grant of Caesar to acquiring it by their favor. After he was accused in such a manner, he made the following reply to these charges: his moving his camp had been caused by the lack of forage, and had been done even by their advice. His approaching close to the Romans had been a measure dictated by the favorable nature of the ground, which would defend him by its natural strength. The service of the cavalry would not have been required in marshy ground, and was useful in that place where they had gone. He, on his departure, had given the supreme command to no one intentionally, for fear an interim leader would be induced by the eagerness of the multitude to risk an engagement, to which he, Vercingetorix, perceived that they all were inclined, owing to their lack of energy, because they were no longer able to endure the strain. If the Romans, in the meantime, had come up by chance, the Gauls should feel grateful to fortune. If the Romans, on the other hand, had been invited by some informer, they should feel grateful to the informer, because he had enabled them to see distinctly from the higher ground how small the number of their enemy was and to despise the courage of those who did not dare to fight, and had retreated disgracefully into their camp. He desired no power from Caesar by treachery, since he could have it by victory, which was now assured to himself and to all the Gauls. Indeed, he would even give back to them the command, if they thought that they conferred honor on him, rather than that they received safety from him. "In order that you may be assured," he said, "that I speak these words with truth, listen to these Roman soldiers!" He then produced some camp-followers whom he had surprised on a foraging expedition some days before, and had tortured with famine and imprisonment. They had been previously instructed in what answers they should make when examined, and said that they were legionary soldiers, who, pressed by hunger and deprivation, had recently gone forth from the camp, to see whether they could find any grain or cattle in the fields, adding that the whole army was distressed by a similar scarcity. No one now had sufficient strength, nor could anyone bear the labor of the work. The general was therefore determined, if he made no progress in the siege, to withdraw his army in three days. "These benefits," Vercingetorix said, "you receive from me, whom you accuse of treason—me, by whose exertions you see so powerful and victorious an army almost destroyed by famine, without shedding one drop of your blood, and I have taken precautions that no state will admit within its territories this army in its ignominious flight from this place."

CHAPTER 21: THE GAULS RALLY AROUND VERCINGETORIX

The whole multitude raised a shout and clashed their arms according to their custom, as they usually do when they approve someone's speech. They exclaimed that Vercingetorix was a consummate general, and that they had no doubt about his honor. The war could not be conducted with greater prudence. They determineed that ten thousand men should be picked out of the entire army and sent into the town, and decided that the general safety should not be entrusted to the Bituriges alone, because they were aware that the glory of the victory would belong to the Bituriges, if they were able to defend the town on their own.

CHAPTER 22: THE SIEGE OF AVARICUM CONTINUES

The Gauls used devices of every sort to oppose the extraordinary valor of our soldiers, for they are a nation of consummate ingenuity as well as most skillful in imitating and making the things that anyone has revealed to them. They therefore turned aside our grappling hooks with nooses, and, after they had caught hold of them firmly, they dragged them off by means of windlasses. They undermined our ramp all the more skillfully, inasmuch as there are in their territories extensive iron mines. As a result, they practice and know every description of mining operations. They had built, moreover, turrets along the whole wall on every side, and had covered the turrets with animal skins. In addition to this, in their frequent sallies by day and night, they attempted either to set fire to the ramp, or attack our soldiers while they were engaged in building operations. Moreover, by splicing the upright timbers of their own towers, they equaled the height of our towers as quickly as our ramp had daily raised them, and, with stakes that were bent and sharpened at the ends, they impeded us from working on tunnels that had opened up, and, with boiling pitch and stones of very great weight, they prevented our men from approaching the walls.

CHAPTER 23: GALLIC WALLS

The form of all the Gallic walls is generally as follows: straight beams, connected lengthwise and two feet distant from each other at equal intervals are placed together on the ground. These are fastened on the inside, and covered with plenty of earth. But the intervals that we have mentioned are closed up in front with large stones. After the beams and stones have thus been laid and cemented together, another row is added on top in such a manner that the same interval may be observed, and in order that the beams do not touch each another, but equal spaces intervene, and each row of beams is kept firmly in its place by a row of stones. In this manner, they consolidate the whole wall until the regular height of the wall has been completed. This work, with respect to appearance and variety, is not unsightly, owing to the alternate rows of beams and stones, which preserve their order in straight lines. Moreover, it possesses great advantages as regards utility and the defense of cities, for the stone protects it from fire, and the wood from the battering ram. Inasmuch as the wooden beams have been joined on the inside with rows of beams generally forty feet each in length, the wall can neither be broken through nor torn asunder.

CHAPTER 24: THE GAULS ATTEMPT A SORTIE

The siege was thus impeded by so many disadvantages, but the soldiers, although they were slowed down the whole time by mud, cold, and constant showers, yet by their incessant labor overcame all these obstacles, and in twenty-five days raised a ramp three hundred and thirty feet wide and eighty feet high. When it almost touched the enemy's walls, Caesar, according to his usual custom, kept watch at the work, and encouraged the soldiers not to discontinue the work for a moment. A little before the third watch [around midnight], they discovered that the ramp was smoking, since the enemy had set it on fire from a tunnel. At the same time, a shout was raised along the entire wall, and a sally was made from two gates on each side of the turrets. Some were at a distance casting torches and dry wood from the wall onto our tower. Others were pouring pitch on it as well as other materials that would feed the flame. As a result, a plan could hardly be formed as to where our men should first run to the defense or to what part aid should be brought. However, as two legions always kept guard by Caesar's orders before the camp, and several of them were at stated times to assist in the work, measures were promptly taken. Some of them opposed the sallying party while others drew back the towers and made a cut in the rampart. Moreover, the whole army hastened from the camp to extinguish the flames.

CHAPTER 25: THE ROMANS REPEL THE GALLIC ATTACK

While the battle was going on in every direction, the rest of the night had been spent, and fresh hopes of victory continually arose before the enemy, and all the more so because they saw that the coverings of our towers burned away, and they perceived that we were exposed, and could not easily go to give assistance. They themselves were continuously relieving those who were weary with fresh men, and were convinced that the entire safety of Gaul rested on this outcome of this crisis. There also happened, in my own view, a circumstance that appeared to be worthy of record, and we thought we should not omit it. In front of the town's gate, a certain Gaul was casting the balls of tallow and fire that were passed along to him into the fire in the vicinity of the tower. He was pierced with a dart on the right side and fell dead. One of those next to him in line stepped over him where he lay, and discharged the same duty. When the second man was killed in the same manner by a wound from a cross-bow, a third succeeded him, and a fourth succeeded the third. Nor was this post left vacant by the besieged until the fire of the ramp was extinguished, the enemy were repulsed in every direction, and an end was put to the fighting.

CHAPTER 26: THE GAULS ATTEMPT A NOCTURNAL ESCAPE

The Gauls had tried every expedient, but nothing had succeeded. They then adopted the plan of fleeing from the town the next day by the advice and order of Vercingetorix. They hoped that, by attempting to do so at the dead of night, they would accomplish it without any great loss of men, because the camp of Vercingetorix was not far distant from the town, and the extensive marsh that intervened was likely to slow down the Romans in their pursuit. And they were in the midst of preparing to execute this plan by night when the matrons suddenly ran out into the streets, and weeping cast themselves at their husbands' feet. They begged their husbands not to abandon them and their common children to the enemy for punishment, inasmuch as the natural weakness of their physical powers prevented them from taking flight. When the wives realized that their husbands (as fear does not generally yield to mercy in extreme danger) persisted in their resolution, they began to shout out loud, and give intelligence of their husbands' flight to the Romans. The Gauls, who were intimidated by a fear that Romans would occupy the passes in advance, desisted from their design.

CHAPTER 27: CAESAR LAUNCHES AN ASSAULT ON AVARICUM

The next day, when Caesar moved the tower forward, and the various works which he had arranged to build were complete, a violent storm arose. He thought that this was not a bad time for executing his designs because he observed that the guards mustered on the walls a little too negligently. He therefore ordered his own men to engage in their work more remissly, and pointed out what he wanted done. He drew up his soldiers in a secret position underneath a protective shed, and exhorted them to reap at last the harvest of victory proportionate to their exertions. He proposed a reward for those who would first scale the walls, and gave the signal to the soldiers. They suddenly flew out from all quarters and quickly filled the walls.

CHAPTER 28: THE ROMANS SLAUGHTER EVERYONE

Alarmed by the suddenness of the attack, the enemy were dislodged from the wall and towers, and drew up in the form of a wedge in the market place and the open streets with the intention that, if an attack were made on any side, they would fight with their line drawn up to receive it. When they saw no one descending to the level ground, and the enemy extending themselves along the entire wall in every direction, they were afraid that every hope of flight would be cut off, so they cast away their weapons, and sought, without stopping, the most remote parts of the town. Some of them were then slain by the infantry as they crowded upon one another in the narrow passage of the gates. Some of them, having made it outside the gates, were cut to pieces by the cavalry. Nor was there anyone who was

eager for plunder. Thus, incited by the massacre at Genabum and exasper-
ated by the siege, they spared neither old men, women, or children. In the
end, out of a number that amounted to about forty thousand, scarcely
eight hundred who fled from the town when they heard the first alarm
reached Vercingetorix in safety. And, as the night was now far spent, he received them in silence after their flight. And, fearing that a sedition might
arise in the camp as a result of their entrance in a group and from the pity
of the soldiers for their plight, he stationed his friends and the chiefs of
the states on the road at a distance from his camp, and took precautions
to ensure that the refugees would be separated, and conducted to their
fellow countrymen in whatever part of the camp had been assigned to
each state from the beginning.

Chapter 29: Vercingetorix Addresses the Gauls

Vercingetorix convened an assembly on the following day. He consoled,
and encouraged his soldiers, telling them that they should not be too much
depressed in spirit, nor alarmed at their loss, as the Romans did not conquer
by valor nor in the field, but by a kind of art and skill in assault with which
they themselves were unacquainted. Whoever expected every event in the
war to be favorable, erred. It was never his opinion that Avaricum should be
defended, and he now had themselves as witnesses of the truth of his opinion. It was owing, however, to the imprudence of the Bituriges, and the too
ready compliance of the rest, that this loss occurred. He, however, would
soon compensate for it by superior advantages, inasmuch as he would, by
his efforts, bring over those states that severed themselves from the rest of
the Gauls, and he would create a general unanimity throughout the whole
of Gaul, the union of which not even the whole earth could resist. He had
already almost accomplished this task. In the meantime, it was reasonable
that he should prevail on them, for the sake of the general safety, to begin
to fortify their camp, in order that they might more easily withstand the
sudden attacks of the enemy.

Chapter 30: The Gauls Rally

This speech was not disagreeable to the Gauls, principally because he
himself was not disheartened by receiving so severe a loss, and had not
concealed himself, nor shunned the eyes of the people. He was also believed to possess greater foresight and sounder judgment than the rest, because, when the affair was undecided, he had at first been of opinion that

Avaricum should be burned, and afterward that it should be abandoned. Accordingly, just as ill success weakens the authority of other generals, so, on the contrary, his dignity increased daily, even though they suffered a loss. At the same time, they began to entertain hopes, on his assertion, of uniting the rest of the states to themselves, and, on this occasion, for the first time, the Gauls began to fortify their camps, and were so alarmed that, although they were men unaccustomed to hard work, yet they were of the opinion that they ought to endure and put up with everything that was imposed upon them.

CHAPTER 31: VERCINGETORIX RECRUITS NEW ALLIES AND TROOPS

Nor did Vercingetorix use less effort than he had promised to gain over the other states, and, as a result, worked to entice their leaders by gifts and promises. For this purpose, he selected fitting emissaries, by whose subtle pleading or private friendship, each of the nobles could be most easily influenced. He took care that those who fled to him on the storming of Avaricum should be provided with weapons and clothes. At the same time, in order that his diminished forces should be reinforced, he levied a fixed quota of soldiers from each state, and defined the number and day before which he wished them brought to the camp, and he ordered all the archers, of whom there was a very great number in Gaul, to be collected and sent to him. By these means, the troops who were lost at Avaricum were speedily replaced. In the meantime, Teutomatus, the son of Ollovico, the king of the Nitiobriges, whose father had received the appellation of friend from the Roman Senate, came to him with a great number of his own cavalry and those whom he had hired from Aquitania.

CHAPTER 32: CAESAR LEARNS ABOUT POLITICAL TURMOIL AMONG THE AEDUI

Caesar, after delaying several days at Avaricum, and, finding there the greatest plenty of grain and other provisions, refreshed his army after their fatigue and deprivation. The winter was almost over, and he was invited by the favorable season of the year to prosecute the war and march against the enemy, and to try whether he could draw them from the marshes and woods, or else press them with a blockade. Some nobles of the Aedui came to him as ambassadors to request urgently that Caesar assist their state in an extreme emergency: their affairs were in the utmost danger, they alleged, because, whereas single magistrates had usually been appointed in ancient times, and had held the power of a king for a single year, two persons now exercised this office, and each asserted that he was appointed according to their laws. One of them was Convictolitavis, a powerful and illustrious youth; the other Cotus, sprung from a most ancient family, and personally a man of very great influence and extensive connections. His brother Valetiacus had held the same office during the previous year. The whole state was up in arms, their senate divided, the people divided. Each of them had his own adherents, and, if the animosity were fomented any longer, the result would be that one part of the state would come to a collision with the other. It depended (they concluded their argument) on Caesar's active engagement and influence to prevent this.

CHAPTER 33: CAESAR SETTLES POLITICAL AFFAIRS AMONG THE AEDUI

Although Caesar considered it ruinous to leave the war and the enemy, yet, he was well aware what great evils generally arise from internal dissensions, and was afraid that a state so powerful and so closely connected with the Roman people, a state which he himself had always fostered and honored in every respect, might have recourse to violence and arms, and that the party that had less confidence in its own power might summon aid from Vercingetorix. Caesar decided to anticipate this development, and because the laws of the Aedui did not permit those who held supreme authority to leave the country, he determined to go in person to the Aedui in order not to appear to infringe upon their government and laws, and he summoned all the senate and those involved in the dispute to meet him at Decetia. When almost all the state had assembled there, and he was informed that one brother had been declared magistrate by the other when only a few persons were privately summoned for that purpose at a different time and place from what he ought to have arranged, whereas the laws not only forbade two who belonged to one family to be elected magistrates while each was alive, but even deterred them from being in the senate at the same time, he compelled Cotus to resign his office. He ordered Convictolitavis, who had been elected by the priests according to the usage of the state after a disruption in the normal succession of magistrates, to hold the supreme authority.

Chapter 34: Caesar Recruits Troops from the Aedui, sends Labienus against the Senones and Parisii, and Sets Out Himself against Gergovia

Having pronounced this decree between the contending parties, he exhorted the Aedui to bury in oblivion their disputes and dissensions, and, laying aside all these things, devote themselves to the war, and expect from him, on the conquest of Gaul, those rewards which they should have earned, and send speedily to him all their cavalry and ten thousand infantry, which he might place in different garrisons to protect his convoys of provisions. He then divided his army into two parts: he gave Labienus four legions to lead into the country of the Senones and Parisii; and led in person six into the country of the Arverni, in the direction of the town of Gergovia, along the banks of the Allier. He gave part of the cavalry to Labienus and kept part to himself. Vercingetorix, on learning this circumstance, broke down all the bridges over the river and began to march on the other bank of the Allier.

Chapter 35: Vercingetorix Follows Caesar's March

When each army was in sight of the other, and was pitching their camp almost opposite each other, enemy scouts were distributed in every quarter to prevent the Romans from building a bridge and bringing over their troops. This was to Caesar a matter attended with great difficulties: he risked being prevented from crossing the river for most of the summer, as the Allier cannot generally be forded before autumn. Therefore, in order to prevent this from happening, he pitched his camp in a woody place opposite to one of the bridges that Vercingetorix had taken care to have broken down. The next day, Caesar stayed behind with two legions in a secret place. He sent ahead the rest of the forces as usual with all the baggage after having selected some cohorts, so that the number of the legions would appear to be complete. He ordered these men to advance as far as they could. When, from the time of day, he then conjectured that they had secured a camp, he began to rebuild the bridge on the same piles, the lower part of which remained intact. He quickly finished the work, and led his legions across the river, selected a fit place for a camp, and recalled the rest of his troops. Vercingetorix, on learning this fact, moved ahead of Caesar by forced marches, in order not to be compelled to engage in battle against his will.

CHAPTER 36: CAESAR ARRIVES AT GERGOVIA

Caesar, in a march of five days, went from that place to Gergovia. After engaging in a slight cavalry skirmish that day, he reviewed the situation of the city, which, because it was built on a very high mountain, was very difficult of access. Caesar despaired of taking the city by storm, and determined to take no steps toward besieging it until he could secure a supply of provisions. But Vercingetorix pitched his camp on the mountain near the town, placed the forces of each state separately and at small intervals around himself, and occupied all the hills of that range as far as they commanded a view of the Roman encampment. Vercingetorix presented a formidable appearance. He ordered the rulers of the states, whom he had selected as his council of war, to come to him daily at dawn to discuss whether any measure seemed to require deliberation or execution. Nor did he allow almost any day to pass without testing in a cavalry action (he sent the archers along with them) what spirit and valor there was in each of his own men. There was a hill opposite the town at the very foot of that mountain, which was strongly fortified and precipitous on every side. (And, if our men could win this hill, it seemed likely that they would be able to block the enemy from a large portion of their supply of water as well as easy foraging. The enemy occupied this place, however, with a weak garrison.) Caesar set out from the camp in the dead of night, and, dislodging the garrison before help could come from the town, he got possession of the place. He posted two legions there, and dug from the larger camp to the smaller camp a double trench twelve feet wide, in order that the soldiers could even individually cross over safe from any sudden attack of the enemy.

CHAPTER 37: CONSPIRACY AMONG CAESAR'S AEDUAN ALLIES

While these affairs were going on at Gergovia, Convictolitavis, the Aeduan, to whom (as we have observed) the magistracy was adjudged by Caesar, was bribed by the Arverni. He held a conference with certain young men, the chief of whom were Litaviccus and his brothers, who had been born of a most noble family. Convictolitavis shared the bribe with them, and exhorted them to remember that they were free and born for empire, that the state of the Aedui was the only one that was slowing down the most certain victory of the Gauls. The rest of the Gauls, he alleged, were held in check by its authority, and, if the Aedui joined the cause, the Romans would have no room to stand on in Gaul. Yes, he had received some kindness from Caesar, but only inasmuch as he won a most just case by Caesar's decision. Even so, Convictolitavis gave more weight to the general freedom of all Gaul, for why should the Aedui go to Caesar to judge concerning their rights and laws rather than the Romans come to the Aedui? The young men were easily won over by the speech of the magistrate and the bribe. After they declared that they would even be leaders in the plot, a plan for accomplishing it was considered, because they were confident their state could not be induced to undertake the war on slight pretexts. It was resolved that Litaviccus should have the command of the ten thousand men who were being sent to Caesar for the war. He should have charge of them on their march, and his brothers should go ahead of him to Caesar. They also arranged whatever other measures were required as well as the manner in which everything should be done.

Chapter 38: Litaviccus Persuades Caesar's Aeduan Troops to Switch Sides

Litaviccus, after he received the command of the army, suddenly called the soldiers to an assembly when he was about thirty miles distant from Gergovia, and, weeping, said, "Soldiers, where are we going? All our cavalry and all our nobles have perished. Eporedorix and Viridomarus, the chief men of our state, being accused of treason, have been executed by the Romans without any permission to defend themselves in court. You may learn the details from those who have escaped the massacre, for I, inasmuch as my brothers and all my relations have been killed, am prevented by grief from declaring what has taken place." Persons were brought forward, whom he had instructed in what he wanted them to say, and in order to make the same statements to the soldiery as Litaviccus had made: namely, that all the cavalry of the Aedui were slain because they were alleged to have held conferences with the Arverni; that they had concealed themselves among the multitude of soldiers, and had escaped from the midst of the slaughter. The Aedui shout aloud and beseech Litaviccus to provide for their safety. "As if," said he, "it were a matter of deliberation, and not of necessity, for us to go to Gergovia and unite ourselves to the Arverni! Or have we any reasons to doubt that the Romans, after perpetrating this atrocity, are now hastening to slaughter us? Therefore, if there be any spirit in us, let us avenge the deaths of those who have perished in a most unworthy manner, and let us slay these robbers!" He pointed to the Roman citizens who had accompanied them in reliance on his protection. He immediately seized a great quantity of grain and provisions, cruelly tortured them, and then put them to death, sending messengers throughout the entire state of the Aedui, and roused them completely by the same lie concerning the slaughter of their cavalry and nobles. He earnestly advised them to avenge, in the same manner as he did, the injustices that they had suffered.

CHAPTER 39: EPOREDORIX INFORMS CAESAR OF LITAVICCUS'S PLOT

Eporedorix, the Aeduan, a young man born in the highest rank and possessing very great influence at home, and, along with Viridomarus, of equal age and influence, but of inferior birth (Caesar had raised him from a humble position to the highest rank after he had been recommended to him by Divitiacus), had come in the number of cavalry after Caesar had summoned them by name. These men had a dispute with each other for precedence. And, in the struggle between the magistrates, they had contended with their utmost efforts on opposite sides: the one for Convictolitavis, the other for Cotus. Of these two, Eporedorix, on learning the plot of Litaviccus, laid the matter before Caesar almost at midnight. He entreated Caesar not to permit their state to swerve from their alliance with the Roman people, owing to the depraved counsels of a few young men. He foresaw what would be the result, if so many thousands of men should unite themselves to the enemy, inasmuch as their relatives could not neglect their safety nor the state regard it as a matter of little importance.

CHAPTER 40: CAESAR RUSHES TO RESTORE DISCIPLINE AMONG THE AEDUAN TROOPS, AND LITAVICCUS ESCAPES TO GERGOVIA

Caesar felt great anxiety about this intelligence, as he had always especially favored the state of the Aedui. Without any hesitation, he drew out from the camp four light-armed legions and all the cavalry. Nor had he time at such a crisis to contract the camp because the affair seemed to depend upon speed. He left Gaius Fabius, his lieutenant, with two legions to guard the camp. When he ordered the brothers of Litaviccus to be arrested, he discovered that they had fled a short time before to the camp of the enemy. He encouraged his soldiers not to be disheartened by the labor of the journey on such a crucial occasion. All were most eager, and, after advancing twenty-five miles, he came in sight of the army of the Aedui. By sending in his cavalry, Caesar slowed and impeded their march. He then issued strict orders to all his soldiers to kill no one. He commanded Eporedorix and Viridomarus, who the Aedui thought had been killed, to move among the cavalry and address their friends. When they were recognized and the treachery of Litaviccus discovered, the Aedui began to extend their hands to indicate submission, and, laying down their arms, to beg that they be spared the death penalty. Litaviccus, along with his clansmen, who, according to the custom of the Gauls, consider it a crime to desert their patrons even in extreme misfortune, fled to Gergovia.

CHAPTER 41: CAESAR RETURNS TO HIS TROOPS AT GERGOVIA

Caesar sent messengers to the state of the Aedui to inform them that he had spared through his kindness those whom he could have put to death by the right of war, and, after giving three hours of the night to his army for repose, directed his march to Gergovia. Almost in the middle of the journey, a party of cavalry who had been sent by Fabius stated in what great danger matters were. They informed him that the camp had been attacked by a very powerful army whose numbers allowed fresh men frequently to relieve the wearied, and thus exhaust our soldiers by incessant toil, inasmuch as, on account of the size of the camp, they had constantly to remain on the rampart. Many had been wounded by the immense number of arrows and all kinds of missiles. The artillery was of great service in resisting their attacks. Fabius, at their departure, left only two gates open, was blocking up the rest, and was adding parapets to the ramparts, and was preparing himself for similar events on the following day. Caesar, after receiving this information, reached the camp before sunrise owing to the very great zeal of his soldiers.

CHAPTER 42: THE AEDUI BACK HOME MEANWHILE ATTACK LOCAL ROMAN CITIZENS

While these things were going on at Gergovia, the Aedui, on receiving the first announcements from Litaviccus, left themselves no time to ascertain the truth of those statements. Some were stimulated by avarice, others by revenge and credulity, which is an inborn character trait in that nation to such a degree that they consider a slight rumor as an ascertained fact. They plundered the property of the Roman citizens, and either massacred them or dragged them away to slavery. Convictolitavis increased the evil state of affairs, and goaded on the people to fury, in order that, after committing an outrageous crime, they would be too ashamed to return to proper behavior. By a promise of safety, they lured from the town of Cabillonus, Marcus Aristius, a military tribune, who was on his march to his legion. They compelled those who had settled there for the purpose of trading to do the same. By constantly attacking them on their march, they stripped them of all their baggage. They besieged day and night all who resisted. After many had been killed on both sides, they excited a great number to armed rebellion.

CHAPTER 43: AFTER THE AEDUI REALIZE THAT LITAVICCUS'S PLOT WAS FOILED, THEY ATTEMPT TO MAKE AMENDS— CAESAR NEEDS ALLIES, SO HE FORGIVES THEM

In the meantime, when intelligence was brought that all their soldiers were in Caesar's power, they ran in a body to Aristius. They assured Caesar that nothing that had taken place had been done by public authority. They ordered an inquiry to be made about the plundered property. They confiscated the property of Litaviccus and his brothers. They sent ambassadors to Caesar for the purpose of clearing themselves. They did all this with a view to recover their soldiers. Because, however, they were contaminated by guilt and seduced by the gains derived from the plundered property, and, inasmuch as that crime was shared by many, and because they were tempted by the fear of punishment, they began to form plans of war and to stir up the other states by messengers. Although Caesar was aware of this proceeding, yet he addressed the ambassadors with as much mildness as he could, indicating that he did not think worse of the state on account of the ignorance and fickleness of the mob; nor would he diminish his regard for the Aedui. Caesar himself feared a greater commotion in Gaul. In order to prevent his being surrounded by all the states, he began to form plans as to the manner in which he could return from Gergovia and again concentrate his forces (he was worried that a departure arising from his fear of a revolt would seem like a flight).

CHAPTER 44: CAESAR SPOTS A WEAKNESS IN GERGOVIA'S DEFENSES

While he was considering these things, an opportunity for success seemed to offer itself. For, after he had arrived in the smaller camp for the purpose of inspecting the works, he noticed that the hill occupied by the enemy had been stripped of men, although, on the former days, it could scarcely be seen on account of the number of men on it. Caesar was astonished. He inquired the reason for it from the deserters, a great number of whom flocked to him daily. They all concurred in asserting what Caesar himself had already ascertained by his scouts. The back of that hill was almost level, but likewise woody and narrow, and it offered a path to the other side of the town. They had serious apprehensions about this place, and had concluded that, because the Romans had occupied one of the hills, if they were subsequently to lose the other, they would be almost surrounded, and cut off from all egress and foraging. Everyone had therefore been summoned by Vercingetorix to fortify this place.

CHAPTER 45: CAESAR DEVISES A TRAP

Caesar, after he was informed of this circumstance, sent several troops of cavalry to the place immediately after midnight. He ordered them to range in every quarter with more tumult than usual. At dawn he ordered a large quantity of baggage to be dragged out of the camp, and the muleteers with helmets in the appearance and guise of horsemen to ride round the hills. To these he added a few cavalry with instructions to range more widely in order to make a show. He ordered them all to seek the same quarter by a long circuit. These proceedings were seen at a distance from the town, as Gergovia commanded a view of the camp. Nor could the Gauls ascertain at so great a distance what the point was of the maneuver. He sent one legion to the same hill, and, after it had marched a little, stationed it in the lower ground, and concealed it in the woods. The suspicions of the Gauls were increased, and all their forces were marched to that place to defend it. Caesar then perceived the camp of the enemy deserted, covered the military insignia of his men, concealed the standards, and transferred his soldiers in small groups from the larger to the smaller camp. He pointed out to the lieutenants whom he had placed in command over the respective legions what he wanted them to do. He particularly advised them to restrain their men from advancing too far through their desire of fighting or their hope of plunder. He set before them what disadvantages the unfavorable nature of the ground carried with it, and that they could be assisted by speed alone. Success depended on a surprise, and not on a battle. After stating these particulars, he gave the signal for action, and sent the Aedui at the same time by another ascent on the right.

CHAPTER 46: CAESAR PUTS HIS PLAN INTO ACTION

The town wall was 1200 paces distant from the plain and base of the ascent in a straight line, if no gap intervened. Whatever detour was added to this ascent, in order to make the hill easy, increased the length of the route. But almost in the middle of the hill, the Gauls had previously built a wall six feet high made of large stones and extending in length as far as the nature of the ground permitted as a barrier to retard the advance of our men. And, leaving all the lower space empty, they had filled the upper part of the hill, as far as the wall of the town, with their camps very close to one another. The soldiers, after the signal was given, quickly advanced to this fortification, and, passing over it, made themselves masters of the separate camps. And so great was their speed in taking the camps that Teutomatus, the king of the Nitiobriges was suddenly surprised in his tent, as he had gone to nap at noon. He escaped with difficulty from the hands of the plunderers with the upper part of his person naked, and his horse wounded.

CHAPTER 47: CAESAR ORDERS THE TROOPS TO RETREAT, BUT THEY CONTINUE TO ADVANCE TO THE WALLS OF GERGOVIA

Caesar, after accomplishing the goal that he had set, ordered the signal to be sounded for a retreat. The soldiers of the tenth legion, by which he was then accompanied, halted. But the soldiers of the other legions did not hear the sound of the trumpet because there was a very large valley between them. They were, however, ordered back by the tribunes of the soldiers and the lieutenants, in accordance with Caesar's instructions. But, excited by the prospect of speedy victory and the flight of the enemy and the favorable battles of former days, they thought nothing so difficult that their bravery could not accomplish it. Nor did they put an end to the pursuit until they drew close to the wall of the town and the gates. But then, when a shout arose in every quarter of the city, those who were at a distance, because they were alarmed by the sudden tumult, fled hastily from the town, inasmuch as they thought that the enemy were within the gates. The matrons began to cast their clothes and silver over the wall, and, bending over as far as the lower part of their naked bosom, with out-stretched hands begged the Romans to spare them, and not to slaughter even women and children, as they had done at Avaricum. Some of them let themselves down from the walls by their hands, and surrendered to our soldiers. Lucius Fabius a centurion of the eighth legion—who (it was

later determined) had said that day among his fellow soldiers that he was
excited by the plunder of Avaricum, and would not allow anyone to mount
the wall before him—found three men of his own company to raise him
up, so he could scale the wall. He himself in turn took hold of them one
by one, and drew them up to the wall.

CHAPTER 48: THE GAULS RALLY TO DEFEND GERGOVIA

In the meantime, those who had gone to the other part of the town to defend it (as we mentioned above) were at first aroused by hearing the shouts
and afterward by frequent reports that the town was in possession of the
Romans. They sent out their cavalry, and hastened in larger numbers to
that area. When each first arrived, he stood beneath the wall, and increased
the number of his countrymen engaged in action. After a great multitude
of them had assembled, the matrons, who a little before were stretching
their hands from the walls to the Romans, began to beseech their countrymen, and, after the Gallic fashion, to show their disheveled hair, and bring
their children into public view. Neither in position nor in numbers was the
contest an equal one for the Romans. At the same time, because they were
exhausted from running and the long continuation of the fight, they could
not easily withstand fresh and vigorous troops.

CHAPTER 49: CAESAR SENDS REINFORCEMENTS

Caesar, when he perceived that his soldiers were fighting on unfavorable
ground, and that the enemy's forces were increasing, was alarmed for the
safety of his troops. He sent orders to Titus Sextius, one of his lieutenants,
whom he had left to guard the smaller camp, to lead out his cohorts quickly
from the camp, and post them at the base of the hill on the right wing of
the enemy, and, if he saw our men driven from the position, he was to de-
ter the enemy from following too closely. Caesar himself, advancing with
the legion a little from that place where he had taken his post, awaited the
outcome of the battle.

CHAPTER 50: THE ROMANS ARE BEATEN BACK FROM THE
WALLS OF GERGOVIA

The fight was going on most vigorously hand to hand. The enemy depended
on their position and numbers; our men on their bravery. Suddenly in the
midst of this, the Aedui appeared on our exposed flank, as Caesar had sent
them by another approach on the right for the sake of creating a diversion.

These Aedui from the similarity of their arms to the other Gauls greatly terrified our men. And, although they were discovered to have their right shoulders bare, which was the customary and agreed on sign, yet the soldiers suspected that the enemy did this very thing to deceive them. At the same time, Lucius Fabius the centurion, and those who had scaled the wall with him, were surrounded, slain, and cast from the wall. Marcus Petreius, a centurion of the same legion, after attempting to hew down the gates, was overpowered by numbers. Despairing of his safety, and already grievously wounded, Petreius said to the soldiers of his own company who followed him: "Since I cannot save you as well as myself, I shall at least provide for your safety, since I, allured by the love of glory, led you into this danger. Save yourselves when an opportunity is given!" At the same moment, he rushed into the midst of the enemy, and, killing two of them, drove back the rest a little from the gate. When his men attempted to help him, "In vain," he said, "you try to bring me to safety, since blood and strength are now failing me. Therefore stop doing this, while you have the opportunity, and retreat to the legion!" Thus he fell fighting a few moments later, and saved his men by his own death.

CHAPTER 51: THE ROMANS SUFFER HEAVY LOSSES

Our soldiers were hard pressed on every side, and were dislodged from their position with the loss of forty-six centurions. But the tenth legion, which had been posted in reserve on ground a little more level, checked the Gauls in their eager pursuit. They were supported by the cohorts of the thirteenth legion, which had been led from the smaller camp, and which had, under the command of Titus Sextius, occupied the higher ground. The legions, as soon as they reached the plain, halted, and faced the enemy. Vercingetorix led back his men from the part of the hill within the fortifications. On that day, a little less than seven hundred of the soldiers were missing.

CHAPTER 52: CAESAR SCOLDS THE TROOPS

On the next day, Caesar called a meeting, and scolded the rashness and avarice of his soldiers: they had decided for themselves how far they ought to proceed or what they ought to do, and they could not be kept back by the tribunes of the soldiers and the lieutenants. Caesar explained what the disadvantage of the ground could bring about, what opinion he himself had entertained at Avaricum, when, although he had surprised the enemy without either general or cavalry, he gave up a certain victory, lest even a trifling loss should occur in the battle, owing to the disadvantage of position. As much as he admired the greatness of their courage, since neither the fortifications of the camp, nor the height of the mountain, nor the wall of the town could slow them, nevertheless, in the same degree, he blamed their disobedience and arrogance, because they thought that they knew more than their general concerning victory, and the outcome of events. Caesar required in his soldiers self-restraint and self-discipline no less than valor and courage.

This 1903 monument celebrates the victory of the Gauls over the Romans in the battle of Gergovia. It stands on the Plateau de Gergovie near Puy de Dôme, France—a site traditionally associated with the battle. Note the Gallic helmet which crowns the monument.

Chapter 53: Caesar Abandons the Siege of Gergovia

After delivering these rebukes, Caesar encouraged the soldiers at the conclusion of his speech. They should not be dispirited on this account nor attribute to the valor of the enemy what the disadvantage of position had caused. Entertaining the same views of his departure that he had previously held, he led forth the legions from the camp, and drew up his army in order of battle in a suitable place. When Vercingetorix, nevertheless, would not descend to the level ground, a slight cavalry action, and that a successful one, took place. Caesar then led back his army into the camp. After he had done this, the next day, thinking that he had done enough to lower the pride of the Gauls and to encourage the minds of his soldiers, he moved his camp in the direction of the Aedui. The enemy did not even then pursue us, and, on the third day, Caesar repaired the bridge over the river Allier, and led over his whole army.

Chapter 54: More Trouble with the Aedui

Caesar then held an interview with Viridomarus and Eporedorix the Aeduans, learning that Litaviccus had set out with all the cavalry to rouse the Aedui. Caesar told them that it was necessary that they too should go ahead of him to confirm the state in their allegiance to Caesar. Although he now saw distinctly the treachery of the Aedui in many things, and was of the opinion that the revolt of the entire state would be hastened by their departure, yet he thought that they should not be detained, lest he should appear either to offer an insult or betray some suspicion of fear. Caesar briefly reminded them at their departure of his services toward the Aedui: in what a state and how humbled he had found them, driven into their towns, deprived of their lands, stripped of all their forces, a tribute imposed on them, and hostages wrested from them with the utmost insult; and to what condition and to what greatness he, Caesar, had raised the Aedui. So much so, in fact, that they had not only recovered their former position, but seemed to surpass the dignity and influence of all the previous eras of their history. After giving these admonitions, Caesar dismissed them.

Chapter 55: The Aedui Revolt

Noviodunum was a town of the Aedui advantageously situated on the banks of the Loire. Caesar had conveyed to that place all the hostages of Gaul, the grain, public money, a great part of his own equipment and that of his army. Caesar had sent to that place a great number of horses, which he had purchased in Italy and Spain on account of this war. When Eporedorix and Viridomarus came to this place, they received information about the current situation in the state. Litaviccus had been admitted by the Aedui into Bibracte, which is a town of the greatest importance among them. Convictolitavis, the chief magistrate, and a great part of the senate had gone to meet him. Ambassadors had been publicly sent to Vercingetorix to negotiate a peace and alliance. They thought that so great an opportunity ought not to be neglected. Therefore, they put to the sword the troops of the garrison at Noviodunum as well as those who had gathered there for the purpose of trading or were on their march. They divided the money and horses among themselves. They took care that the hostages of the different states should be brought to Bibracte and to the chief magistrate. They burned the town to prevent its being of any service to the Romans, as they were of the opinion that they could not hold it. They carried away in their vessels whatever grain they could in a hurry, and they destroyed the remainder by throwing it into the river or setting it on fire. They themselves began to collect forces from the neighboring country, to place guards and garrisons in different positions along the banks of the Loire, and to display the cavalry on all sides, in order to strike terror into the Romans, if they could cut them off from a supply of provisions. They were much aided in this hope from the circumstance that the Loire had swollen to such a degree from the melting of the snows that it did not seem capable of being forded at all.

CHAPTER 56 : CAESAR AND HIS ARMY ESCAPE

When Caesar was informed of these movements, he was of opinion that he ought to make haste, even if he ran some risk in completing the bridges, in order to fight a decisive battle before greater forces of the enemy could be collected in that place. Even then, no one considered it absolutely necessary that he modify his plans, and direct his march into the Province, both because of the infamy and disgrace of such a thing and because the intervening Mount Cevennes and the difficulty of the roads prevented him from doing so. Moreover, Caesar had especially serious apprehensions for the safety of Labienus, whom he had detached, as well as for those legions, whom he had sent along with Labienus. Therefore, Caesar made very long marches by day and night, and came to the river Loire, contrary to the expectation of all. By means of the cavalry, he then found a ford suitable enough, considering the emergency, that was of such depth that their arms and shoulders could be above water for supporting their equipment. Caesar stationed his cavalry at intervals, in order to break the force of the river's current, and led his army across the river in safety, having confused the enemy when they first caught sight of his army. Caesar found grain and cattle in the fields, and, after refreshing his army with these, he determined to march into the country of the Senones.

CHAPTER 57: LABIENUS ON THE MARCH TO LUTETIA IS OPPOSED BY CAMULOGENUS

While these things were being done by Caesar, Labienus left at Agedincum the recruits who had recently arrived from Italy to guard the baggage. He marched with four legions to Lutetia (which is a town of the Parisii, situated on an island on the river Seine). Their arrival was discovered by the enemy, and numerous forces arrived from the neighboring states. The supreme command was entrusted to Camulogenus, one of the Aulerci, who, although almost worn out with age, was called to that honor on account of his extraordinary knowledge of military tactics. Camulogenus, when he observed that there was a large marsh that was connected to the Seine and rendered all that country impassable, encamped in that place, and determined to prevent our troops from crossing.

CHAPTER 58: LABIENUS'S STRUGGLES EN ROUTE TO LUTETIA

Labienus at first attempted to move forward under the protection of sheds, fill up the marsh with hurdles and clay, and secure a road. After he perceived that this was too difficult to accomplish, he issued in silence from his camp at the third watch [sometime after midnight], and reached Metiosedum by the same route by which he came. This is a town of the Senones, situated on an island in the Seine (as we have just before observed of Lutetia). He seized upon about fifty ships, quickly joined them together, placed soldiers in them, and intimidated by his unexpected arrival the inhabitants who had been called out to the war in great numbers. Labienus thus obtained possession of the town without a contest. After he repaired the bridge, which the enemy had broken down during the preceding days, he led over his army, and began to march along the banks of the river to Lutetia. The enemy, on learning what happened from those who had escaped from Metiosedum, set fire to Lutetia, and ordered the bridges of that town to be broken down. They themselves set out from the marsh, and took their position on the banks of the Seine opposite Lutetia and opposite the camp of Labienus.

CHAPTER 59: LABIENUS LEARNS OF CAESAR'S TROUBLE, AND ASSESSES THE DANGERS THAT CONFRONT HIM

Caesar was now reported to have departed from Gergovia. Intelligence was likewise brought to Labienus concerning the revolt of the Aedui, and of a successful rebellion in Gaul. He was also told that Caesar had been prevented from prosecuting his journey and crossing the Loire, and had been compelled by the want of grain to march hastily to the Province. But the Bellovaci, who had previously been disaffected for their own reasons, on learning of the revolt of the Aedui, began to assemble forces and openly to prepare for war. Then Labienus, as the change in affairs was so great, thought that he had to adopt a very different plan from what he had previously intended. He no longer thought of making any new conquests or of provoking the enemy to an battle, but instead how he might bring back his army safely to Agedincum. For, on one side, the Bellovaci, a state that held the highest reputation for prowess in Gaul, were pressing on him, and Camulogenus with a disciplined and well-equipped army held the other side. Moreover, a very great river separated and cut off the legions from the garrison and baggage. He saw that as a result of the very large difficulties thrown in his way he must seek assistance from his own ability and courage.

CHAPTER 60: LABIENUS BEGINS HIS RETREAT

He therefore called a council of war a little before evening, and he exhorted his soldiers to execute with diligence and energy such commands as he should give. He assigned the ships that he had brought from Metiosedum to Romans of equestrian status, one to each, and ordered them to sail down the river silently for four miles at the end of the fourth watch [i.e., before dawn], and wait for him there. He left the five cohorts, which he considered to be the most steady in action, to guard the camp. He ordered the five remaining cohorts of the same legion to proceed a little after midnight up the river with all their baggage, and to make a great commotion. He collected also some small boats, and sent them in the same direction with orders to make a loud noise in rowing. He himself, a little later, marched out in silence, and, at the head of three legions, headed for the place where he had ordered the ships to be brought.

CHAPTER 61: CAMULOGENUS ATTEMPTS TO BLOCK LABIENUS

When he had arrived there, the enemy's scouts, who were stationed along every part of the river and not expecting an attack, because a great storm had suddenly arisen, were surprised by our soldiers. The infantry and cavalry were quickly transported under the superintendence of the Romans of equestrian status, whom he had appointed to that office. Almost at the same time, a little before daylight, intelligence was given to the enemy that there was an unusual commotion in the camp of the Romans, and that a strong force was marching up the river, and that the sound of oars was distinctly heard in the same quarter, and that soldiers were being conveyed across in ships a little way downstream. On hearing these things, because they were of the opinion that the legions were crossing in three different places, and that the entire army, because they were terrified by the revolt of the Aedui, were preparing for flight, they divided their forces also into three divisions. They left a guard opposite the camp, and sent a small body of troops in the direction of Metiosedum with orders to advance as far as the ships would proceed. They led the rest of their troops against Labienus.

CHAPTER 62: LABIENUS DEFEATS CAMULOGENUS

By daybreak all our soldiers had been brought across, and the army of the enemy was in sight. Labienus encouraged his soldiers to retain the memory of their ancient valor and their numerous victorious battles, and imagine that Caesar himself, under whose command they had so often routed the enemy, was present. Then he gave the signal for battle. At the first onset the enemy were beaten and put to flight on the right wing where the seventh legion stood. On the left wing, the position the twelfth legion held, although the first ranks of the enemy fell transfixed by the javelins of the Romans, yet the rest of the enemy resisted most bravely. Nor did any one of them show the slightest intention of fleeing. Camulogenus, the general of the enemy, was present and encouraged his troops. But when the issue of the victory was still uncertain, and the circumstances that were taking place on the left wing were announced to the tribunes of the seventh legion, they turned around their legion to the enemy's rear and attacked it. Even then none of the enemy retreated, but all of them were surrounded and slaughtered. Camulogenus met the same fate. But those who were left as a guard opposite the camp of Labienus, after they heard that the battle was begun, marched to aid their countrymen and take possession of a hill, but they were unable to withstand the attack of our victorious soldiers. In this manner, mixed with their own fugitives, those whom the woods and mountains did not shelter were cut to pieces by our cavalry. When this battle was finished, Labienus returned to Agedincum where the baggage of the whole army had been left. From this place, he marched with all his forces to Caesar.

CHAPTER 63: THE GALLIC REVOLT SPREADS, AND THE AEDUI SUBMIT TO VERCINGETORIX'S LEADERSHIP

As the revolt of the Aedui became known, the war grew more dangerous. Embassies were sent by them in all directions. As far as they could prevail by influence, authority, or money, they strove to incite the state to revolt. After they got possession of the hostages whom Caesar had deposited with them, they terrified those who hesitated by putting hostages to death. The Aedui asked Vercingetorix to come to them and communicate his plans for conducting the war. On obtaining this request, they insisted that the supreme command should be assigned to them. And, when the affair became matter of dispute, a council of all Gaul was summoned to Bibracte. They came together in great numbers and from every quarter to the same place. The decision was left to the votes of the mass. All to a man approved of Vercingetorix as their general. The Remi, Lingones, and Treviri were absent from this meeting; the Remi and Lingones because they attached themselves to the alliance of Rome; the Treviri because they were very remote and were hard pressed by the Germans. This was also the reason for their absence during the whole war, and why they sent auxiliaries to neither party. The Aedui were highly indignant at being deprived of the supreme command. They lamented the change of fortune, and missed Caesar's favors toward them. However, after joining the war effort, they did not dare to pursue their own measures apart from the rest. Eporedorix and Viridomarus, youths of the greatest ambition, reluctantly submitted to Vercingetorix.

CHAPTER 64: VERCINGETORIX PLANS OFFENSIVE MEASURES AGAINST THE ROMAN PROVINCE

Vercingetorix demanded hostages from the remaining states. Indeed, what is more, he appointed a day for this proceeding. He ordered all the cavalry, fifteen thousand in number, to assemble quickly here. He said that he would be content with the infantry that he had previously, and would not tempt fortune nor fight a set battle. On the other hand, since he had abundance of cavalry, it would be very easy for him to prevent the Romans from obtaining forage or grain, provided that they themselves should resolutely destroy their grain and set fire to their houses. By this sacrifice of private property, they would obtain perpetual dominion and freedom forever. After he arranged these matters, he levied ten thousand infantry from the Aedui and Segusiavi, who border on our province. In addition to these, he demanded eight hundred cavalry. He set over them the brother of Eporedorix, and ordered him to wage war against the Allobroges. On the other side, he sent the Gabali and the nearest cantons of the Arverni against the Helvii. He likewise sent the Ruteni and Cadurci to lay waste the territories of the Volcae Arecomici. Additionally, by secret messages and embassies, he tampered with the Allobroges, whose minds, he hoped, had not yet settled down after the excitement of the recent war. To their nobles he promised money, and to their state dominion over the whole province.

CHAPTER 65: DEFENSIVE MEASURES ON THE ROMAN SIDE; CAESAR ENLISTS GERMAN CAVALRY

The only guards offering any protection against all these developments were twenty-two cohorts that had been collected from the entire province by the lieutenant Lucius Caesar, who sent them against the enemy in every quarter. The Helvii, who voluntarily engaged in battle with their neighbors, were defeated, and Gaius Valerius Donotaurus, the son of Caburus, the chief leader of the state, and several others, were slain. They were forced to retreat within their towns and fortifications. The Allobroges placed guards along the course of the Rhine, and defended their frontiers with great vigilance and energy. Caesar perceived that the enemy were superior in cavalry, and he himself could receive no aid from the Province or Italy while all communication was cut off, so he sent messengers across the Rhine into Germany to those states that he had subdued in the preceding campaigns, and requisitioned from them cavalry and the light-armed infantry who customarily fought alongside them. When they arrived, they were mounted on unserviceable horses, so Caesar took horses from the military tribunes and the rest—indeed, even from the Romans of equestrian status and veterans—and distributed their horses among the Germans.

CHAPTER 66: CAESAR RETURNS TO DEFEND THE PROVINCE

In the meantime, while these things were going on, enemy forces from the Arverni and the cavalry requisitioned from all Gaul assembled. A great number of these were collected by Vercingetorix while Caesar was marching into the country of the Sequani through the confines of the Lingones, in order more easily to render aid to the Province. Vercingetorix stationed his forces in three camps about ten miles from the Romans. He summoned the commanders of the cavalry to a council, and told them that the time of victory had arrived: the Romans were fleeing into the Province and abandoning Gaul. This was sufficient for obtaining immediate freedom, but was not enough for acquiring peace and tranquillity for the future. The Romans, Vercingetorix explained, would return after assembling greater forces and would not put an end to the war. Therefore, they should attack the Romans on their march when they were encumbered with their equipment. If the infantry were forced to relieve their cavalry, and were slowed down by doing so, they would not be able to accomplish their march. If, on the other hand, the Roman infantry abandoned their baggage to provide for their safety (the outcome which, Vercingetorix believed, was more likely to ensue), they would lose both their property and reputation. As to the enemy's cavalry, they should have no doubt whatsoever that none of them would dare to advance beyond the main column. In order that the Gauls might act with greater spirit, he would marshal all their forces before the camp, and intimidate the enemy. The cavalry unanimously shouted that they should bind themselves by a most sacred oath, and solemnly swear that anyone who had not twice ridden through the enemy's army would not be received under a roof nor have access to his children, parents, or wife.

CHAPTER 67: CAESAR DEFEATS VERCINGETORIX

This proposal received general approval, and everyone was forced to take the oath. On the next day, the cavalry were divided into three parts, and two of these divisions made a demonstration on our two flanks. The cavalry group in front began to obstruct our march. When this development was announced, Caesar ordered his cavalry to form three divisions as well, and to charge the enemy. At this point, the battle began simultaneously on all sides. The main column halted, the baggage was collected within the ranks of the legions. If our men appeared to be distressed or hard pressed in any quarter, Caesar usually ordered the troops to advance, and the army to wheel round in that quarter. This procedure slowed the enemy pursuit, and encouraged our men with the hope of support. At length, the Germans on the right wing gained the top of the hill, dislodged the enemy from their position, and pursued them even as far as the river where Vercingetorix was stationed with the infantry. The Germans slayed several of them. The rest, on observing this action, were afraid that they would be surrounded, and betook themselves to flight. A slaughter ensued in every direction, and three of the noblest of the Aedui were captured, and brought to Caesar: Cotus, the commander of the cavalry, who had been engaged in the contest with Convictolitavis in the last election, Cavarillus, who had held the command of the infantry after the revolt of Litaviccus, and Eporedorix, under whose command the Aedui had engaged in war against the Sequani before the arrival of Caesar.

CHAPTER 68: VERCINGETORIX RETREATS TO ALESIA, AND CAESAR BEGINS TO DIG IN FOR A SIEGE

After all his cavalry were routed, Vercingetorix led back his troops in the same order as he had arranged them in front of the camp, and immediately began to march to Alesia, which is a town of the Mandubii. He ordered the baggage to be speedily brought out from the camp, and to follow closely behind him. Caesar, after his baggage was conveyed to the nearest hill, left two legions to guard it, and pursued the enemy as far as the time of day would permit. After slaying about three thousand of the rear of the enemy, he encamped at Alesia on the next day. Upon reconnoitering the situation of the city, he found that the enemy were panic-stricken, because the cavalry, on whom they placed their chief reliance, had been beaten. Caesar encouraged his men to endure the hard labor, and they began to draw a line of circumvallation around Alesia.

CHAPTER 69: CAESAR DESCRIBES ALESIA AND THE SURROUNDING AREA

The town itself was situated on the top of a hill in a very lofty position so that it did not appear likely to be captured except by a regular siege. Two rivers on two different sides washed the base of the hill. Before the town lay a plain of about three miles in length. On every other side, hills at a moderate distance and of an equal height surrounded the town. The army of the Gauls had filled all the space under the wall on the side of the hill that looked toward the rising sun, and they had dug in front a trench and built a stone wall six feet high. The circuit of the fortifications that the Romans began constructing comprised eleven miles. The camp was pitched in a strong position, and twenty-three forts were constructed along the Roman line. In these stations, sentinels were placed by day to prevent any attempt at a sudden sortie, and by night the same posts were occupied by watches and strong guards.

CHAPTER 70: THE GAULS MAKE AN UNSUCCESSFUL SORTIE

After the work had started, a cavalry battle ensued in the plain that we have already described as broken up by hills and extending three miles in length. The contest was maintained on both sides with the utmost

PLAN OF ALESIA

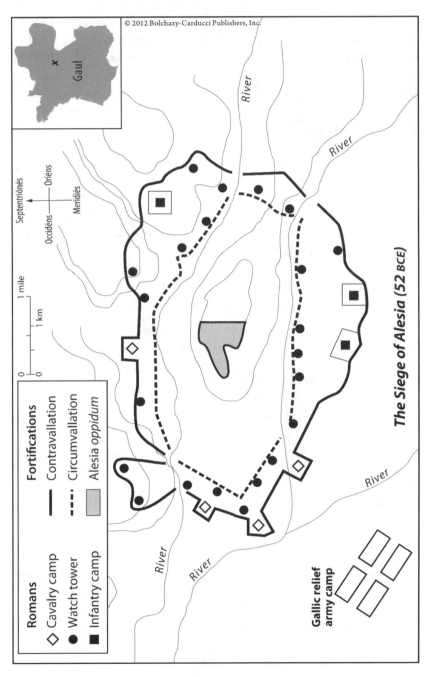

© 2012 Bolchazy-Carducci Publishers, Inc.

Gaul

Septentriōnēs — Oriēns
Occidēns — Merīdiēs

1 mile
1 km
0
0

Romans
◇ Cavalry camp
● Watch tower
■ Infantry camp

Fortifications
— Contravallation
- - - Circumvallation
▨ Alesia *oppidum*

River

The Siege of Alesia (52 BCE)

Gallic relief army camp

vigor. Caesar sent the Germans to aid our troops when distressed, and
he mustered the legions in front of the camp to prevent any sudden sally
by the enemy's infantry. The courage of our men was increased by the
additional support of the legions. The enemy were put to flight, and then
got in one another's way on account of their numbers. And, as only the
narrower gates were left open, they were crowded together in them. The
Germans pursued them with vigor all the way to their fortifications. A
great slaughter ensued. Some left their horses, and tried to cross the ditch
and climb the wall. Caesar ordered the legions whom he had drawn up in
front of the rampart to advance a little. The Gauls, who were inside their
fortifications, were no less panic-stricken than their retreating cavalry,
and believed that the enemy were coming that very moment against them.
They all began to shout at once: "To arms!" Some in their alarm rushed
into the town. Vercingetorix ordered the gates to be shut, so that his camp
would not be left undefended. The Germans retreated after slaying many
and taking quite a few horses.

CHAPTER 71: VERCINGETORIX SENDS OUT HIS CAVALRY BY NIGHT TO SUMMON REINFORCEMENTS

Vercingetorix adopted the plan of sending away all his cavalry by night
before the Romans could complete the fortifications. He instructed them
when departing that each of them should go to his respective state, and
urge all who were old enough to bear arms to join the war. He stated his
own merits, and implored them to consider his safety, and not surrender
to the enemy for torture one who had done so much for their common
freedom. He pointed out to them that, if they failed to do as he asked,
eighty thousand chosen men would perish with him, and that, according
to his calculations, he had barely enough grain for thirty days, but could
hold out a little longer by rationing. After giving these instructions, he
silently dismissed the cavalry in the second watch [i.e., before midnight],
on that side where our fortifications were not yet complete. He ordered all
the grain to be brought to himself. He ordained capital punishment for
anyone who did not obey. He distributed among them, man by man, the
cattle, great quantities of which had been driven there by the Mandubii.
He began to measure out the grain sparingly and in small quantities. He
received into the town all the forces which he had posted in front of it.
In this manner, he prepared to wait for reinforcements from Gaul, and
carry on the war.

CHAPTER 72: CAESAR DESCRIBES HIS LINE OF SIEGE WORKS AROUND ALESIA

Caesar, upon learning of these proceedings from deserters and captives, adopted the following system of fortification: he dug a trench twenty feet deep with perpendicular sides in such a manner that the base of this trench extended as far as the edges were apart at the top. He built all his other siege works at a distance of four hundred feet from that ditch. Because it was necessary to include such an extensive area, and the whole siege works could not be easily surrounded by a line of soldiers, Caesar was afraid that a large number of the enemy suddenly or by night might make a sortie from the town against our fortifications or by day cast weapons against our men while occupied with the siege works. Behind this intervening space, he dug two trenches fifteen feet wide and of the same depth. The innermost of trench, which was located in low and level ground, he had filled with water conveyed from the river. Behind these he built a rampart and wall twelve feet high. To the wall, he added a parapet and battlements with large stakes cut like stags' horns that projected from the junction of the parapet and battlements in order to prevent the enemy from scaling it, and he surrounded the entire work with turrets, which were eighty feet distant from one another.

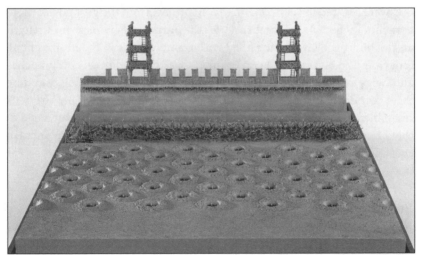

Model of Julius Caesar's siege works before Alesia, made by General Verchère de Refflye for Napoléon III. Caesar sought to contain any Gallic escape with a series of obstacles: a field of lilies—sharpened stakes in pits; trenches of gravestones—impenetrable artificial underbrush; a field of *stimuli*—wood blocks with iron hooks fixed in them; two trenches; and a palisade with towers.

CHAPTER 73: CAESAR DESCRIBES ADDITIONAL FORTIFICATIONS

It was necessary at one and the same time to procure timber for the rampart, lay in supplies of grain, and also build extensive fortifications. The available troops were as a result of this reduced in number, since they had to advance to some distance from the camp, and sometimes the Gauls attempted to attack our siege works, and to make a sally from the town by several gates and in great force. Caesar thought that further additions should be made to these siege works in order to make the fortifications defensible by a small number of soldiers. He therefore had the trunks of trees or very thick branches cut down, had their tops stripped of bark, and then sharpened into a point. He dug a continuous trench everywhere five feet deep. These stakes were sunk into this trench, and fastened firmly at the bottom to prevent the possibility of their being torn up. Only their branches projected from the ground. There were five rows that connected with, and intersected, each other. Whoever entered within them was likely to impale himself on very sharp stakes. The soldiers called these "boundary markers." In front of these, which were arranged in slanting rows in the form of an "x," pits three feet deep were dug, which gradually sloped toward the bottom. In these pits, tapered stakes the thickness of a man's thigh, which were sharpened at the top and hardened in fire, were planted in such a manner as to project from the ground not more than four inches. At the same time, for the purpose of giving them strength and stability, they were each filled with trampled clay to the height of one foot from the bottom. The rest of the pit was covered over with branches and twigs to conceal the deceit. Eight rows of this kind were dug, and were three feet distant from each other. The soldiers called this a "lily" from its resemblance to that flower. Stakes a foot long with iron hooks attached to them were entirely sunk in the ground in front of these, and were planted in every place at small intervals. The soldiers called these "spurs."

CHAPTER 74: CAESAR DESCRIBES HIS OUTER RING OF FORTIFICATIONS THAT PROTECT HIM AGAINST EXTERNAL ATTACK

After completing this inner ring of siege works, Caesar selected as level ground as he could (considering the nature of the country), and enclosed an area of fourteen miles. He constructed against an external enemy an outer ring of fortifications of the same kind in every respect, and separated from the inner ring, so that the guards of the fortifications could not be surrounded, even if attacked by immense numbers (if such a circumstance were to take place, owing to the departure of the enemy's cavalry). Finally, in order that the Roman soldiers would not be compelled to go out of the camp at great risk, Caesar ordered all his men to collect and have on hand forage and grain for thirty days.

Napoléon III, emperor of France from 1852–1870, sponsored archaeological excavations tracing France's roots as he believed the French combined the best of the Gallic and the Roman spirits. On Le Mont Axois near Alise-Saint-Reine, long associated with the ancient Alesia, in 1865 Napoléon III erected this larger-than-life tribute to the Gallic leader, Vercingetorix. As ancient coins show a clean-shaven Vercingetorix, it is believed the statue's flourishing mustache echoes Napoléon's own.

CHAPTER 75: THE GAULS ASSEMBLE TO DISCUSS NEXT STEPS

While those things were happening at Alesia, the Gauls convened a council of their chief nobility, and decided that not everyone who could bear arms should be called out (which was the opinion of Vercingetorix), but instead that a fixed number should be levied from each state. They were afraid that, if so great a multitude assembled together, they would neither be able to govern nor keep their men organized nor have the means of supplying them with grain. They demanded thirty-five thousand men from the Aedui and their dependents, the Segusiavi, Ambivareti, and Aulerci Brannovices. An equal number from the Arverni in conjunction with the Eleuteti, Cadurci, Gabali, and Vellavii, who were accustomed to be under the command of the Arverni. Twelve thousand each from the Senones, Sequani, Bituriges, Santoni, Ruteni, and Carnutes. Ten thousand from the Bellovaci, and the same number from the Lemovices. Eight thousand each from the Pictones, Turoni, Parisii, and Helvetii. Five thousand each from the Suessiones, Ambiani, Mediomatrici, Petrocorii, Nervii, Morini, and Nitiobriges. The same number from the Aulerci Cenomani. Four thousand from the Atrebates. Three thousand each from the Veliocasses, Lexovii, and Aulerci Eburovices. Thirty thousand from the Rauraci and Boii. Six thousand altogether from the states that border on the Atlantic, and which in their dialect are called Armoricae (in which number are included the Curiosolites, Redones, Ambibarii, Caletes, Osismi, Lemovices, Veneti, and Venelli). Of these, the Bellovaci did not contribute their number, as they said that they would wage war against the Romans on their own and at their own discretion, and would obey the command of no man. However, at the request of Commius, they sent two thousand men in consideration of a tie of hospitality that existed between themselves and Commius.

CHAPTER 76: MORE GALLIC DEFECTION (DESPITE CAESAR'S FAVORS!)

Caesar had (as we have previously narrated) availed himself of the faithful and valuable services of this same Commius in Britain in former years, and in consideration of his merits Caesar had exempted Commius's state from taxes, and had conferred on Commius himself the country of the Morini. Yet such was the unanimity of the Gauls in asserting their freedom, and recovering their ancient renown in war, that they were influenced neither by favors nor by the recollection of private friendship, and all of them earnestly directed their energies and resources to the war. They collected eight thousand cavalry and about two hundred and forty thousand infantry. These men were mustered in the country of the Aedui, and a calculation was made of their numbers. Commanders were appointed. The supreme command was entrusted to Commius the Atrebatian, to Viridomarus and Eporedorix the Aeduans, and to Vercassivellaunus the Arvernian, the cousin of Vercingetorix. Each of them was assigned advisors, who were selected from each state, to guide them in the conduct of the war. All marched to Alesia, enthusiastic and full of confidence. Not a single one of them imagined that the Romans could withstand the sight of such an immense host, especially in a battle that would be carried on both in the front and rear, inasmuch as, on the inside, the besieged would make a sortie from the town, and attack the enemy, while, on the outside, the Romans would face great forces of cavalry and infantry.

CHAPTER 77: STARVATION IN ALESIA; THE GAULS CONSIDER CANNIBALISM

But those who were blockaded at Alesia were ignorant of what was going on among the Aedui. The day was past, on which they had expected reinforcements from their countrymen, and all their grain was consumed. They convened an assembly to deliberate on the crisis they faced. Various opinions were expressed among them. Some proposed a surrender; others a sortie, while their strength could support it. The speech of Critognatus, however, should not be omitted on account of its singular and detestable cruelty. Critognatus, who was born from the noblest family among the Arverni, and possessed great influence, said, "I shall pay no attention to the opinion of those who advocate a most disgraceful slavery with their call for surrender. I do not think that they ought to be considered citizens or invited to our council. My business is with those who approve of a sortie. In their advice, as you all agree, the memory of our ancient prowess seems to linger. To be unable to endure deprivation for a short time, however, is disgraceful cowardice, not true valor. Those who voluntarily offer to sacrifice themselves to death can be found more easily than those who are able calmly to endure pain. I would even approve of their opinion (for honor is a powerful motive with me), if I foresaw no other loss except that of our lives. But let us, in adopting our plan, consider all Gaul, which we have summoned to our aid. What courage do you think would our relatives and friends have, if eighty thousand men were butchered in one spot, and they would then be forced to engage in battle almost over our corpses? Do not utterly deprive them of your aid, for they have spurned all thoughts of personal danger for the sake of your safety. Do not, by your folly, rashness, and cowardice, crush all Gaul, and doom it to an eternal slavery! Do you doubt their loyalty and commitment because they have not come by the appointed day? What then? Do you suppose that the Romans work every day on their outer fortifications for mere amusement? If they cannot assure you by their messages, since every possible route is blockaded, take the Romans as evidence that the approach of our reinforcements is drawing near, inasmuch as the Romans, intimidated by their fear of this, labor night and day at their siege works. What, therefore, is my plan? To do as our ancestors did in the war against the Cimbri and Teutones, which was by no means equally momentous. When they were driven into their towns, and oppressed by similar deprivations, they sustained their lives by the corpses of those who appeared useless for war on account of their age. And they did not surrender to the enemy! Even if we had no precedent for such cruel conduct, still I would consider it most glorious that we established it, and delivered it to posterity. For in what way was that war like this war? The Cimbri, after laying Gaul to waste, and inflicting great calamities, at length departed from our country, and sought other lands. They left us our rights, laws, lands, and liberty. But what other motive or wish do the Romans have than, induced by envy, to settle on the lands and in the states of those who, as they have learned, are by reputation noble and powerful in war, and impose on them perpetual slavery? For they have never waged wars on any other terms. But, if you do not know about these things that take place in distant countries, look to the Gaul that neighbors us. That Gaul has been reduced to the form of a province, stripped of its rights and laws, and subjected to Roman despotism. It is oppressed by perpetual slavery!"

CHAPTER 78: THE MANDUBII ARE EXPELLED FROM ALESIA WITH THEIR WIVES AND CHILDREN

After various opinions were expressed, they decreed that those who, owing to age or ill health, were unserviceable for war, should depart from the town, and that they should themselves try every expedient before they had recourse to the advice of Critognatus. They would, however, rather adopt Critognatus's plan, if circumstances compelled them and their allies delayed, than accept any terms of a surrender or peace. The Mandubii, who had admitted them into their town, were compelled to go forth with their wives and children. When these townspeople came to the Roman fortifications, weeping, they begged of the soldiers by every entreaty to receive them as slaves and relieve them with food. But Caesar, placing guards on the rampart, forbade them to be admitted.

CHAPTER 79: GALLIC ALLIES ARRIVE TO RELIEVE ALESIA

In the meantime, Commius and the rest of the leaders, to whom the supreme command had been entrusted, came with all their forces to Alesia, and, having occupied the entire hill, encamped not more than a mile from our fortifications. The following day, they led out their cavalry from the camp, filled the whole plain, which (as we have related) extended three miles in length, and drew out their infantry a little from that place, and posted them on the higher ground. The town of Alesia commanded a view of the whole plain. The besieged ran together, when they saw these reinforcements. Mutual congratulations ensued, and the minds of all were elated with joy. They therefore led out their troops, encamped outside the town, and covered the nearest trench with hurdles, and filled it in with dirt, and made ready for an assault and every eventuality.

CHAPTER 80: CAESAR FIGHTS ON TWO FRONTS

Caesar stationed his army on both sides of the fortifications, in order that, if the occasion arose, each would hold and know his own post. He ordered the cavalry to issue forth from the camp, and begin battle. There was a commanding view from the entire camp, which occupied a ridge of hills, and the minds of all the soldiers anxiously awaited the issue of the battle. The Gauls had scattered archers and light-armed infantry here and there among their cavalry to give relief to their retreating troops, and to resist the impact of our cavalry. Several of our soldiers were unexpectedly wounded by these troops, and left the battle. When the Gauls were confident that their countrymen were winning the battle, and they beheld our men hard-pressed by their large numbers of men, both the Gauls who were hemmed in by the line of circumvallation and the Gauls who had arrived to reinforce them, increased the enthusiasm of their troops with shouts and yells from every quarter. As the battle was carried on in sight of all, neither a brave nor cowardly act could be concealed. Both the desire of praise and the fear of disgrace urged on each side to valor. The fighting lasted from noon almost to sunset, but still victory inclined in favor of neither side. Then the Germans, on one side, made a charge against the enemy in a compact body, and drove them back, and, when their cavalry were put to flight, their archers were surrounded and cut to pieces. In other parts, likewise, our men pursued to their camp the retreating enemy, and did not give them an opportunity of rallying. Those who had come forth from Alesia returned into the town dejected and almost despairing of success.

CHAPTER 81: THE GAULS MAKE AN ASSAULT ON CAESAR'S FORTIFICATIONS

The Gauls, after the interval of a day and after making, during that time, an immense number of hurdles, scaling-ladders, and iron hooks, silently went forth from their camp at midnight, and approached our fortifications in the plain. They suddenly raised a shout to let those who were besieged in the town know of their arrival. They then began to cast down hurdles and dislodge our men from the rampart by slings, arrows, and stones, and executed the other movements which are required for storming fortifications. At the same time, Vercingetorix, having heard the shout, gave the signal to his troops with a trumpet, and led them forth from the town. Our troops, as each man's post had been assigned to him some days before, manned the fortifications. They intimidated the Gauls with slings, large stones, stakes that they had placed along the siege works, and ammunition for the slings. Darkness made it impossible to see anything. Many were wounded on both sides. Several missiles were shot from the artillery. But Marcus Antonius and Gaius Trebonius, the lieutenants to whom the defense of these parts had been allotted, summoned troops from the more remote forts, and sent them to aid our troops wherever they had observed that our troops were hard pressed.

CHAPTER 82: THE GAULS ARE FRUSTRATED IN THEIR ATTEMPTS

While the Gauls were at a distance from the fortification, they had a greater advantage, owing to the immense number of their weapons. After they came nearer, they were caught unawares in the "spurs" or slipped into the pits, and were impaled, or were pierced by the javelins hurled from the ramparts and towers, and thus perished. They received many wounds on all sides, and failed to force their way through any part of the siege works. And, when day was about to dawn, they were afraid that they would soon be surrounded by a sally made from the higher camp on their exposed flank, so they retreated to their comrades. The Gauls on the side of the inner ring, on the other hand, brought forward all the things that had been prepared by Vercingetorix for their assault. They filled up the nearest trenches, but these movements took a long time to execute, which slowed them down. They learned of the retreat of their countrymen before they could draw close to the fortifications, and therefore returned to the town without accomplishing their object.

CHAPTER 83: VERCASSIVALLAUNUS LEADS ELITE TROOPS AGAINST CAESAR'S FORTIFICATIONS

The Gauls, who had been twice repulsed with great loss, deliberated about what they should do. They made use of information from those who were well acquainted with the country. From them they learned the position and fortifications of the upper camp. There was, on the north side, a hill, which our men could not include in their works, on account of the extent of its circumference, and they were compelled to establish their camp on ground almost disadvantageous and pretty steep. Gaius Antistius Reginus and Gaius Caninius Rebilus, two of the lieutenants, with two legions, were in possession of this camp. The leaders of the enemy reconnoitered the country with their scouts, and selected from their entire army sixty thousand men who belonged to those states with the greatest reputation for character and for courage. They privately arranged among themselves what they wished to be done and in what manner. They decided that the attack should take place at about noon. They appointed over their forces Vercassivallaunus, the Arvernian, one of the four generals and a near relative of Vercingetorix. He issued from the camp at the first watch [well before midnight], almost completed his march a little before the dawn, hid himself behind the mountain, and ordered his soldiers to refresh themselves after their labor during the night. When noon now seemed to draw close, he marched hastily against the camp (that we mentioned earlier). At the same time, the cavalry began to approach the fortifications in the plain, and the rest of the forces began to make a demonstration in front of the camp.

CHAPTER 84: VERCINGETORIX LEADS TROOPS FROM ALESIA AGAINST CAESAR'S FORTIFICATIONS

Vercingetorix beheld his countrymen from the citadel of Alesia, and issued forth from the town. He brought out from the camp long hooks, movable sheds, grappling hooks, and other things that he had prepared for the purpose of making an assault. They engaged on all sides at once and every expedient was adopted. They flocked to whatever part of the siege works seemed weakest. The Roman army was distributed along their extensive lines, and with difficulty met the enemy in every quarter. The shouts that were raised by the combatants in their rear had a great tendency to intimidate our men, because they perceived that their safety from that threat rested on the valor of others: for distant dangers generally disturb men's minds more severely than those they can confront directly.

CHAPTER 85: THE GAULS MAKE THEIR ASSAULT AND THE ROMANS THEIR DEFENSE

Caesar, having selected a commanding spot, could see distinctly whatever was going on in each quarter, and sent assistance to his troops where they were hard pressed. The idea uppermost in the minds of both sides was that the present was the time when they would have the best opportunity for a decisive contest. The Gauls despaired of all safety, unless they could succeed in breaking through the Roman lines. The Romans expected an end to all their labors, if they could win the day. The principal struggle was along the upper lines where (as we have said) Vercassivallaunus had been sent. The least elevation of ground, when added to a slope, provides huge momentum. Some were casting missiles. Others were forming a "tortoise" [interlocking their shields above their heads], and advanced to the attack. Fresh men by turns relieved the wearied. The earth, heaped up by all against the fortifications, gave the means of ascent to the Gauls, and covered those works which the Romans had concealed in the ground. Our men no longer had weapons or strength.

CHAPTER 86: CAESAR DIRECTS THE DEFENSE

Caesar, when he observed these movements, sent Labienus with six cohorts to relieve his distressed soldiers. He ordered Labienus, if he found he could not hold the place, to draw off the cohorts, and fight his way back, but not to do this except if it became absolutely necessary. He himself went to the other troops, and exhorted them not to succumb to the strain of the hard labor, telling them that all the profits from all their previous battles depended on that day and hour. The Gauls on the interior side, despairing of breaking through the fortifications in the plains on account of the size of the siege works, attempted to scale the higher parts. They brought in the devices that they had prepared. With the immense number of their missiles, they dislodged the defenders from the turrets. They filled the ditches with clay and hurdles, and then cleared the way. They tore down the rampart and parapet with hooks.

CHAPTER 87: CAESAR CONTINUES TO DIRECT THE DEFENSE, AND HASTENS TO JOIN THE BATTLE PERSONALLY

Caesar sent at first young Brutus with six cohorts, and afterward Gaius Fabius, his lieutenant, with seven more. Finally, as the enemy fought more obstinately, he led up fresh men to the assistance of his soldiers. After renewing the battle, and repulsing the enemy, he marched in the direction where he had sent Labienus, drafted four cohorts from the nearest fort, and ordered part of the cavalry to follow him, and another part to go around the external fortifications and attack the enemy in the rear. Labienus, when neither the ramparts nor ditches could stop the onset of the enemy, informed Caesar by messengers of what he intended to do. Caesar hastened to share in the action.

CHAPTER 88: CAESAR APPEARS IN BATTLE, AND THE GAULS ARE DEFEATED

Caesar's arrival was known from the scarlet color of his robe. The troops of cavalry and the cohorts whom he had ordered to follow him were spotted too, as the low and sloping grounds were plainly visible from the heights. The enemy then joined battle. A shout was raised by both sides, which was succeeded by a general shout along the ramparts and along the whole line of fortifications. Our troops, laying aside their javelins, continued the battle with their swords. Then the cavalry suddenly appeared in the rear of the Gauls. The other cohorts advanced rapidly. The enemy turned their backs. The cavalry intercepted them in their flight, and a great slaughter ensued. Sedulius, the general and chief of the Lemovices, was slain. Vercassivellaunus the Arvernian was captured alive in the flight. Seventy-four military standards were brought to Caesar, and only a few out of so great a number returned safe to their camp. The besieged, beholding from the town the slaughter and flight of their countrymen, despaired of safety, and led back their troops from the fortifications. A flight of the Gauls from their camp immediately ensued after they learned of this disaster, and, if our soldiers had not been worn out from sending frequent reinforcements and the efforts of the entire day, all the enemy's forces could have been destroyed. Immediately after midnight, the cavalry were sent out, and caught up with the rearguard. A great number were captured or cut to pieces. The rest by flight escaped in different directions to their respective states.

Lionel Royer provides a vivid interpretation of Vercingetorix's surrender in this painting of
1899. The Gallic chieftain lays down his arms at the feet of the seated Caesar. Having finally lost
the city of Alesia after a relief force of Gauls, numbering 250,000, could not break through the
Roman lines and left, Vercingetorix surrendered. The Roman siege works and a set of standards
can be seen in the background.

CHAPTER 89: THE GAULS SURRENDER VERCINGETORIX TO CAESAR, AND EACH SOLDIER RECEIVES A CAPTURED GAUL AS PLUNDER

Vercingetorix convened a council the following day, and declared that he
had undertaken that war not for the sake of his own interests and needs,
but for the sake of freedom for all, and, since he had to yield to fortune,
he offered himself to them for whatever course of action they preferred:
whether by his death they wished to atone for their crime against the Romans or to surrender him alive. Ambassadors were sent to Caesar on this
subject. He ordered them to surrender their weapons and to deliver up
their leaders. He seated himself at the siege works in front of the camp. The
Gallic leaders were brought before him. They surrendered Vercingetorix,
and laid down their arms. Caesar kept back the Aedui and Arverni, in the
hopes that he could win over, through their influence, their respective
states, but he distributed the remaining captives one apiece to each of the
soldiers throughout the entire army as plunder.

CHAPTER 90: CAESAR SENDS THE TROOPS TO WINTER QUARTERS AND THE SENATE GIVES THANKS TO THE IMMORTAL GODS

After he made these arrangements, Caesar marched into the country of the Aedui, and recovered that state. To this place ambassadors were sent by the Arverni, who promised that they would obey his commands. He demanded a great number of hostages. He sent the legions to winter-quarters. He restored about twenty thousand captives to the Aedui and Arverni. He ordered Titus Labienus to march into the country of the Sequani with two legions and the cavalry, and he attached Marcus Sempronius Rutilus to him. He placed Gaius Fabius and Lucius Minucius Basilus, with two legions, in the country of the Remi to protect them from suffering any violence at the hands of the neighboring Bellovaci. He sent Gaius Antistius Reginus into the country of the Ambivareti, Titus Sextius into the territories of the Bituriges, and Gaius Caninius Rebilus into those of the Ruteni, with one legion each. He stationed Quintus Tullius Cicero and Publius Sulpicius among the Aedui at Cabillonum and Matisco on the Saone (Arar) river to procure supplies of grain. Caesar himself decided to spend the winter at Bibracte. After learning of these successes from Caesar's dispatches, the Senate decreed twenty days of public prayer and thanksgiving to the immortal gods.

BOOK 8 [51–50 BCE]

The surrender of Alesia represents the dramatic turning point of the war, but Caesar's work of conquest was not entirely done. Book Eight describes the military operations that continue in 51 and 50 BCE to suppress the revolt once and for all. This book was not written by Caesar, however, but instead by one of his lieutenants, Aulus Hirtius.

Appendix: Figures of Speech

This table is a lightly revised version of the one found in Kelsey 1918, pp. 582–584. The section numbers indicate the place of this table in the complete grammatical and syntactical appendix, which may be found online. Indications for pronunciation are only approximate. Many vowels marked short should simply be pronounced as a schwa, i.e., as an unstressed vowel.

301. Caesar uses the following Grammatical Figures:

a. *Asyndeton* (ă-sĭn'-dĕ-tŏn), the omission of a conjunction where a connective might have been used; the effect is terse and clipped (*compare polysyndeton*); as in, **loca, portūs, aditūs cognōvisset**, *should have become acquainted with the natural features, the harbors (and) the approaches* (BG 4.20); **Lūciō Pisōne, Aulō Gabīniō cōnsulibus**, *in the consulship of Lucius Piso (and) Aulus Gabinius* (BG 1.6).

b. *Brachylogy* (bră-kĭl'-ŏ-gē), a condensed form of expression; as in, **cōnsimilis caprīs figūra**, *shape like (that of) goats*, that is, **figūra cōnsimilia figūrae** (dat.) **caprārum** (BG 6.27).

c. *Ellipsis* (ĕ-lĭp'-sĭs), the omission of words essential to the meaning; as in, **Duae fīliae**, for **Duae fīliae fuērunt**, *There were two daughters* (BG 1.53).

d. *Hendiadys* (hĕn-dī'-ă-dĭs), the use of two nouns with a connective where a noun with a modifying genitive or adjective might have been expected; as in, **fīdem et iūs iūrandum**, *a pledge of good faith bound by an oath*, lit., *good faith and an oath* (BG 1.3).

e. *Parenthesis* (pă-rĕn'-thĕ-sĭs), the insertion of an independent sentence or phrase that interrupts the construction with a separate thought, often one that helps explain the main construction; as in, **quam maximum**

potest mīlitum numerum imperat (erat . . . legiō ūna), **pontem . . . iubet** (historical present) **rescindī,** *he levied as many soldiers as possible (there was only one legion, altogether, in further Gaul), and gave orders that the bridge be cut down (BG 1.7).*

f. *Polysyndeton* (pŏl-ĭ-sĭn′-dĕ-tŏn), the use of more conjunctions than the sense requires; the effect tends to emphasize whatever is joined in this way (compare *asyndeton*); as in, **Ceutronōs et Graiocēlī et Caturīgēs,** *the Ceutrones, the Graioceli, and the Caturiges (BG 1.10).*

g. *Prolepsis* (prō-lĕp′-sĭs), or *Anticipation,* the use of a noun as object in a clause preceding the one in which it naturally belongs as subject; as in, **rem frūmentāriam, ut supportārī posset, timēre,** *that they feared that the supply of grain could not be brought in,* lit., *they feared the supply of grain, that it . . . (BG 1.39).*

h. *Synesis* (sĭn′-ĕ-sĭs), construction according to the sense without regard to the grammatical form; as in, **cīvitātī persuāsit, ut . . . exīrent,** *he persuaded the (people of his) state to go out,* lit., *he persuaded his **state** that **they** should go out (BG 1.2).* (I.e., *cīvitās* is singular, so, from a grammatical perspective, *exīrent* should have been singular as well.)

302. Caesar uses the following Rhetorical Figures:

a. *Anaphora* (ă-năf′-ŏ-ră), the repetition of the same word at the beginning of successive phrases or clauses; as in, **nōn aetāte cōnfectīs, nōn mulieribus, nōn īnfantibus pepercērunt,** *they spared not the aged, not the women, not the children (BG 7.28).*

b. *Antithesis* (ăn-tĭth′-ĕ-sĭs), the juxtaposition of contrasted expressions in like order; as in, **Non sēsē Gallia, sed Gallīs sibi, bellum intulisse,** *He did not make war on the Gauls, but the Gauls on him (BG 1.44).*

c. *Chiasmus* (kī-ăs′-mŭs), an arrangement of contrasted words in inverse order (follows a pattern of ABBA) or inverted parallellism; as in, for example, **fāma nōbilēs potentēsque bellō,** *in reputation notable, and powerful in war (BG 7.77).*

d. *Climax* (klī′-măx), an arrangement of words, phrases, or clauses with gradual increase of interest or vigor of expression to the end; as in, **cōnferre, comportārī, adesse,** *that it was being collected, was on the way, was at hand (BG 1.16).*

e. *Euphemism* (yū´-fĕ-mĭzm), the use of a mild expression in order to avoid a word of bad omen or occurrence; as in, **sī quid accidat Rōmānīs,** *if anything should happen to the Romans,* meaning *if any disaster should befall the Romans* (*BG* 1.18).

f. *Hyperbaton* (hī-pĕr´-bă-tŏn), the arrangement of words in unusual order, as the separation of words that belong together, such as the insertion of one or more words between the parts of an ablative absolute; thus, **simulātā Caesarem amīcitiā,** *that Caesar under the pretense of friendship,* the usual order would be **Caesarem, simulātā amīcitiā** (*BG* 1.44).

g. *Litotes* (līt´-ŏ-tēz *or* lī-tō´-tēz), the affirmation of an idea through the negation of its opposite; as in, **neque tam imperītum esse rērum ut nōn scīret,** *and he was not so unversed in affairs as not to know,* meaning *that he was so worldly wise that he very well knew* (*BG* 1.44).

h. *Personification* (pĕr-sŏn´-ĭ-fĭ-kā´-shŭn), the representation of something inanimate or abstract as endowed with life and action; as in **Cōnspicātae nāvēs trirēmēs duae nāvem D. Brūtī,** *Two triremes, having caught sight of the ship of Decimus Brutus* (*BC* 2.6).

— Complete Latin to English Glossary —

I n this vocabulary, the numbers 1, 2, and 4 indicate for regular verbs the conjugation to which the verb belongs, and that their principal parts are formed according to the patterns of the model verbs **laudō**, **moneō**, and **audiō**, respectively; or, if the verb is deponent, according to the patterns of **hortor**, **vereor**, and **partior** (see App. §73).

Words in *italics* are explanatory and are not part of the definition. Words in square brackets are the root(s) from which a word is derived or another closely related word.

The symbol • follows the last letter of the base or stem of the word. To this base, subsequent syllables are added, e.g., **abic•iō, -ere = abiciō, abicere** or **āc•er, -ris, -re = ācer, ācris, ācre.** (NB: In Caesar's day, nouns that ended in **-ius** and **-ium** regularly had a genitive **-ī**, rather than **-iī**, e.g., **auxil•ium, -ī.** For details, see App. §16, c.)

A dagger † follows the entry for those words that appear both on the high frequency vocabulary list and in *italics* in the Latin text.

This glossary is based closely on the vocabulary in the edition of A. T. Walker (see the Acknowledgments at the beginning of this volume for details).

A.

ā (*before consonants*), **ab** (*before vowels and some consonants*), **abs** (*before* **tē,** *and in some compounds*), *prep. with abl., originally denoting separation;* (1) *of place, persons, time, etc.,* from, away from, from the vicinity of; (2) *denoting position, in some phrases,* at, in, on, on the side of; **ā tergō,** in the rear; (3) *with expressions of measure,* away, off;

ab mīlibus passuum duōbus, two miles away; (4) *with the pass. voice often expressing agent (the person by whom the action is performed),* by; (5) *variously translated in other expressions,* from, by, in respect to, after. †

a. = **ante** *adv.,* (1) before, above, previously; (2) *prep. with acc.,* before, in front of, in advance of.

A., *abbr. for* **Aulus,** *a Roman praenomen.*

abic•iō, -ere, abiēcī, abiectum
[**iaciō,** throw. App. §7], throw
away *or* down; hurl.

abs, *see* **ā.**

absum, abesse, āfuī, — [**sum,** be.
App. §78], be away, be absent *or*
distant, be lacking *or* free from.

ac, *see* **atque.** †

ac•cēdō, -cēdere, -cessī, -cessum
[**ad + cēdō,** go], approach, come
near to, arrive at, come to; to be
added.

ac•cidō, -cidere, -cidī, — [**ad +
cadō,** fall], fall to *or* upon; befall;
happen, fall to the lot of, occur. †

ac•cipiō, -cipere, -cēpī, -ceptum
[**ad + capiō,** take], take *or*
receive to oneself, accept;
experience, suffer; learn, hear,
take. †

āc•er, -ris, -re, *adj.,* sharp [App.
§36].

aci•ēs, -ēī (*old gen.* **aciē**), *f.,* sharp
point *or* edge *of a weapon;* sharp
or keen sight, glance; a line (*as
forming an edge*), battle line;
prīma, the vanguard; **media,**
the center; **novissima,** the rear
(guard).

ad, *prep. with acc., originally
expressing motion toward:* (1)
expressing motion, toward,
against, to the vicinity of; (2)
expressing position, at, by, near;
(3) *expressing purpose, with the
gerund and gerundive,* to, for (the
purpose of); (4) *with numbers,*
up to, about; (5) *of time,* up
to, until; at, on; (6) *variously
translated in other relations,* at,
after, for, to, according to, in the
eyes of, among. †

adāctus, *see* **adigō.**

ad•dō, -dere, -didī, -ditum [**dō,**
put], place on, add.

**ad•dūcō, -dūcere, -dūxī,
-ductum** [**dūcō,** lead], lead
to, draw to, bring to; induce,
influence.

adeō, *adv.,* to such an extent, so
much, so very, so; in fact.

ad•eō, -īre, -iī, -itum [**eō,** go.
App. §84], go to, approach, visit,
assail, attack.

ad•ficiō, -ficere, -fēcī, -fectum
[**ad + faciō,** do], affect, inspire;
magnō dolōre afficere, to
annoy greatly.

ad•flictō, 1 [*freq.* of **afflīgō**],
strike repeatedly, harass;
oppress, vex

**ad•haereō, -haerēre, -haesī,
-haesum** [**haereō,** stick], cling
to, stick to.

adhib•eō, -ēre, -uī, -itum
[**habeō,** have], bring to, bring in,
summon; employ, use.

adhortor, 1 [**hortor,** encourage],
encourage, incite.

ad•igō, -igere, -ēgī, -āctum [**ad
+ agō,** move], drive *or* bring by
force, move; thrust, plunge, hurl
(*of weapons*); bind (*by an oath*).

ad•ipīscor, -ipīscī, -eptus sum,
attain to, gain.

adit•us, -ūs, *m.* [**adeō,** go to],
approach, means of approach,
right to approach, access.

ad·iungō, -iungere, -iūnxī, -iūnctum [**iungō,** join], attach, join to, unite, add.

adiūt·or, -ōris, *m.* [**adiuvō,** aid], helper, assistant, abettor.

adminis·ter, -trī, *m.* [**minister,** servant], attendant, priest.

administrō, 1 [**minister,** servant], serve, attend, wait upon; manage, guide.

ad·mittō, -mittere, -mīsī, -missum [**mittō,** send], admit; commit; incur; let go; give reins (*to a horse*).

admodum, *adv.* [**modus,** measure], *literally: up to the measure;* very much, very; *with numbers,* fully; *with negative,* at all.

ad·olēscō, -olēre, -olēvī, -ultum, grow up.

ad·orior, -orīrī, -ortus sum [**orior,** arise], rise against, assail, attack.

ad·scīscō, -scīscere, -scīvī, -scītum [**ad + scīscō,** approve], approve, admit *or* receive (*as allies*).

adsum, adesse, adfuī [**sum,** be, App. §77], be near, be present, be at hand, appear.

Aduātic·ī, -ōrum, *m., a people in Belgic Gaul,* the Aduatici.

advent·us, -ūs, *m.* [**veniō,** come], arrival, approach, coming. †

adversus, *prep. with acc.* [**adversus,** turned against], opposite to, against.

advers·us, -a, -um, *adv.* [perf. part. of **advertō,** turn to], turned to, turned against; opposite, fronting; adverse, unfavorable; unsuccessful; **adversō flūmine,** up the river; **in adversum ōs,** full in the face.

advolō, 1 [**volō,** fly], fly to *or* against, rush on *or* at.

aedifi·cium, -cī, *n.* [**aedificiō,** build], building, house.

Aedu·us, -a, -um, *adj.,* of the Aedui; *as a noun:* an Aeduan; *pl. as a noun:* the Aedui *or Aeduans, one of the most powerful Gallic tribes.*

ae·ger, -gra, -grum, *adj.,* sick, ill.

aes, aeris, *n.,* copper; *anything made of copper,* coin, money; **aes aliēnum,** *someone else's money:* debt.

aes·tās, -ātis, *f.,* summer.

aestimāti·ō, -ōnis, *f.* [**aestimō,** value], valuation, appraisal.

aest·us, -ūs, *m.,* heat, boiling, surging, tide; **minuente aestū,** at ebb tide.

af·ficiō, -ficere, -fēcī, -fectum [**ad + faciō,** do], do to, treat, affect; **magnō dolōre afficere,** to annoy greatly.

ag·er, -rī, *m.,* field, land; district, territory. †

aggregō, 1 [**ad + grex,** flock] *unite in a flock;* assemble; join, attach.

agm·en, -inis, *n.* [**agō,** move], *a moving body;* a marching column; army; **in agmine,** on the march; **prīmum agmen,**

the vanguard (*those in front*); **novissimum** *or* **extrēmum agmen,** the rear (guard) (*those in back*).

ag•ō, -ere, ēgī, actum, set in motion, drive (*animals*); move forward, advance (*military works*); do, transact, carry on (*business*); discuss, speak; hold (**conventum,** a meeting); give, render (**grātiās,** thanks); plead (**causam,** a case); **quod agitur,** the matter in hand; **rēs agitur,** something is at stake.

ala•cer, -cris, -cre, *adj.*, lively, eager, active, ready, joyous, "fired up."

alacri•tās, -ātis, *f.* [**alacer,** lively], enthusiasm, eagerness.

Alesi•a, -ae, *f.*, Alesia; *main city of the Mandubii; now called* Alise-Sainte-Reine.

aliās, *adv.* [**alius,** another], at another place, elsewhere; at another time; **aliās . . . aliās,** at one time . . . at another.

aliēn•us, -a, -um, *adj.* [**alius,** other], of *or* belonging to another, another's; strange, alien, unfamiliar; unfavorable; foreign to the purpose; **aes aliēnum,** debt; **aliēnissimī,** complete strangers.

aliō, *adv.* [**alius,** other], to another place, person, *or* thing; elsewhere.

ali•quis, -quid *and* **ali•quī, -qua, -quod,** *indef. pron.* [**quis,** who. App. §62, *a*], someone, something; anyone, anything, any. †

aliter, *adv.* [**alius,** other], otherwise; **aliter . . . ac,** otherwise . . . than.

ali•us, -a, -ud, *gen.* **alīus** (App. §32) another, other; **alius . . . alius . . . ,** one . . . another . . . ; *in pl.,* some . . . others . . . †

Allobrog•ēs, -um, *m.*, the Allobroges, a Gallic people in the Roman Province.

Alp•ēs, -ium, *f.*, Alps; *the mountains that separate northern Italy from Germany and Transalpine Gaul.*

alt•er, -era, -erum (App. §32), the other (*of two*); second; the one; **alter . . . alter,** the one . . . the other; **alterī . . . alterī,** the one party . . . the other. †

altitūd•ō, -inis, *f.* [**altus,** high, deep], height, depth; thickness (*of timber*).

alt•us, -a, -um, *adj.*, high, deep; *n. as noun:* the deep, the sea.

ambact•us, -ī, *m.*, vassal.

Ambarr•ī, -ōrum, *m.*, Ambarri; *a tribe living to the east of the Arar river.*

Ambior•īx, -īgis, *m.*, Ambiorix, *king of the Eburones.* †

amb•ō, -ae, -a, *adj.*, both.

āment•um, -ī, *n.*, strap *or* thong, *fastened to the shaft of a javelin to aid its propulsion.*

amīciti•a, -ae, *f.* [**amīcus,** friend], friendship.

amīc•us, -a, -um, *adj.* [**amō,** love], friendly, well-disposed; devoted.

amīc•us, -ī, *m.* [amō, love], friend, ally.

ā•mittō, -mittere, -mīsī, -missum [mittō, send], send away, dismiss; let go; lose.

amplē, *adv.* [amplus, large], largely; *comp.,* amplius, more, farther.

ampl•us, -a, um, *adj.,* of large extent, spacious, large; illustrious, splendid, noble; generous, magnificent; amplius, *comparative as noun,* more, a greater number, a greater distance.

an, *conj., used to introduce the second element of alternative questions,* or, or rather.

ancor•a, -ae, *f.,* anchor; in ancorīs, at anchor.

angustē, *adv.* [angustus, narrow], narrowly; in close quarters.

angusti•ae, -ārum, *f. pl.* [angustus, narrow], narrowness; a narrow place *or* pass, strait, defile; straits, difficulties, perplexities.

angust•us, -a, -um, *adj.* [angō, squeeze], compressed, confined, narrow; in angustō, in a critical condition.

anim•a, -ae, *f.,* breath, life, soul.

animad•vertō, -vertere, -vertī, -versum [animus, mind + ad + vertō, turn], turn the mind to; notice; animadvertere in, punish.

anim•al, -ālis, *n.* [anima, breath], animal, living (*and* breathing) creature.

anim•us, -ī, *m.,* mind, intellect; feelings; character; spirit, soul; resolution, courage; animī causā, for amusement; in animō habēre, intend.

ann•us, -ī, *m.,* year. †

ante (1) *adv.,* before, above, previously; (2) *prep. with acc.,* before, in front of, in advance of. †

antecurs•or, -ōris, *m.* [currō, run], forerunner; *pl.,* vanguard.

ante•ferō, -ferre, -tulī, -lātum [ferō, carry. App. §81], carry *or* bear before; prefer.

aper•iō, -īre, -uī, -tum, open, expose.

Apoll•ō, -inis, *m., the god* Apollo.

appellō, 1, call, name, call by name, accost.

appropinquō, 1 [ad + propinquus, near], come near, come close, approach.

Apr. = Aprīl•is, -e, *adj.,* of (*the month of*) April.

Aprīl•is, -e, *adj.,* of (*the month of*) April.

apud, *prep. with acc.,* at, among, near, with; (*with persons*) at the house of, in the presence of. †

aqua, -ae, *f.,* water.

aquil•a, -ae, *f.,* an eagle; a military standard (*the* aquila *was the main standard of the legion*).

aquili•fer, -ferī, *m.* [aquila, eagle + ferō, carry], standard-bearer.

Aquītān•ī, -ōrum, *m.,* the Aquitani *or* Aquitanians (*a people located on the Atlantic*

coast above the Pyrenees, the
mountains that separate the
Iberian peninsula from Gaul).
Aquītān•us, -a, -um, *adj.,*
Aquitanian, of Aquitania.
Arar, -is, *m. (acc.:* **-im**), Arar
(*river*); *now called* Saône.
arbitror, 1, decide, think, believe. †
arcess•ō, -ere, -īvī, -ītum,
summon, send for, invite.
ārd•eō, -ēre, ārsī, ārsum, burn,
blaze, be inflamed, be eager.
argill•a, -ae, *f.,* white clay.
ārid•us, -a, um, *adj.* [**areō,** be dry],
dry; *neut. as noun:* dry land.
Ariovist•us, -ī, *m.,* Ariovistus, a
Germanic king.
arm•a, -ōrum, *n. pl.,* arms,
equipment, weapons; *by*
metonymy: battle, war. †
armāment•a, -ōrum, *n. pl.* [**armō,**
arm], implements, gear; tackle *or*
rigging (*of a ship*).
Arpīnē•ius, -ī, *m.,* Gaius Arpineius,
an equestrian in Caesar's army.
arrip•iō, -ere, -uī, arreptum [**ad**
+ **rapiō,** seize], take *or* seize
hurriedly.
ars, artis, *f.,* skill, art; *pl.* the arts.
arti•ficium, -ficī, *n.* [**ars,** art +
faciō, make], a trade, handicraft;
artifice, trick.
a•scendō, -scendere, -scendī,
-scēnsum [**ad** + **scandō,** climb],
climb up, ascend, mount, climb.
a•scīscō, -scīscere, -scīvī,
-scītum [**ad** + scīscō, approve],
approve, admit *or* receive (*as*
allies).

assistō, assistere, astitī, — [**ad** +
sistō, stand], stand by, stand near.
ascēns•us, -ūs, *m.* [**ascendō,**
climb up], ascent, approach,
climbing up.
asp•er, -era, -erum, *adj.,* rough,
violent.
at, *conj.,* but, at least. †
atque, ac (**ac** *only before*
consonants, **atque** *before vowels*
and consonants), *usually adds*
something especially important,
while **et** *usually adds things of*
equal importance; and also, and
even, and; *after words expressing*
a comparison or difference: than,
as, from. †
Atre•bās, -bātis, *m.,* an
Atrebatian; *pl.* the Atrebates.
at•texō, -texere, -texuī, -textum
[**ad** + **texō,** weave], weave on.
atting•ō, -ere, attigī, attactum
[**ad** + **tangō,** touch], touch *or*
border on, reach, extend to,
arrive at, attain.
at•tribuō, -tribuere, -tribuī,
-tribūtum [**ad** + **tribuō,** assign],
assign, allot.
auctor, -is, *m.* [**augeō,** increase],
one who produces, creates, *or*
originates; promoter, instigator,
advisor, author.
auctōri•tās, -tātis, *f.* [**auctor,**
producer], influence, character,
authority, reputation.
audācter, *adv.* [**audāx,** bold],
boldly, fearlessly, daringly.
Comp. **audācius;** *superl.*
audācissimē.

aud•eō, -ēre, ausus sum (App. §74), dare, risk, venture.

audiō, 4, hear, hear of; **dictō audiēns,** obedient.

auge•ō, -ēre, auxī, auctum, increase, augment, enhance, add to.

aurīg•a, -ae, *m.,* charioteer.

Aurunculēi•us, -ī, *m.,* Lucius Aurunculeius Cotta, *one of Caesar's lieutenants.*

aut, *conj., used where the difference is important or exclusive,* or; **aut . . . aut,** either . . . or. †

autem, *conj.,* but (*a weak adversative*); however, on the other hand; now; moreover. †

auxilior, 1 [**auxilium,** help], help, give aid, assist, render assistance.

auxil•ium, -ī, *n.* [**augeō,** increase], help, assistance, aid; *pl.,* auxiliary troops; reinforcements.

āvert•ō, -ere, -ī, āversum [**ab** + **vertō,** turn], turn away from *or* away, turn aside; turn back, repulse; *perf. part. as adj.:* with back turned.

B.

balte•us, -ī, *m.,* sword belt.

Balven•tius, -tī, *m.,* Titus Balventius, *one of Caesar's centurions.*

barbar•us, -a, -um, *adj.,* foreign (*to Romans and Greeks*), uncivilized; *pl. as noun:* barbarians.

Belg•ae, -ārum, *m.,* the Belgians *or* Belgae (*a people located in northern Gaul along the English Channel*). †

Belg•ium, -ī, *n.,* the territory belonging to the Belgae.

bellō, 1, make war, carry on war, wage war.

Bellovac•ī, -ōrum, *m.,* the Bellovaci (*a Belgic people*).

bell•um, -ī, *n.,* war. †

benefi•cium, -cī, *n.* [**bene,** well + **faciō,** do], benefit, favor, kindness, good deed.

benevolenti•a, -ae, *f.* [**bene,** well + **volō,** wish], goodwill, kindness.

Bibract•e, -is, *n.,* Bibracte; *capital of the Aedui.*

bīdu•um, -ī, *n.* [**bis,** twice + **diēs,** day], space *or* period of two days.

bienn•ium, -ī, *n.* [**bis,** twice + **annus,** year], two years.

bipertītō, *adv.* [**bis,** twice + **partior,** divide], in two parts *or* divisions, in two ways.

Bōi•ī, -ōrum, *m.,* the Boii, *a Celtic tribe in southern Germany and Cisalpine Gaul who had once been powerful.*

bon•us, -a, -um, *adj.,* good, beneficial, profitable, well-disposed; (*with* **animō**) friendly; *as noun,* **bon•um, -ī,** *n.,* profit, advantage; **bon•a, -ōrum,** *n. pl.,* goods, property, estate; **bon•ī, -ōrum,** *m. pl.,* the good (people), good men, good citizens. *Comp.:* **melior;** *superl.:* **optimus** (App. §42).

brev•is, -e, *adv.,* short, brief,
   transitory.
Britanni•a, -ae, *f.,* Britannia,
   Britain. †

C.
C., *abbr. for praenomen* **Gāius.**
C., *sign for* **centum,** one hundred.
cad•ō, -ere, cecidī, cāsum, fall;
   fall in battle, be killed, die.
caed•ēs, -is, *f.* [**caedō,** cut],
   slaughter, massacre, murder.
caelest•is, -e, *adj.* [**caelum,** sky],
   what is in the sky, heavenly,
   celestial; *pl. as noun:* the gods
   (*who live in the sky*).
Caes•ar, -aris, *m.,* (1) Gaius Julius
   Caesar, *general in Gaul and author*
   of the Commentaries; (2) Lucius
   Julius Caesar, *Caesar's relative*
   and one of his lieutenants. †
caesp•es, -itis, *m.,* sod, turf.
calami•tās, -tātis, *f.,* disaster,
   misfortune, defeat.
cap•iō, -ere, cēpī, captum, take,
   capture, seize, catch; take in,
   beguile, induce; take up (*arms*);
   choose, select (*a place*); form;
   adopt (*a plan*); reach; arrive at
   (*a place*); make (*a beginning*);
   collem capere, take a position
   on a hill; **fugam capere,** take to
   flight. †
captīv•us, -a, -um, *adj.* [**capiō,**
   take], prisoner, captive.
Carnut•ēs, -um, *m.,* the Carnutes
   (*a people in central Gaul*).
carr•us, -ī, *m.,* cart, wagon.
car•us, -a, -um, *adj.,* dear, precious.

cas•a, -ae, *f.,* hut, barrack.
Cass•ius, -ī, *m.,* Lucius Cassius
   Longinus, *consul in 107 BCE,*
   defeated and slain in battle by the
   Tigurini.
Castic•us, -ī, *m.,* Casticus, *an*
   important man among the
   Sequani.
castr•a, -ōrum, *n. pl.* [**castrum,**
   fortress], camp, fortified camp;
   castra facere *or* **pōnere,** pitch
   camp; **castra movēre,** break
   camp. †
cās•us, -ūs, *m.* [**cadō,** fall],
   what befalls: accident, chance,
   misfortune, fate; crisis; **cāsū,** by
   chance.
Catamantaloed•is, -is, *m.,*
   Catamantaloedis, *a leader among*
   the Sequani before Caesar's day.
catēn•a, -ae, *f.,* chain, fetter.
Catuvolc•us, -ī, *m.,* Catuvolcus,
   a leader among the Eburones who
   eventually poisons himself when
   things go badly for him.
caus•a, -ae, *f.,* cause, reason,
   grounds, motive; situation,
   condition; a (*legal*) case, cause;
   causam dīcere, to plead a case;
   causā, *following a gen.,* for the
   sake of, for the purpose of, for. †
cēd•ō, -ere, cessī, cessum, go, go
   away; give way, yield, retreat.
celeri•tās, -tātis, *f.* [**celer,** swift],
   quickness, speed, swiftness. †
celeriter, *adv.* [**celer,** swift],
   quickly, rapidly, speedily.
Celt•ae, -ārum, *m.,* the Celts *or*
   Kelts, the Celtae.

centum (C.), *indecl. card. number,* one hundred.

centuri•ō, -ōnis, *m.* [**centum,** hundred], centurion, *the commander of the century, a unit corresponding to one-sixtieth of a legion.*

certām•en, -inis, *n.* [**certō,** struggle], strife, struggle, contest, combat.

certē, *adv.* [**certus,** certain], certainly, at least, at all events.

cert•us, -a, -um, *adj.,* decided, certain, sure, fixed; **certiōrem facere,** inform (*with acc. and inf.*); order (*with* **ut** *or* **nē** *and the subjunctive*); **certior fierī,** be informed. †

cēter•ī, -ae, -a, *adj.,* the rest of, the remainder; *as noun:* the rest, the remaining, the others.

Ceutron•ēs, -um, *m.,* the Ceutrones: (1) *a Belgic people subject to the Nervii or* (2) *a people living in the eastern part of the Roman Province.*

cibāri•us, -a, -um, *adj.* [**cibus,** food], pertaining to food; *n. pl. as noun:* provisions; **molita cibāria,** flour, meal.

Cicer•ō, -ōnis, *m.,* Quintus Tullius Cicero, *brother of the more famous orator and consul of 63 BCE, Marcus Tullius Cicero. He served as one of Caesar's legates.* †

cing•ō, -ere, cīnxī, cīnctum, encircle, surround, invest, encompass; man (*a wall*).

circiter, *adv.* about, around, near. †

circuit•us, -ūs, *m.* [**circumeō,** go around], a going around; a winding path; circumference, circuit.

circum, *prep. with acc.* [**circus,** circle], around, about, near.

circumcīd•ō, -ere, -ī, circumcīsum [**circum,** around + **caedō,** cut], cut around, cut off, cut; isolate.

circum•dō, -dare, -dedī, -datum [**dō,** put], put around, encompass, surround.

circum•sistō, -sistere, -stitī, — [**sistō,** stand], stand, flock *or* rally around, surround, hem in.

circum•spiciō, -spicere, -spexī, -spectum [**speciō,** look], look (*around*) for *or* at, consider, examine.

circum•veniō, -venīre, -vēnī, -ventum [**veniō,** come], come *or* get around, surround, cut off, beset; betray, defraud. †

citō, *adv.,* quickly, speedily. *Comp.* **citius;** *superl.* **citissimē.**

cīvi•tās, -tātis, *f.* [**cīvis,** citizen], citizenship; the citizens (*as forming a community*), state, city. †

clam, *adv.,* secretly.

clāmitō, 1 [*frequentative of* **clāmō,** cry out], cry out repeatedly, exclaim.

clām•or, -ōris, *m.* [**clāmō,** cry out], outcry, noise, shouting, clamor.

clār•us, -a, -um, *adj.,* clear, loud.

clēmenti•a, -ae, *f.* [**clēmēns,** gentle], gentleness, kindness, mercy, clemency.

cliēns, clientis, *m., f.* [clueō, hear, obey], client, vassal, dependent, retainer.

co•emō, -emere, -ēmī, -ēmptum [emō, buy], buy, buy up.

coepī, coepisse (App. §86), began, commenced, undertook; coeptus, *perf. part.,* begun, commenced. †

cōgitō, 1 [co + agitō, consider], consider thoroughly *or* carefully, ponder, reflect; think, purpose, plan.

cog•nōscō, -nōscere, -nōvī, -nitum [co + (g)nōscō, learn], learn, ascertain; study, investigate; *perf., I have learned, and thus:* I know (App. §193, I, *a.*). †

cōgō, cōgere, coēgī, coāctum [co + agō, drive], drive *or* bring together, collect, draw together, assemble, force, compel. †

cohor•s, -tis, *f.,* cohort. †

cohortor, 1 [co + hortor, encourage], encourage greatly, cheer, animate.

commentāri•us, -ī, *m.* [commentor, consider], notebook, sketchbook, memorandum, journal; sketch, memorandum, report; explanation, commentary.

con•iciō, -icere, -iēcī, -iectum [co + iaciō, throw. App. §7], hurl, throw, cast; put; put together (*logically*), conjecture; in fugam conicere, put to flight.

colligō, 1 [con + ligō, bind], bind *or* fasten together.

col•ligō, -ligere, -lēgī, -lēctum [con + legō, gather], gather together, collect; acquire; sē colligere, *collect oneself:* rally, recover.

collocō, 1 [con + locō, place], place, set, station; arrange; nūptum collocāre, to give in marriage. †

collo•quium, -quī, *n.* [colloquor, talk together], talking together; conference, parley, interview.

col•loquor, -loquī, -locūtus sum [con + loquor, talk], speak with, converse, confer, have a conference. †

colō, colere, coluī, cultum, cultivate, dwell in; honor, worship.

comb•ūrō, -ūrere, -ussī, -ustum [con + ūrō, burn], burn up.

commeāt•us, -ūs, *m.* [commeō, go back and forth], trip, voyage; supplies, provisions.

commemorō, 1 [memorō, call to mind], remind one of; state, mention.

commendō, 1 [mandō, entrust], entrust, surrender.

commeō, 1 [meō, go], go back and forth; *with* ad, resort to, visit.

comminus, *adv.* [manus, hand], hand to hand, in close combat.

com•mittō, -mittere, -mīsī, -missum [mittō, send], join, splice; commit (*a crime*), do; allow, permit; entrust; proelium committere, join *or* begin battle.

Com·mius, -mī, *m.,* Commius, *a leader of the Atrebates. He was loyal to Caesar until 52 BCE when he led troops in support of the general Gallic revolt.*

commodē, *adv.* [**commodus,** convenient], conveniently; readily, easily, fitly: **satis commodē,** to great advantage, very easily.

commod·us, -a, -um, *adj.* [**modus,** measure], *in full measure:* convenient, suitable, satisfactory.

commod·um, -ī, *n.* [**commodus,** convenient], convenience, interest, advantage.

commūnicō, 1 [**commūnis,** common], make common, communicate, impart, share.

commūn·is, -e, *adj.* common, general; **rēs commūnis,** the common interest. †

comparō, 1 [**parō,** prepare], prepare, get ready; acquire, gain, secure, prepare for.

com·periō, -perīre, -perī, -pertum [**pariō,** procure], find out with certainty, discover, ascertain.

com·pleō, -plēre, -plēvī, -plētum [*obs.:* **pleō,** fill], fill up *or* completely; complete; cover.

complūr·ēs, -a, *adj.* [**plūs,** more], several, many; a great many.

comportō, 1 [**portō,** carry], carry together, collect, bring.

com·prehendō, -prehendere, -prehendī, -prehēnsum [**prehendō** (=**prendō**), seize], grasp *or* lay hold of, seize, catch, arrest, take, catch (*fire*).

con·cēdō, -cēdere, -cessī, -cessum [**cēdō,** go], go away, depart, withdraw; grant, yield; allow, permit.

con·cīdō, -cīdere, -cīsī, -cīsum [**caedō,** cut], cut down, kill, slay, cut off.

con·cidō, -ere, -cidī, —, [**cadō,** fall], fall down, fall.

conciliō, 1 [**concilium,** assembly], bring together; gain *or* win over, secure; reconcile, conciliate.

concil·ium, -ī, *n.,* assembly, gathering, council.

concitō, 1 [**citō,** put in motion], stir up, rouse, instigate, incite.

conclāmō, 1 [**clāmō,** shout], shout out, call aloud, yell.

con·currō, -currere, -cursī, -cursum [**currō,** run], run *or* rush together; hurry, run, rush; run to the rescue; come, gather.

concursō, 1 [*frequentative of* **concurrō,** run], run about.

concurs·us, -ūs, *m.* [**concurrō,** run], a running together, attack, onset; collision.

condici·ō, -ōnis, *f.,* condition, state; agreement, stipulation, terms:

con·dūcō, -dūcere, -dūxī, -ductum [**dūcō,** lead], lead *or* bring together, assemble, conduct; hire.

cōnfectus, *see* cōnficiō.

cōn•ferō, -ferre, contulī, collātus
[ferō, bring. App. §81], bring
or get together, collect, gather,
carry, bring; crowd together;
ascribe to; put off, defer;
compare; sē cōnferre, betake
oneself, take refuge.

cōnfert•us, -a, -um, *adj.* [*perf. part.
of* cōnferciō, crowd together],
dense, thick, compact, stuffed.

cōnfestim, *adv.*, hastily, at once,
immediately.

cōn•ficiō, -ficere, -fēcī,
-fectum [faciō, make], make
or do thoroughly, complete,
accomplish, finish; finish up,
exhaust, weaken; furnish; dress
or treat (*leather*).

cōn•fīdō, -fīdere, -fīsī, -fīsum
[fīdō, trust. App. §74], trust
completely, rely on, feel
confident, hope; cōnfīsus,
perf. part. with pres. meaning:
relying on.

cōnfīn•ium, -ī, *n.* [fīnis,
boundary], common boundary,
neighborhood.

cōnfirmō, 1 [firmō, strengthen],
establish, strengthen, encourage,
console; declare, assert.

cōn•fi teor, -fitērī, -fessus sum
[fateor, confess], acknowledge,
confess.

cōnflagrō, 1 [flagrō, burn], burn,
be on fire.

cōnflīctō, 1 [*freq. of* cōnflīgō],
strike together; *in the pass.*: be
distressed.

cōn•flīgō, -flīgere, -flīxī, -flīctum
[flīgō, strike], strike against;
contend, fight.

coniūnctim, *adv.* [coniungō,
join], jointly.

con•iungō, -iungere, -iūnxī,
-iūnctum [coniungō, join], join
with *or* together, connect, unite,
bind.

coniūrāti•ō, -ōnis, *f.* [coniūrō,
swear], a swearing together; plot,
conspiracy; secret organization;
confederacy; gang.

cōnor, 1, try, attempt, endeavor.

cōn•scendō, -scendere, -scendī,
-scēnsum [scandō, climb], climb,
mount; go on board, embark.

cōn•scīscō, -scīscere, -scīvī,
-scītum [scīscō, resolve],
resolve upon; sibi mortem
conscīscere, commit suicide.

cōn•scrībō, -scrībere, -scrīpsī,
-scrīptum [scrībō, write], *write
together in a list*: levy, enroll,
enlist; write.

cōnsecrō, 1 [sacrō, dedicate],
dedicate, consecrate.

cōnsecūtus, *see* cōnsequor.

cōn•sentiō, -sentīre, -sēnsī,
-sēnsum [sentiō, feel], *think
together*: agree, combine.

cōn•sequor, -sequī, -secūtus
sum [sequor, follow], follow up;
go after, pursue; reach, overtake;
gain, attain, accomplish; ensue,
succeed.

cōn•sīdō, -sīdere, -sēdī, -sessum
[sīdō, sit down], sit down
together, settle; take a position.

cōnsili•um, -ī, *n.*, consultation, deliberation; counsel, advice; plan, design; measure, course of action; judgement; prudence, wisdom; an assembly for deliberation, council, council of war; **commūnī cōnsiliō,** by, *or* in accordance with, general action; **pūblicō cōnsiliō,** by action of the state; **cōnsilium capere** *or* **inīre,** form *or* adopt a plan; **cōnsilium habēre,** think, consider. †

cōn•sistō, -sistere, -stitī, — [**sistō,** stand], take a stand *or* position, keep one's position, stand, form (*when soldiers make a formation*); stop, halt, remain, stay; (*of ships*) lie at anchor; consist in, depend *or* rest on.

cōnspect•us, -ūs, *m.* [**conspiciō,** look at], sight, view; presence.

cōn•spiciō, -spicere, -spexī, -spectum [**speciō,** look], look at, observe, discern, perceive.

cōnspicor, 1 [**speciō,** look], observe, discern, perceive.

cōnstipō, 1, press *or* crowd closely.

cōn•stituō, -stituere, -stituī, -stitūtum [**statuō,** set up], set up, erect, construct, appoint, decide, decree, determine, establish, set, settle; (*of troops*) draw up (*in formation*); (*of ships*) anchor, station; raise (*a legion*). †

cōn•stō, -stāre, -stitī, -stātum [**stō,** stand], stand firm; depend on; be complete; cost; *impers.*: it is agreed, certain, evident, *or* known.

cōn•suēscō, -suēscere, -suēvī, -suētum [**suēscō,** become used to], become accustomed *or* used to; *perf.*(App. §193, I, *a.*), be accustomed; **cōnsuētus,** *perf. part. as adj.*: accustomed, usual. †

cōnsuētūd•ō, -inis, *f.* [**cōnsuēscō,** become accustomed], habit, custom, practice; mode of life, "lifestyle."

cōn•sul, -sulis, *m.*, consul, *one of the two chief magistrates elected annually at Rome.*

cōnsul•ō, -ere, -uī, -tum, take counsel, consult, consider; *with dat.*: take counsel for, consider the interests of, take care for; spare.

cōn•sūmō, -sūmere, -sūmpsī, -sūmptum [**sūmō,** take], *take together or all at once*: devour, consume, destroy; use up, waste, pass.

cōn•surgō, -surgere, -surrēxī, -surrectum [**surgō,** rise], arise together, arise in a body, arise.

contabulō, 1 [**tabula,** board], floor over, build in multiple stories, build up.

contāgi•ō, -ōnis, *f.* [**contingō,** touch], contact.

contempti•ō, -ōnis, *f.* [**contemnō,** despise], disdain, contempt.

con•tendō, -tendere, -tendī, -tentum [**tendō,** stretch], push forward, hasten; march; strive, contend, fight; be anxious for; maintain, insist.

contenti•ō, -ōnis, *f.* [**contendō,** strive], striving, struggle, contest, dispute.

con•texō, -texere, -texuī, -textum [**texō,** weave], weave *or* bind together, connect.

contigī, *see* **contingō.**

contin•ēns, -entis, *adj.* [**contineō,** hold together], *holding together;* continuous, unbroken; neighboring; *as noun,* mainland, continent.

continenter, *adv.* [**continēns,** continuous], without interruption, continually, continuously.

con•tineō, -tinēre, -tinuī, -tentum [**teneō,** hold], hold together; hold, keep, restrain; bound, shut up, contain; **sē continēre,** *with abl.,* remain in, on, *or* within. †

con•tingō, -tingere, -tigī, -tāctum [**tangō,** touch], touch, reach; extend to; befall, happen to.

continu•us, -a, -um, *adj.* [**contineō,** hold together], holding together, unbroken, uninterrupted, continuous.

contrā, *adv. and prep. with acc.:* (1) *as adv.:* against him *or* them; on the other hand; **contrā atque,** contrary to what; (2) *as prep.,* against, contrary to; opposite, facing.

contrōversi•a, -ae, *f.* [**contrā,** against + **versus,** turned], dispute, argument, quarrel, controversy. †

contumēli•a, -ae, *f.,* affront, indignity, insult; injury, violence.

convall•is, -is, *f.* [**vallis,** valley], enclosed valley, defile.

con•veniō, -venīre, -vēnī, -ventum [**veniō,** come], come together, assemble; convene, meet; come to, arrive; to be agreed upon; *impers.:* be convenient, suitable, *or* necessary. †

convent•us, -ūs, *m.* [**conveniō,** come together], a coming together, meeting, assembly; court.

con•vertō, -vertere, -vertī, -versum [**verto,** turn], turn completely, turn around, wheel around; turn, change; **signa convertere,** (turn) about face.

co•orior, -orīrī, -ortus sum [**orior,** rise], arise, spring up, break out.

cōpi•a, -ae, *f.,* supply, plenty, abundance, number; *pl.:* resources; forces, troops. †

cor, cordis, *n.,* heart.

cotīdiān•us, -a, -um, *adj.* [**cotīdiē,** daily], every day, daily; usual, customary.

cotīdiē, *adv.* [**quot,** how many + **diēs,** day], daily, every day.

Cott•a, -ae, *m.,* Lucius Aurunculeius Cotta, *one of Caesar's lieutenants.*

Crass•us, -ī, *m.,* Marcus Licinius Crassus, *(together with Pompey) political ally and supporter of Caesar, consul in 55* BCE, *is* *killed while leading the Parthian expedition of 53* BCE; (2) *his younger son,* Publius Licinius Crassus, *who served as one of Caesar's lieutenants 58–56* BCE; *died in battle with his father in Parthia in 53* BCE; *and* (3) *an elder son,* Marcus Licinius Crassus, *who served as one of Caesar's quaestors after his brother left Gaul.*

crāt•es, -is, *f.,* wickerwork; fascine (*a bundle of sticks used for filling trenches*).

crēb•er, -ra, -rum, *adj.,* thick, close, repeated, numerous, frequent, at short intervals. *Comp.:* **crēbrior;** *superl.:* **crēberrimus** (App. §40).

crēd•ō, -ere, -idī, -itum, believe, suppose; entrust.

cremō, 1, burn.

cruciāt•us, -ūs, *m.* [**cruciō,** torture; **crux,** cross (*used for crucifixion*)], torture, torment.

culp•a, -ae, *f.,* blame, fault, guilt.

cult•us, -ūs, *m.* [**colō,** cultivate], cultivation, civilization; mode of life, lifestyle; dress; religious worship.

cum, *conj.,* when, as, while; after, as soon as; whenever; since, because; although; **cum . . . tum,** not only . . . but also, both . . . and; **cum prīmum,** as soon as. *See* App. §§238–242. †

cum, *prep. with abl.,* with, along with, together with. †

cūnctor, 1, delay, hesitate, be reluctant.

cupidē, *adv.* [**cupidus,** desirous], desirously, eagerly.

cupidi•tās, -tātis, *f.* [**cupidus,** eager], eagerness, desire, greed, avarice.

cupid•us, -a, -um, *adj.* [**cupiō,** desire], eager, desirous, zealous, fond.

cūrō, 1 [**cūra,** care], care for, take care of, provide for; *with gerundive* (App. §285, II, *b.*): have, order.

curr•us, -ūs, *m.,* chariot.

curs•us, -ūs, *m.* [**currō,** run], running, speed; course, career; pasage, voyage.

D.

D., *sign for* **quīngentī,** five hundred.

d. = diem.

damnō, 1 [**damnum,** damage], declare guilty, sentence, condemn.

dē, *prep. with abl., originally expressing motion from;* (1) *of place,* from, down from, away from, out of; (2) *of time,* just after, about; (3) *variously translated in other relations,* about, concerning, of, from, in accordance with, for. †

dēbeō, 2 [**dē + habeō,** have], *have, or keep from someone:* owe; *with inf.:* ought, must, have to; *pass.:* be due.

dē•cēdō, -cēdere, -cessī, -cessum [**cēdō,** go], go from *or* away, depart, withdraw, leave, forsake; die.

decem (X), *indecl. card. number,* ten.

dē•cernō, -cernere, -crēvī, -crētum [**cernō,** separate; decide], decide, vote, decree.

dēclīv•is, -e, *adj.* [**clīvus,** a slope], sloping downward, declining; *n. pl. as noun:* slopes.

dē•decus, -oris, *n.* [**decus,** honor], dishonor, disgrace.

dēditus, *see* **dēdō.**

dē•dō, -dere, -didī, -ditum [**dō,** give], give up, give over, yield, surrender; devote; **sē dēdere,** submit, surrender.

dē•dūcō, -dūcere, -dūxī, -ductum [**dūcō,** lead], lead down, lead away, withdraw; bring, conduct, lead; influence; launch (*ships*); give in marriage.

dēfecti•ō, -ōnis, *f.* [**dēficiō,** fail], falling away, desertion, revolt.

dēfēnsor, -is, *m.* [**dēfendō,** defend], defender, protector; (*means of*) defense.

dē•ferō, -ferre, -tulī, -lātum [**ferō,** carry. App. §81], bring from, bring down, carry, take; report, disclose; bring before, refer; bestow, confer; **dēlātus** (*sometimes*), falling; coming by chance.

dē•ficiō, -ficere, -fēcī, -fectum [**faciō,** make], fail, desert, fall away, revolt.

dē•fīgō, -fīgere, -fīxī, -fīxum [**fīgō,** fix], fix *or* fasten down, drive in, plant.

dē•fugiō, -fugere, -fūgī, -fugitum [**fugiō,** flee], flee from, run away, shun.

dē•iciō, -icere, -iēcī, -iectum [**iaciō,** throw. App. §7], hurl *or* cast down; dislodge; kill; foil, disappoint.

deinceps, *adv.,* one after the other, in turn, successively.

deinde, *adv.* [**dē + inde,** from there, thence], then, next, after this, thereupon.

dēlīberō, 1 [**lībra,** balance], weigh well; consider, deliberate.

dēligō, 1 [**ligō,** bind], bind *or* tie down, fasten, moor.

dē•ligō, -ligere, -lēgī, -lēctum [**legō,** choose], pick out, select, choose.

dē•litēscō, -tēscere, -lituī, — [**latēscō,** *inceptive of* **lateō,** lie hidden], hide oneself, lurk.

dē•metō, -metere, -messuī, -messum [**metō,** reap], mow, reap.

dē•migrō, 1 [**migrō,** move, migrate], move from, move away, emigrate, remove.

dē•mittō, -mittere, -mīsī, -missum [**mittō,** send], send, thrust, *or* let down; sink; bow (*one's head*); **sē dēmittere,** come *or* get down, descend; **sē animō dēmittere,** lose courage; **dēmissus,** *perf. part. as adj.:* low.

dēmō, dēmere, dēmpsī, dēmptum [**dē + emō,** take], take down, remove.

dēmōnstrō, 1 [**mōnstrō,** show], point out, show, explain, describe; declare, state, say.

dēmum, *adv.,* at length, at last, finally.

dē•pellō, -pellere, -pulī, -pulsum [**pellō,** drive], drive from *or* away, ward off.

dē•pōnō, -pōnere, -posuī, -positum [**pōnō,** put], lay down, put aside, put away, give up; place, station, deposit.

dē•prehendō, -prehendere, -prehendī, -prehēnsum [**prehendō** (=**prendō**), seize], seize, capture, catch.

dē•scendō, -scendere, -scendī, -scēnsum [**scandō,** climb], climb down, go down, descend; have recourse (*to*), resort.

dē•serō, -serere, -seruī, -sertum [**serō,** entwine, join], disjoin; abandon, desert, forsake; **dēsertus,** *perf. part. as adj.*: deserted, solitary.

dē•siliō, -silīre, -siluī, -sultum [**saliō,** jump], jump from, leap down, alight, dismount.

dēspērāti•ō, -ōnis, *f.* [**dēspērō,** despair], despair, hopelessness.

dēspērō, 1 [**spērō,** hope], despair, be hopeless, lack confidence; **dēspērātus,** *perf. part.*: despaired of; *as adj.*: desperate.

de•sum, -esse, -fuī, — [**sum,** be. App. §66], be lacking, be absent from, fail.

dēturbō, 1 [**turbō,** disturb], drive off, dislodge.

de•us, -ī (*nom. pl.*: **diī;** *dat. pl.*: **dīs**), *m.,* god.

dē•vehō, -vehere, -vexī, -vectum [**vehō,** carry], carry away, bring.

dē•voveō, -vovēre, -vōvī, -vōtum [**voveō,** vow], consecrate, devote; **dēvōtus,** *perf. part. as noun*: a sworn follower.

dext•er, -ra, -rum, *adj.,* on the right, right.

dextra, -ae, *f.* [**dexter,** right; *sc.* **manus,** hand], the right hand.

dīcō, dīcere, dīxī, dictum, say, tell, speak, express, mention; name, appoint; **causam dīcere,** plead a case; **iūs dīcere,** administer justice. †

d. = *diem.*

diēs, diēī, *m. and f.,* day; time; **in diēs,** from day to day; **diem ex diē,** day after day. †

differō, differre, distulī, dīlātum [**ferō,** carry. App. §81], scatter, spread; put off, defer; be different, differ.

difficil•is, -e, *adj.* [**facilis,** easy], not easy, hard, troublesome, difficult.

difficul•tās, -tātis, *f.* [**difficilis,** difficult], difficulty, trouble, embarrassment.

dif•fīdō, -fīdere, -fīsī, -fīsum [**fīdō,** trust. App. §74], distrust, lack confidence, despair.

digni•tās, -tātis, *f.* [**dignus,** worthy], worthiness, dignity, (*personal*) merit *or* worth, status, rank.

dīiūdicō, 1 [**iūdicō,** judge], decide.

dīligenter, *adv.* [dīligēns, careful], carefully; with exactness, pains, *or* care.

dīligenti•a, -ae, *f.* [dīligēns, careful], carefulness, painstaking care.

dī•ligō, -ligere, -lēgī, -lēctum [legō, choose], choose *or* single out, esteem highly, love.

dīmicō, 1 [micō, brandish], fight, struggle, contend.

dī•mittō, -mittere, -mīsī, -missum [mittō, send], send in different directions, send away, send off, dismiss; break up; let go, let slip, let pass, give up, lose.

Dīs, Dītis, *m.,* Dis, the god Pluto, *god of the underworld.*

dīs, *see* **deus.**

dis- (**dī-, dif-, dir-**), *inseparable prefix,* apart, asunder, in different directions; *negative:* *equivalent to English* un-, not.

dis•cēdō, -cēdere, -cessī, -cessum [cēdō, go], go away, depart, retire; leave (*especially with* **ab** *or* **ex**). †

disciplīn•a, -ae, *f.* [discō, learn], learning, discipline; instruction, teaching; system.

discō, discere, didicī, —, learn, be taught.

di•spergō, -spergere, -spersī, -spersum [spargō, scatter], scatter, disperse.

dis•pōnō, -pōnere, -posuī, -positum [pōnō, put], place apart, place about; distribute, arrange, station.

disputāti•ō, -ōnis, *f.* [disputō, discuss], argument, discussion.

disputō, 1 [putō, reckon], discuss, debate about.

dissensi•ō, -ōnis, *f.* [dissentiō, think differently], disagreement, dissension.

dis•sentiō, -sentīre, -sēnsī, -sēnsum [sentiō, feel], differ, disagree.

dis•tribuō, -tribuere, -tribuī, -tribūtum [tribuō, assign], assign, divide, distribute.

distulī, *see* **differō.**

dītissimus, *superl. of* **dīves.**

diū, *adv.,* for a long time, long; **quam diū,** as long as; *comp.:* **diūtius,** longer, too long, any longer; *superl.:* **diūtissimē,** for the longest time.

dīves, dīvitis, *adj.,* rich, wealthy; *superl.:* **dītissimus.**

Dīviciāc•us, -ī, *m.,* Diviciacus, *a leader of the Aedui, friendly to the Romans. Caesar pardons Dumnorix at his request.*

dī•vidō, -videre, dīvīsī, dīvīsum, divide, distribute, separate; **dīvīsus,** *perf. part. as adj.:* divided, distributed, separated.

dīvīn•us, -a, -um, *adj.* [dīvus, divine], of the gods, divine, sacred.

dō, dare, dedī, datum (App. §85), give, bestow, present, grant, furnish; offer; yield, give up; **in fugam dare,** put to flight; **dare manūs,** yield; **dare negōtium,**

with dat.: employ, engage, direct. (*Some compounds of* **dō** *are derived from an obs. verb,* **dō,** *put.*) †

doceō, docēre, docuī, docitum, show, teach, instruct, inform.

dol•or, -ōris, *m.* [**doleō,** grieve], grief, distress, pain (*physical or mental*), anguish, annoyance.

domin•us, -ī, *m.,* master.

dom•us, -ūs (App. §29, *d.*), *f.,* house; home; native country.

dōs, dōtis, *f.* [**dō,** give], a marriage present, dowry.

Druid•ēs, -um, *m.,* the Druids, *the priests of the Celts in Gaul and Britain.*

dubitāti•ō, -ōnis, *f.* [**dubitō,** doubt], doubt, uncertainty; hesitation.

dubitō, 1 [**dubius,** doubtful], be uncertain, doubt; hesitate, delay.

dubi•us, -a, -um, *adj.,* uncertain, doubtful.

dūcō, dūcere, dūxī, ductum, lead, conduct, guide, draw; bring, fetch; trace, construct, extend; deem, consider, judge; protract, defer. †

dum, *conj.,* while, as long as; till, until. †

Dumnor•ix, -īgis, *m.,* Dumnorix, *a leader of the Aeduans, brother of Diviciacus, son-in-law of Orgetorix, enemy of Caesar, and leader of the anti-Roman party. Caesar orders his execution in 54 BCE when he tries to escape.*

du•o, -ae, -a (App. §49), *card. num. and adj.,* two. †

duodecim, *card. number and adj.* [**duo,** two + **decem,** ten], twelve.

dūr•us, -a, -um, *adj.,* hard, rough, harsh, difficult, dangerous; severe, inclement.

dux, ducis, *m.* [**dūcō,** lead], leader, commander, general; guide.

E.

ē (*only before consonants*), **ex** (*before vowels and some consonants*), *prep. with abl., originally expressing motion out of;* (1) *of place,* out of, from, away from; *expressing position, in some phrases,* on; **ūnā ex parte,** on one side; (2) *of time,* from, after, since; **ex itinere,** immediately after the march; (3) *variously translated in other relations:* from, out of, of, because of, in accordance with; **ē regiōne,** opposite. †

eā, *adv.* [= **eā viā**], by that way, there.

Eburōn•ēs, -um, *m.,* the Eburones, *a Belgic people who in 54 BCE destroyed troops under the command of Sabinus and Cotta. Afterwards, Caesar almost exterminated them.*

ē•discō, -discere, -didicī, — [**discō,** learn], learn thoroughly, learn by heart.

ē•dūcō, -dūcere, -dūxī, -ductum [**dūcō,** lead], lead out, lead forth; draw (*a sword*).

effēminō, 1 [**ex** + **fēmina,**
woman], make effeminate,
weaken.

efferō, efferre, extulī, ēlātum
[**ex** + **ferō,** carry. App. §81],
bring *or* carry out, carry *or* take
away; raise; spread around,
publish widely, make known;
elate, puff up.

ef•ficiō, -ficere, -fēcī, -fectum
[**faciō,** make], make *or*
do completely, complete,
accomplish, construct; make,
cause, bring about, render.

ef•fugiō, -fugere, -fūgī, —
[**fugiō,** flee], flee from, run
away, escape.

ēgī, *see* **agō.**

egō, meī (App. §51), *first pers.
pron.,* I, me; *pl.* **nōs,** we, us, etc.

ē•gredior, -gredī, -gressus sum
[**gradior,** step], step out, go out,
come forth, depart; march out,
make a sortie; land (*from a ship*),
disembark.

eiusmodī, of such a sort *or* kind,
such.

ē•mittō, -mittere, -mīsī, -missum
[**mittō,** send], let go, send out *or*
forth, release; hurl, discharge;
drop.

enim, *conj.,* in fact, really; for;
sed enim, but in fact,
however.

ē•nūntiō, 1 [**nūntiō,** announce],
report, declare, disclose.

eō, īre, iī (īvī), itum (App. §84),
go, proceed, march, pass.

eō, *abl.* of **is.**

eō, *adv.* [*old dat. of* **is**], to that
place, there (*in the sense of*
thither), to the place (*where,
etc.*), to them (it, him, etc.).

eōdem, *adv.* [*old dat. of* **īdem**],
to the same place, to the same
point (result, purpose, etc.).

epistol•a, -ae, *f.,* letter, epistle.

equ•es, -itis, *m.* [**equus,** horse], a
horseman, a rider; *pl.*: cavalry.
*Roman society was organized by
class or income levels. Originally,
those who could afford their own
horse were assigned to the cavalry.
In Caesar's day, rich men who
belonged to this class, even if they
did not serve in the cavalry, were
called* equestrians. *Rich Gauls
were also called* equestrians. †

equitāt•us, -ūs, *m.* [**equus,** horse],
cavalry, horseman. †

equ•us, -ī, *m.,* horse. †

ē•ripiō, -ripere, -ripuī, -reptum
[**rapiō,** seize], take away, wrest
from, extort, deprive; rescue,
relieve, save.

errō, 1, wander; err, be mistaken.

essedāri•us, -a, -um, *adj.*
[**essedum,** war chariot], a
soldier who fought from a two-
wheeled British war chariot.

essed•um, -ī, *n.,* a two-wheeled
war chariot used by the Britons.

Esuvi•ī, -ōrum, *m.,* the Esuvii, *a
people in northwestern Gaul.*

et, *conj.,* and; also, too, even; **et . . .
et,** both . . . and. †

etiam, *conj.,* and also, also, even,
yet. †

etsī, *conj.* [**et** + **sī,** if], even if, although.

ē•veniō, -venīre, -vēnī, -ventum [**veniō,** come], turn out, result.

ēvent•us, -ūs, *m.* [**ēveniō,** turn out], outcome, issue, result, consequence.

ex, *see* **ē.** †

ex•animō, 1 [**anima,** breath], deprive of breath, render breathless, exhaust; kill.

ex•audiō, 4 [**audiō,** hear], hear (*from a distance*).

ex•cēdō, -cēdere, -cessī, -cessum [**cēdō,** go], go out, go away, withdraw, retire.

ex•cellō, -cellere, —, —, excel, surpass.

excitō, 1 [**citō,** rouse], call forth, excite, animate, arouse; erect, construct (*towers*); kindle (*fires*).

excōgitō, 1 [**cōgitō,** think], think out, contrive, devise, invent.

excruciō, 1 [**cruciō,** torture; **crux,** cross (*used for crucifixion*)], torture severely, torment.

ex•eō, -īre, -iī, -ītum [**eō,** go. App. §84], go from, go out, depart from, leave.

exercitāti•ō, -ōnis, *f.* [*frequentative of* **exercitō,** *from* **exerceō,** exercise], exercise, training, practice, experience.

exercit•us, -ūs, *m.* [**exerceō,** exercise], *a trained or disciplined body of men,* an army. †

ex•hauriō, -haurīre, -hausī, -haustum [**hauriō,** drain], draw out, empty.

exigui•tās, -tātis, *f.* [**exiguus,** scanty], scantiness, meagerness, shortness, dearth, want.

exīstimāti•ō, -ōnis, *f.* [**exīstimō,** estimate], judgement, opinion.

exīstimō, 1 [**aestimō,** reckon], estimate, reckon, think, consider. †

exit•us, -ūs, *m.* [**exeō,** go out], a going out, exit, passage; issue, result, end.

expediō, 4 [**pēs,** foot], set free; arrange, prepare.

expedīt•us, -a, -um, *adj.* [*perf. part. of* **expediō,** set free], unimpeded, free, unobstructed; without baggage; light armed; *as noun*: a light-armed soldier.

ex•pellō, -pellere, -pulī, -pulsum [**pellō,** drive], drive out, drive forth, expel.

explōrō, 1, search *or* find out, investigate, spy out, reconnoiter.

ex•sequor, -sequī, secūtus sum [**sequor,** follow], follow out, enforce.

ex•sistō, -sistere, stitī, — [**sistō,** stand], stand *or* come forth, appear, arise; ensue.

exspectō, 1 [**spectō,** look at], look out for, await, expect; wait to see; anticipate, apprehend.

ex•stinguō, -stinguere, -stīnxī, -stīnctum, put out, quench; destroy.

ex•struō, -struere, -strūxī, -strūctum [**struō,** build], build *or* pile up; construct, build.

extrā, *adv. and prep. with acc.*, out of, outside of, beyond, without.

extrēm•us, -a, -um, *adj.* [*superl. of* **exterus**. App. §44], outermost, utmost, farthest, extreme; the farthest part of; **extrēmī** (*as noun*), the rear ("the ones at the back"); **ad extrēmum**, at last, at the end; as a last resort.

ex•ūrō, -ūrere, -ussī, -ustum [**ex** + **ūro**, burn], burn up.

F.

Fab•ius, -ī, *m.* (1) Quintus Fabius Maximus, *victor over the Gallic Allobroges, Arverni, and Ruteni, in 121* BCE, *after which he was also called* Allobricus. (2) Gaius Fabius, *one of Caesar's lieutenants.* (3) Lucius Fabius, *a centurion of the 8th legion; killed at Gergovia.*

facile, *adv.* [**facilis**, easy], easily, readily. *Comp.:* **facilius;** *superl.:* **facillimē** (App. §41). †

facil•is, -e, *adj.* [**faciō**, do], easy. †

fac•iō, -ere, fēcī, factum, make, construct, form, do, execute (*commands, etc.*); give (*opportunity, etc.*); *with* **ut**, bring about, cause; *intransitive:* do, act. *Pass.:* **fīō, fierī, factus sum** (App. §83), *with pass. meanings, and, used impers.*, result, happen, come to pass. †

facin•us, -oris, *n.* [**faciō**, do], deed; misdeed, outrage, crime.

facul•tās, -tātis, *f.* [**facilis**, easy], power; opportunity, chance; resources, supply.

fals•us, -a, -um, *adj.* [*perf. part. of* **fallō**, deceive], false.

falx, falcis, *f.*, sickle, pruning hook; hook (*for pulling down walls*).

fām•a, -ae, *f.* [**fārī**, to speak], common talk, rumor, report, reputation, fame.

fam•ēs, -is, *f.*, starvation, hunger.

famili•a, -ae, *f.*, household (*including slaves*); retinue (*including all dependents*); family.

familiār•is, -e, *adj.* [**familia**, household], personal, private; *as noun:* intimate friend; **rēs familiāris**, personal property, estate.

fās, *n., indeclin.*, divine law, religiously correct, right, proper, permissable. *Compare:* **iūs**, human law.

fem•ur, -oris *or* **-inis**, *n.*, the thigh.

ferē, *adv.*, almost, nearly, about, for the most part. †

ferō, ferre, tulī, lātum (App. §81), carry, bear, bring; endure, suffer, support, withstand; receive; tell, report, give, render (*aid*); offer, propose (*terms*); **graviter** *or* **molestē ferre,** be annoyed *or* angry at; *passive* (*sometimes*) rush. *In the intransitive, almost* = *verb* to be. †

ferrāment•um, -ī, *n.* [**ferrum**, iron], an iron tool *or* implement.

ferr•um, -i, *n.,* iron; tool; sword.

ferve•faciō, -facere, -fēcī, -factum [**ferveō,** be red hot + **faciō,** make], heat, melt.

ferv•ēns, -entis, *adj.* [*pres. part. of* **ferveō,** be red hot], heated, glowing, hot.

fid•ēs, -eī, *f.* [**fīdō,** confide], faith, confidence; faithfulness, loyalty, trustworthiness; allegiance, protection, dependence; pledge, assurance; **fīdem facere,** convince *or* give a pledge; **fīdem sequī,** surrender.

figūr•a, -ae, *f.* [**fingō,** form], form, shape, figure.

fīli•a, -ae, *f.,* daughter.

fīl•ius, -ī, *m.,* son.

fīniō, 4 [**fīnis,** limit], limit, bound; determine, measure.

fīn•is, -is, *m.,* boundary, limit, border, end; *pl.* boundaries; territory, country. †

fīnitim•us, -a, -um, *adj.* [**fīnis,** limit], bordering on, adjoining, neighboring.

fīō, fierī, factus sum, *see* **faciō.**

firmiter, *adv.* [**firmus,** firm], firmly.

firm•us, -a, -um, *adj.,* strong, stable, vigorous, firm.

flamm•a, -ae, *f.,* fire, blaze.

flectō, flectere, flexī, flectum, bend, turn, direct.

flēt•us, -ūs, *m.* [**fleō,** weep], weeping, lamentation.

flūct•us, -ūs, *m.* [**fluō,** flow], flood, billow, wave.

flūm•en, -inis, *n.* [**fluō,** flow], river, stream. †

fluō, fluere, flūxī, —, flow, run.

fore = futūrum esse, *see* **sum.** †

fort•is, -e, *adj.,* strong, brave.

fortitūd•ō, -inis, *f.* [**fortis,** brave], bravery, courage.

fortūn•a, -ae, *f.* [**fors,** chance], fortune, luck, chance, opportunity, lot, condition; good fortune, success, property, estate. *All* fortuna *was the domain of the goddess* Fortuna, *a deity Caesar and his troops cultivated with great devotion.*

foss•a, -ae, *f.* [*perf. part. of* **fodiō,** dig], trench, ditch.

frangō, frangere, frēgī, frāctum, break, wreck; crush, discourage.

frāt•er, -ris, *m.,* brother.

fremit•us, -ūs, *m.,* confusion, noise, uproar.

frūct•us, -ūs, *m.* [**fruor,** enjoy], fruit; profit, reward.

frūmentāri•us, -a, -um, *adj.* [**frūmentum,** grain], of *or* pertaining to grain; *of places,* fruitful, productive of grain; **rēs frūmentāria,** grain supply, provisions.

frūmentor, 1 [**frūmentum,** grain], get grain, forage.

frūment•um, -ī, *n.,* grain; *pl.:* crops. †

fug•a, -ae, *f.,* flight; **in fugam conicere** *or* **dare,** put to flight.

fūm•us, -ī, *m.,* smoke.

fund•a, -ae, *f.,* sling.

fūn•is, -is, *m.,* rope, cable.

fūn•us, -eris, *n.*, funeral.

fūrt•um, -ī, *n.*, theft.

fūsil•is, -e, *adj.* [fundō, pour], liquid, molten.

G.

Gabin•ius, -ī, *m.*, Aulus Gabinius, consul with Lucius Calpurnius Piso in 58 BCE.

Ga•ius, -ī, *m.*, *a Roman first name, abbreviated* C.

Galli•a, -ae, *f.*, Gaul. †

Gallic•us, -a, -um, *adj.* [Gallia, Gaul], pertaining to Gaul *or* the Gauls, Gallic.

Gall•us, -a, -um, *adj.*, of Gaul, Gallic; *pl. as noun*: the Gauls, *inhabiting Gaul, Northern Italy, etc.* †

Garumn•a, -ae, *m.*, the Garumna *or* Garonne, *a river that formed the boundary between Aquitania and Celtic Gaul.*

Geidumn•ī, -ōrum, *m.*, the Geidumni, *a people of Belgic Gaul, clients of the Nervii.*

Genav•a, -ae, *f.*, Genava, *a city belonging to the Allobroges on the shores of Lacus Lemanus; now called* Geneva.

gen•us, -eris, *n.*, descent, origin, race, class, tribe, family; kind, nature. †

Germān•ī, -ōrum, *m.*, the Germani *or* the Germans. †

ger•ō, -ere, gessī, gestum, carry, bear, wield; (*of war*) carry on, perform, wage, conduct; *pass.*: be done, go on, occur. †

glad•ius, -ī, *m.*, sword.

glān•s, -dis, *f.*, acorn; ball, slug *of* lead.

glōri•a, -ae, *f.*, glory, renown, honor, fame, reputation.

Gnae•us, -ī, *m.*, *a Roman first name, abbreviated* Cn.

Graec•us, -a, -um, *adj.*, of *or* belonging to the Greeks, Greek; *pl. as noun*: the Greeks.

grāti•a, -ae, *f.* [grātus, pleasing], favor, goodwill, gratitude, esteem, influence, popularity; grātiās agere, thank; grātiam habēre, to feel grateful; grātiam referre, to return a favor; hanc grātiam referre, to return a favor in this way; grātiam inīre, to gain favor; grātiā, *following a gen.*: for the purpose of, in order to.

grav•is, -e, *adj.*, heavy, oppressive, hard, severe, serious; advanced (*in years*). †

Grudi•ī, -ōrum, *m.*, the Grudii, *a Belgic people near the Nervii.*

H.

hab•eō, -ēre, -uī, -itum, have, hold, possess; think, consider, regard; deliver (*with* ōrātiōnem); in animō habēre, intend; ratiōnem habēre, have regard for; take care *or* see that (*followed by an* ut *clause*); cōnsilium habēre, form a plan; in numerō hostium habēre, consider as enemies; aliter sē habēre, be otherwise *or* be different; *for* **habēre** *with the perf. pass. part., e.g.,* **vectīgālia redempta habēre,** *see* App. §286, *b*. †

Helveti•us, -a, -um, *adj.,* of the Helvetii, Helvetians; *as noun:* one of the Helvetii, a Helvetian; *pl.:* the Helvetii *or* Helvetians. †

heredi•tās, -tātis, *f.* [**hērēs,** heir], inheritance.

hībern•a, -ōrum, *n.* [*deriving from the adj. that modified* **castra,** fortified camp], winter camp, winter quarters. †

hic, haec, hoc, *demonstrative pron.* (App. §54), *used for what is close in space, time, or thought:* this, this man, this woman, this thing; he, she, it (*more emphatic than* **is, ea, id**); *abl. sing.* **hōc,** on this account, in this respect; the (*with comparatives*); **hic . . . ille,** the latter . . . the former. *See* App. §170, *a.* †

hiemō, 1 [**hiems,** winter], pass the winter, winter.

hiem•s, -is, *f.,* wintertime, winter.

hinc, *adv.,* from that point *or* place, hence.

Hispāni•a, -ae, *f.,* Hispania, Spain.

Hispān•us, -a, -um, *adj.,* Spanish.

hom•ō, -inis, *m.,* human being, person (*as opposed to animals*); *pl.:* humankind, humanity. †

honest•us, -a, -um, *adj.* [**honōs,** honor], honorable, worthy, distinguished, eminent.

hon•ōs, -ōris, *m.,* honor, regard, glory, distinction; honorable position, office.

hōr•a, -ae, *f.,* hour. *There were twenty-four hours in the Roman day, but they divided those hours into twelve hours of light and twelve hours of darkness (between sunrise and sunset). Except at the equinoxes, the hours were thus not of equal length, and varied according to the season.*

hortor, 1, exhort, encourage, incite, urge strongly.

hospit•ium, -ī, *n.* [**hospes,** host *or* guest], the reciprocal relationship that exists between a host and a guest; friendship, hospitality.

host•is, -is, *m. or f.,* (*public*) enemy, enemy combatant (*as opposed to* **inimīcus,** a personal enemy); *pl.:* the enemy. †

hūc, *adv.* [*from* **hic,** this], to this place, hither, here; against these, to these.

hūmāni•tās, -tātis, *f.* [**hūmānus,** human], humanity, culture, refinement.

hūmān•us, -a, -um, *adv.,* human; civilized, cultured, refined, cultivated.

humil•is, -e, *adj.* [**humus,** the ground], *on the ground;* low, humble, abject, weak.

humili•tās, -tātis, *f.* [**humilis,** low], humility, lowness; weakness.

I.

iac•eō, -ēre, iacuī, —, lie; lie slain
or slaughtered.

iaciō, iacere, iēcī, iactum,
throw, cast, hurl; (of an agger,
rampart), throw up or together,
construct.

iacul•um, -ī, n. [iaciō, throw],
javelin, spear, dart.

iam, adv., now, at this time;
already, by this time, at last;
really, indeed, even; neque iam
or iam nōn, no longer; ubi iam,
as soon as.

ibi, adv., there, in that place.

Īd., abbr. of Īdūs.

īdem, eadem, idem (App. §58),
demon. pron. [is, this, that], the
same; this very; īdem atque, the
same as. †

idōne•us, -a, -um, adj., fit,
suitable, adapted.

Īd•ūs, -uum, f. pl., the Ides: the
15th of March, May, July, and
October, and the 13th of other
months.

ign•is, -is, m., fire.

ignōbil•is, -e, adj. [in + (g)
nōbilis, well-known],
unknown, undistinguished,
obscure.

ig•nōscō, -nōscere, -nōvī,
-nōtum [in + (g)nōscēns,
knowing (from nōscō, know)],
forgive, pardon.

ignōt•us, -a, -um, adv. [in + (g)
nōtus, known (nōscō, know)],
unknown, unfamiliar.

illātus, see īnferō.

ille, illa, illud, gen. illīus, dat.
illī (App. §56), demon. pron.
(of what is remote in time, place,
thought, etc.; compare hic), that,
that man, that woman, that
thing; he, she, it; hic . . . ille,
the latter . . . the former, see App.
§170, a. †

illigō, 1 [ligō, bind], attach, hold
together, bind together.

illūstr•is, -e, adj., distinguished,
illustrious.

immān•is, -e, adj., huge, immense.

im•mittō, -mittere, -mīsī, -missum
[mittō, send], send or let into,
insert; send against, direct toward
or against; trabibus immissīs,
beams placed between.

immolō, 1, sacrifice.

immortāl•is, -e, adj. [in +
mortālis, mortal], not mortal,
immortal, deathless.

immūni•tās, -tātis, f. [in +
mūnis, burden], freedom from
public burdens, duties, or taxes;
exemption.

impedīment•um, -ī, n. [impediō,
hinder], hindrance, obstacle,
impediment; pl.: baggage,
luggage (of an army), baggage-
train (including pack animals).

impediō, 4 [in + pēs, foot],
entangle the feet, hamper,
obstruct, hinder, impede, delay.

im•pellō, -pellere, -pulī, -pulsum
[pellō, drive], drive or urge on,
incite, instigate, impel.

im•pendeō, -pendēre, —, — [in +
pendeō, hang], overhang, impend.

imperāt•or, -ōris, *m.* [imperō, order], commander-in-chief, general.

imperīt•us, -a, -um, *adj.* [in + perītus, experienced], inexperienced, unskilled, ignorant.

imper•ium, -ī, *n.* [imperō, order], right to command; authority, supreme power; jurisdiction, dominion, sovereignty; supreme military command, highest official power; command, order.

imperō, 1 [in + parō, procure], demand from, requisition; command, order, instruct, rule.

impetrō, 1, obtain (*by request*), accomplish, succeed in obtaining (*one's request*); impetrāre ā (ab), gain permission from, persuade.

impet•us, -ūs, *m.*, attack, onset, charge; impetuosity, force, vehemence.

impi•us, -a, -um, *adj.* [in + pius, loyal], *without reverence for gods, parents, country*: ungodly, unrespectful, unpatriotic, wicked.

importō, 1 [in + portō, carry], carry *or* bring in, import.

imprōvīsō, *adv.* [imprōvīsus, unforeseen], unexpectedly, without warning.

imprōvīs•us, -a, -um, *adj.* [in + prōvīsus, foreseen], unforeseen, unexpected; dē imprōvīsō, unexpectedly, suddenly.

imprudenti•a, -ae, *f.* [imprūdēns, imprudent], imprudence, lack of foresight *or* forethought, ignorance, indiscretion.

impuls•us, -ūs, *m.* [impellō, impel], impulse, instigation.

in, *prep. with acc. and abl. With acc.:* (1) *of motion, from one place into or toward another place*, into, to; in, among; toward, for, against; at; upon; (2) *of time*, till, into; for; on, at; and (3) *other uses*, in, in respect to, for, under, over, on; in diēs, from day to day; in fugam conicere, to put to flight; in Caesarem incidere, meet with Caesar; summum in cruciātum venīre, be punished with the severest torture. *With abl.:* (1) *of place where or motion within a place*, in, among, over, within, throughout, on, upon; (2) *of time*, in, during, in the course of; on; and (3) *other uses*, in, in the case of; in consequence of, in view of; on, upon; in Ararī, over the Arar; in eō, in his case; in ancorīs, at anchor; in opere esse, be engaged in the work. †

incend•ium, -ī, *n.* [incendō, burn], fire, burning, conflagration.

in•cendō, -cendere, -cendī, -cēnsum, set fire to, burn; inflame, excite.

incert•us, -a, -um, *adj.* [in + certus, decided], undecided, uncertain, untrustworthy; indefinite, vague; disordered.

in•cidō, -cidere, -cidī, — [ad + cadō, fall], fall into or upon; fall in with, meet; happen, arise.

in•cīdō, -cīdere, -cīsī, -cīsum [caedō, cut], cut into.

in•cipiō, -cipere, -cēpī, -ceptum [ad + capiō, take], undertake; begin, commence.

incitō, 1 [citō, put in motion], set in motion; excite, arouse, urge on, stimulate; exasperate; cursū incitātō, at full speed.

incognit•us, -a, -um, adj. [in + cognitus, known], unknown.

incol•ō, -ere, -uī, — [colō, cultivate], inhabit, dwell in, live in.

incolum•is, -e, adj., unhurt, uninjured, safe and sound, unimpaired.

incommodē, adv. [incommodus, inconvenient], inconveniently.

incommod•um, -ī, n. [incommodus, inconvenient], inconvenience, disadvantage, trouble; disaster, defeat, loss, injury.

incrēdibil•is, -e, adj. [in + crēdibilis, believable], unbelievable, incredible, unlikely; extraordinary.

inde, adv., from that place, thence; then, thereupon.

indic•ium, -ī, n. [indicō, disclose], disclosure, information; per indicium, through informers.

indign•us, -a, -um, adj. [in + dignus, worthy], unworthy, disgraceful.

in•dūcō, -dūcere, -dūxī, -ductum [dūcō, lead], lead or draw on, induce; influence, instigate; cover.

Indutiomār•us, -ī, m., Indutiomarus, a leader of the Treveri, rival to Cingetorix, and hostile to Caesar.

in•eō, -īre, -iī, -itum [eō, go. App. §84], go into; enter upon, begin; inīre cōnsilium, form; inīre ratiōnem, make an estimate, decide; inīre grātiam, gain favor; inīre numerum, enumerate.

īnfer•ior, -ius, comp. of īnferus.

īn•ferō, īnferre, intulī, illātum [ferō, carry. App. §81], carry into, import, inflict, cause, produce; cast into; in equum īnferre, mount on a horse; causā illātā, making an excuse; signa īnferre, advance the standards, attack.

īnfer•us, -a, -um, adj., low, below; comp.: īnferior, lower, inferior; ab īnferiōre parte, below, downstream; superl.: īnfimus or īmus, lowest, last with collis (hill), the base of; ad īnfimum, ab īnfimō, at the bottom.

inimīc•us, -a, -um, adj. [in + amīcus, friendly], unfriendly, hostile; as a noun: personal enemy, rival; as opposed to hostis, public enemy.

inīqu•us, -a, -um, adj. [in + aequus, even, just], uneven; unjust, unfair; unfavorable, disadvantageous.

init•ium, -ī, *n.* [**ineō,** go into], beginning, commencement, origin; edge *of a country,* borders.

iniūri•a, -ae, *f.* [**in** + **iūs,** right], wrong, injustice; outrage, injury, harm, damage, violence.

iniussū, *abl. of* **iniussus, -ūs,** *m.* [**iubeō,** order], without command *or* order.

innoc•ēns, -entis, *adj.* [**in** + **nocēns,** harmful], not harmful, innocent.

inopi•a, -ae, *f.* [**inops,** needy], need, lack, poverty; lack of provisions, hunger.

inqu•am, -is, -it, *def. verb used only with direct quotations and following one or more of the words in the quotation,* say.

īn•sequor, -sequī, -secūtus sum [**sequor,** follow], follow up, follow after, follow close behind, pursue.

īnsidi•ae, -ārum, *f. pl.* [**sedeō,** sit], a sitting *or* lying in wait; ambush; treachery; artifice, trick, crafty device.

īnsinuō, 1 [**sinuō,** wind], wind into; make one's way into, penetrate.

īn•sistō, -sistere, -stitī, — [**sistō,** stand], stand upon; stand firm, take a stand; press on, pursue; *with* **ratiōnem,** adopt, use.

īn•stituō, -stituere, -stituī, -stitūtum [**statuō,** set up], set up *or* put in order, draw up; train, educate; procure, prepare; build, construct; begin, determine, decide upon, adopt; **īnstitūtus,** *perf. part. as adj.* (*in addition to the definitions above*): usual, customary; finished.

īnstitūt•um, -ī, *n.,* established plan *or* principle; custom, institution, habit.

īn•stō, -stāre, -stitī, -stātum [**stō,** stand], stand upon *or* near, be at hand, press on; threaten.

īnstrūment•um, -ī, *n.* [**īnstruō,** build], build upon, build, construct; form, draw up *in battle array;* equip, furnish.

īnsuēfact•us, -a, -um, *adj.* [**suēscō,** become accustomed, **faciō,** make], accustomed, trained.

īnsul•a, -ae, *f.,* island.

intel•legō, -legere, -lēgī, -lēctum [**inter** + **legō,** choose, select], select *or* distinguish between; understand; know; see, perceive, realize; find out, learn.

inter, *prep. with acc.* (*sometimes follows its noun*), (1) *of place,* among, between; (2) *of time,* during, within, for; (3) *in other relations,* among, between, in; in among *or* between, in; in among, between; to; over; along with; (4) *with reflex. pron., of reciprocal action* (App. §166), with, to, *or* from each other *or* one another, *as* **inter**

sē differunt, differ from
one another; each other, one
another, *as*, **cohortātī inter sē**,
encouraging one another. †

**inter•cēdō, -cēdere, -cessī,
-cessum** [**cēdō**, go], go *or*
come between, lie between,
intervene, be between; pass.

**inter•cipiō, -cipere, -cēpī,
-ceptum** [**ad** + **capiō**, take], take
or catch between (*one point and
another*); interrupt; intercept;
cut off.

**inter•clūdō, -clūdere, -clūsī,
-clūsum** [**claudō**, shut], shut *or*
cut off, separate, hinder; *with*
itinera, block.

**inter•dīcō, -dīcere, -dīxī,
-dictum** [**dīcō**, say], prohibit,
exclude, forbid, interdict; **aquā
atque ignī interdīcere**, *forbid
the use of fire and water*, exile,
banish.

intereā, *adv.*, in the meantime,
meanwhile.

inter•eō, -īre, -iī, -itum [**eō**, go.
App. §84], perish, die.

inter•ficiō, -ficere, -fēcī, -fectum
[**faciō**, make], make away with,
kill, destroy. †

interim, *adv.*, meanwhile, in the
meantime. †

interit•us, -ūs, *m.* [**intereō**, die],
destruction, death.

**inter•mittō, -mittere, -mīsī,
-missum** [**mittō**, send], send
between; intervene, separate;
abate, cease, let up, discontinue;
delay, neglect, omit; let pass.

**inter•pōnō, -pōnere, -posuī,
-positum** [**pōnō**, put], place
between, interpose; allege;
cause; **fidem interpōnere**,
pledge.

interpr•es, -etis, *m. or f.*,
interpreter; mediator.

interpretor, 1 [**interpres**,
interpreter], interpret, explain.

inter•sum, -esse, -fuī, — [**sum**,
be. App. §66], be *or* lie between,
intervene; be present *at*, take
part *in*; *impers.*: **interest**, it
concerns, it is important; there
is a difference *or* an interval;
magnī interest, it is of great
importance.

intrā, *prep. with acc.* [**inter**,
between], within, inside, into.

intrō•eō, -īre, -iī, -itum [**intrō**,
within + **eō**, go. App. §84], go *or*
come in, enter.

intus, *adv.*, within, on the inside.

inūsitāt•us, -a, -um, *adj.* [**in**
+ **ūsitātus**, usual], unusual,
uncommon, strange, startling.

inūtil•is, -e, *adj.* [**in** + **ūtilis**,
useful], useless, worthless,
disadvantageous.

invent•or, -ōris, *m.* [**inveniō**,
find], inventor, author.

**in•veterāscō, -veterāscere,
-veterāvī, -veterātum**, grow
old; become established.

Iovis, *see* **Iuppiter**.

ipse, ipsa, ipsum, *gen.*, **ipsīus**
(App. §59), *intensive pron.*,
self (*as opposed to, someone
else*); himself, herself, itself,

themselves; he, she, it, they; *as adj.*, very; *in gen.*, his, her, its, *or* their own. (*Not reflexive; for the reflexive pron., compare* **sē**, self, App. §163.) †

ir•rumpō, -rumpere, -rūpsī, -rūptum [**in** + **rumpō**, break], break into, rush into; force a way into, storm.

is, ea, id, *gen.* **eius** (App. §57), *weak dem. pron. referring to some person or object named in the context,* this, that, these, those; he, she, it, they; the, a; **is locus quō,** a *or* the place where; **ea quae,** (the) things which; **eō,** *with comp.,* the; **eō magis,** all the more; **eō ... quō,** *with comp.*: the ... the. †

ita, *adv.,* so, thus, in this way; as follows; **ut ... ita,** in proportion as ... in such proportion as / as ... so; **nōn ita,** not so very, not very; **ita ... ut,** just ... as / so ... that. †

itaque, *conj.* [**ita,** so], and so, therefore.

Itali•a, -ae, *f.,* Italy, *generally Italy below Cisalpine Gaul.*

item, *adv.,* in like manner, so, also, just so.

iter, itineris, *n.* [**eō,** go], route, road; journey, march; passage; **iter facere,** march, travel; **magnīs itineribus,** by forced marches. †

iubeō, iubēre, iussī, iussum, order, command, enjoin, bid. †

iūdic•ium, -ī, *n.* [**iūdex,** judge], judicial proceedings, trial; opinion, judgement; **iūdicium**

facere, express an opinion; **iūdiciō,** by design, purposely.

iūdicō, 1 [**iūdex,** judge], pass judgement on, judge, sentence, decide, determine, think, consider.

iug•um, -ī, *n.* [**iungō,** join], yoke; ridge, crest.

iūment•um, -ī, *n.* [**iungō,** join, yoke], yoke, draft, *or* pack animal, beast of burden.

Iun•ius, -ī, *m.,* Quintus Junius, *a Spaniard who served in Caesar's army.*

Iuppiter, Iovis, *n.* (App. §27), *m.,* Jupiter, *chief god of the Roman state.*

Iūr•a, -ae, *m.,* the Jura *mountains which stretched from the Rhine to the Rhone, separating the Helvetians from the Sequani.*

iūs, iūris, *n.,* human law, law, justice, right; rights, power, authority. *Compare:* **fās,** divine law.

iūs iūrandum, iūris iūrandi, *n.* [**iūs,** right + **iūrō,** swear], an oath.

iūstiti•a, -ae, *f.* [**iūstus,** just], justice, fair dealing, uprightness.

iūst•us, -a, -um, *adj.* [**iūs,** right], in accordance with law *or* right; lawful, valid, just, fair; proper, regular; *with* **fūnera,** appropriate, fitting, proper.

iuvent•ūs, -ūtis, *f.* [**iūvenis,** young], period of youth, *from seventeen to forty-five years;* the youth, the young men.

K.

Kal., *abbr. for* **Kalend•ae, -ārum,**
f., the Kalends, *the first day of the
Roman month.*

L.

L., *abbr. for* **Lūcius,** Lucius, *a
Roman praenomen.*
L., *sign for* **quīnquāgintā,** fifty.
Labiēn•us, -ī, *m.*, Titus Atius
Labienus, *Caesar's most trusted
lieutenant in the Gallic War.
During the Civil War, Labienus
fought on Pompey's side, and died
in battle against Caesar in Munda
(in Spain) in 45 BCE.*
lab•or, -ōris, *m.*, toil, effort,
striving, hardship.
lābor, lābī, lāpsus sum, slip;
go wrong; **hāc spē lāpsus,**
disappointed in this hope.
labōrō, 1 [**lābor,** toil], work hard,
toil; be anxious, troubled, *or*
perplexed; labor, suffer, be hard
pressed.
lacess•ō, -ere, -īvī, -ītum, arouse,
harass, provoke, irritate, attack.
lac•us, -ūs, *m.*, lake.
laetiti•a, -ae, *f.* [**laetus,** joyful],
joy, rejoicing.
langu•or, -ōris, *m.*, weakness,
faintness.
lap•is, -idis, *m.*, stone.
lāpsus, *see* **lābor.**
lātē, *adv.* [**lātus,** wide], widely,
extensively; **longō lātēque,** far
and wide.
lātitūd•ō, -inis, *f.* [**lātus,** wide],
width, extent, breadth.

Latobrīg•ī, -ōrum, *m.*, the
Latobrigi, *a Gallic tribe east of
the Rhine.*
latrōcin•ium, -ī, *n.* [**latrō,**
robber], robbery, brigandage.
lāt•us, -a, -um, *adj.*, wide, broad,
extensive.
lat•us, -eris, *n.*, side; wing *or* flank
of an army.
lāt•us, *see* **ferō.**
laus, laudis, *f.*, praise,
commendation; renown,
popularity, glory.
lēgāti•ō, -ōnis, *f.* [**lēgō,**
delegate], embassy, legation;
commission.
lēgāt•us, -ī, *m.*[**lēgō,** delegate],
one with delegated authority;
ambassador, envoy, legate;
lieutenant. †
legi•ō, -ōnis, *f.* [**legō,** choose], a
legion. †
Lemann•us, -ī (*often with* **lacus**),
m., Lake Lemannus, Lake
Leman, *or* Lake Geneva.
lēn•is, -e, *adj.*, gentle, mild,
smooth.
Levāc•ī, -ōrum, *m.*, the Levaci,
*a Gallic tribe between the rivers
Marne and Moselle.*
levi•tās, -tātis, *f.* [**levis,**
light], lightness; fickleness,
restlessness.
levō, 1 [**levis,** light], lighten, ease,
relieve.
lēx, lēgis, *f.*, law, statute.
līber•ī, -ōrum, *m.* [**līber,** free], *the
non-slave members of a family or
household*; children.

līb•er, -era, -erum, *adj.*,
unrestrained, free; undisputed.

līberō, 1 [**līber,** free], make *or* set
free, release, deliver.

līber•tās, -tātis, *f.* [**līber,** free],
freedom, liberty, independence.

licet, licēre, licuit *and* **licitum
est,** *impers.* it is lawful, one has
permission, it is permitted, one
may, one is allowed; **licet mihi,**
I may; **petere ut liceat,** to ask
permission.

Liger, -ris, *m.* Loire (*river*).

lignāti•ō, -ōnis, *f.* [**lignum,**
wood], the procuring of wood,
collecting of wood.

lignāt•or, -ōris, *m.* [**lignum,**
wood], one sent to gather wood,
wood-forager.

lingu•a, -ae, *f.*, language, tongue.

litter•a, -ae, *f.*, a letter *of the
alphabet, a written* sign, mark,
or character; *pl.*: letters of the
alphabet; letter, written message,
epistle. †

līt•us, -oris, *n.*, seashore, beach,
shore.

loc•us, -ī, *m.* (*pl.* **loc•a, -ōrum,**
n.), place, position, locality,
situation; topic, subject;
condition, state; rank, family;
opportunity; **obsidum locō,** as
hostages. †

longē, *adv.* [**longus,** long], far, far
away, distant, **longē lātēque,** far
and wide. †

longinqu•us, -a, -um, *adj.*
[**longus,** long], far off, distant,
remote; long, long continued.

longitūd•ō, -inis, *f.* [**longus,**
long], length, extent; long
duration.

long•us, -a, -um, *adj.*,distant,
long; of long duration; tedious. †

loquor, loquī, locūtus sum,
speak, talk, converse.

lōric•a, -ae, *f.*, coat of mail;
parapet, breastwork.

Lūcān•ius, -ī, *m.* Quintus
Lucanius, *a centurion.*

Lūci•us, -ī, *m.*, *a Roman
praenomen, abbreviated* **L.**

lūn•a, -ae, *f.*, the moon.

Luteti•a, -ae, *f.*, Lutetia; *city of the
Parisii on an island in the Seine
river; now called* Paris.

lūx, lūcis, *f.*, light, daylight; **prīmā
lūce,** at dawn.

M.

M., *sign for* **mīlle,** one thousand.

M., *abbr. for* **Marcus,** *a Roman
praenomen.*

magis, *adv. comp.* [from **magnus,**
large], more, rather, in a higher
degree; *superl.*: **maximē,**
especially, in the highest degree;
mostly, mainly.

magistrāt•us, -ūs, *m.* [**magister,**
master], public office,
magistracy; public official,
magistrate.

magn•us, -a, -um, *adj.*, large,
big, great (*in size, quantity,
or degree*), abundant, much;
important, extensive; loud
(*voice*); high (*tide*); **magnī** (*gen.
sing. n.*), of great importance;

magnīs itineribus, by forced marches. *Comp.*: **maior;** *superl.*: **maximus.** †

maior, maius, *adj.* [*comp. of* **magnus,** large], larger, bigger, greater (*in degree, size, time, etc.*); older, elder; *as noun*: **māiōrēs natū,** elders, old men; **maiōrēs,** ancestors. †

magnific•us, -a, -um, *adj.* [**magnus,** large + **faciō,** make], magnificent, splendid.

magnitūd•ō, -inis, *f.* [**magnus,** large], size, large size, greatness, extent; stature (**corporum**); violence (**ventī**); severity (**poenae**); **magnitūdō animī,** courage.

magnopere, *adv.* [**magnus,** large + **opus,** work], *with great effort;* especially, greatly, exceedingly, earnestly.

malefic•ium, -ī, *n.* [**malus,** evil + **faciō,** do], evil doing, mischief, harm, injury.

mandāt•um, -ī, *n.* [**mandō,** command], charge, injunction, order, command; message.

mandō, 1 [**manus,** hand], *give into one's hands,* entrust, commit; enjoin, order, command.

maneō, manēre, mānsī, mānsum, remain, continue, abide, stay.

man•us, -ūs, *f.,* the hand; **in manibus,** near at hand; **manū,** by hand, by art; **ferrea manus,** a grappling hook; **dare manūs,** yield; an armed force, troop, band, gang, company. †

Marc•us, -ī, *m., a Roman praenomen.*

mare, maris, *n.,* sea; **mare Ōceanum,** the ocean.

maritim•us, -a, -um, *adj.* [**mare,** sea], of the sea, sea; maritime, naval, on the sea; **ōra,** the seashore.

Mār•s, -tis, *m.,* Mars, the god of war.

mās, maris, *adj.,* male; *as a noun:* a male.

Massili•a, -ae, *f.,* Massilia; *city founded by Greeks in what became the Roman Province (Transalpine Gaul); now called* Marseilles.

māteri•a, -ae, *f.,* material; wood, timber.

mātrimōn•ium, -ī, *n.* [**māter,** mother], marriage, wedlock, matrimony; **in mātrimōnium dūcere,** to marry (*said of the man*).

Matron•a, -ae, *m.,* the *river* Matrona, *now called* the Marne.

mātūrō, 1 [**mātūrus,** ripe], ripen; accelerate, quicken, speed up; hurry up, make haste; hurry, hasten.

maximē, *see* **magis.**

maxim•us, -a, -um, *adj.* [*superl. of* **magnus,** large. App. §42], greatest, largest, biggest.

medeor, medērī, —, cure, remedy.

mediocr•is, -e, *adj.* [**medius,** middle of], ordinary, moderate, average.

medi•us, -a, -um, *adj.,* in the middle of; in the middle, intervening, intermediate; **locus medius utrīusque,** a place midway between the two.

membr•um, -ī, *n.,* limb.

memori•a, -ae, *f.* [**memor,** mindful], the faculty of memory; memory, recollection, remembrance; tradition; **memoriā tenēre,** remember; **patrum memoriā,** in the time of our fathers *or* ancestors.

mēns•is, -is, *m.,* month.

mercāt•or, -ōris, *m.* [**mercor,** trade], merchant, trader.

Mercur•ius, -ī, *m.,* Mercury, *a god especially associated by the Romans with trade.*

mereō *and* **mereor,** 2, deserve, merit, be worthy of; win, earn, incur (**odium**); serve as a *soldier* (*i.e., earn pay*).

Messāl•a, -ae, *m.,* Marcus Valerius Messala, *consul in 61 BCE.*

metō, metere, messuī, messum, mow, harvest, reap.

met•us, -ūs, *m.* [**metuō,** fear], fear, dread, terror, anxiety, apprehension; **metū territāre,** terrify, terrorize; **hōc metū** = **metū huius reī,** from fear of this.

me•us, -a, -um, *poss. adj.* [*of the pron.* **ego**], my, mine, my own.

mīl•es, -itis, *m.,* soldier, private soldier; infantry (as opposed to **equitēs**); **mīlitēs imperāre,** draft soldiers *from,* levy soldiers *upon.* †

mīlia, *see* **mīlle.** †

mīlitār•is, -e, *adj.* [**mīles,** soldier], of a soldier, military, martial; **rēs mīlitāris,** military matters, warfare, the science of war.

mīlle, *indecl. num. adj.,* a thousand; *pl.:* **mīli•a, -ium,** *n.,* thousands (*usually followed by a partitive gen.*); **mīlia passuum,** thousands of paces, miles. †

Minerv•a, -ae, *f., the goddess Minerva, who was associated with wisdom and the liberal arts.*

minimē, *adv.* [**minimus,** least], least, very little; by no means, not at all.

minor, *comp. of* **parvus.**

minuō, minuere, minuī, minūtum [**minus,** less], lessen, impair, diminish; settle (**contrōversiās**); **minuente aestū,** the tide ebbing.

minus, *adv. comp.* [*of* **parvus,** little], less; not at all, too little. †

mittō, mittere, mīsī, missum, send, send off, dismiss, let go, dispatch; hurl, discharge. †

mōbili•tās, -tātis, *f.* [**mōbilis,** movable], movableness, activity, speed; changeability, fickleness, inconstancy.

moderor, 1 [**modus,** limit], manage, govern, control, guide.

modo, *adv.* [**modus,** measure], *with measure or limit;* only, merely; even, just, at least, but; *of time,* just now, recently; **nōn modo ... sed etiam,** not only ... but also.

mod•us, -ī, *m.,* measure, quantity, size; manner, method, style; **ad hunc modum,** in this way; **eius modī,** of such a kind, such; *abl.,* **modō,** *used with a gen.:* in the character of, like.

mol•ō, -ere, -uī, -itum, grind.

moneō, 2, warn, advise, instruct, order.

mōns, montis, *m.,* mountain; mountain range; hill, height.

morb•us, -ī, *m.,* illness, sickness, disease.

Morīn•ī, -ōrum, *m.,* the Morini.

morior, morī, mortuus sum [**mors,** death], die.

moror, 1 [**mora,** a delay], delay, hinder; linger, hang back.

mor•s, -tis, *f.,* death; **sibi mortem cōnscīscere,** commit suicide. †

mortu•us, *see* **morior.**

mōs, mōris, *m.,* manner, custom, practice; *pl.:* customs, habits; character; **mōs māiōrum,** the customs of our ancestors, ancestral tradition.

Mos•a, -ae, *m.,* the *river* Mosa, *now called* the Meuse *or* the Maas.

mōt•us, -ūs, *m.* [**moveō,** move], movement, motion; political movement, uprising, disturbance.

multitūd•ō, -inis, *f.* [**multus,** much], a great number, multitude; the multitude, the common people, the populace. †

multō, *adv.* [*abl. of* **multus,** much], by far, much.

multum, *adv.* [*acc. of* **multus,** much], much, very, greatly,

especially; *comp.:* **plūs,** more; **plūs posse,** be more able *or* powerful; be very powerful *or* influential.

mult•us, -a, -um, *adj.,* much, great; *pl.:* many; *with abl. expressing time when,* late; *as noun,* many *persons or things*; *comp.:* **plūs, plūris,** more; *as noun:* more; *pl.:* more, several, many; *superl.:* **plūrimus, -a, -um,** most; *pl.:* very many. †

Munāt•ius, -ī, *m.,* Lucius Munatius Plancus, *a lieutenant of Caesar.*

mund•us, -ī, *m.,* world, universe.

mūniō, 4, defend with a wall, fortify, defend, protect; **mūnītus,** *perf. part. as adj.:* fortified, defended, protected.

mūnīti•ō, -ōnis, *f.* [**mūniō,** fortify], fortifying; fortification, rampart, works, entrenchments.

mūn•us, -eris, *n.,* duty, service, task; present.

mūrāl•is, -e, *adj.* [**mūrus,** wall], pertaining to a wall, mural; **mūrāle pīlum,** mural javelin, *a heavy javelin that was thrown from the top of a wall.*

N.

nam, *conj.,* for. †

Nammē•ius, -ī, *m.,* Nammeius, *a member of the Helvetian nobility sent as an ambassador to Caesar.*

nancīscor, nancīscī, nactus sum, get, obtain possession of; meet with, find.

nāscor, nāscī, nātus sum, be
born, be produced; rise, spring
up, be raised; be found.

nātāl·is, -e, *adj.* [**nāscor,** be born],
pertaining to birth, natal; **diēs,**
birthday.

nāti·ō, -ōnis, *f.* [**nāscor,** be born],
people, tribe, nation.

nātūr·a, -ae, *f.* [**nāscor,** be born],
nature; natural disposition,
character, constitution.

nāvig·ium, -ī, *n.* [**nāvigō,** sail],
a sailing vessel, ship; sailing,
navigation.

nāvigō, 1 [**nāvis,** ship], set sail,
sail.

nāv·is, -is, *f.,* ship, boat; **nāvis
longa,** galley, ship of war; **nāvis
onerāria,** transport ship. †

nē (App. §188, *b.*) (1), *conj. with
the subjunctive,* that . . . not, so
that . . . not, in order that . . .
not, lest; *after verbs of fearing,*
that, lest. (2), *adv.* not; **nē . . .
quidem** (*enclosing the emphatic
word*), not even. †

ne-, nec-, neg-, *inseparable
negative prefix.*

-ne, *interrog. enclitic: in direct
questions, simply the sign of a
question* (App. §213, *a.*); *in
indirect questions,* whether; **-ne
. . . -ne, -ne . . . an, utrum . . .
-ne,** whether . . . or. †

nec, *see* **neque.** †

necessāri·us, -a, -um, *adj.* [**necesse,**
necessary], necessary, requisite,
pressing; *with* **tempus,** critical; *as
noun:* friend, relative.

necesse, *indecl. adj.,* necessary,
unavoidable, indispensable.

necō, 1 [**nex,** death], put to death,
kill, murder.

neg-, *see* **ne-.**

neg·legō, -legere, -lēxī, -lēctum
[**neg** + **legō,** choose, regard],
not heed, not pay attention to,
disregard, neglect.

negō, 1, say no, refuse, say . . . not.

negōt·ium, -ī, *n.* [**neg-** + **ōtium,**
leisure], concern, business,
undertaking; trouble, difficulty,
labor; **negōtium dare,** employ,
direct; **quid negōtī,** what
business; **nihil negōtī,** no
difficulty.

nēmō, *acc.* **nēminem,** *m. and f.*
[**ne-** + **homō,** human being], no
one, nobody.

neque (nec) (App. §188, *a.*),
conj. [**ne-** + **que**], and not, not,
nor; but not; **neque . . . neque,**
neither . . . nor. †

Nervi·us, -a, -um, *adj.,* of the
Nervii; *m. sing. as noun:* one of
the Nervii; *m. pl. as noun:* the
Nervii, a Belgic tribe. †

nēve (neu) (App. §188, *b.*) [**nē** +
ve, or], and not, nor.

nex, -cis, *f.,* violent death, death,
execution.

nihil, *indecl. noun, n.,* nothing;
with gen., no, none of; *acc. as
adv.,* not, not at all, by no
means; **nōn nihil,**
somewhat. †

nihilō, *adv.,* by no means; **nihilō
minus,** nevertheless.

nisi, *conj.* [ne- + sī, if], if not, except, unless.

nītor, nītī, nīxus sum, rest upon, rely upon, exert oneself, strive, attempt.

nōbil•is, -e, *adj.* [nōscō, know], well-known, distinguished, noted; of noble birth, noble; *as noun*: a noble.

nōbili•tās, -tātis, *f.* [nōbilis, well-known], fame; noble birth, rank; the nobility.

noceō, nocēre, nocuī, nocitum, harm, injure, hurt; nocēns, *pres. part. as noun*: guilty person.

noctū, *adv.* [nox, night], by night, at night. †

nocturn•us, -a, -um, *adj.* [nox, night], at night, nocturnal, nightly.

nōlō, nōlle, nōluī, —, (App. §82) [ne- + volō, wish], not wish, be unwilling; refuse; *imperat.* nōlī *or* nōlīte, *with inf.* (App. §219), do not.

nōm•en, -inis, *n.*, name, title; reputation, prestige; nōmine *with gen.*, in the name of, as; suō nōmine, on his *or* their own account, personally.

nōn (App. §188, *a.*), *adv.*, not; no. †

nōndum, *adv.* [nōn + dum], not yet.

nōnnūll•us, -a, -um, *adj.* [nōn + nūllus, none], some, several; *pl. as noun*: some, several.

nōnnumquam, *adv.* [nōn + numquam, never], sometimes.

Nōrēi•a, -ae, *f.*, Noreia, *a town in Noricum.*

Nōric•us, -a, -um, *adj.* pertaining to Noricum (*a territory between the Danube and the Alps*).

nōs, *see* ego.

nōscō, nōscere, nōvī, nōtum, learn, become acquainted *or* familiar with; nōvī, *perf.*, have learned, *hence* know; nōtus, *perf. part. as adj.*: known, well-known, familiar.

nos•ter, -tra, -trum, *poss. adj.*, our, ours, our own; *in pl. as noun*: our men, our troops. †

nōt•us, *see* nōscō.

novi•tās, -tātis, *f.* [novus, new], newness; strangeness, novelty.

nov•us, -a, -um, *adj.*, new, novel; unusual, fresh; rēs novae, a change of government, revolution; *superl.*: novissim•us, -a, -um, latest, last; *as noun or with* agmen, those in the rear, the rear.

nox, noctis, *f.*, night; media nox, the middle of the night, midnight; multā nocte, late at night. †

noxi•a, -ae, *f.*, crime, offense.

nūdō, 1 [nūdus, bare], strip, uncover, make bare *or* naked, expose.

nūll•us, -a, -um, *gen.* nūllīus, *adj.* [ne- + ūllus, any], not any, no; *as noun*: no one, none; nōnnūllus, some; *as noun*: some, some persons. †

nūm•en, -inis, *n.*, divinity, god; divine force *or* will.

numer•us, -ī, *m.,* number, quantity, amount; account; **in numerō,** *with gen.,* among, as. †

nunc, *adv.,* now, at present, at this time.

nūntiō, 1 [**nūntius,** messenger], announce, send news, report, make known; order, direct.

nūntius, -ī, *m.,* messenger; message, news, report.

nūper, *adv.,* recently, not long ago.

nūt•us, -ūs, *m.* [**nuō,** nod], nod; sign, command; **ad nūtum,** at one's nod *or* command.

O.

ob, *prep. with acc.,* on account of, for; *in compounds,* opposed to, to, forward, against; **quam ob rem,** for which reason, wherefore, why.

obaerāt•us, -a, -um, *adj.* [**aes,** money], in debt; *as a noun:* debtor.

ob•eō, -īre, -iī, -itum [**eō,** go. App. §84], go to *or* towards; perform, attend to.

observō, 1 [**servō,** give heed], observe, mark, watch; regard, obey; celebrate.

ob•ses, -sidis, *m. and f.* [**obsideō,** blockade], *one who is guarded,* hostage; pledge, security.

ob•sideō, -sidēre, -sēdī, -sessum [**sedeō,** sit], sit in the way of, obstruct, besiege, blockade.

obsidi•ō, -ōnis, *f.* [**obsideō,** blockade], siege, investment, blockade; peril, oppression.

obtestor, 1 [**testor,** witness], call to witness; beseech, entreat.

ob•tineō, -tinēre, -tinuī, -tentum [**teneō,** hold], hold, retain, possess, maintain; acquire, obtain.

occāsi•ō, -ōnis, *f.* [**occidō,** fall, happen], occasion, opportunity.

occās•us, -ūs, *m.* [**occidō,** fall, happen], falling down, setting; *with* **sōlis,** sunset; the west.

oc•cidō, -cidere, -cidī, — [**ad** + **cadō,** fall], fall down, set; happen; be slain, perish; **occidēns sōl,** the west.

oc•cīdō, -cīdere, -cīsī, -cīsum [**caedō,** cut], cut down, kill, slay.

occultō, 1 [**occultus,** secret], hide, keep secret, conceal.

occupō, 1 [**ob** + **capiō,** take], take possession of, seize, occupy; engage, employ.

oc•currō, -currere, -currī, -cursum [**ob** + **currō,** run], run in the way of, meet; happen upon; go to, come to; oppose, counteract; occur.

Ōcean•us, -ī, *m.,* the ocean.

octāv•us, -a, -um, *adj., ord. num. adj.* [**octō,** eight], eighth.

offic•ium, -ī, *n.,* service, allegiance, duty; official duty, business; **esse, manēre,** *or* **permanēre in officiō,** to remain loyal.

omnīnō, *adv.* [**omnis,** all], at all; whatever; altogether, entirely, wholly, in all, only.

omn•is, -e, *adj.,* all, every, all the, every kind of, the whole, as a whole; *m. pl. as noun,* all, every one; all the rest; *n. pl. as noun,* all possessions or goods. †

onerāri•us, -a, -um, *adj.* [**onus,** load], equipped for loads *or* fitted for burdens; *with* **nāvis,** transport, freight ship.

on•us, -eris, *n.,* load, burden; weight, size.

oper•a, -ae, *f.* [**opus,** work], work, exertion; service; pains, attention; **dare operam,** give attention, take pains.

opīni•ō, -ōnis, *f.* [**opīnor,** think], way of thinking, opinion; impression; expectation; reputation; **opīniō timōris,** impression of cowardice.

oport•et, -ēre, -uit, —, *impers.,* it is necessary, needful, becoming, proper; *when translated as a personal verb:* must, ought.

oportūn•us, -a, -um, *adj.,* fit, opportune, lucky, suitable; favorable, advantageous.

oppid•um, -ī, *n.,* fortified town, town, stronghold.

op•primō, -primere, -pressī, -pressus [**ob** + **premō,** press], press down, oppress; overwhelm, overpower, destroy; fall upon, surprise.

oppugnāti•ō, -ōnis, *f.* [**oppugnō,** storm], a storming, besieging, siege, assault, attack; plan *or* method of storming. †

oppugnō, 1 [**ob** + **pugnō,** fight], fight against, attack, assault, storm, besiege.

optimē, *superl. of* **bene.**

optimus, *superl. of* **bonus.**

op•us, -eris, *n.,* work, labor; military work *or* works, fortifications, defenses; a work *of engineering or architecture;* **nātūrā et opere,** by nature and art.

opus, *indecl. noun, n.* [*cf.* **opus,** work, deed], need, necessity; **opus est,** it is necessary, there is need; *the thing needed is expressed either by the nom. or the abl.* (App. §146).

ōrāti•ō, -ōnis, *f.* [**ōrō,** speak], a speaking, speech, language, words, address, argument.

ōrāt•or, -ōris, *m.* [**ōrō,** speak], speaker; ambassador, envoy.

orb•is, -is, *m.,* orb, ring, circle; **orbis terrārum,** the world.

ōrd•ō, -inis, *m.,* row, tier, layer; rank, line *of soldiers;* arrangement, order; degree, rank; **prīmī ōrdinis,** centurions of the first rank. †

Orgetor•īx, -īgis, *m.,* a Helvetian noble who conspired to become the supreme leader of the Helvetians. †

orior, orīrī, ortus sum, arise, begin, spring up, rise, start; be born, descend; **oriēns sōl,** the rising sun, sunrise; the east.

ōrō, 1 [**ōs,** mouth], speak; beseech, entreat.

ort•us, -ūs, *m.* [**orior,** rise], rising.

ōs, ōris, *n.,* mouth; face, countenance.

os•tendō, -tendere, -tendī, -tentum [**obs** + **tendō,** stretch] *stretch before;* present, show, bring into view, reveal; tell, declare; point out, mention.

ostentō, 1 [*frequ. of* **ostendō,** show], show frequently; show, exhibit.

P.

pācō, 1 [**pāx,** peace], make peaceful, subdue, pacify; **pācātus,** *perf. part. as adj.:* peaceful, quiet, subdued.

Pad•us, -ī, *m.,* the Padus *river,* the Po, *the biggest river in northern Italy.*

paene, *adv.* nearly, almost.

palam, *adv.,* openly, publicly.

pār, paris, *adj.,* equal, like, similar; equal to, a match for; *with words of number and quantity,* the same; **pār atque,** the same as.

parcō, parcere, pepercī, parsus [**parcus,** frugal], be frugal *or* economical; spare, do not injure *or* harm.

parēn•s, -tis, *m., f.* [**pariō,** bring forth], parent.

pariō, parere, peperī, partum, bring forth; gain, acquire, win.

parō, 1, prepare, get ready; procure, acquire; prepare for, get ready for; **parātus,** *perf. part. as adj.:* ready, prepared; equipped.

par•s, -tis, *f.,* part, share; (political) faction; direction, side, place; district, area †

partus, *see* **pariō.**

pass•us, -ūs, *m.* [**pandō,** extend], a pace, step, stride, *the distance from where the foot leaves the ground to where the same foot again hits the ground, which Romans standardized as a measure of 4 feet, 10 ¼ inches (= five Roman feet);* **mīlle passūs** *or* **passuum,** a *Roman* mile (*4,857 feet*). †

pate•ō, -ēre, -uī, —, lie *or* be open, be passable; stretch out, extend.

pat•er, -ris, *m.,* father; *in pl.:* forefathers, ancestors; **pater familiae,** father *or* head of a household.

patior, patī, passus sum, endure, withstand, suffer; permit, allow.

pauc•ī, -ae, -a, *adj.* (*rarely used in the sing.*), few; *as noun:* few persons or things.

pauci•tās, -tātis, *f.* [**paucus,** few], fewness, small number.

paulātim, *adv.* [**paulus,** little], little by little, by degrees, gradually.

paulō, *adv.* [**paulus,** little], a little, somewhat, slightly.

paulum, *adv.* [**paulus,** little], a little, somewhat, slightly.

paul•us, -a, -um, *adj.,* little; **paulum,** *as noun:* a little; **post paulum,** soon after.

pāx, pācis, *f.,* peace, favor.

pecūni•a, -ae, *f.,* property, wealth; money.

ped•es, -itis, *m.* [**pēs,** foot], foot
soldier; *pl.*: infantry.

pedest•er, -ris, -re, *adj.* [**pēs,**
foot], on foot, pedestrian;
pedestrēs cōpiae, infantry.

peditāt•us, -ūs, *m.* [**pedes,** foot
soldier], foot soldiers, infantry.

pellō, pellere, pepulī, pulsum,
beat, defeat, rout; drive out,
expel.

pendō, pendere, pependī,
pēnsum, weigh, weigh out;
weigh out *money,* pay, pay out;
with **poenās,** suffer.

per, *prep. with acc.,* through,
throughout; by means of,
through the agency of, on
account of, through efforts *or*
influence of; **per sē,** of their
own accord, on their own
responsibility; *sometimes*
with intensive force, in itself,
themselves; *in composition,*
thorough, very, thoroughly,
completely. †

per•agō, -agere, -ēgī, -āctum
[**agō,** lead], lead through;
complete, finish.

per•currō, -currere, -currī,
-cursum [**currō,** run], run along
or over.

per•cutiō, -cutere, -cutī,
-cussum, strike *or* thrust
through, slay, kill.

per•discō, -discere, -didicī, —
[**discō,** learn], learn thoroughly,
learn by heart.

per•dūcō, -dūcere, -dūxī,
-ductum [**dūcō,** lead], lead

through *or* along, conduct, bring
over, bring; construct, extend;
influence, win over; draw out,
prolong.

perendin•us, -a, -um, *adj.,* after
tomorrow.

perequitō, 1 [**equitō,** ride], ride
around, ride about, ride through.

perfacil•is, -e, *adj.* [**facilis,** easy],
very easy.

per•ficiō, -ficere, -fēcī, -fectum
[**faciō,** make, do], make *or*
do thoroughly *or* completely;
complete, finish; construct,
build; achieve, accomplish.

per•fugiō, -fugere, -fūgī,
-fugitum [**fugiō,** flee], flee for
refuge, take refuge; desert.

perīcul•um, -ī, *n.,* trial, test,
attempt; risk, danger, peril. †

perlātus, *see* **perferō.**

per•legō, -legere, -lēgī, -lēctum
[**legō,** read], read through, read.

per•maneō, -manēre, -mānsī,
-mānsum [**maneō,** remain],
stay through *or* to the end, stay,
remain; continue, persist.

per•moveō, -movēre, -mōvī,
-mōtum [**moveō,** move], move
thoroughly; arouse, incite,
excite; affect, influence.

perpauc•ī, -ae, -a [**paucī,** few],
very few, but very few; *m. pl. as*
noun: very few.

perpetu•us, -a, -um, *adj.,*
continuous, uninterrupted;
permanent, lasting, continual;
whole, entire; *n. as noun in the*
phrase **in perpetuum,** forever.

per·scrībō, -scrībere, -scrīpsī, -scrīptum [**scrībō,** write], write out, report, describe.

persev·ērō, 1, persist, persevere.

per·spiciō, -spicere, -spexī, -spectum [**speciō,** look], look *or* see through; view, examine, inspect; perceive, realize, learn, find out, ascertain.

per·suādeō, -suādēre, -suāsī, -suāsum [**suādeō,** advise], *advise thoroughly, and thus convincingly*: convince, persuade, prevail upon; inculcate; **sibi persuādērī,** be convinced. †

per·terreō, 2 [**terreō,** frighten], frighten thoroughly; terrify, terrorize.

pertināci·a, -ae, *f.* [**pertineō,** hold onto], obstinacy, stubbornness, pertinacity.

per·tineō, -tinēre, -tinuī, -tentum [**teneō,** hold], hold *or* reach to, extend; pertain, have reference to, concern; tend, aim at; **eōdem pertinēre,** tend to the same purpose *or* result, amount to the same thing. †

pertulī, *see* **perferō.**

perturbō, 1 [**turbō,** disturb] disturb greatly, throw into confusion, embarrass, disturb; alarm, terrify.

per·veniō, -venīre, -vēnī, -ventum [**veniō,** come], come through; come to, arrive at, reach; *of property,* fall, revert. †

pēs, pedis, *m.,* the foot, a foot (*the Roman measure was 11.65 inches in length*); **pedibus,** on foot; **pedem referre,** retreat.

petō, petere, petīvī, petītum, seek, hunt for, aim at, make for, attack, go to, direct one's course to *or* toward; seek to obtain, strive after; ask, request, beseech. †

Petrosid·ius, -ī, *m.,* Lucius Petrosidius, *a standard-bearer in Caesar's army.*

pie·tās, -tātis, *f.* [**pius,** loyal], loyalty, devotion.

pīl·um, -ī, *n.,* heavy javelin, pike.

pīl·us, -ī, *m.,* century *of soldiers*; **prīmus pīlus,** first century *of a legion*; **prīmī pīlī centuriō** *or* **prīmīpīlus,** the centurion of the first century, the chief centurion.

pinn·a, -ae, *f.,* feather; battlement, parapet.

Pīs·ō, -ōnis, *f.,* (1) Marcus Puppius Piso Calpurnianus, *consul with Messala in 61* BCE. (2) Lucius Calpurnius Piso, *killed in the defeat of Cassius's army by the Tigurini in 107* BCE. (3) Lucius Calpurnius Piso, *Caesar's father-in-law; consul in 58* BCE. (4) Piso, *an Aquitanian.*

plācō, 1, appease.

Plancus, -ī, *m., see* **Munātius.**

plēbs, plēbis, *or* **plēbēs, plēbēī,** *f.,* populace, common people.

plēn·us, -a, -um, *adj.* [**pleō,** fill], full, whole, complete.

plēr•īque, -aeque, -aque, *adj. pl.,* very many, the most of; *as noun*: a great many, very many. †

plērumque, *adv.* [**plērusque,** the greater part], for the most part, mostly, generally; again and again, very often.

Pleumoxi•ī, -ōrum, *m.,* the Pleumoxii.

plūrimus, *see* **multus.** †

plūs, *see* **multus.** †

poen•a, -ae, *f.,* punishment, penalty.

polliceor, 2 [**prō** + **liceor,** bid, offer], hold forth, offer, promise, pledge.

pollicitus, *see* **polliceor.**

Pompē•ius, -ī, *m.,* (1) Gnaeus Pompeius Magnus, *Pompey the Great, political ally with Crassus and supporter of Caesar in 60* BCE, *later joins the Senatorial party against Caesar, is defeated by Caesar in Greece, and murdered in Egypt in 48* BCE. (2) Gnaius Pompeius, *an interpreter who served under Quintus Titurius Sabinus.*

pōnō, pōnere, posuī, positum, place, put, place over; lay down, set aside; station, post; regard, consider; make, build; *with* **castra,** pitch; *pass.*: be situated; *with* **in** *and the abl.,* depend on, *in addition to the above meanings.*

pōns, pontis, *m.,* bridge.

popul•us, -ī, *m.,* the people, the mass, the crowd, *as opposed to individuals*; a people, a nation. †

porrō, *adv.,* farther on; furthermore, then.

port•a, -ae, *f.,* gate.

portō, 1, carry, transport, bring, take.

port•us, -ūs, *m.,* harbor, haven, port.

possum, posse, potuī, — (App. §80) [**potis,** able + **sum,** be], be able, can; to have power *or* influence, have strength, be strong; *with* **quam** *and superl.*: as possible, *e.g.,* **quam plūrimās possunt,** as many as possible; **multum posse, plūs posse,** *and* **plūrimum posse,** *see* **multum.** †

post, *adv. and prep. with acc.* (1) *As adv.,* later, afterward; (2) *As prep.,* behind, after; **post tergum** *or* **post sē,** in the rear.

posteā, *adv.* [**post,** after], after this, afterward.

posteāquam, *adv.* [**posteā,** afterward + **quam,** than], after.

poster•us, -a, -um, *adj.* [**post,** after], after, following, next; *in m. pl. as noun*: posterity; *superl.*: **postrēmus** *or* **postumus,** last.

postrēmō, *adv.* [**postrēmus,** last], finally, at last.

pot•ēns, -entis, *adj.* [*pres. part. of* **possum,** be able], powerful, influential.

potes•tās, -tātis, *f.* [**potēns,** powerful], power, ability, authority; control, sway, rule; chance, opportunity, possibility; **potestātem facere,** grant permission, give a chance.

potior, 4 [**potis,** powerful], become master of, get control *or* possession of, obtain, capture.

prae•cēdō, -cēdere, -cessī, -cessum [**cēdō,** go], go before; surpass, excel.

prae•ceps, -cipitis, *adj.* [**caput,** head], headlong; steep, precipitous.

prae•ceptum, -ī, *n.* [**praecipiō,** instruct], instruction, injunction, command.

praed•a, -ae, *f.*, booty, plunder, spoil.

prae•dīcō, 1 [**dīcō,** proclaim], proclaim publicly *or* before others; declare, report, tell of.

prae•ficiō, -ficere, -fēcī, -fectum [**faciō,** make], make before; place over, put in command of, put at the head of, place in charge of.

prae•mittō, -mittere, -mīsī, -missum [**mittō,** send], send before *or* in advance.

praem•ium, -ī, *n.*, distinction, prize, reward.

prae•sēns, -sentis, *pres. part. of* **praesum.**

prae•senti•a, -ae, *f.* [**praesum,** be present], presence; the present moment; **in praesentiā,** for the present; then.

praesertim, *adv.*, particularly, especially.

praesid•ium, -ī, *n.* [**praesideō,** guard], guard, garrison; safeguard, protection; fortification, stronghold; help, aid; safety.

praestō, *adv.*, at hand, ready; *with* **sum,** meet.

prae•stō, -stāre, -stitī, -stātum [**stō,** stand], stand *or* place before; show, exhibit, supply, furnish; be superior, excel, surpass; *impers.* **praestat,** it is better *or* more advisable.

prae•sum, -esse, -fuī, — [**sum,** be. App. §77], be before *or* over, be in command of, rule over, be at the head of; **praesēns,** *pres. part. as adj.*: present, in person; for the present.

praeter, *prep. with acc.* [**prae,** before], before; beyond, past; contrary to; in addition to, except, besides.

praetereā, *adv.* [**praeter,** beyond], beyond this, besides, furthermore.

praeterquam, *adv.*, besides, except.

prae•ūrō, -ūrere, -ussī, -ustum [**ūrō,** burn], burn in front *or* at the end.

premō, premere, pressī, pressum, press, press upon, press hard; oppress, burden, annoy, harass. †

prīdiē, *adv.* [**diēs,** day], on the day before.

prīmum, *adv.* [**prīmus,** first], irst, at first, in the first place, for the first time; **cum prīmum** *or* **ubi prīmum,** as soon as; **quam prīmum,** as soon as possible, very soon. †

prīm•us, -a, -um, *adj. superl.*
(App. §43), first, foremost; first
part of; *pl. as noun*: the first,
the front rank *or* ranks; leaders,
chiefs; **in prīmīs,** especially. †

prīn•ceps, -cipis, *adj.* [**prīmus,**
first], *taking the first place*; chief,
most prominent, first; *as noun,*
chief *or* principal person, leader,
chief.

prīncipāt•us, -ūs, *m.* [**prīnceps,**
chief], chief place *or* position;
chief authority, leadership.

prīstin•us, -a, -um, *adj.* [*from*
prior, former], former, original;
previous, preceding.

prius, *adv.* [**prior,** former], before,
sooner, previously.

priusquam *or* **prius . . . quam,**
conj., sooner than, before; until.

prīvāt•us, -a, -um, *adj.,* private,
personal, individual; *as noun,*
person, individual.

prō, *prep. with abl.,* before, in front
of; for, on behalf of; on account
of, in consideration of, in return
for; as, in the disguise of; in place
of, instead of; in proportion
to, according to; *in compounds*
(*appears as* **prō, pro,** *and* **prōd**),
for, before, forward, forth. †

probō, 1 [**probus,** good], consider
good, approve; prove, show,
demonstrate.

pro•cēdō, -cēdere, -cessī,
-cessum [**cēdō,** go], go forth *or*
forward, proceed, advance.

procul, *adv.,* far off, from afar, in
the distance, at a distance.

prōcūrō, 1 [**cūrō,** care], care for,
attend to.

pro•currō, -currere, -currī,
-cursum [**currō,** run], run *or*
rush forward, rush out, charge.

prod•eō, -īre, -iī, -itum [**prō** +
eō, go, App. §84], go *or* come
forth, go forward, advance.

prōd•ō, -dere, -didī, -ditum
[**dō,** give], give forth, reveal;
betray, give up; transmit, hand
down; **memoriā prōditum,**
told according to tradition,
handed down.

prō•dūcō, -dūcere, -dūxī,
-ductum [**dūcō,** lead], lead out
or forth, bring forth; prolong,
protract; produce; *with* **cōpiās,**
arrange, draw up.

proelior, 1 [**proelium,** battle],
join *or* engage in battle.

proeli•um, -ī, *n.,* battle, contest,
engagement; **proelium
committere,** join *or* begin
battle, risk a fight, engage in
battle, fight. †

profecti•ō, -ōnis, *f.* [**proficīscor,**
set out], a setting out; start,
departure.

**proficīscor, proficīscī, profectus
sum,** set out for, start out; go,
proceed. †

pro•fiteor, -fitērī, -fessus sum
[**fateor,** confess], admit,
acknowledge, declare, offer.

prōfuī, *see* **prōsum.**

prōgnāt•us, -a, -um, *adj.* [**nāscor,**
be born], born; descended,
sprung.

prō•gredior, -gredī, -gressus sum [**gradior,** step], step *or* go forward, advance, proceed, go.

prohibeō, 2 [**habeō,** hold], keep from, keep, restrain, prevent, prohibit; keep out *or* away from; protect, guard.

prō•iciō, -icere, -iēcī, -iectum [**iaciō,** throw. App. §7], throw forward *or* away; throw, cast; reject, give up, **sē prōicere,** cast oneself; jump.

proinde, *adv.,* hence, accordingly, therefore.

prō•nūntiō, 1 [**nūntiō,** announce], announce, give out publicly, tell, relate, report, say; give orders; *with* **sententia,** pronounce.

prō•pellō, -pellere, -pulī, -pulsum [**pellō,** drive], drive forward, put to flight, rout; dislodge, drive back.

properō, 1 [**properus,** quick], hasten, hurry.

propinqu•us, -a, -um, *adj.* [**prope,** near], near, neighboring, close at hand; *pl. as noun,* relatives.

propius, *adv. and prep. with acc.* (App. §122, *b.*) [**prope,** near], nearer.

prō•pōnō, -pōnere, -posuī, -positum [**pōnō,** put], place *or* put forward, present, offer; relate, tell of, explain; purpose, propose; expose.

propter, *prep. with acc.* [**prope,** near], on account of, because of, in consequence of.

proptereā, *adv.* [**propter,** because of], on this account; **proptereā quod,** because.

propulsō (1) [**propello,** drive forward], to drive off, repel

prō•sequor, -sequī, -secūtus sum [**sequor,** follow], follow, accompany; pursue; *with* **ōrātiōne,** address.

prō•tegō, -tegere, -tēxī, -tēctum [**tegō,** cover], cover, protect.

prō•vehō, -vehere, -vexī, -vectum [**vehō,** carry], carry forward; *pass.,* be carried forward, sail.

prō•veniō, -venīre, -vēnī, -ventum [**veniō,** come], come forth, grow; be produced, yield (*of grain*).

prō•videō, -vidēre, -vīdī, -vīsum [**videō,** see], see beforehand, foresee; care for, provide.

prō•vinci•a, -ae, *f.,* office *of governor of a province*; province, *a territory subject to Rome and governed by a Roman governor*; *especially* the Province, *the southern part of Gaul along the Mediterranean coast.* †

proxim•us, -a, -um, *adj., superl.* (App. §43), nearest, next; last, previous; *with acc.* (App. §122, *b.*), next to. †

pūblic•us, -a, -um, *adj.* [**populus,** people], of the state *or* people, common, public; *n. as noun,* public, public view; **rēs pūblica,** the state, the commonwealth. †

puerīl•is, -e, *adj.* [**puer,** child], childish.

pugn•a, -ae, *f.* [**pugnō,** fight], fight, battle, contest; **genus pugnae,** method of fighting. †

pugn•ō, 1, fight, engage in battle, contend; strive; *often impers., as* **pugnātur,** it is fought, *i.e.,* they fight. †

Pull•ō, -ōnis, *m.,* Titus Pullo, *a centurion in Caesar's army.*

pulv•is, -eris, *m.,* dust.

putō, 1, think, consider, believe.

Pȳrēnae•us, -a, -um, *adj.,* Pyreneian; **Pȳrēnaeī montēs,** the Pyrenaei *or* the Pyrenees Mountains.

Q.

Q., *abbr. for* **Quīntus,** Quintus, *a Roman praenomen.*

quā, *adv.* [*abl. f. of* **quī**], by which way *or* route; in which place, where. †

quadringent•ī, -ae, -a, *card. num. adj.,* four hundred.

quaesti•ō, -ōnis, *f.* [**quaerō,** inquire], inquiry; examination, investigation.

quaest•or, -ōris, *m.* [**quaerō,** seek], a quaestor; (1) at Rome, an annually elected official in charge of state revenues; (2) in the Roman army, a quartermaster in charge of money and supplies, and sometimes employed in commanding troops.

quaest•us, -ūs, *m.* [**quaerō,** seek], gain, acquisition.

quant•us, -a, -um, *adj.,* (1) *interrog.,* how much? how large? how great? what? **quantum,** *as adv.,* how much? (2) *rel. pron.,* as much as, as; **quantum,** *as adv.,* as much as, as; **quantō . . . tantō** (*with comparatives*), the . . . the. †

quant•usvīs, -avīs, -umvīs, *adj.* [**quantus,** as great as + **vīs,** you wish], as great (large, much, etc.) as you wish, however great.

quārē, *adv.* [**quī,** which + **rēs,** thing], (1) *interrog.,* why? wherefore? for what reason?; (2) *rel.,* on this account, therefore, wherefore.

quārt•us, -a, -um, *adj., ord. num.* [**quattuor,** four], fourth.

-que, *enclitic conj.,* and; **-que . . . -que,** both . . . and. †

queror, querī, questus sum, complain, bewail, lament.

quī, quae, quod, *rel. pron* (*see also* **quis**), who, which, what; *often implying an antecedent,* he, she *or* it who, those who; *equivalent of the demonstrative,* this *or* that; **quam ob rem,** for which reason (wherefore); **quem ad modum,** in what manner, how, as; **quō,** *with comparatives,* the . . . ; **quō . . . eō,** the . . . the. †

quīcumque, quaecumque, quodcumque, *indef.* (*or generalizing*) *rel. pron.,* whoever, whatever; whosoever, whatsoever, any . . . whatever; everyone who, everything that.

quid, *interrog. adv.,* why? *with* **posse,** how? *e.g.,* **quid Germānī possent?** how strong were the Germans?

quīdam, quaedam, quiddam *and* **quīdam, quaedam, quoddam,** *indef. pron.* (App. §62 *and b.*), a certain one, someone; a certain, some, a; a kind of. †

quidem, *adv.,* indeed, at any rate, at least, truly; on the other hand; **nē ... quidem,** not even.

qui•ēs, -ētis, *f.,* quiet, rest, repose.

quiēt•us, -a, -um, *adj.,* in repose, undisturbed, peaceful, calm, quiet.

quīn, *conj.* [**quī,** who *or* how + **ne,** negative], that not, but that; *after negative words of doubt or hindrance,* but that, that, from; to; **quīn etiam,** moreover, but actually.

quīnam, *see* **quisnam.**

quīnquāgintā (L), *card. num. adj.,* *indecl.,* fifty.

quīnque (V), *card. num. adj.,* *indecl.,* five.

Quīnt•us, -ī, *m.,* Quintus, *a Roman praenomen.*

quis, quid *and* **quī, quae, quod** (App. §§61–62), (1) *interrog. pron.,* who? which? what? **quam ob rem,** why? **quem ad modum,** how? (2) *indef. pron., especially after* **sī, nisi, nē, num,** anyone, anything, any; somebody, something, some. †

quispiam, quidpiam *and* **quispiam, quaepiam, quodpiam,** *indef. pron.* (App. §62), anyone, any.

quisquam, quicquam, *indef. pron.* (App. §62), any, any person *or* thing.

quisque, quidque *and* **quisque, quaeque, quodque,** *universal indef. pron.* (App. §62), each one, each; everyone, all. †

quō, *adv.* [*old dat. case of* **quī,** who, which], *adv.,* (1) *interrog.* to what place? whither?; (2) *rel.,* to which, to whom; to where, whither; toward which; where, wherein; (3) *indef.,* to any place, anywhere.

quō, *conj.* [*abl. case of* **quī,** who, which], in order that, so that, that.

quoad, *adv.* [**quō,** where? + **ad,** to], to where; as long as, as far as; till, until.

quod, *conj.* [*n. acc. of* **quī,** who, which], as to which, in that, that; as to the fact that, insomuch as; because; **quod sī,** but if; **proptereā quod,** because.

quoniam, *conj.* [**cum** (=**quom**), since + **iam,** now], since now, since, inasmuch as, because, whereas.

quotannīs, *adv.* [**quot,** as many as + **annus,** year], every year, yearly.

quotiēns, *adv.* [**quot,** how many?], (1) *interrog.,* how many times? how often?; (2) *rel.,* as often as.

R.

rati•ō, -ōnis, *f.* [**reor,** reckon],
reckoning, account, estimate;
design, plan, strategy, science;
method, arrangement; cause,
reason; regard, consideration;
condition, state of affairs;
manner, way; condition, terms;
in pl., transactions.

Raurac•ī, -ōrum, *m.,* the Rauraci,
a people along the upper Rhine,
north of the Helvetians.

re- *and* **red-,** *inseparable prefixes,*
again, back, un-, re-.

rebelli•ō, -ōnis, *f.* [**rebellō,** renew
war], renewal of war, rebellion,
revolt.

re•cēdō, -cēdere, -cessī, -cessum
[**cēdō,** go], go back, retire.

rec•ēns, -entis, *adj.* recent, late;
fresh, new, vigorous.

recess•us, -ūs, *m.* [**re** + **cēdō,** go],
go back, retire.

re•cipiō, -cipere, -cēpī, -ceptum
[**re** + **capiō,** take], take *or* get back,
recover; admit, receive, receive in
surrender *or* submission; admit of,
allow; *with* **sē,** withdraw oneself,
retreat, escape, flee, run back;
recover oneself. †

recitō, 1, read aloud.

recuperō, 1, recover, regain.

recūsō, 1, refuse, reject; object to,
make objections, complain; *with*
perīculum, shrink from.

red•dō, -dere, -didī, -ditum [**red-** +
dō, give], give back, return, restore;
give *or* return *something due or*
owed; make *or* cause to be; render.

red•eō, -īre, -iī, -itum [**red-** + **eō,**
go. App. §84], go *or* turn back,
return; come; fall to, descend; be
referred.

red•igō, -igere, -ēgī, -āctum [**red-**
+ **agō,** put in motion], bring
back, bring under; render, make;
reduce.

rediti•ō, -ōnis, *f.* [**redeō,** return],
return.

redit•us, -ūs, *m.* [**redeō,** return],
returning, return.

re•dūcō, -dūcere, -dūxī, -ductum
[**dūcō,** lead], lead *or* bring back;
draw back, pull back; extend
back.

referō, referre, rettulī, relātum
[**re** + **ferō,** carry. App. §81],
bear, carry *or* bring back, report;
pedem referre, go back, retreat;
grātiam referre, show one's
gratitude, make a requital.

re•ficiō, -ficere, -fēcī, -fectum [**re**
+ **faciō,** make], remake, repair;
allow to rest; *with* **sē,** refresh
oneself, rest.

re•fugiō, -fugere, -fūgī, -fugitum
[**re** + **fugiō,** flee], flee back,
retreat; escape.

regi•ō, -ōnis, *f.* [**regō,** keep
straight], line, direction; quarter,
region, country, territory, place;
ē regiōne, *with gen.,* opposite.

rēgnō, 1 [**rēgnum,** royal power],
reign, rule.

rēgn•um, -ī, *n.* [**rēx,** king], kingly
or royal authority, royal power,
absolute power, sovereignty;
despotism, tyranny; kingdom. †

regō, regere, rēxī, rēctum, keep straight; guide, direct, control.

re•gredior, -gredī, -gressus sum [**gradior,** step], go or come back; turn back, return; march back, withdraw, retire, retreat.

re•iciō, -icere, -iēcī, -iectum [**re** + **iaciō,** throw. App. §7], hurl or drive back, repel; cast down or off; drive off or out.

relegō, 1 [**re** + **legō,** delegate], send away, remove.

religi•ō, -ōnis, f., religion; in pl., religious ceremonies, rites; superstitions.

re•linquō, -linquere, -līquī, -lictum [**re** + **linquō,** leave], leave behind, abandon; pass., be left, remain. †

reliqu•us, -a, -um, adj. [**relinquō,** leave], left, remaining, the rest, the rest of; future, subsequent; n. as noun, remainder, rest. †

re•maneō, -manēre, -mānsī, -mānsum [**re** + **maneō,** remain], stay or remain behind, remain.

Rēm•us, -a, -um, adj., belonging to or one of the Remi; pl. as noun, **Rēmī,** m., the Remi, a Belgic people along the Axona (Aisne) whose main city was Durocortorum (now Reims).

re•migrō, 1 [**migrō,** move, migrate], move back, return.

re•mittō, -mittere, -mīsī, -missum [**mittō,** send], send or dispatch back, return, restore, remit; release, relax, give up; **remissus,** perf. part. as adj., mild.

re•moveō, -movēre, -mōvī, -mōtum [**moveō,** move], move back or away, remove, withdraw; **remōtus,** perf. part. as adj., remote, far away.

rēmus, -ī, m., oar.

re•pellō, -pellere, -pulī, -pulsum [**pellō,** drive], bear or drive back, repel, repulse.

repentīn•us, -a, -um, adj. [**repēns,** sudden], sudden, unexpected, hasty.

reperiō, reperīre, repperī, repertum [**re** + **pariō,** procure], procure, find out, discover, ascertain; devise.

reportō, 1 [**re** + **portō,** carry], carry or bring back, convey.

re•poscō, -poscere, —, — [**re** + **poscō,** demand], demand back, exact, ask for.

re•prehendō, -prehendere, -prehendī, -prehēnsum [**prehendō** (= **prendō**), seize], hold back; criticize, blame, censure.

repulsus, see **repellō.**

rēs, reī, f., of indefinite meaning; variously translated according to context; thing, object, matter, event, affair, occurrence; circumstance, case; act, action, deed; reason, ground; **rēs familiāris,** property; **rēs frūmentāria,** supplies; **rēs mīlitāris,** warfare; **novae rēs,** revolution; **rēs pūblica,** state; **rēs actae,** deeds, achievements; **quam ob rem,** see **quī** and **quis.** †

re•scindō, -scindere, -scidī, -scissum [re + scindō, cleave], cut away or down, break down, destroy.

reservō, 1 [re + servō, save, keep], keep back, save up, reserve.

re•sistō, -sistere, -stitī, — [sistō, stand], stand back, remain behind, halt, stand still; withstand, resist, oppose.

re•spiciō, -spicere, -spexī, -spectum [re + speciō, look], look back; look at, take notice of; consider, regard.

re•spondeō, -spondēre, -spondī, -sponsum [re + spondeō, promise], reply, answer.

re•stituō, -stituere, -stituī, -stitūtum [re + statuō, set up], set up again, rebuild, renew, restore.

re•tineō, -tinēre, -tinuī, -tentum [re + teneō, hold], hold back, detain, keep; restrain, hinder; detain forcibly, seize; retain, preserve, maintain.

rettulī, see referō.

re•vertō, -vertere, -vertī, -versum, used almost exclusively in the perf. tenses, and re•vertor, -vertī, -versus sum [re + vertō, turn], turn back, come back, return.

Rhēn•us, -ī, m., the river Rhenus, the Rhine. †

Rhodan•us, -ī, m., the river Rhodanus, the Rhone. †

rīp•a, -ae, f., bank (of a stream).

rogō, 1, ask; request, ask for.

Rōmān•us, -a, -um, adj. [Rōma], Roman; as noun, a Roman. †

Rōsc•ius, -ī, m., Lucius Roscius, one of Caesar's lieutenants.

rot•a, -ae, f., wheel.

rūm•or, -ōris, m., hearsay, report, rumor.

rūrsus, adv. [for reversus, from revertō, turn back], again, back, anew; in turn.

S.

Sabīn•us, -ī, m., Quintus Titurius Sabinus, one of Caesar's lieutenants.

sacrific•ium, -ī, n. [sacer, sacred + faciō, make], sacrifice.

saepe, adv., often, frequently; many times, again and again; saepe numerō, often, time and again, frequently; comp. saepius, oftener, more frequently; time and again, too often.

sagitt•a, -ae, f., arrow.

sagul•um, -ī, n. [dim. of sagum, coat], a small coat; military cloak.

sal•ūs, -ūtis, f. [salvus, safe], welfare, security, safety; preservation, deliverance; place of safety; life (when in danger). †

Samarobrīv•a, -ae, f., Samarobriva (now Amiens), a city belonging to the Ambiani on the river Samara (Somme).

sanciō, sancīre, sānxī, sānctus, make sacred; make binding, ratify, sanction; sānct•us, -a, -um, perf. part. as adj., sacred, inviolable; established.

sap•iō, -ere, -īvī, —, taste; be wise, understand.

satis, *adv., and indecl. adj. and noun,* (1) *as adv.,* enough, sufficiently; rather; very; well; (2) *as adj.,* sufficient; (3) *as noun,* enough.

satis•faciō, -facere, -fēcī, -factum [**satis,** enough + **faciō,** make], make *or* do enough for; give satisfaction, satisfy; make amends, apologize, ask pardon.

sauci•us, -a, -um, *adj.,* wounded.

scāl•ae, -ārum, *f.* [**scandō,** climb], stairs; scaling ladder.

scaph•a, -ae, *f.,* skiff, boat.

scelerāt•us, -a, -um, *adj.* [**scelerō,** pollute], accursed, infamous; *as noun,* criminal.

sciō, 4, distinguish; know, understand.

scrībō, scrībere, scrīpsī, scrīptum, write, record, *or* make mention *in writing.*

scūt•um, -ī, *n.,* shield, buckler; *oblong, convex (2½ x 4 feet), made of wood covered with leather or iron plates, with a metal rim.*

sē- and sēd-, *inseparable prefix,* apart, away.

sē, *see* **suī.** †

secūt•us, *see* **sequor.**

sed, *conj.,* but, but yet (*a stronger adversative than* **autem** *or* **at**). †

sēment•is, -is, *f.* [**sēmen,** seed], sowing.

senāt•us, -ūs, *m.* [**senex,** old], *a body of old men,* senate; *especially, the Roman* Senate.

sententi•a, -ae, *f.* [**sentiō,** think], way of thinking, opinion, sentiment; purpose, design, scheme, plan; decision, resolve; verdict; sentence.

sentiō, sentīre, sēnsī, sēnsum, perceive, be aware of, notice, experience, undergo; realize, know; decide, judge; sanction, adhere to.

septentriōn•ēs, -um, *m.* [**septem,** seven + **triōnēs,** plough oxen], *the seven plough oxen, the stars of the Great Bear (Big Dipper), hence* the North.

septim•us, -a, -um, *ord. num. adj.* [**septum,** seven], seventh.

Sēquan•a, -ae, *m.,* the *river* Sequana, *now called the Seine. It flows across much of northern Gaul, and, more famously today, flows through Paris.*

Sēquan•us, -a, -um, *adj.,* of *or* belonging to the Sequani; *pl. as noun,* **Sēquanī,** the Sequani.

sequor, sequī, secūtus sum, follow, follow after, pursue; accompany, attend; follow *in point of time; with* **poena,** be inflicted; **fidem sequī,** seek the protection.

serm•ō, -ōnis, *m.,* conversation, interview, speech.

sērō, *adv.,* late, too late.

serō, serere, sēvī, satum, sow, plant.

servīl•is, -e, *adj.* [**servus,** slave], of *or* like a slave, slavish, servile.

servit•ūs, -ūtis, *f.* [**servus,** slave], slavery, servitude.

servō, 1, save, preserve; maintain, keep; guard, watch; reserve.

serv•us, -ī, *m.,* slave, servant.

sēsē, *see* **suī.**

seu, *see* **sīve.**

sī, *conj.,* if, if perchance; to see whether *or* if; whether; **quod sī,** but if, now if. †

sibi, *see* **suī.** †

sīc, *adv.,* so, thus, in this manner; **sīc . . . ut,** so . . . that; so . . . as.

sicci•tās, -tātis, *f.* [**siccus,** dry], drought, dryness.

sīcut *or* **sīcutī,** *adv.* [**sīc,** so + **ut(ī),** as], so as, just as, just as if.

sīd•us, -eris, *n.,* star; constellation.

sign•um, -ī, *n.,* mark, sign, signal, watchword; signal for battle, standard, ensign; **ab signīs discēdere,** withdraw from the ranks; **signa īnferre,** advance to the attack; **signa conversa īnferre,** face about and advance to the attack; **signa ferre,** advance *on the march*; direct the attack; **signa convertere,** face *or* wheel about *or* around; **ad signa convenīre,** join the army.

silv•a, -ae, *f.,* forest, woods, a wood.

simil•is, -e, *adj.,* like, similar.

simul, *adv.* at once, at the same time, thereupon; **simul . . . simul,** both . . . and, partly . . . partly; **simul atque,** as soon as.

simulācr•um, -ī, *n.* [**simulō,** make like], image, statue.

simul•tās, -tātis, *f.,* jealousy, rivalry.

sīn, *conj.,* if however, but if.

sine, *prep. with abl.,* without. †

singulār•is, -e, *adj.* [**singulī,** one each], one at a time, one by one; single, alone; singular, remarkable, extraordinary, matchless.

singul•ī, -ae, -a, *distributive num. adj.,* one each, one; one at a time, single, separate; each, every; the several; **in annōs singulōs,** annually.

soc•ius, -ī, *m.*[*compare* **sequor,** follow], companion, confederate, ally.

sōl, sōlis, *m.,* the sun; **ad occidentem sōlem,** toward the setting sun *or* west; **ad orientem solem,** toward the rising sun *or* east.

soleō, solēre, solitus sum (App. §74), be accustomed, be used to.

solvō, solvere, solvī, solūtum, loosen, untie; *with or without* **nāvēs,** weigh anchor, set sail, put to sea.

spat•ium, -ī, *n.,* space, distance, extent, length *of space*: period *or* length *of time, hence* time, opportunity.

speci•ēs, -ēī, *f.* [**speciō,** see], seeing, sight; look, appearance, show, pretense.

spectō, 1 [*frequentative of* **speciō,** see], look at, regard; look, face, lie.

speculātōri•us, -a, -um, *adj.* [**speculātor,** spy], of a spy, spying, scouting.

spērō, 1 [**spēs,** hope], hope, hope for, anticipate.

spēs, speī, *f.,* hope, anticipation, expectation. †

spontis, *gen. and* **sponte,** *abl.* (*obs. nom.* **spōns**), *f.,* of one's own accord, willingly, voluntarily; by oneself.

stabili•tās, -tātis, *f.* [**stabilis,** firm], firmness, steadiness.

statim, *adv.* [**stō,** stand], *as one stands, hence,* immediately, at once, right away.

stati•ō, -ōnis, *f.* [**stō,** stand], standing *or* stationing; a military post *or* station; sentries, pickets, outposts; **in statiōne esse,** be on guard.

stīpend•ium, -ī, *n.,* tax, tribute.

stō, stāre, stetī, statum, stand, abide by.

strāmentum, -ī, *n.,* covering; straw, thatch; packsaddle.

strepit•us, -ūs, *m.* [**strepō,** make a noise], noise, rattle, uproar.

stude•ō, -ēre, -uī, —, be eager *or* zealous; desire, strive after, devote oneself to; pay attention to; accustom oneself to.

stud•ium, -ī, *n.* [**studeō,** be zealous], zeal, eagerness, enthusiasm, desire; goodwill, devotion; pursuit, occupation.

sub, *prep. with acc. and abl.* (1) *With acc.,* (a) *with verbs of motion,* under, beneath; up to; (2) *of time,* just at, about, toward. (2) *With abl.,* (a) *of position,* under, beneath; toward, near to; at the foot *or* base of; (b) *of time,* during, within; *in compounds,*

sub- *or* **subs-,** under; up away; from beneath; secretly; in succession; slightly.

sub•dūcō, -dūcere, -dūxī, -ductum [**dūcō,** lead], draw *or* lead up; lead *or* draw off, withdraw; with **nāvēs,** haul up, beach.

sub•eō, -īre, -iī, -itum [**eō,** go. App. §84], come *or* go under, come up to; come up; undergo, endure.

subitō, *adv.* [**subitus,** sudden], suddenly, unexpectedly, of a sudden.

sublātus, *see* **tollō.**

sub•mittō, -mittere, -mīsī, -missum [**mittō,** send], send up, send, send to the assistance of.

sub•moveō, -movēre, -mōvī, -mōtum [**moveō,** move], move away, drive away, dislodge.

sub•sequor, -sequī, -secūtus [**sequor,** follow], follow closely, follow up *or* on, follow.

subsid•ium, -ī, *n.* [**subsideō,** sit near *or* in reserve], sitting in reserve; reserve force, reserves; help, aid, assistance.

sub•sum, -esse, -fuī, — [**sum,** be. App. §77], be under *or* below, be near *or* close at hand.

sub•veniō, -venīre, -vēnī, -ventum [**veniō,** come], come *or* go to help, aid, succor.

suc•cēdō, -cēdere, -cessī, -cessum [**cēdō,** go], go *or* come under; come up to, come up, advance, be next to; succeed, take the place of; succeed, prosper.

suc•cendō, -cendere, -cendī,
-cēnsum, set on fire below,
kindle, burn.

suc•currō, -currere, -cursī,
-cursum [currō, run], run to
help, aid, assist.

sud•is, -is, *f.*, heavy beam, pile,
stake.

suffrāg•ium, -ī, *n.*, vote, ballot.

suī (*gen.*), sibi (*dat.*), sē *or* sēsē (*acc.
or abl.*), *reflexive pron.* 3rd person
(App. §§163–165), himself,
herself, itself, themselves; he, she,
it they, etc.; inter sē, *see* inter *and*
App. §166. †

sum, esse, fuī,—, be, exist, live;
stay, remain; serve for; *with
gen. in predicate*: be the mark
or sign of; belong to; *with dat.*:
have; *for forms, see* App. §66. †
fore=futūrum esse (*from* sum).†

summ•a, -ae, *f.* [summus,
highest], the main thing *or*
point, sum total, aggregate, the
whole; general management,
control, direction; summa
imperī, the chief command.

summ•us, -a, -um, *adj.* [*superl.*
of superus, high. App. §44],
highest, very high; the highest
part of, the top of; preeminent,
greatest, chief, supreme; all. †

sūmō, sūmere, sūmpsī, sūmptum
[sub + emō, take], take away,
take; assume; *with* supplic•ium,
-ī, *n.* [sub + plicō, bend],
humiliation; sacrificing; humble
request *or* petition, supplication;
punishment, penalty, torture.

sūmptuōs•us, -a, -um,
adj. [sūmptus, expense],
expensive.

superarō, 1 [super, over], go
over; overmatch, be superior
to, surpass, conquer, master,
overcome, prevail; be left over,
remain; vītā superāre, survive.

superior, -ius, *adj.* [*comp. of*
superus, high. App. §44], (1) *of
place*, upper, higher, superior;
(2) *of time*, previous, earlier,
former. †

super•us, -a, -um, *adj.* [super,
above], over, above; *comp., see*
superior; *superl., see* summus. †

sup•petō, -petere, -petīvī,
-petītum [sub + petō, seek,
obtain], be near *or* at hand; be in
store, be supplied, hold out.

supplic•ium, -ī, *n.* [sub + plicō,
bend], humiliation; sacrificing;
humble request *or* petition,
supplication; punishment,
penalty, torture.

suprā, *adv. and prep. with acc.* (1)
as adv., before, previously; (2) *as
prep. with acc.*, above; before.

sus•cipiō, -cipere, -cēpī, -ceptum
[su(b)s + capiō, take], take *or*
lift up; undertake, assume, take
on oneself; begin, engage in.

suspīci•ō, -ōnis, *f.* [suspicor,
suspect], suspicion, distrust;
surmise.

suspicor, 1 [suspiciō, suspect],
suspect, distrust; surmise.

sustent•ō, -āre, -āvī, -ātum, to
build up; to sustain.

sus•tineō, -tinēre, -tinuī, -tentum
[**su(b)s** + **teneō,** hold], hold up
from below; hold up, sustain;
hold back, check, restrain; hold
out against, withstand, endure,
bear; hold out. †

sustulī, *see* **tollō.**

su•us, -a, -um, *adj., reflex.*
pronominal adj. referring to the
subject (App. §§163–167, a.),
[**suī,** himself, herself, *etc.*], of *or*
belonging to himself, herself, *etc.*,
his own, her own, its own, their
own; his, hers, its, theirs; **sua,** *n.*
pl. as noun, one's property; **suī,** *m.*
pl. as noun, their men (*friends or*
countrymen). †

T.

T., *abbr. for* **Titus,** *a Roman*
praenomen.

tamen, *adv.* (*opposed to*
some expressed or implied
concession), yet, nevertheless,
notwithstanding, still, however;
at least. †

tametsī, *conj.* [**tamen,** however +
etsī, even if], although, though,
notwithstanding.

tandem, *adv.,* at last, at length,
finally; *in interrog. clauses to add*
emphasis, as **quid tandem,** what
then?

tantum, *adv.* [**tantus,** so great], so
much, so, so far; only, merely.

tant•us, -a, -um, *adj.,* so much, so
great, so powerful, such; **quantō**
... tantō, *with comparatives, see*
quantō. †

Tasget•ius, -ī, *m.,* Tasgetius, *a*
leader among the Carnutes.

tegō, tegere, tēxī, tēctum, cover,
hide; protect, defend.

tēl•um, -ī, *n., a weapon for fighting*
at a distance, missile, dart, spear,
javelin. †

temerāri•us, -a, -um, *adj.*
[**temere,** rashly], rash,
imprudent, reckless.

temere, *adv.,* rashly, blindly,
without good reason.

tēm•ō, -ōnis, *m.,* pole (*of a*
wagon).

temperō, 1, restrain *or* control
oneself, refrain; **temperātus,**
perf. part. as adj., temperate,
mild.

tempes•tās, -tātis, *f.* [**tempus,**
time], time, season; weather,
usually bad weather, storm,
tempest.

temp•us, -oris, *n.,* a division *or*
section of time, a time, time (*in*
general); occasion, crisis; **omnī**
tempore, always; **in reliquum**
tempus, for the future; **ūnō**
tempore, at the same time, at
once. †

teneō, tenēre, tenuī, tentum,
hold, keep, occupy, possess, hold
possession of; hold in, restrain,
bind; **sē tenēre,** remain;
memoriā tenēre, remember. †

tenu•is, -e, *adj.,* slim, thin; slight,
insignificant; delicate.

terg•um, -ī, *n.,* the back; **terga**
vertere, to flee; **post tergum** *or*
ab tergō, in the rear.

terr•a, -ae, *f.,* earth, land, soil, ground; region, district; **terrae** (*pl.*) *and* **orbis terrārum,** the world.

terreō, 2, frighten, terrify.

terr•or, -ōris, *m.* [**terreō,** frighten], fright, alarm, panic, terror.

terti•us, -a, -um, *adj., ord. number, adj.,* third. †

testimōn•ium, -ī, *n.* [**testor,** be a witness], testimony, evidence, proof.

testūd•ō, -inis, *f.,* tortoise; shed; a testitudo, *a column of men, holding their shields overlapped above their heads* (*which made them look like a giant* tortoise).

time•ō, -ēre, -uī, —, fear, be afraid of, dread; *with dat.,* be anxious about, be anxious for, dread; **nihil timēre,** have no fear.

timidē, *adv.* [**timidus,** fearful], fearfully, cowardly, timidly.

tim•or, -ōris, *m.* [**timeō,** fear], fear, alarm, dread.

Titūr•ius, -ī, *m.,* Quintus Titurius Sabinus, *one of Caesar's lieutenants.*

Tit•us (*abbr.* **T.**), **-ī,** *m.,* Titus, *a Roman praenomen.*

tolerō, 1, bear, endure; hold out; nourish, support; *with* **famem,** alleviate.

tollō, tollere, sustulī, sublātum, lift up, elevate; take on board; take away, remove; do away with, destroy; cancel; **sublātus,** *perf. part. as adj.,* destroyed, elated.

torment•um, -ī, *n.* [**torqueō,** twist], means of twisting; an engine *or* machine *for hurling missiles, e.g., catapults and ballista*; windlass, hoist; device for torturing, *hence,* torment, torture.

torreō, torrēre, torruī, tostum, scorch, burn.

tot, *indecl. adj.,* so many.

tōt•us, -a, -um, *gen.* **totīus** (App. §32), *adj.,* the whole, the whole of; entire, all; *with force of adv.,* wholly, entirely. †

trā•dō, -dere, -didī, -ditum [**trāns + dō,** give], give over, give up, surrender, deliver; entrust, commit; hand down, transmit; teach, communicate.

trāgul•a, -ae, *f.,* a javelin, spear, *or* dart *used by the Gauls.*

tra•iciō, -icere, -iēcī, -iectum [**iaciō,** throw. App. §7], hurl across; pierce, transfix.

trāns, *prep. with acc.,* across, beyond, over; *in compounds,* **trāns-** *or* **trā-,** across, over, through.

trāns•eō, -īre, -iī, -itum [**eō,** go. App. §84], go across *or* come over, cross; march through, pass through; move, migrate; *of time,* pass by.

trāns•ferō, -ferre, -tulī, -lātum [**ferō,** carry. App. §81], carry *or* bring over, transfer.

trāns•fīgō, -fīgere, -fīxī, -fīxum [**fīgō,** fix], thrust *or* pierce through; transfix.

trānslātus, *see* **trānsferō.**

trānsportō, 1 [**portō,** carry], carry across *or* over, bring over, convey, transport.

Trebōn•ius, -ī, *m.*, (1) Gaius Trebonius, *one of Caesar's lieutenants.* (2) Gaius Trebonius, *a Roman of equestrian status.*

trepidō, 1, hurry about in alarm; *pass.*, be disturbed *or* in confusion.

trēs, tria, *gen.* **trium (III),** *card. number, adj.*, three. †

III, *see* **trēs.**

Trēv•ir, -erī, *m.*, one of the Treveri; *pl.* **Trēverī,** the Treveri, *a Belgic people near the Rhine.*

tribūn•us, -ī, *m.* [**tribus,** tribe], tribune; **tribūnus plēbis,** *at Rome, a magistrate elected by the people voting in tribes, originally to defend the interests of the plebs;* **tribūnus mīlitum** *or* **mīlitāris,** *a military tribune.*

tribūt•um, -ī, *n.* [**tribuō,** render, pay], tribute, tax.

tulī, *see* **ferō.** †

Tuling•ī, -ōrum, *m.*, the Tulingi, *a Gallic tribe east of the Rhine.*

tum, *adv.*, then, at this *or* that time; then, secondly; then, also; **cum ... tum,** both ... and, not only ... but also. †

tumult•us, -ūs, *m.* [**tumeō,** swell], uproar, confusion, disorder, tumult; uprising, insurrection.

tumul•us, -ī, *m.* [**tumeō,** swell], swelling; mound, hill.

tunc, *adv.*, then, at that time, at this juncture.

turm•a, -ae, *f.*, troop *or* squadron *of about thirty cavalrymen.*

turp•is, -e, *adj.*, ugly, unseemly; shameful, disgraceful, dishonorable.

turr•is, -is, *f.*, tower. †

tūtō, *adv.* [**tūtus,** safe], safely, securely.

tūt•us, -a, -um, *adj.* [**tueor,** protect], protected, safe, secure.

tu•us, -a, -um, *adj., poss. adj.* [**tū,** you], your, yours.

U.

ubi, *adv.* (1) *of place,* in which place, where; (2) *of time,* when, whenever; as soon as; **ubi prīmum,** as soon as.

ulcīscor, ulcīscī, ultus sum, avenge; punish, take vengeance on.

ūll•us, -a, -um, *gen.* **ūllīus** (App. §32), *adj.*, a single, any; *as noun,* anyone, anybody.

ulter•ior, -ius, *adj., comp.* [**ultrā,** beyond. App. §43], farther, more remote, ulterior.

ultim•us, -a, -um, *adj., superl.* [**ultrā,** beyond. App. §43], farthest, most distant *or* remote; *as noun,* those in the rear.

ultrā, *prep. with acc.,* beyond, on the farther side of.

ultrō, *adv.*, to *or* on the farther side, beyond; of one's own accord, voluntarily, spontaneously, without provocation; besides, moreover; **ultrō citrōque,** back and forth.

ululāt•us, -ūs, *m.*, yell, shriek.

unde, *adv.*, from which place, whence.

undique, *adv.* [unde, whence], from all parts; on all sides, everywhere.

ūnivers•us, -a, -um, *adj.* [unus, one + vertō, turn], *turned into one:* all together, whole, universal; all *as a mass.*

ūn•us, -a, -um, *adj., gen.* ūnīus (App. §32), *card. number, adj.,* one, the same one; single, alone; the sole, the only; the sole *or* only one. †

urbs, urbis, *f.,* city; *especially,* the city, *Rome.*

ūs•us, -ūs, *m.* [ūtor, use], use, experience, practice, skill; service, advantage; need, necessity; ūsus est, there is need; ūsuī esse *or* ex ūsū esse, be of advantage *or* service; ūsū venīre, come by necessity; happen. †

ut *and* utī, *adv. and conj.,* (1) *as interrog. adv.,* how?; (2) *as rel. adv. and conj.,* as, in proportion as, just as; insomuch as; as if; (3) *as conj.* (a) *with the ind.,* when, after; (b) *with the subjunctive,* that, in order that, to; that, so that, so as to; though, although; *after words of fearing,* that not. †

uter, utra, utrum, *gen.* utrīus (App. §32), *adj.* (1) *as interrog.,* which one *or* which one *of two;* (2) *as rel.,* the one who, *of two,* whichever. †

uterque, utraque, utrumque, *adj.* [uter, which *of two*], each *of two,* either *of two;* both. †

ūt•or, -ī, ūsus sum, make use of, employ, use, avail oneself of, exercise; have, enjoy, experience, possess, show; adopt, accept; ūsus, *perf. part. often translated:* with. †

ux•or, -ōris, *f.,* wife.

V.

V, *sign for* quīnque, five.

vacāti•ō, -ōnis, *f.* [vacō, be empty], exemption.

vad•um, -ī, *n.,* ford, shallow, *i.e., a spot where it is possible to wade across.*

vāgīn•a, -ae, *f.,* sheath, scabbard.

vagor, 1 [vagus, roaming], roam around, rove, wander.

valetūd•ō, -inis, *f.* [valeō, be strong], health, poor health.

vall•ēs, is, *f.,* a valley

vall•um, -ī, *n.* [vallus, palisade], wall *or* rampart *of earth set with palisades;* entrenchments, earthworks. †

-ve, *conj., enclitic*=vel, or.

vel, *conj. and adv.* (1) *as conj.,* or; vel . . . vel, either . . . or; (2) *as adv.,* even.

velim, *see* volō. †

vellem, *see* volō. †

vēl•ōx, -ōcis, *adj.,* swift, rapid, speedy.

Venet•ī, –ōrum, *m.,* Veneti; *a Gallic people on the western Atlantic coast.*

veniō, venīre, vēnī, ventum,
come, arrive, go, advance; **in
spem venīre,** have hopes; *pass.
often impers. as* **ventum est,** they
came, it came, etc.

ventitō, 1 [*frequentative of* **veniō,**
come], keep coming, resort; go
back and forth, visit.

vent•us, -ī, *m.,* wind.

vereor, verērī, veritus sum,
revere; fear, dread, be afraid of.

verg•ō, -ere, —, —, look *or* lie
toward, be situated.

vērō, *adv.* [**vērus,** true], in truth,
truly, really, indeed; but,
however, on the other hand.

versō, 1, turn; deal with; *pass.
as deponent,* turn oneself; be,
remain; engage in; fight.

versus, *adv.* [**vertō,** turn], turned
to; toward.

vers•us, -ūs, *m.* [**vertō,** turn],
turning, verse.

Vertic•ō, -ōnis, *m.,* Vertico, *a
high-ranking Nervian.*

vertō, vertere, vertī, versum, turn,
turn around; **terga vertere,** flee.

Verucloeti•us, -ī, *m.,* Verucloetius,
*a Helvetian sent as an envoy to
Caesar.*

verūt•um, -ī, *n.,* dart, spear, javelin.

vi•a, -ae, *f.,* way, road, route;
journey, march.

vīcēn•ī, -ae, -um, *distributive num.
adj.* [**vīgintī,** twenty], twenty
each, twenty.

vicis, *gen.* (*no nom. form*), change;
only in the adv. phrase **in vicem,**
alternately, in turn.

victim•a, -ae, *f.,* victim; a sacrificial
animal.

vict•or, -ōris, *m.* [**vincō,**
conquer], conqueror, victor; *as
adj.,* victorious.

victōri•a, -ae, *f.* [**victor,**
conqueror], conquest, victory. †

vīc•us, -ī, *m.,* village, hamlet.

videō, vidēre, vīdī, vīsum, see,
perceive, observe, examine,
understand; see to, take care;
in pass., be seen; seem, appear;
seem proper, seem best. †

vigili•a, -ae, *f.* [**vigil,** awake],
wakefulness, watching; a watch,
*one of the four equal divisions of
the night, used by the Romans in
reckoning time and organizing
guard duty.*

VII, *sign for* **septem,** seven.

vīm•en, -inis, *n.,* a bendable stick,
switch, osier.

vinciō, vincīre, vīnxī, vinctum,
bind.

vincō, vincere, vīcī, vīctum,
conquer, overcome, vanquish,
prevail; have one's way *or*
desire.

vincul•a, -ae, *f.* [**vinciō,** bind],
bond, fetter, chain.

vir, virī, *m.,* man; husband; a man
of distinction *or* honor; *compare*
homō, a human being, *as
opposed to lower animals.* †

virt•ūs, -ūtis, *f.* [**vir,** man],
manliness, bravery, valor, merit,
worth, courage, virtue; strength,
energy, force; *pl.,* good qualities,
merits, virtues. †

vīs, vīs (App. §27), *f.*, force, might, energy, strength; violence, severity; authority, power; a force, a great number; *pl.* **vīrēs,** strength, force; **vim facere,** use violence. †

vīt•a, -ae, *f.* [*cf.* **vīvō,** live], life; manner of living, lifestyle, living.

vītō, 1, avoid, shun, evade, escape.

vīvō, vīvere, vīxī, vīctum, live; subsist on.

vīv•us, -a, -um, *adj.* [**vīvō,** live], alive, living.

vix, *adj.,* with difficulty, barely, hardly.

vocō, 1 [**vōx,** voice], call, summon; invite.

volō, velle, voluī, — (App. §82), wish, be willing, want, desire; prefer, choose; intend; mean; **quid sibi vellet,** what did he intend *or* mean? †

volun•tās, -tātis, *f.* [**volō,** wish], wish, will, desire, inclination; goodwill, favor; consent, approval.

Vorēn•us, -ī, *m.,* Lucius Vorenus, *a centurion in Caesar's army.*

vōs, *see* **tū.**

voveō, vovēre, vōvī, vōtum, vow.

vōx, vōcis, *f.,* voice, tone; outcry, cry, shout; word; *pl.,* words, language, *variously translated according to context, as* entreaties, complaints, tales, etc.

vulgō, *adv.* [**vulgus,** the crowd], commonly, everywhere.

vulg•us, -ī, *n.,* the common people, the multitude, the public, the masses; a crowd.

vulnerō, 1 [**vulnus,** wound], wound.

vuln•us, -eris, *n.,* a wound.